HISTORY OF ASSYRIA

PALACE GATE AT DUR SHARRUKIN

HISTORY
OF
ASSYRIA

A. T. OLMSTEAD

THE UNIVERSITY OF CHICAGO PRESS

Chicago and London

THE UNIVERSITY OF CHICAGO PRESS, CHICAGO 60637
THE UNIVERSITY OF CHICAGO PRESS, LTD., LONDON

© 1951 by Cleta P. Olmstead. All rights reserved
Published 1923. Midway Reprint 1975
Printed in the United States of America

International Standard Book Number: 0-226-62776-4
Library of Congress Catalog Card Number: 23-17167

TO

NATHANIEL SCHMIDT
THE MASTER WHO TAUGHT
NIHIL JURARE IN VERBA MAGISTRI

PREFACE

ASSYRIANS deserve to be studied by and for themselves. Current practice has bracketed them with the Babylonians and has seen in their culture but a pale reflection of Babylonian civilisation. As the student of ancient history has come to realise that there is no such thing as "classical" culture or history, that the Romans were worlds distant from the Greeks, so he must carefully differentiate between Assyrians and Babylonians in his record.

And what a story it is that the historian of Assyria has to relate! Only a Parkman could do full justice to its colour and movement. Primarily it is a war, a war for the civilised world of its day, and a war which almost succeeded. One need not belong to the much-abused school of fife-and-drum historians to realise that a narrative in which the wars did not play a large part would not be true to the character of the people themselves.

Yet, at the very beginning, a warning should be uttered. The Assyrian was frankly and honestly an imperialist; there was bloodshed and cruelty in his warfare and he did not understand why he should not relate what he did. In this he was simply following current practice and his example has been followed in turn to recent days. Historians of Assyria in modern times have carefully tabulated each horror and have given the Assyrian a reputation for frightfulness. The present writer believes the truth should be told about war and none of his evil doings has been concealed, save as closer investigation has sometimes shown that the sin is against the truth and not against the human body.

But this practice of telling the truth about the Assyrians has distorted the popular conception of the Assyrian character, for other historians have not told with equal fulness the truth about the peoples whose histories they have written. A certain school of historians before 1914 seems to have de-

WAR

termined to legislate war out of history, another found it only
a convenient peg on which to hang diplomatic contests, a third
eulogised the powder cart on which history advanced, but
all were alike in refusing to tell their readers about the horrors
of war they read in their sources. The historian of Assyria
has one consolation, the blood of millions is not on his skirts.

The truth is that the Assyrians were no worse than other
imperialists. One might gather from the pages of many writers
that the Assyrians were the only people who ever cut off enemy
heads or used torture; the student of history who has gone
beyond the manuals to the sources can prove atrocities in
every period and against every people whose records have
been preserved. Modern imperialism differs in one respect
fundamentally from ancient, it is not so honest; such an innocent term as "punitive expedition" may cover a multitude
of sins, from flat-nosed bullets to men blown in shreds from
cannon, from the horrors of the Belgian rubber country to the
horrors inflicted on Belgian peasants. Imperialism and imperialists are always terribly alike.

With all its grimness, the story of Assyrian war has a fas-
cination. Even when dealing with frontier raids against petty
tribes the very specialist does not long remember, there are
presented illuminating instances of political policy, or insight
is afforded into the lives of strange and unknown peoples,
hidden away in wild valleys and forested mountains which the
geographical research of our own day has still fully to explore.

Day by day our horizon widens. We behold Elam develop
from prehistoric times, the Hittite sphinx speaks at last and
in broken Indo-European, we trace the spectacular rise of
Haldia where a generation ago thought only of a savage Armenia, we assist at the very beginnings of the Median and
Persian invasions of the Fertile Crescent. Familiar faces are
there also, peoples and individuals known from our Greek
texts, and the Greeks themselves appear for a tantalising moment or two. Best of all, we have at last a background for
the Chosen People. The Old Testament no longer stands by
itself; every page is illuminated, and the evolution of Israel

is seen to be but an episode in the great drama wherein Assyria played the chief part.

War was not the only interest of the Assyrian. First of all imperialists, he developed a real empire. No longer was the conqueror to rule a mass of semi-independent states; he organised a provincial system which did more than we suspect to weld the peoples he controlled into a unity with international outlook. Whether we love or hate imperialism, we must recognise that the firm foundation of modern imperial organisation was laid by the Assyrians.

Warrior first and then administrator, the Assyrian was not without a deeper culture, and if we have not as yet credited him with non-military activities, it is because we have confined our reading to his war annals. Now we may visit his ruined capitals, stroll about his city ramparts, observe the architecture of his palace, enter his once closely guarded harem. We may read his record on his palace walls, often in the ornamental cuneiform writing, but we will learn more of his civilisation if we turn to the beautiful bas-reliefs which likewise clothe his walls. From his sculptures we may learn his method of making war or of fishing, the manner in which a palace or a bird's nest is constructed, the foods he ate, the animals he kept in his stables. We may assist in the introduction of novelties in technology, such as a new method of casting bronze, or in the discovery of a new plant, the tree wool men shred for garments.

As the empire enters the last century before the tragic crash, the interest grows in intensity and the sources multiply. Fifteen hundred business documents testify to the economics of the empire, and the same number of letters take us behind the scenes. Here are the defeats so carefully glossed over by the official propagandist; we may estimate exactly the extent of the boasted victories, sympathise with the worries of a provincial governor as he bears the civilised man's burden among the savage tribes or attempts to conciliate a cultured but degenerate people. We uncover the intrigues of the officials or of the harem women. Some speak of cutting timber, the transport of stone, the building of a palace, the securing of horses, the tribute from the provinces; others are from astronomers and report eclipses, fortunate and unfortunate days, the progress of the stars in the heavens. Many are religious, more are ecclesiastical in tone.

Revealing as they are, even the letters do not give us ultimate truth. That we find in all its nakedness in the appeals to the deity for knowledge of the future, or in prayers, where the heart is laid bare in agony before the divine ones whose decisions for ill it cannot reconcile with its own known righteousness. There are few periods of the ancient or of the earlier mediæval history which can compare with this last Assyrian century in fulness of source material and in variety of incident. Once we read these letters and prayers, we can no longer consider the Assyrian merely a brutal man of war; he stands forth in all his humanity as a man like unto ourselves.

The most subtle yet the most telling cultural evidence is that which comes from psychological reaction to language. A falsely modern appearance is often given to the past by the use of the pet phrase of the hour; this false atmosphere can be avoided no better than by the large employment of the actual words of the Assyrian writers. Much of the delicate flavour must perforce evaporate in the transfer from one language to another, but enough remains to give some faint suggestion of the mind behind the translation or the paraphrase.

In the same fashion, extensive use has been made of the Biblical quotations; the English versions have not been avoided when they seemed to have the right word, but there has been no hesitation in departing from them, even to the point of paraphrase, if it seemed necessary in the interest of clearness. The translations rest on the results of modern scholarship; in numerous cases where the text is in disorder, the right word has been found in the versions or by necessary conjecture. Later interpolations, especially those proved as such by their absence from the Greek translations, have been left one side without comment.

Every published source has been read in the original. The

latest translations have been in every case compared and made
the basis for that here given.. These translations are of all
dates, some made a generation ago, while even the comparatively late ones need to be brought up to date. For the reigns
of Tiglath Pileser III, Sargon, and Sennacherib, the author
has employed the draft translations he is preparing for the
new series of cuneiform texts by American scholars.

That these renderings may be improved is to be expected,
for so vast is the literature and so difficult its investigation
that even repeated readings with this purpose in view have
not always normalised the text and translation. This for
the expert; for the intelligent, perhaps still somewhat sceptical reader, it may be emphatically stated that the points
at issue are of much the same character as those which still
agitate the students of the classics, with this advantage to
the Assyriologist—that his material is increasing so rapidly
that every day sees new problems of translation solved.

The book is not intended as a mere cento of uncorrelated
translations. Every effort has been made to apply modern
methods of historical criticism. Source problems have been
investigated in detail and the sources have been asked the
standard questions. If often we can only confess our ignorance and our hope for future information, in others results
of first-class value have been secured.

Special attention has been paid to human geography. The
greater part of the lands described has been seen by the author in person. As Fellow in the School for Oriental Studies
at Jerusalem in 1904–1905 he traversed Syria in detail from
Hamath to the borders of Egypt; as director of the Cornell
Expedition he visited in 1907–1908 the sections of Asia Minor,
north Syria, Mesopotamia, Assyria, and Babylonia which are
of most interest to the historian of the Assyrian Empire.
Geographical descriptions are in most cases based on personal
observation. Classes and seminars in the later history of these
regions and war work dealing with the problems of the present-
day Near East have added background.

Bibliography has been reduced to a minimum and so have

the discussions on moot points. In a subject so rapidly changing, most bibliographical aids quickly cease to have value for others than the expert, and as for questions in dispute, it has been observed that the vast majority are solved by the discovery of new material and not by the genius of the interpreter.

All this bibliographical material has been listed and the moot points have been discussed in a series of preliminary studies. The standard books on the history of Assyria and of neighbour countries are listed with critical comment in the chapter on the ancient Near East in the *Manual of Historical Literature* about to be published under the auspices of the American Historical Association. A full study of the sources and of the problems, with a complete bibliography of Assyrian historical inscriptions, is given in the *Assyrian Historiography*.[1] The entire political history of Babylonia is presented in a series of articles in the *American Journal of Semitic Languages*,[2] and the Chaldæan Dynasty will be found in a forthcoming article in the *Annual of the Hebrew Union College*, volume II. A similar series for the earlier portion of Assyrian history may be found in the *Journal of the American Oriental Society*.[3] A detailed history of the reign of Sargon may be seen in the author's doctoral dissertation,[4] and a briefer account of that of Sennacherib in the *Proceedings of the American Historical Association*.[5] The Assyrian data for Asia Minor are collected in the Ramsay Memorial volume,[6] and the complicated balance of power as

[1] Olmstead, *Assyrian Historiography*, *Univ. of Missouri Studies, Social Science Ser.*, III, 1, 1916.

[2] *The Political Development of Early Babylonia*, AJSL., XXXIII, 283 ff.; *The Babylonian Empire*, ibid., XXXV, 65 ff.; *Kashshites, Assyrians, and the Balance of Power*, ibid., XXXVI, 120 ff.; *Babylonia as an Assyrian Dependency*, ibid., XXXVII, 212 ff.; *The Fall and Rise of Babylon*, ibid., XXXVIII, 73 ff.; cf. *A History of Babylon*, Amer. Jour. Theology, XX, 277 ff.

[3] *The Assyrian Chronicle*, JAOS., XXXIV, 344 ff.; *Tiglath Pileser I and His Wars*, ibid., XXXVII, 169 ff.; *The Calculated Frightfulness of Ashur-nasir-apal*, ibid., XXXVIII, 209 ff.; *Shalmaneser III and the Establishment of the Assyrian Power*, ibid., XLI, 345 ff.; cf. *Chaldæans and Chaldians in Armenia*, AJSL., XVII, 250 ff.; *Assyrian Chronology*, ibid., XXXVIII, 225 ff.

[4] Olmstead, *Western Asia in the Reign of Sargon of Assyria*, 1908.

[5] *Western Asia in the Reign of Sennacherib of Assyria*, Proc. Amer. Hist. Assn., 1909, 91 ff.

[6] *Anatolian Studies Presented to Sir William Mitchell Ramsay, The Assyrians in Asia Minor*, pp. 283 ff.

recovered from recent Hittite, Egyptian, and Assyrian sources in the *Journal of Egyptian Archæology*.[1] The question of oriental imperialism is discussed in the *American Historical Review*,[2] the Assyrian government of dependencies in the *American Political Science Review*.[3] Fundamental problems of the text of the Old Testament in their relation to the source criticism are presented in a new light in a series of articles in the *American Journal of Semitic Languages*.[4] Relations of geography with human life are discussed in the *Bulletin of the American Geographical Society* and the *Journal of Geography*.[5] Certain questions connected with legal matters are taken up in unsigned reviews in the *American Law Review*.[6] The Hittite inscriptions secured by the Cornell Expedition have been published;[7] it is hoped that other results may be published in the near future.

For the illustrations of the volume, heartiest thanks must be given to the friends who have so generously placed their material at the author's disposal. The new material from the excavations at Ashur, in the hands of scholars only in the last few months, has been utilised through the kind offices of the publishers, Messrs. J. C. Hinrichs, and the Deutsche Orient-Gesellschaft (Figs. 14–28). From their publications also the maps and plans from Ashur have been redrawn. Until the appearance of the recent catalogue, the beautiful reliefs from Dur Sharrukin have been known only in drawings two generations old; through the kindness of the editor of the catalogue, M. E. Pottier, for the first time a general history can present them in all their art (Figs. 90, 110–114, 117–118, 140, 149, 150, 162–166, 171). While in Babylon, Doctor Robert Koldewey

---

[1] *Near East Problems in the Second Pre-Christian Millennium, Jour. Egypt. Arch.*, VIII, 223 ff.

[2] *Oriental Imperialism, Amer. Hist. Rev.*, XXIII, 755 ff.

[3] *Assyrian Government of Dependencies, Amer. Pol. Science Rev.*, XII, 63 ff.

[4] *Source Study and the Biblical Text, AJSL.*, XXX, 1 ff.; *The Earliest Book of Kings, ibid.*, XXXI, 169 ff.; *The Greek Genesis, ibid.*, XXXIV, 145 ff.; cf. *The Reform of Josiah and Its Secular Aspects, Amer. Hist. Rev.*, XX, 566 ff.

[5] *Climatic Changes in the Nearer East, Bull. Amer. Geog. Soc.*, XLIV, 432 ff.; *Climatic Changes, ibid.*, XLV, 439 ff.; *Climate and History, Jour. of Geography*, X, 163 ff.

[6] Cf. especially *Amer. Law Rev.*, L, 316 ff.

[7] Olmstead, Charles, Wrench, *Hittite Inscriptions*, 1911.

was good enough to permit us to photograph the Hittite Relief there discovered (Fig. 84).

Virtually every Assyrian object now in America has been placed at the disposal of the author. Of the numerous examples of the reliefs of Ashur-nasir-apal scattered through the country, selections have been made from those in the New York Historical Society (Figs. 54, 55, 57), the Metropolitan Museum (Fig. 80), Auburn Theological Seminary (Fig. 53), through the kindness of Professor W. J. Hinke, and Bowdoin College (Fig. 58), through the kindness of Professor H. E. Andrews. Professor A. T. Clay secured for me the photograph of the earliest Assyrian annals, that of Arik-den-ilu, from the library of Mr. J. P. Morgan (Fig. 33), and, with the Yale University Press, gave permission for the reproduction of the copies of the Babylonian Dictionary (Fig. 34), the Prism of Esarhaddon (Fig. 169), and the Assyrian Vase with Relief (Fig. 159). The series of photographs from casts, showing the details of the sculptures more clearly than the now weathered originals, have been secured from the Metropolitan Museum (Figs. 45, 46, 50, 77, 155, 156, 157, 158) and the University of Illinois (Figs. 44, 49). The precious prism of Sennacherib, now in Haskell Museum of the University of Chicago (Fig. 126), has been secured through the courtesy of Professors J. H. Breasted, D. D. Luckenbill, and J. M. P. Smith, and of the University of Chicago Press, as was Fig. 91 and the photograph of Ashur (Fig. 11), where we were not permitted to take pictures at the time of our visit.

Illustrations not otherwise credited come from the photographs made by the members of the Department of Semitic Languages of Cornell University who spent the year 1904–1905 in Palestine and Syria under the direction of Professor Nathaniel Schmidt, or from those by the Cornell Expedition in 1907–1908. They were all taken by Doctor B. B. Charles, Professor J. E. Wrench, and the author. Doctor B. B. Charles has further placed the author under obligation by securing such excellent results from the films, taken so often under the most difficult circumstances. To the labours of these two friends, the greater part of the illustrations is due.

Complete acknowledgment of favours received would fill
many pages. The book owed its first inspiration to the classes
in Oriental history given by Professor Nathaniel Schmidt of
Cornell University; to him the author owes his knowledge of the
Oriental languages; with him, when director of the Jerusalem
School, he spent his first year in the enchanted East. It is no
less than his due that this book bears his name in dedication.

History without historical method is not history; it is to
the patient care exercised by Professor G. L. Burr, from fresh-
man class to doctoral dissertation, that the historical point
of view is owed. The late Professor J. R. S. Sterrett was responsible for the second trip to the Near East and his devoted
sacrifices in the securing of funds and his personal knowledge
of the field made the work of the Cornell Expedition possible.
Nor would acknowledgment to his Cornell instructors be complete without mention of the late Professor H. A. Sill in Greek
and Roman History, Professor C. H. Hull in American History, the late Professor C. L. Bennett in Latin, Professor G.
P. Bristol in Greek, Professor E. P. Andrews in Archæology.

Whatever of value was obtained from his visits to the Near
East was due in the first instance to the loyal co-operation of
his companions, Professor J. E. Wrench of the University of
Missouri and Doctor B. B. Charles of Philadelphia. Ambassador Leishman and his staff, Consuls Merrill and Magels-
sen, now deceased, and Consuls Harris, Jackson, and Young,
eased many difficulties with the authorities, and a host of
missionary friends gave their aid. Two who are now at rest,
Mr. J. E. Fowle of Talas and Doctor A. N. Andrus of Mardin,
demand special mention.

Aid has often been asked in this country and the author
has not been disappointed. In so far as was possible with
so different a people, this book has been modelled on the *History of Egypt* by Professor J. H. Breasted of the University
of Chicago; through his kindness arrangements have been
made for its publication as a companion volume, and the author has often "gone down to Egypt for help," and with better
success than the ancient Hebrews. Professor D. D. Lucken-

bill has read the manuscript and his unrivalled knowledge as editor of the *Assyrian Dictionary* has saved many annoying slips or worse. From the same institution much aid has been secured from Professor I. M. Price, Doctor T. G. Allen, and Professor J. M. P. Smith, who as editor of the *American Journal of Semitic Languages* has welcomed his articles, suffered his peculiar notions, and given him good advice.

With other Orientalists the author has debated common problems, especially at the meetings of the American Oriental Society. Professor A. T. Clay of Yale University, the late Professor M. Jastrow and Professor J. A. Montgomery of the University of Pennsylvania, Professor T. J. Meek of Bryn Mawr College, President Julian Morgenstern of Hebrew Union College, such are some of the names to be remembered.

Among professed historians, Professor L. M. Larson of the University of Illinois has read the entire manuscript and made valuable suggestions. The unrivalled knowledge of the more modern phases of Near Eastern history owned by his colleague, Professor A. H. Lybyer, has illumined many an older problem. With Professor M. Rostovtzeff of the University of Wisconsin valued debates on the land system have occurred.

This history would have been in the press years ago had it not been desired to use the Assyrian letters; that it appears thus early is due to Professor Leroy Waterman of the University of Michigan. With unhoped-for generosity, the manuscript of his edition *Correspondence of the Assyrian Kings*, which is soon to appear in the *University of Michigan Humanistic Studies*, was placed at the author's disposal. Passages which for fifteen years had defied understanding slipped into their historical niches after his insight had made all things clear. To no other scholar does the book owe so much.

This preface should not close without at least brief mention of the illuminating discussions with the author's wife.

URBANA, ILLINOIS,   A. T. OLMSTEAD.
 September, 1923.

CONTENTS

xvii

CONTENTS

ABBREVIATIONS

AJSL.   *American Journal of Semitic Languages.*

BA.   *Beiträge zur Assyriologie.*

CIS.   *Corpus Inscriptionum Semiticarum.*

CT.   Cuneiform Texts in the British Museum.

H.   R. F. Harper, *Assyrian and Babylonian Letters;* the translation has been in large part based on the manuscript by Leroy Waterman, *Correspondence of the Assyrian Kings,* to be published in the *University of Michigan Humanistic Studies.*

J.   C. H. W. Johns, *Assyrian Deeds and Documents.*

JAOS.   *Journal of the American Oriental Society.*

JRAS.   *Journal of the Royal Asiatic Society.*

KB.   *Keilinschriftliche Bibliothek.*

KU.   Kohler and Ungnad, *Assyrische Rechtsurkunden.*

MDOG.   *Mittheilungen der Deutschen Orient-Gesellschaft.*

MVAG.   *Mittheilungen der vorderasiatische Gesellschaft.*

OLZ.   *Orientalistische Literaturzeitung.*

PSBA.   *Proceedings of the Society of Biblical Archæology.*

R.   H. Rawlinson, *Cuneiform Inscriptions of Western Asia.*

RA.   *Revue d'Assyriologie.*

RT.   *Recueil de Travaux.*

TSBA.   *Transactions of the Society of Biblical Archæology*

VS.   *Vorderasiatische Schriftdenkmäler.*

ZA.   *Zeitschrift für Assyriologie.*

ILLUSTRATIONS

MAPS

CHAPTER I

AT HOME IN THE DESERT

Ashur, the tiny city-state on the middle Tigris, gave its name to the mighty empire which grew from its first rude beginnings, even as it took its name from the imperial deity before whom all other national gods were to bow the knee; for the first history of the Assyrians we must go hundreds of miles and thousands of years away from the earliest Ashur. The Assyrians were Semites and as such found their first historical home in the Arabian peninsula.

Speculation as to the first home of man, where he was differentiated from his Simian cousins, is for the present vain, but we may be sure it was not Arabia. It is equally vain to speculate as to the manner in which man was divided into so many races and as to how one particular group became fixed in a land so unfavourable to the development of a high material civilisation. All we can say with assurance is that the Semites did come to live in the Arabian peninsula and it is there we can trace their first history in the days before history came to be written.

The constant tribal struggles which make the greater part of Arabia always a "No Man's Land" have permitted no student of prehistoric archæology to penetrate the sandy wastes, and we cannot as yet speak of prehistoric man on the firm basis of his material remains. We do find wonderfully flaked flints in the Sinaitic peninsula, under as unfavourable climatic and soil conditions as in Arabia proper. The same types of flaked flints occur on the highlands of Palestine to the north and along the equally sterile rims of the Nile canyon. The

1

most early man known had a considerable range, and the circumstances of that range afford some support to the theory that in remote ages when man was first emerging from the non-human state, the now desert areas of the Orient enjoyed a more genial climate.

Whatever the conclusions we draw as to the times before the invention of writing, our earliest written records show us the Semite already in Arabia. Here, so far as our information permits us to go, was his "first home," and here certainly a large part of his character was formed. What special characteristics he brought with him. who shall say? Certain knowledge begins with Arabia.

The Arabian peninsula is by no means all desert. In the southwest, Yemen is to-day a land of high breezy plateaus and running waters, with a large and industrious population; in the days before Muhammad, back almost three thousand years ago, there was a settled civilisation which has left us an abundance of monuments. Across the centre extends a belt of comparatively fertile land with towns of some size and wealth. Such spots, are, however, the exception. In the southeast is the Dahna, whose waste no human foot has been known to penetrate; in the northwest is the Lesser Nefud, not impossible of crossing, but yet of much difficulty. Equally repellent are the "burnt places" one finds in certain sections.

The remainder of Arabia is simply arid, with fertile soil which only needs the life-giving water to produce the most luxuriant vegetation. The tiniest spring causes a verdure to arise whose beauty is not all due to the contrast with the near-by sands, and the terribly scanty rains of the winter bring a truly marvellous growth in the few days the torrid sun permits it to endure. In these few days and at these few oases, the herdsman feeds and waters his flocks. Then he must be off, following the spring rains north and the autumn showers south.

So the normal civilisation of Arabia is the nomadic. Now and then a family may settle in an oasis and set up a claim to private ownership. The amount of land fit for cultivation

FIG. 1. BLACK GOAT'S HAIR TENT OF THE ARAB.

FIG. 2. ARAB OF THE TAI TRIBE, THE
NOBLEST TRIBE OF ARABIA.

FIG. 3. MORE THAN HALF SAVAGE
SHEPHERDS OF THE MESOPO-
TAMIAN PLAIN.

FIG. 4. ANAT, THE BEAUTIFUL ISLAND TOWN ON THE
EUPHRATES.

FIG. 5. FLOWER–COVERED PRAIRIE IN SPRING.

FIG. 6. PALMS AGAINST THE SETTING SUN.

is strictly limited by the few drops of the oasis spring or the water which can be retrieved from the winter torrent before it is absorbed by the never-satisfied sands. The further growth of the settlement is as strictly limited by the amount of food which can be produced on this strictly limited amount of soil.

In the rare cases where there is enough soil and water to permit the dwelling of a few thousand souls, the desert still cannot be ignored. When the native ascends the housetop in the evening, the desert gleams before him, and its rapid radiation gives him the bitterly cold nights which permit him to endure the fierce heats of the day. Its sands are ever in motion and ever threatening to overwhelm the toil of centuries. From its wide spaces may at any moment descend the Bedawi, whose threat is of a more sudden though not of a more certain danger than the sands.

Now and then the Bedawi is successful in killing or driving out the settler, and sometimes he decides to settle down for himself. The dispossessed householder finds no difficulty in resuming the nomadic life his ancestors abandoned. He speaks the same language, accepts the same ideas, and in his heart of hearts he had already admitted the superior attractiveness of the nomad life, especially when in his green oasis the wild bard of the desert chanted the raids of past heroes. So he takes to the desert once more, perhaps to gain renown as a robber, perhaps merely to be a caravan leader.

The effect of the nomad life is easy to recognise. Every citizen was at least potentially a wanderer. Under such conditions, we do not expect a high material culture. While nearly six thousand years of written history have surged around his home, while man has progressed from the first use of metals to the age of steel, the Bedawi of to-day is essentially the same as he was at the beginning of that long period of development. To-day he does carry a gun worthy a place in any antiquarian shop, he smokes a pretended tobacco, he may occasionally bring to his tent a bit of cloth from Manchester or some knick-knack made in Germany, but his material life has changed as little as his intellectual outlook. His home is still the long tent of black goat's hair. His wealth is still in his goats and sheep, his camels and his mares, and the kids still nuzzle the traveller as he sleeps under the flap raised to catch the breeze. No spot of land is his own, save as he claims the areas where his ancestors and kinsmen were wont to pasture their flocks, the north and south passages along which they follow the march of the seasons.

And at that, he does not possess these areas in security. He plunders the half-sedentary peasant, and in turn is attacked by the other tribes who would enjoy his flocks and herds, who could raise their scanty crop of barley better in his oasis, and so he must be ever on his guard. No civilised state has such a record of constant warfare as the Arab tribe close to a "state of nature." However, this is not so blood-curdling a statement as might appear at first glance. The chief end of Arab war is booty, not slaughter, for the side which lets the most blood must pay indemnity for the difference. The reason for this most uncivilised attitude is the blood revenge; he who kills must be killed, if not in his own person, then in that of his next of kin. Bloodshed in war may therefore be considered an unfortunate accident.

Periodically, in a year when the scanty crops fail of drought, when the rains are not sufficient for the pasturage of the flock, when there is an excess of population, when a genius arises to lead them to a promised land, when some accident beyond our ken rouses the Bedawi or the peasant from his lethargy, there comes an outpouring of the nomads. In this period of confusion and turmoil, there is turned a new page of history.

Then indeed we have a surprise. The nomad of the desert changes his character. He becomes a great warrior and builds up a mighty domain. His son is an able administrator, and the empire grows into a living organism. His grandson is a patron of culture, under whose protection a new civilisation is born.

The change in character is only apparent, for he is still the nomad at heart. As a ruler, he is never content with what he possesses, he must always advance his armies. As a patron of civilisation, he borrows from the older races the entire basis of his culture, but when he has done with it every phase shows important modification. With it all goes a certain instability of character. Like his ancestor in the desert, quick to fly to arms, endowed with marvellous patience in enduring fatigue and in carrying on the most mighty labours, and then relapsing into the languid life of complete cessation of activity around the tent-pole, the civilised Semite is quick to act, patient to execute, sudden to stop. The same is true of his mental life. Often indeed he transmits and improves, but rarely does he put the seal of even approximate finality on his intellectual productions. He has been the caravan leader, the middle-man, who has furnished the transportation for the idea or the technology.

Religion, it is often said, is his special contribution. Seen in his own desert environment, one wonders at the attribution. The truth is that the Bedawi is as nearly without religion as any man of similar grade in civilisation. To our sophisticated minds, he should hear the voice of God in the desert. He in truth hears but the faintest whispers, and he is as free of super-stition as of formal religion. His life is a struggle in which nature contributes but little, and to himself must be assigned credit for what he secures. It is his own craft which brings him flocks, his own skill that defies the terrors of the desert. Thus he is a rationalist because he knows the worst, and he also knows that within himself lies such slight amelioration as may come. His life is a struggle against the extreme and it is the barest of existences. Therefore, the economic element is the clearest and religion is secondary.

Such religion as he has is of the elements. His chief god is the sun, and wherever he goes the basis of his religion is solar. The moon, too, is a chief deity, as is the god of the weather and the atmosphere. All are familiar friends, whom he invites to the common meal, where he eats with them the lamb he has sacrificed, and offers to his divine companions the same luxuries which appeal to their fellow clansmen. For each god has his special favourite among the tribes, and they in turn honour him most without denying the right of others to a place in their esteem. They operate on the basis of give and take, and they willingly assist those who honour and feed them. The clear blistering air of the desert rarely favours illusion, and the mirage shows the reality that exists elsewhere. The nomad comes to look upon his gods with something of this sanity. They are not vague and mysterious, with ill-defined powers and functions; each is carefully assigned to his proper sphere, and they can be treated as men grown large. As for the dead, they are dead and that is about the end of the matter. Nomad faith is a simple faith, which nevertheless has in it potentialities of a real fanaticism, especially when it is combined with the idea of nationalism and with the hope of victorious war.

CHAPTER II

MEN OF THE EARTH MOTHER

ARABIA moulded the character of the Semite; it was the Fertile Crescent which made him civilised and gave him a part in world history. Indeed, the whole story of the Mediterranean area is that of a struggle between the nomads, whether from the Arabian desert or the northern grasslands, and the earlier settled population.

The Arabian desert is not an isolated phenomenon; crossing the narrow Red Sea it is continued in the Libyan desert, broken only by the green thread of the Nile, and this in turn merges without boundary into the vast Sahara which ends only with the Atlantic. Eastward it passes over the Persian Gulf, traverses sterile hills, and turns north over the salt wastes which comprise the eastern half of Persia. Inside this line of salt desert is a range of mountains. At first their direction is not far from north and south, but ultimately their western trend becomes more pronounced until at last they turn straight west through Armenia and Asia Minor to the Ægean. With the fourth side, the sea, there is formed the Fertile Crescent.

Egypt is a part, though an isolated part, of the Fertile Crescent, for a tongue of desert reaches the sea at its northeast corner and separates it from Syria. Two straight north and south mountain systems divide Palestine and Syria into various almost equally isolated areas. Only in the extreme north does Syria open into the great plains of Mesopotamia which stretch to Assyria and to the eastern boundary ranges, or to the Persian Gulf, where, at the beginning of human settlement, Babylonia was in process of formation. This is the Fertile Crescent, varied indeed in character, but with one factor common to all parts: it is a narrow strip of land which repays cultivation while on all sides is mountain or desert. In it was first developed civilisation. From the desert bay to the south and the encircling ring of hills to the north and east came the barbarians who would destroy it.[1]

Man came early to the Near East. Palæoliths or flaked flints are found in the Nile valley and scattered over the desert on either side, in the Sinaitic peninsula, along the ridge of Palestine, through Syria, and well down the Euphrates; none have as yet been found in the Assyrian country proper, but doubtless that is due to lack of investigation. Such geological evidence as we have would indicate the first interdiluvial period as their date, and this would correspond to the first interglacial age of the north. Prehistory still means to most students merely the prehistory of western Europe, but we are beginning to suspect that its culture was derived from the primitive culture of the Near East.[2]

Palæolithic man has left us his handiwork, but not himself; at the very beginning we have an unknown quantity in the racial equation. Neolithic man in Egypt was short, slight, dark, with a rather immature skull; local variations in the neolithic culture make it doubtful whether we are to expect the same physical type elsewhere. Palæolithic man seems not to have formed communities, and his relics are scattered; neolithic men collected in villages and surrounded them with walls for defence. They possessed a sure eye for location, for with them begins the first occupation of virtually every important city of the Near East. Ashur, Nineveh, Arbela, all show their traces.

Flint still continued to be the chief material for their implements, and now and then, especially at Arbela, we find the rare polished stones so familiar in western Europe. Peculiar to the Near East is the large use of obsidian, a natural glass of volcanic origin, which was especially adapted to small objects and made excellent arrow-heads. Their fireplaces dot the ruins. Pottery had been invented, and food might be

---

[1] Cf. especially Breasted, *Ancient Times.*
[2] Breasted, *Scientific Monthly,* 1919, 289 ff.

FIG. 7. PALM GARDEN WITH MUD BRICK WALL BY SIDE OF CANAL.

FIG. 8. AN AFFLUENT OF THE TIGRIS, THE DIYALA.

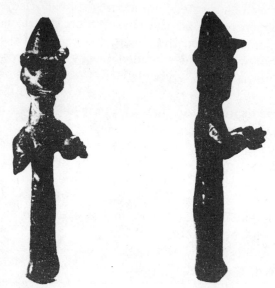

Fig. 9.   PREHISTORIC IDOL.   (Armenia.)

Fig. 10.   NEOLITHIC OBJECTS FROM ASIA MINOR.

boiled as well as roasted; liquids might be carried. No longer was man dependent on the chase or on the casual discovery of wild plants; the ox, the sheep, the goat had been domesticated; split wheat and six-sided barley were grown near the village. Skins were giving place to wool as material for clothing.

As agriculturists, the men of the neolithic age had reached a definite stage of psychical development. Their welfare centred about the planted field where the women did the work, and this factor became especially apparent in religion. Primitive animism still exerted its malign influence, with its millions of spirits, all evil and ready to pounce upon defenceless humanity. But there had been an advance. Woman, who made fertile the fields by her labour, was herself the best example of fertility; through the mysteries of her physical life might best be propitiated those good spirits who brought her labour to fruition. Thus there sprang up the worship of the earth mother, the goddess of fertility. To our more developed sensibilities, there was much in her worship that is most repulsive; we must not forget that it meant for the first time the recognition of the divine mystery of motherhood.

Meanwhile, in the hills northeast of the Persian Gulf, long straight lines as if drawn by a ruler, and in the hot valleys between, there had evolved a higher form of the neolithic civilisation. Its centre was at Susa, and the marvellously beautiful decorations of its painted pottery afford some idea of its high culture. Across the Persian Gulf was an outpost of this neolithic culture in the seashore city of Eridu.

The neolithic settlement at Eridu comes from the days when Babylonia was not yet in physical existence, when men were settling at the mouths of the Tigris and Euphrates and along the shores of the sea into which Babylonia was to be moulded. As the silt brought down by the mighty rivers began to push out into the Gulf, say some five thousand years before our era, mountaineers from the Susa region commenced their descent into the alluvium. In most respects Babylonia was then anything but an attractive land, a huge bottom with lagoons at the river mouths, with swamps along the lower course, with pools left here and there by the receding flood, with stratified soils ranging from gravel and sand to the finest silt. Its rivers had already reached grade, and there was the tendency to meander, to cut off corners, to turn into a new channel at the slightest obstacle in the course, to overflow the surrounding country with every flood.

But one thing might be said in favour of Babylonia, though that made surpassing appeal to ever-hungry primitive man. Its type soil was a light loam, washed down from the mountains where its two rivers found their source, and rich in the lime extracted from their limestones. The special plant foods, nitrogen, potash, phosphorus, were there in unusually large quantities. The rainfall, rarely over eight inches per annum, was enough to prove its fertility by the plants which sprang up after the pouring showers, but irrigation was absolutely necessary to bring in permanent cultivation. Water was furnished in abundance by the rivers, the Euphrates in particular, whose lazily moving chocolate-coloured stream may be induced with the greatest ease to spread its fertilising solution of silt over the surrounding fields. With irrigation, the great stretches of alkali land might be washed out, for the soil was porous and easily handled. Babylonia furnished an ideal outlet for mountaineers who had already outgrown the narrow confines of their cramped valleys.

Far as the eye can reach, the land is level, the sky-line flat. The one element of beauty is the palm, which forms a long fringe along the rivers and canals or hides the village with its shapeless blocks of mud huts and its gardens surrounded by mud walls. A palm-grove against the setting sun or reflected in the sluggish waters does make an appeal to the æsthetic sense of the traveller, but he soon tires of the eternal sameness of the fruit, whose cloying sweetness is so unhealthy in a torrid clime. Yet he should not forget that it does afford much energy in small bulk, and so is an ideal food for the poor. As time went on, the fields of barley, millet, and wheat produced great patches of green where before were sun-baked plains.

Babylonia then tends to monotony, to the development of a certain mediocrity of character. As a natural result, its conquerors, no matter how energetic, soon fall under its malign spell. All too soon they become true Babylonians, good business men, devoted to their every-day occupations, highly religious, unenterprising, and the prey of each successive invader.

As one's caravan marches northward from Babylonia, the blistering heat and mirage-laden air of the never-ending level give way to the rolling prairie. Only along the Tigris and Euphrates are narrow strips of bottom-land. Back a mile or so from the streams are low bluffs of loose conglomerate resting on sandstone, and back again from these on the low plateau between the rivers stretch the prairies. Although the soil is residual rather than alluvial, it is scarcely inferior to that of Babylonia for fertility. After the spring rains, the country blossoms like the rose. Day by day the colour changes with the flowers—one day red with huge tulips, another blue, another yellow, and the air at times is almost sickeningly odorous. In spite of all this beauty, the general effect is that of desolation, broken only by the solitary Arab camp or the equally solitary flock of sheep.

At first sight, one is persuaded that all this desolation is due to modern mismanagement, for such fertile soil must have been cultivated in antiquity. A few hours' march is sufficient to show this a delusion. Rarely, indeed, does the traveller behold any sign of earlier occupation, barely a dozen sites in all the long stretch of the middle Tigris, perhaps a few more along the middle Euphrates, while in the territory away from the streams they are practically non-existent. The reason is clear: like the alluvium, the prairie has a rainfall too scanty to bring the crops to maturity; unlike the alluvium, its surface lies just too high for canals to be drawn from the deep-sunk beds of the boundary rivers.

Signs of occupation are detected only along the few streams the prairie boasts. Those which take their start from the Armenian mountains that compose the northern rim succeed in passing south for a certain distance, and along their banks is a continuous line of ruin mounds. Only two, the Balih and the Habur, finally reach the Euphrates, and these two connect the north with the south by close-set villages. The others are absorbed into these two, are swallowed up by the hungry earth, or are evaporated into the dry air. Typical is the fate of the one great stream bed west of Ashur, the Tartara. In spring, the rains of the Singara mountains fill it so full that it cannot be forded, and it has cut a valley from five to twenty feet deep and into the underlying gypsum and limestone. By April, an Assyrian king found no water in its bed save as he dug wells to the water-level twenty-five feet below.

The remainder of the arid country, ever growing broader as we pass to the south, is still roamed as it was in earlier days by wandering and more than half-savage shepherds, when they are not forced to retreat before the inroads of the powerful tribes of north central Arabia, for the Mesopotamian prairie has always been the abode of the wandering Semitic nomad as was our own of the American Indian. Without adequate protection, even the small amount of cultivation practicable has not always been attempted, and the fertile prairie has remained desolate throughout the ages for want of the two essentials: water and a strong government.

Trade was well advanced in neolithic times, as the finds of objects from distant points amply show. Already the great trade route of the ancient Orient was being traversed. Starting from Egypt, it crossed the narrow strip of desert into the Philistine plain, turned inland through Hollow Syria, and in north Syria sent a branch northwest into Cilicia and by the Cilician Gates to the plateau of Asia Minor. The main route met the Euphrates and then divided. The shortest line was down the Euphrates, but much of it ran between desert and steppe, and it was always in danger from the raiding Arabs. Caravans generally preferred to march due east along the foot-hills of the northern rim to the Tigris; down-stream the river could be utilised by means of the kalak, the floating

Fig. 11. ASHUR, FIRST ASSYRIAN CAPITAL, FROM THE NORTH.

To the left is the Tigris, then **the ruins** of the Ashur temple, the temple tower, the north wall. In the middle distance **are** the city walls, in the far distance the Ialman Mountains.

Fig. 12. ARBELA, HOME OF THE PROPHETIC GODDESS ISHTAR.

Fig. 13. NINEVEH, THE LATE ASSYRIAN CAPITAL.

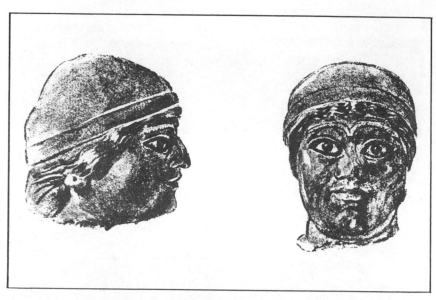

Fig. 14. HEAD OF NOBLE LADY FROM ASHUR. (Restored.)

Fig. 15. POTTERY AND OTHER SMALL OBJECTS FROM GRAVE.
(Early Ashur.)

platform built on inflated skins.   Its terribly swift current and hidden obstacles made it dangerous for all but the professional boatman, while passage up-stream against the current was a simple impossibility.   Merchants, therefore, regularly preferred the land.

In the northeast corner of the Fertile Crescent, where the route turned sharply to the south to avoid the mountains, lay the Assyrian Triangle, between the Tigris, the Upper Zab, and the hills.   The greater roll to the land indicated its nearness to the rough country which had run well into it spurs of conglomerate with serpentine veins.   Its soil was as good as that of the prairies, and a greater rainfall and numerous streams made its complete cultivation possible.   Even the olive might be grown, though not with complete success.   In the centre of the west side of the Triangle, on the east bank of the Tigris, lay its chief capital, Nineveh.

From Nineveh the road ran across the Triangle and over the Upper Zab to another important centre, Arbela, in the midst of a broad plain at the base of the eastern mountains.   Skirting these, it forded the majority of the Tigris affluents not far from where they leave the eastern foot-hills.   It was a route favoured by nature, which had planted at intervals of easy marches sites for villages rejoicing in running waters, but it was exposed to the raids of fierce mountaineers, and the southern half was the debatable land, always in dispute between the men of the alluvium and the men of Assyria.

A shorter branch ran direct from Nineveh down the west bank of the Tigris.   At the northern exit from Mount Abeh, the only hills of importance which it must cross, a tiny pocket of soil is commanded by a low bluff, solid sandstone with a capping of conglomerate, which rises eighty-five feet above the river.   Under its scarp runs the Tigris, always an impressive stream, and in the spring floods rising twenty feet in a few days until it forms a mile-wide sea.   Its swift current strikes the wall from the east, and the rapids thus formed force a backwater under the steep northern slope.

From the bluff one has a wide view in fine weather even to

the far-away snow-capped mountains beyond the Assyrian Triangle; the border ranges of Persia are in sight; just outside the walls one may look down into Babylonia. But the view is attractive only in its sweep. When cultivated, the bottom-lands are a thread of green with a still more narrow thread of tamarisk-bushes by the river; but the great plains to the east lose their green before the spring rains have more than ceased, the near-by hills are rough and barren, the prevailing colour is a dirty grayish brown. Winter is short but rather sharp; once in a generation the ground is covered with snow, the temperature sinks almost to zero, and remains a whole day below the freezing-point. Spring and autumn are also short, and for half the year summer reigns. In the shade the temperature may reach a hundred and fifteen. If the wind is still, the heat is unbearable; if it blows, the earth dissolves into dust and life becomes miserable. No longer does one hear the whirr of the red-legged partridge or the song of the lark on the neighbouring hills.

The men of Susa were not long content with the swampy, monotonous alluvium. Hillmen as they were, they felt the same attraction which thrills the present-day traveller when he leaves the baking alluvium for the grassy open prairies. So the neolithic inhabitants of Ashur, Nineveh, and Arbela were dispossessed or made subject, and the northwest corner of the Fertile Crescent became an integral part of the territory under the sway of the Susa culture.

For the culture found in Ashur is essentially the same as that of Babylonia or Elam, and everywhere the aristocracy have the same physical appearance. The men are of medium height and build, perhaps a trifle stocky. Their heads and faces are long, sometimes reaching an extreme, their fore-heads are retreating, their cheeks are full, their eyebrows are bowed, their eyes are large, their nose is generous and slightly hooked though broad at the base, their lips are thin, their mouth is small, their chin is double. Their neck is nearly absent, for the head is set almost directly on the broad shoulders; the lower body is well though not over developed.

These peculiarities are clearly exposed by the almost universal habit of shaving the face and head. Like the men are the women, far from slim, but not quite too robust to pass our extreme limit for beauty. In general, the women of the statues have a higher forehead than the men. The striking difference in representation must indicate a different convention of feminine beauty; there would have been few women among the invaders, and when their chiefs married the aristocratic ladies of the older race, it was their appearance which convention considered the norm of female beauty.

Treatment of the hair is a striking feature. The men almost without exception shaved the face and head completely. This has been considered proof that we have here a race with little bodily hair, but the earliest representations seem to be those where the hair is simply combed back from the forehead and knotted at the nape of the neck, and other examples show bald-headed men with all but the chin-beard shaved. Women parted their hair in the middle and combed it back with a rippling effect, catching it up in a net at the back of the neck. A bandeau was worn over the brow or a close cap covered the entire head. Ladies of the higher class wore a turban elaborately intertwined from a single long strip of cloth.

Before the gods in the earliest times, men appeared in sacrificial nudity. By the date when the Ashur statuettes were carved, the men wore in the god's presence a simple skirt, while the women added an upper garment which left the right shoulder and breast exposed. Sometimes this dress was plain, more commonly it consisted of rows of ruffles sewed upon a lining; in the case of the women, this was shaped under the right arm and had a binding. The fair sex was much decorated with bead necklaces, bracelets, and armlets, but their simpler husbands were adorned neither with such effeminate ornament nor with more martial weapons.

The men who introduced this civilisation spoke the Shumerian language, so called from Shumer, or south Babylonia. It belonged to the agglutinative group, and is roughly paralleled by such modern languages as Turkish, with which some scholars find connections in vocabulary and grammar. Before entering Babylonia, the Shumerians had invented a system of writing. Originally it was pictographic, and in the last Assyrian century scholars still preserved the memory of the older signs. Our earliest written records, from the middle of the fourth millennium, show that the meaning of these signs had been completely lost. A considerable literature had already sprung up in Babylonia; not only royal dedications and business documents, but more ambitious compositions, religious hymns and incantations, even legends of some length. Nothing of this sort has been discovered at Ashur.

That Shumerian was, however, actually the spoken language of the land is proved by such Shumerian names as that of E-harsaggal-kurkurra, Ashur's own temple in his native city, with the good Shumerian meaning of "House of the great exalted mountain of the lands," or such as E-mishmish and E-gashan-kalama, the shrines of the mother goddess at Nineveh and Arbela respectively. Doubtless, Assyria was connected as closely with Babylonia politically as it was culturally, but we know too little of its history in this period to say to which of the warring city-states of the alluvium it belonged. It is not certain whether we may attribute to this period our earliest inscription, the dedication of a certain Ititi in the temple of the mother goddess at Ashur.

Life in Ashur was of the simplest. The house of a typical citizen would consist of one or two large rooms and several of smaller extent, all of mud brick, and around a small court. Their floors would be likewise of adobe. Possibly a raised seat might extend along the wall; more likely the visitor would squat on the reed mats. Virtually all the furniture, if we may employ such a word, was of clay. Survivals of the neolithic red and black geometric painted pottery are found at first, but the typical pottery is adorned with designs added in relief or by geometric incisions, often made with a comb. Virtually every form is represented from the huge pithoi used to collect rain-water, the pitcher, the bowl, to the saucer. Of clay, too, was beaten out the fireplace or the charcoal brazier

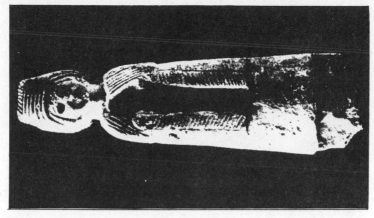

Fig. 18. GYPSUM STATUE OF A LADY. (Ashur.)

Fig. 17. COPPER STATUETTE OF A LADY. (Ashur.)

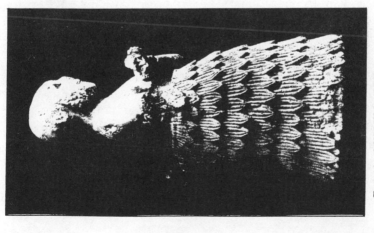

Fig. 16. GYPSUM STATUE OF A NOBLE. (Ashur.)

or the jar used as fireless cooker. Woman's chief adornment, beads, were of clay dipped in a glazing solution which made them almost glass in appearance.

Although the foundation of all life in Ashur was agricultural, we have but a single indication of it, a copper sickle, and that was quite appropriately dedicated in the temple

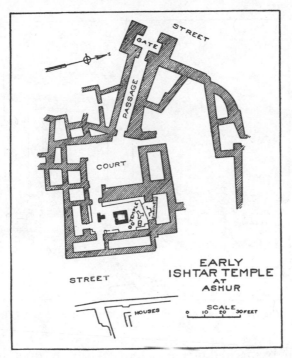

MAP 1. THE ISHTAR TEMPLE AT ASHUR.

of the goddess of fertility. It is no mere accident that it is her temple which is the one building that is preserved from such early times, that it is her cult which is the best-known fact of the period.

When a citizen would worship his goddess, he must dress accordingly. Ceremonial nudity had given place to a skirt for men, and women added the upper garment which left one shoulder and breast exposed. The worshipper took his goat or sheep in his left arm, raised his right in adoration, and was conducted by priests clad in the robes of minor divinities. From the street he passed through the open gateway with its guards lounging upon the clay benches of the guard-room, marched down a long narrow passage, and across the courtyard saw the plain adobe front of the temple, with its

Fig. 19. SHRINE OF ISHTAR TEMPLE AT ASHUR (EARLY PERIOD).

flat roof of beams and pressed clay. Within its door, he turned to his left and looked down the room to the shrine at the far end. On a low bank around the wall stood or sat statuettes of the worshippers, but no inscription gave their names. Directly before him was a square altar of clay with hollowed top on which his animal was sacrificed and a smaller square pan of terra-cotta to catch the blood. Beyond was a large jar to catch the rain-water, and smaller vessels with which to dip it.

An attendant next took from the side-wall one of several three-foot models of houses. Strange to say, the houses repre-

Fig. 20. EARLIEST TEMPLE OF THE MOTHER GODDESS AT ASHUR.

sented were of wood; clearly these are the houses in which
the Shumerians lived before they left the mountains. The
structures are two-storied, a front and a back room on the
first floor, one room opening out on the flat roof for the upper.
Windows are high and narrow, but above them is a second tier
of smaller openings, triangular or arched. Sashes surround

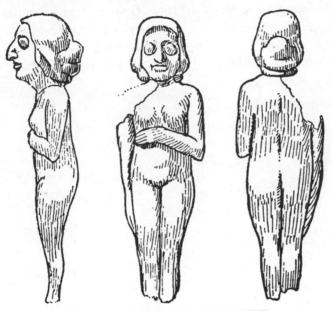

FIG. 21. IVORY FIGURE FROM ASHUR.

each window, and studding-beams on the outside mark the
separation of the rooms. All these are pitted by dots. At
the top of the houses are snakes, lions, or doves, the creatures
sacred to the mother goddess. On these the worshipper set
his offerings: on the topmost story the deity's portion of the
victim, placed on flat round cakes, on the lower a tall holder
in which were flowers or branches with fruit upon which the
worshipper poured out water in sympathetic magic, with the
hope that thus the deity would grant the fruit-producing rains.

Still farther to the front was a T-shaped bank of clay, in
whose corners were large jars, and a saucer filled with beads

was near by.　Here, too, were other stands for incense, or for other plants.

In a niche at the end of the room, perhaps closed by a veil or some such mat of woven reeds as was actually found not far off, and elevated half a man's height above the floor, was the image of the goddess.　We may guess her appearance only from the extraordinarily crude clay images which the priests sold for a trifle to the faithful.　Generally she is naked and her maternal features are accentuated, her hands hold her breasts, and she is standing.　Occasionally she is seated; more rarely she is clothed.　The more gorgeous accessories are missing.

CHAPTER III

THE WINNING OF THE SOWN

LIFE in Ashur, to judge from the absence of warlike finds, was peaceful. Suddenly the city was overwhelmed. Palace and temple alike were plundered, the statues were shattered, the buildings were committed to the flames, the settlement was covered with a deep layer of ashes and half-burnt débris. A similar catastrophe overwhelmed Shuruppak, the oldest city in Babylonia. The Shumerian civilisation had come to an end.

No other explanation seems possible; we must connect this with the inroad of the Semitic barbarians. Ashur was indeed resettled, but the scanty traces of the walls at the temple of the mother goddess, adobe on a base of small stones, the miserable character of the few objects scattered through this stratum, indicate a period of deepest decadence. Later tradition related that the first city wall had been erected by a certain Kikia, whose name has been thought Asianic; possibly the small towers with rough stone base and small burnt bricks for the superstructure may be ascribed to him, for they were erected before the foundation of the Ashur temple. Possible also is the attribution to the end of this period of the construction of the first temple to Ashur by another man whose name sounds Asianic, Ushpia, for above the tower ruins are a few adobe fragments.

Gradually the Semites learned their lesson from the Shumerians they had subdued. For the open tribal warfare, they substituted the close, heavy-armed phalanx of their predecessors. The loose tribal organisation where the chief had little power passed rapidly through the city-state stage into the loosely compacted empire. In the Shumerian mind the real ruler of his city-state was its chief god, and the king was merely his vicegerent on earth; the more practical Semite

21

called himself a god, and thus brought into his own person the prestige which the Shumerian had shared with his deity. By the Shumerian theory, title to the land was vested in the god, and rent was paid instead of taxes; with the Semites we find our first examples of land held in fee simple.

Shumerian culture was taken over en bloc, Shumerian was still the language of the educated, royal inscriptions and business documents were in most cases written in it. Semitic Akkadian was fitted to the cuneiform signs; the fit was not a close one, for certain of the Semitic sounds had been unknown to the older language.

Greatest of all the adjustments which the Semite was called upon to make was that in the field of religion. Chief of the deities was the mother goddess from whom came the instinct of life, whether manifested in grain, in animal, or in man himself. Another goddess ruled the shadowy underworld. Below these goddesses and their less-important male counterparts were the evil spirits, kept from injury to weak man only through incantations, the property of the magicians and conjurers. This was their practical religion, tempered only by magic and the hope of the earth mother.

Practical as ever, the Semite admitted himself a stranger in a strange land. He admitted the necessity of conciliating the deities of his new home, especially those who were guardians of the soil from which he must now gain his livelihood. In Arabia he had possessed no regular priesthood, so he took over the magicians and the conjurers. He had no temple and he made himself at home in the squares of mud brick with their steeple-like temple towers, memorials of the days when Shumerian gods yet dwelt on mountain peaks. His ritual was taken bodily from the older cult, with its ceremonies of cleansing and purification. Shumerian became his sacred language, whose intricacies he learned by means of vocabulary and phrase-book; he was the first inventor of interlinear "trots"; his own religious compositions were modelled on those in the sacred tongue. In seeming, then, the cult was completely absorbed.

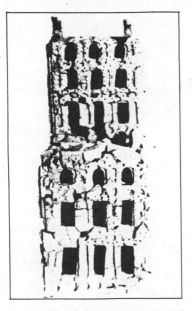

FIG. 22. CLAY MODEL OF HOUSE
USED IN ISHTAR CULT.
(Ashur.)

FIG. 23. MODEL OF CHARIOT. (Ashur.)

FIG. 24. METAL MOULD. (Ashur.)

Figs 25–28. CLAY MODELS OF ISHTAR USED IN THE CULT. (Ashur.)

In the ultimate analysis, things were, after all, not quite the same. The mother goddess was doubtless needed to furnish fertility for the soil, but she was identified with the Semitic goddess Ishtar. Nergal, the Arab sun-god in his more maleficent aspect, descended to the land of the dead and forced the unwilling Eresh-kigal to be his wife, and a subordinate, as a good Semitic wife should be. Other deities in the same fashion gradually lost their predominant position or were identified with the desert gods, some manifestation of sun, moon, or elements. Their names were substituted for those used by the Shumerians, their functions became increasingly Semitic, a new hierarchy under the control of the king-god demoted the magicians and conjurers to a lower rank, the temples became adjuncts of the palaces. Shumerian began to drop out of general use and became a dead language, used only in the ritual.

What the Semites could accomplish was indicated by Sargon of Agade and his successors. For the space of a century, there was a perfect blaze of civilisation, when the first great Semitic dynasty of Asia forced the whole eastern half of the Fertile Crescent, from the Persian Gulf to the Mediterranean, to recognise one supreme ruler.[1]

Assyria was within the empire, but Assyrian culture lagged far behind. Nevertheless, this was the time when Assyrian character was being formed. When we turn from the Babylonian to the Assyrian records, we are at once conscious of a new atmosphere. We pass from the presence of mediocrities into a group made up of individuals. As individuals, they may be far from likable, but we never fail to realise that they actually lived and were vital forces in their world. Their literature may lack in breadth, it gains in vividness. The monotony of Babylonian art merges into the splendid Assyrian bas-reliefs with their feeling for nature. Although their home country was rougher and more diversified and the natural obstacles to union correspondingly greater, there first appeared here the beginnings of organised empire, where foreign

[1] For detailed history of early Babylonia. cf. *AJSL.*, XXXIII, 283 ff.

lands were not merely subdued but were reduced to the form of provinces, where deportation of captives resulted in an assimilation not so different from that resulting from the American "melting-pot." This, too, is contrary to what physical environment would lead us to expect. Earlier environment, conditions beyond our ken, must have played their part in forming the Assyrian people.

The low bluff at Ashur, in the hands of the right people, might become the strategic point on the most important route of the civilised world. Its situation was that of Rome in even stronger form, and the Semitic characteristics already matured in the desert were hammered into national features in this formative period. Open to easy attack on all sides, it was a position to be held only by constant warfare. If it was a post of danger, it was also a post of opportunity. The desert which came to be a terror to its citizens was a still greater terror to the merchants. A narrow bridge-head between Tigris and desert, armies thundered back and forth along the trace; toll-giving caravans of necessity, and still more often, must pass under its walls. Like Rome once more, it might block to its own advantage the march of caravans and armies, but only by constant preparedness for war. Through such necessity of being always on the alert, the natural warlikeness of the Semite was not lost, as so generally happened when the nomad became sedentary; rather it was heightened to an extreme which sometimes became unjustified delight in human suffering.

After an era of decline, Assyria again fell under the sway of Babylonia when Shumerian reaction was represented in the dynasty of Ur (2431–2361). Its greatest king, Dungi, reports the destruction of Urbillum or Arbela in 2409, and his son Bur Sin must again destroy it six years later. His mighty sukallu, Arad Nannar, power behind the throne, was governor of Urbillum,[1] among other cities. Ashur, too, was under Bur Sin's control, for he promoted a certain Zariku from the governorship of Susa to that of the Assyrian city. As gover-

[1] Cf. *AJSL.*, XXXV, 65 ff.

nor of Ashur, he built the temple of the "Palace Lady," the mother goddess, for the life of his master Bur Sin. The Babylonian records of Bur Sin are in Shumerian; curiously enough, the Ashur dedication is in Semitic.

A huge mound had now arisen from the ruins of the older temple structure, and on its summit was erected the new building of five rooms, isolated on every side. Again the walls were without stone foundations, and the ground plan of the chief hall was the same as that used five centuries before. From the now low-lying courtyard rose broad steps between jutting towers. Ashes from the sacrifices were used to fill up the court, and thus preserved for us precious relics.

For the first time we find in Zariku's inscription the city called Ashir, and before it is placed the sign of divinity. Images of Ashir, to use the earlier form of Ashur's name, have also been found in this stratum. He is here double-headed, each head with the turban and long beard. He is seated, and carries the sacred boomerang. But he is still the interloper; four well-built temples of the mother goddess had been constructed, and Ashur was still to have an adequate house.

Changes had taken place in the fashions. Long-bearded males with turbans were now as common as those with hair entirely shaved and bareheaded. Men ordinarily dressed in a long fringed robe which descended to the knees and left one shoulder uncovered; women differed only in that their garments reached the ankles. They were buried in covered vases, if children; if adults, in the earth direct. Warriors were accompanied to the after-world by models of their chariots and by their bronze-shod and bronze-pointed spears, by bronze battle-axes and knives.

Aside from the inscription of Zariku, our only writing occurs on the impressions of seals on the lumps of clay which closed the mouths of jars. Their design is the one common to the Ur period, the moon-god Nannar of Ur seated on his throne while a minor deity introduces the worshipper. One bears the name of Izi Dagan, governor of Mari on the middle Euphrates and servant of Bar Dagan. Now, strangely enough, a letter has been found in Babylonia which Iadiri, the son of Izi Dagan, wrote in company with six men of Hanat, the island town a little down the river, to the aklu official of Amurru: "In trust of those fugitives who have returned from Mari, they have destroyed the shrine of Marduk who loves you." [1]

Not long after, the west Semites of Mari put an end to the dynasty of Ur, and Ishbi-urra founded the dynasty of Nisin (2361); perhaps Ashur was included at first in their kingdom. A rival dynasty secured north Babylonia in 2225, and Sumu-abu raised Babylon from obscurity. During the wars of the period, Ashur appears to have become independent. Very appropriately, Puzur Ashir I heads the list, for in his name is found the name of Ashur in its earlier form. His son Shalim-ahum wrote an inscription, and his son in turn, Ilu-shuma, made an unsuccessful foray into Babylonia; as his opponent was Sumu-abu of Babylon, we may date Ilu-shuma not far from 2225.

Ilu-shuma is better known for his rebuilding of the temple of the mother goddess, Ishtar the Assyrian, as she was now regularly called. The foundations seem to have been laid with stone, and the main hall was more than a hundred feet long, three times that of the earliest structure. Erishum is said to have been contemporary with Sumu-la-ilu (2211–2175), the next king of Babylon. He tells us how he restored the temple of Ashur, and his bricks still prove his work on the solid stone walls, pavement, and asphalted drains and canals. It was Erishum, too, who first built at the *mushlal*, the great buttress north of the Ashur temple, finding his base in the gray-green sandstone half-way down the hill below the conglomerate level. He was also the founder of the temple of Adad, the weather-god and the most characteristic west Semitic deity. Ikunum erected the temple of the underworld goddess Eresh-kigal and rebuilt the city wall, where his towers and stone bases, his adobe structure, and his mud mortar and layers of reeds still remain.

Sargon of Agade, the renowned hero, was imitated by the

[1] *CT.*, IV, 1; Ungnad, *OLZ.*, XVII, 343.

FIG. 29. THE EUPHRATES, A LAZILY MOVING, CHOCOLATE–COLOURED
STREAM IN THE ALLUVIUM.

FIG. 30. THE MIDDLE TIGRIS AT AMEDI.

FIG. 31. SNOW-CLAD SUMMIT OF ARGÆUS

FIG. 32. MOUNT ARGÆUS, THE HIGHEST MOUNTAIN OF ASIA MINOR.

Assyrian Sharrukin, both in his name and in his insistence that his subjects should place the sign of divinity before it. A tablet sealed with his seal has been found among the tablets from Cappadocia, and this raises the most difficult question of Assyrian relationship.

North from Mount Argæus, the highest summit of Asia Minor, extends a fertile plain. At its upper end lay the city of Ganish, from whose ruined mound have come the Cappadocian tablets so called. Already there was a colony of Semites at this spot by the beginning of the third millennium, for Sargon of Agade was invited to assist its citizens, since, as they confessed, they were not men of war. They were writing letters and making business agreements in the days of the Ur dynasty, for one of their tablets is sealed with the cylinder of a servant of Ibi-Sin, the last king of that family (2386–2361). They use Semitic, but it is a distinct dialect, with analogies to the Assyrian. Their names are sometimes Asianic, there is reference to their neighbours the Hittites, Hittite pictographs appear on their seals, some of the Semites bear west Semitic names. But the commonest single element is that of the god Ashir or Ashur as he is indifferently called; the proportion of names in the lists which have the Ashur element is amazing, and we even have Mannu-ki Ashur, "Who is like the god Ashur?" Some of these business men are called Shalim-ahum or Erishum, as the contemporary rulers at Ashur itself, or the later king Ashur-rabi is anticipated, in .. ..t a majority belong with Assyrian personal names. They used the eponym to date the year before the Assyrians themselves, and their months were those employed by the Assyrians before they were led to substitute the ones from Babylonia which ultimately conquered western Asia. ✓ Connection with Ashur and the Assyrians there must have been, whether as a trading colony from Ashur or whether they and the Assyrians had separated before the Assyrians reached Ashur.[1]

After Puzur Ashir II and Ahi Ashir, the city of Ashur fell

[1] For summary of the present situation as regards the question of the Cappadocian tablets, cf. G. Contenau, *Trente Tablettes Cappadociennes*, 1919.

under the sway of Rim Sin (2154–2093), the well-known ruler of Elam, who has gained an unearned notoriety by the common identification with the Arioch of Genesis. When Rim Sin fell before the lawgiver Hammurabi (2124–2081), a second Erishum was made governor in Ashur. In the preface to his famous code of laws, Hammurabi relates how he returned to that city its grace-giving lamassu; this is the term applied to the human-headed bulls which guarded the palace gates, and would seem to connect Ashur with the bull-worship. He likewise informs us that he made the face of Ishtar to shine in E-mishmish of Nineveh.

Under the reign of Hammurabi's incapable son, Samsu-iluna, south Babylonia was lost to the so-called Second Dynasty of Babylon, which henceforth, weak as it was, was accepted as the chief power of the alluvium. The empire built up by Hammurabi rapidly disintegrated in the incapable hands of his descendants, Ashur slipped away, but later tradition left the period a blank so far as names of rulers were concerned.

In 1926 the first dynasty of Babylon glimmered out, and Marduk, chief god of Babylon, and his consort Sarpanitum went into captivity to Hanat, on the middle Euphrates. Shamshi Adad I seems to have been the man who brought the end. He calls himself "King of the Universe," an old title formerly connected with the extreme north of Babylonia, and what is the territory to which he wishes it to be specifically applied is made clear by his next claim, "who devotes his energies to the land between the Tigris and the Euphrates." He received tribute from the kings of the Tukrish and from the king of the upper land, and he set up a memorial tablet in the city of Laban by the shore of the great sea. A ruler who controlled the Fertile Crescent from Babylon to the Lebanon and the Mediterranean enjoyed a mighty empire, but it was not Assyrian. His father, Igurkapkapu, is not counted in the Assyrian lists. and he himself does not take his royal title from Ashur. A mighty empire of which we have only glimpses elsewhere is indicated.

In these days of the high cost of living, it is consoling to learn that it was a problem nearly four thousand years ago. The incorporation of Ashur in a larger empire, the increased civilisation, the consequent rise in the scale of living, were all producing rising prices.   To meet the outcry against profiteering, Shamshi Adad promulgated a decree by which he announced the standard prices which were to obtain in his domain.   It is of interest to compare them with the tariff decreed at almost the same time by Sin-gashid, one of the independent princes who had arisen in south Babylonia.   In Uruk the shekel buys three measures of wheat; in Assyria but two are given.   This is as we should expect, for Babylonia was the granary of the world, and the territory around Ashur could not for a moment compare with it in fertility.   In the same manner, we are not surprised to find that in Uruk the shekel will purchase thirty measures of oil, in Ashur only twelve.   On the other hand, we should suppose that the city which had at its very doors steppes across which roved vast flocks of sheep would furnish cheaper wool than Babylonia, and again we are not disappointed, for twenty-five pounds of wool cost no more at Ashur than twelve at Uruk.

Ashur owed its beginnings as a great city to Shamshi Adad. The great wall was fortified and its base was now of gypsum blocks, though the upper portion was still of mud brick, rough and uncleansed of impurities.   Instead of mud mortar, "earth of Ubase," rock asphalt from one of the springs a day's journey north of Ashur, was laid cold; it gives one a shock to realise that this spring is one of the indications of petroleum which has caused the Mosul oil-fields to be in dispute between Turks and British.   Canals of unhewn limestone and gypsum drained the walls.   To him are also to be ascribed the first ramparts along the Tigris, with stone facing and broad bastions instead of towers, which for the first time brought the enlarged city within the fortifications.

For the first time, likewise, Ashur owned a worthy abode. The structure, adobe upon a stone foundation, formed a parallelogram, something over a hundred yards in length by about half that width, and surrounded a central court with its sacred well, and extended as far into the northeast point as possible. On three sides were rows of long, narrow rooms, on the fourth was the temple proper, a long, rather narrow forehall, a smaller shrine, and four little storerooms behind. To northwest and southeast were openings through which traffic might pass. Many additions were made in later times, but the original core was never changed in ground plan. Southwest of the temple was the temple tower, a solid mass of brickwork laid on the native rock, two hundred feet on the side and at least a hundred and fifty feet high. The monotony of the façade was broken only by vertical lines. Farther west was a new palace, and, since he worshipped the sun-god Shamash in his name, a temple for Shamash and Sin, divinities of the sun and moon.

The great Shamshi Adad was followed by Ishme Dagan, by a man whose name ends in Ashshat, and by Rimush. Another group is headed by Adasi and his son Bel-ibni, to whom Esarhaddon pointed with pride as ancestors. He calls Adasi "the founder of the kingdom of Assyria," which can only mean that he freed Ashur from subjection to the kingdom on the Euphrates. The remainder of this group, Shabai, Sharma Adad I, Gizil Sin, Zimzai, Lullai, have unusual names; one edition of the ruler list omits the whole group and thus indicates a doubt as to their legitimacy.

These kings fill the last half of the nineteenth century and the first half of the eighteenth. They are names and nothing more, and they are characteristic of the period throughout the Near East. In Babylonia, the so-called Second Dynasty was recognised as holding the hegemony, but its power was confined to the southern half, and even here such rulers as Sin-gashid of Uruk challenged its rights to the land. In the north there was anarchy, closed at last by the sack of Babylon by Gandash, the Kashshite (1745).

Elam had seen great changes. The original Shumerians had been supplanted as a ruling race by new hordes from the north and east, and with them appears on the historical stage a new and little recognised group, the Caucasian. So called because to-day their only representatives have found a last refuge in the Caucasus mountains, in antiquity there were notable peoples who spoke these tongues. If we may judge from their names and from a vocabulary of Kashshite words which the Babylonian scholars compiled, they were Caucasian. To the south were the tribes we specifically call Elamite. Traces of their pecular language are found as early as the days of Naram Sin of Agade, with whom an unknown ruler struck a treaty; by this time they were independent and writing their own records, and their successors were to be the last serious enemies of Assyria.

North of Assyria the tribes who were to form the later Haldian empire were settling in the rough hills of Armenia. Caucasian seems also the native language of Mitanni, though the aristocracy bear Iranian names. The original Hittites in Asia Minor had been Caucasian in speech, though by this time an incoming Indo-European aristocracy had profoundly modified the Hittite vocabulary, though hardly the syntax. The two most enigmatic languages of Europe, Etruscan and Basque, may be found to belong to this group.

A third dynasty of Babylon had been founded by these Kashshites, whose earlier kings placed "King of the Kashshites" first in their titularies. In Egypt, the glorious twelfth dynasty had closed a generation earlier (1788), and only local princelings contended with each other in never-ending struggles.

During this period of utter darkness, there appear the Hyksos; if there is still much obscurity about their race, we may at least assert that they were west Semites and that their chief centre of power was north Syria. A statue of their greatest king, Khian, has been found in north Babylonia, an alabaster with his name in Cnossus of Crete.

About the time that the third dynasty begins in Babylonia, a new dynasty commences in Ashur. The names of the rulers are Pan Ninua, Sharma Adad II, Erishum III, Shamshi Adad II, Ishme Dagan II, Shamshi Adad III, an unknown, Puzur Ashir III, Enlil-nasir I, Nur-ili, Ishme Dagan III.

Again we have names and nothing more, but the names are at least west Semitic, with their frequent invocation of the chief gods, Adad and Dagan. Two Shamshi Adads and two Ishme Dagans can only be named in imitation of the mighty Shamshi Adad and his son. The connection with the Euphrates settlements was probably renewed, and perhaps the empire did not pause here. It is tempting to identify this empire with that of the Hyksos.[1]

[1] For early Assyria, cf. *AJSL.*, XXXVI, 120 ff.; XXXVIII, 225 ff. The Ashur excavations publisbed in preliminary form *Mittheilungen der deutschen Orient-Gesellschaft;* of the final publication, only *Der Anu-Adad Tempel, Die Festungswerke, Die Stelenreihen, Die archaischen Ischtar-Tempel,* all by W. Andrae, have thus far appeared; the inscriptions are given in the *Keilschrifttexte aus Assur* in various series edited by L. Messerschmidt, O. Schroeder, and E. Ebeling; for the king lists, cf. E. Weidner, *Die Könige von Assyrien.*

CHAPTER IV

THE BALANCE OF POWER

AFTER such obscurity, we are blinded by the sudden step into the full light of history. Without warning, the hitherto politically isolated states of the Near East come into close, even intimate, relations, which are witnessed to by full Egyptian annals, by a diplomatic history from Assyria, and by the archives of the Egyptian and Hittite chancelleries. Through these, we are able to work out the intricacies of a veritable balance of power.[1]

Beyond a doubt, the colossus of this world was Egypt. In the old days she had been far from militaristic, content to send an occasional band of soldiers to mine turquoises or copper in the Sinaitic peninsula, or to plunder the tribes of the upper Nile of their scanty hoard of gold. The inroad of the Hyksos had changed all this. They had conquered the Nile valley and had insulted all the oldest and most cherished convictions of its inhabitants. So severe was the effort to expel the Hyksos that the energy generated was sufficient to carry the Egyptians without pause to the Euphrates and to make Egyptian influence dominant throughout the civilised world. Syria and Palestine were definitely within her empire, and obeyed her orders implicitly; the states beyond retained a precarious independence, and sought to postpone the day of reckoning with gifts.[2]

Babylonia was much fallen from her former estate. There could be no denial that she was still the second great power, but at what a distance! Her territory was strictly limited to the alluvium, or, at best, to the few square miles of debatable country to the north, her prestige had suffered under the weak

[1] Cf. *Near East Problems in the Second Pre-Christian Millennium, Jour. Egypt. Arch.*, VIII, 223 ff.

[2] Cf. Breasted, *History of Egypt*, 211 ff.

Kashshites, her young kings had been reduced to begging gold from the Pharaoh, and to seeking marriage with Egyptian princesses, even if they were not quite genuine.[1]

Out of the north, a new competitor had suddenly appeared full grown. Archæology informs us that from the most remote times there had been a branch of the neolithic civilisation in Asia Minor. In the twenty-eighth century before Christ, there was a settlement of Semitic merchants in Cappadocia who invoked the aid of the elder Sargon. The colony was still near the foot of Mount Argæus four hundred years later during the Ur dynasty. There is no hint of war in their writings, which consist of business documents and business letters. They left a highly important legacy, for through their agency cuneiform writing was introduced into Asia Minor and became the common system of the next period.

Without more preliminary preparation, the year 1500 finds a great empire in Asia Minor. Its capital was in the north-central part of the peninsula and was known to foreigners as Hatte, to the natives as Hattushash. As so often in the ancient world, capital and folk had the same name, whence came the Biblical Hittites, the term we employ to-day for this race. Their capital, with its mighty temples and palaces, its sculptures, and rock-cut pictographs, its huge wall sprawling down the sloping hill on which the city was perched, has recently been excavated, and its hoard of tablets is now in process of publication. Many are in the diplomatic language of the age, in Babylonian, and are now available to the historian.[2] The larger number are in the cuneiform character but in the language of the land. Thanks to the vocabularies prepared to assist the scribes in the mastery of the foreign Babylonian and Shumerian, thanks even more to the ideographic writing common to the various languages which used the cuneiform, the general sense of the annals can already be made out.[3]

[1] For Babylonia under the third and fourth dynasties, cf. *AJSL.*, XXXVI, 120 ff.

[2] *Keilschrifttexte aus Boghazköi;* Luckenbill, *AJSL.*, XXXVII, 161 ff.

[3] F. Hrozny, *Hethitische Keilschrifttexte aus Boghazköi,* 1919

The language of the higher classes shows extraordinary similarities to the Indo-European languages, and especially to the Latin, combined with other elements which seem equally non-Indo-European. Five other languages, of the most diverse character, are represented in the archives; while the philologists are puzzling over their interpretation, it is futile for the historian to attempt to assign them to a definite portion of the empire. Finally, we have the still undeciphered pictographs on the rocks.[1]

Judged by their portraits, the Hittites were a very mixed people. Some appear decidedly Mongolian, with slant eyes, snub noses, and sloping foreheads, and wearing a veritable pigtail; others may be those of the men who introduced the Indo-European language.

About the year 1500 the first known king of the Hittites, the father of Hattushilish I, conquered a whole list of towns in Cappadocia, the most important of which was Tyana, to be famous as the home of the anti-Christ Apollonius. The third of these kings, Murshilish I, claims the capture of Aleppo, which has always been the most important city in north Syria when oriental influences have been in the ascendant. He does not mention it, but the capture of Aleppo brought him into contact with Egypt, and the intricate diplomacy of the balance of power begins.[2]

Ahmose (1580–1557) had reached central Syria and the Phœnicians, Amenhotep I raided all Syria, Thutmose I was at Niy and hunted elephants in Naharina within the Euphrates bend. Thus the Egyptians might set up a claim for all Syria. Queen Hatshepsut ruled less firmly, and when Thutmose III began his first Syrian expedition in 1479, even Sharuhen on the extreme southern boundary was in revolt, though the decisive battle with the king of Kadesh was fought at Megiddo. The next year, 1478, we have Thutmose listing the "tribute" of the "Chief of Ashur," lapis lazuli, vessels of coloured stone, horses, wagons, valuable woods.

[1] Olmstead-Charles-Wrench, *Hittite Inscriptions*.
[2] Forrer, *MDOG.*, LXI, 20, now places this group in the twentieth century.

The Egyptian pompously speaks of "tribute"; to understand what it really meant, we must turn to Assyrian history again. We reach firm ground in the middle of the sixteenth century with Ashir-nirari I, son of Ishme Dagan III, who gave the capital a new wall, while palaces and temples to Sin, Shamash, and Enlil testify to a certain prosperity. Puzur Ashir IV continued the work on the *mushlal* wall and built a new one to surround the "New City," the suburb to the south. We have the first report of formal treaty relations with Babylonia, for he and Burna Buriash I "swore an oath and established their boundary in friendly agreement." The successor of Enlil-nasir II, Ashur-rabi I, may be dated about 1490–1470, and is probably our desired "Chief of Ashur," but he is quite an independent king, and he would have been bitterly resentful had he known that Thutmose had been mean enough to speak of his "tribute." He desired aid against Babylon and protection against Mitanni; Egypt would welcome an enemy in the rear of Mitanni, who might even avail against the Hittites.

Thutmose did not consider it wise to attack Naharina, the Mitannian country, until 1469, by which time it might be assumed that Assyria had seriously weakened her rival. The same year he claims to have received the "tribute" of Babylon and the Hittites, but he hesitates to give the names of the kings in question. So far from the Hittite admitting his tribute to Egypt, Murshilish actually claims the conquest of Aleppo, and, not to be outdone by his rival, he goes him one better by claiming a similar capture of Babylon with much booty! Conquest of Mitanni by Egypt was impossible if Aleppo was in Hittite hands, while Hittite and Egyptian claims over Babylon were equally absurd. Rarely can we catch two rivals in such a beautiful series of lies.

Thutmose made an expedition against Naharina-Mitanni in 1467; the "chief" of the great Hittites is mentioned in 1461; in 1460 he again fought with Naharina. The scene of the exploits of the hero Amenemhab was near Aleppo and Carchemish. By this time, one of his officials, Hantishilish, had murdered Murshilish and had married his daughter. Not content with advancing his frontier into the anti-Taurus region, where he took Arabissus and Togormah, on the road to the Euphrates, he captured Carchemish, which Thutmose had just claimed for himself.

Conquest of Carchemish gave the Hittites a bridge-head on the Euphrates. Situated at the upper end of a fertile flood-plain, its chief importance lay in its control of the most direct road across the river from Assyria to Syria and the empires beyond. Its peaceful population in neolithic times lived without walls; their scanty wealth of hand-made pots attracted no enemy; no wall would include their barley-fields. Their dead found safety under the house wherein they had lived, doubled up in jars.

Copper was just being introduced when a new race arrived; that they were warriors is shown by the prompt fortification of the mound which had gradually arisen by the riverside from the débris of their predecessors. Their pottery was now made on the wheel, but this advance in technic was countered by the slight use of coloured decoration. Their dead were interred in stone-lined coffins, the body was extended at full length, there was store of implements and weapons for the life to come.

Advantageously placed at the Euphrates crossing, the city grew apace, and the time came when it had covered so much ground that a new wall was demanded. Along the river, it was constructed of mud brick laid on stone foundations; the greater part of the land defences consisted of a simple rampart of earth which was led arbitrarily to include certain important buildings and paid no attention to the topography. It was this city which fell into the hands of the Hittites.[1]

The accession of Amenhotep II found all central Syria in full revolt, which can only mean that the cities had gone over to the Hittites. Again the defeat of Naharina is proclaimed, and for the first time we have direct mention of Mitanni. Without doubt, the tribute claimed from Mitanni marks the

[1] Woolley, *Carchemish*, 38 ff.

alliance of the two countries, for between them Hittite territory intervened.

At the height of its power, Mitanni included almost all the
grain-growing territory within the great bend of the Euphrates,
and it had begun the annexation of a few square miles beyond
that stream. Harran, reputed home of the Hebrew patriarch
Abraham, would appear to have been the chief city, and its
nobility went by the name of Harri, in whom some have professed to see the first Aryans, or Mariani, connected by others
with the Sanscrit Marya. Some of the names of its chief
personages do seem Iranian, but the specimens of the language
preserved in the letters connect it rather with Caucasian.

As a result of his alliance with Egypt, the Mitannian king
Saushshatar invaded Assyria, and "by his might and power"
took the palace doors of silver and gold and set them up in his
palace at Washshukkani. The Assyrian king can hardly
have been Ashir-nirari II; more probably it was Ashir-bel-
nisheshu, or his brother Ashir-rim-nisheshu, who made a
friendly agreement with the Babylonian Kara Indash I. The
Hittite rulers of this period were Huzziash, the result of another palace revolution, and Telibunush, the author of the
inscription which has told us all that has gone before. His
own exploits were in the later Isauria.

Thutmose IV (1420–1411) began the series of marriages with
Mitannian princesses which were to show that that country
was definitely allied with Egypt. This was with the daughter
of Artatama, who had just succeeded his father Saushshatar,
and the letter in which it is mentioned indicates that it came
after a series of peaceful negotiations; Thutmose, however,
claims that he won spoil on his first campaign against Naharina!
One can only wonder what his new-made bride thought of such
a compliment! He also established "true brotherhood" with
a king of Babylonia, perhaps Kara Indash I (1420–1408).

Through the Mitannian marriage, Amenhotep III (1411–
1375) was the grandson of Artatama of Mitanni, and so was
half Asiatic himself. It was therefore natural that he should
be on good terms with his uncle, Shutarna of Mitanni, and that

in true Asiatic fashion he should receive his cousin Giluhipa in marriage (1401). Shutarna died shortly after this, and was succeeded by Tushratta, whose daughter Taduhipa became the wife of the coming Amenhotep IV. Amenhotep III was also on good terms with Ashur-nadin-ahe (1410–1390) of Assyria, and sent him a subvention of gold, but this did not prevent his cousin Tushratta from filling his palace with gifts brought as "tribute" by "the Assyrian." Nineveh was ruled by his sukallu Nabu-li, and in his insolence he went so far as to exile Ishtar from her beloved city that she might visit with her healing his mighty cousin. As for Ashur himself, he was accorded a subordinate position among the gods of Mitanni.

With Babylonia begging for gold, with Assyria receiving a subvention and under the control of his cousin of Mitanni, with Syria his in greater part, with the king of Alashia or Cyprus entreating him not to ally himself with the Hittites, the position of Amenhotep might seem secure.

An example illustrates the untruth of this supposition. Nuhashshe in north Syria pretended to be Egyptian, but was in reality independent under its king, Sharrupsha; Tushratta ignored the claims of his cousin and quietly made the attempt to bring it over to Mitanni. Sharrupsha hurried off a messenger to Shuppiluliuma, saying: "The servant of the Hittite king am I, save me." Shuppiluliuma, who had recently succeeded his father, Hattushilish II, hurried off troops and Tushratta was driven away, all Mitannian territory west of the Euphrates was quickly overrun, the Euphrates was crossed. Tushratta led out his army but did not dare to attack the invader, who recrossed to the right bank and took possession of Aleppo. Akit Teshub had raised a conspiracy against his brother Takuwa, the Egyptian nominee for king of Niy. Then the Hittite turned against Nuhashshe, and Sharrupsha escaped with his life, leaving his servant Takib-sharri to be appointed in his place.

Tushratta claimed the return of the Hittite king as a victory and sent a gift to his Egyptian relative from the spoil. The natives of Mitanni were less certain of the victory. When his son Artatama "waxed strong with his servants," he displaced his father. He remained content with the title "King of Harri," and handed over Mitanni to his son Shutarna, to the prejudice of another son of Tushratta named Mattiuaza. Shuppiluliuma expresses a righteous indignation over the manner in which outside aid was invoked. All Mitanni went to ruin, and the Assyrians and the men of Alshe divided it between them. The Mitannian possessions were wasted by being given to Assyria. The palace designed by Tushratta was wrecked by his grandson, and the treasures with which it had been filled were assigned to the Assyrian who had been the servant of his father and had brought him tribute. The doors of silver and gold which Saushshatar had plundered from Assyria were removed from his palace and returned to the Assyrians; in his meanness Shutarna returned them to Assyria. Alshe, the fertile triangle just south of the Armenian mountain rim, received gold and silver vessels. The houses of the Harri were ruined, and the nobles were deported to Assyria and to Alshe; when they attempted return, Shutarna crucified them. Akit Teshub fled with two hundred chariots and his Harri to Babylonia, but its king confiscated all their possessions and sought to kill the refugees.

Romance now further complicated the already tangled threads. Shutarna lifted up his hand to kill his brother Mattiuaza, but he tore himself out of his hand and escaped to cast himself at the feet of the Hittite "Sun." The youthful royal exile made romantic appeal to the heart of the king's daughter, who "looked upon Mitanni with favor" and persuaded her father to give her in marriage to the stranger. Another daughter of the "Sun" had been married to another royal exile, Biashshilim of Carchemish. Together, the two bridegrooms set forth to reclaim their heritage. Carchemish was quickly recovered; from this time on the Hittite pictographs were always employed in inscriptions, and the Hittite art was followed with such success that the later productions of Carchemish rival those from the capital of her former mistress.[1]

[1] Hogarth-Woolley, *Carchemish.*

From his friend's capital Mattiuaza sent to the men of
Irrite, just across his border: "Shutarna alienated the Harri
with the riches of Tushratta and made them of one mind."
The reply was less polite: "Why have you come? If you come
to fight, come on!" Despite additional troops sent by Shutarna, Irrite fell, and the men of Harran accepted Mattiuaza's
rule. The Assyrian also sent a messenger to implore peace.
With the delimitation of the boundary between the two bridegrooms, the political story ends.

The new wife of the Mitannian ruler had no intention that
her romance should fade so quickly. In highly practical
fashion, she caused her father to lay down the rules that should
govern the house of Mitanni. Ten women were permitted
in her husband's harem, but the daughter of Shuppiluliuma
was to be the only queen; only her children might succeed to
the throne; no woman should be her rival.

In all this long account "the Assyrian" frequently appears,
but his name is deliberately suppressed by Shuppiluliuma.
"The Assyrian" was Ashur-uballit, son of Eriba Adad, the
first of the men who created the Assyrian empire. A few
square miles about Ashur was its extent at his accession; at
its close Assyria had won recognition as one of the great powers.
By taking advantage of the troubles in Mitanni, he gained
his freedom and extended his territory. Ashur might no longer
be invoked among the gods of Mitanni. Ishtar of Nineveh
once more became an Assyrian, and her recovery was celebrated by the restoration of her temple. A governor of Nineveh appears by the side of the "governor of the land," the ruler
of Ashur. The independent state of Singara known to the
Egyptians disappeared, and the provinces of Isana and Nimit
Ishtar are found west of the Tigris. The wide-extending
Shubari represented a part of the spoils extorted from Mitanni;
the first line of mountains to the north and east of the Triangle, the region of Musri, followed.

Thus was added the third part of Assyria, the hill country,
deep, well-watered, fertile valleys, hidden away by snow-
capped ranges. The temperature in Ashur might rise to a

hundred and fifteen degrees; it was now possible to spend the summer in comfort in the mountain, and thus keep up the physical tone. ✓Quiet vacation rest was not for the Assyrian. He needed occupation, even in the summer, and there were ever more valleys beyond whose local "kings" had not yet paid tribute. So the summer campaign in the mountains northeast of the Triangle became a regular institution.

The letter by which Ashur-uballit replied to the coming of Egyptian ambassadors has been preserved in the Egyptian archives. He calls himself "King of Ashur, the Great King," and insists on full equality by addressing the Egyptian as brother. He tells Ikhnaton to his face that when his grandfather Ashur-nadin-ahe sent to Egypt, presumably in connection with Mitannian raids, they presented him in return with twenty talents of gold, and he delicately suggests the like for himself. Burna Buriash II of Babylon protested vigorously to the Egyptian court against the recognition accorded the Assyrians, his vassals, but his own predecessors had made many treaties of equality with their former subjects, and the recent loss of autonomy was to Mitanni and not to Babylon.

Ashur-uballit earned a sweet revenge on Burna Buriash by persuading his successor, Kara Indash II (1367–1355), to marry his own daughter and to agree upon a new set of boundary regulations. This was not the last of the matter, for the son of this union, Kadashman Harbe (1355–1344), was barely ten years of age when he began his rule, and the successes claimed for him, annihilation of the Aramæan Sute and the fortification of a site on the Elamite border, were in reality confessions of weakness. That the tribesmen could invade Babylonia at all is the probable reason why the Kashshites rose against the half Assyrian youth and put him out of the way. In his stead they chose Nazi Bugash, the "son of a nobody." This was the very quintessence of revenge that in his old age Ashur-uballit might settle the succession of the haughty power which in his youth had dared call him vassal. For the first, but far from the last, time Assyrian armies appeared in the alluvium and placed on the uncertain throne

FIG. 34. ASSYRIAN DICTIONARY.
(Yale Babylonian Collection.)

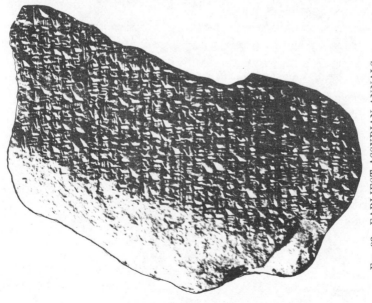

FIG. 33. EARLIEST ASSYRIAN ANNALS.
(Arik-den-ilu.) (Morgan Library.)

the infant son of Kadashman Harbe, Kurigalzu the Younger (1344–1321).

Rarely in this earlier period do we find a native Assyrian document which more than mentions a conquest, a wall, or a temple. A unique tablet comes from Marduk-nadin-ahe, the scribe of Ashur-uballit. Although his name is Babylonian and that of his father and grandfather as well, he is a true Assyrian, who can refer to "the houses of his fathers." He is our first example of a Babylonianised Assyrian, that type which was to become so common in later centuries. His residence was under the shadow of the Marduk temple, which dated back to the days when Ashur was a part of Babylonia and the god Ashur was Marduk's vassal. In his house was a well, a storeroom, and underground apartments such as to-day protect the wealthy and the foreigner from the unbearable summer's heat.

That he could see his descendants on the throne of Babylon argues a long rule for Ashur-uballit (1370–1340). When his own was occupied by his son Enlil-nirari (1340–1325), the nascent empire was forced to meet an attack by Kurigalzu. Encouraged by his capture of the Elamite Hurpa-tila, he demanded the northern kingdom through the combination in himself of both claims. The battle was contested on the Tigris; the Babylonian historian asserts that the enemy king was slain in a great defeat, the Assyrian that his master won the victory, destroyed the hostile camp, and caused the territory to be divided. A minor discovery in the Assyrian capital proves the latter true, a votive eye with a dedication to Enlil by Kurigalzu which formed part of the booty. To secure Babylon from expected attack, Kurigalzu built the "Wall" named after himself, which is to-day the most striking landmark in the neighbourhood of Baghdad, and is one of the two traditional rivals for the traditional "Tower of Babel."

Babylonian practice had been thus far followed in the preparation of the records intended for the edification of posterity. A few words indicating descent, a few as dedication to a god, a word as to the buildings, possibly at the very end a line or two mentioning the countries conquered, such was their simple form. Intercourse with other nations had taught them that no self-respecting king was without his annals. Our first example comes from the reign of Arik-den-ilu (1325–1310), and the very crudeness shows how new was the form. Lines divide the tablet into sections which represent five separate campaigns, but the account is barely more than a list of names, united by a few formulas.

The greater part of his advance was made at the expense of Mitanni. Her breakdown was permitting the entrance of Aramæans, Ahlame and Sute, into southern Mesopotamia; Assyria checked them and formed a small province in the Iauri region with Tabite as capital and the turtanu as governor. From the east of Mitanni, the Assyrians detached Halah, the later home of the "Lost Ten Tribes of Israel," and to the north Kutmuh was secured; both were added to the province of Nineveh. The Qute in the Armenian foot-hills were invaded, and seven thousand men were defeated on the Elamite frontier.

CHAPTER V

THE FIRST EMPIRE

A DECIDEDLY strenuous period of activity is opened by Adad-nirari I (1310–1280). Particularly noteworthy were his additions of territory to the northwest. The long reign of the Hittite Shuppiluliuma had been followed by those of his sons Arnuwandash I and Murshilish II. Aleppo with its king, Rimsharma, was bound anew by treaty. Kissuwadna, or Cilicia, was recovered from the Harri to the advantage of its king, Shuna Ashshura, whose name bore the same acknowledgment of the might of Ashur that we find in the Cappadocian tablets of a thousand years before.

The last act of Murshilish was a war with Seti I of Egypt (1313–1292). The conflict was not confined to these two combatants, for Nazi Maruttash (1321–1295) of Babylonia threw down the gage of battle to the Assyrians, presumably as a Hittite ally. The inevitable battle was contested at Kar Ishtar, and the camp and the priests of the Babylonians fell into their rivals' hands. By the boundary, drawn east and west through the battle-field to the junction of the Balih with the Euphrates, all claim to Mesopotamia was surrendered. Adad-nirari could assume the title "King of the Universe" which he so pointedly denies to his father.

Peace was shortly made between Seti and the new Hittite monarch, Muwattallish, but the truce was not of long duration, for under Ramses II (1292–1225) the war broke out with renewed violence. The new king of the Hittites wrote the new king of Babylon, Kadashman Turgu (1295–1278), that he had been forced to wage a defensive war against the Egyptians, and a sympathetic answer was returned, but no action was taken. Ramses might celebrate the battle of Kadesh (1288) in song and temple relief, but in his heart he recognised that he was fighting a losing battle and appealed to the Assyrian

45

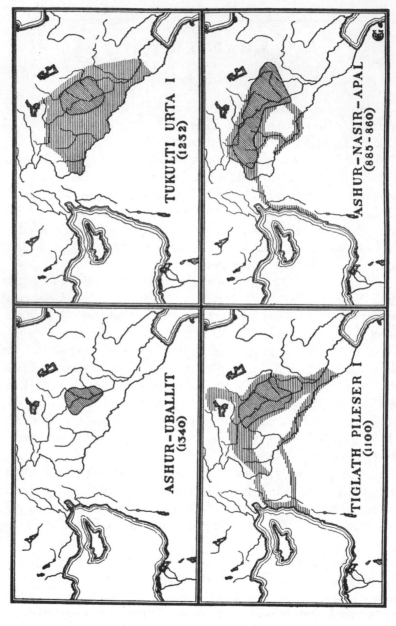

TUKULTI URTA I
(1252)

ASHUR–NASIR–APAL
(885 – 860)

ASHUR–UBALLIT
(1340)

TIGLATH PILESER I
(1100)

MAP 2. DEVELOPMENT OF THE ASSYRIAN EMPIRE (1340-860).

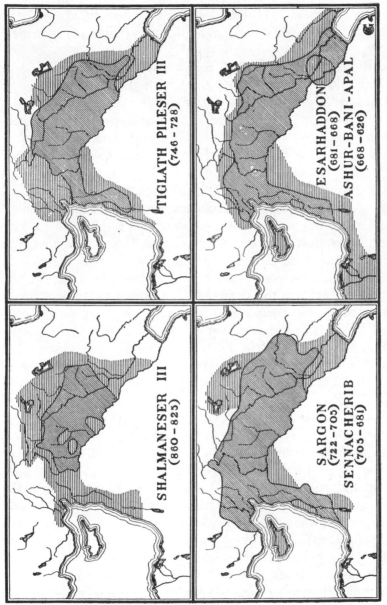

MAP 3. DEVELOPMENT OF THE ASSYRIAN EMPIRE (860-626).

TIGLATH PILESER III
(746 – 728)

SHALMANESER III
(860 – 825)

ESARHADDON
(681 – 668)
ASHUR-BANI-APAL
(668 – 626)

SARGON
(722 – 705)
SENNACHERIB
(705 – 681)

king. Adad-nirari replied by sending gifts and a promise of
aid; like Thutmose III, Ramses took a mean advantage of the
occasion and in his annals used the ugly name of "tribute"
(1282).

Did Adad-nirari learn of this verbal treachery? He was
of little aid to Egypt in her fight with the Hittites, but the
withdrawal of Hittite aid to Mitanni was a godsend to Assyria.
The writer of a letter in the Hittite archives tells his correspondent that in the days of Adad-nirari, Hani Galbat, that
is, Mitanni, was invaded and destroyed. The king himself
chronicles the capture of Shubari, of Kashiari, the rough country south of the west Tigris, of Harran, the most important
city in Mitanni, of Washshukkanni, once proud of the palace
doors of an Assyrian, of Carchemish on the Euphrates. Adad-
nirari's proudest title was "Founder of Cities"; he deserved
the magnificent bronze sword of state which bears his name.

His two predecessors had been too busy building up the
empire to build in the capital; Adad-nirari did both. Space
around the Ashur temple was becoming scarce, and the movement west along the northern slope began with his construction of the "Court of the Peoples" some distance beyond the
temple tower. A shrine to Marduk indicated that the wars
with Babylon were not to prevent the steady advance of Babylonianisation.

The whole circuit of the city walls was rebuilt. The great
terrace which protected the Ashur temple to the north was
pushed out to secure more space. Instead of the earlier clay
mortar, Adad-nirari sent to the bitumen springs a few miles
north and secured "earth of Ubase" to bind together the
cut stone. Baked bricks with asphalt were common, and
where adobe was used the bricks were larger, better cleansed,
and yellow rather than gray. Since its first erection by Puzur
Ashir IV, the wall of the southern suburb had twice needed
repair, at the hands of Ashir-bel-nisheshu and of Eriba Adad,
but by this time some parts were fallen and others weak, so that
they demanded renewal. The wall of the suburb was in still
worse condition on the river-bank. Mighty blocks from the

mountain were cast in as base, above was hewn stone and baked brick, but the spring floods have been so successful in their attack that not one stone survives. His retaining wall along the river side of the main city was continued without essential change by his successors, but again the river has been victorious, and we have only a short stretch to testify to the truth of his statement that he did make these walls of limestone, baked bricks, and asphalt, and that he prepared memorial tablets, each hidden in its little room.

Shalmaneser I (1280–1260) determined to follow his father's example by lopping off some more territory from the Hittite possessions. Unfortunately for him, just at this moment there came a change in affairs. The anti-Egyptian Muwattallish was put out of the way by his brother Hattushilish III. A son of Muwattallish, Urhi Teshub, fled to Ramses, who surrendered him as the price of a peace, to be confirmed by his marriage to the Hittite monarch's daughter (1272).

This peace was most unfortunate for Shalmaneser. When the Mitannian king began to suspect the next Assyrian objective, he sent his Hittite overlord a letter, telling how Hani Galbat had been destroyed by Adad-nirari. He complains that a king of Shupria has been invited by his lord as protection against the writer and has seized his throne, so that now the king of Shupria is destroying the land by oppression.

So when Shalmaneser had penetrated the difficult defiles into what was left of Mitanni land, he found its ruler supported by his Hittite master. This was more than Shalmaneser had bargained for, and when the Hittites seized the passes, the invaders began to suffer from lack of water. Shalmaneser admits that it was their thirst and the need of a camping-ground that caused his army so bravely to advance into the masses of the enemy troops; he claims, however, that he killed their soldiers to a countless number, waged war against his chief enemy at the point of the spear to the setting sun, reduced numerous cities to mounds and ruins. His sweeping victories from Taidi to Carchemish are verbal repetitions of his father's.

His accession year had been devoted to chastising the re-volted Uruadri, our first mention of the Urartu which was so to plague the Assyrians and, as Ararat, was to be known to Bible readers as the resting-place of the Ark. He raised his hands in prayer, mustered his armies, and climbed up against their mighty mountain fortresses; in three days the whole land was made submissive to the feet of Ashur; their men were brought down dead; for servitude and fear he chose them; tribute that was heavy for a mountain country was for all time imposed upon them. The strong mountain fortress of Arina had revolted, despising the god Ashur; over its site was sown stones, its dust was gathered and poured out at the gate of Ashur as witness for future days.

Before they had broken into open revolt, the Qute, whose numbers were as countless as the stars of heaven, had stirred up enmity against Assyria. Shalmaneser raised his hands to Ashur and the great gods in witness: "Faithfully they prom-ised their good faith." The camp was left behind, and with only the choicest of the chariots he rushed into battle. The bodies of the wide-spreading hosts were poured out like water from Uruadri to Kutmuh, remote regions and distant and inac-cessible plains. A wedge was driven into the former territory of the Hittites; to make its control more sure, Shalmaneser planted at Halsi Luha, in the triangle of fertile land north of Amedi, a colony which endured four centuries.

Further advance was prevented by the troubles which Hat-tushilish had stirred up on the southern boundary. The Hittite had been allied with Kadashman Turgu; as soon as he learned that a new king had ascended the throne in Baby-lonia, he sent a letter of condolence on the death of his "brother," and described the copious tears he had shed when he heard the sad news. He unfortunately added that if the nobles did not recognise the claim of Kadashman Enlil, the son of his old ally, he would follow up his messenger with an army. Innocent and even praiseworthy as this would seem at first glance, such action might well establish a precedent for Hittite interference. The Babylonians deeply resented it, and Itti Marduk-balatu, the prime minister, bluntly replied that Hattushilish was not addressing the Babylonians as brothers, rather as slaves was he making them subject.

Intercourse was renewed when Kadashman Enlil came of age, but the newly found brotherhood was soon endangered when information filtered in of an agreement between the Hittites and Egyptians. Kadashman Enlil inquired if it made any change in his relation to the contracting parties. The Hittite reply was ambiguous. The former enemies have indeed become brothers; with a common enemy they will fight, and with a common friend will they be at peace. Rebels or enemies who flee to each other's lands will be given up on demand.

Having thus gently but forcefully left the Babylonians outside the new entente, Hattushilish proceeds to calm down his friend. After all, there are certain contingencies through which the new alliance might be broken. For instance, if the extradition clause does not work, the kings will be angry with one another; if Ramses aids his enemy, there will be war. If Egypt has prevented the transmission of official letters from Babylonia to the Hittite land, then Kadashman Enlil should take action. Hattushilish is properly shocked by such a confession of weakness as that his messengers have been discontinued because of attacks by the Ahlame along the Euphrates. Such a word is not good, and by it the sovereignty of his brother suffers detraction.

Assyria is the most serious sinner. If its king detains a Babylonian ambassador in his land, that is an act of war, and surely Babylonia is not a conquered land. What king of Assyria is powerful enough to restrain his messengers? Kadashman Enlil is a mighty man of valor, a youthful wild bull. At last Hattushilish comes out plainly and begs his young brother to go and spoil the hostile land, kill his enemy, for the king who lays aside his weapons is sure to suffer in the end. Though the enemy land be three times or four as great as his own, let him march against it.

Such an attack against Assyria did actually take place.

After a brief reign (1278–1270), the greater part of it in his minority, Kadashman Enlil disappeared. Hattushilish had worked upon his youthful vanity to his destruction.

With all the booty collected in the wars, Assyrian building went on apace. The Ashur temple had been burned, and its ruins were still untouched. Shalmaneser respected the ground plan of Shamshi Adad I, but set up new stone foundations and basalt sockets for the gate-posts. The long sides of the temple were continued into a forecourt with surrounding rooms and a great gate with broad towers in front. Near by was a reservoir, with a capacity of eighty cubic yards. Shalmaneser occupied the addition as a palace, but since its walls were in alignment with the temple, later rulers handed it over to religious use. Had it been priest-ridden Babylonia, the palace would have been far from the temple; Assyrian kings were their own chief priests, and took up their abode under the shadow of the sacred edifice.

Nineveh, too, possessed a palace, and the Ishtar temple was restored. We hear for the first time of another city, destined to be an Assyrian capital, Kalhu, the Biblical Calah, a day's journey south of Nineveh, near the junction of the Tigris and the Upper Zab.

Connected with the new additions to Assyrian territory goes a change in the titulary. Characteristic of the preceding period was "governor of Bel and priest of Ashur." To this Shalmaneser added "the mighty king," which was to be henceforth a permanent attachment, and "King of All," a modification of the Babylonian "King of the Universe." The full form appears under Tukulti Urta I, "King of the Universe, King of Assyria, Mighty King, King of the Four World Regions."

His accession was greeted by the invasion of twenty-seven thousand Hittites from beyond the Euphrates crossing; they were thrown back into their own land, and Dudhaliash, successor of Hattushilish III, sent a peaceful letter to Tukulti Urta (1260–1232). His first full year he devoted to the north. Qute and its neighbours took his hands; the wealth of their mountains and their highlands yearly they brought to Ashur; a long list of lands, Qurhi, Kutmuh, and the wide-extending Shubari, were burned over. Highlands and valleys, impassable places, whose path no king had before known, in the power of his abounding strength he traversed. Four kings of Nairi land stood forth in mighty array to make battle and conflict, but the ravines and gullies of the mountains received their blood. In the course of these expeditions, he reached the shore of the Upper Sea, Lake Van, and no Assyrian king went farther; on his eastern border his wars led him across the Lower Zab and into the mountains.

The Euphrates settlements, Mari, Hana, and Rapiqu, next claimed his attention, and with them over thirty of the "lands" occupied by the nomad Ahlame. On the line of the Tigris he added Arrapha, a few years before an autonomous state in relation with Egypt. Thus both roads into Babylonia came under his control.

Babylonia had suffered a series of minorities, those of Kadashman Enlil (1278–1270), Kudur Enlil (1270–1261), Shagarakti Shuriash (1261–1248), and Kashtiliash III (1248–1240), four generations with an average of less than ten years each. Assyria had been more fortunate, for six generations had the normal average of twenty. Such a condition invited aggression. Without apparent excuse, Tukulti Urta invaded the lands of his southern neighbour. The boy Kashtiliash was brought in fetters to the presence of the lord Ashur, there to be sacrificed. His place was assigned to Enlil-nadin-shum, but when the pressure of Babylonian patriots became too strong to be resisted, even by an Assyrian nominee, and he revolted, Tukulti Urta returned to Babylon, levelled the city ramparts, and slaughtered the citizens. "The treasures of the temple Esagila and of Babylon profanely he brought forth, the great lord Marduk he removed from his abode, he carried him off to Assyria, governors he established in the land."

Tukulti Urta was the first Assyrian monarch to face the dilemma of effectively ruling a hostile country and at the same time respecting it as the motherland of his own culture. His first experiment, a vassal king, was a failure; his governor, Kadashman Harbe II, was considered an independent ruler by the patriots, though Tukulti Urta had no doubt in his own mind as to who was the true monarch. He claimed sovereignty over the Four World Regions, Kar Duniash, Shumer, and Akkad, and to these he added the rule of the cities of Sippar and Babylon. At the close, he calls himself king of Shubari, Qute, and Nairi. Between he lists two ancient lands, Dilmun and Meluhha; the former was an island in the Persian Gulf, noted for its pearls, where once the creation was localised; the other, in the Arabian peninsula, was the source of much-prized products to early rulers of Babylonia. Why he might claim these titles is unknown.

He was devoted to Ashur in his earlier days. The weakest portion of the fortifications was at the northwest where a saddle connected with the main ridge. With bronze axes he cut down to the water-level and constructed the first city moat. Only at the Gate of the Metal Worker was there a ramp, and this was protected by an outwork with arched postern gates so low that one must stoop to enter. A square of sloping rock was left before the gate as a trap for any enemy who might succeed in crossing the moat. Everywhere the walls were repaired and based on the solid rock.

For the double purpose of commanding this gate and of securing a free space farther west, a huge platform was erected, an irregular quadrangle some six hundred feet on the side, which filled almost the whole northwest corner of the city between the temple tower of Adad and the Gate of the Metal Worker. One angle extended out from the north cliff, and made unnecessary further walling. The name assigned it was "Palace of the Royalty of the Lands."

The temple of Ishtar the Assyrian was largely restored. Several of his foundation deposits have been laid bare. A huge block of lead, weighing some eight hundred pounds, on which was a building inscription, was covered with glass beads of various colours, sea-shells, semiprecious stones, and bits of lead, copper, and iron. A layer of reeds and clay mortar, and more beads, formed a bed for a tiny square each of silver and gold, and for somewhat larger plates in the precious metals with the foundation narrative. The same inscription appeared on the five-ton block of limestone and the second lump of lead which topped the whole.

All too soon he tired of his old capital and began to long for a city which should immortalise his name. To the north on the opposite shore of the river, the new capital grew up almost overnight. The fertile plain surrounding was irrigated by a new canal, around it rose massive city walls, within was a mighty palace, a new temple for Ashur, shrines for the other gods.

Tukulti Urta might indulge the hope that his Kar Tukulti Urta was "established forever"; the nobles whose memories centred about the older city could not be so easily reconciled. The hatred of the Babylonians was not lessened when they perceived the inability of their new master to protect them against foreign invasion. The first of a new line of Elamite kings, Kitin Hutrutash, had already entered the alluvium in the days of Enlil-nadin-shum and had carried off men from Nippur, Der, and Harsagkalama. No success had been won against them by the Assyrian nominee, and Adad-shum-iddina had found them at Nisin and had fought with them on the Tigris.

Kashshites and native Babylonians alike rallied to the support of the son of the last legitimate king, Adad-shum-nasir (1231–1201), and after seven years of rule Tukulti Urta was driven out of Babylonia. Failure abroad furnished the needful excuse for those at home to demand his deposition. Ashur-nadin-apal led the revolt against his father, Kar Tukulti Urta was besieged, and its founder perished by the sword. So sudden was the abandonment of the city that its excavators found in the ovens the pottery which the makers had failed to complete.[1]

Assyria had become a world-power under a series of able kings; Tukulti Urta was the last. His unworthy son did

[1] King, *Records of the Reign of Tukulti Ninib I*, 1904; Bachman, *MDOG.*, LIII, 41 ff.; Schroeder, *Keilschrifttexte aus Assur*, II, 60 f.

nothing to justify his parricide, save to make a peace with the Babylonians which acknowledged their overlordship and rectified the frontier in their favour. Ashur-nirari III (1213–1207) shared his lands with Nabu-daiani, and both received a letter from the Babylonian "Great King" in which he simply calls them "two kings of Assyria." Some one has repeatedly given them orders for grain and fish; this was without command from their lord. They are to inform the unknown that Adad-shum-nasir will bring ruin upon him, since what he has done is contrary to the orders of the gods.[1]

The very name of Enlil-kudur-usur, "O Enlil, protect the frontier," shows the extremity into which Assyria had so rapidly fallen; after five years of doubtful control (1207–1202), he, too, was assailed by Adad-shum-nasir and left dead on the field of battle. Equal lack of success characterised the first year of a usurper, Saggal-apal-ekur[2] (1202–1175), the son of Eriba Adad. He was besieged in his capital and was in dire danger; then the tide turned, the Assyrians won a battle in the vicinity of Ashur, and Adad-shum-nasir was compelled to return home in disgrace. For thirty years he had upheld the old traditions of Babylonian dominance over Assyria; his failure was followed by his death, and his son Meli Shipak took his place (1201–1186). Merodach Baladan I (1186–1173) claims the title "King of the Universe," which should mean another retreat of the Assyrian frontier.

Had the throne of Babylon been filled by a young and vigorous dynasty, the fate of Assyria might have been sealed. Fortunately for her future, this period of exhaustion was marked by even more serious weakness throughout the whole Near East Egypt was slowly decaying under the later Ramessidæ of the nineteenth dynasty, less and less able to hold their own at home. Arnuwandash II, son of Dudhaliash, still retained Aleppo and Carchemish within the Hittite sphere of interest, though Tukulti Urta had challenged their ownership. Ramses III reports that the " peoples of the sea" broke

[1] *H*. 924.
[2] Cf. Luckenbill, *AJSL.*, XXXIX, 63.

the back of the Hittites, and then our knowledge of Asia Minor becomes a literal blank for centuries.

As the older powers disappeared from the Fertile Crescent, barbarism descended. The recent excavations at Carchemish have illustrated the process in one of the older centres of culture. Complete destruction marked the trail of the invaders. They were men of the northern grasslands, for their weapons were now of iron; their armour might have been worn by the Athenian hoplite of the days of Pericles. Their dresses were northern, for they were fastened by the fibula or safety-pin in the shape of a bow. They burned their dead and placed the ashes in urns. Their coarse pottery was adorned with painted black designs of a geometrical character and similar to contemporary types discovered in Cyprus; that this similarity is due to contact as well as to likeness in race is indicated by the presence of imported wares from Cyprus, from the Greek islands, and even from the Greek mainland of the days when Mycenæ was at her height.

In still another respect, these new inhabitants of Carchemish were men of the north and so unlike their predecessors. While the earlier dwellers had been content with crude earthworks which defied the very elements of military defence, the northerners cleverly seized every advantage which could be won by higher ground or by a rock foundation for their walls. No longer was a moat demanded, for the entire circumvallation was double, and rectangular salients swept the line of the straight wall. Once military principles were followed, the defenders cared little for appearances, and the older Hittite sculptures were refaced and cut down or the inscriptions turned against the inner core.[1]

Along the edge of the desert new hordes of Semitic nomads were at the same time pouring out. Aramæan tribes, Ahlame, Sute, and the like, settled in Mesopotamia, and then, as disintegration continued, even in Babylonia. The kingdom of Amurru in north Syria, opposite Arvad, which we last see as a Hittite vassal under Bantishinni, endured long enough to fur-

[1] Woolley, *Carchemish*, 48 ff.

nish later writers with a picture of a great Amorite empire,[1] and then it went down before attacks of invading Aramæans. By the beginning of the fourteenth century, isolated Hebrew tribes, the Habiri of the Amarna correspondence, were working their way into Palestine; with the breakdown of Egyptian rule, there ensued those struggles so vividly portrayed in the Book of Judges. Before they could secure the coast land, along the northern section of which the Phœnician cities were just beginning to prosper, they met an enemy who combined greater aptitude for war with a higher material culture. Driven from their home in Crete by the mail-clad Greek barbarians, and foiled in their invasion of Egypt, the Philistines settled down on the fertile plain to which they were to furnish the name of Palestine. All these conclusions must be conjectured in the light of later events, for the Hebrews alone told their tales of the "period of the Judges."

Six centuries the Kashshites had ruled Babylonia, and the line was worn out. Just then Ashur-dan I began his long reign (1175–1140) in Assyria, while Babylon could only place opposite the one-year reign of Zamama-shum-iddina (1173). The Assyrian king made a dash into the debatable land and won back Akarsallu and Zaban, where the Ur dynasty had devastated Simurru. The boundary stood not far from the Iaiman mountains, due east of Ashur itself, and that this could be considered a gain is the best testimony to the terrible losses of the last half-century.

The year was not to be marked for Babylonia by this loss alone, for in it the Elamite ruler Shutruk Nahhunte I, accompanied by his son Kutir Nahhunte I, marched into Babylonia and put its king to death. His successor, Bel-nadin-ahe (1173–1169), managed to keep himself on the throne three years, and then he, too, was forced to succumb to the Elamite flood. Kashshite rule came to an abrupt end, and the kings who followed seem actually to have been vassals of Elam.

These rulers form a new dynasty, the fourth, whose ancestral home was in Nisin, a few miles south of Nippur, and which

---

[1] Clay, *Empire of the Amorites.*

had already furnished Babylon with one dynasty. Marduk-shapik-zer (1169–1152) and Urta-nadin-shum (1152–1146) were indeed of little account, but the son of the second, the first Nebuchadnezzar, is one of the great figures in history. After a series of picturesquely narrated campaigns, by which Elam was prostrated and Marduk was recovered for Babylon, he met in the third year an invasion of peoples whom he calls "Hittites," and who may actually be northern barbarians from the region of Carchemish. The whole force was impaled or made prisoner. He then turned his attention to Assyria, where the long reign of Ashur-dan had ended in disaster.

With a modicum of imagination we may reconstruct the story behind two letters, sadly mutilated now and already somewhat illegible when they were copied by the scribes of Ashur-bani-apal. One is from a Babylonian king, Nebuchadnezzar himself. The story begins with a certain Ashur-shum-lishir, who in the time of the writer's father had been driven from his country and had found refuge in Babylonia. No such name is found in the official lists of rulers, and the writer of the letter likewise refuses to him the title of king. He is only "lord of lands," and while he was in exile, in his "not lordship," Urta-tukulti Ashur ruled Assyria, and his name is found in the official lists. He invaded Babylonia but was unsuccessful; perhaps it was at this time he was forced to return to Babylon the statue of Marduk which Tukulti Urta had carried off ninety-two years before. Ashur-shum-lishir was restored with Babylonian help, but no sooner was he back in Assyria than he forgot his former humiliation and began to speak words of majesty.

When Nebuchadnezzar became ruler in Babylonia, he sent a great noble to take charge of the petty kinglets on the northern frontier. With him went a certain Harbi-shipak, a Habiri by title and a Kashshite by name, who had come into Babylonia with an official of Ashur-shum-lishir at the beginning of that prince's exile, and had entered the Babylonian service. He stood in the presence of the governor and acted as inspector. Suspicion seems to have been roused that Harbi-shipak in reality recognised Urta-tukulti Ashur as his true lord. He arrived at court with a rather testy letter from the great feudal noble: "One day only didst thou (the king) await me in Zaqqalu, long enough to send those who were counsellors and prudent. I was angry, for only one day did he await us in Zaqqalu."

The Babylonian monarch had a reply ready to his hand: "Have I not been gracious to thee, have I not blessed thee with blessings, and have they not put thee in charge of the kings on thy frontier? Why then are your words like those of a mere ordinary official?" The former career of Harbi-shipak is known to the king, the governor has had him on his personal staff, and ought likewise to know his character. "Who among you," the officials on the frontier, "like a king gives orders? On him may Ashur-shum-lishir, lord of lands, fall, and may the word of Assyria be similar to that of a mere official, and may they disagree with each other. May Ashur-shum-lishir dwell in that one's land. Since Harbi-shipak came to Akkad, he has been a sinner, and since he came, his lord, Urta-tukulti Ashur, is ravaging the land." The governor has proposed a meeting with the Assyrian ruler, he will attend to the matter, for "the good of Akkad and of Assyria the god desires." The king answers: "Do thou as thy heart desires," attend to the necessary arrangements, "let us see each other, send thy deputy with the following instructions: 'The good of Akkad and of Assyria he desires.' Such should be the word of kings."

A further suggestion is that the governor cross over and visit Urta-tukulti Ashur, who has been ravaging the land. However, he did not fight that year in that land, though an attempt has been made to keep it quiet. The Babylonian king writes sharply on this point: "Since thou hast received the power, why hast thou not entered? And what is this about taking Urta-tukulti Ashur to the land of Iriqa?" This, by the way, is our first reference to Iraq, the Arab name of Babylonia. Then he gives his own opinion of his opponent: "Thou hast said of Urta-tukulti Ashur: 'He is a servant, he is not a true man.' In fact, he is just like you. Why does he not finish his task? The men of Assyria are women."

Judging from the fragment of the reply which has survived, the governor was great enough a noble that he could afford to speak plainly: "It is my slanderer who is full of wrath, he is the one who is turning things upside down. Urta-tukulti Ashur only makes divinations and sees dreams, he does not turn things upside down." The king had written with evident sarcasm: "Who among you gives orders like a king?" With equal sarcasm the governor counters with remarks about "old men who are kings and fathers who are" rulers. He makes it clear that the words spoken to Nippur, Sippar, and Babylon, perhaps their charters of privileges, have not been forgotten by them. No one, either the enemy, his sons, or his great ones, shall cause hostility to the kingship of his master. As to the great men of Assyria, the report is of Enlil-kudur-usur.[1]

Shortly after Nebuchadnezzar wrote this letter, Urta-tukulti Ashur disappeared, and his place was taken by Mutak-kil Nusku (1137–1127), who restored the line of Eriba Adad. Ashur-resh-ishi I (1127–1115) claims to be the "Avenger of Assyria." He took the initiative against Babylon, but Nebuchadnezzar, fresh from his triumphs in Elam, quickly forced the invader to decamp. The Babylonians then collected their siege-engines to beleaguer Zanqi, but the new Assyrian levies fell upon them and he retreated hurriedly, burning his siege-train behind him. Nebuchadnezzar collected a fresh army and made a second attempt upon Assyria, but again the defenders were successful, forty chariots were taken, and the leader fell into their hands. Ashur-resh-ishi could now think of restoring the empire. He claims to have subdued the Ahlame, the Lulume, and the Qute. The stage was set for Tiglath Pileser.

[1] Pinches, *JRAS.*, 1904, 407 ff.

CHAPTER VI

TIGLATH PILESER I AND THE NEW WORLD

TIGLATH PILESER I does not begin a new dynasty or inaugurate a new policy. Superficially, the chief reason for assigning him a separate chapter is the fact that for the first time in Assyrian history we possess detailed annals from which we can reconstruct a lifelike picture. Actually, we must recognise that these full annals are possible only because there has been a complete change in the parts played by the chief actors in western Asia.[1]

Egypt was no longer a foreign power, and was itself falling into the separate parts which its long length along the Nile constantly threatened. The Hittite empire was broken into numerous units, Mitanni was gone, Philistines and Zakkalu had taken over the seaports of Palestine, and the Hebrews were securing the hill country, Aramæans were settling in Syria, pressing into Mesopotamia, and threatening Babylonia, the men who had perfected the Minoan art were in flight across the seas before the mail-clad Greek barbarians. The mountains of Armenia and Persia housed a perfect chaos of tribes without hint of organisation. The polished international world of the balance of power was long since gone and a welter of small and hostile states had taken its place. The outlook was discouraging for civilisation, yet it is in such periods of disorder that are laid the foundations of the great empires of the future.

The whole history of Tiglath Pileser is the attempt to bring some sort of order into this chaos. It is not always interesting to trace his movements in detail, to attempt to remember names of persons and places of small significance in the world's

[1] The reign is fully discussed, *JAOS.*, XXXVII, 169 ff.; *Historiography*, 10 ff. Chief source, the Cylinder, Budge-King, *Annals*, I, 27 ff.; new material in Schroeder, *Keilschrifttexte aus Assur*, II, 68; 71.

development, but it is worth our while to study typical illustrations of the policy which brought Assyria reward.

On the northwest frontier, for example, the half-century of
decline had seen Asianic peoples, the débris of the Hittite
empire, forcing their way into regions which had once owed
allegiance to Assyria. Among these were the Mushki, from
whom the Cappadocian capital of Mazaka took its name.
From the corner of Armenia, they had come down into Alzi,
the fertile triangle stretching down from near the source of
the west Tigris to the great bend at Amedi which we have
already learned to know as Alshe.   It was bad enough to lose
this rich agricultural plain, not to speak of the copper-mines
just to the north, but when to this there was added Kutmuh,
the yet more fertile country between the Tigris and Mount
Kashiari, it was clearly time to act.

Hastening through Mount Kashiari, the first range of hills
which stretch from east to west along the northern edge of
the plain, he engaged the twenty thousand Mushki warriors
in Kutmuh.   "The bodies of their warriors like the storm-god
I hurled to earth, their blood in the ravines and on the heights
of the mountains I made to flow down.   Their heads I cut off,
by the side of their cities like grain heaps I piled up.   Their
spoil, their property, their possessions, to an unnumbered
quantity I brought out."

The wretched inhabitants fled across the Tigris to the fortress
of Shereshe, but the Assyrians pursued them "through the
difficult mountains and the blocked ways," hewing a passage
with bronze axes, and took the stronghold.   The River Name
carried to the Tigris the bodies of the Qurhi hordes hastening
to their aid, and a booty of bronze unguent vessels and great
copper sacrificial bowls worthy the Assyrian deities prove the
mines near by.

The objective of the fourth campaign was "the lands of the
distant kings who were on the shore of the Upper Sea, who had
never known subjection."   By difficult trails and steep passes,
which no former king had known in their recesses, by blocked
roads and by paths which were not open, he traversed sixteen

mighty mountains. In the good country he marched with his chariots, in the difficult he opened a way with bronze axes. Plane-trees, the wood of the mountains, he cut down to make pontoons for the advance of his troops. The line of march was up the east Tigris to the south shore of Lake Van, and then west through the fertile plain to the north of the moun-ains. Crossing the east Euphrates, Tiglath Pileser fell upon a confederacy of twenty-three princes, who were ordered to furnish hostages and a regular tribute of horses and cattle. At the farthest point of advance, at Melazgerd, one can still see the inscription he carved.

His fifth campaign drove the Ahlame "in one day" from the Habur River to Carchemish, and across the river, and followed them up on rafts laid on inflated skins. In the same region of Harran and of the Habur, he slaughtered ten mighty male elephants and took four alive. When we compare this with the hundred and twenty that the Egyptian Thutmose III hunted in this same section, we may argue that change of climate has decreased the number of elephants—or suspect that the earlier scribe was the more skilful flatterer. Four wild aurochs were put to death in Mitanni land, a hundred and twenty lions were killed on foot and eight hundred from the chariot. Tiglath Pileser was a mighty hunter—if the statistics are correct.

His vacation ended, he must march against a new enemy on the northwest frontier, the Musri, about the east branch of the Tigris. Allied were the Qumani; Hunusa, one of their strongholds, was fortified with a triple wall of burnt brick, but this did not save it from utter destruction. Salt was sown on the site, and a chapel erected in which was placed a bronze thunderbolt, and written on it the decree that the city should never be rebuilt. The royal city of Kibshuna lost its great wall with piers of burnt brick, and the three hundred families which had supported the revolt were handed over to the tender mercies of the pro-Assyrian party.

Soon after, Tiglath Pileser made a trip still farther west which had in it the elements of the spectacular. Crossing the

Fig. 35. BYBLUS, THE OLDEST PHŒNICIAN CITY, WHENCE CAME
OUR WORD FOR BIBLE.

Fig. 36. THE EARLIEST SITE OF TYRE, BEFORE THE PHŒNICIANS
SECURED CONTROL OF THE MEDITERRANEAN.

It bears now the shrine of the "Beloved Prophet," the Mohammedan form of Adonis.

FIG. 37. THE GARDENS OF SIDON.

FIG. 38. ALTAR IN A PHŒNICIAN TEMPLE AT SIDON.

Euphrates and establishing on its right bank the settlement of Mutkinu, he swept through north Syria to the sea, first of Assyrian monarchs to behold the Mediterranean. The citizens of Arvad, secure on their island in the midst of the sea, gave him a ride in their ships, three double hours to Simirra, and assisted him in killing a whale, the "horse of the sea," on the trip. Byblus and Sidon followed Arvad in the payment of dues, and on his return he placed a tribute of cedar beams for the temple of Anu and Adad upon Ili Teshub, the king of the "great Hittites."

At this very time, Wenamon, sent by Hrihor, Amon priest of Thebes, was visiting Byblus; his report, with its grim humour and its realistic descriptions, reveals Syria divided into small states whose rulers were entirely independent of Egypt and highly contemptuous of claims set forth on the basis of earlier Egyptian successes. Absurd as they now had become, they were still insisted upon, and the appearance of an Assyrian army in country claimed by Egypt could not be permitted to go without protest. An embassy was accordingly prepared, presumably by Nesubenebded, the Delta prince visited by Wenamon. Tiglath Pileser revenged Assyria for the "tribute" claimed by Thutmose III and Ramses II by reversing the claim; he merely states that the king of Egypt sent a crocodile, which he exhibited to his people.

Not for long could Tiglath Pileser enjoy himself on the blue Mediterranean, hunting whales and dreaming of a conquest of Egypt. Aramæans were pouring like a flood across the Euphrates, and only a hurried retreat prevented his being cut off. Month by month, even in the intense heat which reigned over the barren steppes in summer, the records show him turning this way and that to attack them, and ever the Aramæans are found farther north. Harran was lost and the road to the Mediterranean was closed. He crossed from Tadmar of Amurru and Anat of Suhi to Rapiqu of Kar Duniash. The last reference shows how far up the Euphrates Babylonia extended; in the first we are tempted to find the Biblical Tadmor and the Roman Palmyra.

Already in the third year of his reign, the Babylonian Marduk-nadin-ahe had fallen upon Ekallate, "the Palaces," but a few miles south of Ashur, and carried away the local gods Adad and Shala (1107). Despite this disaster, Tiglath Pileser continued to call himself "King of the Four World Regions," which should imply rule of some portion of north Babylonia, but his frontier was at the Lower Zab when war was declared.

Sufficient time had been allowed Marduk-nadin-ahe for consolidating his possessions in the debatable land, yet when Tiglath Pileser turned from the bootless wars with the Aramæans to seek an easier and more profitable victory, he was not prepared. A skirmish between the chariotry of the contending parties above Zaban was favourable to the Assyrians, but the next year they decided to follow the west bank of the Tigris to Dur Kurigalzu, where they met their first resistance. This overcome, they continued south to Sippar, to Babylon, and to Opis. Twice Marduk-nadin-ahe was defeated, and the palaces of Babylon were burned.

Such conquests need no interpretation. All the Babylonian possessions north of the alluvium were lost, and all the important cities of north Babylonia had felt the hand of the invader. Babylon herself might hope soon to be freed, but her imperial position was gone forever.

The first step towards an efficient imperial organisation was taken by Tiglath Pileser. It was still an empire of the crudest type, with no bond of union other than a common master of the various subject kings, and his title is "king of all princes, lord of lords, mighty one, king of kings, who hath ruled the peoples and hath been proclaimed over princes." Provincial organisation was confined to Assyria proper.

Its theocratic character is evident. Ashur and the great gods command that he should extend the boundary of the land, enemies are those not subject to the lord Ashur, the conquered are numbered with those subject before the lord Ashur, and pay his tax and tribute. On complete reduction of a land, the gods are carried captive to Ashur; when kings are set free they are forced to swear the oath of the great gods for servanthood forever, and a captive king on whom Tiglath Pileser has mercy is sent home to be a worshipper of the great gods.

Those who came out on the royal advance and embraced the royal feet were bidden to give hostages, furnish an indemnity, and promise a regular yearly tax, to be paid in the city of Ashur in the presence of the king. It is this yearly tribute, sharply to be distinguished from the extraordinary contribution with which the king must be greeted when he appears in subject territory on his annual expeditions, which gives the first hint of effective imperial control. Through the personal knowledge of the high state of military preparedness and through the impression the glitter of wealth must make, the client princes were made to realise that revolt was suicidal.[1]

The decline of Assyrian power under his ancestors had brought about decay and desertion. Much labour was demanded to restore palaces, and many of the cities were no longer protected from the nomad enemy by their ruined town walls. The first building taken in hand was the "Palace of the King of the Four World Regions," which was completed in the fourth year. The palace has left few traces, but there are fragments of its decoration; in particular bulls and lions in basalt. Especially to be noted is the eye for a basalt bull which was fixed with an iron spike.

Adad was the greatest of the west Semitic gods, and naturally held a high place in early Ashur. He occupied the site alone in the days of Erishum, but when Ashur fell under the rule of Babylon, the sky-god Anu, a comparatively new head of the pantheon, became "father" of Adad and was given an equal share in the shrine. In spite of his very name, Shamshi Adad I, for example, honours in his building Anu equally with Adad. Of these constructions, we have a stone wall, gypsum with rubble filling, at the southeast corner of the sacred area. The later plan of the temple was due to Ashur-dan I, who began the rebuilding, and to Ashur-resh-ishi I, rather than to

[1] *Amer. Pol. Science Rev.*, XII, 64 ff.

Tiglath Pileser, who brought the task to completion and has given us the literary data for its reconstruction.

In the centre of the northern wall the curious double temple towers, a hundred and fifty feet high, could be seen far to the north. The main building material was adobe, the bricks somewhat over a foot square and baked almost to the hardness of stone by the intense sun. Rubble and sand filled the terraces, the lower courses and the corners were faced with limestone or gypsum. The usual double gate on the southeast side led into a courtyard of some size, ninety-three by a hundred and sixty feet, around which were grouped small rooms in the thick walls. At the opposite end were three entrances, the middle one leading into the small corridor which separated the two temples, the others into the sacred places themselves. In front of each were two small rooms and two others opened into the corridor; the shrine itself was next the temple tower with a niche at the far end in which was placed the life-sized cult image. How splendid these must have appeared may be conjectured from the discovery of Adad's trident thunderbolt, a wooden core over which was laid gold of unusual fineness and of a coin value to-day of some two hundred dollars.

Tiglath Pileser increased the terraces, raised the level of the rooms, and pushed out the line of the walls. Close-grained yellow limestone, in blocks five feet long, was added to the facing, and mason's marks on them, made with bitumen and including the swastika, can still be observed. Slightly plano-convex paving-blocks, an imitation of the pre-Sargonid use in Babylonia, were laid down, and sunburnt bricks, in L shapes, half-cylinders, and segments of circles, still more adorned the portals.[1]

Nor was Tiglath Pileser without due regard for the welfare of the country as a whole. The water-wheels in all Assyria were repaired, and there was a resultant increase in the taxes paid in kind to the great advantage of the royal treasury. The horses, cattle, and asses, driven away on the various raids, were collected together, and the deer, stags, and ibexes taken

[1] W. Andrae, *Der Anu-Adad-Tempel*, 1909.

in the chase were reared for sacrifices. Cedars and other trees, all sorts of garden-truck, were carried away and planted in the gardens of Assyria. The picture is idyllic.

In summing up his reign, Tiglath Pileser boasts: "I have made good the condition of my people; in peaceful habitations have I made them dwell." It is the irony of fate that to us Tiglath Pileser is known almost exclusively by his wars, while the later history was to show that conflict and decline were to be the destined lot of his people.

CHAPTER VII

DARK CENTURIES

THE glories of Tiglath Pileser were but fleeting. Before his reign was closed, there were signs of coming trouble, and if from the succeeding period we possess no annals, we may assert that there were no further glories to unfold. Perchance his reign was ended by assassination, for he was not followed by a legitimate heir, but by the usurper Saggal-apal-ekur II (1102–1092). A son of Tiglath Pileser, Ashur-bel-kala, finally succeeded in reclaiming his ancestral heritage, but only for a time, when another usurper, Enlil-rabi, appears.[1]

In Babylonia the son of Marduk-nadin-ahe, named Itti Marduk-balatu (1097–1088), had been forced to cede his place to the usurper Marduk-shapik-zer-mati (1088–1080), who held his throne only by a personal visit to Assyria to promise dependence on the north. When Ashur-bel-kala was driven from home, he found refuge in Babylonia, where the king with the long name had yielded to Adad-apal-iddina (1080–1058), who restored the line of Marduk-nadin-ahe. Babylonian aid was purchased by the marriage of Ashur-bel-kala to the daughter of Adad-apal-iddina, and the Assyrians are so careful to regale us with the rich dowry which the bridegroom brought home, that we ask in suspicion whether they would have us forget gifts presented by a groom to a father-in-law who had become his suzerain.

An almost life-size figure of the nude goddess is the earliest Assyrian statue in the round we can exactly date. Although mutilated by the loss of head, hands, and feet, the proportions are good; Ashur-bel-kala's artist has well represented the solid though not overstout bodies of the women of Ashur. Ashur-bel-kala found his last resting-place in the capital. An

[1] For period covered in chapter, cf. *JAOS.*, XXXVIII, 209 ff.

arched underground passage led to a massive stone door set in stone sockets. Deep under the south wing of the palace lay the vault, unusually large and solidly constructed. The floor was formed of asphalted bricks, above which was a layer of basalt slabs. In a niche was a lamp. The body was placed in a massive coffin of basalt with cover, the only ornament of which was the royal inscription. An unornamented coffin of limestone probably held his queen.[1]

The seventeen years (1092–1075) of interrupted rule by Ashur-bel-kala were followed by those of Eriba Adad, perhaps his son. A half-century after the death of his father, Shamshi Adad IV, a second son of Tiglath Pileser, ascended the throne.

A most regrettable failure of the gods properly to reward filial piety is the loss from the record of the name of the one man in all Assyrian history most noted for his care in preserving the memory of an ancestor; we know not whether it was Shamshi Adad or his brother. Among the restorations of the pious unknown were the palace wall, the cemetery, and the great northern terrace. The ruined city moat was cleansed from the Gate of the Metal Worker to that of the Tigris, and the fallen doors of the former were replaced with bronze valves. The city wall was rebuilt and a rampart heaped outside it. Thirty years the canal dug by Ashur-dan had been abandoned, now it was reopened and orchards planted in its vicinity. The quay wall of the Tigris was raised, the palace terrace of Tukulti Urta rebuilt.

An obelisk, topped with two sloping steps and with an inset panel in the upper centre of one side, contains the narrative just quoted. On the left stands Tiglath Pileser, with short, square-cut beard, and with heavy hair reaching to the neck. He is clad in a single long robe, with a girdle in which is inserted a dagger. His right hand is outstretched, his left holds a bow and ropes which lead to the nostrils of four captives who lift their hands in supplication. The heads of the first two are covered by round caps with hanging points, the others wear flat round hats. All have pointed beards. Over long, cling-

[1] Strong, *JRAS.*, 1892, 338; Andrae, *MDOG.*, LIV, 37 ff.

ing robes hangs an upper garment which reaches a little below the waist. In the field above are symbols of the five great gods. The winged disk of Ashur plainly shows its Egyptian origin; from it extend two hands, the right with open palm, the left presenting the bow to the king. Already the chief characteristics of Assyrian relief are illustrated in this first dated example, the position of monarch and captive, the treatment of hair and drapery, the solid figures, the emphasis on muscular development.[1]

Shamshi Adad IV was followed by a son, Ashur-nasir-apal, the first of the name (1049–1030). Through the devotion of a later-day copyist, we may read a composition which he addressed to the Ishtar of Nineveh, "the mother of wisdom, the lady of majesty, who dwells in Emashmash, the goddess who hath made brilliant my fame, the queen of the gods, into whose hands are given the mandates of the great gods, she who reigns over all kingdoms, who determines decrees, the goddess of the universe." The hymn then turns to the matter in hand: "To the lady of heaven and earth who receives prayers, to her who hearkens unto pleading, who accepts beseeching, to the merciful goddess who loves justice, Ishtar, to whom all that are confounded bring their distress."

Having thus paved the way for the specific cry for help which is to follow, the prayer proceeds: "The afflictions which I behold, before thee I bewail; to my words full of sighing, let thy ears be directed. To my afflicted speech let thy mind be opened; look upon me, O Lady, that through thy turning to me thy servant's heart may become strong. Ashur-nasir-apal am I, the afflicted, thy servant, humble and fearing thy divinity, provident and thy favourite, who hath established thy offerings, who without ceasing offers thy sacrifices, who is eager for thy festivals, who brings abundance upon thy shrine, who makes plentiful the wine, the desire of thy heart, which thou lovest. The son of Shamshi Adad, who adores the great gods, I was begotten in the midst of mountains which none knoweth, I was without understanding and to

[1] Budge-King, *Annals*, LI.

thy Ladyship I never did pray, the people of Assyria did not
know and did not receive thy divinity. But thou, O Ishtar,
mighty princess of the gods, in the lifting up of thine eyes
didst teach me and didst desire my rule; thou didst take me
from out of the mountains and didst call me to the threshold
of the peoples. Thou didst preserve for me the sceptre of the
temples until the growing old of mankind. And thou, O
Ishtar, didst magnify my name, and thou hast granted to the
faithful salvation and mercy. Out of thy mouth came forth
the command to renew the statues of the gods which had been
burned. The temples which were fallen into ruins I repaired,
the overthrown gods I restored and brought back to their
places; they were exalted, thy offerings I established forever.
I caused to be made a throne of boxwood, a divan of costly
work, affording rest to thy divinity, whose interior was lined
with gold, with precious stones of the mountains I adorned
it. I set it up in Emashmash, the dwelling of its splendour."

All these good deeds are recited by Ashur-nasir-apal to make
more strange his need for complaint.

"In what have I done thee wrong? Why hast thou allotted
me disease, boils, and pestilence? As one who doth not
honour thy divinity am I tormented. If I have not incurred
sin and evil, why am I thus afflicted? To my very foundations am I unloosed; I am broken to pieces and rest I find not.
On the throne of my kingdom I fasted, and to the feast I had
prepared I drew not nigh. The wine of the temple service
has been changed into gall, from the joyful shout I am withheld, from the beauty and pleasure of life am I debarred. My
eyes are sealed and I cannot see, I do not raise them above
the face of the earth. Until when, O Lady, shall the disease
continue without cessation, bringing my members to destruction?

"Ashur-nasir-apal, the sore afflicted, who is in fear of thee,
who grasps in supplication the staff of thy divinity, who prays
to thy Ladyship am I. Look upon me with compassion, and
let me pray to thy mightiness. For that about which thou
art angry, grant me forgiveness, and let thy heart be appeased;

let thy heart in mercy strengthen me. Make thy disease come forth and restrain my sin; let tranquillity for me be ordered by thy mouth, O Lady. To the Patesi, thy favourite, who varies not in his devotion, do thou grant mercy and cut off his affliction. Intercede for him with thy Beloved, the father of the gods. Then, till the end of time, shall I exalt thy Ladyship." [1]

This is a cry from the depths of a human soul. He may be simply following the forms set down by the pious of long ago when he begs relief of the goddess, and declares his ignorance of the sin which has brought disease upon his body; the details fit only his own case. In view of his long royal ancestry, his statement that he was begotten in the midst of unknown mountains is passing strange until we recollect that his father did not come to the throne until a half-century after the death of the grandfather, and that his uncle did not immediately succeed to the paternal throne, nor was he able to hold it continuously. Ashur-nasir-apal must have been born in one of these periods of exile.

Still more puzzling is his declaration that king and people alike knew not the goddess until she taught them to pray to her Ladyship. The temple of Ishtar had, for centuries, furnished the only claim to distinction for Nineveh, his own ancestors had often brought their offerings to her shrine; why then was a revival of her worship demanded? But there is nothing surprising in the story of divine statues which had been burned or thrown down from their places, of temples falling to ruin. Whether due to internal quarrels or foreign invasion, the cry of the sick monarch might well be the cry of the sick land.

The darkest days of Assyria come with the son of Ashur-nasir-apal I, Shalmaneser II (1030–1018), and with Ashur-nirari IV (1018–1012). These two monarchs are followed by a group which for length of rule and for ability to transmit the succession without a break has no rival. Two centuries and a half the throne passed from father to son, from the second Ashur-rabi (1012–995) to a second Ashur-resh-ishi

---

[1] Brünnow, ZA., V, 66 ff.; Jastrow, Religion, II, 111 ff.

(995–966), a second Tiglath Pileser (966–933), another Ashur-dan (933–911), the second Adad-nirari (911–890), the second Tukulti Urta (890–885), the great Ashur-nasir-apal, counted the second of the name (885–860), the third Shalmaneser (860–825), the fifth Shamshi Adad (825–812), the third Adad-nirari (812–782), the fourth Shalmaneser (782–772) and Ashur-dan III (772–754); Ashur-nirari V (754–746) also belongs to the family.[1]

Ashur-rabi began his reign with misfortune, for the kings of the Aramæans deprived him of the cities of Pitru and Mut-kinu, in the great bend of the Euphrates, which had been colonised by Tiglath Pileser I. Aroused by this loss, Ashur-rabi forced his way to the Mediterranean and erected a stele on Mount Atalur, where it was later seen by Shalmaneser III. Ashur-resh-ishi II and Tiglath Pileser II we know only from the inscription of Ashur-dan II, who restored the Gate of the Metal Worker; the decay must have been great when the most important defence of the city lay in ruins.

Adad-nirari II begins once more Assyrian expansion. His recently recovered annals are simple enough, without a hint of striving for literary effect, but his conquests deserve attention. In the "beginning of his reign" he invaded the lands of the Qumani, made captive their king Iluia, and dragged their gods before Ashur. Kirhi was devastated with the cities on the Shupuru River of Mehri. Across the Lower Zab he invaded Lulume, Zamua, and Namri. Uradri, or Urartu, was subdued, and Kutmuh was made Assyrian.

Following the example of his predecessors, Adad-nirari pushed on to Mount Ialman, the last range of hills before the Babylonian plain was reached, and there put to flight Shamash-mudammiq when he attempted to make a stand in the pass. Arrapha and Lubdu, lost to Babylonia, were recovered, the whole region from Lahiru to Sulum was made Assyrian, the land of the city of Der was ravaged.

Taking advantage of this defeat, Nabu-shum-ishkun I killed the discredited monarch, but enjoyed no better fortune,

[1] For remainder of chapter, cf. *JAOS.*, XXXVIII, 211 ff.

for he, too, suffered a humiliating reverse, and saw his enemy make himself master of Bagdadu, our first narrative reference to the city made famous by the *Arabian Nights*. Complete alliance was contracted between them, and each married the daughter of the other.

Four times Nairi and Kirhi were attacked; the land of Alzi was destroyed until it was like the ruined mounds from before the flood. The nomad Ahlame and Aramæans were reduced, the cities they had taken were restored to Assyria.

Six expeditions in successive years and a later seventh were directed against the land of Hani Galbat. Nur Adad of Temanna collected his troops and set his line of battle in Pazi at the foot of Mount Kashiari; from Pazi to Nasibina he was defeated. By the third year, Mamli had become ruler of Temanna; he took the royal feet, and his palaces were reckoned to Adad-nirari. In those days the Assyrian received a great and a small animal called a *pagutu* from the land of the son of Adini, our first contact with the new Aramæan state in the bend of the Euphrates. By the fourth year, Muquru had become king of Temanna; he forgot the oath of Ashur, and Adad-nirari brought back territory lost since the reign of the first Tiglath Pileser. The sixth expedition, Nur Adad was back in Temanna and in his capital Nasibina. Seven cities round about were taken by Adad-nirari and placed under Ashur-dini-amur, the turtanu.

Cities lost since the days of Tukulti Urta I were forced by defeat to take his feet, and twice he went to the aid of Kumme against the Kirhi, who had burned it. Adad-nirari made sacrifices to the local Adad of Kumme, and burned in return the cities of the Kirhi.

He then crossed the Habur River and passed into Guzana, where Abisalamu, son of Bahianu, was forced to pay tribute. His last recorded trip was down the Habur to the Euphrates, and the cities, Tabite, Qatni, Laqe, Hindanu, are the same conquered in more detail by his son and grandson.[1]

With the accession of Adad-nirari II (911), later scribes begin

[1] Schroeder, *Keilschrifttexte aus Assur*, II, 83 f.; 87.

FIG. 39. THE GATE TO THE KASHIARI. (Mardin.)

FIG. 40. A VILLAGE HIDDEN IN THE KASHIARI. (Kullith.)

FIG. 41. KURDS OF ASIA MINOR.

FIG. 42. A MAN OF THE
KASHIARI.

FIG. 43. PEASANT GIRL OF
MESOPOTAMIA.

their list of eponyms. This system, by which each year was in turn named from a high official, was in use centuries before his day; his annals have made clear to us that they were justified in taking his reign as marking an era.

The first narrated expedition of Tukulti Urta II (890–885) is that of 889 against the Nairi; the next, the son of Amme Baal of Zamani begged his aid, and appeared before the king in Nineveh with family, goods, and gods; in the third, a campaign was carried on in the eastern mountains while the king remained at home. In the fourth, Tukulti Urta took the field in person, and the loss of two of his cities forced Amme Baal to sue for peace. Commodious villages were granted him, he was installed in a "residence of peace," and when he took the oath in the name of the lord Ashur, he was told: "If you furnish horses to my body-guard, Adad the god who loves me will bless you also." Two-thirds of the booty went to the god, the other third was laid up in the palace.[1]

The expedition had begun in May; so quickly was its object attained that in October Tukulti Urta undertook another, against the Kirruri region, on the verge of the Assyrian hill country, shut off from the world by snow-filled passes for the greater part of the year. In the Lullu land he subdued thirty villages, where he must negotiate on foot mountains that the king calls emphatically a "place of perdition, which the eagle of the sky could not penetrate in his flying." The fugitives found safety only when they had placed the Lower Zab behind them.

In the last year of his reign (885), Tukulti Urta made a sudden dash into Babylonia. His detailed itinerary is not without interest to the casual reader; to the geographer it is a precious source for the topography of the middle Euphrates country. Ashur was left in the midst of April. The first night, camp was pitched in the prairies; the next day the army reached the Tartara, the dry stream bed which runs south from the Singara hills. No water was flowing, but a little digging disclosed it near the surface, and from these water-holes, all

[1] Scheil, *Annales de Tukulti Ninip II*, 1909.

night long, the army drew up its water like a gardener. Four days they followed the road of the desert where there was no sweet water, only nine wild bulls for the king to slay. Fresh water was found at the "mouth" of the Tartara, where it ended in a swamp. Another waterless stretch led them to canals, where a whole day and night was spent in camp securing the precious fluid. The banks of the Tigris were reached and the army was in Babylonia; so fertile was the country that the soldiers lost their way amid orchards which appeared veritable forests.

Sippar marked the farthest south of the expedition; from this point the Assyrians turned west to the Euphrates and began the advance up-stream. Soon they were opposite Id, "the fountainhead of bitumen, the place of gypsum, where the great gods speak." Travellers from the days of Herodotus have celebrated the wonders of Hit and of its petroleum deposits; it is quite in the nature of things that early man should make it the seat of an oracle.

Continuing up the Euphrates, the long line of towns unrolls. When the meadows along the stream were reached, a day and a night were consumed in loading up with a supply of water, for after that came the rocky desert, where no forage could be found. Succeeding camps brought the invader to Anat, the capital of Suhi land.

The beautiful island town was not appearing for the first time in history. Under its earlier name of Hana, it is frequently mentioned as autonomous in the days of the first dynasty of Babylon, and when Babylon fell, Marduk and his wife were carried off to it. Tiglath Pileser I and Adad-nirari II claimed its conquest. Some time during the Assyrian decline, an independent prince named Shamash-resh-usur set up his stele. Clad in a simple robe whose fringe falls to his ankles and with only a plain fez for head-dress, his beard is square and of medium length, his hair reaches his shoulders, a sceptre is in his left hand, his right is raised in adoration, but with the thumb upright. Behind him a deity lifts his hand in blessing; before him are Adad and Ishtar. The god holds the thunderbolt in either hand, and in addition a ring in his right; the goddess carries her star and bow in her right, her left is extended in the gesture of blessing. All three deities are elevated above their worshipper by mountains, each wears an elaborate girdle, a skirt with five flounces, and three overlapping bosses in front.

The prince rules the ancient Mari as well as Suhi, and his inscription is dated by his thirteenth year as if he were king. While engaged in a sacred feast at Baqa, he tells us, Talbanish was attacked by the Tumanu tribe; three hundred and fifty of them he killed, the remainder begged for mercy. Talbanish was planted with palm-trees, for this is the northern limit at which they bear fruit; the palace garden of the new city was made the abode of Adad and of his son, of his wife Shala, and of the divine judge. The Suhi canal had become silted up by age, but Shamash-resh-usur summoned many of his people, dug the length of a thousand canes, and opened the bridge of the canal gate so that it admitted a boat thirty-seven feet long into a canal thirty-three feet wide.

His most curious information is reserved for the close. Bees which collect honey and wax, which were never before known in Suhi, were brought down from the mountains of the Habha people and were placed in the gardens of Gabbari-ibni. He and his gardeners understood the preparation of the honey and also of the wax. In future days a ruler will inquire of his elders whether it is indeed true that Shamash-resh-usur introduced bees into Suhi land.

At this time the prince was Ilu-ibni; he thought it wise to meet the invader with gifts of precious metals, bricks of gold, a throne of ivory, tables of the same. Amme-alaba of Hindanu added a whole talent of myrrh, precious aromatics, camels, great birds which may perchance be ostriches. So close did the mountains now come to the river that it was necessary to cut a road with iron axes. As the Assyrians were encamped in the meadows, Mudadu of Laqe reached them with food for man and beast, another Aramæan chief presented his gifts at noon, a third at nightfall. No attempt to follow up the

Euphrates beyond the Habur was made, for the state of Adini blocked the way.   Contributions were exacted from the Aramæans settled along the Habur; the last conquest was Nasibina.   This is the last time Nasibina appears as enemy territory; thirty-two years later it heads the list of the provinces.

A sudden raid into the land of the Mushki closes the story of the year's operations.   The narrative continues with the works of peace, the building of palaces, the making of irrigation machines, the securing of food for the people, the hunting exploits; above all, the reconstruction of the great wall first built by Ashur-uballit.   The account was composed towards the end of September, 885; not many days later the end came, and Ashur-nasir-apal, his son, reigned in his stead.

CHAPTER VIII

THE CALCULATED FRIGHTFULNESS OF
ASHUR–NASIR–APAL

THE long reign of Ashur-nasir-apal II (885–860) marks
another epoch in our knowledge as well as in the actual history,
for once more we have annals of the fullest sort.[1] The two
centuries which had elapsed since the death of Tiglath Pileser
I had seen twelve monarchs on the throne, less than a score
of years each. The age of each successive ruler, therefore,
tended to be less and less at his accession. Ashur-nasir-apal
must have been a decided youth when his father died after a
reign of but six years. So young a prince might be expected
to possess a warlike temper.

The march of Tukulti Urta had shown that the moment was
opportune for renewed advance, and Assyria possessed once
more resources in men and in wealth. The country actually
administered from the capital was small enough, the provinces
of Ashur, Isana, Nimit Ishtar, Kalhu, Nineveh, Kakzu, Kutmuh, so that Assyria comprised a tract seventy-five miles on
the side, and half of that mountain or unirrigated prairie.

In the hands of an efficient ruler, this compact country could
do wonders. A thorough overhauling of the military system
had been carried out and a new army developed. The core
still remained the native Assyrian infantry, but the chariots
were supplemented by a cavalry made up largely of allies, a
curious anticipation of the Roman custom. With this went
the art of besieging cities and an increase in the use of battering-
rams and of similar types of machines.

So far as her neighbours must be taken into consideration,
there was no cause for concern. Babylon was too strong for

The records, including the Monolith, the Kurkh Stele, and the Annals, are
published Budge-King, *Annals*, I, 155 ff. For source criticism, cf. *Historiography*,
15 ff.; for history of reign, *JAOS.*, XXXVIII, 217 ff.

safe attack, and in turn was unwilling to indulge in open war. On no other side was Assyria threatened by a first-class power. It is true that there was constant pressure all along the frontier, but it was the pressure of disunited tribes, which could be no great menace to a strong government, though any relaxation of vigilance might subject the state to grave danger. Already the Indo-European tribes were close to the Assyrian boundaries, and the petty frontier states were being crushed between more-civilised and less-civilised neighbours. Farther to the north-west this same pressure was driving the Haldians south, and the state which the Assyrians called Urartu and the He-brews Ararat was being welded together behind the masking line of the loosely organised Nairi tribes. Before the end of the reign, their conquest was to bring Urartu and Assyria face to face.

The road to the Euphrates and the sea was blocked by the Aramæans, who, since the days of Tiglath Pileser I, had swept over the whole steppe. They were rapidly taking over the civilisation of the peoples they had subjugated, and were al-ready laying the foundation for that supremacy of the Ara-mæan language and customs which was to be the dominant factor in the history of Mesopotamia for the next fifteen hun-dred years. Beyond the Euphrates lay Syria, still largely Hittite in its northern portions, but with the current of Ara-mæan migration already running strong. All these disunited groups offered an easy victory to an ambitious king, who might well hesitate to measure his strength with Babylon.

A considerable part of the year 885 had been taken up with the expedition of Tukulti Urta, but there were still left some months fit for campaigning. There had been no contest for the throne, and Ashur-nasir-apal burned to accomplish great exploits.

For the first time in Assyrian history the bas-reliefs come to our aid, and we may revivify the narrative through their de-tails. Ashur-nasir-apal appears in his chariot ready for the march. The side is decorated with crossed quivers which contain arrows, a small bow, and the iron hatchet so often

FIG. 44. ASHUR–NASIR–APAL HUNTING THE LION.

(Cast at the University of Illinois.)

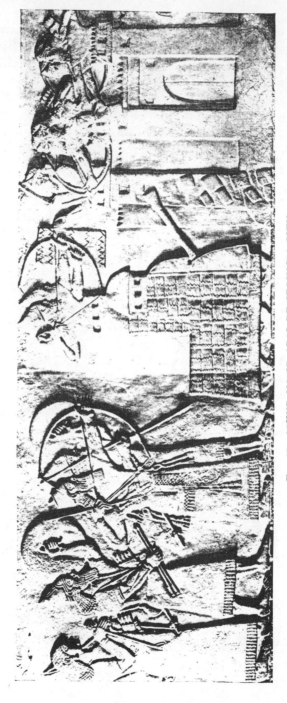

Fig. 45. ASHUR–NASIR–APAL BESIEGING A CITY.
The battering-ram is destroying the walls. (Cast in Metropolitan Museum.)

needed to cut a path for the armies. At the rear hangs the bossed shield, and in a human-headed socket is the spear. The bar at the end of the chariot-pole terminates in a swan's head, and between the two horses is a huge, elongated, and richly decorated board. A third and reserve horse gallops by their side. Bands over the chest harness the horse to the yoke, and the reins are carried through a single thong. Rosettes with flying tassels adorn the horses' flanks, beads are ringed about the neck, the long tails are tied half-way up their length. In the chariot stands the king, sometimes under a parasol, sometimes fitting an arrow to the bow, his forearm shielded with a strap against a recoil of the bowstring. Before him floats the winged figure of Ashur, also letting fly his arrows against the enemy.

The two standards of the army are guarded by archers in chariots; other archers are on horseback, their whole strength devoted to the fighting, for a companion rides by the side of each and holds the rein. The sturdy infantry is likewise armed with the bow, which in the days of Ashur-nasir-apal was indeed the chief reliance of the Assyrians and of the most of their enemies. Needless to remark, the scenes always show Assyrian successes and the enemy is usually in flight.

After the conflict comes repose in camp, a circular enclosure with battlemented walls and divided into four equal sections by broad streets crossing at right angles. Within may be seen the slaughter of the steer, the preparation of the food, the baking of the bread, the drawing of the wine from jugs set in supports. Outside is the royal pavilion, entered between posts on whose tops stand ibexes ready to spring, and before it tethered horses surround the manger or are being curried down. Before it, too, stands the eunuch chamberlain, who receives and checks up the miserable captives with arms bound behind them and threatened by a soldier armed with a mace. Just above, and with the contrast beloved by the Assyrian artist, two buffoons clad in lion-skins caper to the strains produced by a third on a guitar with exaggerated length of fingerboard.

The king returns in triumph and at ease in his chariot, his royal standard in the lead. Before the successful troops are the musicians plucking with long plectrum the nine-stringed harp or thrumming with bare fingers the drum hung from the neck. In ghastly contrast to their melodies are the severed heads of the slain which the soldiers are carrying to be counted. Our last memory is of a vulture with a dripping human head in its claws.[1]

Ashur-nasir-apal launched his career of conquest by an invasion of the territory directly east of Assyria, where the frontier was always too close for comfort. Steep mountains, which were not prepared for the progress of chariots and foot-soldiers, did not check his advance to the land of Tumme. He seized its chief fortress, Gubbe, in the heart of the hills, but its defenders escaped to a very steep mountain, which rose like the point of an iron dagger, and no flying bird of the heavens could reach its midst. Like the nest of the vulture within the mountain was set their stronghold, into which none of the kings his ancestors had penetrated, but in three days the warrior overcame the mountain, he climbed up on his feet, he cast down the mountain, he destroyed their nest, their host he shattered, with their blood he dyed the mountains like crimson wool.

None of the sculptures of Ashur-nasir-apal contains labels which permit its exact location, but we can often make a shrewd guess. One scene certainly belongs in this general region. In the preliminary skirmish, we see one of the enemy falling backward from his chariot, another falling forward over the front. An Assyrian is about to kill a prostrate soldier while his friend attempts to drag him to safety. The city is in a wooded country and its outworks extend to a small stream; it is fortified with double wall and battlemented towers, and the defence is carried on behind wicker shields with arrows and stones. A man with unstrung bow is offering surrender, and the pursuit is continued through the woods, which are filled with decapitated corpses.

[1] Budge, *Assyrian Sculptures in the British Museum,* 1914.

The army next turned north and went down into Kirruri, already admittedly under Assyrian influence, and ready to furnish horses and mules, cattle and sheep, bronze vessels and wine.   Before the end of the reign, it seems to have been made a province.   Horses and metals, both crude and worked, came from Gilzan and Hubushkia, for to-day iron, lead, and copper have been reported in large quantities in the hills northeast of Assyria.

By the Hudun pass Ashur-nasir-apal entered Kirhi, west of the east Tigris, and met his first serious resistance.   Names familiar from the conquests of Tiglath Pileser I are encountered.   Nishtun, the capital, was occupied, and the inhabitants fled to the lofty mountain opposite.   Though it hung like a cloud from heaven, the Assyrians flew like birds and conquered the nest on the rocks of the mountain.   When the fugitives saw the devastation of their villages, they descended and promised to pay in future their dues.   Their chief, Bubu, was carried off to Arbela, where he was flayed and his skin spread on the wall of the city.

Spring comes late in the countries lying directly under the Armenian boundary range, and Ashur-nasir-apal did not lead out his troops from Nineveh till August.   Operations were resumed where they had been left off the previous winter, and the towns at the foot of the mountains and between the east and west branches of the Tigris were secured.   There still remained the great block of rough volcanic land south of the west Tigris; once Kutmuh, the fairly level tract north and east of this, was made Assyrian, the hill country could be isolated and reduced at leisure.   The Tigris was crossed, and the states on the farther bank vied with the Mushki in presenting bronze vessels and wine.

This well-devised plan to isolate Kashiari came to an abrupt pause when information was received that the Aramæans on the lower Habur had assumed an anti-Assyrian attitude. Here, on a strip of territory which to our own day is considered the most beautiful and most fertile portion open to the nomad, had grown up a number of important Aramæan states.   One

of these, Sha Dikanni, we know somewhat from excavation.
The settlement was but six feet above the water's edge.
Around it ran mud-brick walls faced by cement, good baked
bricks, and fragments of well-dressed gypsum, a welcome link
between the gypsum construction of Asia Minor and that of
Crete. Earlier western connections are indicated by scarabs
bearing the names of the Egyptian Thutmose III and Amenhotep III, while from the Assyrian period come bricks marked
with cuneiform characters in yellow or white outlines on a
pale-green ground, terra-cotta pine-cones and a terra-cotta
bull's head.

The sculptures, in particular, show a similarity to the Assyrian, but with it a provincial character of their own. At
what must have been the water-gate of the palace was a pair
of winged bulls, with the pavement slab between. The Assyrian style was followed, the square-cut, carefully curled
beard and mustache, the hair to nape of neck, though the
wings were shorter, the legs more stumpy, the muscles more
exaggerated. The animal had double ears, human ones with
elaborate earrings, and above them bull's horns on a flat cap.
The large flat nose and thick, overhanging lips give a distinctly
negroid expression to the face. A lion was equally Assyrian,
even to the fifth leg. From the interior of the mound came a
relief, a full-sized male figure staring out at us with square-
cut beard, hair massed on the neck and bunched out on either
side, with much the same effect as in the bulls. A round
spiked helmet is on his head, a flowing robe falls to his ankles,
armlets and bracelets complete the costume. The right arm
swings at the side and carries a dagger, the other clasps something to his breast.

Thanks to the excavations, we know best Dikanni, whose
present ruler was a certain Shalmanu-nunu-shar-ilani, a curious name, "the god Shalman, the fish, is king of the gods,"
which suggests connection with the sacred fish still revered in
the modern Urfa. The most important city of the region in
the days of Ashur-nasir-apal was Halupe, not far from the
junction of the Habur with the Euphrates. Hamataia had

shown his devotion to Assyria by coming a long distance with supplies for the army of Tukulti Urta.   During the period of Assyrian weakness, there had been growing up in the west another Aramæan state of considerable magnitude, which had become the virtual successor of Mitanni, since it included the entire tract within the great bend of the Euphrates, and extended down the river at least as far as the Balih.   Such a state was little if any inferior to the shrunken Assyria of the ninth century.   Adini might hope to outplay Assyria at her own game, by supporting a pro-Adinian party in territory under Assyrian influence.   So it came to pass that Hamataia was put to death, and a certain Ahia-baba, the son of a nobody whom they had brought in from Adini, persuaded the cities of the Habur to join the cause of a common Aramaism.

Ashur-nasir-apal hastened direct from Kutmuh to the Habur, where his presence secured the upper hand for his partisans.   The existing government was overthrown and the friends of Adini handed over.   The pro-Assyrians embraced the feet of the monarch, saying: "If thou wishest, slay; if thou wishest, let live; as thy heart wishes, do."   Aziel, their leader, was made prince, the regular tribute was increased, the royal figure was set up in Hindanu as part of the cult.

The unfortunate Ahia-baba was carried off to Nineveh and flayed.   His rebel followers had shorter shrift.   With a cool delight in the recital of tortures which has not a parallel in Assyrian literature, the young king tells the story: "I erected a pillar opposite his city gate, all the chiefs who had revolted I flayed, with their skins I covered the pillar, some in the midst I walled up, others on the pillar on stakes I impaled, still others I arranged around the pillar on stakes.   Many within the borders I flayed, with their skins I covered the walls.   As for the chieftains and royal officers who had rebelled, I cut off their members."

In this same "year of my name," when the king himself was eponym, bad news came from the northwest frontier. Shalmaneser I settled a large body of Assyrians in Halsi Luha.   Ashur-nasir-apal was too anxious to assert the reality of control by the central power, and Hulai, their governor, raised the standard of revolt and marched against another royal city named Damdamusa. Ashur-nasir-apal began his activities with the erection of a royal stele, fragments of which have survived, beside those of Tiglath Pileser I and Tukulti Urta II at the source of the Subnat River. While there, he received the wine of Izalla, famous from the days of the great Nebuchadnezzar to those of Christianity. The same route through Kashiari as that taken by Tiglath Pileser was followed, and Hulai was flayed and his skin exposed at Damdamusa. The triple-walled Tela was taken by storm, and the expected atrocities were varied only by deprivation of hands, noses, eyes, and ears, by heaps of living beside the heads, by the binding of heads to the vines in the city gardens.

Tushhan, which had seceded in sympathy with Hulai, saw a palace "for the dwelling of my royalty" built in its gate, and the city became the capital of the Nairi province and the centre of operations against the northern peoples for the next century. A memorial tablet was inserted in the reconstructed city walls. A stele of white limestone still tells how the Assyrians who had been forced to flee across the river to Shupria no longer suffered want and hunger, but were brought back and reoccupied Tushhan, which was made a store city for grain and chopped straw.

Further efforts to restore his authority in the level country between the Kashiari hills and the Tigris were checked by the news that all Zamua, the country in the hills due east of Ashur, had leagued under a chief with the Semitic name of Nur Adad. The pass of Babite had been closed by a wall, but a battle in the defile opened it. Fortress after fortress was taken by assault, until the Assyrians were rewarded with the sight of Mount Kinipa, an isolated peak almost ten thousand feet high, "like the point of an iron dagger." Ashur-nasir-apal felt a great pride in being the first Assyrian king to behold it, for his scholars informed him that this was indeed the Mount Nisir on which the Babylonian Noah was supposed to have landed after the deluge.

FIG. 46. OFFICIALS CONDUCT TO ASHUR-NASIR-APAL A CAPTIVE KING, HIS DAUGHTER, AND HIS TWO SONS.
Tusks of ivory and other objects of value are represented above. (Cast in Metropolitan Museum.)

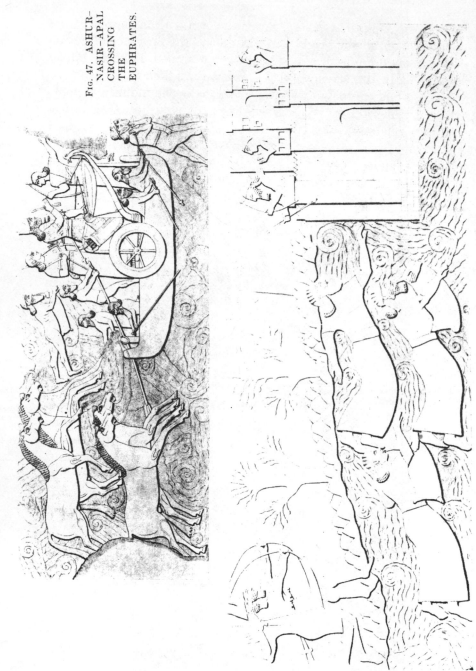

FIG. 47. ASHUR-NASIR-APAL CROSSING THE EUPHRATES.

FIG. 48. SHADUDU ESCAPING BY SWIMMING THE EUPHRATES.

From Arakdi as centre, a series of expeditions spread their terror over all the neighbouring lands.   The province of Mazamua was organised, and Arakdi was renamed Tukulti Ashurasbat, "In the strength of Ashur I have taken it."

A second campaign was needed to make the mountain chiefs pay their tribute.   Its leader seems to have been the crown prince Shalmaneser.   The beardless youth is royally dressed and stands in a chariot of royal design.   The hostile leader, already pierced by two arrows, grasps the bridle of the chariot horses, and other enemies shoot at the crown prince from behind.   An Assyrian drives his sword into the kneeling enemy; a second beats down with his wicker shield a mountaineer who has taken refuge on a hill.   Slinging their shields on their backs, some ·of the invaders hold their companions' horses, and one mounted· bowman has hung a head from the harness of his mount.   The crown prince abandoned his chariot in the rough country and on horseback pursued the infantry.   Then the line of communication was cut by the enemy, and it was necessary for the army to construct a way through the difficult mountains with iron hatchets and bronze axes.

Discouraged by this failure, the Assyrians next turned their attention to the opposite frontier, and in June of 880 the steppes were invaded.   Five lions were killed opposite Maltena, and some of the finest of the palace reliefs are devoted to the theme. The helmeted Assyrian foot-soldiers smite short sword against small rounded shield and thus act as beaters up.   One lion, with enormously exaggerated claw in tail, already lies mortally wounded under the feet of the prancing chariot horses; the other has been barbed by the royal arrows, and rises with widely distended mouth, a magnificent figure as he clutches the chariot axle.   The driver with flying hair hastens on his three steeds, but the king scorns escape and, bending backward with drawn bow, is ready to give the king of beasts his coup de grâce.   The king leans on his bow in triumph, his cup raised in his right hand, ready to pour out his libations over the dead lion.   Around him cluster his attendants and high officials, while bearded men pluck the nine-stringed harp to celebrate his might.

The army then turned northeast to Kutmuh, where a palace was consecrated at Tille, which became the capital, and henceforth gave its name to the extended province. A wedge of unconquered territory yet remained, the Kashiari, and through this the Assyrians forced their way, storming many a hamlet on its almost inaccessible height. A satisfactory excuse for intervention in Zamani was now afforded. Amme Baal by his tribute had openly acknowledged Assyrian tutelage, and to the same degree had made himself obnoxious to the patriotic party which was being stirred to activity by the rapidly growing power of Urartu. Amme Baal suffered death at the hands of his nobles, and Bur Raman took his place.

The site of Amedi, near the great bend of the west Tigris, was magnificent—a cliff three hundred feet above the broad river, and blocks of black basalt everywhere. No less than four walls had been erected, low where the river ran, elsewhere with beetling towers. The king lets fly his arrows against the doomed city, and his protection is a parasol! Soldiers covered with scale armour from neck to ankles are drawn up before the city in pairs, one of whom shoots against it; the other, armed with a dagger, upholds the shield. Men falling from the walls testify to the accuracy of the Assyrian fire, but their main reliance is in their siege-engines, which sometimes permit the capture of a town in a single day. One hardy Assyrian ascends a ladder; others dig holes with knives under the wall and dispute the possession of the treasure hidden in its cracks; again some take their place in the high movable towers, covered with hides, which assure them an equality with the men on the ramparts. Most terrible is the battering-ram, which can be wheeled up to the very foot, and when its projecting beam with its head of iron begins to batter the foundations, not even the grappling-irons let down by the defenders can long save the city. For the besiegers throw their whole weight on hooks which hold the ram in place, and when the besieged hurl down fire the men in the towers extinguish it with water poured from long spouts. The palace is seen, with round openings below the battlements, and the captive women of the harem, their dress a jacket over long skirt with zigzag pattern and hem at bottom, raise hand to filleted head in lamentation.

The inventory of booty has an interest as showing what was the treasure of one of these second-rate Aramæan kings. As might be expected from a people so close to the desert in ancestry, first came the horses, chariots, cattle, and sheep. Metals were fairly common, though the two talents of silver as against the same of gold suggest that the white metal was still of relatively high value; the three hundred talents of iron as compared with the hundred of lead and the two hundred of bronze excite our notice because of the unusually high ratio of the comparatively new metal. That the Aramæans were already settling down to the industrial life they later so completely dominated is indicated by the vessels, pans, bowls, and caldrons of bronze, the couches of ivory overlaid with gold. The chief's sister and the daughters of his nobles were entered in the royal harem, and an additional "aid" was exacted under the pretence of the dowry demanded for so august a marriage.

Bur Raman was flayed alive and his skin displayed on the city wall of one of his towns. His brother Ilanu took his place, and a tax of four pounds of gold and twenty-six of silver, of a thousand sheep and two thousand measures of barley, was laid upon him. Such a rate was far from oppressive. Fifteen thousand Ahlame mercenaries, who had been in the service of Amme Baal, were incorporated into the royal army.

Attacks on the Aramæans settled farther south marked the year 879. The army passed down the Habur, collecting tribute as it went, and to the Euphrates, where another prince of Suhi named Shadudu had trusted to his neighbour of Babylon, Nabu-apal-iddina. The three thousand soldiers sent under the leadership of his brother Zabdanu availed as little as did the equally valuable aid furnished by the Babylonian seer Bel-apal-iddina.

An unusually vivid picture is the flight of Shadudu. Unde-terred by his all-enveloping cloak, he has seized a goat-skin, inflated it, and, puffing away for dear life through the orifice still in his mouth, is being rapidly carried down the stream. Behind him floats his son, similarly buoyed up by a skin, and an unfortunate elder who has been wounded by an arrow must swim for his life without even this frail aid. On the other shore rises the towered and battlemented town of Suru with an anxious old man who has laid aside his bow, while, with two women, he watches the struggle. Assyrian archers have lined up among the palms and olives along the river-bluffs, and from their shelter aim at the unfortunates in the stream. It is consoling to learn from the annals that they all escaped.

The next recorded campaign was in the same territory, but against a different Suru, that of Halupe. Ships were con-structed at this point, and the army drifted down-stream or followed on shore till the narrows of the Euphrates were reached. At Haridi the river was crossed in skin vessels, and the Assyrians gave battle to the allied Aramæan tribes who had gathered on the desert side of the stream. Accord-ing to the arithmetic of our truthful scribe, six thousand five hundred souls were slaughtered out of a total of six thousand, leaving a considerable remnant to die of thirst in the Eu-phrates desert. Their leader was forced to take refuge on a steep mountain, for two days the Assyrians marched after him, and slaughtered the remainder of his troops. Pursuit was continued to the northern narrows of the Euphrates, where for a third time it was necessary to slaughter the rem-nant of his troops. The traditional feline had barely more lives than this minus five hundred enemy soldiers.

Pursuit of the wild auroch is mentioned for the last time in history. Fifty were killed and eight taken alive. A parallel to the lion-hunt pictures the chariot again in full course, but only a single attendant follows with an extra horse. He rides sidewise on a richly fringed blanket and carries tufted spear and bow in either hand. One bull has fallen under the horses, the other has sprung at the chariot. The king seizes the beast

FIG. 49. ASHUR–NASIR–APAL HUNTING THE WILD BULL.

(Cast at the University of Illinois.)

FIG. 50. ASHUR–NASIR–APAL RETURNS IN TRIUMPH.
His god Ashur hovers above. (Cast in Metropolitan Museum.)

by a huge horn, and with a dagger strikes between the second and third vertebræ and into the spinal cord.

Direct contact was now established with Adini, and two guard cities were established on its borders, at the upper narrows. The first direct attack in 877 was against Kaprabi, the "Great Rock," probably Edessa, for "the city was very strong, like a cloud it hung down from heaven." Protected by round shields raised high by his body-guard, the king began the siege with his arrows; his followers wheeled up a tower against the walls of solid stone. The lower parts were of wicker, with curved projections in front, beyond which extended the ram. Above and below were loopholes, and soldiers filled the top, one hurling stones, the other protecting both with his shield. When resistance was finally broken, the general in charge denoted his desire for surrender by his unstrung bow and his lifted hand with thumbs held straight up beside the fingers. The city was committed to the flames, and its inhabitants dragged off to increase the population of the new Assyrian capital.

Later in the year, Ashur-nasir-apal set forth along the mercantile route known as the Carchemish road. Adad-ime, the new ruler of Izalla, was ordered to provide the great king with chariots, horse, and foot. Already the foreign cavalry was taking the place of the chariotry, that was to be expected on the analogy of other nations; that it was necessary to supplement the disappearing native infantry with "allied" foot was an omen of portent for the future.

The approach of the Assyrian army forced Ahuni of Adini to come to terms. Ashur-nasir-apal descended from his chariot and received his rival as he was presented by the Assyrian general and kissed the feet of his conqueror. Another chief, with decorated fillet, short, rounded beard, girdle, and robe to feet, fared less well, for his arms were tied behind his back, and the soldier who held the rope beat him on the head with his fist. There followed one of Ahuni's daughters, a girl with short hair and of a sufficient stoutness to reach the oriental minimum of female beauty. The golden ring and buckle, the golden necklace and sword, the elephant tusks and ivory thrones overlaid with gold and silver, indicate his wealth and show how far he was above the ordinary ruler.

The winter of 877–876 was spent in quarters in Adini. In the spring, while the Euphrates was still in flood, the army crossed. Under the eyes of the monarch on shore, the soldiers place their clothes and weapons on the reed boats, inflate goat-skins, and launch them on the current. With much prying and heaving, the chariot is dismantled; with much use of the whip in the hands of a eunuch official, it is placed on a raft laid on inflated skins. The king sits bolt upright in the chariot and clad in full regalia, even to the fez-like tiara. A eunuch of his staff stands behind him, two boatmen, nude save for the breech-clout, tow the raft along the shore, three more paddle energetically, a naked fourth guides it with a longer oar. The eunuch in the bow is pointing to the approaching west shore, whence men rush into the stream and drag out the raft by ropes slung over their backs.

For the first time in years, an Assyrian force was in north Syria. Carchemish was even more important than in the days when it was part of the Hittite empire; indeed, its ruler, Sangara, had assumed for himself the title "King of the Hittite Land." The enormous wealth accumulated by this trading city at the most important crossing of the Euphrates into Syria is indicated by the tribute Sangara presented. Twenty talents of silver, a hundred of bronze, two hundred and fifty of iron, couch, buckle, rings, and swords of gold, jugs, bowls, a censer, images of the gods in bronze, such was the wealth in metals. Beds, thrones, and tables were of ebony, which must have been imported clear from the Sudan. They were inlaid with ivory, in the fashion so common in the East to-day, though now the elephant has disappeared and mother-of-pearl has been substituted. Mantles and other weaves in wool testified to a rather large industrial population.

North Syria proper formed another fragment of the Hittite empire which still retained the name Hattina and still used the Hittite writing. Lubarna, its ruler, received Ashur-nasir-apal in his capital of Kunulua, and brought tribute as rich as his predecessors. Passing the Orontes River, the great sea of the Amorites, the Mediterranean, was reached somewhere about the site of the later Laodicea.

Further advance to the south was not needed, for all Phœnicia hastened to send him gifts—Tyre, where there reigned Ethbaal, the father-in-law of the Israelitish Ahab; Sidon, which once gave its name to the Phœnicians; the age-old Byblus, famous in Egypt for its ships as early as the Early Empire, for its connection with the myth of Osiris and Isis, for its papyri trade which made our sacred book called the Bible; Mahalata, Maisa, and Kaisa, the three towns which were to amalgamate into the Phœnician Tripolis; Amurru, the ancient city which had given its name to the "Westland," to the Amorite people, and to the sea on whose shores it stood; its later representative, Arvad, whose inhabitants had moved out to their island home after Phœnician control of the sea had made it safe from pirate raids.

Phœnician merchants saw in the Assyrian advance not the danger of conquest but the opportunity of securing valuable commercial concessions through their connection with what they rightly foresaw was to be the coming empire of the Near East. Their contributions are of extraordinary interest, for they afford our earliest detailed information regarding the Phœnician commerce. Of the precious metals, we miss only iron; their cloths must have included the famous purple; the box, ebony, and ivory spoke of their trade. Ashur-nasir-apal describes a perfect menagerie. Fifteen mighty lions from the mountains, fifty cubs for the cages in the Assyrian palaces, a great and a little dolphin, wild bulls, elephants, francolins, male and female pagate, wild asses, gazelles, stags, panthers, were collected in the zoological gardens of Kalhu.

The campaign of the year 876 marks the definite close of regular warfare, for half a score of expeditions had weakened the power of the still small kingdom. With the exception of one or two trips for building material, unbroken peace reigned until 867, when there followed one more campaign of the old-fashioned sort. Ashur-nasir-apal is careful not to refer to Urartu in his regular annals, and a casual mention of it in one of his standard inscriptions is an inadvertence of the scribe. But we cannot doubt that an expedition which hastily started in September against regions soon to be closed by the snows was an attempt to check Haldian influence in the north.

Its results were curiously unimportant. The line of march was to Qummuh, thence up-stream along the Euphrates, past the Adini boundary, into Kirhi, and around to Zamani. The army stormed Damdamusa and Parza Nishtun. Amedi was invested, and we are told of a pile of heads opposite the city gate, of captives impaled about the town, of plantations cut down, of a conflict within the gate. But nowhere are we told that Amedi was captured, and it seems not improbable that Ashur-nasir-apal abandoned his last siege in disgrace.

The successes of this monarch may as easily be under-estimated as exaggerated. He took up his task when only a beginning had been made to redeem a long period of inactivity, during which virtually all Assyria's foreign possessions had been lost. He took advantage of the upward trend of Assyrian fortunes, and his father in his brief five years had laid the foundations for a career of conquest. Granting all these initial advantages, Ashur-nasir-apal used them well. The campaigns of the first ten years were arduous, and the map proves that their strategy was excellent.

His failure to attack Babylon left his glory less than that of many of his predecessors, but he was wise to ignore Baby-lonian attempts to stir up disaffection on the middle Euphrates. He did not penetrate to Lake Van, but he did prevent the advance of Haldia south of the mountains. He did not subdue completely the Kashiari hills, but he might well argue that so poor a region was not worth the cost of conquest, and constituted no great danger if properly garrisoned along its border.

His most serious mistake was his western policy. If Assyria was satisfied to be a mere robber principality, plundering where spoil was easiest found, it might be considered good policy to collect such booty from the rich Hittite states of north Syria

Fig. 52. KNIFE-EDGE ROCK IN THE KASHIARI, WITH CASTLE ABOVE AND INSCRIPTION BELOW.

Fig. 51. ROCK-CUT TOMB MONUMENTS AT AMURRU.

or the still richer cities of Phœnicia, and hope for the day when the conquest of Egypt, equally wealthy and defenceless, would be more than a splendid dream. If a true empire were in process of formation, consolidation of the lands east of the Euphrates was absolutely necessary before further advance was safe.

Ashur-nasir-apal was not without some appreciation of this necessity. The official narratives are indeed in large part recitals of war and rapine, of such statements as: "I cut off their heads, I burned them with fire, a pile of living men and of heads over against the city gate I set up, men I impaled on stakes, the city I destroyed and devastated, I turned it into mounds and ruin heaps, the young men and maidens in the fire I burned." He still claims to be "king of all princes, king of kings," but just before he tells us, "in the lands which I have subdued I have appointed governors, service, labour, and serfdom I inflicted upon them.'

With all his wars, the amount of territory actually added to Assyria was small. Kutmuh had been separated from Nineveh and made a separate province by his father. He tells us himself of the foundation of the Tushhan province, and its governor does appear in the lists. The same is true of Amat, the province in the foot-hills northeast of the Triangle. Kirruri, just beyond, appears to have suffered the same fate. His attempt to form a province in Mazamua ended in failure. The Assyrian Empire was still to be formed.

CHAPTER IX

IN THE PALACE OF THE KING

WE are still far from the opportunities of the later empire, when the mass of letters and other documents gives us clear insight into court life, but we can at least visit the palace and call upon the sculptures to restore in imagination the daily life of the men who acknowledged Ashur-nasir-apal as their lord. For he was no mere man of war; he delighted as much in architecture, and a main object of his military enterprises was the securing of the needful wealth to construct and adorn his new buildings.

His earlier years were spent at Ashur, which had much for which to thank him. The city moat from the Gate of the Metal Worker to the Tigris Gate, the entire land circuit of the city, was cleansed of the earth which filled it, and the former gate was given higher doors of wood, covered with copper. The walls were renewed in every part, and the great terrace of the New Palace of Tukulti Urta I as well.

The modest palace he erected here has been almost completely levelled. "The Court of the Nations" prepared by Adad-nirari I formed the entrance, and the orientation was the same, a little to the north of east. A towered gate with reliefs of bulls and lions opened directly into the upper end of the broad but shallow audience-chamber, whose wall was decorated with various inset objects. The room behind was almost as broad; the others, about twenty in all, were small and ranged around an inner court. An outer room had a deep well, of connected lengths of terra-cotta pipe, from which channels carried the water through the palace, and another large room on the inner court was a bath, with a large stone in a niche, and a hole in the centre for the exit. Perhaps to him belongs an alabaster figure of double human size.

Characteristic of the most energetic rulers was their regular refusal to rebuild a palace in a former capital, their insistence on a new establishment in a new centre, where they might be free from the memories of former generations. Ashur-nasir-apal is careful to mention the colonies of Shalmaneser I in the north, and he named his son after the ancient hero. The fact that Kalhu had been the residence of his patron saint may have been the real reason why he chose that city for his new capital.

When he turned his attention to the site, it was a mere mass of ruin heaps. Digging down a hundred and twenty courses to the water-level, he first rebuilt the city wall. Within its limits arose a great palace, with apartments finished in cedar and cypress, juniper and ebony, pistachio and tamarisk. In the gates were "beasts of the mountains and of the seas," fashioned of white limestone and alabaster. Thrones of all precious woods and covered with ivory and the metals, the spoil of the lands, were set up within. By its side stood the temple of Urta, under whose special protection were the new structures. A canal was brought from the Upper Zab, and along its course could be seen plantations of fruits.

In proof of these statements, we have the excavations. We know the ground plan of the palace, can enter in imagination the various halls, even of the harem; above all, we can study at our leisure the sculptured scenes upon the walls. In them we find our chief source for the culture of the middle Assyrian period, and can write from them a full chapter in the history of civilisation.

Had we been travellers in the days we are attempting to bring back, we should have seen first and afar off the temple tower. As we approached, we should have discovered that Kalhu was defended by the Tigris on the south and west, and on the other sides by moats filled with water brought from a stream which came from the northwest. Great dams prevented the flooding of these moats when the river was high, and bridges led across the Tigris and the Upper Zab. Passing a gate in the massive walls, we would reach the temple tower, a huge square of a hundred and fifty feet on a side, jutting out from the palace platform. The stone basement was twenty feet high, with battlemented top, the only ornaments the shallow pilasters and the small circular projection to the north that once retained the statue of the king. Thus the massiveness of the huge roughly dressed blocks, destitute of mortar, could be felt in all its strength. Above rose the adobe core, for the casing of burnt bricks is the work of his son.

A paved court next led to a small temple, whose main entrance looked east, and was flanked on either side by a huge human-headed lion, sixteen and a half feet high. On each was the divine turban; the face was the common Assyrian type, bearded and with the hair curled in a mass upon the neck. Great wings with a triple line of feathers curved over their backs, wavy hair covered the remainder of their bodies, around their middle was a ribbon tied with a tassel. The tail had the claw of the Asiatic lion. Legs with strongly emphasised muscles supported them, two solidly planted feet appeared in front, while three more gave the impression of irresistible movement when seen from the side. Underneath was the Standard inscription, a beautiful example of calligraphy when seen once, wearisome when encountered sprawling across the sculptured slabs for the hundredth time.

Before each of these divine guardians of the gate was a square altar. By their sides were three small slabs, one above the other; the upper and lower presented winged human figures in low relief, the middle one was eagle-headed. The winged man had two pairs of wings, one upraised, the other drooping; on his head was the triple-horned cap; a fringed cloak to his heels covered a fringed tunic which reached only to his knees. Around his middle was a tasselled girdle; on his feet were thonged half-sandals. His braceleted right hand was raised towards the colossi in blessing, his left grasped the short mace with fringed end. Paint can be yet perceived on the hair and beard, the eyes and the sandals. Between were the eagle-headed figures, with huge beaks, lolling red tongues, stiff high crests, their dress and posture like that of their more

FIG. 53. WINGED GENIUS FERTILISING THE SACRED TREE WITH
PALM SPATHE.
(Auburn Theological Seminary.)

FIG. 55. EAGLE-HEADED FIGURE
(PALACE OF ASHUR-NASIR-APAL.)
(New York Historical Society.)

FIG. 54. TREE OF LIFE. (PALACE OF
ASHUR-NASIR-APAL.)
(New York Historical Society.)

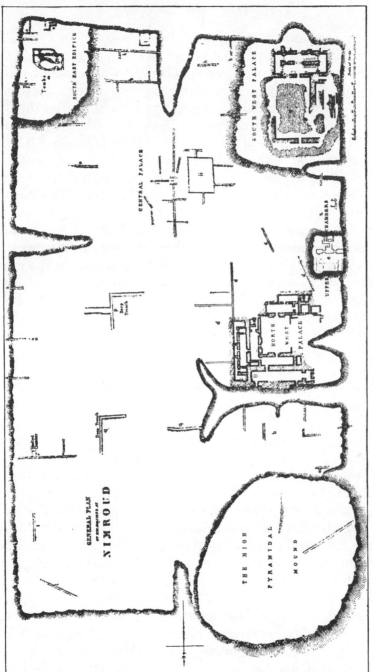

MAP 4. THE CITY OF KALHU.

"Northwest Palace" (Ashur-nasir-apal); "Central Palace" (Shalmaneser III and Tiglath Pileser III); "Upper Chambers" (Adad-nirari III); "Southwest Palace" (Esarhaddon); "Southeast Edifice" (Sin-shar-ishkun).

human companions, save that their weapon was a knife struck into their girdle; their right hand held aloft the spathe which was to fertilise the palm, in the left was a small basket. Typically Assyrian as this scene appears, it was borrowed from the south, for the palm bears no fruit so far north.

This was the main entrance. To either side were others, flanked by a representation of the battle between Marduk of Babylon and Tiamat, the personified Chaos. Tiamat has started towards the entrance of the temple, but has halted to snarl back at the approaching Marduk. His mouth, with its huge sharp teeth, is wide open, his long ears stand erect, his eyebrows bristle. His body is feathered, his wings and tail are those of a bird, but his fore feet are the paws of a lion and the hind feet eagle's claws. Marduk, in the dress of the gods, pursues in such haste that one foot is lifted from the ground. His sword hangs useless from the shoulder-belt, in each hand he bears against him the thunderbolt, the double-headed trident.

On the walls within the portals were two huge human figures, garlanded and their right hands raised in prayer, in their left were branches ending in three flowers, plucked from the tree of life for the blessing of the king. In the room itself were sculptured figures of Ea, the fish-god. He, too, raises the fertilising palm spathe, but over the usual costume is the head and body of a scaly fish, with tail reaching to the waist.

Beyond this entrance, in a corner of the courtyard, appeared the figure of the king. On a stele of limestone, within an arched frame and in more than human size, Ashur-nasir-apal stands out in high relief. On his head is the fez-like cap, the fringed ribbon falls to the shoulder, his raised right arm is bare save for the tunic, his left is so swathed in the outer garment that it appears as if in a sling, and even his legs are covered. His girdle is broad, and across the front of the skirt is a fringe. His adornment is profuse, a bracelet on either wrist, a huge ring in the ear, a necklace with egg-and-dart effect, and below this hang the divine symbols, the crescent, the trident, the Maltese cross, and the encircled star; in his left hand he bears

the mace, in his girdle the three poignards.   His eye is large
and vacant, his nose bulbous and down-hanging, his forehead
low, his beard short.   This last proves that he was indeed
young when he came into possession of the royal power, and

FIG. 56. EMBROIDERY ON ASHUR-NASIR-APAL'S DRESS.

on the back and sides, as well as in the field in front, is inscribed
the earliest form of his annals.   He looks out at other sacred
emblems, the winged globe, the crescent, the star, the two-
pronged fork, the horned cap.   This splendid stele stood on a
long pedestal, and before it was a low triangular altar resting
on lion's feet and with a circular hollowed top.   We are in

the presence of the central fact of the empire, the worship of
the deified ruler.

Returning to the main entrance, we pass through portals
guarded by human-headed lions and into a vestibule whose
mud-brick walls were once covered by plaster painted with
various figures. Another portal ornamented with winged
beings led to the inner shrine, at whose farther end was a recess paved with a single alabaster slab, no less than twenty-
one by sixteen and a half feet, and containing the annals of
the reign. The cult statues of Urta and of his associates which
once were worshipped here have disappeared, but not without
traces. Enamelled ornaments or parts of the body, the hair,
and beard, black marble eyes inlaid with ivory and with eye-
balls of bright-blue enamel, arms and legs of wood, now charred
by the fire in which the gods of Assyria met their doom, are
all that remain. Small blue figurines reproduce Urta's consort,
a nude woman with outstretched arms and horned and battlemented crown. Fragments of glazed and pictured bricks, of
agate, lapis-lazuli, and cornelian, bits of glass, beads, and cylinders, one of which is Egyptian, a chalcedony ointment-box
or a casket in the blue glaze borrowed from Egypt, with the
holes around the rim still showing where once the gold was inlaid a glazed vase carved with the usual scene of a battlemented town with women stretching out their hands in supplication and a captive with inverted kettle over his head,
such is the débris from which we must attempt the impossible
task of imagining the riches of the temple in the days of its
greatest glory.

A short hundred feet to the east, on the platform edge, we
come to another temple whose entrance this time faced the
south. Unlike the first, this portal was guarded by true lions,
eight feet high, and with much of that success in reproducing
animal figures which is the glory of Assyrian art. Aside from
the realism of the mouth with its wide-open jaws, the thick
mane, and the erect hair, the work is rougher and gives even
more of the sense of solidity. This temple was the replica of
the other, in its inner chamber, its huge inscribed block of

Fig. 58. ASHUR-NASIR-APAL WITH ATTENDANT.
(Bowdoin College.)

Fig. 57. ASHUR-NASIR-APAL WITH OFFERING BOWL.
(New York Historical Society.)

alabaster, and its niche. The clew to its purpose is discovered through a statue found in the room. On a pedestal of reddish limestone, above the great inscribed slab, rises a figure of the king. It differs from the other examples of Kalhu sculptures in that it is entirely in the round. The ruler is here little more than half size and he is far less adorned. His head is bare, his hair is plainly treated, and ornaments are conspicuous for their absence. His long dress sweeps the ground, permitting only the toes to be seen. In his left hand he carries the fringed mace, in his right a long rounding teethed sickle, the descendant of the boomerang carried by the Shumerian princes. The king is in his priestly robes, humble before his god. As a work of art, it has one defect, it is too flat viewed from the side. Across the breast is an inscription from the middle years of his reign, and indeed his beard is longer and his figure more mature.

A great paved open space was closed at its southern end by the palace facade. The river flowed at the west, and to it descended two broad flights of steps. The entrance to the north was flanked with two smaller gateways, guarded by the human-headed lions. That to the west was bordered by a series of slabs with sculptures of unusual interest. The central figure on one side is the king with his bow in his left hand and the two arrows in his right, and behind him stands his eunuch attendant with his mace and a reserve bow and quiver. Opposite is his turtanu or chancellor, Ashur-iddina, his hands crossed in the common attitude of respect, and likewise followed by a eunuch. Over these figures, themselves eight feet high, towered to twice the height a gigantic winged genius with the fertilising palm spathe. Across the open passageway could be seen a second turtanu and servant and then a unique group of dependents. The men's faces are painted black, which should imply that they are negroes, but their bodies are short and stocky, their shoes are of the upturned fashion we have come to associate with the Hittites, and they wear a conical head-dress formed by winding folds of the turban or a simple fillet. Some are clad in long sweeping robes with cape effect, others with a tunic reaching only to the knee, the artistic fringes and borders break the monotony, and bracelets, armlets, and necklaces afford further ornament. Hands are raised in supplication by some groups, some carry trays with armlets, bracelets, and earrings.   On the shoulder

FIG. 59. TRIBUTE OF MONKEYS.

of one is crouched a monkey, an arm is over the rope, his tiny hands clutch the fillet which binds his master's hair.   A second is led by a rope but rises to his hind legs and looks regretfully backward.   Monkey nature was never more faithfully depicted.

Through the entrance flanked by human-headed bulls, the visitor came into the lower end of a long, narrow hall, one hundred and fifty-four by thirty-three feet, the peculiar form of which was due to its roofing, a barrel vault.   The walls of mud

FIG. 60. ENTRANCE WITH HUMAN-HEADED BULLS, PALACE OF
ASHUR-NASIR-APAL.

FIG. 61. CORNER OF ROOM IN PALACE OF ASHUR-NASIR-APAL.
Note the use of the dowel holes.

brick reach to fourteen feet in height, and where exposed were covered with a plaster on which were painted complicated designs in brilliant reds and blues. Up to eight feet, the walls were panelled with the slabs of gypseous alabaster on which were carved the scenes already described. In the long gallery of art, which was in reality the throne-room, historical events predominated. This type of relief was in two stories, with a band of inscription between. Originally, there was much colour, especially the hair and beard, the eyes and the sandals. Here were ranged in order the flight of Shadudu, the lion-hunt, the royal camp, the transport of chariots across the river. At the upper end of the room stood the throne, resting on a great stepped slab of alabaster over a foundation sacrifice of animals and gold-leaf. A shallow recess behind showed in the centre the sacred tree, a highly conventionalised mass of branches tipped with floral designs. Above floated the winged disk within which appeared Ashur. On either side stood the royal figure, grasping the ceremonial mace in his left hand, his right raised in adoration, thumb between first and second fingers, while at his back the winged being held aloft the fertilising palm spathe.

A somewhat smaller chamber with the lone figure of the king, emblems of the gods on his breast and attended by pairs of eagle-headed demons, leads the guest to the banqueting-room with its magnificent series of reliefs. Again we behold the richly clad figure of the monarch, this time seated on his throne, if we may apply that name to what is, in spite of its rich decoration, little more than a couch. There is no back, but a cushion adds somewhat to its comfort, bronze rams' heads decorate the corners of the seat, double reversed volutes the frame. The royal feet rest on a footstool supported by lion's claws. Ashur-nasir-apal gazes at the uplifted bowl of wine with a pleasure which the artist delights to depict. In front of him stands a eunuch, a ram-headed fly-flapper in one hand, a long ram-headed handle in the other, and over his shoulder the same immense fringed napkin which to-day is presented the guest after he has eaten and washed his hands. Behind is another eunuch with upraised fly-flapper and the royal bow, quiver, and sword, followed by a second with the same furniture, save that the fly-flapper is replaced by the thonged staff with the disked star at the opposite end. On both sides, the scene is concluded by winged creatures bearing the now well-known palm spathe. Elsewhere the king is to be seen leaning on his bow, holding in his uplifted hand the arrows or a bowl of wine, or worshipping his gods with raised hand and firmly held twig with the triple-flowered branch.

The remainder of the great structure had little to offer. Everywhere was irregularity, for no attempt was made to balance rooms and courts. The other sides of the great court were surrounded by rooms of mud brick, but they are rarely painted. Sometimes they are faced with slabs of inferior design or containing the simple repetition of the standard inscriptions, but gradually they tail off to the servant's quarters.[1] Thus Ashur-nasir-apal showed his love for Kalhu; but he was buried in Ashur.

Save for Ashur-nasir-apal himself, the men who walked these courts must remain nameless for us. Our only recourse is the long list of officials who year by year gave their names to date events. In his second full year, Ashur-nasir-apal followed the normal custom and held the eponym office in person. He was succeeded in this by Ashur-iddina, who should by the same rule be the turtanu whose majestic figure faced the king on the palace walls. In the men who follow, Shimutti-aku, Sha Nabu-damqa, and Dagan-bel-nasir, we have the highest court officials, who must be represented in the eunuch attendants of the king. In no case are the officials those who held similar rank under his predecessors; the young king was a man of strong individuality, and it is manifest that he followed not the advisers of his father.

Fate was kind to Ashur-nasir-apal in that he was not entirely forgotten by later peoples, but this was by no means an unmingled good fortune, for he owed it to confusion with the

---

[1] Layard, *Nineveh and its Remains*, I, 70 ff.; 117 ff.; 271 ff.; *Nineveh and Babylon*, 123 ff.; 348 ff.; Budge, *Assyrian Sculptures*.

Ashur-bani-apal whose name was so familiar to the Greeks as Sardanapallus. The earlier Greeks knew him best; Hellanicus, one of the first Greek historians, in his *History of the Persians*, declared that there were two monarchs of the name, and the much-maligned Ctesias approximated his date with startling accuracy. The three hundred years before Cyrus put an end to the Median power, round number as it is, brings his death to 850, barely ten years too late. But one may be permitted to imagine the sensations of Ashur-nasir-apal could he learn that for so many millennia he was to be remembered only as an unwarlike and effeminate prince!

CHAPTER X

THE THREAT OF ARARAT

SHALMANESER III was no longer a young man when he ascended the throne in 860.   His father had reigned no less than twenty-five years, and he himself owned a son already old enough to accompany him on distant journeys.   His first step was to make a complete sweep of the palace officials, who were replaced with men nearer his own age.   Ashur-bel-ukin was appointed turtanu, and Ashur-bania became the chief cellarer.   Abi-ina-ekalli-lilbur, whose name, "May my father grow old in the palace," indicated a hereditary position, very appropriately was chosen chamberlain of the palace.   Not one of the men who surrounded the person of the king or ruled in the provinces had previously held office high enough to be entered in the eponym lists.

Thanks to the efforts of his father, the foreign situation was by no means threatening; rather it offered encouraging opportunities for war if the new king cherished such ambitions. During the entire quarter-century peace with Babylonia had never been formally broken.   The Aramæan invasion had been brought to a standstill, and the Median tribes just appearing on the eastern sky-line threatened no danger as yet.   Syria promised much booty at little cost.   The brief glory of the Hebrews under David and Solomon had disappeared with the disruption into Israel and Judah (938), while the invasion of Palestine by the Egyptian Shishak a few years later had not been followed up by his weak successors of the Libyan twenty-second dynasty.

On the north alone was cause for concern.   Behind the protection of the Armenian mountains, a formidable power was developing.   The natives used the name Haldians for themselves and Biaina for the land; the Assyrians called their country Urartu, whence the Hebrews derived the form Ararat, which, in their tradition, they made the region where the ark of Noah landed.[1] A reluctant notice had already been forced from the scribes of Ashur-nasir-apal; indeed, the last recorded campaign of his reign had been necessitated by the growing influence of that state, and the failure of the official historians to mention the part played by Urartu was simply confession of failure to win back the lost laurels.

Nor did his son dare a direct attack on Haldia at first. In the very beginning of his accession year, for he had been enthroned early, Shalmaneser collected his foot-soldiers and his chariots and entered the defiles of Simesi land, the rough Tiyari region where almost to our own day the Christian mountaineers preserved a hardly won independence. No opposition had been previously encountered, mute evidence that the wars of his father on this frontier had not been without result, that the Assyrian domain had been extended to include the country to the immediate northeast of Nineveh.[2]

The royal annalists furnish a more or less coherent narrative; for the life-giving details we turn to the scenes represented on the bronze bands of a palace gate. It is here we behold the Assyrian army in its full array, the heavy and light infantry, regularly associated in pairs, and clad in helmet and short cloak. The light-armed have a sword on the left side, a small round shield is carried on the left arm and a javelin in the right hand; the heavy-armed use spear, bow, and quiver. The cavalry bear sword and javelin, bow and quiver, ride bareback with hunched-up knees, hold the reins in their left hand, and each possesses in addition a led horse.

The first acquisition of the reign was Aridi, commanding the Upper Zab. The scene of plunder, the pillar of heads, the holocaust of youths and maidens, indicated that the new king was to be no less harsh than his terrible father in repressing

[1] Gen. 8 : 4; Isaiah 37 : 38; II Kings 19 : 37; Jer. 51 : 27.
[2] Detailed narrative of reign, *JAOS.*, XLI, 345 ff.; *AJSL.*, XXXVII, 217 ff.; sources, N. Rasmussen, *Salmanasser den II's Indskriften,* 1907; gate reliefs, Pinches, *Bronze Ornaments of the Palace Gates of Balawat,* 1880; King, *Bronze Reliefs from the Gates of Shalmaneser,* 1915; discussion, Billerbeck, *BA.*, VI, 1 ff.

disorder.   The result was seen when all the chiefs from whom Ashur-nasir-apal had exacted tribute appeared before his son to make trial of his clemency.

Climbing out of the Zab valley, Shalmaneser descended into Hubushkia by a mountain pass and over hills which reached to heaven like the point of an iron dagger, where a passage for the chariots could be made only by much labour on the part of the pioneers.   The capital of the same name was soon a smoking ruin, and its Nairi princes begged the royal pardon. The Haldian border was reached at Sugania, a tiny fortress perched on a high rock at the junction of two affluents of the upper Tigris.   Around the arched bridge it commanded, the Assyrians constructed a circular camp, with a gate at either exit of the road.   The king set forth in his chariot, attended by others in which were carried the standards.   Arrived at the doomed city, he dismounted and, still surrounded by his body-guard, shot his arrows against the fortress.   The main attack was launched by archers, but sappers, protected by long leather robes, were employed to loosen the stones in the walls, and other soldiers attempted an assault with ladders.   The natives resisted desperately with bow and spear until the houses were fired, when they abandoned the struggle.   Opposite the town, a pillar of heads was erected, and the survivors, naked, save for the peculiar "liberty caps" and uptilted shoes, their necks bound to a yoke with a long rope and their hands tied behind their backs, were dragged before the official who stood, club of office in hand, to receive them.

Operations recommenced with a skirmish in the open.   The king stepped down from his chariot, the standards remained. In marked contrast to the stalwart Assyrians were the little Haldians, clad in scanty robes or entirely nude, armed with long or short lance and defended by the small round shield and greaves.   In their formation, pairs of archers and shield-bearing lancers, they had followed the Assyrian system. Fourteen of the surrounding villages went up in smoke, the men were impaled on stakes set in the wall, the severed heads were hung in the gates.   The invaders cut down the palm-trees, surprising so far north until we remember that to-day they still flourish fruitless on the warm shores of Lake Van, and captive horses recall to our minds that Armenia has always been famous for the fineness of its breeds. The strangest trophy was a rough platform on wheels, so ponderous that eleven men were needed to pull it along by means of ropes over their shoulders. On it was a huge jar, no less than eight feet high, held in place by a man mounted behind it, and guarded by poles in the hands of the three men who followed. The eunuch camp prefect made frequent trips in his chariot to oversee the collection of the booty, which was packed in camp under his businesslike direction.

The army descended to a plain for its next encampment, a rectangular walled enclosure, studded with battlemented towers within whose protection in one corner stood the royal tent. Quitting this place, the army pushed on over mountains so steep and by roads so execrable that it was necessary for the attendants to drag the chariot horses up the slope by main force. Without encountering further resistance, Shalmaneser reached Lake Van at a village where the mountains ranged about the curving shore. The procession to the water's edge was formed: first the two royal standards, then the monarch on foot, his high officials, the musicians playing on harps, finally the bulls and rams destined for the sacrifice. The royal effigy had been carved on a low cliff overhanging the water, where Shalmaneser appeared as he was wont to be seen on state occasions, richly robed and with sceptre and tiara, but unarmed, in token of the peaceful nature of his mission. The standards were set up, with a tall candlestick by their side, the king assumed the attitude of devotion, two bulls and four rams were slaughtered and presented on the three-legged altar before the stele, the libations were set forth in a jar on an ox-footed support. Portions of the slain animals were thrown by the soldiers into the lake to be consumed by the fish, turtles, and wild swine that swarmed the shore or the waters.

Considerable damage had been caused to a corner of Haldia, but it was only a corner, and Arame, the first Haldian king of whom we have record, had not even been engaged. Winter was approaching and the passes would soon be closed: Shalmaneser decided to return and by the same route.   On his way Asau of Gilzan brought his gifts, including two humped camels of the Bactrian breed.   The reconnaissance in force had indicated with sufficient clearness that it would be no easy matter to develop successes on this frontier, and it suggested that the material returns might not meet the expense of equipping an army.   Shalmaneser turned to north Syria, where Haldian influence was strong, and it was not until after he had subjugated Adini that another effort was made to punish his Armenian ally.   Turning back from the Euphrates in 857, the Assyrians filed along the slopes of the huge extinct volcano of Sumu into Zamani and thence through wild mountain paths to the source of the Tigris, where, amid the most savage of scenery and tribes as wild to-day as when their ancestors resisted the march of Assyrian armies, the full-grown river emerges in a gorge whose walls had already been adorned with the figure of Tiglath Pileser.   At this time Shalmaneser carved the first of the reliefs which were to commemorate his visit to so astounding a spot.

The border range was penetrated by the Enzite pass, the Assyrians crossed the eastern branch of the Euphrates, and appeared before the Haldian capital, Arzashkun, on a rocky elevation north of Lake Van.   The little Haldians, armed with swords and javelins and wearing helmets, short skirts, and pointed shoes, put up a good resistance, and even dared to seize the bridles of the cavalry and chariot horses in the vain attempt to delay the Assyrian approach.   Their discomfiture was completed by the mounted archers, they were stabbed by the footmen, or their legs were hacked off as they lay on the ground. The gates were reached, and under the protection of their companions' shields the soldiers set fire to the city.   Arame, hurrying through the mountains with the main body of the Haldians, found that he had arrived too late, and his forces were driven back to the hills in confusion.   The accustomed pillar of heads, the stakes with impaled prisoners, the stele on the near-by mountain were followed by a march down to the lake and the repetition of the ceremonies which had marked the beginning of the reign.

Over mountains so high that the attendants must needs lead the chariots, the army continued to Gilzan, where camp was pitched before the chief castle, situated on a high hill beyond a stream. The inhabitants, led by their chief, Asau, were clad in the long double robe, upturned shoes, and filleted hair which characterised the Hittite peoples and contrasted so strangely with their Semitic countenances. Some brought kettles on their heads or skins of wine slung over their shoulders, their companions drove horses, cattle, sheep, and goats, not to forget the seven two-humped camels. To judge from the bronze-gate representations, they were barely the size of ponies; after the lapse of a generation, the Obelisk presented them grown to twice the height of a man, and the tribute had likewise grown, adding all sorts of metals and royal robes. Asau was ordered to receive within his palace a stele of Shalmaneser, and the army returned by the pass of Kirruri above Arbela.

Thirty years before, Anhite of Shupria had paid tribute to Assyria, but the close presence of the Haldians had made him lapse from the Assyrian allegiance. In 853 his capital of Uppume was besieged. The main fortification was in three sections, each with a gate, the central portion on a high hill, the suburbs on one somewhat lower, and there were two outforts. The attack, under the personal direction of the king, was carried on entirely by archers, on foot or in chariots. An unnamed city was likewise situated on three hills. On one was an outfort, with the wall extending down to lower ground. From the crest of the next, the walls of the main settlement stretched across a gully and covered all the third elevation. What the captives had already suffered is indicated grimly by the high isolated pillar before which were heaped three piles of heads. The crown prince had already appeared in the battle, well protected by the tall shield in the hand of his attendant; he now took charge of the train of captives, the men naked and yoked, the women in long robes, though the only hint of booty was a lone horse. The captives were presented to the governor of Tushhan as he stood at the gate of the walled city on a low hill.

The Assyrians continued up the river until they reached the "source of the Tigris, the place whence the waters flow," the "cave of the river" pictured in the sculptures. In one scene the mountains sweep in a long curve around the water, on the far side of which is a fortress, with square gateways between the towers. Stone pillars with round balls on their tops flank the opening. A sculptor works in the water, mallet on chisel, at a representation of the king which is complete save that the surrounding cartouche is still to be incised. So perfect is the royal figure that an official already has taken his position on a platform erected among the rocks and adores his master's effigy. Other Assyrians lead up a ram for the sacrifices and drag on his back a reluctant bull destined to meet the same end.

A long parade of soldiers, foot and horse, up the course of the stream fills the second scene. At their head is the king, whose sad lack of horsemanship is indicated by his riding straightlegged and with huge stirrups tied to the horse-blanket, not, in the only fashion known to the oriental expert, with hunched-up knees and bareback. The royal chariot and those which bear the standards are naturally a part of the picture and so are the sacrificial calf and ram. Through three openings we see trees and soldiers, waist deep in the icy waters, who uphold torches to lighten the gloom. On the rock at the entrance is the niche with the conventional royal figure, while on a smaller rock in the water the sculptor is putting on the finishing touches under the direction of the officer at his side. The accuracy of the picture is proved by the reliefs surviving unto this day, one on the wall of the passage where the Tigris for the moment comes to light before again plunging into the mountain, the second in a huge upper cave decorated with stalactites and stalagmites, where in prehistoric times the river found its outlet. Above still towers the cliff up which lead

Fig. 63.   OLDER TIGRIS TUNNEL,
NOW CLOSED.

To left is the inscription of Tiglath Pileser I.

Fig. 62.   THE PRESENT TIGRIS TUNNEL.

The white squeeze paper shows the location of the inscription of Shalmaneser III.

FIG. 64. THE EXIT FROM THE TIGRIS TUNNEL.

FIG. 65. EDESSA, PERHAPS KAPRABI.

rock-cut stairs to the terraces on the summit that mark the site of the settlement that once dominated the sacred stream.

With the exception of a brief trip to the sources of the Tigris and Euphrates in 845, when Lala of Melidia paid his first tribute, there is a total absence of references to the Haldian region until 832   This cannot be accidental, for the truthful map indicates that Assyria was losing ground during these years.   The growing power of Urartu was reflected on the eastern frontier.   Several times it was visited by the troops of Shalmaneser; the details would be unworthy our attention were it not that we have our first references to several peoples of the first importance in the later period.

Mazamua, now replacing the older Zamua, was invaded in 856; the natives took refuge in boats upon an inland sea, but the invaders followed them on rafts and "dyed the sea with their blood like wool."   By 828 Mazamua was a province. The year 844 saw a brief campaign into Namri land.   Marduk-mudammiq, whose name indicated Babylonian influence in the neighbourhood, retired to the hills, and his authority was given to a new ruler whom we know only as Ianzu, the native Kashshite word for king.   By 835 he had become hostile, had been driven to the hills, and had been made prisoner.   Paru of Elli was established in Tupliash.   Twenty-seven kinglets of Parsua land paid their dues when Shalmaneser appeared in their country, and in the Missi land he found a possession of the Amadai.   This at least is worthy our most careful notice, for it is the first appearance of the Medes in history.

A change of dynasty in Haldia replaced Arame by Sardurish I, the son of Lutipri.   His are the first Haldian monuments, but the cuneiform had not yet been adapted to the vernacular, and Sardurish writes in Assyrian.   His imitation of the Assyrian royal formulas might be innocent enough, but his title "King of the World, King of Nairi," was a direct challenge to Shalmaneser.

An expedition was prepared, but Shalmaneser did not himself undertake to meet the challenge; stranger still, the official annals admit that it was led by Daian Ashur, the turtanu. Haldia was entered by the Ammash pass, and the Euphrates was crossed, but Sardurish was safe on the rock of Van, to which he had transferred his capital, and a great wall to the lake permitted the bringing in of provisions. The barren claim to victory hides a defeat, for when two years later it was necessary to raid Kirhi and Ulluba, there can be no doubt that there had been retrocession of the Assyrian sphere of influence.

Daian Ashur crossed the Upper Zab in 829, forced tribute from Datana of Hubushkia, and drove out Udaki from Zirta, capital of the Mannai. Though not so well known to the general reader as the Medes, this reference likewise has its interest to the student of Assyrian history, for the Mannai were close and respected allies of Assyria in the last century of her existence. The last campaign of the reign (828), the unwearied old turtanu made a swing around the circle. After the capture of Musasir, another state destined to play a most important part in the next century, he fell upon the border of Haldia, but failed here and returned through Gilzan and the Parsua towns that he might have some conquests to narrate. Such "victories" of the last few years need no interpretation; the border states might be sure that the immediate future was not with Assyria, but with Haldia.

Assyrian influence had been made supreme in western Mesopotamia by Ashur-nasir-apal, but the growth of Haldia had seriously weakened her prestige, and control of the Euphrates bend must again be won by the sword. After the virtual failure of the Armenian expedition of 860, Shalmaneser turned to the west. Lucky and unlucky days played a large part in Assyrian life; we realise the difference between ancient and modern superstition when we discover the army leaving Nineveh on the lucky 13th of Airu, the beginning of May. The chief objective was wealthy north Syria, but it crossed the northern limits of Adini, whose new master, Ahuni, was driven by a skirmish to take refuge behind his fortifications. When the horrible spectacle of a pillar of heads was seen before the Aramæan settlement of Bur Marna, the "Spring of our

Lord," the threat was sufficient to bring in the contributions of Habini of Til Abni and of Gauni of Sarugi, whose name is to be compared with that of the Hebrew patriarch Serug.[1] Assyrian control was marked by the erection of a palace; a surviving slab bears a lion which might be the twin of those in the palace of Ashur-nasir-apal.

Conquest of Syria was impossible with Adini in the rear, and in the next year Shalmaneser invited the crown prince to leave with him Nineveh on the lucky 13th of Airu. He hastened by the direct road to the capital of Adini, Til Barsip, which commanded one of the most important fords of the Euphrates, where the islands show in summer and a ferry crosses to-day. The city was large as such cities went, the ramparts on the land side were strong, a quay cut through the conglomerate testified to commerce by water, and the Hittite substratum in the people was indicated by the Hittite sculpture in basalt. Ahuni attempted to block the passage of the river, but was driven back into the city, and the Adini cities on the Syrian bank were plundered.

The third year (857) Shalmaneser was forced to devote more special attention to Adini, for, inspired by the growing power of Haldia, Ahuni actually led the whole of his army against the Assyrian border. The Assyrian general sent out by Shalmaneser found the enemy drawn up on a mountain; he blew like the fierce wind-storm that breaks down trees, let fly his troops like a hawk against his opponents, and drove Ahuni out of the camp like a thief, so that his master might despoil the royal treasures. The name of Til Barsip was changed to Kar Shulmanasharidu, in honour of the sovereign whose "fort" it became. Two mighty lions of basalt, inscribed with a record of the warfare, were placed in the south gate, while inside the walls was a stele where Shalmaneser might be seen addressing the rival prince with his conical cap. The occupied cities were given similar names. But Adini was not completely Assyrianised, for a century later the Hebrew Amos saw the cutting off of the sceptre-bearer of Beth Eden still in the future, and its

[1] Gen. 11:20.

captivity was remembered as late as the days of Sennacherib.[1]

With Adini Assyrian, it was absurd to permit a little Mesopotamian state to retain its independence at the River Balih, in the heart of that territory. The partisans of Assyria were passed the word, and on the royal approach in 854, they assassinated their lord, Giammu. No new king was named, but the Assyrian gods were placed in the temple and a ceremonial feast was celebrated in the palace of the late ruler. The incorporation, long ago demanded by the necessities of the case, was at last carried into effect, and the Balih region became a part of the Harran province.

Strangely enough, the still smaller state of Til Abni in the semiarid region due east was permitted to retain its independence. Without the sculptures, we should never have suspected the favoured place it held. The reception accorded Habini was very different from that to any other conquered ruler. He did indeed make obeisance, bowing his head before the king, but he made his approach from his fully fortified camp in chariots which, in form as in trapping, were in the best Assyrian style, and he was accompanied by attendants who exemplified all the latest fashions of the Assyrian upper class. Their hair hung in a mass at the nape of the neck, and their beards were long and square cut, like that of Shalmaneser himself, and in sharp contrast to the pointed beards affected not only by the princes of the subjugated peoples but by the lower-class Assyrians as well. Habini himself wore the long-fringed robe and the fringed jacket with diagonal opening, and had just laid aside his ornamented Assyrian sandals. He was thoroughly Assyrianised and valued by his masters.

The official scribe who compiled the record for the Obelisk has carelessly omitted the campaign for 838; the sculptor has seen to it that we learn it was against Marduk-apal-usur, the last prince of Suhi on the middle Euphrates. The scene in the most conspicuous position shows what made strongest appeal to the artist, the palm-covered hills along the river in which the lion hunted the stag. The natives, assigned to second

[1] Amos 1 : 5; II Kings 19 : 12.

Fig. 66. MESOPOTAMIAN WATER–WHEEL.

Fig. 67. LION FROM SARUGI, A PROVINCIAL IMITATION OF THE
LIONS FROM KALHU.

place, barely permit their beards to appear; the most conspicuous article of apparel was a fringed girdle of such length that it hung down the side. Similar fringed girdles of various colours were draped over a pole resting on the shoulders of two citizens of Suhi, the remainder were laden with elephants' tusks, golden pails, bowls, and bars of lead. No king appears in the various scenes to bow before Shalmaneser and no *shaknu* is again mentioned in Suhi. Four years before, Nimit Ishtar was still the capital of a small province; there was now formed the most extensive province of the empire, Rasappa. Its capital was at the head of the Tartara under the Singara range; it included Apku north of the mountains, Nimit Ishtar to the east, Mari to the southeast, and the whole steppe region to the south and southwest, Qatni on the Habur, and the entire length of the Euphrates, so far as it was Assyrian, from Dur Karpati, "Pot Wall," opposite the fort Ashurnasir-apal had located against Adini and had named from himself, through Sirqu, Laqe, Hindanu, Anat, Suhi, to Ashurisbat, the new designation of the bitumen pits at Id.

With the reign of Shalmaneser III the history of Babylonia becomes inextricably bound up with that of Assyria, and Assyrian records are henceforth our chief source of information. The ruler of Babylon was, at this time, Nabu-apal-iddina, known to all students of Babylonian religion and of art for his beautiful relief in commemoration of the finding of the Sun-God's image. Too weak to war directly against Assyria, he had yet sent aid to a rebel in Suhi, and no sooner was Shalmaneser on the throne than he enforced a treaty which was euphemistically entitled a "treaty of complete alliance," but in reality marked the subjugation of Babylonia to Assyria. This subordination became perfectly evident when Shalmaneser marched south and in Babylon and Borsippa offered the sacrifices to Marduk and Nabu which only the suzerain of those cities might present (860). In due time Nabu-apal-iddina "stood upon his mountain," and his place was filled by the Assyrian nominee, Marduk-zakir-shum I. The anti-Assyrian forces rallied around his younger brother, Marduk-bel-usate, who seized the upper part of Akkad, and thus cut off Marduk-zakir-shum from his overlord.

Shalmaneser was only too glad to rescue his subordinate. He sacrificed to Adad at Zaban, and then marched south against Daban, the temporary capital of the rebel (853). Marduk-bel-usate was shut up in Gananate, his crops and orchards destroyed, his canals dammed, but it required a second year's campaign before he was driven out "like a fox from his hole." The fugitive hastened along the road to Elam, but in the mouth of the pass he was overtaken and put to death as a rebel.

Freed from the rivalry of his brother, Marduk-zakir-shum had still to reckon with his overlord, who was in no haste to surrender the advantages he had won. As the acknowledged suzerain of Babylon, he filled the city with his gifts and pure offerings to Marduk, sacrificed to Nergal in Kutu, and appeared in Borsippa, where even more gracious treatment was accorded Nabu and his consort, their temple Ezida, and their inhabitants, who were banqueted, richly clothed, and presented with wondrous gifts.

Having thus won over the priestly class and having learned that the gods looked graciously upon him and had heard his prayers, he determined to clear Babylonia of the pest of Aramæan tribes which was bringing the land to ruin. Under the inspection of a seated eunuch, a bowman of the body-guard supervised the construction of the pontoon bridge across the Euphrates. Inflated skins were tied together, beams connected them with the shore, an earthen causeway was heaped up at either approach. The superstructure was formed of stones, brush, and clay, carried by soldiers with swords at their sides, ready to repel a sudden attack. The enemy were not far away, for the bowmen were still shooting in their direction.

Once the chariot horses had been led across the shaky bridge, the Assyrians were in the territory of the powerful Dakkuru. Like their descendants in modern times, these wanderers possessed little mud castles where they deposited their scanty wealth in times of danger. Baqani was a small, double-walled fort with two gates, situated on a fair-sized artificial mound by the stream and in a country filled with palms. The nomads were soon in flight, and Shalmaneser dismounted to receive Adini, the Dakkuru chief, a tall, beardless youth. His nobles followed swathed in trailing fringed robes, while the higher officials were brave with their long Assyrian beards. Tribesmen, clad only in short skirts and in their bare feet, brought bars and pigs of various metals and large and small kettles to the edge of the stream, where they were transferred to two small flat-bottomed boats, laden with bales of goods and steered by a rude oar while naked men dragged them along. Already the skin of a wild beast and a tray filled with ivories had been landed and were ready for the conqueror.

From his camp Shalmaneser passed over a second pontoon bridge and approached a town surrounded by double walls, each with two gates. This was the abode of Iakinu, king of the Sealands, a man with a pointed beard and long fringed garments. His present lack of importance was emphasised by his following of but two servants, one bearing a small kettle and leading two calves, the other with a jug and a lamb under his arm. None might guess that he was to give his name to a land and a race which was to furnish the most redoubtable opponents to the later empire until it went down before them and the dynasty of Nebuchadnezzar made Babylon the wonder of the world.

CHAPTER XI

FIRST CONTACTS WITH ISRAEL

THE reconnaissance of Ashur-nasir-apal indicated that Syria was wealthy and not too difficult of conquest; Shalmaneser took it upon himself to secure the proof. North Syria was in a transition period, half Hittite, half Aramæan. To the former belonged the most northerly state of Syria—Gurgum, with its ruler, Mutallu. A short distance south lay the Aramæan Samal, already known to the Egyptians, and two ancestors, Gabbar and Bamah, had preceded its present king, Hayya. The territory directly west of the Euphrates crossing and the line to the sea was held by Hattina, though it was sometimes also called Unqi, from the great swamps in the centre. The reigning monarch was Sapalulme, whose name drew attention to an assumed descent from the mighty Shuppiluliuma of the real Hittite empire, whose remembrance was preserved in Hattina. The actual crossing of the Euphrates was controlled on the west bank by the Hittite Sangara of Carchemish; Agusi with its capital Arne was under the Aramæan Arame.

Because of its closer connection with the Greeks, we welcome gladly the most casual references to Asia Minor, though it is doubtful if contemporaries were aware that a frontier had been passed when they entered the anti-Taurus or the Cilician plain. The kings of these portions of Asia Minor always considered their territory an integral part of north Syria, they regularly entered the alliances formed against Assyrian invasion, and in the Assyrian records they are mixed indiscriminately with the chiefs of north Syria.

Four distinct divisions are now recognised, and with certain slight modifications and changes of name, they continue to the end of the Assyrian period. Well up the Euphrates was Melidia, or Melitene, already made tributary by Tiglath Pileser

I, and now ruled by Lala. In the anti-Taurus to the west was Tabal, generally divided among independent chiefs, one to each of the mountain valleys. In the rolling country later called Lycaonia was Hilaku, whose name was to be transferred to Cilicia after the Hilakai had descended through the Cilician Gates into the plain, which during the whole of Assyrian history was to be called Que. The latter was now under the control of Kate, the former of Pihirim.[1]

Rafts laid on inflated skins carried the Assyrians across the Euphrates in 859, only to be met by a confederacy which included the whole group of previously mentioned kings. A tactical victory was won, but Shalmaneser was forced to content himself with the barren honour of erecting a stele under the Amanus at the sources of the Saluara River. The siege of the Hattinian Alisir, not far from where was to be one day the site of the mighty city of Antioch, was checked by another attack from the allies, but the Assyrian victory was again followed by no important results.

The tribute of the "kings of the seacoast," the Phœnicians, alone recompensed him for his trouble. The quadrangular Assyrian camp with its overhanging towers was pitched by the seashore, and the king took his place under his parasol. He was surrounded by his guards and attendants, in particular the three turtanus. The master of ceremonies, facing backward, beckoned for the ambassadors to approach. The two representatives of Tyre and Sidon, accompanied by their sons, advanced, their hands in the attitude of adoration. Their beards were pointed, their double robes were long and clinging, their turbans were wound with ribbons which fell to their necks, their shoes were upturned. Behind these merchant princes came the tribute-bearers, some bearing trays filled with oriental sweetmeats, some with boxes on their shoulders or huge caldrons carried like caps on their heads. The last of the procession unloaded their boat in the water, too shallow to permit reaching land.

---

[1] Cf. *The Assyrians in Asia Minor*, in *Anatolian Studies presented to Sir William Mitchell Ramsay*, 283 *ff.*

Their boats were long, narrow craft, each with two men who steered and rowed, or rather poled them along by oars without oar-locks. Ropes attached to the upstanding figureheads of camels at the high prows and sterns held them fast to the shore. They were piled high with bales of dark-blue wool, with cloths the colour of the precious lapis lazuli carried on poles suspended from men's shoulders, with ingots of gold and silver, lead and copper. One great jar required special attention as it was handed from the boat to the shore. Whole trees and beams of cedar, in themselves sufficient to repay the Assyrians for their long trip, were brought down and piled up. Across the bay could be seen a rocky islet which bore a town with high battlemented walls and possessed two gates. Their hands laden with gifts, the chief and his wife came forth, her hair flowing, her skirt tucked up to avoid the water.

A second stele was carved at Atalur, on a cliff by the seashore, where one day Antioch's seaport, Seleucia, was to be located, and where his predecessor, Ashur-rabi II, had already left a memorial of his presence. The return journey was equally prosperous. The Hattinians, clad in short girdled tunics and protected only by round helmets and neck-pieces, were easily defeated in detail, while the Assyrians seized them by the hair, stabbed them, and decorated the chariots with the severed heads. Hazazu was a good-sized fort on a low artificial mound which witnessed to the respectable antiquity that already lay behind it. When the troops in heavy armour began the escalade and the town was already on fire, the townspeople could no longer resist. The king received his prisoners under a canopy held by servants before the round camp. Great was the contrast between the richly clad officials who introduced them and the long file of captives, some without a stitch of clothing, their necks in a rope and their hands tied behind them, the women with their hair hanging down their backs and in gowns which reached only to elbows and ankles.

The year following, Shalmaneser began the systematic reduction of the Adini towns west of the Euphrates. At the investment of Til Bashere, the king seated himself under a

Fig. 68. SHALMANESER AND HIS SOLDIERS.

Fig. 69. TRIBUTE OF TYRE. BRONZE REPOUSSÉ WORK ON PALACE GATE.

Fig. 70. IN THE GREAT SWAMP OF NORTH SYRIA.

Fig. 71. THE ORONTES AT ANTIOCH.

Fig. 72. SAMAL, CAPITAL OF THE NORTHERN JUDAH.

canopy to watch the operation of a new contrivance, a ram on six wheels, operated by a man in a sort of cupola on the top, which was attacking the tower that protected the lone gate in the long wall. The defenders dropped stones upon it but in vain, and the city on the low mound which gave so commanding a position to the crusading Turbessel, and above whose walls projected the gable roof of the palace of Hittite fashion, became Assyrian. The citizens of the upper town, bearded men wearing liberty caps, with long, double robes open at the sides and pointed shoes, were led with ropes about their necks; the matrons, their hair below the waist and barelegged, followed meekly; and dromedaries and mules brought out the couches and such other furniture as was considered worthy of removal. The whole convoy was under the direction of the crown prince, whose uncertain stand in his chariot was made easier by the protecting arm of his squire, and his presence was also indicated by the smaller tent at the side of the larger and by the double guard which watched the camp.

Changing his direction, Shalmaneser fell upon the territories of Carchemish, and the reduction of Sazabe brought the coalition to terms. The remaining narrative for the year is made up of the tribute furnished by the various princes. That the numbers have grown in the process of transmission is to be expected, but when all allowance is made, the lists still afford us a most instructive insight into the economic life of north Syria.

The ruler of Hattina offered three talents of gold and a hundred of silver, three hundred of copper and the same of iron, a thousand articles in the last metal, a thousand cloaks, twenty talents of one kind of purple and two of another, five hundred cattle and five thousand sheep. For the collection of this tribute, it was necessary to penetrate the great swamp of Unqi, access to which could be gained only by flat-bottomed boats that could pass anywhere in the shallows. Two men, their long hair bound with fillets and their clothes as abbreviated as might be expected of an aquatic folk, rowed and steered them by oars hung in thongs. Shalmaneser did not trust himself to their uncertain protection, but contented himself with a position on the shore across from where, on a low mound in the midst of the swamp, stood the capital, a double-gated fortress with battlements on its walls.   Under the parasol which the damp heat demanded, he received the Hattinian monarch, aping the Assyrian with his long fringed robe and shawl. With him were his nobles, their hair long on head and face, their sweeping robes carefully draped, and the inevitable Hittite upturned shoes.   Among them was to be observed a man with a strongly negroid face, unsuspected witness to race mixture.

The plundering was thorough, and the soldiers carried off their loot in baskets and sacks, skins filled with wine, trays heaped with valuables, tusks of elephants.   From a smaller castle, also on a mound in the water, came other suppliants bearing the same gifts, but with different dress, short robes which exposed their bare limbs and the regulation shoes, Aramæans who had forced themselves in by the side of their Hittite neighbours.   A third furnished horses and cattle, the latter still driven in huge herds along the watery ways, though rare enough in other parts of Syria.   One of these Aramæans trudged along, on his back a huge wine-jar that was destined to be placed later on a tripod by the table and under the tent which Shalmaneser had ordered to be pitched some distance back from the shore.   The tragedy behind the curt statement of the annals—"his daughter with her rich dowry I received"—is revealed in all its pathos in the half-grown Hittite maiden, her hair barely reaching to her neck, who stretched out her hands in vain supplication to the relentless conqueror who had determined to immure her in his harem.

Sangara was not so rich as the king of Hattina, for the commercial predominance of north Syria was yet to be gained by Carchemish.   His gifts were but three talents of gold, seventy of silver, thirty of copper, a hundred of iron, twenty of purple, five hundred weapons, and cattle, five thousand each of sheep, horses, buffaloes, and goats, but he made up the account by presenting five hundred noble maidens, whom the scribe cyni-

cally lists between the cattle and the weapons. Four of his
castles, all located on the bank of the Euphrates, on low mounds
and without the usual overhanging platforms, were forced to
disgorge. The citizens, headed by Sangara himself and his
two beardless sons, were not unattractive—profiles less sharp
than those of the Assyrians, noses straight, short hair and
beards. The common sort had retained their ancestral garb,
the conical twisted turbans, the long double robes, the upturned shoes, but Assyrian fashions had conquered the nobility, who wore the long single robe and the coats with
plain sleeves which characterised the victors. Hayya of Samal
offered ten talents of silver, ninety of copper, thirty of iron,
three hundred articles of clothing, the same number of cattle,
and ten times that number of sheep, two hundred cedar beams,
as well as his daughter.

Whatever we may think of these indemnities, the direct result if not the direct incentive of the expedition, we have no
reason to doubt the amount of the yearly assessments, for
their modesty is the best argument for their authenticity.
Hattina gave a talent of silver, two of purple, a hundred cedar
beams; Samal, twenty pounds of gold, a hundred cedar beams;
Agusi, twenty pounds of gold, six talents of silver, five hundred
cattle, and five thousand sheep; Carchemish, but two pounds
of gold, a talent of silver, and two of purple; Qummuh, forty
pounds of silver and three hundred beams.

For those who are not affrighted by statistics, the interest of
this passage is great. Previously we have been furnished more
or less exact accounts of the booty collected in the course of a
raid, and sometimes a general statement as to the infliction of
a regular tribute. Here for the first time we are presented
with a formal tribute list. There is the greatest disproportion
between the indemnity, the contribution paid when the king
must go to the trouble and expense of collecting and equipping
an army, and the yearly tribute handed over in the capital.
The indemnity often gives huge amounts of copper, iron,
clothes, which are never included in the yearly tribute. In
Hattina, for example, the yearly tribute in precious metals

was less than one per cent of the indemnity. The system tended to favour submission, since it was far cheaper to furnish a yearly tribute instead of an indemnity. The populace was compelled to pay for the support of their own princes in addition, but even with this included, the taxation was certainly not so grinding as in Sargonid times.

The objective of the next year's campaign was Halman, or Aleppo. He received the tribute of the kings of north Syria again, the only change being that Gurgum and Hattina were now under Gabbarud. Shalmaneser sacrificed to the local Adad; his offerings accepted, he might believe his title made good, with gods as with men, to the rightful rule of Syria.

His way was paved for further advances to the south. At the end of the long road lay the greatest prize with a mighty past, a present wealth, and a future which at its best was most dubious. With all its manifest weakness, the barbarous Libyan kings still claimed a vague suzerainty over the whole of Syria in memory of the days of Thutmose III and Ramses II. Shishak I, the founder of the twenty-second dynasty, had actually enforced his rights in Palestine by his arms, and the Zerah the Ethiopian who is reported to have invaded the Philistine plain was probably Osorkon I. The second Osorkon was precariously seated on the Egyptian throne, and, imperilled though he was by internal dissensions, was keenly interested in what was happening in Syria. We cannot blame Egypt for doing all she could to postpone the day when Assyria should stand on the north side of the desert and look with desire to the Nile valley. We should blame the states of Syria and Palestine, whose eyes were so blinded by the glorious past that they could not recognise the ever-lessening promise of the future.

Hamath and Damascus were the two greatest powers in central Syria. The enormous ruin mound and the numerous and impressive Hittite inscriptions discovered within show how long the former had been a leading centre. Its king, Toi, had cemented friendship with David, and now Irhuleni was the head of a fair-sized confederacy. Damascus had been an

Fig. 73. SINGARA, AT THE HEAD OF THE TARTARA.

Fig. 74. ALEPPO, CHIEF CITY OF NORTH SYRIA.

FIG. 75. THE MOUND AT HAMATH.

FIG. 76. WATER-WHEEL IN THE ORONTES AT HAMATH.

important oasis mart long before the Aramæans had made it their own, and it is mentioned several times in the days when Egyptian control of Syria was more than a name.   The Aramæans had secured it by the days of David, and when its inhabitants brought aid to Beth Rehob, David garrisoned the city.   In the confusion at the end of Solomon's reign, one of the generals of Hadadezer of Zobah set up for himself, expelled the Hebrew guards, and as Rezon I began the history of Damascus as a state of the first magnitude.   Ben Hadad I was developing a real empire.

Tyre was a small settlement on a tiny rock not far from the sea in the Egyptian period.   With the decline of the Egyptian and Minoan sea-power, the Mediterranean became Phœnician. Hiram I abandoned this site, which was henceforth called Old Tyre, and was marked only by the ancient shrine of Tammuz and his mother-mistress.   Since the sea was safe, the capital was transferred to the more convenient Haven Tyre.   A series of successors known only in their names came to an end through the assassination of the last by Ethbaal, the priest of Astart.   Looking about for advantageous connections, he determined to renew the alliance consecrated by Hiram with David and Solomon.

The two Hebrew kingdoms had seen evil days since the death of Solomon.   His descendants ruled one after the other a few square miles of rocky soil, and even thus did not always retain full independence.   The north was larger, more fertile, more on the line of the great road to Egypt, but it was cursed by ever-changing dynasties, with internal wars and much bloodshed.   The accession of Omri (885-874) brought prosperity and comparative peace.

The dynasty which Omri founded was the most important in Israel's checkered history, and so great was his repute that the Assyrians henceforth gave the name of Bit Humri, the "House of Omri," to Israel, long after the line was ended. Ethbaal married his daughter Jezebel to Ahab, Omri's son, to seal the alliance.   Another alliance permitted the merchants of Damascus to occupy quarters in his capital.   Chemosh, patron deity of Moab, was angry with his country, so Mesha tells us, and Omri was permitted to afflict Moab many days, to capture and colonise Medeba, and to level to the ground other cities. A huge tribute, a hundred thousand lambs and a hundred thousand rams, was paid to the Israelite monarch.

Increased prosperity demanded a new capital, which was found on the high isolated hill of Samaria. Cup-holes and similar markings testified to the sacred character of the summit on which Omri erected his palace. The rock was carefully smoothed, and from it were taken the massive limestone blocks which formed the walls. Great open courts, around which were smaller rooms, furnished a ground plan modelled on the palaces of Kalhu or Babylon, and its size, an acre and a half in all, betokened a wealth which can only be called surprising.

Imposing as it was, Ahab (874–852) and his Tyrian wife were not satisfied. Against the walls and covering its quarries, down the slopes to the west and south, extended the new quarters with still finer joints, smoother surfaces, and better construction. On its southern face the palace abutted on the massive city wall which ran along the cliff and which had a gateway flanked by frowning towers at the point where Herod placed the gate of the Romanised Sebaste.

Not content with a palace, Jezebel demanded a temple, and the new capital soon saw a shrine to her patron saint, Baal Melkart, "the Lord, King of the Tyrian City." A strange testimony to the popularity of his cult has been unearthed. Excavators have uncovered some seventy-five fragments of jars on which the scribe with a reed pen and in a flowing hand which speaks volumes for his practice has jotted down data in regard to the oil and wine which have come in, the date in the ninth or tenth year (865–864), the notation of fine oil or old wine, the wine from the vineyard of the ancient ruin mound, the cities or individuals from which or whom the jars came, and those to whom they were sent.

Analysis of the names shows many interesting features. The national deity is well represented by such names as Joash and Jehoiada, for Yahweh names first appear in Israel during the dynasty of Omri. Aramaic names such as Abda and Sheba probably are those of the traders for whose sakes Ben Hadad I had insisted on Damascene bazaars in Samaria. Asa is the king of Judah who was reigning at this time, though we cannot believe that the Elisha whose name we read was related to the prophet who was so bitterly opposed to the dynasty.

Our keenest attention is directed to the group which commemorates the interloping god, such as Abibaal, who bears the name of Hiram's royal father. The predominance of Baal names is no accident; the men of the court were deliberately giving them to their sons, and we cannot doubt that they were thinking of Baal Melkart and not of the "Lord" Yahweh.[1] Such a situation, where nearly as many of the younger generation were named from the Tyrian deity as from the national divinity, could not but arouse the hostility of the more conservative religious leaders, and the unfortunate enthusiasm of Jezebel for the god of her youth brought against the house of Ahab the continued opposition of those who followed the prophet Elijah.[2]

The line of Ben Hadad I was continued by an unknown son and by a grandson, Ben Hadad II, who succeeded in building up an empire of so considerable a size that thirty-two "kings" were in his train. To his summons, "Thy silver and thy gold are mine; thy wives and thy children are mine," Ahab replied with surprising meekness: "Be it according to thy saying, my lord king, I am thine and all I possess." Still more insulting words met this abject surrender: "By this time to-morrow I shall send my servants to thee; they shall search thy house and thy servants' houses and whatever they please they shall take away." Ahab's council of elders advised resistance. Ben Hadad swore an oath: "The gods punish me thus and yet more if the dust of Samaria shall provide a handful for each of the host at my feet." The contest at repartee was fittingly closed

---

[1] Yahweh is a more correct pronunciation of the name of the Hebrew deity than Jehovah.

[2] Reisner, *Harvard Theological Rev.*, III, 248 ff.; Lyon, *ibid.*, IV, 136 ff.

by Ahab: "Let him who girdeth on his armour not boast as he that putteth it off." He likewise won the more important wager of battle, for when Ben Hadad celebrated the anticipated victory by a drinking-bout, the Israelites made a sudden onset, and only a portion of the cavalry found escape with the king.

Ben Hadad returned the next year, for his courtiers had found the explanation for his defeat. Yahweh was a hill god, and naturally prevailed in the hill country; let the next battle be contested in the plain, and the Damascene gods would be successful. Disillusion came at Aphek, where a crushing defeat was suffered by the invaders. Immured in the city, Ben Hadad sent ambassadors with sackcloth on their loins and ropes around their necks to bear the humble request: "I pray thee, let me live."

In all his dealings, Ahab showed himself a man of strong common sense. He realised that incorporation of Damascus in Israel was beyond hope, and he saw the danger from Assyria. He ignored the former insults and answered, "Is he yet alive? He is my brother." By employing this term, he indicated that he had no intention of using his unexpected success to reduce Ben Hadad to a confession of vassalage. Peace was made on the basis of the return of the cities taken from his father, Omri, and the concession of such markets in Damascus as Ben Hadad had formerly enjoyed in Samaria. The moderation of Ahab was bitterly condemned by the prophetic group which followed Elijah, but these men had no conception of foreign affairs; the underlying cause of the peace was the threat of Assyria.

Ample warning of what might be expected had been afforded by the campaign in north Syria. So when in 854 Shalmaneser took the next step south, a coalition had been brought together to block his advance. Behind the alliance stood Egypt, whose participation in the negotiations is indicated by the finding of the name of Osorkon II in Ahab's palace, but the Egyptian contribution was negligible, a mere thousand men. The Assyrians knew well enough that Egypt was a broken reed, for they list it far to the end of the roll. The headship is assigned to Adad-idri, that is, Hadadezer, who seems to have ascended the throne of Damascus through the deposition of the ruler defeated by Ahab.[1] According to the Assyrian statistics, his troops consisted of twelve hundred chariots, the same number of cavalry, and twenty thousand foot. Irhuleni of Hamath comes next, with seven hundred chariots and cavalry and ten thousand foot.

Somewhat to our surprise, the third place is taken by Ahabbu of Sirla, or Ahab of Israel. The sacred book does not mention this particular incident, though our knowledge of it explains the whole foreign policy of Ahab. Exaggerated the two thousand chariots and the ten thousand soldiers assigned to him may be, they do prove the relative position of Israel. Recent fashion has tended to emphasise the smallness of Israel as compared with the historical world-powers, and in especial with Assyria or Egypt. A different standard of comparison is required; we do not, for example, compare Athens with Persia or Rome, but with Sparta or Thebes. If in the same manner we compare Israel with the other states of Syria, we reach another conclusion. Ahab held high rank in the coalition which gathered at Qarqara, and he is assigned the largest number of chariots; a rather remarkable statement, since the Biblical narrative of the war with Ben Hadad implies that Israel was particularly deficient in this respect.

Among the less-important nationalities which sent contingents to this epoch-making contest, we have five hundred men from Que, a clear indication that the inhabitants of the Cilician plain were becoming alarmed at the closeness of the Assyrian approach to their borders. Several were sent by the various Phœnician states: ten chariots and ten thousand foot from Irqanata, two hundred from Mattanbaal of Arvad, the same from Usanata, and ten thousand from Adonibaal of Shiana, though these estimates are far too high, since no city-state of this period could muster such a force. A thousand camels were contributed by Gindibu, the Arab, first indication that the true Arabs were following the Aramæans in their in-

[1] Luckenbill, *AJSL.*, XXVII, 267 ff.

vasion of the Fertile Crescent. The list ends with the ten
thousand foot of Baasha, the son of Rehob, the Ammonite.
Properly interpreted, the hitherto dry statistics enlighten many
a dark page of history.

No difficulty was experienced in looting the frontier cities of
Irhuleni and in burning the palaces. Parga, for example, stood
on a low artificial mound, defended by a stream and by high
battlemented towers above whose walls appeared to the wayfarer tall buildings with flat roofs and many windows. The
assault was launched under the protection of a small movable
fort and was assisted by a movable ram, or rather sow, with
staring eyes, projecting snout, and heavy necklace, moved forward by a kneeling man, behind whom stood archers encased
in the rear. The defenders were unusually brave, for they
fought from the open space in front as well as behind the protection of their ramparts.

Without meeting open resistance, the invaders continued
up the Orontes valley through orchards laden with figs to
Qarqara. The fort was small and its mound not particularly
elevated, but its battlemented towers were much above the
average height and its position strategic, for its loss would permit direct attack on Hamath. The king ensconced himself in
a tent set up on a rock near the river. The battle did not begin auspiciously for the Assyrians, for the sculptures make a
very unusual admission when they show the troops of Hamath,
archers with pointed helmets or in chariots much like the Assyrian, pressing over the Assyrian dead to meet the main forces
of the enemy. The written records claim a complete victory.
The blood of the vanquished was made to flow over the passes
of the district, the field was too narrow to throw down their
bodies, the broad plain alone sufficed for their burial, their
corpses blocked the Orontes like a dam. The number of the
slain grew with the passage of time, from fourteen thousand to
twenty thousand five hundred, to twenty-five thousand, to
twenty-nine thousand. Pursuit was continued from Qarqara
to the Orontes—and the Monolith Inscription comes to a sudden end.

With perhaps equal justice, Osorkon declared that all lands and all countries, Upper and Lower Retennu in particular, all inaccessible countries, were under his feet.[1] Had this famous conflict, because of its connection with Israel, the best known of all Assyrian battles, been the overwhelming victory claimed by Shalmaneser, we should not have to record the careful avoidance of Syria which marks the next few years.

Immediately after the battle the coalition fell to pieces. Ahab no longer feared Assyria, and determined to attack his late ally. The Judæan Jehoshaphat (875–851) had already been made subject, and when the siege of Ramoth Gilead was broached, he meekly made reply: "I am as thou art, my people as thy people, my horses as thy horses." Even with this assistance, the siege was a failure and Ahab met his death. The cry was raised, "The king is dead, every man to his city and every man to his country," and the host disbanded.[2]

Not until 849 did Shalmaneser find courage to visit again this frontier. Capture of certain additional cities belonging to Carchemish is reported, and after that came the turn of Arame of Agusi, who had already paid tribute but whose territory had not yet been invaded. His capital, Arne, was unusually well defended. It lay on a high mound, its walls were high, and stone was employed in its construction instead of the usual adobe. The resulting slope presented very real difficulties to the attacking party, but the city fell a prey with all its animal wealth after an assault.

First of Irhuleni's cities to be attempted was Ashtamaku. The attack was confided to the crown prince, who rode at the head of his cavalry and chariots over the dead and in pursuit of the fleeing leaders of the enemy. One of them escaped up the slope to the city, the horse of his companion stumbled, and he was compelled to stretch out his hands for mercy. Archers shot at the city until the dead hung over the walls and the defenders begged for peace.

Hadadezer and the allies who had come to the help of Hamath were defeated and ten thousand of their troops destroyed.

[1] Breasted, *Records*, IV, 372.　　　　[2] I Kings 22.

Irhuleni took refuge in his double-walled fortress, with its gable-roofed houses, where he had made himself comfortable on a couch of Assyrian form, with the flapper and shawl of the eunuch servant, and with the long fringed robe and drapery of an Assyrian monarch. These could not protect him from the Assyrian fury, and he, too, was reduced to ask quarter. He was permitted to retain his Assyrian dress, even to the pointed helmet, provided he bowed down in worship, and the youthful prince destined to be his successor was allowed to approach in his chariot and surrounded by his fellows; the common people were treated more roughly, their clothes stripped off, their necks inserted in yokes, their women in too scanty clothing bewailing their disgrace with hand raised to head. Even to Assyrian monarchs, the sins of kings were not as serious as those of the ignoble crowd!

The defection of Irhuleni had not destroyed the alliance, and the year 846 found the Assyrians again fighting its members in central Syria. The "numberless levy of the troops from the whole of his wide-extending dominions was called out," to the number of one hundred and twenty thousand, a maximum for the size of Assyrian armies and an indication of the gravity of the situation.

Conditions had become more propitious by 842. At the instigation of the Hebrew prophet Elisha, the reigning king of Damascus had been smothered while sick, and Hazael, the usurping son of a nobody, had taken his place.[1] The confederacy completely broke down, and the war with Israel entered a more active phase with the attempt of Jehoram to win back Ramoth Gilead. This time Shalmaneser met with no resistance until he entered the territories of Damascus. Where the Barada breaks through the Lebanon, under Mount Senir,[2] Hazael made his stand, but his fortified camp was stormed, the orchards which filled the fertile valley were felled, and the Assyrians appeared before Damascus. The walls were too strong for assault, and Shalmaneser had not the patience for a formal siege, so was forced to content himself with a plunder-

[1] II Kings 8:7 ff.   [2] Deut. 3:9; I Chron. 5:23; Ezek. 27:5; Cant. 4:8.

ing raid into the Hauran mountains to the east and south, whose rich volcanic soil made it, then as now, the granary of the Syrian area.

Shalmaneser then struck back to the coast, through that plain of Esdraelon which has always been the direct route from Damascus and the Hauran to the sea. On a projecting cliff which he calls "Baal's Head," and which may well be intended for the projecting headland of Carmel where Elijah had contended with the priests of the Tyrian Baal a few years before, he affixed a stele. Shortly after, he received tribute from the Tyrians, the Sidonians, and from Iaua of Bit Humri, or, being interpreted, from Jehu of the house of Omri!

Important changes had indeed taken place in Israel in the twelve-year period which had elapsed since Ahab had faced the Assyrians on the stricken field. After Ahab's death before Ramoth Gilead, his weakly son, Ahaziah, lasted but two years (852–850), and in want of issue was followed by his brother Jehoram (850–842). The long reign of Jehoshaphat (875–851) came to an end the next year, and another Jehoram (851–843) ruled Judah. Jehoshaphat had been a loyal vassal of the north, as the name of his son bore witness.

Mesha of Moab made his revolt good on the death of Ahab. The lost Medeba was soon recovered. Baal Meon had become so Israelite that a citizen who bore its ethnic had been prominent at the court of Ahab; now Mesha restored it and made it a reservoir. From of old the men of Gad had occupied Ataroth, and the king of Israel had rebuilt it for his own purposes; Mesha took it by assault, made its inhabitants a gazing stock to his god Chemosh and the men of Moab, carried off the altar hearth and dragged it before Chemosh, and settled men in the city. Then said Chemosh, "Go, take Nebo from Israel"; so Mesha went by night and fought against it from break of day to noon. The whole of the population, seven thousand men, besides the women, the slaves, and the resident aliens, were devoted to Ashtor-Chemosh, that is, were ceremonially slaughtered before the deity. The vessels of Yahweh were made a spoil. Jahaz had been used as a base by the Israelite king in his warfare against the near-by capital, Daibon; Chemosh drove him out from before the face of Mesha with the aid of the two hundred chiefs of Moab. Walls and citadels were built by the Israelite prisoners, the ruined cities were restored, the Arnon highway constructed.[1]

Mesha declared that he saw his pleasure on Omri's son and on his house, so that Israel perished with an everlasting destruction. Those who recognise the uniqueness of this record in a dialect of Hebrew will be selfishly thankful that he caused it to be inscribed before the episode was completed. Jehoram had no intention of allowing the contest to go by default. Augmented by the troops of his namesake of Judah, the army marched along the wilderness route into Edom, where they were joined by the subject king of that country. After much suffering from want of water, Moab was reached. The Moabites were worsted in a pitched battle, the cities were beaten down, the arable land covered with stones, the fountains stopped up, the trees felled. Kirhareseth was besieged by the slingers until only ruins were left. Mesha with seven hundred picked men attempted to break through into Edom but failed. As a last resort, he adopted the desperate expedient of offering up his eldest son upon the wall. Terrified by this awful sight, which would bring upon them the immediate wrath of the local deity, the invaders hurriedly decamped.[2]

Jehoram of Judah, as was fitting a vassal, had married Athaliah, a daughter of Ahab. His Israelite connections availed him little, for after the failure of the Moabite expedition the Edomites revolted, and a night raid with his chariots to Seir did not restore his control. Libnah likewise fell away to the Philistines, and the Arabs of the Sinaitic peninsula were even able to make an inroad as far as Jerusalem, where they plundered the palace and took all the royal family but his youngest son, Ahaziah. It was this son, named from his cousin of Israel, who shortly succeeded (843–842).

The usurpation of Hazael seemed to offer an excellent opportunity for Israel to recover Ramoth Gilead. The city was

[1] Moabite Stone.   [2] II Kings 3.

FIG. 77. BLACK OBELISK OF SHALMANESER III.
The second row represents Israelites, whose king, Jehu, is
seen bowing before the conqueror to the left.
(Cast in Metropolitan Museum.)

FIG. 78. THE SYRIAN GATES, A VILLAGE OF A SINGLE LONG
STREET. (BEILAN.)

FIG. 79. WASHING OUT SILVER AT THE "BULGARIAN MINES," WHICH
MADE THE WEALTH OF TARSHISH OR TARSUS.

successfully taken, but Jehoram was wounded, and retired to Jezreel to recuperate. Danger from Damascus was still imminent, and Jehoram left behind him a garrison under his best general, Jehu. Suddenly there appeared a member of the prophetic guild who had been commissioned by Elisha to anoint him king. Driving furiously to Jezreel, Jehu met Jehoram and Ahaziah coming forth to meet him, shot the former and pursued the latter to Megiddo, where the wounded Judæan died. The body of Jehoram was cast into the field of Naboth, in deliberate fulfilment of the prophecy by Elijah. Jezebel arrayed herself in her best as for a sacrifice, hurled reproaches at her would-be murderer, and met her death at the hands of her treacherous eunuch attendants with the bravery to be expected from such a queen.

Aided by the Kenite Jehonadab, whose whole family followed the custom of their ancestor Rechab and refused to drink wine or live in a house, Jehu arrived at Samaria, pretended to be a zealous worshipper of Baal Melkart, assembled the devotees of the foreign god, and put them to death. The shrine was defiled and Yahweh reigned supreme, if not in the hearts of men, at least in the palace of the king.

The drastic wiping out of the two royal families had lessened the number of his enemies, but the position of Jehu was still insecure. Tyre was of necessity opposed to his rule, and Judah was no longer even a nominal vassal. With the manly spirit of her mother Jezebel, Athaliah took over the inheritance of her murdered son, and Baal's house received the dedications hitherto owed to the Yahweh temple. There were many advantages, so it seemed to the short-sighted Jehu, in securing the support of the powerful intruder. As he passed through Israelite territory Jehu appeared before him, and the reliefs of the Black Obelisk immortalise the Hebrew ruler as he kissed the ground before Shalmaneser and his eunuchs. His beard is short and rounded in the ancient fashion, a liberty cap is on his head. An almost sleeveless jacket and a long fringed skirt with girdle are all he wears. A group of Israelites is next depicted. Over the undress costume of Jehu they have draped a long robe open at the left, where a bit of the skirt fringe is allowed to appear, while the end of the robe is thrown over the right shoulder in a shawl-like effect. They bring huge ingots of unworked metal, gold, silver, and lead, small golden pails of not inartistic design, bowls, cups, and ladles. On the backs of some are sacks filled with precious objects, one holds a sceptre, another raises aloft a tall thin drinking-goblet, others bear bundles of weapons, and the last carries on his head a flat basket filled with fruit.

Following the submission of Jehu, the Obelisk pictures "tribute" of Egypt. Men whose only dress is a fillet and a short tunic, belted high and fringed, and with short square beards, conduct two double-humped camels. The sculptor has made a special effort to depict a bull different from the variety with which he is acquainted, stockier and without the familiar hump. His rhinoceros is merely a bull with a single horn. The gazelle is probably intended to represent the oryx which gave its name to an Egyptian nome. The elephant is rather well done, and leaves no doubt that we are dealing with the African species; but the monkeys which follow are the crudest imitations of the truly lifelike specimens in the palace of Ashur-nasir-apal. "Tribute" of course they were not in any sense. The nearness of Shalmaneser to the Egyptian frontier had caused the Egyptian ruler, Takelet II or Shishak III, to send gifts of greeting. Doubtless somewhere in his records, did we have them all, we would find mention of the "tribute" presented by his vassals, the Assyrians.

Damascus, though badly shaken, was still unconquered, and in 838 Shalmaneser made a last effort to complete the reduction of central Syria. Tyre, Sidon, and Byblus furnished fresh proof that the Phœnicians were prepared to pay any reasonable price if their control of the trade routes should be free from interference. Hazael was a different proposition, and Shalmaneser must content himself with placing on a bit of black marble the ludicrously inappropriate inscription: "Booty from the temple of the god Sher of Malaha, residence of Hazael of Damascus, which Shalmaneser, son of Ashur-nasir-apal, king of Assyria, brought within the walls of the city of Ashur."

The complete failure of Assyria in the west meant ruin for those who had espoused her cause. Freed of fear from the north, Hazael again began to harass Jehu. The whole of the east Jordan country, Gilead and Bashan, the tribal territories of Gad, Manasseh, and Benjamin, clear to Aroer on the Arnon which a few short years ago Mesha had claimed for his own, fell into his hands.[1] With bitter wrath Amos condemns Damascus. For three rebellions of Damascus and for four, Yahweh will not turn away his punishment, for they threshed Gilead with threshing implements of iron. Therefore will Yahweh send a fire into the house of Hazael and it shall devour the palaces of Ben Hadad. The bars which close the gate of Damascus will be broken, the inhabitants of the Aven valley, Hollow Syria, will be cut off.[2]

Jehu was more successful in the southern kingdom. Athaliah (842–836) by her insistence on the Baal cult had alienated the priesthood of her adopted country. The infant son of Ahaziah had been saved by his aunt Jehosheba from the slaughter of the seed royal, and had now reached the age of seven. Her husband, Jehoiada, the chief priest of Yahweh, persuaded the foreign body-guard of Cretan mercenaries to support the legitimate claimant, Jehoash, and Athaliah was slain as she attempted to penetrate the cordon around the temple. The enraged populace sacked the Baal temple, the Tyrian priest Mattan was killed, and Yahweh was acknowledged sole God in Judah, as he had already been in Israel.

The Assyrians waited fourteen years before they made any attempt to chastise the presumption of the men of Que who took part in the battle of Qarqara, and it was not until three years later (837) that they enjoyed any success. Then they marched through Nairi to Tunni, a mountain of silver and of various rocks, took cut stone from the quarries, and left in return a stele. They ended with Tabal, where twenty-four kinglets handed over their quota, and with Que, where the

[1] II Kings 10 : 32 ff.   [2] Amos 1 : 3 ff.

lands of Kate were ravaged. The next year Uetash, the fort of Lala of Melidia, was assaulted, and kings of Tabal again presented their tribute.

Que was entered through the Amanus Gates in 834, and Timur was taken from Kate who was shortly after deposed by Tulli. The new ruler surrendered when he saw his fort of Tanakun in Assyrian possession, and was supplanted by Kirri, brother of the former king. The inhabitants of Lamena found refuge in the hills. The year 833 closed with the capture of Tarzi, or Tarsus, which at this time was taking the place of Mallus as the central point in the Cilician plain, as the terminus of the great route which led through the Cilician Gates to the plateau of Asia Minor, and as the outlet of the famous Hittite silver-mines to the north of the mountains whose wealth was to make the name of Tarshish world-famous.

The failure of Shalmaneser to follow up the raid of 842 in Palestine led to the conviction in north Syria that Assyria had shot her bolt. Agusi took a hostile attitude, and on his return from Cilicia Shalmaneser captured Muru, one of Arame's forts, but he himself was untouched. The raid of 832 into Haldia was likewise a failure, and Sardurish induced the Hattinians to dethrone their pro-Assyrian prince Lubarna in favour of a usurper named Surri. Surri died a natural death, which the historian ascribes to the offended majesty of Ashur, and his erstwhile followers handed over his sons and accomplices to Daian Ashur for impalement. Sasi declared his adherence to the Assyrian cause and was made king, subject to heavy tribute of metals and ivory. The royal figure was installed in the temple at Kunulua, and Syria ceased to interest the Assyrians.

CHAPTER XII

THE GREAT REVOLT

THE military machine constructed by Tukulti Urta and Ashur-nasir-apal remained in good working order, and the new territory opened up to Assyrian influence was notable. Babylonia was brought under effective control and a portion of her territory annexed. Assyrian armies penetrated far within the Median mountains, and the failure to fix the frontier permanently was due more to the support offered by Haldia than to the resistant qualities of the tribesmen themselves. Haldia was the great problem with which Assyria was confronted, and Daian Ashur grappled with it to the best of his ability; if he had not checked its advance, it was not because he had feared to lead his armies within its confines and to the very gates of the capital. His lack of success was one more illustration of the time-honoured principle that Semites with their desert ancestry never succeeded in the mountains.

Shalmaneser's most serious mistake was in following his father's example in the west. The attempt on Que was a new development of that policy, and could be still less justified, for the Cilician plain was in no sense an integral part of the territory which nature seemed to have destined for the Assyrian empire. Once in Syria, it must be granted, there was no strategic barrier fixed by nature until the desert northeast of Egypt was reached. With the growing menace of Haldia so close at hand, it would have been the part of wisdom to have left Damascus, Hamath, and Israel to their mutually destructive wars.

Despite the successes of the reign, no small portion of the territory acquired was still autonomous, under princes of doubtful loyalty, ready to rise at the first suggestion of outside aid, or, if themselves loyal at heart, liable to deposition when

145

the anti-Assyrian party gained the upper hand. Within this ring of client states the number of provinces had largely increased, though we cannot say exactly how many had been added. All the palace officials were nominally in charge of a province, though the turtanu Daian Ashur, for example, could have spent little time in Harran; the territories governed by the others cannot be precisely defined. At the head of the named provinces was Nasibina, still unconquered in the days of Shalmaneser's grandfather; it doubtless owed this position to the fact that its governor was also in charge of Ashur. After Kalhu, the list breaks off and we have only the lesser provinces, Ahi Zuhina, or Arzuhina, Nairi, Amat, Kirruri, Ninua, Kakzu, Arrapha, and Mazamua. Nimit Ishtar is testified to by an eponym stele, and Tushhan appears as early as the reign of his father.   Others doubtless are hidden among the provinces of the other palace officials; among these we may perhaps place some or all the provinces listed in the revolt: Shibaniba, Shimu, Shibhinish, Parnunna, Kurban, Arbela. Nimit Ishtar had been enlarged into Rasappa and Kutmuh into Tille, while the name Nairi had been transferred from Tushhan together with two of its subdistricts, Tidu and Sinabu, to a new province which also included Suhni, Alzi, and the capital Mallanu.

Placed on the map, Ashur represented the original Assyria, Nineveh and Kalhu the Triangle proper, Kakzu and Arbela its continuation east of the Upper Zab, Arzuhina and Arrapha the debatable land extending to the Ialman hills, Mazamua what remained of Ashur-nasir-apal's conquests in the mountains due east. Shibaniba, Kirruri, Rimusi, Shibhinish, Parnunna, Kurban, Amat, Shimu, formed a series of provinces northeast of the Triangle, illy located as yet and small in size but of the utmost importance because they alone held off the warlike mountaineers from too close approach to the capitals. Tille, Nasibina, Tushhan, and Nairi blocked the exit from the Armenian mountains. Strictly speaking, these two groups were primarily of a defensive character, as their restricted area shows.   On the other hand, the two huge provinces of

Harran and Rasappa were not merely the result of their location on the Mesopotamian plains; they needed little military supervision because they were protected by the mountain outposts.

Whatever our doubts as to the exact time certain sections were given the provincial form of government, it is evident that the reign of Shalmaneser represents the great period of incorporation. It was only his due that with his reign begins the so-called Assyrian Chronicle. What we really have is a chronological table in three columns: in the first the official who gave his name to the year; in the second the office he held or the province he governed; in the third the most important event of the year, generally a military expedition. It is the backbone of our chronology, and from its seemingly dry statistics we may learn the actual working of the provincial system and discover many a clew to the more formal history.[1]

A curious silence as to building operations is noted in his annals; nevertheless, Shalmaneser built much. Regularly he marched forth from Nineveh, but each year saw the booty deposited in Ashur. · He makes much of his kindness to the old sacred city, and mentions earlier royal builders, but ignores completely what his own father had done. Through the two long reigns, a space of sixty years, Ashur was completely remade.

Important improvements were made in the two earliest temples, those of Ishtar and of Ashur. For Ashur the temple tower near by was entirely rebuilt, a huge edifice whose mass has been estimated at six million bricks, each as large as eight of ours. At the corners was a foundation deposit, between two layers of reeds. A thousand beads of glass, round and bright blue, or cylindrical with layers in light and dark, a hundred blanks of agate or quartz, a thousand shells, mostly of the snail, lead and iron foil with incised dedications to Ashur, formed the deposit.

---

[1] Edition, *JAOS.*, XXXIV, 344 ff.; for the provincial system, "Assyrian Government of Dependencies," *Amer. Political Science Rev.*, XII, 63 ff.; Forrer, *Die Provinzeinteilung des assyrischen Reiches*, 1920.

So ruinous was the Anu-Adad temple that through long stretches the very walls could not be traced. Where possible, Shalmaneser built on the older foundations and reused the inscribed pavement stones and bricks which bore the name of Tiglath Pileser I. Where the workmen cut through the adobe walls of his predecessors, the marks of the picks can still be traced, sharply distinguished from those made by the modern implements. When forced to use new materials, the work of Shalmaneser is much inferior, but the decline is best shown by the difference in size. On every side the enclosed limits shrank, and the temple towers now covered but two-fifths of the ground occupied by those of Tiglath Pileser. Some improvements are to be attributed to Shalmaneser: the hundred-foot well in the courtyard, the inscribed basalt door-sockets, the cedar beams, the bronze covering for a gate whose procession of officials is so like that of the better-known pictures. New to Assyrian temples was the device of the triple indentation which adorned the temple towers, and the ground plan of the double temple where the broad room precedes the long, for the future to be the most holy place and the abode of the cult statue. At the southeast corner a paved road led to the isolated gate where justice was executed, as we may judge from the legal tablets found within.[1]

The new circuit of the land walls began with the ruined Adad tower of the temple. The inner wall swung around the restored New Palace terrace of Tukulti Urta I, which thus became a huge bastion overlooking the weak corner. The Gate of the Metal Worker had already been given higher doors of wood and had been plated with copper, some of which has survived. While other gates were double, this was triple, and the whole gate structure was askew to the wall, a narrow entrance with towers on either side and a ramp across the moat. Round inscribed plates of lead, two hundred pounds in weight, were foundations to the inscribed sockets of basalt on which rested the bronze shod posts of the gates, and around were packed small stones. The roofs were of cedar, and some of it

[1] Andrae, *Anu-Adad-Tempel*, 39 ff.

has been preserved hardly scorched.   Access to the roof was
by ramp or stairway.

Bricks inserted in the walls of the inner gate picture the low
rounded ramp, the arched gateway, the battlemented and overhanging towers on either side.   The valves of the gate were

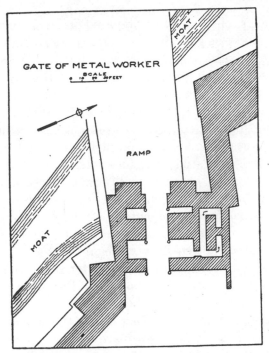

MAP 5. GATE OF THE METAL WORKER AT ASHUR.

covered with copper, fastened with bronze nails and with
iron.   Decoration was of various coloured knobs, some enamelled in colours, some in the native clay but with inscriptions,
which were pressed into the wall.   One was elaborately decorated with a circle of alternate buds and fruit of the pome-
granate in gray-blue, white, yellow, and red, in another the
colour scheme was black, white, and black.   A peculiar adornment inserted in the wall consisted of rude hands with the
five fingers close together.   The wall decorations showed a

colour scheme of a delicacy one can scarcely credit as Assyrian. The battlements themselves were of enamelled bricks of pale blue with light-yellow edging; below was a double row of the blue bricks edged on top and bottom in yellow, and between was a course with the herring-bone pattern in alternate black and cream.

Shalmaneser tells us that he prepared an image of his majesty and placed it in this gate; in the second gate room, on opposite sides of the passage, the statues were found. A fragmentary standing figure in the round is closely modelled on the similar statue of his father. The seated figure in black basalt shows the king solidly placed on a simple cube, without arms but with a projecting foot-rest; the head is lost but the usual beard falls to the breast, the body is completely covered by a girdled robe, the hands rest stiffly on the knees.

Beyond this gate the outer wall now followed closely along the slope of the moat, no longer leaving space for the enemy under the walls, for the invention of the battering-ram had made this too dangerous. The posterns and bastions like-wise disappeared, and towers at regular intervals took their place. The inner wall followed the outer more or less closely and at an average distance of about sixty-five feet along the western side of the city. It did not attempt to include the southern suburb, but turned east along the line of the older structure, cut through the open place where the stelæ of kings and eponym officials had been set up, and reached the Tigris. Although the walls were so pretentious, the technic was by no means an improvement. The base of the wall was faced with stone, but the bricks above were not so well formed, and the clay was often mixed with potsherds.

Shalmaneser took up his abode in Ashur after 848, but he soon tired of its charm and in 832 removed to Kalhu, there to remain to the end. His palace was begun southeast of his father's, and its scanty ruins manage to contribute something to the art of the reign. Most impressive were the bulls, huge cubes of fourteen feet, on whose backs were inscribed the narra-tive which is our main recourse for the middle period. A pair of small winged lions forming an entrance to a chamber and a nine-foot figure with right hand uplifted and a branch of poppies in the left may be mentioned.

His Black Obelisk has enjoyed wide popularity because of its portrait of Jehu; to the artist it makes as little appeal as does its badly garbled annals edition to the historian. Its height is six and a half feet, and it has been cut from a hard black limestone, but so little care has been taken that a diagonal white streak mars its perfection. Five sets of reliefs cover each of its sides, but the execution is rough and scarcely a line which is supposed to be straight has attained its object. Where we can compare its work with that of the preceding period, as in the case of the monkeys, the decline is most evident.

The period is redeemed from artistic banality only by the repoussé work of the palace gates and by the tiling. Bow and shield bearers in white on a deep-blue ground with bows and battlements in golden yellow bear his inscriptions at Ashur, and red marks on them show how they were to be put together. One of the finest examples of this technic comes from Kalhu. The king stands under an awning to receive a high official, who wears a rich yellow dress and carries over his left shoulder a balance with a long slender scale pan. In his right hand the king holds a bowl which he has just received from his subordinate, his left hand grasps the bow whose straight tip touches the ground, while under his left arm he carries the double-edged sword in its sheath adorned with the herring-bone pattern. On his head is perched the white fez-like tiara, with band rising in front, and with two flaps which fall to the waist behind. His glossy black beard is short and so is the coil of hair resting upon his neck. He wears a short-sleeved jacket of dark yellow and a dark yellow skirt with double row of fringes, a third rounding to show where the end of the skirt has been tucked away into the belt. His garments, like those of the other officials, are adorned with huge rosettes, and on his feet are black sandals. Behind is a eunuch, similarly dressed, save for his bare head, carrying under his right shoulder a reserve bow and under his left a quiver with arrows and a sword. Still further to the left, a bearded soldier, barelegged and in short tunic and pointed helmet, wears his sword at his side and holds his spear in his right hand.[1]

Shalmaneser is a colourless figure. The very works of art which were intended to hand down his fame to the after-world only make this the more clear. They show him at his best in the audience-chamber, where he could hold the arrows gracefully in one hand and the bow resting on the ground in the other with the ornamental sword at his side. His tiara and fillet, long hair-ribbons, fringed shawl and robe coming down to his sandalled feet, all give him a certain look of effeminacy.[2]

The gate reliefs depict him in the field but the story is the same, though it must be stated at once that in several of the cases where his annals claim he exercised the leadership in person the reliefs fail to represent him. When he does appear, he rarely descends from the chariot to engage actively in the fighting, and he needs the parasol to shoot against the besieged city. In the chariot both he and the crown prince require an additional man beside the driver to hold the shield and by an arm thrown about the waist prevent them from falling to the ground. The one occasion on which Shalmaneser appears on horseback, it is with the awkwardness of a man not accustomed to ride and not quite certain that he can keep a firm seat.

At his accession, he selected a new group of officers entirely different from those who had been associated with his father. Of these the chief was Ashur-bel-ukin, the turtanu, assisted by Ashur-bania-usur, the chief cellarer, and Abi-ina-ekalli-lilbur, the chamberlain. After five years, there was a palace revolution which made Daian Ashur the turtanu and substituted Belbania for the official of the long and flattering name. That there was something not quite creditable to the actors in this revolution seems indicated by the care with which all trace of it was covered up. The earliest inscription for the reign, the Monolith, gives no warlike expedition for the year 855; the later editions place in this year one against Shupria. Just once the

---

[1] Layard, *Monuments*, II, 55.   [2] *TSBA.*, VI, pl. 8.

latest edition, the Obelisk, breaks its custom of dating by the regnal years. This is in 856, which is called the eponymy of Daian Ashur, though the official from whom the year was actually named, Ashur-bania-usur, still held that office as he had thirty years before.

In contrast with the colourlessness of Shalmaneser, Daian Ashur stands out as a real personality. A large proportion of the highest officers at court, many of the commanders in the field, the prefect of the camp, all the men most closely connected with the royal person, were on the testimony of the reliefs eunuchs, and there is good reason to assume that Daian Ashur himself was one of these unfortunates. For a quarter of a century, a term almost without parallel in the east, he ruled the empire in the name of his nominal master, and so notorious was his usurpation of the supreme power that it was he and not his lord who was credited with the glory of successful campaigns on the monument which was to commemorate the reign. It must be admitted that the Obelisk gave honour where honour was due, for while Daian Ashur must have been at least as old as Shalmaneser, in his later years the king took his ease at home and abandoned the mountain campaigning to the unwearied old man.

On his earlier expeditions, from 858 onward, Shalmaneser had been accompanied by his son, the crown prince, and thenceforth the reliefs represent him with considerable frequency. If we are to identify him with Ashur-daian-apal, he must by this time have been no less than forty-five years old. A prince of such mature age could scarcely be expected to suffer in silence a usurpation of power so great that the turtanu's name should be glorified in the official records destined for posterity, while his own exploits, represented anonymously in the earlier reliefs, were in later years entirely lacking.

The unanimity with which Assyria rose is in itself proof of the general feeling that the rebel's cause was just. At the head of the revolt stood Nineveh, which might find some excuse in the neglect of the king; Ashur had been his special protégé, yet Ashur too became disloyal. Arrapha with its control of the debatable land, the sacred city of Arbela, six of the provinces on the northeast, the most dangerous frontier, with isolated districts here and there in the other provinces, Amedi, which still retained a measure of independence—all are placed on the roll of dishonour. The Aramæans of Hindanu and Til Abni came to a definite understanding with Ashur-daian-apal, while his scribe Kabti wrote his master concerning the rebel whose son had spoken to him about the words the king might speak.[1]

To meet the reproach that the turtanu and not Shalmaneser was the actual ruler, the king took upon himself the eponym office the next year, but the revolt continued unabated. In the midst of the great uprising, Shalmaneser passed away and his son Shamshi Adad V (825–812) entered upon a heritage which must still be made certain by force of arms.

With his own resources, the task seemed impossible. Since the rebel had secured the aid of the Aramæans, the only available ally for Shamshi Adad was Babylon. A few short years ago Marduk-zakir-shum had been his father's vassal; in his need Shamshi Adad purchased Babylonian assistance by even more humiliating concessions. The treaty specifically placed him under Babylonian domination. Akkad is placed before Ashur, Marduk-zakir-shum alone bears the title of king, the oaths are in the name of Babylonian gods. Troops are promised but at a price: "If Shamshi Adad hearkens to the wicked words of Marduk-rimani, to the king he shall say: 'Kill, destroy, make captive.'" The booty is to be restored, the fugitives seized and judgment made by the king; whosoever shall sin and take for himself the dues which pertain not to him shall find his kingdom destroyed by Marduk and the other Babylonian gods.[2]

Aided by the troops of Marduk-zakir-shum, Shamshi Adad assailed Ashur. The city wall still preserves the memory of this assault. Near the great bend in the circumvallation of the southern suburb, we can see where the tower was breached, and beyond huge masses of brickwork lie overturned in the

---

[1] H. 872, copy of an ancient letter sent to Sargon.
[2] Peiser, MVAG., 1896, 6, 14 ff.

ditch. Near by are five bronze pick-heads, used in making the breach, and scattered about are over a hundred and fifty bronze arrow-heads, with two or three sides, and the majority with a tang turned backward on which blazing tow might be fixed before it was shot against the wooden roofs.

Assyria was brought within control by the end of his first full year. Shamshi Adad even found time to despatch forces to restore Amedi to its allegiance and to teach the Nairi kinglets that it would be wise to send in their neglected gifts of horses. Amedi lost its independence and was made the capital of the Nairi province. Comparison of the territory claimed with that actually controlled by his predecessors made only too clear the disastrous consequences of the revolt. The empire had been shaken to its foundations: all the country west of the Euphrates—Syria, Palestine, and Asia Minor—all the lands so often raided beyond the Armenian mountains, a good share of the territory along the eastern frontier, had slipped away during the fratricidal struggle, the greater part never to be restored before the arrival of a new dynasty.

Shamshi Adad attempted to bring back at least the nearest of the former Assyrian possessions. His second campaign was intrusted to his commander-in-chief Mutarris Ashur, "wise, knowing in warfare, a man of discernment." With such encomium, we look for his name among the eponyms, but we find it not. The career of Daian Ashur had shown only too clearly the danger of combining military and civic functions; no longer was the turtanu to lead armies in the field—his duties were divided among subordinates.

Haldia was again the chief inciter to revolt. Sardurish had been succeeded by his son Ishpuinish, and he in turn had almost immediately associated with himself his son Menuash. The land of Etiush, the Araxes region, was taken from its king, Uderuhinish, the eastern mountains were penetrated through Parsua to the Sea of the Setting Sun, Lake Urumia, and a stele was left in Kelishin, to-day the most dangerous of the frontier passes. Mutarris Ashur likewise reached the Sea of the Setting Sun, recovered the territory taken by Ishpuinish, and on a third expedition received horses from Hubushkia, the Mannai, and Parsua, so that the unfortunate mountaineers must now pay double tribute. Past the antimony mountain, the Assyrians moved on to the territory of the Medes, drove the natives to refuge on the White Mountain, won their capital, Sagbita, burned hamlets estimated at one thousand two hundred, and made such an impression that thirty Nairi chieftains came in with their gifts. The list is too long for insertion, but Iranian scholars find it most precious, the first collection of Iranian proper names.

By June of 821 Shamshi Adad was prepared to test the validity of oaths extorted by force of necessity. Marduk-zakir-shum had just passed away, and his son Marduk-balatsu-iqbi had taken his place. The Babylonian frontier was now at Zaddi, almost due east of the city of Ashur itself. The direct route into Babylonia was, therefore, blocked by enemy garrisons, but the road farther east along the mountain slopes was passable and afforded an opportunity to outflank the enemy. Pausing only long enough to kill three lions on Mount Ebih, Shamshi Adad crossed the range and occupied Me Turnat, whose inhabitants were carried off to be reckoned Assyrian citizens.

The crossing of the Turnat and the Ialman mountains brought the submission of four hundred "cities," whose size we can conjecture when we note that all told they mustered just three hundred and thirty warriors. The palm-groves were cut down, and the Babylonians retired to Dur Papsukal, which lay on an island in the midst of the stream, and so seemed a city of refuge to the four hundred and forty-seven "cities" placed on the map by the official eye-witness of Shamshi Adad. It was captured with heavy loss to the defenders, the royal bed and other palace furniture came into the possession of the king, and so well satisfied was he that he handed over the remainder of the booty to the common soldiers. Too late Marduk-balatsu-iqbi arrived with a relieving army and took up his position on the River Daban. Shamshi Adad claims the victory, describes the dead and wounded and the immense spoil—and the narrative closes abruptly. We need the Babylonian story to learn what happened next.

That all was not as Shamshi Adad would have us believe is made evident by the careful avoidance of Babylonia in the years immediately following. During 820–818 expeditions were directed against Tille, whose name thenceforth takes the place of Kutmuh in the list of provinces. Babylonian problems again claimed attention in 815 when the great god went to Der; two years later the Chaldæan land was the object of his attentions, and in 812 Babylon. This second campaign proved fatal to Shamshi Adad.

Of his brief reign, there is little to remark, either of reproach or of commendation. The carved figure he left behind represents the conventional Assyrian monarch. He resided in the southeast palace at Kalhu, his annals were set up in the court of the Anu-Adad temple at Ashur over a human head, he was buried with his fathers in the royal sepulchres at Ashur. His inscribed coffin of basalt was even less pretentious than that of his grandfather.

CHAPTER XIII

WOMAN'S RULE, APPROACH TO MONOTHEISM, AND DECLINE

THE reign of Shamshi Adad was short and its significance small. Yet it was his fate to marry a princess whose name was to go down the ages, long after his own was forgotten, as the most beautiful, most cruel, most powerful, and most lustful of Oriental queens, Sammuramat, or, to give her the more familiar Greek appellation, Semiramis.[1]

Had Sammuramat died as the wife of Shamshi Adad, Oriental legend would have bestowed on her no immortality. Such fame as was hers was due to the premature death of her husband, for as queen mother woman has always found her best opportunity in the Orient, and Ashur had called her son to be king of Assyria in his childhood.

So powerful was Semiramis at first that she made dedications in her own name, erected a stele in the Square of the Stelæ as if a king, placed her name before that of her son, and emphasised rather that she was the widow of Shamshi Adad and daughter-in-law of Shalmaneser than that she was the mother of the reigning monarch. The conquests attributed to Semiramis are indeed but exaggerations of those which must be assigned to her period of rule. The real credit should go rather to Nergal-ilia, who had risen from a mere governorship of Arrapha in 831 to a position but four grades below the turtanu in 818, and reached this coveted post with the accession of Adad-nirari.

The most important expansion of territory was made on the eastern frontier, where the Greeks located the most spectacular triumphs of Semiramis. After the year "in the land" needed by the queen for the settling of her power, the imminent

[1] Cf. especially Lehmann-Haupt, *Die historische Semiramis*, 1910.

danger from the Median hordes forced operations against them
in 810.   Incorporation of Mesopotamia into the Assyrian
Empire was completed in 809 when Guzana, the territory
about the headwaters of the Habur, was pacified and placed
on the list of provinces.   Expeditions in 808 and 807 against
the Mannai mark the most easterly extension of the Assyrian
arms and afford a slight basis for the fabled conquests of
Semiramis in Bactria and India.

   In his fifth year Adad-nirari reached maturity and took upon
himself the burden of empire.   Semiramis lost her power, but
her brief reign had been sufficient to give her a unique reputation.   She was one of the few orientals the Greeks remembered,
and down to the nineteenth century poems and operas were
composed in her name.   In her son Ninyas, whom she was reported to have married, we have all the Greeks knew of Adad-
nirari.

   Adad-nirari celebrated his coming to age by an expedition
into Syria, against Arpad, the capital of Agusi, and against
Damascus.   His success was commemorated by one of his
governors, Nergal-eresh of Rasappa, who set up in Zabani
south of the Singara mountains a stele which represented in
rude provincial style the king before the divine emblems.
The next year Hazazu was besieged, the city of Bali was invested in 804, and the year following the march was directed
against the Upper Sea.

   Menuash of Haldia, associated with his father Ishpuinisn,
became sole king about 815, and promptly set about reconquer-
ing the Mannai from the Assyrians.   More fortunate than they,
his monuments are still found in Mannai land, at the foot of
Lake Urumia, and they thus prove that he had better control
of these wild passes than have the governments of our own day.
Then Menuash was in the Nipur hills due north of Assyria, and
the Assyrian records speak of expeditions against Hubushkia
in 802, in 792, in 785, and in 784.   The immediate result of
this shutting off of the Mannai by the Hubushkians was the
loss of the Parsua region to Adad-nirari.   Menuash slaughtered
two thousand odd soldiers in Alzi, and the Assyrian expedition

into Lusia proved a failure. He even claims the conquest of the Ashurini land, that is, territory belonging to Assyria proper. The various peoples along the upper Euphrates are named, and inscriptions were erected in their territory. Beyond its bend, he reached to the Hittites and to Melidia, and a conquest of the Urume may be our earliest reference to the Armenians, perhaps now settled in Cappadocia. North of this far-stretching line all Armenia was his, clear to the Araxes River. He was justified in adding "mighty king" to his titulary.

Everywhere we find his inscriptions and his building, but his heart was especially devoted to Tushpash. The east and west range between Mesopotamia and Armenia had already been proved in many a hard-fought struggle to be one of the most impenetrable barriers in existence. On the other side, a mile above sea-level, was a great lake, without outlet, and un-drinkable because filled with alkali. The mountain rim which shut it in on the south was equally marked on the other side of the triangle, with Nimrud reaching almost ten thousand feet in height and with Sipan almost fourteen thousand, whose gleaming snows and pointed craters were magnificent when viewed from afar.

On the third, or eastern, side of the triangle was a broad plain surrounded by hills, and in the centre a long rock of extraor-dinarily hard limestone three hundred feet high, and which formed a most striking landmark. The plain was extremely fertile and irrigation was easy. Menuash built a canal to which he gave his name, and the garden city began the career which still continues, thanks to the beneficent waters first made to flow by Menuash. Poplars grew up, as well as apples, peaches, pomegranates, melons, cucumbers; we have records of the establishment of vineyards and of temples with many units of seed land. The bare Van rock, with its wonderful view, was covered with buildings, but only rock-cut steps, rock-hewn inscriptions, and the caves for the dead have survived. Else-where we find accounts of canals, palaces, forts, and temples, for the age of Menuash is the golden age of Haldian architec-ture.

Punitive expeditions were directed by Adad-nirari against
the Medes in three groups of two years, beginning with 801,
795, and 790, and in 787 as well; Namri was invaded in 798,
and about the same time Elli, Harhar, Arziash, and Mesu
were attacked. The collapse of Assyrian influence in the
barren mountains of Media seemed for the moment more than
offset by successes obtained in the south and west. A more or
less valid claim to Babylonia might be put forward by Adad-
nirari on the basis of his mother's Babylonian birth, but no
attempt was made to render it effective until after Semiramis
was deposed. Already in 796 and 795 we have expeditions
to Der, but no serious attack was made until 786. It was a
matter of little difficulty to carry off the new ruler, Bau-ahi-
iddina, and with him went an impressive spoil of gods: the
"Great God" who went in procession to Der, Humhummu,
the Mistresses of Babylon and Akkad, Shimalia, Nergal,
Annunitum, Mar-biti of the city of Malki. Thence Adad-
nirari continued to Kutu, Babylon, and Borsippa, where he
made the pure offerings of a sovereign prince, and the cities
supported the decrees of Bel, Nabu, and Nergal. The kings of
the nomad Chaldæans were devastating the settled country;
their forays were checked for the time being by the strict
measures taken by the Assyrians. A new boundary was delimited, and the next year the "Great God" went to Der in
state under Assyrian auspices.

Progress of the Assyrians west of the Euphrates was checked
by the pestilence, and it was not until 797 that Mansuate, now
the dominant city in north central Syria, was in danger. The
whole Hittite land, Amurru, Tyre, Sidon, Israel, Edom, and
Palastu, the first instance of the use of the Philistine name in
the sense of the later Palestine, recognised the Assyrians as
their masters. The willingness with which Israel and Edom
made submission was further increased by their desire to see
their revenge on their enemies Judah and Damascus.

So low had Hazael brought Israel in the last days of Jehu
that his son Jehoahaz (814–800) possessed but fifty horsemen
and ten chariots out of the two thousand Ahab had led into

battle at Qarqara. Passing without fighting through a thoroughly cowed Israel, Hazael won for himself the whole of the Philistine land from the western sea to Aphek. The equally Philistine Gath was taken from Judah, and Jehoash (836–799) saved himself from complete ruin only by sending to Hazael all the treasures of temple and palace. Hazael's son, Bar Hadad III, was a man of lesser caliber, and Jehoahaz resumed his independence. Bar Hadad made another attempt to restore Aramæan control when the young Jehoash became king in Israel (800–785). Samaria was besieged, and for a time the famine was severe, but there came to the camp of the invader a rumour that Hittite and Egyptian kings had been hired against them, a great panic befell, and they fled in dismay. In three pitched battles, the greatest at Aphek, all the cities taken by Hazael were recovered.[1]

Foiled in the south, Bar Hadad turned his attention to north Syria, where Irhuleni had been succeeded by a certain Zakir whose original home was Laash. Thanks to his god Baal-shamain, the "Lord of Heaven," he was made to reign in Hazrek[2] on the Orontes, a short distance south of Hamath. If Hazrek had before this belonged to Damascus, we can understand why Bar Hadad formed an alliance against him. Of the ten kings, we have mention of Bar Gush, king of Agusi, the king of Quweh or Cilicia, the king of the Umq we have learned as the equivalent of Hattina, the king of Samal, the king of Meliz or Melitene—it is the usual catalogue of the kings of north Syria and of Asia Minor.

All these kings fell upon him suddenly and laid siege to Hazrek, raised a wall higher than the wall of that city, and dug a ditch deeper than its moat. Then did Zakir lift up his hands to Baal-shamain, and Baal-shamain answered him and sent by the hand of seers and men expert in numbers, and thus did Baal-shamain say: "Fear not, for I have made thee king and I will stand by thee and I will rescue thee from all those kings who have made siege against thee." So Zakir appointed men of Hazrek for charioteers and for horsemen to guard her king in

[1] II Kings, 12 f.; 6 f.   [2] The biblical Hadrach, Zech. 9 : 1.

the midst of her, he built her up and added a district to her, and made it her possession and made it his land. And he filled with men all these fortresses on every side and he built temples in all his land. The stele, written in a curious mixture of Aramaic and Phœnician, did he set up before Al Ur and his other gods, Shamash and Sahar, and the gods of heaven and earth, and upon it he wrote that which his hands had done.[1]

A year after the Israelite Jehoash had ascended the throne, the Judean Jehoash was followed by his son Amaziah (799–782). His reign began with a great success, the slaughter of the Edomites in the Valley of Salt and the capture of their rock-girt metropolis Sela. The youthful victor sent a message to the equally youthful Jehoash: "Come, let us look each other in the face." Jehoash replied with the fable of the thistle that asked the cedar of Lebanon for a marriage alliance. Battle was joined at Beth Shemesh, commanding the entrance to the valley up which runs now the railroad to Jerusalem; Judah was completely defeated, Amaziah was made prisoner, the wall of Jerusalem was broken down for two hundred yards. Amaziah was permitted to continue his rule, but as a subject.

Bar Hadad had been supplanted by Mari, and on him the Assyrians made a spectacular assault. Established in his palace, Adad-nirari received an enormous indemnity—twenty-three hundred talents of silver and twenty of gold, three thousand of copper and five thousand of iron, cloths, linen, a bed of ivory, a litter inlaid with the same precious material, full compensation for the many defeats suffered by his predecessors at the hands of Damascus.

A sinister hint has survived as to the means employed to bring to an end the dynasties of Syria. An Aramæan dedication to Hadad is set up by the eunuch Akrabu, son of Gabbarud. His father was the king of Hattina who had opposed Shalmaneser III, and he had been saved from a fearful death when an end was made to his father's state only because he

---

[1] Pognon, *Ins. sémitiques*, II, no. 86; Torrey, *JAOS.*, XXXV, 353 ff.

had been so mutilated that he could never become a pretender to the throne.[1]

The returning armies carried home from Syria more than the rich booty. The plague has always been at home in the Nile valley, and about this time, as Amos puts it, Yahweh sent among the Hebrews pestilence after the manner of Egypt.[2] It spread throughout the country, and the first series of expeditions in that direction were checked by the ravages of the fell disease. After another visit to Syria, it broke out in 765 and again in 759. During the entire period it must have been endemic, and to no small degree it contributed to the weakening of the empire.

Little is known of the culture. Decline is indicated by the structure Adad-nirari erected in Kalhu, south of the palace of Ashur-nasir-apal, a group of four upper chambers, the material of adobe, the interior walls plastered and painted. Pavement slabs before the two entrances gave the genealogy of the king through five generations, or, no small jump, to the semi-mythological heroes of the earliest Assyrian history.

Excavations have been carried on at Guzana, at the magnificent source of the Habur still called the "Springhead." A group of private letters to its governor Mannu-ki-Ashur, eponym in 793, will be interesting when published. Another work of art from the reign is the stele from Rasappa.

The conquests of Semiramis, real or fabled, yield in interest to her religious reforms. While the earlier centuries had seen much Babylonianisation in religion, there had been a remarkable ignoring of Nabu, god of Borsippa. A single early example of a Nabu name is the Sha Nabu-damqa who was chamberlain for Ashur-nasir-apal; we wait until the present reign before we have the name of another official compounded with Nabu. Then we have a group, and particularly illuminating is the Nabu-shar-usur, "May Nabu protect the king," for we may rest assured that no courtier would so have named his son unless the god had been a prime favourite of the king he wished to flatter.

[1] *CIS.*, II, 75; Sachau, *ZA.*, VI, 432 ff.   [2] Amos 4 : 10.

FIG. 80. EUNUCH OFFICIAL OF ASHUR–NASIR–APAL.
(Metropolitan Museum.)

FIG. 81. STATUE OF GOD NABU, PALACE OF
ADAD–NIRARI III.

If we were to judge contemporary art by the Nabu statues dedicated by Bel-tarsi-iluma, the governor of Kalhu, "for the life of Adad-nirari, king of Assyria, his lord, and for the life of Sammuramat, lady of the palace, his mistress," our opinion would be low indeed. The huge horned head and box-like lower body point back to a god in pillar form, the hair is roughly waved, the eyes and eyebrows are most primitive, the arms so bloated that they cause one to suspect dropsy, but the clasped hands are rather well done, and the fine finger-nails indicate of what the artist was capable when not bound by his ancient original.

On the statue is a long hymn of praise to the god, who is said to be the powerful, the exalted, son of Esagila, the majestic leader, the mighty prince, son of Nudimmut or Ea, whose command is exalted, the messenger of cunning things, ruler of all heaven and earth, who knoweth all things, whatever their names, whose ear is open, who holdeth the pen of the tablet, who taketh the hand of the prisoner, the merciful, who weaveth spells, who cleanseth or casteth a spell upon the beloved of Enlil, lord of lords, whose power hath no equal, without whom no decision is made in heaven, the compassionate, the forgiving, whose condescension is good, who dwells in Ezida in Kalhu. Thus far the writer has been quoting an earlier hymn, with its frank recognition of other gods friendly to Nabu. At most we may compare the cases where the devotee, in his ecstasy, declares his patron the only god worthy of worship. The author of this profession of faith has left henotheism behind and has almost reached pure monotheism with its intolerance of other gods, for he solemnly concludes: "Thou who shalt follow after, trust in Nabu, trust not in any other god."[1]

Times were no more ripe for monotheism than they were in the days of the Egyptian Ikhnaton, and the intolerance of Nabu worshippers produced its inevitable reaction. The Nabu temple was restored in Nineveh as late as 787, but the inscriptions which date from the time when Adad-nirari was his

[1] *IR.*, 35:2; Rogers, *Parallels*, 307 ff.

own master are as conspicuous for their silence in regard to
Nabu as they are for the emphasis on the supreme position of
Ashur. Nabu names disappear, and the propaganda ended in
failure. Perhaps we do wrong to compare the movement
with that of Ikhnaton; a few years before, the nationalist
Elijah had successfully protested the introduction of the Tyrian
Baal into Israel; in each case nationalism was victorious.

Adad-nirari III (812–782) was still a young man, well under
forty, when death transferred his throne to his son Shalmaneser
IV (782–772). Actual power was vested in the turtanu
Shamshi-ilu who had been governor of Ashur as early as
805 and had retained it until his promotion. In him we have
the third of the dominating personalities who set the tone for
the age; that he exercised that dominance in weaker fashion
than did his predecessors must be reckoned a chief cause for
the decline of the dynasty and for the revolts which disturbed
its latest days.

Assyria's greatest enemy was now Haldia. The petty Armenian power whose Arame and Sardurish I had checked the
Assyrians under Shalmaneser III had grown apace. Shamshi
Adad had found the traces of Ishpuinish close to Lake Urumia,
Menuash had pushed the border west to the Euphrates, and
with the growing wealth had erected palace after palace.
Argishtish I anticipated Shalmaneser IV in becoming king by
about a year (783), and soon made Haldia the first power in
the Near East. His own annals, carved on the precipitous
cliffs of his isolated citadel of Tushpash, overlooking Lake
Van, repeat with wearisome monotony the names of unknown
lands with their equally monotonous list of sheep and goats
carried off as booty. Here and there we are able to pick out a
city whose location is sure, and thus we may correlate in some
degree the fourteen years of the annals with the data of the
Assyrian Chronicle.

The Araxes region held the attention of Argishtish his first
two years, but in 781 he turned south and fought with the Hittites, Niriba, and Melidia. This very year the Assyrians place
an expedition against Urartu, and in the next a letter to the

god Ashur refers to Pan Ashur-lamur, governor of the ancient
capital, but it is too mutilated to have preserved the events in
detail.   More expeditions date from the two years following
and from the eighth and tenth as well.   In his fifth year
Argishtish makes mention of an Assyrian general Harsitash,
in his next he fought in Bushtush and Parsua, in 777 against
the Assyrians and the Mannai, against the Mannai in 776 and
775, and Assyria and Alzi are mentioned together, in 774 he
was close to Lake Urumia, near the end of his reign he could
mention Syria as part of his conquests.   In Sargon's time men
remembered that Ushhu and Quda had not been obedient to
Assyrian kings since the time of Shamshi-ilu.[1]   Perhaps the
best evidence can be found of the danger to which Assyria
was exposed by the location of a monument barely twenty-
five miles north of Nineveh which mentions Argishtish,
Shamshi-ilu, and the judge Mushallim Urta, and is probably
the witness to a battle on this site.

First place in the records is contested by the Ituai with the
Haldians.   They make their earliest appearance on the north
Babylonian frontier when their territory was invaded by the
second Tukulti Urta, they were a part of the Ashur province
early in the reign of Adad-nirari III (805), but they were again
hostile to Assyria in 791, expeditions were demanded against
them in the first two years of Shalmaneser, and once more in
his seventh.   The third year of his successor saw an attack
against Gananate, on the northeast of Babylonia; the fourth
was against the city Marrat in the Sealands; the fifth was
against the Ituai; the sixth was spent "in the land," sure sign
of a reverse; in the seventh the Assyrians were back again
fighting Gananate.   The Assyrian frontier had obviously retreated all along the south; it was to the advantage of local
communities and not of Babylon, for the kings we may place
here, Nabu-mukin-zer, Marduk-bel-usate, and Marduk-apal-
iddina II, were utterly powerless.

As might have been expected, the growing weakness of the
central power was reflected in the growing independence of

[1] H. 246.

the nobility.   A condition almost feudal is illustrated by the case of Bel Harran-bel-usur, whose very name, "May the Lord of Harran protect the lord," declared dependence on the non-Assyrian god of the rival Mesopotamian metropolis.   How great were his pretensions is shown by the city he founded in the desert west of Ashur, not far from where to-day stretch the ruins of Romanised Hatra.   He is sculptured in the royal attitude of devotion before the sacred emblems, though his beardless, puffy face shows him a eunuch.   He appeals to the gods, first the Babylonian Marduk, "who settles cities and founds towns," then to the equally Babylonian Nabu, to Shamash who "judges all the cities and protects the world regions," to Sin and to Ishtar, but Ashur is deliberately ignored.   It is these gods and no human overlord who have given orders for the building of the deserted city and for its change of name to Dur Bel Harran-bel-usur, for the construction of the temple, the shrines, and the road to the city.   We see the figures of these deities and not of his nominal master on the stele he caused to be carved, and it is in their dwelling that it is dedicated.

There is no mention of the king when Bel Harran-bel-usur describes the revenues, free-will offerings, incense offerings which he has granted for the eternal worship of the gods, though such technical terms should have been reserved for the royal finances.   The blessings and curses which end the stele are positively insulting.   They are directed to the individual whom Ashur, Shamash, Marduk, and Adad shall call to rule the land, and he is ordered in so many words not to suppress the revenues, take away the freedom from dues which Bel Harran-bel-usur has established for that city, he is not to carry off the grain when it is reaped or requisition the straw, its waters he is not to divert to another plot, boundary and boundary-stone are not to be changed, seizure of cattle and sheep is not to be made, the inhabitants who dwell therein are not to bear tax or forced labour, nor any other due which may be inflicted, nor shall the levy be exacted from them.

Usurpation of rights which, even when the Kashshite kings

ruled a feudal Babylonia, were reserved to the king alone is shown at its worst in the concluding passage: "Do not move the boundary-stone from its place, do not set it up in another place, do not set it up in another locality, do not put it in a house of lead, do not break it, do not hide it in the earth, do not cast it into the water, do not cover it with asphalt, do not burn it in the fire, do not erase the writing. The gods whose names are written on this stele, when in war, battle, fight, in sickness, disease, pestilence, plague, you raise your hands, will hear your prayer and will come to your aid. Whoso changes my writing and my name, Ashur, Shamash, the pest god Dibbara, and Amurru, the great gods, without limit will be unpropitious." [1]

Amazing as it may seem, with all this breakdown of the central power, in the face of the constant encroachments of Haldia and of the defections in the south, the Syrian policy was not abandoned. The Assyrians marched to the cedar land in 775, and two years later they reached Damascus. The sudden death of Shalmaneser, perhaps from the plague, made no change in the policy, for the troops of Ashur-dan III (772–755) attacked Hazrek in 772 and again in 765, but pestilence intervened and Shamshi-ilu turned his thoughts from war.

Syria was left to follow her own devices, which, unfortunately for the historian, did not include the chronicling of what she did. The Hebrew narrator loses interest at this point and devotes but a few lines of condemnation to the long reign of Jeroboam II (785–745). One statement alone is vouchsafed, that he restored the borders of Israel from the city Libo in the Hamath country to the sea of the Arabah, the Dead Sea.[2] Granted that this assertion is approximately correct, the Assyrian retreat had permitted a great increase of Israelite power.

The wealth secured and the pride engendered find illustration in the prophecies of Amos. The student of Hebrew religion gives to the first writing prophet a definite place in that

---

[1] Scheil, *RT.*, XVI, 176 ff.; Unger, *Stele des Bel Harran-bel-usur.*
[2] II Kings 14 : 25.

great evolution; the historian of the Assyrian Empire quotes him as illustrating certain social and economic changes which, he is sure, must have taken place universally, but whose clearest evidence is found in the sermons recorded by the Hebrew prophets.

Amos began his career with visions. Yahweh formed the locust to devour, but the plague was stayed when the prophet prayed their withdrawal. Next came devouring fire, and a second time his intercession was successful. The third vision was of the wall shown untrue by the plumb-line, and Yahweh could no longer pass in patience the disobedient Israelites.

To the pilgrims assembled at Bethel, Amos made this proclamation. He was reported to the king by the chief priest Amaziah, who gave him this advice: "Soothsayer, run back home to Judah, for there only can you earn your daily bread by carrying on the prophetic business"—in other words, condemnation of Israel would be popular enough in the south —"but prophesy no more at Bethel, since there is the royal sanctuary and palace." The answer of Amos contains the essence of the new prophecy: "I was no prophet, not even a prophet's son; I was but a herdsman, a dresser of scyamores. Despite such lack of qualification, Yahweh took me away from following the flock and gave me order: 'Go, prophesy against my people Israel.'" Amaziah is to suffer in person the doom impending on Israel, his wife is to be publicly dishonoured, his sons and daughters shall fall by the sword, his land shall be divided by a measuring-line, he himself shall be buried in unclean soil.

The upper classes are to be deported because their worship of Yahweh lacks an ethical element. They trample upon the needy and deprive the poor peasant of life itself. They long for the new-moon festival to be over that they may again sell grain, and the Sabbath that they may offer wheat in the bazaars. They make the measure by which they sell small but the weight is great, so that they cheat the people with false balances. They are care-free in Mount Zion and reckless in the hill of Samaria, and the agriculturalist Amos is particularly disgusted because these newly rich traders consider themselves the chief men in the nation. It is they and not the nobility by birth who lie on the ivory couches we have so frequently met in the Assyrian tribute lists, they recline at ease at banquets, and feast on chosen lambs from the flocks and calves stall-fattened. They bawl out idle songs to the sound of the lyre, they invent new musical instruments like David. They pour down huge caldrons of wine, they anoint themselves with the best oils. Their women are as heartless as the men. They are cows of Bashan who oppress the poor, but their time will come, they shall be dragged away with hooks, each straight ahead from the enemy's breach in the walls, and into the land of Harmon.

Should not the whole earth tremble in fear of this, should not every inhabitant mourn? Should not the invasion rise like the inundation of the Nile and recede like the same river of Egypt? Yahweh will make the sun set at noon, he will make the earth dark in the clear day, as had happened in the awful eclipse of 763. The pilgrimages to Bethel will be turned into mourning, the songs into dirges, like the mourning for an only son.

Nor is Israel alone to suffer. Punishment is to come upon Damascus for her sins. Tyre has forgotten the covenant of brotherhood made by Hiram with David and Solomon and has handed over the Hebrews as slaves to the Aramæans. Ammon has destroyed expectant mothers with unspeakable cruelties in their desire to enlarge their territory in Gilead; Rabbah shall be fired and their divine king shall be taken captive with his priests. Moab burned the bones of a ruler of Edom, so shall her city Kerioth be fired. In the background we always feel the presence of Assyria, but never a word is uttered in condemnation of the hostile empire.[1]

A mind beyond the ordinary was demanded to realise the inevitable rebound of Assyria, for at the moment nothing seemed more unlikely. The Syrian armies brought back the pestilence, sure sign of the wrath of the pest god Nergal,

---

[1] Of the commentaries, cf. especially Harper, *Amos and Hosea.*

and two years after Shamash caused a total eclipse of the sun. To us its occurrence in 763 fixes by exact astronomy the Assyrian chronology; to contemporaries it was proof of divine anger. Amos saw in the sun setting at noon and the earth dark on a clear day Yahweh's wrath; to the Assyrians it was the last manifestation needed to prove the necessity of a change in dynasty.

Ashur, abandoned long since as a capital, had fallen into the hands of a great feudal noble, Aplia, who added to the territories he ruled as governor two of the most important frontier provinces, Mazamua on the east and Amedi on the north. The sun was eclipsed on the 15th of June; before the end of the year Ashur raised the standard of revolt. Two years later Arrapha was in rebellion, and in 759 Guzana cast off the yoke of Shamshi-ilu. A second expedition against Guzana in the next year brought "peace in the land" and two years of quiet. Aplia disappears.

Ashur-dan died in 755 without issue. His two predecessors, like himself, had reached the throne at an early age, and Shalmaneser IV had left no other son. Shamshi-ilu placed the uneasy crown upon an uncle of the last king, Ashur-nirari V, the son of Adad-nirari, and so a mature man of at least thirty years of age. No sooner had Shamshi-ilu possessed himself of the viziership, at the accession of Shalmaneser IV, than he made a clean sweep of the former officials, and only Nergal-eresh of Rasappa survived. So clearly was it recognised that the reigns of Shalmaneser IV and Ashur-dan III were one that the cursus of eponyms was broken only to insert the new king and the old turtanu. The cursus begins anew with Ashur-nirari, and of all the hierarchy of the last two reigns, Shamshi-ilu is the only one who continues in office. The others had been sacrificed to the revolution, whose leader we may see in the new chamberlain, Marduk-shallimanni.

The first year of Ashur-nirari's reign (755–746) was graced by an expedition against Hazrek, and in the second the Assyrians marched against Arpad in north Syria, where Haldian influence was becoming increasingly pronounced. Mati-ilu, king of Arpad, was forced to sue for peace, the terms of which were embodied in a formal treaty:

"Mati-ilu, his sons, his daughters, his nobles, the men of his land, shall not sin against the oaths. This goat is not brought forth from his flock as an offering, either for the war-loving or the peace-loving Ishtar, either for illness or for slaughter as food; it has been brought that Mati-ilu should take the oath of loyalty to Ashur-nirari, king of Assyria. If Mati-ilu sins against the oaths, then as this goat is brought from his flock and shall never return to his flock, to the headship of his flock shall not return, so shall Mati-ilu, with his sons, his daughters, and the men of his land be brought out of his land, to his land shall he not return, to the headship of his land shall he not return. This head is not the head of a goat, it is the head of Mati-ilu, it is the head of his sons, of his nobles, of the men of his land. If Mati-ilu transgresses these oaths, then as the head of this goat is cut off and his teeth laid in his mouth, so shall the head of Mati-ilu be cut off.

"At the command of Ashur-nirari shall he go against his enemies; Mati-ilu with his nobles and his military forces shall not go out or march according to the pleasure of their own hearts, else shall Sin, the great lord who dwells in Harran, clothe Mati-ilu, his nobles, and the men of his land with leprosy like a garment, that they camp outside in the open fields and receive no compassion. Increase of cattle, asses, sheep, horses, shall there not be in his land. May Adad, the prince of heaven and earth, cut off Mati-ilu, his land, and the men of his land with want and hunger; may they eat the flesh of their sons and daughters and may they be savoury as goat's flesh or mutton; may Adad cut off their wells and may rainfall cease; may dust be their food, on the bare ground may they seek repose. If Mati-ilu, his sons, his nobles, sin against the oaths to Ashur-nirari, king of Assyria, may his cultivators not sing in the fields the harvest song, may not a plant of the field spring forth. If they bring an offering for remembrance of any one, but it be not an offering for thy life, if they bring it for thy sons and daughters but bring it not for the life of Ashur-

nirari, his sons and his nobles, then may Ashur, father of the
gods, who grants kingship, reduce thy land to a desert, thy
subjects to skeletons, thy city to ruined mounds, thy house
to a ruin.

"If Mati-ilu sins against these oaths to Ashur-nirari, king
of Assyria, may Mati-ilu become a common prostitute, may
his men become women, as a prostitute in the squares of his
city may he find his support, from land to land may they drive
him, as a mule may he have neither wife nor children.   May
Ishtar, queen of women and mistress of wives, take from them
their bows.   May their wailing be bitter: 'Woe is us, against
the oaths to Ashur-nirari, king of Assyria, have we sinned.'"
In witness are the gods, a long list headed by Ashur and concluded by the local deities, the Adads of Kurban and of Hallaba
or Aleppo.   Terrible as was this oath, its effect was transient.
Before the brief reign had come to an end, Mati-ilu had denounced the treaty and had entered into an alliance with
Haldia, whose king, Sardurish II, claimed the defeat of Ashur-
nirari.

Four years of inactivity ensued and then came two expeditions against the Namri land, not wars of offence, but attempts
to beat back the mountain tribes from Assyria itself.   That
destruction did not come from this frontier so early was due
to the fortunate circumstance that, after one more year "in
the land," Kalhu revolted.   On the lucky 13th of Airu, in
the beginning of May, 746, Tiglath Pileser, perhaps the city's
governor, sat upon the throne.

All was going to ruin in Ashur.   The inner walls erected only
a century before by Shalmaneser III had completely fallen;
already houses were being built from the débris and little streets
and alleys were taking the place of the broad avenues which
had led to the city gates.   Our records are completely silent
as to any form of cultural life, for the period marked a decline
in material prosperity no less than in population and in military power.

CHAPTER XIV

THE RESTORATION—TIGLATH PILESER III

WITH the advent of Tiglath Pileser III (746–728), we enter upon the last period of Assyrian history. Our sources rapidly become more and more abundant and the importance of the events chronicled increases in the same ratio. It is this period of little over a century which justifies a detailed history of Assyria.

Tiglath Pileser was a usurper, though he boasts of the kings his fathers.[1] He appears but once before his accession, on the occasion when Adad-nirari granted him a field with the immunities customarily conceded to high officials. His name was a reminiscence of the first Tiglath Pileser; when he reached the throne, he promptly adopted no small part of his traditional policy.[2]

The authority of the new ruler was firmly established by the beginning of May. Ample time was left for war, Babylonia promised an easy victory, so to Babylonia he hastened. A great darkness had fallen upon that country. After Marduk-apal-iddina II, for two years there was no king, and then Eriba Marduk, son of Marduk-shakin-shum, seized the hand of Bel, and justified his usurpation by restoring to their rightful owners, the citizens of Babylon and Borsippa, the fields settled by hostile Aramæans.

Some ancient scholars begin the ninth dynasty with Nabu-shum-ishkun (760–747), though probably he was the son of his predecessor; at any rate he was a member of the Dakkuru

[1] We can hardly accept the suggestion of Schnabel, *OLZ.*, XII, 530, that he was son of Adad-nirari IV and brother of Ashur-nirari, for that would make him too young.

[2] Detailed study of reign, A. S. Anspacher, *Tiglath Pileser III*, 1912; cf. *AJSL.*, XXXVII, 223 ff.; latest edition of inscriptions, Rost, *Keilschrifttexte Tiglat-Pilesers III*; new edition by writer in preparation; source criticism, *Historiography*, 32 ff.

tribe. His rule outside Babylon was nominal, for in the
suburb of Borsippa was the Assyrian Nabu-shum-imbi as
mayor and housekeeper of Nabu, and by his side was a priestly
college, also largely Assyrian. He fears the great godhead of
Nabu, rebuilds the temple in his own name, and we sense the
royal formula under the statement that no official from of
ancient days before his time had undertaken it. Before he
could complete the work ordered him by Nabu, lord of lands—
this appellation of right belongs alone to Marduk, god of the
suzerain Babylon—there arose a state of anarchy. The men of
Babylon, Borsippa, Dushulti on the Euphrates, the Chaldæans,
Aramæans, and men of Dilbat, contended for long with one
another. Then up rose Nabu-shum-iddina, whose father,
Dannu Nabu, once held that office of housekeeper which
Nabu-shum-imbi had usurped, and asserted his ancestral
claims. Ezida fell into his hands, whereupon he assailed the
house of Nabu-shum-imbi by night. The only defence known
to Nabu-shum-imbi was prayer to his patron saint, but the
citizens of Borsippa were more warlike. All night long they
stood with their bows and lances about the house, and in the
morning Nabu-shum-imbi was safe and ready to ascribe his
salvation to the city god.

A new era, that of Nabu-nasir, begins with 747; the native
chronicle and the so-called Ptolemaic Canon of Rulers alike
begin with his accession year. The next saw the enthronement of Tiglath Pileser, whose support Nabu-nasir was only
too glad to purchase. So it was with the alluring prospect of
being welcomed by the propertied classes as a deliverer that
Tiglath Pileser set forth to inaugurate his reign with cheaply
bought laurels.

A few days' march east of the Tigris brought the Assyrians
to the outpost of Til Kamri, defended by a great coalition of
Aramæan tribes. The river which protected the allied front
was crossed on rafts, and the battle showed that the vitality
of Assyria was still unimpaired. Tiglath Pileser seized the
first opportunity to make it apparent a new policy was to
obtain in the administration of dependent states. Over

against the rebel city, an entirely new settlement was established, Assyrian from foundation to coping; its name Kar Ashur, "Wall of Ashur," indicated its purpose as guard-house against the nomads. A palace was constructed within and it was garrisoned by the "men of the lands, the booty of my hands," henceforth to be considered native Assyrians, and so subject to tax and gift. The whole northern quarter of Babylonia seems to have been included in the new province.

All the old-time centres, Sippar, Kutu, Kish, Babylon, opened their doors, and their Assyrian saviour offered his ritually pure sacrifices in these "cities without parallel." The eastern border along the banks of the Surappu and Uknu Rivers to the seacoast was reduced and made to use one tongue, and the deported inhabitants were assigned to the provinces of the turtanu, the chamberlain, the chief cellarer, and the governors of Barhalza and Mazamua. Dur Tukulti-apal-esharra was built, and the captives settled in his "Wall" were commanded to worship the royal image which his lord Ashur had ordered him to set up "as a sign of victory and might."

His second campaign was against Parsua, whose chieftain Tunaku had seized districts claimed for Assyria. The numerous tribes to whose eponymous founders the scribes regularly prefixed "House" were overrun, and the men of Harshu, long ago hostile to the kings of Ur, were burned out of the mountain forests. A relief depicts Nikur, Tunaku's capital, on the crest of a high mountain, its double walls battered down by the wheeled ram with its projecting spears, which is driven up a prepared ramp. The archers carry a new type of shield, wicker and head high, with covering top. The dead and the impaled living were stripped of their clothes in further ignominy. Parsua and Bit Hamban were the provinces formed from this territory. One further land we must notice because it is called the "Land of the Rooster"; he may be on his way from the Iranian plateau, for the Greeks called him the Persian bird, though the Syrians named him the Akkadian.

No small part of the extant annals is filled with the expedition of 737 against the Medes. A queer mixture of races is indicated with "houses" of tribes bearing Iranian, Kashshite, or Aramæan names, and all inextricably mingled. Assyrian influence is seen in a "ruin of Ashur," and place names with Kengi remind one of how in earliest Shumer Kengi meant the "Land." Ashur-daninanni, governor of Mazamua, was the leader, and the house of Ishtar in the province of the goddess Bau was made the centre.

Continued absence of Tiglath Pileser on the Syrian frontier left Babylonia too much to her devices. Nabu-nasir remained the nominal ruler, and in far-away Uruk men dated by his fifth year as they restored an ancient festival whose very name had been forgotten and the lines of the edifices had lapsed from men's memories. King, resident, and nobles alike promised aid, and so the lady Usur-amatsu enjoyed a new abode. How little Nabu-nasir excelled his predecessors is shown rather by the separation of Borsippa from Babylon. Nabu-nasir was not content to allow the contest to go by default, but, as the author of the Babylonian Chronicle sadly confesses: "The battle which Nabu-nasir waged against Borsippa is not recorded." Fourteen years he ruled in quiet, if not with power. His son Nabu-nadin-zer was shortly deposed by a provincial governor, Nabu-shum-ishkun II; after a little more than a month, the rebel met his fate, and the ninth dynasty came to an inglorious end (732).

The new pretender was Nabu-mukin-zer, chief of the Aramæan Amukkanu, and there is significance in the fact that from his reign we have the first use of Aramaic in an explanatory note to the cuneiform Babylonian which was still the one language in which business transactions could be legally written. Union of Babylonia under a strong Aramæan ruler was a serious danger to Assyria, so in 731 Assyrian armies were once more marching along the old war-path east of the Tigris. The Puqudu and Lahiru were added to the province of Arrapha, and various other tribes were punished.

All this was preliminary to an attack on the *de facto* king of Babylon, now confined in his native Sapea, a triple-walled city the lowest circuit of which is higher than a full-grown palm-tree.   Archers in an abbreviated and girdled dress form the defence, but many of their nude bodies lie in the encircling stream across which the invaders have constructed an approach for the battering-ram with its double spears.   In the distance

Fig. 82. SPOIL OF SAPEA.

a palm-tree is seen falling through the exertions of a soldier. Two rams stand idle before a deserted city with double walls, while from a side-gate issue ox-drawn carts, each bearing a family into exile.   Before a palm-tree in full bearing is a high official with raised staff, while his two eunuch scribes register the spoil of sheep and goats.   It is appropriate that in this war against Aramæans we have our first example of the second scribe with the papyrus roll to supplement the use of tablet and stylus.

While the siege of Sapea dragged on, there appeared in camp embassies of unusual interest. Balasu, the Dakkuru chief, was to be remembered by those who read Greek as Belesys, the Chaldæan priest who assisted the Median Arbaces to overthrow the first Assyrian empire.[1] Nadinu had settled at Larak, an old city on the lower Tigris, abandoned so many centuries that its ruin mound was in popular fancy supposed to date beyond the universal flood.

Much more important in actual history was Marduk-apaliddina, "son" of that Iakinu who had paid tribute to Shalmaneser III, and real son of the late king of Babylon, Nabushum-ishkun. His gifts were royal, gold, the "dust of his land," golden vessels and necklaces, precious stones, the product of the seas, probably the pearls for which in every age the Persian Gulf has been famous, beams of ebony, and spices.

The siege of Sapea was prolonged to the fourth year, when the reign of Nabu-mukin-zer ended with his life. There was no legal ruler in Babylonia, and Assyria could hardly accept as of divine right half-barbarian Aramæan chiefs, while revolutions with monotonous regularity had shifted actual rule from tribe to tribe. Tiglath Pileser was a foreigner and usurper, but he represented a higher degree of culture, he reverenced the older civilisation, he stood for law and order. Assyrian peace might mean stringent military rule and high taxes, but anything was preferable to the anarchy which Babylonia had endured for generations. Native Babylonians had long since forgotten warfare, and thought only of trade and the cult; they might prefer Assyrian peace at a price, but the choice was rarely theirs. If Assyrian kings were strong and wise, Babylon enjoyed security; if not, Babylonia was plundered by Aramæan tribes.

If Babylonia was not to become an international menace, it must be policed from Assyria, lest the intolerable confusion should infect Assyria from across the border. We might, therefore, have expected that the Assyrians, with their hard common sense in political affairs, would have reduced Baby-

[1] Ctesias, in Diod. II, 24.

lonia to a province.   There was little unity even this late in
the alluvium, and from early times parts of Babylonia had been
Assyrian.   The conqueror might adorn himself with his choice
of titles which represented his lordship over some city-state of
hoary antiquity whose local pride still clung to some shreds of
its former greatness.   It was somewhat different with the title
"King of Babylon."

Babylon had been the last capital of a united Babylonia, and
the title carried some claim to rule over the whole country,
which in these degenerate times rarely corresponded with the
actual situation.   During Babylon's hegemony, the literature
had been systematically revised in honour of Marduk, and this
was the literature in the hands of the Assyrians.   Babylon in
their eyes became the heir of all the glories of earlier civilisation.

Only one obstacle stood in the way of assumption of the
title.   According to the theory of the Marduk priests, no one
could be rightfully king until he had "seized the hands of Bel,"
and thus had become his "man" in truly feudal relation.
This ceremony must be gone through with, not only on the
first New Year's Day, but on each and every.   The king might
be needed at the head of his troops; the residents only considered that his absence would rob them of the greatest show
of the year.

Despite these evident disadvantages, Tiglath Pileser determined to secure for himself the prestige which was connected
with the title.   On the 1st of Nisan, 729, he seized the hands
of the Lord Marduk and became king of Babylon in name as
in fact.   To save the tender susceptibilities of the citizens,
he even permitted them to use a separate name, Pulu, and
this is the reason why he is once called Pul in the Book of
Kings.[1]

[1] II Kings 15 : 19.

CHAPTER XV

ARARAT IN SYRIA AND THE NORTHERN JUDAH

HALDIA was now at the height of its power. All Armenia was under the sway of Sardurish well up towards the Caucasus, the eastern mountains were his to the Mannai and Lake Urumia, his rock inscription near the Euphrates crossing to Melidia stated the conquest of that city. Ashur-nirari had been defeated, and the territories on the southern slopes of the Armenian mountains, so toilsomely brought under by Tiglath Pileser I and by Ashur-nasir-apal II, were entirely lost to Assyria, and the same was true of the northeastern mountains where the operations of Shalmaneser III and Adad-nirari III had been conducted. Haldian control of these regions was dangerous but not particularly costly; since Sardurish had seduced Mati-ilu of Arpad from his oath to Ashur-nirari, the wealth of Syria was no longer at the disposal of Assyria.

Sardurish had revised his titulary to fit his wider territory. He already had precedent for the "King of the World" which Assyrians had wrested from Babylonia; "King of Shuraush" challenged Assyrian overlordship of Syria, and there was another challenge in the title "King of Kings."

With the situation in the south temporarily adjusted by his first two campaigns, Tiglath Pileser prepared to attack the Haldian problem. Not daring to follow Sardurish behind his mountain rampart, he determined to oust him from north Syria, where the renegade Mati-ilu was supported by Sulumal of Melidia, Tarhulara of Gurgum, and Kushtashpi of Qummuh. The coalition chose a position in the rough hills on the northwest corner of Mesopotamia, in the district of Qummuh. The Sinzi canal was dyed with their blood, and Sardurish eluded pursuit by a solitary flight on a mare, sure symbol to the Eastern mind of a disgraceful rout. The royal bed, tent, chariot, and camp furniture were dedicated to Ishtar, and the prisoners numbered nearly ninety-three thousand. Chase was continued to the boundary of Haldia proper, the bridge across the Euphrates, and the territory thus recovered was organised in the manner which by now had become usual.

Mati-ilu resisted for three years in Arvad as might be expected from a man who had foresworn his oaths. The punishment inflicted was long remembered. A half-century later, the rab shaqe of Sennacherib could ask the Jewish subjects of Hezekiah "Where are the gods of Arpad?" "Where is the king of Arpad?" in the confidence that the terrible fate of Mati-ilu had not been forgotten,[1] and when Isaiah wished to make the Assyrian king emphasise the total destruction of Hamath, he puts in his mouth the question "Is not Hamath as Arpad?"[2]

Kushtashpi and Tarhulara transferred their allegiance, and with them came Uriaik of Que, Pisiris of Carchemish, Rezon of Damascus, and Hiram II of Tyre. Of the last we have bronze bowls, dedicated by his governors in Qartihadast to Baal Lebanon as first-fruits of the bronze. These governors are called *sakans*, a term borrowed from the Assyrian *shaknu*, they rule the Cyriote Carthage, they dedicate first-fruits of the artificial metal based on the native metal which received its name of copper from Cyprus. They dedicate them to the lord of the mountains whose towering crests are in sight from every village in their homeland, and they call their earthly lord "King of the Sidonians," not of Tyre.[3]

From these bronze bowls we may gain some conception of the rich gifts which the durbar at Arpad brought to the Assyrians, the metals, priceless laden spices, elephant hides, ivory, coloured stuffs. All north Syria was represented save Tutamu, the reduced ruler of what had once been Hattina, who kept up a futile resistance in the Unqi swamp, while the royal throne was set up in his palace at Kunulua and his possessions choked the treasury of the invader.

---

[1] II Kings 18 : 34; 19 : 13; Isaiah 36 : 19; 37 : 13.
[2] Isaiah 10 : 9; cf. Jer. 49 : 23.

[3] *CIS.*, I, 5.

Hebrew tradition told of early Aramæan connections, as when Jacob found among that people a wife; Hebrew Judah in the south was closely paralleled in language, in thought, in the name of a ruler, most startling of all, in his commemoration of Yahweh in his name, by a country in north Syria called by the scribe Iaudi.   Humour is not a characteristic we ordinarily attribute to these ancient worthies, but the Kalamu who so jauntily appears on his stele, a flower in his hand instead of the expected weapon, gives us a history of his predecessors which is, to say the least, unconventional: "Gabbar ruled Judah, but not a thing did he; so did Bamah, and not a thing did he; and so did Father Hayya, and not a thing did he; and so did Brother Saul, and not a thing did he.   But I, Kalamu, son of integrity, that which I accomplished not even one of these before me had done.   My father's house was in the midst of mighty kings and every weapon humbled them.   And I was in the hand of the king as one eating my beard or as one eating my hand.   And the king of the Danunim"—unconsciously we call to mind the contemporary Greek Danians— "was mighty against me, and I hired against him the king of Assyria.   A virgin was sold for a sheep and a hero for a garment.   I, Kalamu, son of Hayya, sat on the throne of my father.   In the presence of the former kings, the Mushkabim"—the lower classes—"had gone about like dogs, but I, to one I was a father, to one as a mother, and to one as a brother. He who before my time had not seen a sheep, I made the master of a flock; he who before my time had not seen an ox, I made the master of cattle and the master of silver and the master of gold.   And he who had not seen a coat from his youth, in my days was clothed in fine linen.   And I took the Mushkabim by the hand and gave them an affection for me like the affection of the orphan for his mother.   And whoever of my sons shall sit on the throne after me and injures this inscription, may the Mushkabim"—the older subject population—"not honour the Baririm"—the Aramæan nobility— "and may the Baririm not honour the Mushkabim.   And whoever shall destroy this inscription, may there destroy him

Fig. 84. TESHUB, THE HITTITE WEATHER GOD.
Relief found at Babylon.

Fig. 83. ROCK–CUT INSCRIPTION OF SARDURISHI,
THE HALDIAN KING, ON A CLIFF BY
THE EUPHRATES.

Fig. 86. PALACE FAÇADE. (SAMAL.)

Fig. 88. BEEHIVE VILLAGE IN NORTH SYRIA.

Fig. 85. PAVED STREET, COLUMN BASES, AND FAÇADE
OF PALACE. (SAMAL.)

Fig. 87. CARVED FIGURE. (SAMAL.)

Baal Semed"—the lord of the ox-team, represented on the stele by the horned head-dress—"the god of Gabbar, and Baal Haman"—the new moon with the old in its arms—"of Bamah, and Rekub-el, the lord of our house," who as the chariot god was symbolised by the bridle.[1]

Not long after this monarch, with his keen sense of social justice and his contemptuous hiring of the decadent kings of Assyria, there ruled in the northern Judah a certain Panammu, son of Qarel, whose inscription is on a huge round figure of the god Hadad. It is Hadad who gave into his hands the sceptre when he sat on the throne of his fathers; Reshef, the war-god, stood by his side, he was aided by El and Rekub and Shamash. His land is a land of barley, wheat, and garlic, where men till the soil and cultivate vineyards. In his days did Judah both eat and drink. The gods received offerings from his hands and in return they have abundantly granted whatsoever he has asked from them. Hadad ordered him to build and he did so, and he has also prepared a statue for Hadad and a burial-place for himself.

An undercurrent of uneasiness runs through all this rejoicing. The gods have at last given him seed, and a son may be expected to hold his sceptre and sit upon the throne in his stead. Then he may hope that his son will sacrifice to Hadad and will remember his father, will say: "May the soul of Panammu eat with Hadad and may the soul of Panammu drink with that of Hadad." There lurks the fear that this hope will not be realised. In such an event, Hadad is begged to refuse favourable opinion as to the sacrifices of the negligent one, deny his requests, suffer him not to eat, and withhold sleep from him by night. There is danger that some member of the royal family, some personal friend of the king, may slay his son and reign in Judah, and if this happens, he is urged not to kill in anger, put to death by his bow, slaughter kinsman or kinswoman, steal this memorial. But if he does sin in such manner, even though the evil-doer say "I have put these orders into

[1] F. von Luschan, *Ausgrabungen in Sendschirli*, IV, 237 ff.; Torrey, *JAOS.*, XXXV, 364 ff.

the mouth of a stranger," the reader is not to allow his eye to be wearied, he is to slay in wrath or instruct a stranger to kill him.[1]

His fears seem to have been justified. There is reason to assume that Bar Sur was his son, and of Bar Sur we are told that there was a conspiracy which slew him together with seventy of his kinsmen. With the remainder the usurper filled the prisons and made desolate cities to be more numerous than those inhabited. The native record omits the name of the murderer; from the Assyrian we discover that it was Azriau. This is so certainly an Azariah that it is small wonder he was identified by earlier scholars with the almost contemporary king of the better-known Judah to the south. The failure of the identification only leaves the wonder the greater; how are we to explain the worship, postulated by his name, of the same Yahweh who was the one national deity of the biblical Judah?

The anger of Hadad was incurred because the usurper had raised the sword against his house and had murdered Bar Sur, one of his sons. Was the Yahweh worshipper Azariah an opponent of the cult of Hadad? For Hadad did make the sword to be in Judah and showed his anger by a great dearth of wheat and barley, so that a peres of wheat and a shatrab of barley and an esnab of oil all stood at a shekel. The elder Panammu had closed his admonitions to his descendants with these significant words: "Instruct a stranger to kill him." His younger namesake took the hint and called in the one stranger who might avail, Tiglath Pileser.

Little aid came from the allied princelets, and Judah was soon reduced. Panammu II was made king over his father's house, the prisons were put out of commission, the captives were set free. Then up rose Panammu and released the women of the harem, and his father's house he made better than before. Wheat and barley, millet and spelt were plentiful in his days, his people might eat and drink because of the lowness

---

[1] Sachau, *Ausgrabungen in Sendschirli*, IV, 1 ff.; Cooke, *North-Semitic Inscriptions*, 159 ff.

of their cost. Tiglath Pileser appointed lords of villages and lords over chariots, but Panammu was esteemed among the mighty kings. Whether he possessed silver or whether he possessed gold, he was wise enough to lay hold of the skirt of his lord, the king of Assyria, and his lord, the king of Assyria, was gracious to him more than to mightier kings. He ran at the chariot wheel of his lord, Tiglath Pileser, king of Assyria, in the campaigns he waged from the east to the west, even the four world quarters. And the daughters of the east did Tiglath Pileser bring to the west and the daughters of the west to the east. The borders of Judah were extended so that cities from the border of Gurgum were added. Thereafter, the title "King of Samal" took the place of Judah.

Panammu gave final proof of the loyalty he had asserted for Tiglath Pileser by death in the Assyrian camp when it was pitched before Damascus (732). The sad event was bewailed by the whole camp, and Tiglath Pileser made a funeral feast for him and brought him home for burial. Because of his father's righteousness and for his own righteousness, Panammu's son Bar Rekub was placed by Rekub-El and Tiglath Pileser on the ancestral throne. He proudly informs us that his father's house excelled all in its labour for its lord; he ran at the wheel of his lord, the king of Assyria, even in the midst of most mighty kings, lords of silver and lords of gold. He took the house of his father and made it far better than the house of any one of the most mighty kings, so that the kings his brethren envied all the prosperity of his house.

One stele he set up is dedicated to the Baal of Harran, whose identity with the moon-god Sin is proved by the symbol of the old moon in the new moon's arms. Bar Rekub sits on a throne which closely imitates the Assyrian in its pine-cone base, its ornament of tied double volutes, its ox-headed terminals. On his head is a round cap with large button, his short hair and beard are in elaborate ringlets, a ringlet falls to his neck in front of his large ear, to which his extraordinary mustache extends. A long fringed robe is looped over his left arm, in his left hand he holds a lotus, his right is raised to address

his eunuch scribe. The papyrus roll under the scribe's arm
and an Egyptian pen-box in his hand illustrate the progress of
the new method of writing to the East.

After the deposition of Azariah, Tiglath Pileser took up the
case of his allies. Kullania, the Calneh of Isaiah and Amos,[1]
Byblus and the nineteen regions which belonged to the territory of Hamath, including the coast cities of Usanata, Shiana,
and Simirra, with their villages up to the mountains in the
rear, the old enemy city of Hazrek, all were restored to the
Assyrian fold. The new province was given the name Simirra
and was placed under the crown prince Shalmaneser. More
than thirty thousand of its inhabitants were removed to the
province of Que and some twelve hundred to Ulluba, recently
conquered by his generals on the Armenian frontier.

To take their place, large numbers were imported from the
southern and eastern portions of the empire. Twelve thousand
Ahlame from the Zab region were ordered to Syria in 739,
others were sent by the governors of Lulume and of Nairi,
fifty-four hundred were deported from Der by the chief commander of the fortress; all these were settled in north Syria.
Little groups, a few hundred each, were collected from the
various tribes on the eastern frontier and colonised farther
down the coast in the Phœnician cities.

With the aid of such data, we begin to realise the movements
involved in the system of deportation. We can form some
conception of the immense amount of discomfort if not of
actual suffering which resulted, the settlement of mountaineers
in the hot plains and vice versa, the deaths from the unwhole-
some surroundings or from the brutality of the military escort,
the complete breakdown of the economic system when highly
skilled bankers and artisans were placed in countries which
afforded a bare existence and rude nomads took their place in
the old culture lands. In a word, we have the same phenomenon as that reproduced twenty-six centuries later with an
added horror in these same unhappy lands. Of such and

[1] Amos 6 : 2; Isaiah 10 : 9.

through such action was made the mingled people that was to be the later Syrians.

His task achieved, Tiglath Pileser sums up those who brought him tribute. Beside the rulers already named, we have Menahem of Samaria, Sibitti Baal of Byblus, Eniel of Hamath, Dadilu of Kasku, Uassurme of Tabal, Ushhitti of Tuna, Urballa of Tuhana, Tuhamme of Ishtunda, Urimme of Hurikna, and Zabibe, queen of the Arabs. We can forgive the long list when we find among the names from Asia Minor the first references to Ciscessus, Tyana, Aspendus, and Characene, all so well known to the reader of the later classics. Nor can we regret the first appearance in history of the older form of the matriarchal authority current in Arabia, the classic example of which is the legend of the visit of the Queen of Sheba to Solomon. Included among the tribute was the "bird whose wings are coloured blue"; was it the peacock whom Indian records report as being sent to Babylonia?

Now that the Haldian forces had been driven out of Syria, it was decided to carry the war into Armenia. An Assyrian governor was operating in Ulluba, under the barrier range, as early as 739, and three years later the official designation was "against the foot of Mount Nal." A long recital of the conquered "forts of Urartu" follows, but a considerable number had been taken by Tiglath Pileser I and Ashur-nasir-apal II. Ulluba was made a province, with a new foundation named Ashur-iqisha as capital. Kirhu was handed over to the chief cellarer, the lands along the Ulurush or west Tigris to the governor of Nairi, and the region which stretched to Qummuh and the Euphrates to the turtanu.

The frontier had been thrust back sufficiently to permit a rapid dash into the heart of Haldia. Tiglath Pileser came home from Syria for this year 735. Without molestation, he penetrated to the fertile plain which surrounded the Haldian capital of Tushpash. He set up a stele opposite the city gate and marched majestically without a rival for the distance of seventy double hours, but his main object was unattained. The great citadel rock at Van remained impregnable and

Sardurish suffered but a temporary loss. Affairs had reached a stalemate; the Haldians had failed in the lowlands, the Assyrians in the mountains, and this was to remain the situation for the future.

CHAPTER XVI

THE LAST DAYS OF ISRAEL

SATISFIED with having inflicted humiliation on Haldia, Tiglath Pileser was back in Syria in 734. The line of Jehu in Israel had ended, as prophecy had declared,[1] with the fourth generation, when Zechariah was murdered at Ibleam by Shallum after a reign of six months. Shallum held his precarious seat but eight days and then gave way to Menahem, whose chief claim was that he came from the old capital of Tirzah (744–735). At the first entrance of the Assyrians into Syria, Menahem hastened to make his peace, levying fifty shekels each on his sixty thousand men of wealth that he might offer Tiglath Pileser a thousand talents of silver. So the hand of the king of Assyria was with him, and he turned back and stayed not there in the land.[2]

Not all Hebrews approved this action. The tragic experience of Hosea with his erring wife had fixed men's attention upon him. Through his trial, he had come to recognise that when Israel worshipped the local Baals, with their licentious cult, she was untrue to her husband Yahweh. Soon he began to realise the social implications of the new prosperity and thundered against the sins of swearing and breaking faith, of killing and stealing and commiting adultery, though for this the priests were primarily to blame, since they fed on the people's sin.

Equally did Hosea condemn the revolutions which were sapping the strength of the land at the very moment when all was needed to resist the aggressor. The political history of the period is not preserved in sufficient fulness to permit our understanding of all the prophet's allusions, but the general tenor cannot be mistaken.

[1] Amos 7 : 9; cf. Hos. 1 : 4.　　　　　[2] II Kings 15 : 8 ff.

The priests, the house of Israel, and the house of the king must hearken to the judgment, for they have set up a snare at Mizpah and spread a net on Mount Tabor and they have made deep the pit of Shittim.   Ephraim and Samaria practise fraud, the thief enters the house, the robber bands roam without.   They anoint kings in their wickedness and princes through their lies; on the royal birthday they make their king sick and the princes with the heat of wine, while the monarch himself has stretched out his hand with loose fellows.   Their hearts burn like an oven while they lie in wait; their anger is damped during the night, but in the morning it blazes again like a flame of fire.   They are all red hot like an oven, they devour their chieftains; all their kings are fallen, yet there is none of them that calleth upon Yahweh.   They have set up kings, but they were not approved by Yahweh; they have made princes, but he has not recognised them.   All their princes are in revolt, therefore Yahweh does not love them.   They say "We have no ruler, for we fear not Yahweh; and as for the king, what is he able to do for us?"

By such internal feuds, Ephraim has been forced to mix with the peoples; he is as a cake not turned.   Strangers devour his strength and he knows it not; gray hairs begin to appear and he does not realise it.   Yet a little while and the blood spilled at Jezreel will be avenged upon the house of Jehu; and with this the kingship will cease in Israel.

The pro-Assyrian policies of the rulers furnished special cause for the prophet's anger.   When Ephraim saw his sickness and Israel his sore, instead of going in repentance to Yahweh, Ephraim went to Assyria and Israel to the Great King, though he could neither heal nor cure the wound.   They have gone to Assyria, as a wild ass roving alone, and Ephraim has sent love gifts.   He is feeding on wind and is following after the east wind, he is continually multiplying lies and desolation.   He is like a silly dove, devoid of understanding; they call unto Egypt and then go to Assyria; they make a covenant with Assyria and then oil is brought into Egypt to buy aid.

Therefore blow the horn in Gibeah and the trumpet in Ramah, the high places whence the advance may be first seen; sound an alarm at the House of Idols, raise the ancient war-cry: "After thee, O Benjamin!" Yahweh himself will be to Ephraim as a lion and as a young lion to the house of Israel; he will tear and stride away, he will carry off his prey and none may deliver. Whether their ambassadors go to Assyria or to Egypt, Yahweh will spread his net upon them and shall bring them down as birds of the heavens. No longer shall they dwell in Yahweh's land, but Ephraim shall return to Egypt and eat unclean food in Assyria. Egypt shall gather them up, Memphis shall bury them; their precious objects in silver shall nettles possess, thorns shall spring up in their tents. The inhabitants of Samaria shall tremble for the calf which is housed in the abode of idols, the representation of Yahweh in bull form which Jeroboam set up in Bethel, "the house of God"; the people shall mourn it, and the shaveling priests who serve there shall writhe over its fate. It shall be carried as a gift to the Great King; Ephraim shall be disgraced and Israel shall be ashamed for its idol.

Samaria is cut off with her king, like a bit of flotsam on the wave. The high places of the City of Idols shall be destroyed, the thorn and the thistle shall grow upon their altars; they shall say to the mountains "Cover us" and to the hills "Fall upon us." Therefore shall a tumult arise among the peoples, and all the fortresses shall be destroyed as Shalmaneser destroyed Beth Arbel in the day of battle, when mother was dashed in pieces with her children. So shall it be done unto Israel in Bethel, because of their great wickedness; at dawn shall the king of Israel be utterly cut off.[1]

Menahem slept with his fathers after ten years' rule, and his incapable son Pekahiah reigned in his stead. Scarcely two years (735–734) elapsed before Pekah, one of his generals, put him to death in the citadel of Samaria, with the assistance of fifty Gileadites, his fellow clansmen. Hosea made bitter comment: "Gilead is a city of men who work iniquity, it is stained

---

[1] The badly damaged text has been corrected and the order made more logical according to Western notions; cf. especially Harper, *Amos and Hosea*.

with blood; as bands of robbers lie in wait for a man, so the priests hide on the road, they murder those who go up to Samaria.''

Pekah's native country was east of the Jordan and in close touch with Damascus; we can understand how he came to introduce a pro-Damascene policy, and combined with Rezon against Judah, where the succession of incapable rulers in the northern kingdom had permitted it to cast off the Israelite yoke and to expand its territory. Swayed by a patriotic impulse, Hosea prophesied the wrath of Yahweh against the princes of Judah who had removed the boundary marks and thus had freed themselves from Israelite domination.[1]

The conservative country nobles assassinated Amaziah (799–782) at Lachish, whither he had fled for refuge, and placed on the throne the sixteen-year-old Azariah, better known as Uzziah (782–751). His long reign restored the glory to Judah. Shortly after his accession, he fell upon Edom and secured Elath, the port on the northern extension of the Red Sea which gave access to the lucrative trade along the Arabian coast.[2] The Ammonites paid him tribute, and he warred against the Arabians that dwelt in Gur Baal and against the mysterious Meunim, whom some have identified with the Minæans of southwest Arabia. The now decadent Philistines lost Gath, which of all their five cities most threatened Judah, since it was placed on the hills which commanded one of its exits. Jabneh and Ashdod furnished ports on the Mediterranean. Azariah loved husbandry as well as commerce and possessed husbandmen and vine-dressers in the mountains and the cultivated fields, while cattle pastured in the low hills bordering the Philistine plain and on the table-land east of the Jordan. In the waste places of Judah he erected towers to protect the herds and flocks which were watered at the wells he dug. Jerusalem received from this wealth new towers at the corner gate, the valley gate, and the angle of the wall.[3]

Azariah became a leper in the middle of his reign and his duties were taken over by Jotham. During the regency, or in

[1] Hos. 5 : 10.   [2] II Kings 14 : 19 ff.   [3] II Chron. 26.

the short time he ruled alone, Jotham warred with the Ammonites and forced them to pay a yearly tribute of a hundred talents of silver and ten thousand cors of wheat and of barley. The building programme of his father was continued with the upper gate of the temple and the wall of Ophel, the original site of the city.[1] A youth of twenty, Jehoahaz by name but in the Biblical writings abbreviated to Ahaz (736–721), received the bequest of the state. Judah's prosperity rapidly disappeared under his feeble rule. Rezon succeeded in reasserting his control over the port of Elath, the Edomites aided in the attack, the Philistines wrested away the recently conquered territory, invaded the hill country and the Negeb, and secured such truly Hebrew cities as Beth Shemesh, Aijalon, Timnah, and Socoh.[2]

There now came upon the scene the greatest of Hebrew prophets, Isaiah the son of Amoz. Already in the last year of Azariah, he had felt the prophetic call, had been ordered to preach inevitable destruction until the land should be utterly waste. In token thereof, his son received the name of Shear-jashub, "Only a remnant shall return." He began his career with an attempt to right social injustice at home, where a child was king and the women of the harem bore rule. The people had forsaken Yahweh, the national deity, the Holy One of Israel, and it was in the train of this national apostasy that there had followed all the horrors of a corrupt culture. The decline of Israel had been the opportunity of Judah, and now there was to be found in the latter country all the evils of a more complicated civilisation which had been felt in Israel a century before. The rich joined house to house and lay field to field, and ground the faces of the poor. Bribery was common, justice could not be secured. All this was apostasy from Yahweh, and there was to come a day when the Lord, Yahweh of Hosts, was to take away from Jerusalem and from Judah stay and staff.

Assyria once more appeared on the horizon, and Isaiah found himself forced to consider the broader questions of inter-

[1] II Kings 15 : 32 ff.; II Chron. 27.   [2] II Kings 16 : 1 ff.; II Chron. 28.

national relation. The traditional hostility between Damascus and Israel led the prophet at first to expect that they would destroy each other. Yahweh hath sent a "word" against Jacob, it hath descended upon Israel; all the people shall understand, both Ephraim and the inhabitant of Samaria. They say in the pride and stoutness of their hearts: "The bricks have fallen but we will rebuild with hewn stones; the scyamores have been cut down but we will replace them with cedars." Instead, Yahweh will raise up his adversary Rezon and will stir up his enemies; the Aramæans before and the Philistines behind shall devour Israel with open mouth.[1]

Isaiah was disappointed, for the two made common cause against Judah. Ahaz was defeated in a battle before Jerusalem, and tradition long remembered how Zichri, a mighty man of Ephraim, slew the brother of Ahaz, Maaseiah, the chamberlain Azrikam, and Elkanah, the second in command under the king[2] (735). No wonder the hearts of Ahaz and of his people trembled as the trees of the forest tremble with the wind.

The crisis brought Isaiah definitely into his position of adviser, however unwelcome, in diplomatic affairs. Taking with him his son Shearjashub, whose ill-omened name had been amply justified by the recent catastrophe, he set forth to meet Ahaz. He found the youthful ruler at the end of the conduit of the upper pool, on the highway that passed by the fuller's field, and bade him not to fear these two tails of burnt-out firebrands who had purposed to set up in his place the son of Tabeel. Instructed to ask a sign, Ahaz refused, for he would not tempt Yahweh. A sign he was given none the less, the sign of Emmanuel; the young woman now with child, the wife of Ahaz, should bear a son to be named "God with us." Before he should have knowledge sufficient to refuse evil food and choose the good, the land whose two kings were the terror of Ahaz should be forsaken. But there was an addition. From

---

[1] Isaiah 9 : 8 ff.; for the various problems of Isaiah, cf. especially the commentary by G. B. Gray, *Isaiah*, in "International Critical Commentary."
[2] II Chron. 28 : 7.

the day that Ephraim should return from vexing Ahaz, Yahweh would bring upon Judah days worse than those which had gone before, when the king of Assyria should arrive in person.[1]

Isaiah spoke the literal truth when he declared that he and the children Yahweh had given him were for signs and wonders. Before the birth of his next son, he took a great tablet and inscribed it "For Maher-shalal-hash-baz," with Uriah, the chief priest, as witness. With this ominous name, "Hasten spoil, hurry booty," the new-born child was christened, and with it went the oracle, "Before this child shall have knowledge to cry 'My father' or 'My mother,' the riches of Damascus and the spoil of Syria shall be paraded before the Assyrian monarch." The people have refused the softly flowing waters of Shiloah and fear Rezon and Remaliah's son; Yahweh is bringing upon them the water of the River, strong and many, the king of Assyria in all his glory. It shall flood all its channels and overflow all its banks; it shall sweep onward into Judah, it shall reach to the neck.[2]

Despite these prophecies or perhaps because their value was discounted in his eyes by the threats of punishment for Judah as well as for Ephraim, Ahaz still refused to believe Isaiah, and offered up his eldest son in the fire to Yahweh. On the failure of this supreme sacrifice, he stripped the gold and silver from palace and temple and sent them to Tiglath Pileser, saying: "I am thy servant and thy son, come and save me." [3]

The appeal of Ahaz fitted exactly the plans of Tiglath Pileser. Rezon was driven into his city gate like a mouse, his chief advisers impaled, his gardens and orchards hacked down. The siege of the city was long, and Panammu of Samal lost his life in the attack; Rezon was killed, and the line of kings extinguished. The inhabitants were deported to Kir, and central Syria became a definite dependency of Assyria.

Isaiah hailed the fall of Damascus as fulfilment of prophecy. Damascus is taken away from being a city and has been made a ruin heap. The cities of Aroer are forsaken, they have become an abode for flocks, where they may lie down and none

[1] Isaiah 7.   [2] Isaiah 8.   [3] II Kings 16 : 5 ff.

may make them afraid.   The fortress shall cease from Ephraim
and the kingdom from Damascus, the remnant of Syria is as the
glory of Israel.   It is as when the harvester gathers the standing grain and his hands reap the ears; only gleanings are left
as at the beating of an olive-tree, two or three olives in the top
of the uppermost bough, four or five in the outermost branches
of the fruit-tree.[1]

Ahaz paid no attention to the words of the prophet, but
hastened to Damascus to meet his lord, the Assyrian king.
In Damascus he saw a certain altar, connected with the worship of Ashur and the king.   The pattern was promptly sent
to the chief priest of the royal temple at Jerusalem, that same
Uriah whom Isaiah had taken to witness that Damascus
should be destroyed, and by the return of Ahaz the altar was
ready for use.   On this altar, now called the "great altar" par
excellence, Ahaz ordered that there should be burned the
morning burnt offering and the evening meal offering which had
formerly been the perquisite of Yahweh alone, the royal burnt
and meal offerings, the burnt, meal, and drink offerings of all
the people, and here should be sprinkled all the blood of the
burnt offerings and all the blood of the sacrifices.   The brazen
altar which had formerly stood before the temple of Yahweh
was moved to the north of the new altar, and henceforth was
to have no offerings, it was to be used only for the purpose
of divination.

No longer was Yahweh to rule as king in Judah, he must be
content to be counted a minor deity, whose chief function was
the delivery of oracular responses.   The brazen oxen which
supported the great sea and represented the power and majesty
of Yahweh were no longer appropriate, so the laver was placed
on a stone pedestal.   A throne for the new divine king was set
up in the house where once Yahweh had reigned in power, and
the royal entry was turned about by Ahaz from before the
face of the statue of the Assyrian king.   Isaiah denounced
with vigour the men of Judah, but Ahaz was logical according
to his lights.   He had appealed to Yahweh, even to the sacri-

[1] Isaiah 17.

fice of his first-born, and Yahweh had failed him; Ashur and the Assyrian king had brought him salvation; therefore, they were mightier gods than Yahweh and were worthy of supplanting him in the house which had been formerly his alone.[1]

Ashur's anger was next poured out against the Arabs who had aided Damascus. Samsi had succeeded Zabibe as queen,

FIG. 89. PURSUIT OF AN ARAB.

and, like her predecessor, had transgressed against the oath or the god Shamash, whose name she bore. Severe were her sufferings if we trust the Assyrian statistics of loss, a hundred thousand men, thirty thousand camels, twenty thousand cattle, but such a census has never been known in Desert Arabia, at least outside the pages of the *Arabian Nights*. On the reliefs, two spearmen mounted on horses trample dead Arabs as they pursue a nomad clad only in a high-girdled tunic who guides a fleet dromedary by a rope about the nose. The artist intended to indicate that the nomad realised he was about to be caught and was stretching out his hand in supplication; to the irreverent modern, he seems to be turning back in mockery and waving his pursuers such a derisive farewell as only an Arab can make. Like a female wild ass, we are told, Samsi fled to the city of Bazu, a place of thirst, and a relief professes to

[1] II Kings 16 : 10 ff.

show her barefoot and tearing her hair, the while she carefully balances one of the eleven sacrificial jars she is said to have presented after her spirit had been broken by hunger.

Gifts from other tribes well known to later history ended the campaign. The Sabæans were just wresting the hegemony of south Arabia from the Minæans and desired Assyrian recognition. The Haiappai find their eponymous ancestor in the Ephah, son of Midian, whose former location was east of the Gulf of Aqaba and along the eastern shore of the Red Sea; the name also occurs among the Calebites, in the south of Judah.[1] Tema is another son of Midian[2] and from its oasis paradise has come a stele which reveals the strong Assyrian influence exerted through these invasions and through the more peaceful march of the caravans. On one side stands the god Salm of Hajam, with conical hat, fringed and draped robe of the Assyrian fashion, his staff in his left hand, and above him the Assyrian winged disk. Below is the dedicator, Salm-shezib, the priest, with his hand raised in prayer before the altar. The inscription on the front gives the reason for its erection, the introduction of a new deity, for in the twenty-second year Salm, god of Mahram, and Shingala and Ashira, gods of Tema, endowed Salm of Hajam with sixteen palms from the field and five from the royal estates, yearly. Neither gods nor men shall drive out Salm-shezib, son of Petosiri, from this home, neither his seed nor his name, priests in this house forever.[3] The father of Salm-shezib bears an Egyptian name, but his own is Assyrian, the figures betray traces of Assyrian connections, the winged disk has the Assyrian form, and perhaps Ashira is for Ashur; the words for "grant," for "royal estate," for "stele" itself, all are borrowed from the technical terminology of Assyria. Such traces of Assyrian influence furnish what basis there is for the claim that Tiglath Pileser formed a province, constructed a palace, and appointed the Idibailai tribe over the others.

[1] Gen. 25 : 4; Isaiah 60 : 6; I Chron. 2 : 46 ff.
[2] Gen. 25 : 15; Isaiah 21 : 14; Jer. 25 : 23; Job 6 : 19.
[3] *CIS.*, II, 113; Cooke, *North-Semitic Inscriptions*, 195 ff.

Tiglath Pileser himself turned against Pekah, whose native country, Gilead, was easily reached from Damascus, and then to northeast Galilee, the home of the Naphtali tribe—Ijon, the beautiful valley between Hermon and the northern extension of the Galilean hills; Abel of the house of Maacah, its most important town on the western slopes, the "city and mother in Israel" which Sheba raised in the vain attempt to unite Israel against David and Judah; Kadesh, the sacred city of refuge, the home of Barak, where he and Deborah collected the tribesmen against Sisera; Hazor, whence proceeded King Jabin, whose general Sisera was; and finally Janoah.[1] From Bara came two hundred and twenty-six captives, six hundred and twenty-five from another whose name has been lost, four hundred and thirty from Hanaton, whose name had kept in memory the heretic monotheist, Ikhnaton of Egypt, long after he had been forgotten at home,[2] six hundred and fifty from Cana, where the Gospels place the marriage feast, the same from another lost city, thirteen thousand five hundred and twenty from Jotapata, six hundred and fifty from Iron. Pekah (734–732) was deposed and Hoshea (732–723) was given his place.

Passing by the cities of Aruma and Marum, the latter connected with those waters of Merom by which another Jabin was said to have been defeated by Joshua,[3] Tiglath Pileser marched to free Ahaz from the danger of his other serious enemy, the Philistines. Mitinti of Ascalon had disavowed the agreement and sinned against the oath; on the news of Rezon's defeat he disappeared, and his son Rukibti came out to the Assyrian camp for investiture. Hanun left Gaza as the Assyrians approached, but the threat of his country being made a province forced him to desert the Egyptian cause. By this success, the last important town on the Syrian side of the desert was brought under Assyrian influence and Egypt lay exposed to invasion.

While Tiglath Pileser was making his position firm in Baby-

---

[1] II Sam. 20; Judges 4; Joshua 11; II Kings 15 ff.
[2] Joshua 19 : 14; Breasted, *History of Egypt*, 355 ff.   [3] Joshua 11.

lon, his generals were busy on the western frontier, where Uassurme of Tabal was deposed and his place taken by the son of a nobody named Hulli; the commander-in-chief was then sent on to Tyre, where Metten won absolution for a temporary lukewarmness by the enormous sum of a hundred and fifty talents of gold (728). The next year, the last embers of revolt were stamped out in Damascus.

Assyria was never more a military monarchy than under the last Tiglath Pileser. The reign was dominated by military considerations, and culture played a decidedly secondary part. He did build a palace at Kalhu, and we possess his enthusiastic description. Its site was the Tigris bank and its area was greater than those of the kings his fathers. Before it stood a colonnade like a palace of the Hittite land. Not the model alone was Western, for the construction was of sweet-smelling cedar and of other woods from the Lebanon, the Anti-Lebanon, and the Amanus. Doors of cedar and cypress, double-leaved, whose entrance is blessed, whose scent refreshes the heart, with plating of bronze and silver were covered and fixed in the gates. Lions and bull colossi, whose figures were wrought with exceeding cunning, clothed with power, were set up in the entrance for a wonder. Thresholds of white alabaster made glorious the exit. A relief of stone, the guard of the great gods, the product of the world abyss, encompassed the side walls. "The palace of joy, granting abundance, blessing the king, bringing their builder a good old age," they were called. The gates were named "Gates of Righteousness, ordering aright the judgment of the princes of the four world regions, making old the tribute of the mountain and the sea, bringing the fulness of the land before the presence of the king their lord."

Of all this glory, but a few fragments are preserved. The reliefs already described are poorly executed and contrast most unfavourably with those brought from the palace of Ashur-nasir-apal. The beginnings and ends of the slabs which bore the royal annals have been chiselled off by instruction of a successor who planned to use them for building material. Thanks to the vandalism of Esarhaddon, there are whole years for which we lack the official records, for others we have barely a word preserved here and there. The actual loss may be easily exaggerated, for the missing portions would have added more names of cities plundered and tribes subdued, but the remainder would have consisted of the same formulas with which we have become so wearisomely familiar. There has been certainly no loss to literature.

Historical imagination is nevertheless sadly lacking in the writer or reader who cannot see behind the formulas, for these matter-of-fact statements, so statistical in their monotony, breathe the very spirit of the practical administrator. We need only observe how the moribund empire came to life to realise that Tiglath Pileser was a military genius; that he was equally fitted to cope with the most difficult administrative problems should be equally obvious. In every sense, the regeneration of the empire was his personal achievement.

He did not initiate the provincial organisation, but he made one important change, so much so that he may well be considered the second founder. Previously, the provinces had been rather large, and in a few cases, such as Harran and Rasappa, almost enormous; they were subdivided into *urasi*, always centring around an important town and in some cases representing in themselves former "kingdoms" of considerable size. If Tiglath Pileser had been himself the governor of Kalhu, we can understand how it was that he quickly reduced the area of these provinces until they ceased to be powerful enough to be a danger. Hitherto it has been possible to name each province as it was formed and to trace its general history; hereafter the new provinces have little more significance than the counties of the average American state. A large proportion cannot be located on the map, few of their chiefs ever attained the rank of eponym, the cursus of eponyms after a time was abandoned. Most significant of all, no longer were the officials who named the year permitted to set up their stelæ in the old capital of Ashur.

How the new system of consolidation worked is illustrated by the case of Bel Harran-bel-usur. Tiglath Pileser was none too sure of his throne in his first years, and so great a territorial magnate must be handled gently. He was appointed chamberlain of the palace, in rank second only to the turtanu himself, and in 741 he was eponym and named the year. The stele on which he had insulted the weak Shalmaneser IV remained unchanged, save that the single reference to his nominal ruler was chiselled out, and the name of his master took its place. Tiglath Pileser bided the time when the central government might be restored. The last year of Tiglath Pileser shows one of the rare instances of demotion in the Assyrian lists. Bel Harran-bel-usur was no longer chamberlain of the palace; he had been assigned to one of the decidedly lesser governorships, that of Guzana. Centralisation was completing its work.

Nevertheless, the system of granting chartered rights was too strongly intrenched to be entirely rooted out. As late as 730, we find Tiglath Pileser inditing for Zakur a charter with full immunities. If the estate had been taken from Mutakkil Ashur without adequate compensation, this would explain how he came to be a supporter of Sargon, who rewarded him with the province of Guzana, of which the eunuch Bel Harran-bel-usur was now deprived.

Shalmaneser was called from his province of Simirra to be the fifth and last monarch of that name (728–722). No sooner had he left the Phœnician coast than one of the Delta Kings of Egypt, Sibu or So, began a series of intrigues which resulted in the disaffection of Tyre, of its vassal, Sidon, and of Accho and Samaria. The mere appearance of Shalmaneser was sufficient to induce the majority to surrender, more especially as surrender brought freedom from the financial control of Tyre. Eager to avenge their wrongs and to destroy a dangerous trade rival, the pro-Assyrian Phœnicians furnished Shalmaneser with sixty ships manned by eight hundred oarsmen; Tyre could muster but twelve, but so well were these served that she utterly defeated her opponents and captured five hundred sailors. Shalmaneser hastened back, but Tyre was safe on her island and the Assyrians no longer possessed a fleet. They were reduced to blockading the streams and the magnificent springs southeast of the city. The wells within the walls were sufficient for actual needs, and the quality was not bad. The five years' siege ended in failure, and Shalmaneser made a treaty with Tyre which remained for long the basis for future exactions. Luli of Tyre was even able to bring back the rebel city of Citium on the island of Cyprus, which had been deluded by the appeal of independent trade relations with the empire.[1]

No mercy could be expected by the inhabitants of Samaria, and even if they might, ravaged Israel could not pay a crushing indemnity. They resisted bravely for three years, but were at last forced to admit the besiegers (723). Shalmaneser had no joy of his victory, for a few months later he himself fell before the usurper Sargon.[2]

[1] Jos., *Ant.* IX, 283 ff.   [2] II Kings 17 : 1 ff.; 18 : 9 ff.

CHAPTER XVII

SARGON AND THE SYRIAN SETTLEMENT

SARGON THE YOUNGER might well boast himself a self-made man; instead, he boasts the three hundred and fifty kings who ruled Assyria before him. Further details of his ancestry are hidden by a discreet silence. His son Sennacherib claimed descent from such heroes as Gilgamesh, Enkidu, Humbaba, and the like. This was going a little too far, and Esarhaddon discovered the genealogy which was thereafter accepted as standard and according to which Sargon was a scion of that Bel-bani, son of Adasi (1826–1806), who founded a new and perhaps non-Assyrian dynasty.[1]

Many centuries before, some thirty according to the chronological scheme accepted in his day, there had lived a mighty hero named Sargon, first to make sure the rule of the Semite in Babylonia and to report conquests reaching to Syria. In assuming his name, Sargon made him a sort of patron saint. The archaism in art and religion, the development of the birth legend, so close to that of the child Moses, the pious preservation of the liver omens through which the elder sovereign had won his victories, all showed that the new monarch considered himself the "later" Sargon the legend had seemed to prophesy.

A slight laid upon the city of Ashur by Shalmaneser proved his undoing. Ashur became angry at the sacrilegious wretch who feared not the lord of all, overthrew his rule in the wrath of his heart, called Sargon to the kingship, lifted up his head, gave him sceptre, throne, and crown. To establish his royalty,

[1] For detailed sketch of the reign, cf. *Western Asia in the Days of Sargon of Assyria*, 1908; the excavations at Dur Sharrukin (Khorsabad), Botta and Flandin, *Monuments de Nineve*, 1849–1850; V. Place, *Nineve et l'Assyrie*, 1867–1870; latest edition of inscriptions, H. Winckler, *Keilschrifttexte Sargons*, 1889; new edition in preparation by author of this history. Discussion of sculptures, Bonomi, *Nineveh and Its Palaces*, 147 ff.

Sargon granted freedom from tribute to the sacred cities of
Ashur and Harran, and every citizen found his privileges increased as never before.   They were freed from the levy of the
whole land for military purposes, from the summons of the
levy master; like the other temple cities of Assyria, they were
freed of all dues.   The charter containing the grant of privileges was written on a great silver tablet which was set up
before the image of Ashur.   Thus Sargon, the seed of Ashur,
the city of knowledge, assumed the burden of empire, and the
priests received the dues he owed as feudal vassal of the gods
Anu and Dagan.

Syria was neglected for three years, and by 720 the whole
country was aflame with revolt.   The centres were Gaza, still
ruled by Hanun, and Hamath, under Iaubidi, whose name
furnishes as startling proof of the north Syrian worship of
the Hebrew Yahweh as does Azariah of Samal.   The northern Judah was ruled by Bar Rekub, whose boasted love for
Tiglath Pileser did not extend to the supplanter of his dynasty.
Simirra had been the capital of the province whence Shalmaneser had passed to the kingship.   Arpad, Damascus, Tyre,
and Samaria had been recently independent.

The allies did not act in concert, for the Assyrians were too
quick for them.   Iaubidi took up his position at Qarqara on
the historic spot where once before Syrians had met Assyrians
in the field.   The omen did not hold good, for this time the
patriots were defeated.   The loss of the battle meant the loss
of Hamath, whose low-lying site in the great valley trench
offered little opportunity for defence.   The flower of its troops
was added to the standing army with which Sargon was replacing the antiquated feudal levy, and a colony of six thousand
three hundred Assyrians under an Assyrian governor took their
place.   Samal was fired by its conquerors and made a province
also.

Hanun was defeated before the gates of Gaza and fell back
toward Egypt.   Sibu summoned his lieutenant, and the two
armies met at Raphia, where before the Great War was the
formal boundary between Egypt and Palestine.   Sibu fled "as

a shepherd deprived of his flock," and Syria knew his intrigues no more.

The leading rebels were brought to Assyria to face their enraged lord. The first success of the reign needed to be emphasised. A horrible punishment, only too common among all nations in these rude times, was decreed for Iaubidi. Pegged to the ground spread-eagle fashion, the executioner seized a short curved knife and, beginning with his right arm, flayed him alive. Hanun was chained hand and foot with ring and bar. The remaining rebels, short-bearded, with tasselled caps and short coats over long fringed garments, knelt in abject submission, and at least saved their lives. A vivid bas-relief on the walls of the new capital served as warning against imitation of revolt. The relief was unknown in far-away Palestine, where the natives, in despite of their former Christianity and their present Islam, reverence the hero as the Prophet Hanun in the village which is still his house, Bet Hanun.

No attempt was made to follow up the advantage secured and attack Egypt. Sargon was at Ashur, and no subordinate dared risk the responsibility. Five years later (715) the annals speak of a tribute from Piru of Musri, that is, Pharaoh of Egypt, which by the usual rule would indicate that peace had been declared between the former antagonists.[1] Further advance upon Egypt was unwise until a firmer hold was secured on Syria; therefore, the next few years saw much attention devoted to settlement of its affairs. The city-states which had not been implicated directly in the revolt were allowed to retain their autonomy under their local kings. Those which were—Samal, Simirra, Damascus, the mainland Tyre, and Samaria—soon appear with Assyrian governors.

In the case of the last, the native records tell us a little more of this process of settlement. The storming of the city took place at the very end of Shalmaneser's reign, and all further arrangements were left to Sargon. Twenty-seven thousand of the leading citizens were deported to Mesopotamia and

[1] Or it may have been made with Bocchoris, son of Tefnakhte. Breasted, *Egypt*, 550.

Fig. 91. BAR REKUB OF SAMAL AND HIS SCRIBE.

Fig. 90. SARGON AND HIS CHIEF OFFICIALS. (Louvre.)

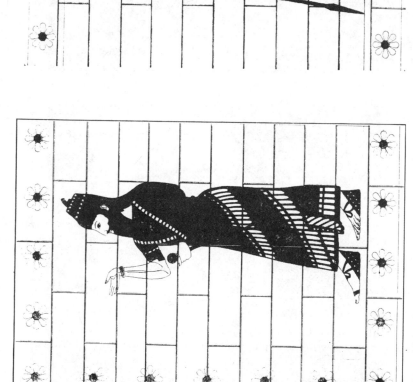

Fig. 93. ASHUR-ISQA-DANIN. HIS TURTANU.
(PALACE OF SARGON.)

Fig. 92. SARGON THE KING. (PALACE OF SARGON.)

settled in Guzana, Halah, and the country along the Habur River.[1] Thus was formed the nucleus for that community of Jews which long made Mesopotamia the real focus of Jewish thought. Not long after, Tab-sil-esharra, governor of Ashur, reports a field in Halah whose revenues were given to the Nabu temple of Dur Sharrukin.[2] The serfs who paid these dues were probably Hebrews.

Samaria was too important a site to be abandoned. The survivors were treated as Assyrians and ordered to pay the usual tribute to their governor. The system of deportation was in full swing and no less than four instances occur in this reign. Immediately after the uprising of 720, two Aramæan tribes from Der were settled. Three years later, two Hittite tribes were placed in Damascus, two Arab tribes were assigned to Samaria, and Deioces of Media and Itti of Allabria were interned in Hamath.

Again the Hebrew scriptures illustrate the process. The men of Hamath who were settled in Samaria were doubtless participants in the revolt of 720, and perhaps the same is true of the men from Sepharvaim in north Syria and the unknown Avva. The men of Cutha and Babylon must have been forced to emigrate at a later period. At the first, so the naïve account runs, they feared not Yahweh; for this, Yahweh sent lions among them, and some of them were killed. So they sent to the Assyrian king, saying: "The nations which thou hast carried away and placed in the cities of Samaria know not the law of the god of the land; therefore hath he sent lions among them, and behold they slay them, because they know not the law of the land."

Sargon recognised the reasonableness of this request and ordered one of the exiled Hebrew priests sent back to teach them this very necessary religious system. At Bethel, where the eponymous ancestor of Israel had seen the ladder and where Israel's first king had set up the golden bull of Yahweh, the cult was reorganised. One of his sacred sites was thus preserved for Yahweh, the remainder of the high places were

[1] II Kings 18 : 11. [2] H. 480.

handed over to the gods brought in by the new settlers.   The
men of Babylon made Succoth-benoth, the men of Cutha made
Nergal, the men of Hamath made Ashima, the Avvites made
Nibhaz and Tartak, while the men of Sepharvaim burned their
children to Adrammelech and Anammelech.   "So," concludes
the chronicler, "they feared Yahweh but made priests for the
high places from their own people to sacrifice for them in the
temples on the high places; they did indeed fear Yahweh, but
they also served their own gods, after the manner of the nations from whose midst they had been carried away." [1]

How great was the disturbance to the economic life caused
by these deportations is indicated by the sudden drop in the
culture as found in the excavations in Palestine.   More understandable is this if the settlement of the Arab tribes is mere
acknowledgment of the accomplished fact.   As the Syrian
localities became gradually deserted, less through the rare
Assyrian attacks than through the incessant and murderous
civil wars, resistance to the never-ceasing pressure from the
desert weakened, and the Arabs pushed in, as they are doing
to-day in the disorganisation which has followed the Great
War.   If only they paid a nominal tribute, the government in
distant Assyria offered no objection.

Of the four desert tribes mentioned, Tamudi, Ibadidi, Marsi-
mani, Haiappai, the first enjoyed a peculiar fame in later legend.
Thamud, so ran the oft-repeated story of the Koran, was a
great tribe in the Days of the Ignorance, the successor of the
prehistoric Ad.   In the pride of their hearts, they made from
the plains castles and dug out the mountains into houses.
Unto them came the prophet Salih, preaching the doctrine of
the Unity.   They rejected the manifest sign of the she camel,
sprung from the rock in witness against them, they hardened
their hearts and hamstrung her.   A great earthquake brought
upon them their judgment, and when morning broke they lay
on their faces, dead in their houses.[2]   Such was the tale so often quoted by the prophet Muhammad to point the moral to
those who would not accept his own teaching; Thamud was in

[1] II Kings 17 : 24 ff.   [2] Sura 7 : 71 ff.; 14.

reality a minor tribe in both Assyrian and Roman times and their reputed glory was due only to their conjectured association with the imposing ruins of the Nabatæan Hegra.

Other Arabs were of greater present importance. Samsi, queen of the Arabs, continued her tribute, for once her headsmen presented a hundred and twenty-four white camels.[1] Itamra of Saba must be one of the Yathaamars who appear as princely *mukarrib* or as kings in the Sabæan inscriptions from southwest Arabia. It goes without saying that Saba sent no tribute, for Assyrian troops were never within a thousand miles of its capital. If from equal to equal, reason for mutual exchange of gifts can be found in the feeling that the two civilised countries must needs unite against the barbarous nomads between; in the desire to exchange goods directly instead of by the roundabout route through Syria; and in the hope that Saba might displace her rival Main. Assyria was in control of Gaza, the port through which the south Arabian commerce must reach the Mediterranean; if the Minæans had assisted Gaza in the late troubles, we can understand why Assyria took the side of Saba.

Six years after the settlement of 720, Syria remained quiet. Meanwhile, conditions had completely changed in Egypt, where a strong unified government had taken the place of the Delta Kings. About the time that Shalmaneser III was warring with the Syrian states, say about the middle of the ninth century, the chief followers of Amon left their home in Thebes for the freedom of the upper Nile. Around their capital Napata, the Biblical Noph,[2] there grew up a powerful state called Ethiopia. Its culture was purely Egyptian, and its rulers never forgot the days when Amon had been supreme over a united Egypt which had spread his worship throughout western Asia.

Piankhi followed his father Kashta and began the realisation of these hopes. For the moment, he was able to force submission from all the Egyptian kinglets, including Osorkon III, an unimportant relic of the twenty-third dynasty, and the much more serious competitor, Tefnakhte of Sais in the delta.

[1] *H*. 631. [2] Isaiah 19 : 13.

His return to the upper Nile permitted Tefnakhte to secure
Lower Egypt for his own, and his son Bocchoris was considered
to form the twenty-fourth dynasty. He it was, perhaps, who
had made the agreement with Sargon which the Assyrian ruler
called tribute.

In the sixth year of Bocchoris, so we are told, a lamb spoke
and predicted the Assyrian conquest of Egypt; the immediate
danger to Bocchoris came not from the north but from the
south. Piankhi had been followed by his brother and son-in-
law Shabaka as king of Ethiopia, and the new king quickly
marched north, burned Bocchoris alive, and founded the
twenty-fifth dynasty. To all appearance, Egypt was once more
her old self, and all the Syrian states promptly began plotting
revolt against Assyria in reliance on Egyptian support.[1]

In Judah, the pro-Assyrian Ahaz had been succeeded by the
child Isaiah had predicted as Emmanuel; he had been named
Hezekiah, "Yahweh strengtheneth" (721–693), in memory of
the deliverance. Since Ahaz had ousted Yahweh from his ancestral abode, and had given precedence to Ashur and the
Assyrian king, the policy of Assyria had been brought home
in all its ugliness, and the most devoted follower could with
difficulty find argument in favour of her treatment of Samaria.

At this moment, a new prophet arose to add repeated
emphasis to the preaching of Isaiah, Micah of Moresheth.
The little village was on the lower slopes of eastern Judah,
not far from the Gath which Azariah had restored to the Hebrews. From the near-by hills, he could see the Assyrian armies marching south, and their presence caused him to break
silence:

"Hear, all ye nations, heed, earth and all your peoples;
Yahweh is witness against thee, the Lord from his holy
temple. Behold, Yahweh goes forth from his place, has gone
down and treads on earth's heights; the hills melt before him,
the valleys cleave in sunder.

"This has come for the wrongs of Jacob, for the sins of the
house of Judah; the wrong of Israel? Samaria; and the sin of

---

[1] For the period, cf. Breasted, *Egypt*, 537 ff.

Judah? Jerusalem. I made for this Samaria a field mound, as places for planting vineyards; her stones to the valley poured down, her foundations laid open. For this will I weep and wail, I will go stripped and naked; like jackals will I mourn, like ostriches make lamentation.

"Woe to those who devise iniquity on their beds; in the morning, they execute it, since their hands have the power. Fields they covet and seize them, houses too and they take them. They oppress a man and a house, even a man and his heritage. Behold, I devise an evil, your necks you may not move from it; neither walk upright, for it is a time of evil. In that day shall they sing a taunt, over you they shall raise a dirge: 'The field of my people is measured by the rod, there is none to restore it; our captors divide our fields, we are undone completely.' 'Prophesy not,' they demand, 'such things one should not prophesy; the reproach of a talker will not reach the house of Jacob. Is Yahweh's temper short? doeth he thus? are not his words gracious to him who walks uprightly?' No, ye rise up as a foe, against those who walk in safety; the robe ye tear off from peaceful passers-by. Ye drive my peoples' women from their pleasant houses; ye take away my glory from their young children forever. Rise ye and depart, for this is no resting-place for you; for uncleanness bringeth ruin, even a grievous destruction. As though a man should walk in wine and in falsehood and should lie: 'I will prophesy to thee of wine and strong drink,' he would be prophet for this people.

"Hark, Yahweh cries to the city, hear, tribe and city assembly; can I forget the wicked's house treasures, the short measure that is accursed? Can I make pure her wicked scales, her bag of weights unlawful; her riches full of violence, her inhabitants speaking falsehood? But I indeed do smite thee, for thy sins thy house is ruined; thou shalt eat and not feel full, thou shalt save but not retain it. What you save I will give to the sword, thou shalt sow but thou shalt reap not; thou shalt tread olives but not with oil anoint thee, thou shalt make sweet wine but not drink it. The statutes of Omri hast thou followed, all the works of the house of Ahab; that I may make thee a desolation, ye shall bear the reproach of the nations."[1]

Powerful support for Micah's preaching was found in Isaiah's prediction that the young Hezekiah must put his house in order, since he must die and not live. To his earnest prayer, Isaiah brought back the promise of Yahweh's relenting, and, what was of equal import, that Yahweh would deliver king and city from the hand of the Assyrian monarch. But this could be secured only at a price, and a later generation of nobles recalled to remembrance the remarkable manner in which Hezekiah had hearkened to the prophet Micah when he declared in the name of Yahweh of Hosts: "Zion shall be ploughed like a field and Jerusalem shall become mere heaps of stones and the temple mount as wooded heights." The contemporaries of Jeremiah also remembered how they entreated Yahweh and how he repented him of the evil he had pronounced against them.[2]

Rejection of the Assyrian rule was emphasised by greater stress laid once more on the worship of Yahweh and the *masseboth*, among which we may see surely the figures of Ashur and of the king, were broken in pieces. The high places were removed, the Asherah cut down, and the brazen serpent to which the people had long sacrificed in memory of a story of salvation in the wilderness[3] was likewise reduced to fragments. The temple, defiled by the presence of images of the hateful foreigner, was purified, as was the great altar which had been deflected from the service of Yahweh. The passover was celebrated, and an attempt was made to extend Judæan influence to the north by the invitation to the Israelites to take part in the ceremonies. Centralisation of the religion, already begun by David and Solomon, was brought a step nearer by the destruction of shrines outside the now sacred city.[4]

[1] Cf. J. M. P. Smith, *Micah*, in "International Critical Commentary."
[2] Jer. 26.: 16 ff.   [3] Num. 21 : 4 ff.
[4] II Kings 18 : 1 ff.; II Chron. 29 ff.

Other measures did not receive such approval from Isaiah. Merodach Baladan, the new Babylonian king, sent an embassy to congratulate Hezekiah on his recovery from his illness, and, quite incidentally, to suggest alliance. The members were received most hospitably and shown all the resources of the kingdom. Isaiah was anti-Assyrian enough, but he was not pro-Babylonian. To his mind, Yahweh was the all-sufficient source of strength for Judah, and alliance with foreign nations merely tempted him to wrath. "Hear the word of Yahweh," he exclaimed in answer to the defiant reply of Hezekiah that the ambassadors had seen all that was in his house; "behold the days will come when all that is in thy house and that which thy fathers have laid up in store unto this day shall be carried to Babylon. And thy sons that shall issue from thee, whom thou shalt beget, shall they take away, and they shall be eunuchs in the palace of the king of Babylon." [1]

Egypt was as little approved as Babylonia: "Ah, the land of the rustling of wings, which is beyond the rivers of Ethiopia; that sendeth ambassadors by the sea and in papyrus boats on the waters. Go, swift messengers, to a nation tall and smooth, to a people terrible from their beginning, a nation of might and of treading down, whose land the waters divide. All ye inhabitants of the world and ye dwellers on the earth, when a signal is lifted on the mountains, see ye; and when the trumpet is blown, hear ye. I will be still and will look on from my dwelling, when there is clear heat in sunshine and a cloud of mist in the heat of vintage. For before the vintage, when the blossom is over and the flower becometh a ripening grape, he will cut off the branches with pruning-hooks and the young shoots he will cut down. They shall be left together unto the carrion birds of the mountains and to the beasts of the earth; and the carrion birds shall summer upon them and all the beasts of the earth shall winter upon them." [2]

"Woe to the rebellious children, who carry out a purpose which is not from me and strike a treaty, but not according to my spirit, that they may add sin to sin; that set forth to go

[1] II Kings 20; Isaiah 39.   [2] Isaiah 18.

down to Egypt and have not inquired at my mouth, to flee to the fortress of Pharaoh and take refuge in the shadow of Egypt. Therefore shall the fortress of Pharaoh be your shame, and the refuge in the shadow of Egypt your confusion. For though his princes are at Zoan and his ambassadors come to Hanes, yet shall they all be brought to shame by a people that cannot aid them, that bring not help but shame and disgrace. By the beasts of the Negeb, through a land of trouble and distress, from whence come the lioness and the lion, the viper and the flying dragon, they carry their riches on young asses' shoulders, their treasures on the humps of camels, to a people that cannot aid them, for Egypt's help is vain and to no purpose."

This was unpopular language to use before crowds enthusiastically debating the speedy arrival of an Egyptian army which should free them forever from the Assyrian yoke, and it was strongly resented. The reply was as uncompromising as before: "Go, write it on a tablet before them, and inscribe it on a scroll, that it may be for the time to come a witness forever. For it is a rebellious people, lying children, children that will not hear the teaching of Yahweh, that say to the seers, 'See not' and to the prophets, 'Prophesy not unto us right things, speak to us smooth things, prophesy illusions, leave the way, turn aside from the path, abolish out of our sight the Holy One of Israel.' This is why the Holy One of Israel saith: 'Because ye reject this word and trust in wile and guile, therefore this guilt shall be to you as a breach ready to fall, bulging out in a high wall, whose breaking cometh suddenly in an instant.' And he shall break it as a potter's vessel is broken, breaking it in pieces without sparing; so that there should not be found among the pieces a sherd wherewith to take fire from the hearth or to dip up water out of the cistern. In returning and rest should ye have been saved, and in confidence should have been your strength, but ye would not. For ye said: 'No, but we will fly upon horses,' therefore shall ye flee; and 'We will ride upon the swift,' therefore swift shall be they that pursue thee. A thousand shall flee at the shout of one or of five, till ye be left as a pole on the top of the mountain and as a signal on a hill." [1]

"Woe to them that go down to Egypt for help and rely on horses; who trust in chariots because they are many and in horsemen because they are very strong, but have not looked unto the Holy One of Israel, and have not asked oracle of Yahweh. Yet he too is wise and can bring to pass evil and will not recall his words but will rise against the house of evil-doers and against the helpers of those who work iniquity. Now the Egyptians are men and not gods, and their horses are not spirit, and when Yahweh shall stretch out his hand, he that helpeth shall stumble and he that is helped shall fall, and they shall all be consumed together. As the lion with his young cub growleth over his prey, and even though a multitude of shepherds be called forth against him he will not be dismayed at their shout nor be cast down for their noise, so will Yahweh of Hosts come down to fight against Mount Zion and upon its hill." [2]

The leader in this pro-Egyptian movement was a certain Shebna whose Aramæan name and lack of parentage point to his being a foreigner, while his position as chamberlain of the palace makes one suspect that he was a eunuch. "What right hast thou" as a foreigner "to be here, and whom hast thou here" as fellow kinsman to give him a recognised status, "that thou hewest thee out a sepulchre on high, carving a habitation for himself in the rock. Behold, Yahweh will hurl thee, will hurl thee away, O man, into a country wide extending; it is there thou shalt die, and thither shall be the tomb of thy glory, O thou shame of thy lord's house! And I will thrust thee from thy office and from thy station shalt thou be pulled down. Then shall I call my servant Eliakim, the son of Hilkiah, and I will clothe him with thy robe and bind him with thy girdle and thy authority I will commit to his hand and he shall be a father to the inhabitants of Jerusalem and to the house of Judah and the key of the house of David will I lay on his back, so that he shall open and none shall shut and he

[1] Isaiah 30. [2] Isaiah 31.

shall shut and none shall open.　And I will drive him as a peg into a sure place and he shall be for a seat of honour to his father's house; and they shall hang upon him all the honour of his father's house, the offspring and the issue, every small vessel from the bowls to the flagons." [1]　In part, Isaiah's prediction was successful, for Shebna, though not entirely removed, was demoted to the office of secretary, while Eliakim actually did become chamberlain. [2]

In spite of the treaty, then, Egypt continued to intrigue with the enemies of Assyria in Palestine.　About 714, alarmed by the continuous colonisation of Syria, Azuri the king of the Philistine Ashdod withheld his tribute and his example was followed by his neighbours.　The uprising was quickly put down and his brother Ahimiti elevated to the throne.　Again the anti-Assyrian party gained control and the place of Ahimiti was taken by a mercenary Greek soldier from Cyprus who is simply called by Sargon Iamani, the "Ionian."

This first appearance of the Greeks in Assyrian history is significant of the new developments in Greek lands.　The almost complete cessation of direct intercourse between the Orient and Greece which marked the end of the Mycenæan period proper was now past, and the century 750–650 is noted for the ever-extending settlement of the Hellenes.　The Odyssey shows us Cretan pirates plundering the coasts of Egypt, until the king was forced to come out in person, one of the Delta Kings who divided the sovereignty of Egypt. [3]　Within the half-century, there were to be purely Greek settlements in Egypt itself.　Farther north Greeks were settling in Cyprus and on the mainland of Cilicia.　It was the most natural thing in the world that in this great outpouring of the Greek peoples, a Greek pirate should turn up in Ashdod, and, in virtue of his superior armour and military training, should assume charge of affairs.

Ascalon remained quiet under Rukibti, but the revolt spread to Gath and then to Judah, Moab, and Ammon. Judah was by no means a unit in entering the new combina-

---

[1] Isaiah 22 : 15 ff.　　　　[2] Isaiah 36 : 3.　　　　[3] Odys., XIV, 257 ff.

tion, for Isaiah protested strongly. He loosed the sackcloth from his loins and the sandals from his feet and delivered
this oracle: "Like as my servant Isaiah has walked naked and
barefoot for three years, a sign and an omen against Egypt
and Ethiopia, so shall the king of Assyria lead away the captives of Egypt and the exiles of Ethiopia, young and old,
naked and barefoot, to the shame of Egypt. And they shall
be dismayed and confounded, because of Ethiopia their expectation and of Egypt their boasting." [1]

How dangerous this outbreak was considered is shown by
the haste with which Sargon acted. Although it was too early
for the feudal levy to be called out, he hurried off his turtanu
Ashur-isqa-danin with but four hundred and twenty of his
own body-guard. The Assyrians suddenly appeared and invested Azekah, high upon its isolated hill with a far view to
the west and fortified with the great walls which recent excavation has laid bare.[2] The Ionian had surrounded low-lying
Ashdod with a trench and secured a water-supply from the
outside; the capture of Azekah made him lose heart, and he
fled to Egypt, whence he was extradited and handed over to
Sargon.

Ekron appears on a low hill near the water; its archer defenders wear a single long robe and helmets with neck-pieces.
An apparent negro makes more probable its location on the
border of Egypt. The Baal of Gezer, a little north, is larger,
and its acropolis is on a high isolated rock in the rear. Two
rams are driven up a made road, under the supervision of a
eunuch general. The captives, both men and women, wear a
fringed blanket which covers the head and falls down over the
left shoulder. One woman carries a small skin in her hand,
the other has a child sitting on her shoulder. The chief is
brought by the eunuch before the king seated in his chariot,
another seizes the unfortunate by the throat and draws the
sword to slay him. Several other towns on hills are taken by
escalade. Another relief shows the booted, short-bearded

[1] Isaiah 20.
[2] Joshua 10 : 10; I Sam. 17 : 1; II Chron. 11 : 9; Jer. 34 : 7; Neh. 11 : 30.

men, with shaved heads, abbreviated dress and sleeves, short curved swords and pointed oval shields, fighting a charioteer. One is under, one above, the horses, a third turns to flee, two others still await the approach of the enemy.

Too important to remain long desolate, the captured towns were rebuilt and settled with loyal colonists. A certain Mitinti was intrusted with their rule. Sargon now held the cities of the Philistine plain and controlled the main routes, he could afford to permit a precarious liberty to the mountaineers of Judah, Moab, and Ammon. The sudden punishment of the Ionian much impressed the Syrian imagination; Syria remained quiet, and contributed nothing to the history for the next dozen years.

CHAPTER XVIII

RUSASH OF HALDIA AND "GOLDEN" MIDAS

REACHING in a great arc from northeast to northwest were the provinces and appanages of the Haldian empire. No longer the most powerful in western Asia, the reign of Shalmaneser had allowed new growth. Although the son of Sardurish, its present ruler Rusash boasted on the equestrian group he had-dedicated in one of his provincial capitals: "With my two chariot horses and my charioteer alone my hands conquered the kingdom of Urartu." The older Menuahina, founded by Menuash, had been completely destroyed; Rusash restored it, but farther north, and called it Rusahina after himself. Since the waters of Lake Van are not potable, he constructed to the east among the barren and desert wastes an immense reservoir, and a canal which, under the name "Stream of Semiramis," still carries the water to Van. The next step was to build temples to Teishbash, the storm-god.

Building interests could not for long exhaust the energy of so live a monarch. To the north of Lake Gokcha, an inscription told of the twenty-four countries, lost since the days of Argishtish I, whose inhabitants had been deported to Haldia. The southeast, as far as Musasir, was in his hands, but on the southwest his frontier no longer touched the Euphrates. Haldian influence was not confined to the territory ruled directly by Rusash; with Merodach Baladan, to whom he may have been allied, he was the cause of almost every war of the reign.

Great changes had occurred in eastern Asia Minor since Tiglath Pileser had sent his armies into its recesses. A new power had arisen which, if a potential rival to Haldia, for the time being might prove a valued ally against Assyria. The Assyrians spoke of Mita the Mushkian, but we know him as Midas the Phrygian, the golden Midas of Greek legend whose touch transformed all to the precious metal.

About the time the Hittite empire was falling to pieces, say in the twelfth or eleventh century before Christ, there was a people in Thrace called the Bryges who spoke an Indo-European language, employed the Aryan political institutions, and adored a paternal nature-god, Men, the moon. Other tribes of similar character were forcing them onward, until they crossed the narrow straits into Asia, following the example of their kinsmen, the defenders of Troy against the Homeric Greeks. In west central Asia Minor they found a land which seemed to them homelike. On one side were low plains, blazing hot in summer, flooded with water in spring, fertile but always unhealthy; on the other elevated treeless prairies with fierce sun in summer and windswept in winter. Between were pine-clad hills, running water, fertile valleys, and a bracing climate.

Little of their history has survived through the mist of Greek legend. The fierce Indo-European nomads settled down, until later writers could declare that the Phrygian life was primarily agricultural. As such, they came to adore the earth mother and her lover-son in all their manifestations, of which Cybele and Atthis were the chief. The material culture of the natives was likewise taken over, but so profoundly was it influenced by their racial genius that whether we look at their tomb façades, cut from the living rock, or at their humblest sherds of pottery, we see the same geometric patterns which connect them with the later prehistoric civilisation of central Europe.

We know still less of their political history. Legend merely states that their first king was a Gordius, from whom the first capital took its name, and that his son was the famous Midas. We are likewise told that the names of Gordius and Midas alternated in the royal line, but which Midas was the Mita of the Assyrians is quite uncertain. The occurrence of typically Phrygian names of places in distant parts of the peninsula has rightly been taken to indicate the extent of the Phrygian power. By the end of the eighth century they were firmly

Fig. 94. COMANA, HOME OF THE CAPPADOCIAN MOTHER GODDESS.

Fig. 95. TOMB OF MIDAS AT THE MIDAS CITY IN PHRYGIA.

FIG. 96. HITTITE KING BEFORE
HIS GOD. (IVRIZ.)

The god, clad in the native costume, holds
grapes and the barley stalk; the king is
in Assyrian dress.

FIG. 97. SACRIFICE TO THE GOD TESHUB. (MELIDIA.)

The weather god stands on his bull, whose bellow is the thunder, the thunderbolt
is in his hand. The priest-king pours a libation of wine, the boy brings the
goat for sacrifice.

fixed in Cappadocia, and so thoroughly had Midas come to be identified with Asia Minor that the Assyrian scribes revived for him the title of Mushkian, unknown since Tiglath Pileser I and Ashur-nasir-apal II had fought these redoubtable tribes-men.

It is hardly to be questioned that this was the Midas who moved the capital from Gordium, a miserable little village of rude houses in an open valley,[1] to the heart of the pine-clad hills. On a high flat-topped rock, commanding the main passage through the hills, he established the settlement which we still call the Midas City because on one of its supporting cliffs is a magnificent tomb façade, one of the finest examples in the geometric style, whose Phrygian inscription contains the name of King Midas. Of the city within the two-mile circuit of walls, we have only a double throne of the gods with Phrygian inscription, an altar at the gate where the wheel-tracks can still be traced, the scarped rocks where once the walls were set. A city with half the circuit of Sargon's new capital was the centre of no small empire.

The weakness of Haldia and the short and ineffective reign of Shalmaneser presented opportunity which Midas was not slow to seize. The little state of Shinuhtu, just north of the Gates, was led to revolt; by order of Sargon it was annexed to Tyana, whose king Matti had already paid Assyrian tribute. Much more serious was the revolt of Carchemish.

Long since the northern barbarians had succumbed to the lure of Hittite civilisation and to the advantages of the site. Their language was written in the older pictographs, their art can scarcely be distinguished from that of the Hittite capital. Particularly in architecture was the earlier influence to be noted. The same use of mud brick for the main walls, the same dado of sculptured slabs, the same battlements decorated with rosettes, the same employment of enamelled brick, all testified to the conquest of the Hittite culture. As for their sculptures, only a close scrutiny reveals any marked difference from those found at Hatte, and the similarity is virtually com-

[1] Körte, *Gordion*.

plete with the contemporary states of north Syria and Asia Minor which carried on the traditions of Hittite technic.

Warlike character had disappeared before the opportunities of money-making presented by its position on the Euphrates crossing. Mercantile in its interests and careless of politics, it had been spared incorporation, and in the period of Assyrian decline it had gone its own way. So it resented its loss of freedom to Tiglath Pileser III, and although Pisiris had paid his tribute meekly enough in 740, when Midas urged him to throw off the yoke, he was perfectly willing to compromise himself. To those who have considered Midas almost a Greek, there is something incongruous in the thought of his stirring up revolt on the far-distant Euphrates; when we remember that four centuries previous, northerners had occupied Carchemish, we begin to suspect that it was some belated memory of common origins which might have led to the alliance.

Midas a second time failed to afford adequate support, and Rusash proved no more dependable. Carchemish was made a province, and the Assyrians held the great western road. Like other mercantile cities, Carchemish had her mercenary troops; taken over in a body, they swelled the ranks of the new standing army. The sack of so great a city, perhaps the greatest trading centre of its time, produced enormous booty, eleven talents of gold, twenty-one hundred in silver, bronze, ivory, and elephant hides.

Carchemish was the greatest Hittite centre surviving, but its Hittite character, never strong, had been much diluted by Aramæan infusion. Sargon rebuilt it, and the relative rank of its eponyms under his successors shows its recognition as one of the greatest cities. Some of the sculptures executed under Assyrian influence, the exquisite relief of the mother goddess, for example, have a delicacy and a sureness which is absent in the purely native work. Its commercial influence likewise continued; throughout the later empire, no small number of commercial documents were reckoned by the "mina of Carchemish," our actual pound.

Forward movement from the Tarsus base next attempted
Iconium, an age-old city where the fabled Nannacus had ruled
before the flood, and at this moment, as its mound proclaims,
at the height of its prosperity. Midas and Rusash fought a
battle on the coast, where mountains and sea came together,
and certain towns long held by the Phrygian were detached
by the Assyrians, but Iconium was still free. The Ionian
Greeks, who had long troubled the seacoast, were driven back.

The great trade route from Tarsus through the Gates to
Hatte and to Sinope on the Black Sea was commanded by
Tyana, already a religious centre. Matti had come to recognise the real meaning of Assyrian policy, and made terms with
Midas, who left behind one of his Phrygian inscriptions.[1]
Matti was deposed, and the Assyrians moved on to Tabal,
where the Hulli of Tiglath Pileser's time had been followed by
his son Ambaris. Sargon married him to his daughter Ahat-
abisha, whose steward kept the Assyrian court informed as to
what was going on. As dowry, Ambaris was assigned Hilaku,
the temporary halt of the Cilicians on their way from the Troad,
where they had furnished Andromache to the Homeric epic.[2]
Midas and Rusash proved the usual broken reeds to Ambaris,
and Tabal for a few short years was an Assyrian province.

His example had been followed by Tarhunazi, ruler of Kam-
manu, or Comana, but the Assyrians drove him from Melidia
to the isolated rock of Til Garimmu, the Togarmah where the
Hebrew prophet looked for horses and mules,[3] and carried him
off to Ashur. By the fortification of the towns in the Anti-
Taurus, a wedge was thrust forward between Haldia and
Phrygia. One year later, the Assyrian territory was rounded
off in north Syria by the acquisition of Marqasi and Gurgum,
where Tarhulara had been murdered by his son Mutallu.
Que was pacified in 711–709, and the two practicable passes
over the Taurus were closed to Midas. "Tribute" was received from Midas, which presumably marks a treaty, and the
war in the west came to a full stop.

[1] Myres, *Liverpool Annals*, I, pl. XIII.   [2] *Il.*, 6 : 395; 415.
[3] Ezek. 27 : 14; 38 : 6; cf. Gen. 10 : 3; I Chron. 1 : 6.

Well to the north of where we last found it, Qummuh abandoned friendly relations with Sargon and went over to Argishtish, the recent successor of Rusash in Haldia. Mutallu retired to the wild mountains and was safe, but his men were deported to the swamps of the south and inhabitants from Bit Iakin were settled in their place. The country was famous for its weaves, and shortly after Sennacherib reports to his father that the Qummuh chiefs had arrived with their tribute and seven female mules. They were assigned to the "house of the Qummuh land" but fed at their own expense. They desired to bring their tribute in person to Sargon, but Sennacherib was of the opinion that it was unnecessary to go to Babylon, they should be received by him in Kalhu. Let them bring quickly their cloth and fruit. The official brokers of the royal palace claim they have received but seven talents from that region, and that the men of Qummuh are not satisfied, declaring that their produce has been scanty and that they should bring the royal weavers.[1]

Ionians had already been making trouble in Que; perhaps this is the time when Soli was founded by Argives and Rhodians. Cyprus was largely theirs. As enemies of the Phœnicians, who had colonised Cyprus before them, they were inclined to be friendly with the Assyrians, who were also hostile to Midas, who, in turn, was none too kindly disposed to the Greeks on his western borders. The Assyrians had no fleet, and friendship with the great empire would mean commercial privileges throughout the whole of its provinces.

We can therefore understand why, while Sargon was in Babylon, he received an embassy and gifts from the seven kings of the land of Ia, a region of Iatnana, as the Assyrians named Cyprus, which lay seven days distance in the midst of the sea. In return for their gifts of gold and silver, ebony and box, he sent an "image of his majesty," which the Greeks preserved so carefully that it has endured to the present. It was set up in Citium, as the Greeks named the Cypriote Carthage which in the reign of Tiglath Pileser was still dedicating its

[1] H. 196.

FIG. 98. THE LEVEL LINE OF THE TAURUS FROM THE NORTH.

FIG. 99. A VILLAGE IN A NOOK OF THE TAURUS.
Ivriz with its Hittite inscriptions and reliefs.

first-fruits of the bronze to the Baal of Lebanon; in the meantime the Greeks had deprived the Phœnicians of its possession. Thenceforth the Greeks of Cyprus continued to keep up friendly relations with the Assyrians, and once in a while they sent presents; to the end they preserved their independence untouched. One result of the connection there may be; later chronologers transferred the rule of the sea from the Phrygians to the Cypriote Greeks about the date of Sargon's death.

More than once, in our study of the problems of the northwest boundary, we have felt the sinister influence of the Haldian Rusash. Still more serious were the results he produced in the north and east. When in 719 Sargon turned his attention to this sector, he found his best base the large and influential tribe of the Mannai who lived around the southern part of Lake Urumia. As next-door neighbours of Haldia, from whom they had suffered much, they naturally threw in their lot with Assyria. To their south lay Zikirtu, whose chief, Metatti, just as naturally allied himself to the Haldians.

Trouble began when Metatti persuaded two of the Mannai towns to revolt against their lord Iranzu. Iranzu appealed to Sargon, and the invaders were driven out. Aza, son of Iranzu, was also a "lover of the yoke of the god Ashur." Ashur's yoke was anything but light, and Rusash persuaded the commons to strike for liberty and less taxes. Aza was slain by Metatti and Bagdatti of Uishdish, and his dead body was exposed on Mount Uaush; Bagdatti reigned but a moment, for the Assyrians returned, flayed him alive, and exposed his bleeding corpse on this same Mount Uaush. Ullusunu, Aza's brother, soon realised that Rusash was the nearer and more dangerous foe, and his example was followed by Ashur-liu of Karalla and Itti of Allabria.

A hasty expedition in 716 brought Ullusunu to his senses, and he was reinstated. Not so easily did the two who had followed his leadership win off. Bound hand and foot, they were carried to the king. Rings were inserted in their lips, and the monarch grasped the cord; even as one was on his knees imploring mercy, he was blinded with the spear-point. Ashur-liu was flayed alive, while his men were deported to Hamath, where they were soon joined by Itti and his family.

CHAPTER XIX

PURPLE PATCHES OF A HISTORIAN

BEST known in all Assyrian history is the campaign of 714. At its conclusion, the great scribe of the king, Nabu-shallim-shunu, son of Harmakki, the royal scribe, sent in the name of Sargon to the capital of Ashur, to all the great gods who dwelt therein, to its palaces and its citizens, a huge tablet, whose wealth of rhetoric and of detail puts it in a class by itself. Thanks to this official "news from the front," we may envisage the campaign in all its details.[1]

In the month of July, Urta wrote on an ancient tablet that the time was propitious for the assembling of an army and for the formation of a camp. The troops set forth from Kalhu and crossed the Upper Zab at its flood. On the third day, there were ceremonies in honour of Enlil and Ninlil, and the Assyrians leaped across the Lower Zab as if it had been a ditch. The passes of Mount Kullar of Lulume brought them to Sumbi, where a grand review was held and the numbers computed of the charioteers, cavalry, archers, spearmen, pioneers, the camels and asses of the convoy.

The yoke of the chariot of Nergal and Adad, the divine standards which marched before the army, was directed towards Zikirtu and Andia. Into the midst of the mountains they advanced, between high summits which were clothed with all sorts of woods, whose interior was chaos and frightful their passes, where the shadows extend over the country like a forest of cedars and the wayfarer sees not the splendour of the sun. Twenty-six times they crossed the Buia in its wanderings.

They then faced Mount Simiria, a great mountain peak, which stands like the point of a lance, and uplifts its head from

[1] Thureau-Dangin, *Relation de la Huitième Campagne de Sargon*, 1912; Schroeder, *Keilschrifttexte aus Assur*, II, 141.

the mountain home of the mistress of the gods, which upholds
the heavens on its summit, while below its roots reach to Arallu,
the abode of the dead.   From side to side there was no passage,
like the back of a fish its ascent was difficult, on its sides extended down caves and precipices, and when the eye looked

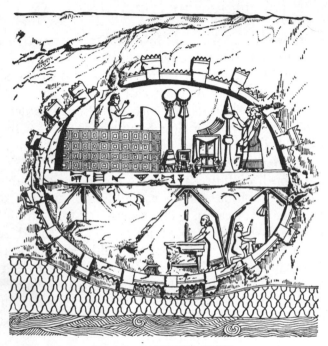

Fig. 100. SARGON'S CAMP.

upon it fear was evoked.   The very body-guard could not traverse its difficult paths, so with mighty axes of bronze the men
of pain, the pioneers, were loaded, and they broke the rock of
the mountain like cut stone.   Thus the road was opened and
the body-guard flew up like eagles, the camels and asses ascended like the wild ibex, the offspring of the mountain.

Camp was pitched on the summit, seven thousand feet high.
The reliefs label the "camp of Sargon," no longer round as in
the old days, but oval, and with the royal tent, the standards,
the altar, the huts of the cooks, the two scribes we have learned

to expect. Seven long-extending mountains, covered with verdure whose scent was good, were climbed, and the rivers which ran down their sides must be crossed in flood before the army might descend into the Mannai provinces.

With rejoicing of heart and gladness of countenance, because Sargon had not ceased yearly from avenging him, Ullusunu met Sargon at a frontier fortress. Soon after he received the dues of Bel-apal-iddina, who two years before had been made prince of Allabria. The village chiefs of Namri, Sangibutu, Abdadani, and the mighty Medes heard of the approach of his army, the devastation of their land in the former year remained in their memory, stupefaction was poured out upon them. Dalta of Elli and a long list of Median chieftains whose strongly Iranian names prove the Mazdian worship brought their gifts to Parsua, fast horses of open knees, raging mules, the camels peculiar to their land.

Ullusunu had gone on to Sirdakka, waiting in perfectness of heart to perform a vassal's duty. As though an Assyrian governor, he had heaped up granaries with food and wine against the coming of his master, he had sent his eldest son with tribute and the greeting gift, without delaying for orders he had set up a stele. He and his nobles crawled on all fours like dogs into the royal presence and besought Sargon to avenge the Mannai on the Haldian, to restrain the Kakme, most evil of men, from entering the midst of their land, and to restore the ruined Mannai to their places. The words of supplication were heard and Sargon replied: "It is enough." Restoration and victory were promised them and they took confidence. A magnificent banquet was spread for Ullusunu—the author does not add that it was prepared from Ullusunu's stores—and more than in the case of his father Iranzu was his throne elevated. The Mannai sat with the men of Assyria at a common table of joy, and before Ashur and the men of their own land they blessed the royal rule.

Village chiefs of Gizilbundu, situate in the isolated mountains, a distant place, closed like a bridge, whose citizens trusted in their own strength and recognised not the Assyrian sovereignty, none of the Assyrian kings had before seen their abode, received their gifts, or so much as heard their name, prayed for a safe life and that their walls should not be destroyed, and abjectly kissed his feet. For the good of their land—the phrase is quite modern enough to recall the notorious "White Man's Burden"—a resident was intrusted with their care, though general supervision was to be exercised by the governor of Parsua.

A march of thirty hours along the frontier between Mannai and Media brought the army to Panzish, where Ullusunu had erected a fort to restrain the feet of the hostile Zikirtu and Andia from entering and to prevent the escape of fugitives. In full sympathy with this undertaking, Sargon strengthened its casing and ordered oil, wine, and weapons of war to be accumulated within.

Metatti of Zikirtu had thrown off the yoke of his lord Ullusunu, had forgotten his service, and had trusted to Rusash, who, like himself, knew no prudence and was a helper who could not protect his life. When Metatti saw the Assyrians, his double-walled city of Parda with its hill and river defences had no value in his eyes. A ram was run up the steep road, another passed over a made causeway, the archers, spearmen, and sappers advanced to the attack. The men of his land in their sheepskin dress ascended the difficult mountain whose exaggerated steepness is pictured in the relief. With paralysed limbs they saw from afar three strong cities and eighty-four hamlets destroyed as if by the waters of the primeval flood. His hill guards were slain, but of Metatti himself Sargon could only report that his place of abode was not found.

With Uishdish was reached that part of the Mannai land which had been ravaged by Rusash the mountaineer, the seed of murder, who knows not prudence, whose lips speak words of strife and injustice, who guards not the weighty words of Shamash, and yearly, without ceasing, rejected his statutes. Not content with his former sins, he had added the greatest of crimes, meriting the ruin of his land and the defeat of his men, for he had summoned his troops and had dared to meet the Assyrians face to face. The conflict began in Mount Uaush, the same which had seen the bodies of former Mannai rulers exposed, a mighty mountain, which like the form of a cloud in the midst of heaven lifts up its head, where, from distant days, no one had passed its place and no one had seen its road, and the winged bird of heaven on high had not gone, with great storms and the strength of cold, upon which the snow is heaped day and night. News was brought by messenger that the Haldian army was drawn up in the depths of the mountain, and Sargon changed his course to the Haldian frontier.

"The unhappy troops of Ashur, who had marched by a distant route, were moaning and exhausted. They had traversed many mighty mountains, whose ascent and descent were difficult, and they had changed their appearance. Their fatigue I did not soothe, water for their thirst I did not pour out. I did not set up my camp, I did not fortify the wall of my camp. I did not send my warriors forth, I did not collect my army, those who were at my right or my left did not return to my side, I did not look back, I did not use the greater part of my troops, I did not raise my eyes. With my own chariot alone and with the cavalry who march at my side, who never leave my side in a hostile and unfriendly land, the troop and squadron of Sin-ahi-usur, like a mighty javelin I fell upon Rusash, his destruction I accomplished, I routed him. The bodies of his warriors like malt I brewed. His warriors who bore the bow and the lance before his feet, the confidence of his army, I slaughtered. Two hundred and fifty of the royal seed, his governors, his officials, and his cavalry in my hands I took and I broke his battle-line. I shut him up prisoner in his camp, and his horses, trained to the yoke, with javelins and arrows I destroyed under him. To save his life his chariot he abandoned, he mounted a mare, and before his troops he fled. Metatti of Zikirtu and his neighbour kings I defeated, like ants in distress they travelled the difficult roads. For the distance of six double hours, from Mount Uaush to Mount Zimur, the jasper mountain, at the point of the javelin I pur-

sued them.   Against the remnant I had left that they might
glorify the success of Ashur my lord, Adad the mighty thunderer
sent forth his powerful voice and by the flooding clouds and
stones from heaven he completed their destruction.   Rusash
feared the report of my mighty arms, and like a bird of the
glen who flees before the eagle his heart trembled.   As a man
who has poured forth blood, he left Turushpa (Tushpash), his
royal city, like one fleeing the hunter he reached the flank of
his mountain.   As a woman in travail, he laid himself down on
a couch, food and water he refused, an incurable disease he
inflicted upon himself."

Thus the tribesmen of Zikirtu and Andia were shut off from
attacking the Mannai.   The heart of Ullusunu was made glad,
and for the miserable inhabitants the light was brought forth.
In joy of heart and gladness, with singers and harpers and tam-
bourine-players, Sargon returned to camp and splendid sacrifices for the gods magnified their godhead.

The great battle had taken place on Mount Sahend, to give
it its modern name, and probably where that mountain mass
all but blocks the way along the swampy eastern shore of Lake
Urumia.   The first result of the victory was the recovery of
Uishdish for the Mannai.   The cities which Rusash had
founded, numerous as the stars of heaven, were won over,
their mighty walls were smashed like pots to the foundations
and levelled to the ground, their granaries were opened, and
barley without reckoning was given to the soldiers to eat.
With the great fortress of Ushqaia, the head of the boundary
of Haldia was reached, which closed like a door the province
of Zaranda, shut off the Assyrian messengers, and like a boundary mark gleamed, and above the territory of Subi land was
clothed with glory.   On the great plain which is to-day dominated by the trading centre of Tabriz, there dwelt the men who
had no equal in the knowledge of riding horses, and every year
they sent their young stallions to be used in the Haldian army.
When the inhabitants beheld the defeat of their king, their
legs became weak like the root on the bank of a stream; when
the fugitives arrived with the news and stooped to tell them,

they fell down like dead men in a faint. Ushqaia was abandoned and its occupiers took the "Road of No Return." Its mighty wall, set on the solid rock, eight cubits in thickness, was completely destroyed, the high beams of the houses were fired, with the smoke the heavens were covered as with a cloud. Like an inroad of grasshoppers, the cattle in the Assyrian camp were sent into the fields and all the forage was consumed. The citizens of Sangibutu abandoned their double-walled and deep-ditched cities in whose midst were stalls for the horses in the royal army, and fled to a dry land, a land of thirst like a desert. Crossing Mount Kishpal, Sargon saw at its foot the city of Ulhu.

Oriental despotism had here shown how it might ameliorate the hard lot of the common people. Where before there was not enough water for drinking purposes, Rusash brought down a veritable stream of water, in abundance like the Euphrates. From its breast he made canals without number to go forth, and fruits were as plenteous as rain. Plane-trees he made to bear shad as a forest, like a god the king made the dwellers to give forth joyous cries. Three hundred *imers* of arable land were cultivated in grain, the desolate fields were turned into meadows, herb and pasturage ceased not summer or winter. The men were taught by the good king to erect dikes, and to overlook all this work of his hand Rusash built a palace of sweet-smelling cypress.

Into this paradise came the news of Sargon's approach. With cries of despair and with beating of breasts, the wretched inhabitants abandoned their goods and fled to their mountain slopes by night. Like an earthen pot, the invaders destroyed, the treasures of barley were carried off from their hidden grain-pits, the wine-skins, filled with the precious liquid like river water, were slit open, the wine-jars, huge pithoi of a hundred gallons or more such as have been excavated near Van, were smashed, and the sun looked down on the empty fragments, the skins dripped wine like the downpour of heaven. The sound of the axes thundered like Adad as the trees and walls were cut down. Not a stalk was left to cover the ruin, the meadows in which they had grazed horses were made desolate, their great fortresses and the fifty surrounding hamlets were burned to the ground. And the whole recital of this advance of Assyrian culture is taken from their own narrative!

The next centre of Haldian civilisation was in the heart of the mighty cities of Sangibutu. Again we have the irrigation system, which in their territory never knew cessation, but the twenty-one villages were better guarded with walls of a hundred and twenty courses of bricks, with deep ditches and strong towers. On the slopes of the surrounding mountains were watch-towers, whence morning and evening the approach of an enemy could be observed. Again the inhabitants fled and took their position on the mountainside. Like a dense cloud of the night, the Assyrians covered the land, the cities like grasshoppers they devoured, their troops swarmed up the slope like wild sheep. The sappers climbed the walls, and with axes cut down the cypress beams of the palaces. Their cleverly built houses were fired, the grain was loaded on pack animals for the return to Assyria, their luxuriant vineyards were destroyed, and the great forests, which covered the mountains like reeds, were hacked down.

Turning due west, Sargon made for Lake Van. The capital Tushpash was at this point but a few miles away, but he dared not attack it. Veering to the north, he crossed Mount Uizuku, over seven thousand feet high, and the mountain of cypresses, whose product is coloured breccia. Thirty cities stretched along the shore of the "shaking sea"; the others were abandoned, and their inhabitants took refuge in Argishtiuna and Qallania, solidly set on the mountains where they gleamed like stars. The capital founded by Argishtish on the northern shore of the lake's northeastern bay gave them no safety.

Haldian territory was left at Uaiais (Uesi), the province of their confidence, the foot of the frontier of the land of Urartu, which is on the boundary of Nairi, which above all the fortresses of Rusash was strong and cleverly constructed in work, where his valorous soldiers, the spies, brought in the news of the lands round about as they dwelt in its midst, and the governors with their troops were brought into it by the king and were protected by its mighty walls.   That this is no exaggeration is shown by a view of the modern Bitlis, clustering around its castle at the junction of two streams, in the narrow gorge surrounded by mountains, and commanding the only direct egress to the south from the Haldian capital.   The rear of the fort was secured and Haldian troops crushed like lambs before the gate, the vineyards and forests were destroyed, but the citadel remained untouched, a centre for espionage or for sudden surprise attacks upon Assyrian lands.

Down the valley of the east Tigris, and through the tunnel attributed by modern legend to Semiramis, Sargon marched to the land which the archaising historian names Nairi, though in this century it was usually called Hubushkia from its royal city.   Four hours to the north, he was met by the Ianzu, and was conducted to the capital to receive the annual tribute.

At Hubushkia, the modern Sert, Sargon was well beyond the mountain barrier, and the territory properly Assyrian was not far distant.   His wearied troops might well expect an end to an unusually strenuous expedition.   But Sargon willed otherwise.   If he had in truth expected to receive the submission of Musasir, he was disappointed, for Urzana sent not a single messenger to ask the royal peace.   The entrails were examined, and Shamash indicated that defeat should be the lot of the Guti.   The scholars who followed the royal train identified this ancient mountain race with the more northern Musasir, and Sargon was content with the omen.

The greater part of the army and all the camp impedimenta were sent direct to Assyria, while Sargon, accompanied only by the thousand cavalry and spearmen who formed his bodyguard, advanced due east up the valley of the modern Bohtan Chai and into the very heart of the frontier range.   Leaving the valley, he led, in his chariot, his men over Mount Arsiu, whose summit could be no more ascended than the height of a peak and down into the valley of the Upper Zab.   This river crossed, there came another difficult road.   "Between the high mountains, the elevated ravines, the peaks of the difficult mountains, which pass all describing, and in their recesses was no road for the advance of my body-guard, mighty torrents of water traverse its midst, and the voices of its mountain slopes thunder for an hour's distance like the voice of the god Adad. All useful trees, fruits, and desirable vines cover it, but in its narrow defiles it is full of fear, where no king had passed, and no prince who preceded me had seen their road. Their great trunks I cut down and their difficult peaks with axes of copper I cut. A narrow road, a passage, a street, where the body-guard could pass by the side, for the advance of my troops between them I constructed. My own chariot I placed on the necks of men, and I mounted my horse at the head of my troops. My warriors with the horse-men who went by my side marched in single file, and with difficulty I made them traverse it." Exaggeration there is little, for the modern traveller still sees the same combination of fruitful valley and savage mountain surrounding.

Mighty cattle and sheep without number were being sacrificed in Musasir before the national god Haldia, who was crowned with the royal crown and bore the royal sceptre of Urartu. In vain were the sacrifices, for Urzana barely escaped and alone, leaving his family and his subjects to what mercy might be shown by the invaders. The old men and the women ascended to the roofs of their houses, weeping sadly, and crawling on their four paws to win a safe life for themselves. But Sargon had no mercy, and the sins of the king were visited upon his helpless subjects. "Since Urzana had not submitted himself to the word of Ashur but had cast off the yoke of my lordship and had refused to do his service, I determined that the men of that city should be made captive, and I ordered that the god Haldia, the confidence of Urartu, should go forth, before his city gate I placed him as a conqueror."

With all due allowance for the inevitable overstatement, the booty was obviously enormous, and the details are of equal value in affording an insight into the resources of such a mountain ruler and into the peculiar civilisation of the suzerain Haldia. The captives are given as six thousand one hundred and ten, probably not far from the true population of the city; the number of animals, twelve mules, three hundred and eighty asses, five hundred and twenty-five cattle, one thousand two hundred and thirty-five sheep, is surprisingly moderate. From the heaped-up chambers, gorged with hidden treasures, whose seals had been opened, were taken thirty-four talents of gold, one hundred and sixty-seven of silver, pure bronze, lead, carnelian, lapis lazuli, sceptres of ivory, ebony, and box, inlaid with gold and silver, vases of all sorts, among which are especially mentioned caldrons of Tabal with handles of gold, ablution vessels of bronze, golden daggers and poignards, fly-flappers of gold, silver incense-burners of Tabal, many other objects of bronze "the setting down of whose names for the purpose of writing is not easy," as the wearied scribe confesses, a confession echoed most heartily by the modern translator as to many of the objects whose meaning he must determine, many objects of iron such as lamps, coloured cloths, and chitons, the product of Urartu and Kirhi.

When the ridia officials approached the Haldia temple, they found there the deity with his consort Bagbartu, whose Iranian name hints that she was once a god, made female when the land was brought under the sway of the supreme Haldia. Still richer spoil was afforded by the temple treasures. Much gold, one hundred and sixty-two talents of silver, three thousand six hundred of crude copper were but a beginning. Golden bucklers stood at either side of the temple, of a weight of five talents each, red like flame, and within them gleamed the heads of menacing dogs. The golden shields have disappeared, but the great sanctuary near Van has preserved bronze shields of the second and third Rusash, with concentric bands of lions and bulls who might have been taken from the Assyrian monuments. Two talents of fine gold went into a portal for his doors, in the likeness of such a horned animal as we observe on the shields. The lock was in the form of a human hand, a talisman such as has been found in gypsum, while the bar which closed the door had a winged "Deluge" crouching like a dragon. Two golden keys were in the form of female colossi, crowned and bearing the spiked club and the divine circle, while the base was guarded by menacing dogs.

Here too were deposited the golden sword that Urzana wore at his side, bucklers embellished with the deluge dragon, lions, or wild bulls, basins, and vessels of silver encrusted with gold, two great horns of the wild bull inlaid with gold, the signet ring which brought to completion the orders of the goddess Bagbartu, her ivory bed ornamented with gold and precious stones, ivory wands, poignards of ebony and tables of box, lances and daggers of bronze which actually have been recovered in great numbers, a great laver of bronze that held eighty measures of water and which was filled with sacrificial wine when the kings of Urartu sacrificed before Haldia.

A regular statuary hall is described. Four in bronze represented the great guardians who protected his gate, and one of them was in prayer. The small bronze models are roughly Assyrian in design, but with face turned to side, flat crown, and human hands grasping each other over the breast, a link between the fully animal bodies of the Assyrians and the Greek centaurs with four animal feet and two human hands. Sardurish, predecessor of Rusash, was here, and if we would realise how he looked, we turn to the statue found near the Van sanctuary. The body is bronze gilt, the head is of white stone, the eyes and necklace were of precious gems. To our minds, this is a strange combination, but the effect must have been much similar to the chryselephantine statues of the best Greek period. The right hand holds a palm-leaf fan, the left grasps tightly a long narrow band which falls over the left shoulder and ends in a looped cord. The face is beardless, and we may see here a eunuch attendant.[1] Likewise to be seen was the group of the bull, the cow, and the calf, into which Sardurish had changed the accumulated bronze of the temple. Argishtish was standing in a house of sixty talents' weight, his head crowned with the starry diadem of the gods, his right hand extended in benediction. Rusash himself was there with his

---

[1] For excavations at Toprakkaleh, cf. Lehmann-Haupt, *Abh. Ges. Göttingen, NF.*, IX, 3; Lynch, *Armenia*, II, 62 ff.

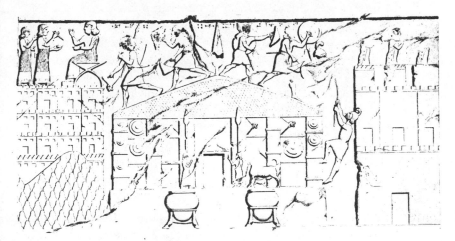

FIG. 101. PLUNDER OF THE "GREEK" TEMPLE AT MUSASIR.

FIG. 102. WEIGHING OUT THE BOOTY OF MUSASIR.

two chariot horses, his charioteer, and this boastful inscription: "With my horses and my single charioteer, my hands have conquered the kingdom of Urartu."

On the wall of Dur Sharrukin a city with triple circumvallation lies in the midst of steep mountains. From its towers women stretch out their hands in supplication. On the opposite side of the city an official sits on a camp-stool placed upon the inner wall, and the two scribes with stylus and clay tablet or pen and papyrus reckon up the spoil. In the centre is the temple, with its almost Greek pediment, its hexastyle front, its two outer pillars hung with shields, its middle ones banded, the two on either side the low door adorned only by the statues in front. One is indeed a figure with hand raised to bless, its companion is helmeted and stretches out his arm in a more menacing manner, but behind each is a spear, double man length. From the columns extend gargoyles like the threatening heads of beasts, in the court is the calf suckled by the cow, and in front are the two huge lavers with their ox-footed support. Assyrian soldiers swarm up the column by the aid of a rope, or run across the sloping roof with its tall spearlike acroterium, and throw down the lion-bossed bucklers which adorn the summit. The huge bronze statue in long robe and pointed helmet is being hewn to pieces while two eunuchs weigh the fragments in the scale-pan.

Not the least pleasing result of this wholesale spoliation was the recovery of the objects, in every sort of metal, which the enemy had plundered from Assyrian cities. The inhabitants of the little town were counted as Assyrians, and dues and the corvee were inflicted upon them. Affliction was sprinkled over all Urartu, and tears for eternity established over Nairi. The "chief tongues," the captives, were sent to Ashur by Tab-shar Ashur, the great abarakku. After all this campaigning, against such enemies and through such territory, we are asked to believe that the total loss was one charioteer, two cavalrymen, and three pioneers!

When the Haldian heard the news, he crouched on the ground and rent his garments, he ripped off his fillet and tore his hair, flat on the ground he threw himself, his heart was angry, his liver burned, in his mouth were fixed bitter words. This should mean, if anything but rhetoric, that he was ill. Before many years, the story was much improved. The sheep, for example, in seven years increased from one thousand two hundred and thirty-five to one hundred thousand two hundred and twenty-five. Legend now told how when Rusash heard of the capture of his god Haldia, with his own iron dagger, like a pig, his heart he pierced, his life he ended. It is all most pathetic.

A bilingual stele, Haldian and Assyrian, stands near one of the eastern passes, where some have placed the site of Musasir. On it Rusash tells how Urzana entered the temple of the gods before him, how Urzana's troops took the oath of loyalty in the temple of Haldia. Rusash went to the Assyrian mountains to fight, then grasped Urzana by the hand and made him king in Musasir, or, rather, in Ardinish, as the Haldian version has it. Fifteen days he delayed in Musasir, while he restored the former offerings. His last success was in the Lulu land which the Assyrian version calls the land of Akkad. The record ends with the assurance that the gods gave days of joy. For a suicide, Rusash appeared somewhat troublesome still to the Assyrians.

The truth of the matter is that the expedition so elaborately reported was a mere raid, spectacular and destructive, but entirely destitute of enduring results. If it has been quoted at length, it is because of its literary interest, for the light it sheds on Sargon's character, and for its surprising revelation of the height reached by civilisation in the northern lands.

CHAPTER XX

DEIOCES AND THE MEDIAN FOUNDATIONS

The veracious "Father of History" sponsors an entertaining tale about the origins of the Median power. After the Assyrians had ruled Upper Asia for five hundred and twenty years, he says, the Medes first of all their subjects revolted and in a single battle completely freed themselves. The other dependent peoples followed their example, and thereafter all enjoyed what the Greek believed the greatest of all blessings, complete autonomy.

Such happiness was too great to last. In due course tyranny arose and in the following manner: Once upon a time there was a man named Deioces, the son of Phraortes, and he was a very wise man and a village chief. The Medes lived scattered here and there in villages, and if one wronged another, there was none to do justice. So Deioces set up as a wise man, rendering righteous judgments till his fame grew nation-wide and all came to him to right their wrongs. Now Deioces found that this was wasting all his time, so he craftily refused to act longer as judge. He might be retained as judge in one only manner, and the Medes, perceiving this, called an assembly and offered Deioces the kingship. Like a good Greek tyrant, he refused to accept unless he were permitted to enroll a body-guard and was given a palace. Once in power, he forced the Medes to abandon their villages, and with them founded the great city of Ecbatana. After a reign of full fifty-three years, Deioces was followed by his son Phraortes, but not until he had laid the foundations of the Median empire that was to be.[1]

Reality was in almost every respect different. The original home of the Medes had been that Iranian plateau whose im-

[1] Herod., I, 95 ff.

243

portance as a centre of racial and cultural diffusion we are only beginning to appreciate. They seem to have been akin to the later Persians ethnologically, and their language may be considered a Persian dialect. Their culture was still essentially nomadic, though they had been settled long enough in the mountains to have taken on some of the characteristics of a sedentary people. Their cities were regularly on a hill commanding a stream. On the highest point was a citadel, and two or even three walls were not uncommon. Towers and battlements had been borrowed from their neighbours, and the gates were frequently arched. In dress and arms they had learned less from the Assyrians. Their hair was short and held by a red fillet, their short beard was curled. Over a tunic they wore a sheepskin coat which the Assyrian artist considered so curious that he repeated it times without number. High laced boots formed another conspicuous part of their costume, and occasionally we detect those same upturned shoes that we have come to consider Hittite. Unlike the desert nomad, they carried no bow or sword; their regular weapon of offence was a long spear, of defence a rectangular wicker shield.

Not the slightest sense of unity can be detected. Some leaders appear a little more important than others; in the typical list of Median names, no village chief appears superior to his companions. These names are perfectly good Iranian, and in meaning agree with the quasi-nomadic culture still the background of the earlier hymns of the Avesta. Mazda worship is already in existence, but the more developed deity, Ahura Mazda, is never invoked in their names, and this seems to prove that the prophet Zoroaster, the sacred books of the Avesta, and Ahura Mazda himself are yet in the future.

There was too much nomadism in the Median blood to permit them to be content in mountains more conspicuous for picturesqueness than for fertility. As early as 835, Shalmaneser had discovered them ousting the earlier tribes on the eastern frontier, and succeeding monarchs filled their annals with unmeaning lists of village chiefs and of the hamlets or tribes they ruled. Often they sent gifts which the Assyrians

Fig. 103. MEDIAN CHIEF PRESENTING
CITY MODEL.

Fig. 104. SIEGE OF A MEDIAN CITY.

called tribute, sometimes the presence of an Assyrian general produced a temporary acceptance of the Assyrian yoke; if the Medes were never effectually controlled by the Assyrians, no more did they revolt and defeat them in one great battle.

A Deioces there was in truth and he was a village chief, but he did not end his days as the revered founder of a new Median empire in his splendid metropolis of Ecbatana; Daiaukku was a "governor of the Mannai" who had given his son as hostage to Rusash, fell into the hands of the irate Assyrians, and was deported to Hamath in Syria (715). Name, time, place nevertheless prove that this petty princeling is the historical Deioces. His "house" survived to a later date, and he may after all have been an ancestor of the dynasty which ultimately made Media the greatest power in the world.

Thanks to the exertions of Tiglath Pileser III, Sargon was well situated on this frontier. Northwest and beyond the Mannai lay Andia, whose king sent tribute. An unknown correspondent tells how his son Iala has arrived with this tribute of fifty-one horses, and with him Abit-shar-usur, a Mannai official, who later writes that Nabu-eresh, the Chaldæan who had been sent in honourable exile to this far border with orders that he be watched secretly, has suddenly left with the statement that he was going to bear his greetings to the palace.[1]

Between Arbela and Musasir was Kirruri, a province since the ninth century, whose governor was Shamash-upahhir. South of it was Parsua, and again to the south of this last, between the Zab and Diyala Rivers, on the first outliers of the eastern mountains, lay Arrapha under Ishtar-duri. East of this was Lulume, the later representative of Mazamua, an ill-defined district in the Median highland, whose governor, Sharru-emuranni, bore the brunt of the conflict.

Shamash-upahhir writes of the village chiefs who are under his feet, and the chiefs themselves complain of the king's order to work in the mountain ravines; they are obeying his commands, but the work is heavy upon them, heavy exceedingly,

[1] H. 466; 411.

and they cannot perform their task.   May they receive their ration of oil and food as they enter the land.[1]

The governor of Parsua, under the protection of the wicker shield held by his squire, sent his shower of arrows against the city of Kishesim, the postern gate was fired, and on the relief the flames appear as huge stag's horns.   The city's name was changed to "Fort of Nabu."   Harhar had entered into close relations with Dalta of Elli, who had not yet earned the fame of a "vassal who loved my yoke."   This was sufficiently serious to bring out the king in person.   The triple-walled city was commanded by an isolated rock citadel, and around it flowed a good-sized stream.   The sheepskin cavalry was driven into the city, a frieze of fourteen impaled citizens was lined along its unbroken lower wall, the city was taken by escalade.   In honour of the royal visit, the name was changed to Kar Sharrukin, the "Wall of Sargon."

Instructions were given Mannu-ki Ninua, the new governor, to go against the Medes.   He reports that the royal officers established peace and returned in safety.   He is building a great house in Kar Sharrukin and bringing the land under cultivation.   The walls will be extended according to the written recommendations.   The Medes round about are quiet and he is carrying on his work.   The king has ordered him to go to the aid of Sharru-emuranni, governor of Lulume.   The son of Ludu is to direct him, but no one is to be permitted to see him, since he is one of the supposed enemy.   This manœuvre has been successfully executed, and he is now back at the capital.   His royal master has demanded what he meant by not sending the grain; his reply is that the rains fall continually and the grain in consequence is cut off from the granary.

There is news of Dalta.   The people of Zabgaga have left his house and are now with their brethren.   Mannu-ki Ninua, therefore, went to their town and imposed the oath upon them. The governorship has been restored and they are at peace, but they have besought him about the city of Zabgaga.   Nabu-bel-ukin has been placed over them, and the governor has ad-

[1] H. 136; 526.

vised them: "As Nabu-bel-ukin has poured out the libation
at the time of the oath-taking, I will watch over you and your
words, I shall summon the men before the king.   Whatever
news they hear of these people, they will send to me."   The
men are to attend to the welfare of the messengers and are to
receive clothing and silver rings in return.   They say: "The
king has given us command, before the governor we stand."
The city of Sanir has likewise taken the oath, and he spoke
kind words to them, such as the king his lord loves.   As for
those who would not come down to take oath, their brethren
have promised that they should be forced to descend.

Fifteen of the fifty soldiers who went to Nikur before him
are dead, but they went from the houses of the enemy and
took cattle and sheep.   When raiders started out from the
Median country, he learned of it, and sent for aid to the Mannai
and Mazamua, yet the king has chided him: "Seize the for-
agers."   The king should know whether he is careless or
whether he has executed his tasks.[1]

Details of the campaign of 716 are shown in the reliefs.
A eunuch led the attack, aided by a body of most peculiar
auxiliaries.   Here they have a shirt of fringed cloth with stepped
pyramid ornament on the lower portion.   Under a cap their
hair is short and so is their beard, their girdle is broad, they
wear sandals.   Elsewhere, they have only a strip around their
hips which is adorned with serrated lozenges.   Their bows and
arrows are red, the iron tip is blue, the long quivers are intri-
cately decorated.   An unknown city shows a royal stele inserted
in the wall.

In 714 we begin to hear of Sharru-emuranni of Lulume.   He
insists most strenuously that he is not the son of a village chief,
but a high official; the king has assigned him his position, and
whatever he hears and whatever he sees he will report to the
king his lord.   He has in part stationed his troops as ordered,
but the son of Bel-iddina has refused to take the road with him,
the nobles hold back, only the baser sort went with him; if
the king will only send an official of the mule's stable to go with

[1] H. 126–129; 1008; 556.

him, then will they desert and revolt. As to what the king
has written, "If the horses of which a rumour has arrived fall
into your hands, come and bring them," the merchants of
Kumesa are upright, he is awaiting them. When the sheep
did not arrive, he sent the servants of the king to Kibatki,
the people were terrified and laid down their weapons. When
they send to him, he will put them in a net and bring them to
the king. The king has demanded: "Why have you delayed
and not awaited the governor of Arrapha?" Ishtar-duri has
left Zaban and has taken the road to Parsua. They went up
to Mount Nipur together. He agrees that the son of Bel-
iddina should go with him. Let Nabu-hamatua do the king's
task in repairing the breaches of the royal forts.[1]

Nabu-hamatua has himself received a personal letter from
the governor of the Median country requesting that his messenger bring the people to the palace. He has spoken kindly
words to them and set their minds at rest. But as for the son
of Bel-iddina, he is a scoundrel and a liar, who will not hearken.
In reality, Nabu-hamatua has made the natives abandon their
six forts and has said to them: "Go to, let each man build his
house upon his field, and let him dwell there; let each of you
do his work in his field. Let your hearts make you joyful,
for you are the servants of the king." They are at peace and
do their work, while the king's servants have entered the forts
and have made the watch strong. He has tabulated according to their flesh the five horses Ullusunu handed over to
Asharidu. Three times a year the official of Asharidu of
whom the king inquired has fled from Nabu-hamatua, let them
bring down his land as a district. The king has also inquired
about Bel-ahe the trader, the writer has sent secretly and will
bring him.[2]

Nabu-ahi-iddina is in trouble. The king gave him orders to
transmit to various officials, but there has been little result.
When he informed Nabu-hamatua, and he in turn the chieftains, they refused, since their land had been assigned to the
second officer of Hamban. The king had ordered that fifty-

[1] H. 319; 317; 310–312.   [2] H. 208; 1058.

two riding horses should be given to certain chiefs and the remainder sent on to the king, but they say: "He has asked an
evil thing, they shall all go with us." [1]

Dalta had now changed his policy with the loss of five border
towns to the Elamites; Assyria recovered them for him, and
the letters of Nergal-etir, the chief hostler, show him sending
his horses to the palace, though once he is reported for failure
to pay his dues.[2] He had departed this life by 708, and his
sons Nibe and Ishpabare contested the throne. Nibe called
in the Elamite Shutruk Nahhunte, his brother summoned
Assyrian aid. Ishtar-duri of Arrapha regretted that the
Assyrian troops were few in numbers and scattered in Media,
but they will obey orders. He has observed the heavenly
bodies, and has sent word for troops to take their position with
Marduk-shar-usur. This Marduk-shar-usur has been asked
by the king for news from Nagiu. The king of Elli on his own
initiative declared that Sangibutu has been given to Marduk-
shar-usur. The Assyrian has assured Kibaba: "Your cities
will be cared for, they have been taken away; if you attempt to
attack them or try to overthrow them, I shall fall upon you."
These men have a hundred horsemen and they are continually
opposing the king. Twenty horsemen of Iptu and the remainder of the horsemen of Ishpabare who go with them, they
cannot have.[3]

Four thousand five hundred bowmen were sent from Elam
to garrison Elli, but the seven generals of Sargon won the day,
stormed the capital Marubishta on a high mountain, made
Nibe a prisoner, and placed Ishpabare on the throne. His
revolt a bare six years later is only one indication among many
of the untenable position of the Assyrians in Media. The
attempt to dam back the Median tribes was an impossible
one, but Sargon did what he could, and at least postponed the
evil day.

[1] H. 884.   [2] H. 226 f.; 236.   [3] H. 159 ff.; 174.

CHAPTER XXI

MERODACH BALADAN THE CHALDÆAN

"An ancient nation" the prophet Jeremiah calls the Chaldæans.[1] The prophet was justified, for already they had a respectable antiquity behind them when he delivered his oracle. Modern scholars, however, were not justified in assuming from this statement and from the references in the classical writers that Chaldæa was the earliest name of the alluvium and that the Chaldæans were the earliest inhabitants.

The Chaldæans were an Aramæan tribe who entered Babylonia some thousand years before our era, and who first appear in written history in 851 when Shalmaneser III met in west-central Babylonia a sealand king named Iakinu. His two lone attendants and the scantiness of his tribute marked him as a minor personage, but he gave his name to the "house" of Iakin, which was to be the future title of the Kaldu family. Adad-nirari III found the Chaldæans plundering Babylonia, and shortly thereafter the throne itself was held by Marduk-apal-iddina II (804–802), who bears the same name as the Biblical Merodach Baladan, and was probably one of his immediate ancestors. Certainly to be counted among them was Eriba Marduk (800–760), son of Marduk-shakin-shum, and his own father was Nabu-shum-ishkun (760–747), Eriba Marduk's immediate successor, though later scholars began with him a new dynasty.

Since then, the family had been in eclipse, and when Tiglath Pileser received gifts from Merodach Baladan in 731, only the unusual richness of the objects presented differentiated him from the other Aramæan chiefs. The weaker reign of Shalmaneser V permitted him to extend his machinations far beyond the limits of Iakin in the Sealands and to win the confi-

---

[1] Jer. 5 : 15.

dence of the citizens of Babylon. With the usurpation of Sargon, Merodach Baladan struck, and Babylon was his.

A new era opened in Elam with the accession of Humbanigash I, son of Humbandara, in 742. During his first years, there was peace with Assyria, for the long line of Aramæan buffer states protected Elam from her most dangerous neighbour. These states once reduced by Tiglath Pileser III, the personal union of Assyria and Babylon became an immediate danger; a right instinct assured Humbanigash that it was preferable to fight the battles of Elam on the plains of Babylonia. An Elamite army was hurried to the aid of Merodach Baladan, and when the Assyrians appeared they were driven from the field and the near-by parts of Assyria were ravaged, though Sargon still managed to retain possession of Der. So long as he held it, he might employ it as a base for intrigues with the anti-Chaldæan party or for actual military operations.

Twelve years passed quietly enough in Babylon. Sargon attempts to win our sympathies by the tale of how the Chaldæan usurper imprisoned the leading men and confiscated their property, innocent of crime though they were. Merodach Baladan has his story of lands torn from their rightful masters, of forgotten boundaries and destroyed boundary stones, when the Assyrian enemy devastated the land and there was no king in Babylon. Peaceable folk must have suffered when the alluvium was torn between the two factions.

A nephew of his predecessor, Shutruk Nahhunte II, the son of Intata, who became king in 717, did not alter the Elamite policy. Shamash-bel-usur, governor of Ahi Zuhina, was erecting a temple in his capital Der and complaining that there were no inscriptions for its walls, when news came that he was to prepare a campaign against the Elamite border. The king's first inquiry was why the equipment was not ready, and Shamash-bel-usur had a long tale of woe. When he went to Urzuhina, he saddled a mule and found a stable for mules in one village of Mazamua and in another one for asses. Although, as the king knows, Urzuhina lies in the woods and the road from thence to Arakdi is impassable for riding beasts, yet he made

the trip. No one has come with news from the place whither
the fugitive officials have deserted. The king has declared: "If
you seize the shatammu officials, you will do me a favour." The
liars of Arrapha, a delicate allusion to Ishtar-duri, its governor,
have collected in the house of the chamberlain of the palace and
have set themselves up in it. Now he has brought them together, he protects them. Could Shamash-bel-usur but seize
them, he would bring them to the king's presence. The youths
have revolted against their lords, he will immediately send their
names and bring them before the king. Let them be collected and judged, quickly the troops will tramp them down.
The king should know he is bringing in the fodder from the
storehouse, the ship will not carry it. The king has asked
news of the king of Elam; on the 11th of July he went to Bit
Bunaki, on the 13th he went out to the mountain, and he is
fortifying the strongholds.[1]

The army of Shamash-bel-usur proceeded from Der to the
outposts which Shutruk Nahhunte had fortified against Iatbur,
the stretch of level land at the foot of the mountains, took
towns in Rashi, and drove their inhabitants into Bit Imbi.
A second army cut in between Elam and Babylon and reduced
the swamp tribes preliminary to attack on the home territory
of Merodach Baladan. The fort of Dur Athara commanded
the direct route from Babylon to Susa. Its walls were raised,
a canal drawn about it, but it was taken before nightfall, and
as Dur Nabu became the chief city of the new province of Gambulu.

In the marshes of the lower Uknu, the tribes dwelt in reed
huts among the reed beds; a cash contribution was imposed
over and above the tax of one out of twenty from their flocks.
The Tupliash was dammed and guarded by two strongholds,
but their surrender was forced by starvation. Their land was
made a part of the Gambulu province and their future loyalty
secured by hostages. Of the fate of one, Nabu-zer-ibni, chief
of the Rua, we learn from a letter of Ishtar-duri. He had
been exiled to far-away Damascus, but was brought back by

[1] H. 157; 408; 537; 802; 799.

the king's order and was now in Abdudi under charge of Bel-duri. All his brothers have been brought to confer with him. Attempt has been made to persuade them to flee, but they have refused, and express regret that he had not come before. They will bring about the defeat of Merodach Baladan.[1]

Proclamation is made to the citizens of Babylon. They are begged to speak with their brethren. Truly Babylon is in fear of slaughter. Let them remember their words and speak to their brethren: "The city we shall rescue from the hands of the foe, there will be no destruction." If they speak good words, speak good words to them; if words of evil, then words of evil with them speak.[2]

Merodach Baladan is in Babylon. Nabu-hamatua went with his army to the Litamu and then to the cities of the Dak-kuru. The report which has come from them is not good. When they entered Babylon, so it is said, they slaughtered each other. The ship of the governor of Ashur, Tab-sil-esharra, is stationed at Bab Bitqa and is being used by the abarakku to bring down silver, the ship of the governor of Arrapha is ferrying at Opis and bringing across oil, straw, and fodder. He suggests an exchange of places, especially as the men in the service of the Arrapha governor are already ferrying at Bab Bitqa. Tab-shar Ashur, the architect, has written from the palace: "Let them pass the rivers, let them go to Birtu, let them make a ferry." Arbailai, the third mounted messenger, has arrived with the news that the Tigris has risen so high that he could not bring the stallions. Let them make a bridge there and pitch camp on the ground seen by Arbailai. To-morrow, let them settle their pastures, let them bring over their camp until it is complete. To-morrow, the bridge will be finished and the king can pass over.

The king has advised Tab-sil-esharra that the commander-in-chief is going to Kar Shamash, and the governor of Ashur inquires the reason, since the governor of Arrapha is doing very well, and he himself needs him. The Ituai of the governor of Arrapha are available; a hundred are in Sipte, let fifty go

[1] *H*. 158.   [2] *H*. 571.

with their commander and remain with the carpenters as guard until his return.   Then we find that the Ituai have crossed the river and keep watch in Sinni.   Haldi-usur, the charioteer, whose name shows his Haldian ancestry, has sent a letter about Birtu; he has come with a letter to be forwarded to the king. Twelve days he was held back, now Marduk-shum-iddina has come to his side.[1]

Passing down the west bank of the Tigris, Sargon found his first enemy in Dakkuru.   Complaint came in from the officials in the neighborhood, for the king had not hearkened to their many former words.   All the minor officials of Dakkuru turned to Merodach Baladan with one voice and sent the qadu officer Nabu-li to him.   He brought back with him to Bab Bitqa the shaku and the troops of Iakin.   The shaku and the swordsmen of the Dakkuru, the Aramæans and the infantry of Dakkuru turned to him, the prefects feared and were silent, wailing they heard, to the rear they retreated.   The troops that were formerly with them did not put their booty in order.   They made strong their cities and the king did not await them.   The troops should have gone to Bab Bitqa, but up to now they have not set forth.   Let him take a message from the king to the shaku and to Ana Nabu-taklak as follows: "When I heard of Merodach Baladan, the canal of the sealand I closed, and Hamani, son of Iashumu, with his clan and his Aramæans, in the midst I settled.   Now I send you his troops, let Shaini and the Sealanders who are with you go into the Sealands."   The king has declared that the land of Rabiti has returned and that he has cut off mighty forts, but they reply: "The land of Akkad is not in thy hands."[2]

The position of Merodach Baladan was fast becoming untenable.   Sargon portrays with deep feeling the scene when he learned that he had been betrayed by Elam, how he threw himself on the ground, tore his clothes, and filled the air with his loud lamentations.   The king of Elam had his own troubles and could not come; shut off from his ally, Merodach Baladan could only fall back along the Tigris.

[1] H. 436; 89; 100; 95; 482; 396.   [2] H. 542.

In long procession, the citizens of Babylon and Borsippa, magistrates, trade guilds, artisans, carried to Sargon in his camp of Dur Ladina the greeting of their local deities. The pious monarch graciously received the envoys. New Year's Day was approaching, when some one must seize the hands of Bel. Sargon determined to follow the example of his immediate predecessors. The old canal to Borsippa was restored and again served as festival road on which Nabu might travel to greet his father and lord. On the auspicious first of the new year, Sargon was recognized by the lord Marduk as King of Babylon.

The priests, at least, had no complaint of the new order of affairs. In three years, Sargon gave the Babylonian gods over a hundred and fifty talents of gold and sixteen hundred of silver, not to speak of the bronze, iron, stone, and clothing. He caused burnt bricks to be struck, he built a fortress with tar and asphalt, on the side of the Ishtar Gate, to the bank of the Euphrates in the depth of the water, and he founded Imgur Bel and Nimitti Bel, mountain high, firm upon it. Bits of this old double wall still survive, the earliest existing portions of this famous group of city defences.

One of the helper tribes of Merodach Baladan, the Hamranu, had retreated into Sippar. An Assyrian force was detached from the main army and sent under the qepu of Birtu, Nabubel-shumate, of whom the governor of Ashur has this to report: On the 7th he arrived at Ashur, and when Tab-sil-esharra inquired "Why have you come here?" he replied, "A command came to me from the king: 'The qepus, all of them, have come, before my face they appear; you did not come at the same time. Why is all the land of the Uppai plundered, who has plundered Sippar? Why have you gone out with your servants and carried off the booty?' So," says Nabu-bel-shumate, "on account of this matter I was disturbed and have come." [1]

Sargon was ready to come to grips with his foe in May. Merodach Baladan fell back before his advance to Dur Iakin,

[1] *H*. 88.

his ancestral home, in the marshes of the "Bitter River" at the head of the Persian Gulf, where he prepared to make his last stand. The nomad troops were collected, earthworks thrown up outside the walls, the whole encircled by a canal from the Euphrates. The bridges were torn down and the dam broken to make the country a morass.

Like eagles, the Assyrians crossed the stream and advanced to the attack. The nomads were forced back and a hand-to-hand struggle followed under the walls. Merodach Baladan was wounded in the arm, but his troops resisted to the last and were slaughtered before the gate. Rich booty fell into the hands of the conquerors, including the royal furniture and plate. Three days the city was given over to sack, then it was burned, its towers thrown down, its very foundations torn up, and the place given over to utter ruin. Withal, the prime object of the expedition was unattained; Merodach Baladan escaped to a refuge in the swamps of the extreme south.

Settlement of affairs in south Babylonia was taken up in earnest. The political prisoners from Babylon, Borsippa, Sippar, and Nippur were freed from their confinement in Dur Iakin and were restored to their houses and lands. The captive gods were likewise returned to their cities and new edifices were erected in their honour. Captives from Qummuh were settled along the whole Elamite border; the change from the cool bracing highland to the fever-laden swamps, we fear, must have been fatal to the majority.

While Sargon was in Babylonia he received gifts from Uperi of Dilmun, which lay a distance of thirty double hours, like a fish in the midst of the sea; Dilmun, already known in one of the earliest Shumerian myths of beginnings, is the chief of the Bahrein Islands, whose almost unparalleled heat is compensated by the pearls which are recovered from the shallow waters over the coral reefs. No reference has been found to Uperi, but the inscription which marked the palace of Rimum, servant of the god Enzag, is known.

In the centre of the island are some thousands of mounds, with encircling walls and reaching to the height of forty feet.

A stoned passageway leads to the tomb made of two rooms, one above the other. Huge stones cover the roof and equally huge stones close the entrance. Worthy of special notice is the great use of ivory, pendants, statuettes, the bull hoof of a chair. Ostrich shells were coloured and scratched with rough banded copper. Bones of a horse speak for some sort of sacrifice. The lower chamber had its walls covered with cement, and poles and drapery were used to shroud the dead.[1]

[1] Bent, *Proc. Royal Geographical Society*, N. S., XII, 1 ff.; *JRAS.*, 1880, 192.

CHAPTER XXII

LETTERS FROM THE ARMENIAN FRONT

A CRISIS of an unusually serious character called Sargon from Babylon in 707. The death of Rusash had brought no peace with Haldia; rather, it had produced in his son Argishtish a younger ruler, who was untried in war and anxious for the trial. The opportune moment seemed to have arrived in 712. Sargon was in Babylonia with his best troops and the northern frontier was denuded of soldiers, for of those who had not accompanied their monarch to the south many were engaged in the construction of Dur Sharrukin. Assyria was administered by an untried crown prince, Sennacherib, who had taken up his post at Kalhu, whence he made frequent report to his father.

As part of his duty he was intrusted with the various hostages and ambassadors who came from the subject peoples. Certain Sidonians seem to have been inclined to ignore him, for they made him no report and did not even take their place in the watch of Nineveh, but, as Nabu-eriba informs the king, they wandered about the streets of the city and abode each in the dwelling of his desire. The chiefs of Qummuh were more respectful to the crown prince, but they too evidently thought they could do better by coming to Babylon to behold the king, although Sennacherib did not see the matter in the same light.[1]

Kalhu was far from an ideal station for the crown prince. It was distant from the seat of operations, and reports must be relayed from governor to governor, then to Sennacherib, and finally to Sargon in Babylonia. Such a condition was hardly conducive to efficiency in operation, but it has preserved to us a mass of authentic records which compensate for the complete omission of the events in the official histories.

Our first letters date from the winter of 710–709. Argishtish had already summoned his dependents to his new capital

[1] *H*. 175; 196,

at Argishtihina, which lay on the north side of the Lake of
Van and might therefore be supposed out of sight of the Assyrians. Fortunately, Sargon had a good intelligence service
and rumours soon began to come in. Ashur-risua, former
head scribe of the harem, was at present in charge of the
Tille region. His chief activity had hitherto been the cutting
of beams for Dur Sharrukin. Sha Ashur-dubbu, governor of
Tushhan, farther west, was also engaged in timbering, and the
majority of his men were busied at Dur Sharrukin. Upahhir
Bel, governor of Amedi, had scattered his men inspecting
beams. Tab-sil Ashur was with Kisir Ashur above the Zanani
River and was likewise engaged in logging.[1]

Threats of the coming trouble were frequent. Ishtar-shum-
iqisha writes that the chiefs of Zikirtu have just been in conference with him. They have reported that the Urartians
have come against their land and carried off spoil, and are
about to advance against the Assyrians themselves. Alarmed
by this news, he has taken the silver and has deposited it in
the stronger protection of the forts, while he is sending the
horses away to a safer region. He urgently advises that it be
placed between the eyes of the chiefs, that is, that it be made
perfectly clear to them, for they have spoken rebelliously, saying: "We have not heard concerning the governor." Let the
king ask the deputy chief, for he was present when the report
was given to the turtanu.[2]

Nabu-usalli sends in word that three nobles of Kumai
have come to him and are with the guardsman Mar Ishtar.
They demand that they be taken direct to the king as he has
ordered, for only to him in person will they declare the matter
of the foreign land. They will say nothing to the guardsman,
for they have spoken to the governor and the guardsman and
neither will pay any attention to them or bring them into the
palace.[3]

Ashur-risua was ordered to send spies to T'irushpa (Tushpash), still the most important city in Haldia and the centre
from which raiding armies set forth. He has learned that the

[1] H. 490; 138; 705; 424; 732; 485.   [2] H. 205.   [3] H. 206.

king of Urartu has entered Turushpa and has shut them up. The remaining people who went with him, officers and men to the number of a hundred, have been killed. Ursine has been captured in Turushpa, and his brother, Apli-uqnu, went to the same city. When they did not come near him, he fell upon them. Another missing official was Isaiae; after investigation Ashur-risua can only reply to the king's inquiry that no one could tell whether he was dead or alive. The near approach of the Haldians naturally led to disaffection among the soldiers of Sargon, many of whom had seen their homes destroyed and their relatives killed by the orders of the man who now forced them to fight under his standards. Narage, a captain, plotted revolt, and twenty of his men followed him, but Ashur-risua detected it in time and the rebels were seized.[1]

Another example of disaffection may be seen in a letter from Sha Ashur-dubbu, governor of Tushhan. He had sent two of his captives, two of his underofficers, and six men, seal in hand for authentication, in pursuit of deserters. While on the road they paused at the Haldian border to eat of the supplies they brought with them and were joined by the brother of a certain Shuprian, who partook of their food. This was the most treacherous misuse of the laws of hospitality, for while they were off their guard, they fell into an ambush set by the Shuprian himself. The subalterns and privates escaped the snare and rescued the captains. Ashur-risua has sent them word to establish a military post on the spot; he will investigate and if they are still in his territory, he will lay hands on those highwaymen. He has already occupied the fortress of the Shuprian, but a good part of his troops has been withdrawn to assist in the building of Dur Sharrukin, and the cavalry alone are at his immediate disposal. Let the king send order that the royal Taziru and Ituai should come and guard the timbers which are already prepared, while he is away from headquarters. Following the royal instructions, he has assembled people and a hundred men have been released to bring by the river the five hundred logs freshly cut by the

[1] *H*. 148; 144.

Urartian, the remainder according to their watch he has made stay in the house of their abode, but he fears an uprising. The governor of Pulu has demanded why his brother's messenger has held back.[1]

A certain captain of Ashur-dur-pania was instructed to proceed to the chief of Muturna, which was within his assigned territory. Instead of carrying out his work with his brethren, he was fearful, took fifteen of his fifty men, and went off to Urartu. Meanwhile, Ashur-dur-pania had sent Ilu-dala to gather tribute in Shupria, and now gave him orders: "This captain of fifty of mine is smiting the land and all who enter against him. Overcome his violence, go, he has retreated to Shupria, go." The rebel captain entered Marhuha and the forest of Shupria; Ilu-dala saw him and the prisoners with him. With a hundred shield-bearers from Marhuha, he went against Ilu-dala and attacked him on the road; none of the king's men were killed but he himself was wounded and was forced to return to Marhuha. He has not yet been secured, though they have surrendered the men who claim the king's service.[2]

He has further to report that on the 23d the chiefs of Shupria came to seek letters. The men of the land who were in the service of the king three and four times fled from the service and servitude of the king, they have written each other and have established condition. Since Ashur-dur-pania and his associates have gone out for the king, let him hear them and force the return of the troops that have fled. The king of Urartu has received them, he has given them fields, plantations, and houses, and among those who have bowed down to him are the chiefs who came for the letter. That letter of theirs to the king is not true, let the king hear his servants. Seven men, one and three mules, were with the men who came. Bag Teshub is sick. As to the inspectors, about whom the king has given orders, he has sent sixteen to the palace chamberlain.[3]

The king has made inquiry about the priest of Penza and

[1] *H*. 138; 705.   [2] *H*. 251.   [3] *H*. 252 f.

what the king of Urartu wrote him. He has written: "Peace to Bag Teshub; thou shalt not make a treaty, thou shalt not receive him, I beseech you." Yet he has sent the messenger of Bag Teshub with his own messenger to Urartu. Bag Teshub himself forwards the news of Urartu, the wicked deeds he has heard, the state of Andia, the going into the Mannai land, and the setting up of control in the land of Zikirtu.[1]

News secured from the spies sent into Haldia was forwarded by Upahhir Bel from Amedi. The governor of the Haldian district opposite is in Harda, under the very tip of the barrier range. Opposite the territory held by the messenger, they keep watch from city to city, as far as Turushpa garrisons are established. No immediate attack need be feared, for an intercepted letter from Argishtish to the governor of Harda ordered: "As to the work for which I furnished instruction, do not do it; feed the horses until I send the messenger." Sargon had ordered that the Ituai should hold their land by the bow tenure, their straw and barley should be tax free, they should be counted as fields belonging to true Assyrians. Upahhir Bel withdrew them from inspecting timbers and sent them to fight under the charge of the local chief. His lieutenant and nine of his men were wounded by the bow, while the enemy suffered a loss of two dead and three wounded. The palace Ituai have come back from the Euphrates with his messenger, and have been sent out again with one or two "houses." Let the king send against the princes, let them keep watch in Shuruba, so that by harvest they may be conquered. He informs the crown prince that he has ordered out a certain governor, telling him: "We are your protection, for your part seize the fortresses." His collected troops are with him and he keeps watch in Harda.[2]

Gabbu-ana Ashur entered his province of Kurban the 16th of July. The 20th of the next month, he informs the king that he was about to send a record of the men to be requisitioned to the other governors, Nabu-li, Ashur-bel-dan, and Ashur-risua. Nothing has been neglected; the task has been exe-

[1] H. 139; 215.　　　　　　　　　　[2] H. 201; 424; 548.

cuted in every particular; nothing has been omitted. The latest news is that the Urartians have not yet left Turushpa. The king has promised him that the men who belonged to Arzai shall be in his charge, in so far as they are listed in the appropriate tablet. They have all fled and come over to the side of the king. He has sent all his chopped straw to Dur Sharrukin, and now there is not enough for two soldiers. As for the reeds, though they are plentiful, whenever the guard sees a prospect of booty, he neglects the feasts.[1]

While Argishtish remained in Turushpa, carrying on his sacrifices and with his governors all around him, the Mannai in the Haldian cities on the shores of Lake Urumia revolted and Ashur-risua sent Ana-luqunu, governor of Musasir, and Tunnaun, governor of Karsitu, to their border to garrison the revolted cities. Ten governors are co-operating with Ashur-risua. The messenger of the Ukkai went up to the land of Urartu, he came down to Assyria, and now is in Musasir. "These statements are truly so," he urges the abarakku, "and whatsoever there is in this letter to the palace I shall send it. These are trustworthy reports which I send to my lord."[2]

The year's events had been most favourable to Haldia. Mutallu of Qummuh had been drawn away. Although the Haldian king had failed to move from his capital, his troops had secured important accessions and disaffection was widespread. The operations of 708 were no more calculated to restore confidence. At the beginning of April, Argishtish moved out at last. His turtanu, Qaqqadanu, in charge of the border opposite the Ukkai, went with four other generals to Uesi, whence they were preparing to invade territory actually within the Assyrian limits. Meanwhile, Argishtish was collecting other armies. Their troops were already in garrison.[3]

A letter from Ashur-risua was received by Tab-sil-esharra; it arrived at Ashur on the 6th at evening and immediately he forwarded the news to the king. The Ukkai messenger has gone to Urartu, the Ukkai themselves have taken the oath to Arne. His city has come over to him, and proclaims the tablet

[1] *H.* 121 ff.   [2] *H.* 381; 619; 145.   [3] *H.* 492; 444.

of the Ukkai at the entrance of the cities of Kumai and Eliski. The Ukkai have come and are settled in it. Tab-sil-esharra has levied troops, but he has not yet learned where they are needed. Ashur-risua replies that Are and Arisa have directed their weapons against him, but have not yet set their troops in motion; when they begin, he will be warned by his messengers. Let his correspondent send the Ituai of Dur Shamash and the men of Parza Nishtun, let these be the ones to go up, let them be set free. As to the fifty soldiers offered from the city of Ishtar-duri, let them be ordered to Shulmu-bel-lashme.[1]

Sennacherib sends a long despatch to his father, quoting the pertinent portions of several letters addressed to himself. Ariae repeats the orders of the Urartian king to his governors: "With the troops in your hands seize the governors of the Assyrian king in Kumai and drag them before me." They have not yet succeeded in cutting them off, but Ariae is very anxious and begs that troops be quickly forwarded. On the 11th of September came a letter from Ashur-risua. When the men of Zikirtu brought gifts to the king of Urartu, they received nothing in return, but went back empty. Now he is in Uesi, at the exit from Haldia. The Mannai have come but they brought no definite information. The governor he appointed is not in Uesi and the Haldian king has been driven out of the city. He avoided the main roads and they have repaired the bridges. The men of Arzapia have requested Sennacherib to withdraw the Ukkai from before them, asking: "Why should he slay me? I call upon you for aid." Sennacherib despatched his own body-guard against the Ukkai, but they and the Mannai have sent messengers to Kalhu.[2]

News of Urartu is also sent by Bel-iddina. Messengers from Andia and Zikirtu have entered Uesi; they have reported to the Haldian king that the land of Assyria is opposed to them. He has gone against them in Zikirtu with his troops and with the Hubushkians in five divisions. He has also inquired of his nobles as to whether their troops are prepared.[3]

Before the winter closed in, while Argishtish was still in Uesi,

_____
[1] H. 101; 147.   [2] H. 198.   [3] H. 515.

he had ordered against Musasir a body of three thousand foot-
soldiers, accompanied by baggage camels, under Setinu, the
governor who had been located opposite Ashur-risua.   They
crossed the Salmat River and joined with Suna, the governor,
opposite the Ukkai.   Upon this, the Assyrian chamberlain
wrote to Urzana, who had regained his throne in Musasir since
Sargon had invaded his fastnesses, and asked him whether the
king of Urartu had moved with his troops, and if so, where he

Fig. 105. SEAL OF URZANA, KING OF MUSASIR.

was staying.   Urzana replies with a missive which can only
be called impudent.   For salutation, he barely condescends to
give a perfunctory "Peace to thee."   To the question as to
whether Argishtish had retired with his army, he answers with
the one word "Gone."   "Where is he staying?"   The governors of Uesi and the Ukkai came to Musasir to sacrifice in
the Haldia temple and they say that the king has gone off and
is staying in Uesi.   As for himself, the governors have met,
they have come, they have offered sacrifices in Musasir, and
Urzana implies that this is the end of the matter as far as he
is concerned.   As to the chamberlain's order, "Without permission of the king of Assyria let no man put his hand to the
temple ceremonies," Urzana flippantly replies: "When the king
of Assyria comes, should I be hostile to him? What I have
always done, that shall I do; as to that, how should I be hostile?"   In other words, the king of Assyria has always acknowl-

edged the autonomy of Musasir, and in this status its king will remain, neutral between the warring parties.[1]

To Sargon he was less belligerent. The king knows from the reports that there are no cattle or sheep. He has seized the roads in the reed thickets and is awaiting patiently the expected Assyrian support, but no one comes. He cannot appear before the king, but those who fled from him are there, so that he is in the enemy land. The pious hope that the gods will conquer Sargon's enemies and establish his dominion over the lands closes the letter. Sennacherib, at least, knew better, for the frontier garrisons had sent him the information that Urzana, his brother, and his son, had all gone to the Haldian king to seek his peace. Shulmu Bel locates him at Alammu; this was half-way between Uesi and Nineveh, and on the direct road, a position threatening to Assyria.[2]

Barely had the spring campaign of 707 begun when Argishtish was suddenly called north by a terrible danger which now began to threaten the civilised countries of western Asia. Another branch of that Iranian race which already so hardly pressed the eastern border of Assyria had poured across the Caucasus. Striking out from their "Cimmerian darkness," the Gimirrai, as the Assyrian called them, struck the Haldian frontier obliquely on their way to Cappadocia. Thus seated, they could on the one hand fall upon Phrygia or the rising power of Lydia; on the other, Assyria or Haldia might be attacked. The last felt the presence of the barbarians most severely, and Argishtish determined to stop them before they actually crossed his boundary. At first the Haldians enjoyed a certain success, and forced payment of tribute from Guriana in the Tabal region.[3]

The advantage did not long remain on the side of Argishtish. Soon after he entered the Cimmerian land, in May, the decisive battle was fought. Ashur-risua, Nabu-li, and the Ukkai reported the news to Sennacherib, who sent the abstracts on to his father. Argishtish fled from the battle-field to Uasaun, and thence to the mountains, where he hid alone; his turtanu,

[1] H. 409.   [2] H. 768; 197; 891.   [3] H. 146.

Qaqqadanu, was made prisoner, nine of his governors were done to death, and included among them was the governor of Uesi, the great frontier post. "A great slaughter has taken place, now his land is quiet." The whole of Urartu is exceedingly afraid because of the men of the cities of Pulu and Suriana; they are assembling troops and they say: "Our forces at once become like reeds, shall we set foot against him?" [1]

Anxious to regain Assyrian favour, Urzana passed on the news to the deputy of that same chamberlain he had not long since flouted, and it finally reached Sargon through the intermediary of Ashur-risua and Sennacherib. The Assyrians made capital of the defeat, and we have a rather sharp royal word to Nabu-dur-usur, without greetings or even the statement of the king's peace. Sargon has just sent Mannu-ki Ashur, the guardsman, to the Urartian leaders, and Nabu-dur-usur is to hand over "those prisoners who eat before you" to the guard who will bring them to Urzuhina; he is also to write down their sum on a tablet. Let the women be located in Arrapha, let them supply grain and fodder for the beasts of burden. [2]

Roused by the news, Sargon left Babylon in 707, and the next year, old as he was, he took the field in Tabal. His death is shrouded in mystery. In 705 he marched against Eshpai, the Kullumite, ruler of a petty land near Elli on the eastern Assyrian border; his camp was taken, and he himself met his death. Such was the obscure end of the greatest of Assyrian rulers.

[1] *H.* 112; 197; 646. [2] *H.* 1079; 306.

CHAPTER XXIII

SARGONSBURG

Sargon's annals follow Assyrian forms and give us military history; his city and his archives open to view a culture which was as worthy of observation. Military reforms did indeed play an important part in his reign. The low chariot of the earlier period gave way to one much higher, and carrying three instead of two fighting men. Bowmen appear first in this reign as the most important element in the infantry. "Troops of the feet," the royal body-guard of cavalry under the leadership of Sin-ahi-usur, were more and more used in emergencies in place of the provincial levies, and individual members were often sent on confidential errands. The feudal levy of the people in arms had proved a failure, and to Sargon belongs credit for frank recognition that a standing army was demanded. After a state was brought to an end, the usual procedure was to enroll the forces of the deposed prince in the royal army.

Provincial organisation had ceased development and became fixed; the reign contributes much to our knowledge of the imperial free city. Ashur was given a charter, yet we find a governor, Tab-sil-esharra, formally set over it. How the new freedom worked may be perceived from a letter he wrote the king in answer to an inquiry about rebuilding. Since the king freed Ashur, he has been responsible for the dues. When the walls of the palace at Ekallate collapsed, they were not repaired; he would now undertake the restoration of the breaches. Shall they summon the bought slaves or the freemen of the palace chief? He is forwarding the register of the bought slaves and of the sons born to the maids in the palace. Three hundred and seventy are serfs, subject to corvee, ninety are their sons, the same number belong to the side palace. Let a hundred and ninety do the king's labour. If a body-guard or a guard commander come, he will furnish these men to them that they may perform the king's work.[1]

Even better does Harran illustrate Sargon's worldly religion. Like Ashur, it was an old capital, and like Ashur it was granted a charter. Nabu-pashir seems to have been Sargon's personal representative, and we have a number of letters from him. For example, on the 17th Sin went out from the city and entered his New Year's House; the royal offerings were made in peace. When Sin re-enters the temple he will dwell in peace and bless the king. The treasures of Sin under seal are sixty-six pounds of gold and much silver. The king has written about the casting down of the god's emblems; there has been destruction, there is no funeral pile, and no putting out of its burning. When they make the funeral pile they are troubled; they will make a lower structure. Sargon's architect, Tab-shar Ashur, discusses the divine symbols of Sin at Harran. At this time, too, Sargon presented Sin of Harran with a manorial estate. Later he changed his mind, took it away, and used it for his own purposes. Thereupon, says a later king, Sin made the Assyrians to suffer.[2]

Industry was in a bad way, and we hear of decaying villages, of agricultural apparatus out of commission, of canals choked up and unfit for use. All this Sargon tells us he changed. The villages he rebuilt, the canals he opened, the waters he restored were a very real blessing to the country. Civilisation was once more becoming complex, and the rise in prices was accentuated by the large amount of the precious metals brought in by the wars. Sargon, entirely ignorant of economic laws, naturally assumed the increase in the cost of living was due to conspiracy on the part of the Aramæan merchants into whose hands the internal trade of the empire had fallen. One of his proudest boasts is the promulgation of a tariff that made the necessities of life accessible to all—wine for the sick, incense for joy of heart, oil for wounds, while sesame was to sell at the same price as grain. One wonders just how much this edict of the benevolent despot improved the lot of the proletariat.

[1] H. 99.   [2] H. 134; 131 f.; 701; 489; Johns, PSBA., XL, 117 ff.

First of Assyrian kings, so far as we know, Sargon began the formation of a library. Tablets exist with his library mark, and others were written in his reign. To one scholar or patron of scholars, Nabu-zuqup-kini, we can attribute several. The great astronomical work, *When Anu, Enlil, etc.*, forecasts, observations of the moon and stars, prayers, cult directions were included, and there began the renewed interest in the legends of the elder Sargon. The influence of all this literature was soon felt, and the official histories are as far from the dull routine style of the last Tiglath Pileser as can be imagined. The extreme of rhetorical writing is reached by the report of the eighth campaign, and Sargon so appreciated the artistry of this effort that he permitted Nabu-shallimshunu to attach his name to his composition.

Sargon's capital was movable. At first he resided in Ashur, repaired the walls, paved the side temple, and covered the ramp and sides with glazed and pictured bricks, azure blue in ground, yellow rosettes in circles, the centre a projecting and pierced bulb, blue with a white ring. Then he moved to Kalhu and restored the palace of Ashur-nasir-apal, which later he handed over to the crown prince. The middle period saw Sargon at Nineveh and restoring a temple to Nabu and Marduk.

Finally, he determined to found a city which should bear his name. An appropriate site was found at Maganuba, a half-ruined town to the northeast of Nineveh, at the foot of the barren Musri hills. The soil was largely clay, thus furnishing a good and cheap building material. The ground was fertile and trees were then more frequent—palms, olives, figs, and oranges, according to the reliefs. Near by were alabaster quarries, from which slabs for the sculptures might be taken. The waters are strongly charged with sulphur, perhaps an additional advantage in the eyes of an aging ruler.

Three men had been made a grant of the land by Adad-nirari III; in return for the desired site, Sargon gave the owners ninety-five *imers* of land in a priestly city near Nineveh, on the same easy terms as the original grant, ten imers of barley to Ashur and Bau. Those who would not accept an exchange

FIG. 106. DUR SHARRUKIN, CAPITAL OF SARGON.
The temple tower is seen to the left, the gates of the city to right.

FIG. 107. THE HILL OF OPHEL. (EARLIEST JERUSALEM.)

of land were not so fortunate; they were paid in cash, but at
the original cost of the estates, the title-deeds furnishing the
evidence.   In view of the marked decrease in the value of the
precious metals, this worked an undoubted hardship; we may
be sure the wise preferred to receive their pay in land.

City and palace were the work of Tab-shar Ashur, the chief
architect, who as great abarakku had been eponym in 717.
The city was laid out in the form of a rough rectangle, nearly
two thousand yards on the side, and was oriented with its corners approximately to the cardinal points.   Up to the city led
a roughly paved road, forty feet wide, which was continued
within the gate as a street of the same dimensions.   On one
side of the roadway was a half-circle and a stele used as a
mile-stone.

Around the whole rectangle was a high wall, its base of rub-
blework between two stone facings, the upper portion of un-
baked bricks.   The poor building material made them of necessity enormously thick, over eighty feet in all.   More than
a hundred and fifty towers studded the walls, which were
pierced by eight gates bearing the names of the eight great
Assyrian deities.   Three were used for vehicles; the others for-
bade wheeled traffic by steps in their midst.   Huge winged
bulls with human heads guarded the entrance; above the arch
were enamelled bricks, within were slabs carved with the figures bearing palm spathes and baskets.   Under each gate, on
a bed of sand, was hidden away a large number of cheap
trinkets, amulets, figures of menacing spirits, and the like,
while the roof was vaulted above with crude bricks, a piece of
work calling for no small skill.   Here the peasants would pass
in with their produce or expose it for sale in the cool halls, the
venders of sweetmeats or of snow-cooled drinks would be on
hand, inquisitive citizens would congregate to learn the news
from the front or the latest court gossip.   Here, too, were soldiers on guard and the judge, ready to expose the unfortunate
captive to the jeers of the idle mob or to consign him to the
lightless prison-hole sunk in the midst of the wall.

Construction had its difficulties.   The king demanded of

Tab-shar Ashur why the governor of Arrapha had neglected the half of the gate assigned him. Tab-shar Ashur hastened to the spot on the third day and was requested by the governors of Kalhu and Arrapha to arbitrate their differences. If the king should ask the details, the former is to be under the approach to the "Great Gate" and thence to the "Rejoicing of the People." The portion of the other is to be for twelve hundred feet, to the foundation of the "Shining Gate." That disposes of the wall to the middle of the gate and the remainder is assigned, three hands to the governor of Arrapha and one to him of Kalhu in co-operation. He has done this on his own initiative, though he has had no direct orders from the king, but each of the governors has accepted his arbitration and is at work on his appropriate assignment.[1]

Little has been preserved of the city proper. Its long, straight streets crossed at right angles, there were no sidewalks, but the roadway was paved. They were lined with long, staring walls of mud brick, with scarcely a break for window or door; once within, there was more life in the courts, perhaps even gardens, but of the town life, whether of temple or of bazaar, we have little trace.

The palace was the one reason for the existence of Dur Sharrukin and the one survival of importance. Ships were sorely needed for the transport of the material to be used. Tab-shar Ashur is asked by the king why the necessary ships have not been completed by the beginning of the month, since all the months are now ended, while the ships remain incomplete. He has already written the king that three of the ships will be complete by the 1st of March, four more like them by the 1st of the next month, and these seven are already sheathed. On the first day they left the palace they arrived at Ubase. The ships are safe. On the second day they guarded the gods of the king and entered in safety.[2]

A whole group of letters deal with the cutting of logs in the northern hills, and the governors, who were soon to be engaged in the Armenian wars, are frequently led to complain that all

[1] *H*. 486.   [2] *H*. 330; 433.

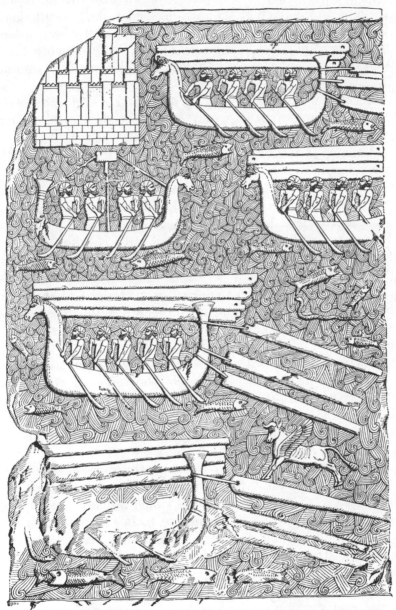

FIG. 108. BRINGING CEDAR FROM THE LEBANON.

their men are busy in the forests cutting down trees, floating them down the river, or actually engaged in the construction of Dur Sharrukin. Tab-sil-esharra, for example, has been ordered to number and send living logs, and the total reaches fifteen thousand two hundred sound logs and thirteen thousand one hundred and fifty-seven which are old or worm-eaten. Sha Ashur-dubbu writes from Tushhan that his men are now at Dur Sharrukin, and asks that other officials help him guard his timber till its removal thither.[1]

Armenia furnished the beams for the main structure; for the roofs Sargon went to the Lebanons for the sweet-smelling cedar which tradition had long since made the royal wood. Before us the reliefs depict the sea, and beside its natural scaly denizens float winged bulls, human-headed lions, and the sea-god Ea, with half-fish, half-human form. Ships with horsehead bows and fish-tailed sterns skim about with mast upright and oarsmen sculling without oar-locks, or return with their decks laden with the heavy planks or dragging them in the water behind. High towers on a hill projecting into the sea represent Old Tyre, a double wall of good ashlar marks the island home of the later city. Huge beams are piled on the rocky shore by labourers with skirts tucked high, though elsewhere they wear long dresses with tassels, short-sleeved overdresses, and laced boots. Their head-dress is wound tight around the head, permitting short curls to escape, their very short beards are continued to their ears. Beside the timber, they present cups, sacks, or models of their cities.

Large quantities of stone must be transported. Tab-shar Ashur speaks of the bringing of stone colossi in six ships, or replies to an inquiry as to blocks which are to be carried by water. He complains of the failure to furnish him with carpenters, potters, and workmen. Gabbu-ana Ashur asks that the three stone thresholds and the stone colossi of the protecting deities be sent him, since his men have no work to do.[2]

The palace stood on a platform situated on the line of the western city wall and extended partially outside. Erected in

[1] H. 92; 138.   [2] H. 103; 105; 125; 1065.

FIG. 109. WINGED GENIUS. GLAZED BRICKS OF
ARCHIVOLT. (PALACE OF SARGON.)

FIG. 110. WINGED GENIUS. (Louvre.)

Fig. 112. GILGAMESH AND THE LION. (PALACE OF SARGON.) (Louvre.)

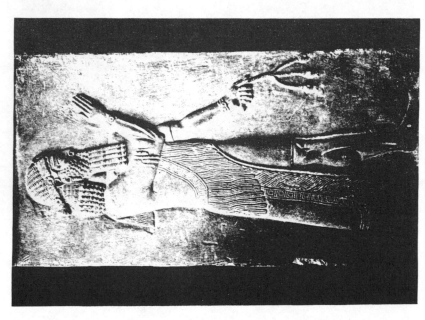

Fig. 111. FIGURE OFFERING. (PALACE OF SARGON.) (Louvre.)

imitation of Babylonian models, it had more practical justification. It was the most difficult part of the city for the enemy to assail, and it was a refuge from a possible revolt of the
heterogeneous collection of captives settled within. The huge
mass was not a mere lump of earth, but was constructed of
carefully prepared crude brick with a well-executed drainage
system. The pressure of this enormous body was resisted by
a retaining wall of massive, well-dressed stone, some of whose
blocks weighed over twenty tons and were laid with mathe-
matical accuracy. On the city side a ramp probably ascended
to the parapeted top.

On this elevated mass was a series of buildings, large enough
to contain the population of a fair-sized town, with their fourteen courts and eighty-seven rooms. There were two main
entrances, the one which faced the city in the style of the city
gates, but more elaborate, the central archway flanked by great
bulls and adorned with tiling. This triple gateway was the
ancestor of the triumphal arch.[1]

Around the largest of the courts were storerooms, each with
a tiny cell for its keeper. In some were iron implements,
pottery, or similar supplies; others contained foodstuffs or
drinkables preserved in jars whose pointed ends rested in supports. A sudden rain during the excavations revealed to the
astonished workmen wine more than twenty-five centuries old.
Near by were the kitchens, where cooking was carried on under
conditions much the same as in the East to-day. Rows of jars
turned on one side contained the fire, the bread was baked by
plastering the dough on the outside, or the fire was removed
and the meat sealed inside, an anticipation of our fireless
cookers.

Not far off were the stables and the open courts where the
horses were hobbled to rings in the pavement. The keeper of
these royal stables under Sargon was Nergal-etir, who is constantly reporting the arrival of horses and mules and their
general condition. Among them are horses from Barhalza,
Arabians; horses from Elli, whence came later the famous Nis-

---

[1] Breasted, *Proc. Amer. Hist. Assn.*, 1914, I, 107.

sæan breed; horses of Asia Minor or north Syria, the famous Cappadocian stock, small but sturdy; great horses from Egypt or Ethiopia.

Entering through a still more magnificent gateway, one found oneself in a court somewhat smaller than that of the servants and adorned in the same style, but more richly. Various gateways opening out from it were guarded by the human-headed bulls, but between them stood a figure of the ancient hero, Gilgamesh, whom courtly belief held the ancestor of the reigning monarch. Clad in royal garments and with hair and beard elaborately curled, in his right hand he holds the sacred boomerang and his left clutches a snarling lion to his breast. Around the walls of this main court are the scenes representing the king with his chief officers, the securing of timber for the palace construction, the sacred winged figures with palm spathe and basket. A long passageway filled with figures of tributary Phœnicians and Medes, their chiefs bearing models of turreted cities, has on its right rooms with reliefs illustrating the famous swing around the circle of 714. We cross the corner of a still smaller court, turn to the left, and pass through three long, narrow rooms, which show respectively scenes of punishment, the Syrian campaign, and the banquet.

These were the richly adorned public rooms where the king received his prisoners for punishment, his vassals to accept gifts, his officials for consultation. Near the centre of the platform and as retired as possible were the private apartments of the king. Their simple, unpretentious character speaks in no uncertain terms of the almost Spartan simplicity affected by the warrior king.

Skirting along the wall to the southwest, one came to the third quarter. Two doors at right angles prevented even a glimpse into the interior to the casual passer-by, and a servants' court was another obstacle before one might reach the grand central court. Opening into this last were two suites of rooms, entirely isolated and each with its own smaller courtyard; a third suite opened directly into the servants' court. It has been generally assumed that this carefully shut-off quarter was the harem, that the two suites of rooms belonged to Sargon's two wives, and that the third was for Zakutu, wife of Sennacherib.

The central enclosure is rich with tiling and remarkable for sculptures in the round, horned gypsum figures of the gods, clad in enveloping robes and with slabs on their heads. If they are gods, then we may stress the resemblance in ground plan to the Ashur temples; if we do so, then we assume the temples more carefully shut off than the harem. Also, we still have a fourth quarter devoted to the priesthood, around the temple tower, a solid mass of brick nearly a hundred and fifty feet high. Each of its seven stories bore the colour of the planet to which it was dedicated, around it ran a ramp of easy ascent, and on its summit were two altars on which sacrifices were offered. Near by was a small temple with basalt reliefs, and other buildings for the private quarters of the priests, scribes, and physicians. The temples were all endowed and Tab-sil-esharra writes of a town in Halah which was to be an endowment of the Nabu temple at Dur Sharrukin; Hebrews had just been settled here and they may well have been among the serfs on Nabu's manor.[1]

Outside the city lay the great park, also under the charge of the chief architect, Tab-shar Ashur. As in the case of the wall, the officials attempted to scamp their work, and Tab-shar Ashur has to report that Paqaha has brought his own men to restore the canal, but the radianu who was to have collected men for the corvee has not turned up. So he has taken a hundred of his own to carry on the whole for a month. Let the king force the negligent one to a reckoning. He has one piece of good news, the governor of Rimusi will shortly arrive with three thousand men.[2]

By the side of a tiny lake filled with fish and bearing two equally tiny pleasure-boats rises a little building of almost purely Greek character. On a high podium is a dystyle temple with antæ. The columns are unfluted, but the torus and fillet which form the base and the convex necking, volute, and

[1] H. 480.　　　　　　　　　　[2] H. 102.

abacus of the capital are purely Ionic.   The plain epistyle is crowned with a wide cornice whose overhang is unusually pronounced.   The flat roof must have been covered with tiles, for palmette-shaped antefixes appear above the cornice.   Such a building is totally un-Assyrian, and it must have been borrowed from the Greeks direct and recently, so exact is its form. Is it possible this is the "Hittite" bit hilani, the so-called porch, about which Tab-shar Ashur writes in connection with the housekeeper of the bath-house? [1]   The term "Hittite" was in these late days applied especially to north Syria, and Sargon received tribute from near-by Greek kings of Cyprus.

Fig-trees with purplish fruit and reddish leaves surround the foreign structure and give place to tall firs as a hill is reached. Within the recesses partridges walk, and on the summit is a monument on a high podium, with channelled column, rectangular and channelled entablature, above which are stepped acroteria.

Sargon hurries in his chariot towards the park.   In his hand is a blue lotus and two buds, and his red-striped parasol covers his red-striped fez.   Spearmen and mace-bearers march before, his two beardless sons and their mounted attendant gallop after.   Next struts the master of the hunt, a mace stiffly held over his right shoulder, his left holding his sword horizontal with equal stiffness.   The dismounted servant now quiets his master's young stallion and retains the hare, which is the proof of the youth's archery; the royal prince has transfixed a flying bird and is now drawing bow at the target, whose bull's-eye, or, rather, lion's head, he has neatly pierced.

In the banquet-room of the palace twenty-eight of the highest nobles, four to the table and in their richest dress, raise high the capacious goblets as they drink the toast to their royal master.   The tables are lion-footed over pine-cones, table-cloths cover each, and rich food is placed upon them. Their seats to us would be uncomfortable, for they have no backs, but the ringed feet and the bronze heads of bulls at the corners give them decoration.   A eunuch with fly-flapper

[1] *H*. 487.

Fig. 114. THE ROYAL STUD. (PALACE OF SARGON.) (Louvre.)

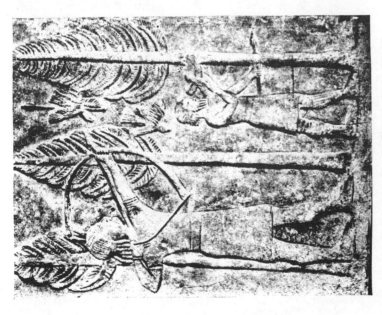

Fig. 113. ASSYRIAN ARCHERY. (PALACE OF SARGON.) (Louvre.)

FIG. 115. GARDEN SCENE: THE "IONIC" TEMPLE.

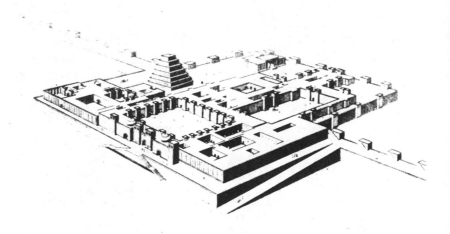

FIG. 116. PALACE AT DUR SHARRUKIN. (RESTORATION.)

In front is the royal gateway and service court, to left the "harem," to right the official
quarters, in the rear the temple tower.

stands behind each group of two, affording the feasters royal state. Four officials less richly dressed but carrying thonged maces have deposited the remains of their feast on the floor and drink their toast standing. Music is contributed by a harper who carries by a broad belt slung over his left shoulder an eight-stringed instrument, much like the Greek lyre. Tracing back the eunuchs, who carry in each hand one of the large-handled drinking-cups ending in a huge lion's head with open jaws, the ancestor of the Greek rhyton, we find them dipping into the source of supply, a huge mixing-bowl set on a cone with convex slope topped by a reversed rosette.

Sargon and the men who walked his halls are presented with almost photographic truth. On his head the monarch wears the golden tiara studded with red jewels; it is much like the modern fez, but with a stiff spike instead of the tassel. At the back fringed red ribbons with rosettes fall nearly to his waist. His chief garment is a long robe ornamented with rosettes inside squares and fringed at the bottom with four rows of beads. Over it is a mantle with opening down either side, with double rosettes and fringe. The sandals have heels with red and blue stripes and are held in place by a toe thong and a strap over the foot. His broadsword is ornamented with lions and he also carries a staff. His bracelets are of linked rosettes, his armlets of coiled wire, his earrings are beaded. The turtanu, Ashur-isqa-danin, is dressed much like his master, save that his head has only the fillet, his sandals are blue, his sword is tipped by a hemisphere, a ball with flat disks, and a lion's jaw. Did we know the exact order of precedence at this time, we might identify by name the other six officers who regularly appear on the walls by the side of their lord.

A special place is always given to the eunuchs. All wear robes extending from neck to ankles, with rosettes in squares along the lower portion, with fringes and beads, their sleeves are short, a diagonal fringed band crosses their chest, their sandals are flat, their bracelets bands of wire, their earrings imitate the Egyptian symbol of life. The objects they carry are equally to be noted, fly-flappers ending in lions' heads, the feathers inserted in a lotus-bud, napkins red with the Phœnician "purple," bows ending in the heads of birds, maces with wrist-loop and topped with a ball, a crown, and the jaws of a lion.

Dur Sharrukin enables us to realise the great advance in art made during the period. The artistic ability of the nation had been almost ruined in the period of decline, but with Tiglath Pileser III we have a change for the better. Assyrian art found its highest expression in its bas-reliefs; they extended for a mile along the walls of Sargon's palace, and their beauty is undeniable. A new experiment, or, rather, the revival of an older method under the influence of Hittite Carchemish, was attempted, the use of basalt for the oversoft alabaster, but it was soon abandoned. Vivid colours, in accordance with the general rule in ancient art, were used to bring out the details. Sculpture in the round is rare; a good example is the figure bearing the plinth, and the twenty-six human-headed bulls, each weighing forty tons, were half in the round. Only fineness of finish could avail here, for the general outline, even to the fifth leg, was ordained by the accepted canons of art; comparison with similar figures from the palace of Ashur-nasir-apal shows a wonderful increase in lifelikeness.

Painting was placed directly on the crude brick wall, and but one or two fragments afford some slight conception of an art little inferior to the reliefs. Tiling has always been a specialty of the Near East, and some of its finest specimens may be found in the palace of Sargon. On the gates we have courses where figures with the mystic palm spathe face each other across a circular ornament intended for the sun, the whole enclosed within rows of conventionalised white and yellow daisies. Other friezes in tile show conventionalised but vigorous lions, bulls, and eagles, the ancestors of the better-known figures prepared by Nebuchadnezzar for the Processional Road of Babylon. A rude fig-tree and a more complicated plough than the one in use to-day are of more interest for subject than for execution, while the series reaches its highest development in the truly magnificent figures of Sargon and his turtanu.

Their best efforts were no longer lavished on ceramics, for

alabaster, the metals, and glass had relegated mere pottery to a secondary place.   One room showed a complete nest of jars, one within the other, and ranging from pithoi four feet high to tiny pipkins.   Glass, known in Egypt from at least the times of the twelfth dynasty, twelve hundred years before, now appears in Assyria.   One beautiful and elaborate glass bottle was found in a storeroom, the sole perfect survival of a large collection, and Kalhu furnished a fine example with Sargon's name actually upon it.   Babylonian seal cylinders were still being manufactured in large numbers, but the seal impressions on the Assyrian business documents indicate that the stamp seal so common in later times was already beginning to be employed on a large scale.

Metal working was at a high stage.   Fragments of bronze reliefs from the supposed harem, remains of facing on a wooden door, make us regret the loss of a second Balawat history in pictures.   Lifelike bronze lions, miniature replicas of those in the palace of Ashur-nasir-apal, furnish the exact weights used in Assyrian metrology and illustrate a curious bit of economic history.   Previously the Assyrians had employed the heavy mana or double pound, while Babylonia and Syria preferred the light or Carchemish mana, about our own pound.   Other kings had simply tolerated this light mana, but Sargon, conqueror of Carchemish, made it as "royal" or official as the "mana of the land."   Thus possible obstacles to western trade were removed.

Well as they handled copper and bronze, the Assyrians had long ago entered the age of iron; indeed there was an iron furnace in the palace in Ashur.[1]   Much of their success in warfare, as in the arts of peace, was due to the extensive use of the metal.   How commonly it was employed may be surmised from the fact that one storehouse in Dur Sharrukin preserved nearly two hundred tons, all worked up into implements. Among these was a huge iron chain, hammers, pickaxes, mattocks, and ploughshares, of the same sort as used by modern peasants but of larger size.   Some of the picks weighed over

[1] H. 91.

twenty-five pounds, and their peculiar resonance is especially noted.

Rush the building as the architect might try, the construction was slow. The dedication was celebrated in 706 with a great feast, at which the princes of the blood royal, the higher officials, and the scribes were invited guests. Within the year Sargon was no more. His great building venture was left incomplete. One gate was without its bulls, the inscriptions in it were merely painted, the temple was half finished, partially carved slabs were abandoned in the workshop. Natural decay was not permitted to complete the slow destruction. The descendants of Sargon were vandals who no more respected the edifice erected by the founder of their dynasty than they did those of the one he had supplanted. Many of the bas-reliefs have been mutilated beyond hope of recovery, and that by no barbarian's hand, for the mutilation was caused by the chisel of the expert. Many others were carried off to the too-near Nineveh, there to adorn the new abode of Sennacherib.

With its brief glory gone, the city still lingered, and is occasionally referred to. At the downfall of the empire it was burned over and then went to ruin. In the Arab middle ages Sarghun was not quite forgotten, but a new name was coming into use. Persia had twice ruled the world, and the second empire was fast joining the first as the happy hunting-ground of legend. One of the few Sassanid heroes still remembered was Chosrhoes, and to him was ascribed the ruin, now called Khosraubad, the "town of Chosrhoes."

To-day the surly peasants of the vermin-filled little village of Khorsabad pick their way through mud by the aid of bricks bearing the name of Sargon. But for long ages none could read the writing, and the only proof of his existence was due to the accidental fact that a prophet in a petty western kingdom happened to have dated a sermon by the year when his turtanu took Ashdod.[1] So little did this establish his identity, such is the irony of fate, that scholars long argued that he was the same as that Shalmaneser whose throne he had usurped.

[1] Isaiah 20 : 1.

FIG. 117. BRINGING THE TABLES FOR THE BANQUET.
(PALACE OF SARGON.) (Louvre.)

FIG. 118. DRINKING CUPS AND THE STATE CHARIOT.
(PALACE OF SARGON.) (Louvre.)

Fig. 119. CROW AND BULL IN GLAZED BRICKS. (PALACE OF SARGON.)

Fig. 120. TREE AND PLOUGH IN GLAZED BRICKS. (PALACE OF SARGON.)

CHAPTER XXIV

SENNACHERIB AND THE BABYLONIAN PROBLEM

SENNACHERIB was no novice in ruling when in August of 705 he entered upon his inheritance. There is no likelihood that he was born to the purple; he appears so early as heir presumptive and is found in such responsible positions that he must have been in the prime of life at his father's accession. While Sargon was annexing Babylonia, his son remained as regent in Kalhu, and by his conduct of the Armenian operations accustomed men to his personal rule.

All the courage and ability possessed by the new ruler was needed. His father, so the priests informed him, had sinned against the gods and had incurred the curse of the king of the gods, therefore he should not be buried in his own house. The pious son inquired of the oracle and learned what was needed to cleanse his father's sin; the cost was high—elaborate ceremonies, an image of the god Ashur, restoration of Assyrian temples. Sennacherib paid, but thereafter he was more than cool to the priests.

The news that an Assyrian king had fallen in battle brought about an immediate uprising of the subject states. Incited by Egypt, Hezekiah of Judah openly defied Assyria in spite of the threats of Isaiah, and this was typical of the unrest which had gripped all Syria, for even Phœnicia forgot commercial expediency and revolted under Tyre's leadership. Those who still clung to Assyria suffered like Padi of Ekron, who was handed over to Hezekiah by the populace. The Cappadocian province, so laboriously formed by Sargon, slipped away almost without notice. The defeat of the Haldian king laid open the whole northern and eastern frontiers to the Indo-Europeans, and the Medes were driving the Elamites and their kindred towards Assyria. Babylonia remained but half pacified, and, with much of Assyria proper, was infested by Aramæan tribes.

283

Babylonia offered the most pressing danger. Sennacherib refused to follow his father's policy in making himself king, but handed over Babylon to his younger brother, while retaining such control that the king lists could actually call him the ruling monarch. Chauvinistic writers, however, marked the years 704–703 as "kingless." [1]

After two years the Assyrian rule came to an end, and a former official of Merodach Baladan, Marduk-zakir-shum II, succeeded in holding the throne against the attacks of Marduk-bel-ushezib and Marduk-balatsu-iqbi. Merodach Baladan reappeared and retrieved his old position with the aid of Shu-truk Nahhunte of Elam. Six months he was allowed to reign in peace. Then the Assyrian commander-in-chief began the siege of Kish, but received the worst of it and begged aid from his monarch, who was now engaged before Kutu. Urged to haste by this appeal, Sennacherib assaulted Kutu with fire and took it, and forced to surrender Nergal-naṣir, the Sute leader, and ten Elamite captains.

The sculptures of Sennacherib were labelled on the extreme upper edge, and the subsequent burning of the palace has almost without exception destroyed these epigraphs. A scene dominated by a huge river which fills a third of the reliefs may represent the siege of Kutu. Grooms unharnessed the horses and led them down to the water or unyoked those attached to the royal chariot. The charioteer still clung to his reins, and the eunuch was just raising the parasol above the king's head. The skins were being prepared for the raft which was to be used for the crossing. Some of the skins were already inflated and were being brought to the water's edge, others were being blown up and the openings tied. The river was filled with soldiers swimming on their individual goatskins, shield on

---

[1] For history of reign, cf. "Western Asia in the Reign of Sennacherib," *Proceedings of Amer. Historical Assn.*, 1909, 93 ff.; for relations with Babylon, *AJSL.*, XXX-VIII, 73 ff.; bibliography and source criticism, *Historiography*, 43 ff. The greater part of the records may be found in Bezold, *KB.*, II, 80 ff.; the present account is based on the new edition by the author of this history. Valuable supplements are to be found in the bas-reliefs, described by Layard, *Nineveh and its Remains; Nineveh and Babylon;* reproduced, Layard, *Monuments of Nineveh;* Paterson, *Palace of Sinacherib.*

back and spear tightly clasped in hand. While the king remained safe on the near bank, his warriors laid siege to an outpost which was vigorously defended by the archers. Mounted cavalry shot their arrows from horseback, those on foot found refuge behind the high, curving shield, and one infantryman, kneeling under a short wicker shield, dug out stones from the wall. The city proper was guarded by high battlements and lofty stage towers, while five square gates gave access to a smaller stream. The main town fell an easy prey when the outwork was taken, for all the warriors had been concentrated for its defence. Women captives, with filleted hair, long outer robe, and inner shirt, were conveyed on ox-carts, the men wore a fillet and a short tunic fastened at the waist by a broad belt. More than a dozen statues of the gods, some as much as three feet high, their hands raised and a staff in their left fists, were clasped tightly about their waists by the soldiers who removed them.

Sennacherib then hastened to Kish, represented as on the near side of the river and surrounded by a reed-filled ditch, which had been crossed by infantry and cavalry. Behind his huge circular shield, an Assyrian was attempting to fire the city gate with a torch, and the enemy was begging for mercy. Merodach Baladan hastily decamped, but among the captives were his stepson and a brother of an Arab queen.

To Sennacherib, watching the proceedings from the safer side of the river, his soldiers carried the heads of the slaughtered foes and heaped them up in a reed arbour, slung between palm trunks. Here, too, were deposited the caldrons and drinking-bowls, the bed and throne, the spear bundles and swords. One group stands out with unusual vividness, the little calf trotting blithely ahead, the patient cow, the bull hanging back and roaring protest, his head tossed high in air. The male captives were handcuffed in pairs and loaded with skins of food and water for the long march to their new homes; the majority of the women were placed on mules or ox-carts. Our sculptor shows a real sympathy for the deported wretches in the scenes where the mothers hold out the water-skins for their children

to drink or the fathers plod along with their little ones on their
shoulders.   Lest we should fail to realise that the march was
forced in the midst of the fearful Babylonian summer, the

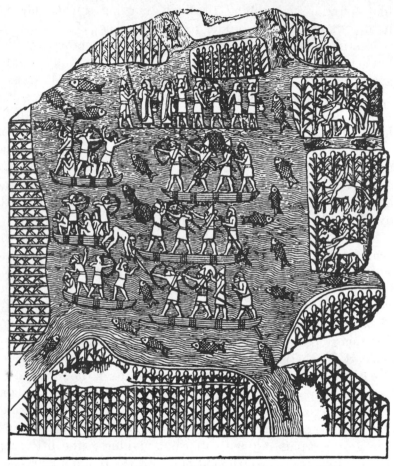

Fig. 121. FIGHTING IN THE BABYLONIAN MARSHES.

artist has indicated the season by the huge clusters of ripe
dates which load the palm-trees.

Babylon, with its accumulated treasures, fell into Assyrian
hands without further fighting.   By this time the Chaldæan
ruler had taken refuge in the swamps whose junglelike recesses

are pictured in the reliefs. Up the watery ways, almost like narrow streets, the startled inhabitants pushed their rafts, squatted behind their reeds, several times man height, or from their shelter shot arrows at their invaders, who pursued them in light wicker boats. In hand-to-hand struggles the enemy were decapitated and thrown to the fishes. One unfortunate was ordered by his captor to swim on a skin and by a rope drag a skiff in which his family was being led into captivity.

Once on firmer ground, the women were bundled into rude four-spoked ox-carts or mounted on asses, the wagons were heaped with furniture, vessels, and weapons. Especially to be noted is a tall casket of some precious metal, battlemented and towered walls resting on rosettes and a primitive sort of Ionic volute, a round column with base, ox-footed legs, the whole on a stool with cone-shaped supports. On their heads the captives carry wicker baskets or large leather water-bottles. Very graceful is the figure of the woman giving a skin of water to her child. An idyllic touch ends the recital, the hungry soldiers roasting a leg of lamb before the fire, and the happy warrior who will diversify his supper by the wild duck he has caught around the neck. After but five days' search in the marshes, it was reported that no trace of the Chaldæan could be found and all pretence of pursuit was abandoned.

Eighty-eight mighty cities and eight hundred and twenty smaller towns of their territory were occupied. One of the few sets which has preserved its label represents Dilbat surrounded by its palm-trees and with a river on either side, but the palms are being hacked down by the Assyrian soldiery. A second depicts the captivity of a riverine tribe, their millet-fields surrounded by reed swamps and palm-trees, their towns graced by a peculiar wedge-shaped ornament on the walls. The captive women bore vases and caldrons, the men large wicker baskets, and some drove ox-carts. These were the tribesmen of the Dakkuru, Saalli, Amukkanu, and Iakin, and we have an elaborate list of their towns; every possible hamlet is given and the still smaller "cities" cited cannot even be farmsteads. That these nomads should be settled in the oldest cities of

Babylonia is the saddest commentary on the degree to which the country had fallen from its former estate.

The attempt to hold Babylon as a separate dependency under the rule of a member of the royal family had proved a failure. Sennacherib was still patient and hoped to win over the dissatisfied Babylonians by giving them a native Chaldæan, Bel-ibni by name, whom he calls "the son of the chief architect, the seed of Babylon," but who in reality seems to have been a member of the family of Merodach Baladan. He had passed the greater part of his life in Sargon's palace in Kalhu, and might therefore be supposed safely pro-Assyrian.

On his homeward way, Sennacherib slew the Hirimme who had never paid tribute to his fathers until not one survived the sword. On the inhabitants who were newly settled in their place was placed the duty of furnishing "forever" one ox, ten sheep, ten homers of sesame wine, twenty homers of fine dates, as the stated dues of the god Ashur. We are a long, long distance from the eighty thousand and fifty oxen and the eight hundred thousand one hundred sheep he claims to have brought back to Assyria.

He is telling the literal truth when he declares that the Iasubigallai were not submissive to the kings his fathers, for six centuries before Arik-den-ilu had taken up arms against them. The Assyrian column passed through lofty wooded mountains, where the king must mount a horse while his chariot was carried on men's backs, and there were spots where the king must climb on his own feet like a wild bull. The district was annexed to Arrapha.

Shortly after, he received a letter from the governor of Kar Sharrukin, probably still Nabu-bel-ukin. The whole garrison is well and the village chiefs have asked for peace. Ishpabare has revolted against him and killed his troops.[1] He was quickly defeated, and a section of Elli was detached and formally organised by the governor of Harhar. A single epigraph which identifies the plunder of Bit Kubatti places the group of mountain backgrounds on the eastern frontier. The Assyrian army

[1] *H.* 645.

marches out in great numbers, archers, slingers, and spearmen, each in his appropriate company. A mountain torrent, filled with fish, turtles, and eels, is near a city surrounded by trees. Spearmen scale the rocks, archers shoot from the foot of the hill, footmen climb the walls and slay the fugitives as they seek escape over the flat housetops.

Striking tribute to the artist's keenness of observation is afforded by one scene. On the summits of the mountains are pine-trees, those same strata of pine-bearing sandstone so conspicuous in the Lebanon. Vineyards fill the centre along the river, only scrub-oak grows in the lower portions, in close contact with the villages. Literally hundreds of his soldiers in regular order accompany the king in his chariot through the forest. In regular Indian fashion, Assyrians fight in the woods the natives, with reversed liberty-caps and lappets; trees are felled to build a ramp against the walls; the walls are climbed, the sheep slain, the captives dragged off.

Images of the gods, small figures with high conical hats, their hands joined in front of them, sit uncomfortably on poles laid on the shoulders of their new worshippers. Heavy loads are borne on the backs of the captives and placed on the kneeling camel, whose groans of protest can be prevented from culminating in determined revolt only by the uplifted foot of the driver. We are then shown the loaded camel on the journey, the captives bent under their burdens, the cart heaped with planks. There is a pause in the march, the horses are fed from portable mangers, the father sits on the cart-pole and eats while the mother on a bale of goods holds her wearied boy on her lap. In the contrast the sculptor so well loved, we are shown the lone fisherman, wading in his mountain pool, playing one fish caught on his line, the wicker hamper on his back filled with previously acquired trophies.

The absence of Sennacherib in the west (701) simply furnished another opportunity to the Chaldæans. Bel-ibni recognised the claim of kinship and united with Merodach Baladan and with Nergal-ushezib, who, from his home in the swamp-land, was intriguing for the throne he was later to fill.

Nergal-ushezib went down to sudden defeat at Bit Tuti (700) and Merodach Baladan was driven to a desperate step. Collecting the gods in their shrines and the bones of his ancestors from their last resting-place, the incongruous cargo was shipped to Nagitu in the midst of the sea. Reverence for the dead outweighed regard for the living, and many of his kinsmen, including even his brother, were left behind on the shore. The policy of conciliation which had borne such evil fruit was definitely abandoned, and the crown prince, Ashur-nadin-shum, was brought from the palace his father had recently constructed for him in Ashur, and was made king of Babylon (699–694). Bel-ibni was carried back to Assyria, where he was leading a quiet life as late as 682.

Before long the conviction became a certainty that there was no hope of Babylon remaining content with Assyrian rule while Merodach Baladan remained alive, and Sennacherib determined to attack his refuge by sea. Neither Assyrians nor Babylonians possessed fleets on the Persian Gulf and Sennacherib was forced to rely on the Phœnicians. Orders were given them to construct great ships at the head of navigation of the Tigris and Euphrates, at Nineveh and Til Barsip. Their crews, too, were foreigners—Tyrians, Sidonians, and even Ionian Greeks. The Tigris ships descended to Opis, whence they were dragged by rollers through the reeds to the Arahtu at Babylon, and so into the Euphrates. Troops were embarked, and they were joined by the Euphrates ships, with barley and other grains for the horses, collected from the fertile plains about Til Barsip.

Camp was pitched at Bab Salimeti, the "Gate of Peace," two hours distant from the coast-line, but soon the tide came up and began to enter the tents. There was actual danger that the entire expedition might be wiped out, and Sennacherib confesses that he was forced to take refuge on the fleet, where he remained five days shut up as in a cage. We can understand how the Phœnicians from the virtually tideless Mediterranean should not know the action of the tides; it seems hardly credible that there was no responsible person in the army who possessed the requisite information. So alarmed was Sennacherib that he determined not to take charge in person of further operations.

The ships continued on to the swamps at the mouth of the river where the Euphrates then discharged its waters direct into the receding sea. Ea, god of the deep, whose wrath might be seen in their misfortune, was propitiated by elaborate sacrifices. A fish, a ship, and a figure of the capricorn, all of gold, were thrown into the sea; a century ago the same custom was observed in entering the Persian Gulf, when mariners sent forth a cocoanut boat with rice and prayers.

We should naturally assume from the account of these formalities that a trip of some length lay before the fleet; as a matter of fact, it was merely the crossing of a corner of the gulf to the Ulai River, probably not more than a single day's journey for the slowest of the boats. Curious, too, is the thought that for many centuries the part of the map they sailed has been solid land far north of the present shore-line.

Once more the inexperience of the armada proved its undoing. The invaders landed at a most unsuitable place, where the shore was marshy. Wading through the shallow water, they found a huge army drawn up on the Ulai. The Assyrian tells the usual tale of cities laid waste, but the return of the ships to Bab Salimeti marked the abandonment of the effort to take Merodach Baladan, dead or alive (694).

The expedition did have one unexpected consequence. The year 699 had seen in Elam the downfall of Shutruk Nahhunte and his imprisonment at the hands of his brother, Hallutush In Shushinak II. Everything was propitious for war with Assyria, and in the spring of 694 he moved straight against Sippar, massacred the inhabitants, and sent Ashur-nadin-shum to Elam to meet his fate. Babylon fell into his hands, and Nergal-ushezib, the son of Gahul, realised at last his ambition, though with Elamite aid. At the end of the year 694 north Babylonia was garrisoned by Elamite armies and the invasion of Assyria had begun; by the following July the central point of Babylonia, Nippur, had been secured.

Such rapid progress of the enemy was sufficient cause for alarm. The crown prince was a captive, if not already mercifully relieved by death, the north was in Elamite hands, the greater part of the Assyrian regular army was in the south and completely encircled. A whole year they remained without movement; then, towards the end of September, they took the offensive, but by that time Uruk had been handed over by its citizens to the enemy. In retaliation, the Assyrians executed the son of the Elamite king, who had fallen into their hands in the first battle and Uruk was recaptured, only to fall almost immediately into Chaldæan control. One week later the final battle of the campaign was contested at Nippur. A second time the Assyrians gained the upper hand, but the capture of Nergal-ushezib was not due to Assyrian prowess, as Sennacherib claims. A later letter tells how he was betrayed and how the traitor was laid upon a balance and the other pan weighted with the silver which was the reward for his treachery.[1] Nergal-ushezib was exposed in the great gate at Nineveh, but this was only revenge; it could not restore Sennacherib's first-born.

Checked up by the topography, these victories barely won a safe retreat for the imperilled army, and the alluvium was in no sense Assyrian. A successor to Nergal-ushezib was found in the Chaldæan Mushezib Marduk (692–689), who had been driven to Elam when he resisted the governor of the newly established province of Lahiru, and now came back in the train of the foreign conqueror. That conqueror was not to triumph long, for on the 26th of the same month which had seen the fall of Uruk and the captivity of Nergal-ushezib, Hallutush In Shushinak met his death in an uprising, and his place was taken by Kutir Nahhunte II.

Taking advantage of the change in Elam, Sennacherib sought his revenge, late as was the season. The boundary posts of which the Elamites had deprived Sargon were easily won back and placed under the fortress chief of Der. When Kutir Nahhunte heard the report of the long list of cities which

[1] H. 292.

had fallen prey to the invaders, he left Mataktu, with its palm-covered groves between the rivers, and retreated to the far-distant mountains. It was now the month of January, and the terrible cold, the rain, and the snow proved too much for the Assyrian morale; Sennacherib frankly admits that he feared the brooks and torrents and hastily returned to Nineveh.[1]

Defeat for the Elamite king was followed by the expected revolution, and after but ten months of power Kutir Nahhunte was succeeded in August of 692 by his younger brother, Humbanimena. Invited to assist Mushezib Marduk, the allies mustered an army of rarely composite character. They came from Parsua by Lake Urumia, far to the north of Elam and from Anzan, equally far to the south along the Gulf; in their ranks were Aramæans headed by Samuna, the son of the now deceased Merodach Baladan, the houses of Adinu, Amukkanu, Gambulu; to continue the roll is to repeat the census of the Aramæan tribes in Babylonia.

No stand was made by the Assyrians until the motley host had reached Halulina on the Tigris, well within the debatable land. The official account is picturesque enough. Shuzub, as Sennacherib contemptuously abbreviates the name of Mushezib Marduk, is wicked, base, without knees, a fugitive Aramæan, a deserter, a murderer, a plunderer, and even when he fled to Elam infamy and crime followed him there. Like the onset of numerous locusts in the spring of the year, the enemy came together to make battle. The dust of their feet, like a heavy storm-cloud pregnant with mischief, covered the face of the broad heavens.

Sennacherib called upon his gods and they came to his aid. Like a lion he raged and put on his cuirass; with a helmet, the sign of war, he covered his head. In his splendid war-chariot, which overthrows the enemy, in the anger of his heart he drove furiously. The mighty bow with which Ashur had intrusted him he grasped in his hand, the javelin which destroys life he seized in his fist. Against all the wicked enemy like a

---

[1] Preliminary draft of official narrative for seventh expedition, *Keilschrift-texte aus Assur*, II, 142.

storm he raged and like Adad he thundered. By order of
Ashur he attacked on front and on flank, like the onset of a
terrible storm.   In the strength of Ashur and the onset of the
mighty battle, their front he destroyed and their retreat he
caused.   The troops of the enemy he cut off with bow and
arrow, through the mass of their corpses he cut his way as if
splitting it open.   Humbanhaltash, the nagir of the king of
Elam, energetic and careful, the leader of his troops and his
great confidence, whose girdle dagger was inlaid with gold and
whose arms were bound with double rings of pure gold, Sennacherib quickly hewed down like a fat steer hobbled with
chains, their necks he cut as if they had been wild animals,
their dear lives he divided in two like a cord.   Like a heavy
rain-storm, their trophies and their arms he scattered over the
broad field, the prancing steeds in the clotted blood of the
slain swam as in a river.   On the wheels of his chariot of battle, which overthrows both good and bad, blood and filth
dropped down.   With the corpses of their warriors, like herbs
he filled the fields, like seeds of ripe cucumbers he cut off their
hands.   The double rings of gold and bright silver on their
arms he seized, with sharp swords he cut down their governors,
their girdle daggers he took.   The remnant of his nobles, with
Nabu-shum-ishkun, son of Merodach Baladan, gathered their
auxiliaries, but the royal hands seized them alive in battle.
The chariot-horses whose drivers had been killed in the mighty
battle were wandering about without direction; they were collected together, and when the battle had continued to the
fourth hour of the night, Sennacherib bade the slaughter cease.
The fury of his battle overwhelmed like a wild bull that Humbanimena, king of Elam, with the king of Babylon and the
Chaldæan princes who had come to his support; their tents they
abandoned, and to save their lives they trampled upon the
bodies of their troops and took to flight; like captive young
birds their hearts failed.   He bade his horses and chariots to
pursue after them, and in the place where they were taken,
there they were run through by the sword.

The account is a notable contribution to Assyrian literature but hardly to the political history of Assyria. Details are as vague as they are picturesque, and it scarcely needs the definite statement of the impartial Babylonian Chronicle to persuade us that this is no evidence for Assyrian cruelty; the recital is simply a clever bit of propaganda, and in reality Sennacherib suffered a crushing defeat.

Yet two more years of preparation were required until Babylon fell at the end of November, 689, before the Assyrian mines and escalade. The patience of Sennacherib was exhausted. He had treated Babylon with unsuspected forbearance, and proof of his kindly feeling is still to be seen in the splendid breccia pavement of the Procession Street. Conciliation and firm rule had alike been futile; nearly the whole reign and much treasure and blood which could ill be spared from an empire already bled to the limit of safety had been wasted in the vain effort to conciliate the fanatic patriotism of its citizens.

No longer could the most optimistic pro-Babylonian dream that Babylonia would ever accept Assyrian rule so long as Babylon had an existence. Sennacherib was only human, and it was asking too much that he should forgive the subjects who had betrayed his first-born to Elam, the age-long enemy of their own city. He determined to destroy Babylon completely. After the reduction of the defences, the carnage continued until the corpses filled the public squares. All the treasures which Babylon had accumulated, often by the plunder of still earlier capitals, were taken as spoil by the soldiers, who even went so far in their impiety that they crushed into fragments the very statues of the gods themselves. While so engaged they discovered Adad and Shala, stolen from their homes in Ekallate by Marduk-nadin-ahe when he had bested Tiglath Pileser I, four hundred and eighteen years before. The turn of fortune which restored them to their homes sent Marduk in his turn a captive to Ashur.

Every house in the city was destroyed from foundation to roof and fired. The inner and outer walls, the temples and temple towers were torn down and thrown into the Arahtu, canals were dug through the site, the city was overwhelmed with water, the brickwork foundations were scattered more than if they had suffered from an inundation, the site was annihilated as if a swamp; in future days none might find ground of the city, the temples, or the gods.

In the view of the orthodox Babylonians, "for eight years there was no king in the land." A son of the king, Ashur-ahi-iddina, or Esarhaddon, was intrusted with the actual administration of the country around Babylon, and his name was changed to Ashur-etil-ilani-mukin-apal. We still have the record of the gifts, buckles of gold, a crown of gold, a golden necklace inlaid with precious stones, weighing four pounds, spoil of the Amukkanu, which was presented by his father after the naming.

We need not deny the cruelty with which Babylon was wiped out, and the loss of cultural elements was indeed great. Neither should we forget that she suffered the same punishment she had so often meted out to others. She had been treated with an indulgence without parallel in the history of the ancient Orient, and she had returned these favours with the worst ingratitude. Even Assyrians who worshipped Babylonian culture must at last conclude that all good citizens of Babylon were long since dead. Sennacherib was followed by a sentimental son, who undid his father's work. It was only human nature that the Babylonians forgot Esarhaddon but remembered Sennacherib. Had Assyria been more mercilessly consistent, the fall of the Assyrian empire might have been indefinitely postponed.

CHAPTER XXV

ISAIAH AND THE SIEGE OF JERUSALEM

THE lull in Babylonia after the re-establishment of Assyrian rule seemed to permit an effort to win back the Egyptian frontier. So far as the Hebrews were concerned, the route to Egypt was in the safe-keeping of the Assyrians, for Samaria was a province, but Hezekiah was still in position to cut the line any time he wished to order a descent from the mountains. Twice he had taken part with the enemies of Assyria, in 720 and in 713, and had escaped special punishment. That for twenty years he could have retained his independence in direct defiance of Assyria is striking commentary on the weakness of her standing in Palestine.

The truth of Isaiah's predictions was put to the test in 701. A league of the Syrian states had been formed with the purpose of preventing further encroachments. Chief of the Phœnician allies was Tyre, and Judah developed with her the same close relations which had obtained in the days of David or Omri. The citizens of Ekron recognised the leading part played by Judah when they handed over their deposed king to be guarded in the safer mountains. Ashdod, made a province in 713, proclaimed her independence by a new king, and Ascalon added to her territories the villages around Joppa.

Isaiah alone was pessimistic. "Rejoice not," he cries to Philistia, "because the rod which smote thee is broken, for from the serpent's root shall come forth an asp, and his fruit shall be a fiery flying serpent." Isaiah had accurately gauged the character of Sargon's successor; therefore "Howl, O gate; cry, O city; let all Philistia faint; for there cometh a smoke from the north, in his ranks there is no straggler." [1]

Plunging into the recesses of the Lebanons, Sennacherib came upon a city surrounded by vineyards, its two and three

[1] Isaiah 14 : 29 ff.

storied houses with flat wooden roofs, square doors, and numerous tiny upper windows. In the centre was the royal palace, of well-cut ashlar blocks and with open upper balcony. Flames were soon pouring from its windows, and the horses and chariots, furniture and vases were made a spoil. The Assyrians painfully climb the mountain with the aid of their spears or of clubs cut for the purpose, or win a moment's repose in the shade of the sacred cedars. A castle in the heart of the forests is attacked, and the prisoners led to the camp where Sennacherib sits on a high throne. The commander stands before him, without the walls are the prisoners with manacled hands. About the tents the servants are busy at their tasks, and the water-jugs are hung to the tent-poles that the water may cool by radiation.

Descent was by the Dog River route. On the promontory to the south of the stream, where already were the rock-cut reliefs of the kings of the nineteenth Egyptian dynasty, the invader left the memorial of his presence. Sidon the Great, Little Sidon, perhaps the island off the coast where is now the crusading castle, Beth Zeth, the "house of oil," another suburb to the southeast, Zarephath, where Elijah dwelt with the widow woman, just around the bend of coast to the south, all were methodically reduced.[1]

Tyre was next to be besieged. Assyrian archers hide behind their wicker shields and aim at the citadel, located at the foot of the mountain and with battlements hung with shields. At the arched water-gate, with its flanking of Ionic columns, a man is just handing over a child to the outstretched arms of a woman aboard one of the ships. It is Luli, about to flee from his ancestral home to Cyprus.

The scene then shifts to the open sea, indicated by the artist with wavy lines, and filled by him with fish, crabs, turtles, and starfish. Here float the ships of the fugitives, biremes with eight or twelve oarsmen to each bank and with sharp, wicked-looking rams, ships with masts and triangular sails, clumsy tubs with high, uplifted stem and stern. On the lower deck

[1] Joshua 11 : 8; 19 : 28; I Kings 17 : 8 ff.

FIG. 122. BURNING OF A CITY IN THE LEBANON.

FIG. 123. PHILISTINES WITH FEATHERED HEAD-DRESS.

FIG. 124. CEDARS OF LEBANON.

FIG. 125. TERRACED SLOPES OF THE LEBANON.

sit the rowers, on the shield-hung upper deck are spear-bearing warriors and noblewomen, with high head-dress and long veils. The inevitable touch of humour is not forgotten; this time it is rather grim, a huge crab clasping a fish in his claws, a not inept comparison of the Assyrian and of his unfortunate prey.

Isaiah burst forth in a pæan of rejoicing at the fall of the city which stood for the hated Baal worship and alliance with Egypt. "Howl, ye ships of Tarshish," he cries, for as they cross the narrow sea from Tarsus to Cyprus, "from the land of Cyprus it is revealed to them that it is laid waste, so that there is no house, no entering in. Be still, ye inhabitants of the coast, thou whom the merchants of Sidon passing over the sea have replenished; on great waters was the seed of the Shihor, the harvest of the Nile was her revenue, and she was the mart of the nations. Be thou ashamed, O Sidon, for the sea hath spoken, the stronghold of the sea: 'I have not travailed or brought forth, neither have I nourished young men or brought up virgins.'" While the sea denies her own daughter to her ruin, "when the report comes to Egypt, they shall be surely pained at the rumor concerning Tyre," for Egypt had hoped to come to her aid and now it is too late. "Pass over to Tarsus, howl ye inhabitants of the coast; fareth it thus with thee, O joyous one, whose origin is of ancient days and whose feet carried her afar off to sojourn? Who hath purposed this against Tyre, the bestower of crowns, whose merchants were princes, whose traders were the honorable of the earth? Yahweh of Hosts hath purposed it, to profane the pride of all glory, to disgrace all the honorable of the earth. Overflow thy land as the Nile, O daughter of Tarsus, there is no longer any girdle. He hath stretched out his hand over the sea, he hath shaken the kingdoms; Yahweh hath given commandment concerning Canaan, to destroy the fortresses thereof." Then, in a passage which might almost have been modelled on the Assyrian narrative: "Thou shalt no more rejoice, O thou ravished virgin daughter of Sidon; arise, pass over to Cyprus, even there shalt thou find no repose." As a fitting conclusion, Isaiah turns to the fate of that Merodach Baladan

who so recently had induced Hezekiah to revolt: "Consider
the land of the Chaldæans; this people exists no more, since
the Assyrians appointed it for the abode of wild beasts.   They
set up their siege towers against them and overthrew their
palaces and made it a ruin; therefore, howl ye ships of Tarsus,
for so is your fortress laid waste." [1]

A second Ethbaal was set up in the place of Luli, but there
is no mention of the capture of either Old Tyre or Island Tyre;
the submission of the new ruler was sufficient.   Once south of
the Tyrian territory and the notorious Tyrian Ladder, which
only in our own day has been destroyed for the passage of
British troops, the list of subject states continues—Mahalliba,
Achzib, Acco, on the north shore of the bay of that name,
and Ushu, under Mount Carmel and not far from the present
port of Haifa.[2]

At the last-named place there came into the royal presence
a number of subject kings to pay their devoirs: Menahem of
Samsimuruna, Abdiliti of the island Arvad, Urmelech of Byblus; Mitinti of Ashdod appeared in the hope of disassociating
himself from the other rebels, and Pudiel of Ammon, Chemosh-
nadab of Moab, and Malikram of Edom secured their position against their more settled brethren by kissing the royal
feet.

Isaiah beheld the Assyrian advance with mingled feelings.
The invaders were about to defeat the much-trusted Egyptians, and henceforth there would be ample recognition that
she was a broken reed to lean upon.   This was a positive gain,
yet Judah was herself involved in the revolt and might expect
the horrors of a sack.   No Jewish patriot, however doctrinaire,
could view such a fate with equanimity.   This mingling of
feelings appears in the next oracle: "Ho, Assyrian, rod of my
anger, the staff of my indignation.   I sent him against an im-
pious nation and against people who had incurred my wrath
gave I him charge to make spoil and seize prey and to trample
them down like mire in the street.   Notwithstanding this, he
does not intend so to limit his plan, for it is in his heart to de-

---

[1] Isaiah 23.   [2] Judges 1 : 31; Joshua 19 : 29.

stroy and to cut off yet more numerous nations. For he has said in his heart: 'Are not all my princes kings? Has not Calneh become as Carchemish and Hamath as Arpad and Samaria as Damascus? As my hand was able to seize the kingdoms which worshipped images, though their number exceeded those in Jerusalem, can I not treat Jerusalem and her images as I have Samaria and her images? By the strength of my own hand have I done it, and by my own wisdom, since I have full understanding; I have obliterated the boundaries of the peoples and have made spoil of their treasures and as a mighty hero have I cast down all who sit on thrones. My hands have searched out the riches of the nations as if they were in a nest, and as one gathers eggs that have been abandoned in fright have I gathered the whole earth. There was none that fluttered a wing or opened a beak or chirped.'"

Sennacherib may boast in his inscriptions that he is wise and that through his own understanding new processes were invented; Isaiah knows the truth: "Shall the ax boast itself against the man that wields it? Shall the saw magnify its own importance as against the man who draws it to and fro? As if a rod could impart motion to the man who lifts it up, as if a wooden staff could lift up one who is not wood! Send leanness against his fattest parts, and kindle a burning fire under his glory; it shall consume the glory of his forest and his garden alike, as when a sick man pines away. So the remnant of his forest trees shall be so few that a child may write down their number.

"He is coming to Ai, he is passing through Migron, at Michmash he is storing his baggage, they are crossing the gorge, they are lodging at Geba; Ramah is trembling, Saul's city of Gibeah is in flight; cry aloud with thy voice, daughter of Gallim, listen, O Laishah, answer her, Anathoth. Madmenah is a fugitive, the inhabitants of Gebim are fleeing to save their goods; he is halting in Nob, he is shaking his fist against the mount of Zion's daughter." Let not Jerusalem fear because of this: "Behold, the Lord, Yahweh of Hosts, will lop off the boughs with a terrible crash, and the high of stature shall be hewn down and the lofty shall be brought low. He shall cut through the thickets of the forest with iron and Lebanon shall fall down through a Glorious One. Surely as I have planned, so shall it come to pass; as I have purposed, that purpose shall stand, to break the Assyrian in my land and on my mountain to tread him under foot. This is the purpose which is purposed concerning the whole earth, and this is the hand that is stretched out over all the nations. It is Yahweh of Hosts who has purposed and who shall annul it? His is the outstretched hand and who can turn it back?" [1]

When, however, the Assyrian march was resumed, it was not along the ascending backbone of the country south to Jerusalem, but around Carmel and down the plain of Sharon. With the neighbouring cities of Beth Dagon, Bene Barak, and Azur, which the Philistines had long since won from the tribe of Dan,[2] the port of Joppa was taken without difficulty. The army of the Egyptian and Ethiopian kings under Taharka, Shabaka's nephew, had arrived by this time and had taken up their position at Eltekeh, back of the stream of Jamnia.[3] The commander of the Egyptian chariotry, the sons of the Egyptian kings, the generals in charge of the Ethiopian chariots, all were taken alive, and the cities of Eltekeh and Timnah fell into their hands.[4] Ekron was now defenceless. The governors who had sinned received condign punishment, and their bodies hung on poles around the cities. Their followers were imprisoned, the remainder who had not committed sin or wickedness, whose was not the guilt, were pardoned.

Padi of Ekron was still held in chains by Hezekiah. Scorning to waste his own energies on the mountain chieftain, Sennacherib sent his rab shaqe or commander-in-chief. He took up his position by the conduit of the upper pool on the highway passing the fuller's field, where once Ahaz had met Isaiah, and there negotiated with the Judæan ambassadors, Eliakim the son of Hilkiah, who was over the household, Shebna the royal scribe, and Joah the son of Asaph, the recorder. The

---

[1] Isaiah 10; 14 : 24 ff.   [2] Joshua 19 : 45.   [3] Cf. Breasted, *Egypt*, 552.
[4] Joshua 15 : 10; 19 : 43; Judges 14 : 1; II Chron. 28 : 18.

speech which follows in the Hebrew narrative may not have been written down by Joah immediately after; it was composed by a man who well understood the theory of Assyrian rule and is nearly if not quite contemporary.

"Say to Hezekiah: Thus saith the great king, the king of Assyria: In what hast thou trusted? Is not thy strength for war but useless talking together and vain words? On whom then dost thou trust that thou hast rebelled against me? Behold, you have trusted to Egypt, this staff of a shattered reed, which has pierced the hand of him who leaned upon it. But if you say: 'It is Yahweh our God in whom we trust,' then exchange pledges with my lord the king and I will give you two thousand horses if you can place riders upon them. In truth, it was by order of Yahweh himself that I have come up against this land to war against it."

This last statement completely destroyed the equanimity of the Jewish representatives and they hastily besought him to continue the conversation in Aramaic, the diplomatic language, lest the men crowded on the wall might understand. This proved that his words were striking home, and the rab shaqe quickly seized the advantage: "Was it to your master and to you that my lord sent me? No, it was to these very men on the wall." Then, in a loud voice he shouted to the crowd hanging over the battlements: "Do *you* hear the words of the great king, the king of Assyria. Let not Hezekiah deceive you with empty words, for he cannot deliver, neither let him tell you that the gods will deliver you so that this city will not fall into the hands of the king. For he says: Make a treaty with me and every man shall eat of his own vine and fig-tree and drink the water of his own cistern until I come and take you away to a land like your own, a land of grain and wine, of bread and vineyards. Let not Hezekiah seduce you by saying that the gods will deliver you. Has any of the gods of the other nations delivered his land from the hands of the Assyrian king? Where are the gods of Hamath and Arpad? Where is the god of Sepharvaim? Have their gods delivered Samaria out of my hand? Who of all these nations has delivered his land out of my hand that the gods should deliver Jerusalem out of my hands?"

Overawed by the king's orders, the crowd made no response, but there were doubtless many to whom a separate peace made a strong appeal and who would gladly have purchased security by the murder of a now unpopular ruler. With rent garments, the Jewish representatives approached the king, who in his turn rent his clothes, covered himself with sackcloth, and entered the temple in supplication. Eliakim, Shebna, and the priestly elders were sent in humble guise to Isaiah, who replied with one of his most impressive prophecies:

"Thus saith Yahweh, Israel's God: I have heard that which thou hast prayed unto me concerning Sennacherib, king of Assyria, and this is the word which God hath spoken against him:

"The virgin daughter of Zion hath despised thee and laughed thee to scorn; the daughter of Jerusalem has shaken her head behind thee. Whom hast thou reviled and reproached, and against whom hast thou raised thy voice? Hast thou not lifted up thine eyes on high against the Holy One of Israel? By thy servants hast thou reproached Yahweh and hast said: 'With the multitudes of my chariots have I ascended to the heights of the mountains and to the recesses of the Lebanon; I have cut down its highest cedars and choicest cypresses, I have entered its topmost height. I have made a bridge, I have drunk waters and the whole assemblage of waters.' Hast thou not heard how I created it long ago and formed it in ancient times? Now I have brought it to pass, to make desolate the nations in fortified places, and those dwelling in fenced cities were of small power. They dried up and became as dry grass upon the houses and as fodder. But now I know thy sitting down and thy going out, thy coming in and thy rage against me. For this thy rage against me and because thy arrogance has come to my ears, it is thy nose I will ring and thy lips I will bridle, and by the way thou hast come I will turn thee back.

"For you," turning to the delegation, "this shall be the sign

of your salvation: This year ye shall eat the aftergrowth, in
the second that which groweth of itself, in the third sow and
ye shall reap, plant vineyards and ye shall enjoy the fruit.
The king of Assyria shall not come into this city or so much
as shoot an arrow against it or come before it with shields or
heap up a mound against it; by the way that he came, by that
shall he return, for I will protect this city and deliver it." [1]

None the less, Hezekiah was not to win off scot-free. From
his safe refuge, he looked on helplessly while the villages lower
down the slopes fell one after the other before the Assyrian
rams and mines. Sennacherib claims that he took forty-six
walled cities with their numberless suburbs, and two hundred
thousand one hundred and fifty captives. There are scholars
who defend the accuracy of this last figure; those who know
the country in person will recognise the absurdity of such a
census for the few square miles of rocky country which comprised the western boundary of Judah. Doubtless we have
the authentic figure in the one hundred and fifty suffixed to the
huge round number. One of these luckless Jewish exiles was
the next year sold by his captors to the slave-dealer Bahianu,
and though his father commemorated Yahweh by his name of
Ahijah, the son was renamed Mannu-ki Arbaili, "Who is like
the sacred city of Arbela?"

In a sense, the conflict was a draw. Sennacherib could not
capture Jerusalem, and his utmost boast is that he shut up
Hezekiah "like a bird in his cage in the midst of his royal city;
fortresses against him I erected and those who came forth from
his gates I turned back." On the other hand, Hezekiah had
learned that Egypt was indeed a broken reed, and determined
to make his peace with Sennacherib. The terms were not
easy. Such cities as he possessed along the edge of the Philistine plain must be ceded to Ekron, Ashdod, and Gath. His
mercenary bowmen and spearmen were incorporated in the
Assyrian army, his women in the Assyrian harem. To his former tribute was added a special gift, thirty talents of gold,

---

[1] For reconstruction of Isaiah 36–39 and II Kings 18 : 13–20 : 19, especially on
the basis of the Greek version, cf. *AJSL.*, XXXI, 196 ff.

eight hundred of silver, precious stones, stibium, lapis lazuli, couches and seats of ivory, elephant hide and raw ivory, ebony and boxwood, cloths and chitons of various colours, implements of various metals, all brought by his ambassadors after the Assyrian return. Yet it could not be denied that Hezekiah was still on the throne, however chastened in spirit; Jerusalem remained inviolate, and through the prestige thus won steadily tended to supplant in reputation the sanctuaries of an older day.

In the meantime Sennacherib had been moving south. His sculptures show us that the Philistines had changed their costume little since the days when the Thekel had been represented on Egyptian monuments. Their portly leaders wear the same Indian-like head-dress of high-standing feathers which their ancestors long since had used in Crete, and the long robe with many-folded girdle; their hair was bunched on the neck and they carried a torch in the hand. In the same room was a scene which we may locate at Ashdod, where Mitinti had already proffered submission. We have now a double-walled city, the gateways arched and approached by ramps from the outer wall. Within are warriors, without is a narrow canal with trees on either side, which finds its outlet in a large river on whose waters are skin rafts and double-headed boats. From the former a man drops a line which has just been swallowed by a fish and two of his companions are investigating the food found in a kettle. Horses are ferried on the double-headed craft and their drivers swim across on skins. In the rocky gardens outside the city, with their regular rows of trees, a man is being lowered by a rope into the water. At the extreme end is a hanging garden, supported by entablatures and columns which are not far from the Corinthian. The submission of Sil Bel of Gaza soon followed and Zedekiah of Ascalon was carried off with his gods, while his place was taken by Sharru-ludari, son of their former king, Rukibti.

Turning sixteen miles eastward from Gaza over a rolling country, Sennacherib pitched his camp under the hundred-foot hill by the side of a dry river bed, where stood Lachish, our

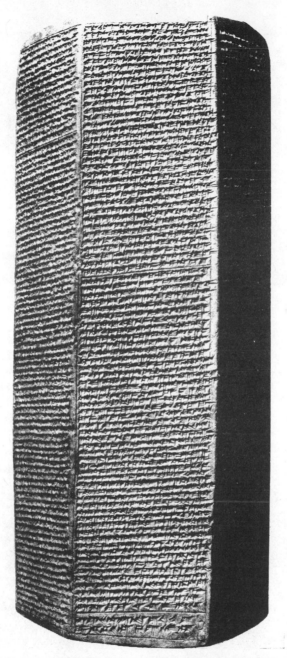

Fig. 126. PRISM OF SENNACHERIB, CONTAINING
THE STORY OF HIS WAR WITH HEZEKIAH
OF JUDAH. (University of Chicago.)

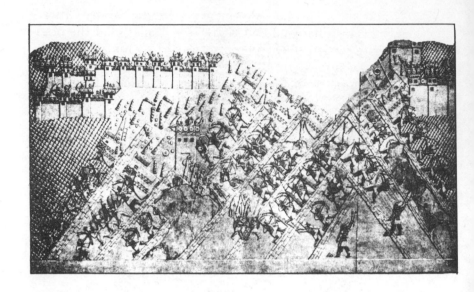

Fig. 128. SIEGE OF CITY IN ASIA MINOR.

best-known example of a Palestinian "Mound of Many Cities."
Already Lachish had suffered many vicissitudes, and the original Amorite settlement had been succeeded by four more when
the Assyrians appeared.   This so-called fifth city did not have
the heavy north wall found in the earlier periods, for a huge
barracks with indented outer walls and many-columned hall
furnished protection on this side.[1]

We turn to the sculptures to continue the story, ıor the
slabs which picture the siege of Lachish are no product of the
artist's fancy; they are based on careful sketches made on
the spot.   We know the view was taken from the south, for
the increasing steepness of the three slopes, from the left to the
centre and then to the right, exactly corresponds to the degree
of slope in the mound to-day.   In the cliff to the right we
recognise the place where it was worn away by the undercut-
ting torrent.   The Assyrian camp, oval and with a broad road
along its main axis, was pitched on a tongue of land between
two stream beds, across from Lachish and accessible to the
water-holes in the dry summer bed of the stream.   In addition
to the usual tents and huts, it contained an altar with two
cone-hatted eunuch priests standing before it.   Near by, their
horses at ease, were parked the chariots which bore the royal
standards.   The royal tent, guyed with ropes, had been set up
outside, and the royal riding-horses, chariots, and parasol were
not far distant.   Sennacherib was enthroned before the doomed
city, on a smaller artificial mound.   The feet of the throne
were pine-cones, the arms were supported by three rows of
bearded caryatids, a fringed cloth decorated with rosettes was
thrown carelessly over the high back.   For footstool was a
metal seat with lions' paws resting on pine-cones.   Sandals,
fringed robes with rosettes, bracelets, fez-like cap, streamers
to waist, Sennacherib was the conventional king in his dress,
while in his right hand he upheld two arrows and his left rested
on the curved bow.   Behind stood the two eunuchs with fly-
flappers and napkins.

The scene before him was animated to a degree.   Lachish

[1] Petrie, *Tell el Hesy;* Bliss, *Mound of Many Cities.*

was strong and the number of soldiers required to win it correspondingly great. The main body of troops was in three lines: the first a rank of kneeling archers, the second crouching forward, the third, intermingled with spearmen and slingers, standing upright. In reserve were horsemen and charioteers in large numbers. The groves of palms and olives were cut down to furnish material for the ten banks and the seven strangely modern battering-rams, or, rather, tanks which trampled the vineyards as they crept towards the walls. Along the summit and above the battlements, the men of Lachish had erected wooden platforms on which hung a row of round shields, even as in Solomon's House of the Forest of Lebanon. The same shields were part of the defender's armour, as were the pointed helmets with ear-lappets; some wore merely a turban with the end reaching down to the shoulder and their robes girded to their thighs.

From the battlements and towers the citizens shot down the men who attempted to raise scaling-ladders, or hurled stones and lighted torches against the wicker shields and wooden sheds of the attacking parties. To save them from this catastrophe, those within the sheds continually poured out water over the roofs with long-handled ladles. Prisoners were impaled alive, flung naked upon the ground preliminary to being flayed, or had their heads struck off by swords. In the centre was a gateway, whose steps, found by the modern excavators, witnessed the march of the captives as they cowered before the king. He, however, was more interested in the spoil, bundles of scimitars and long spears, chariots, tall candlesticks and metal vases, ox-drawn carts with women and children, all presented by the commander-in-chief.

Sennacherib next marched on Libnah, but before he could reach it he received information that the Egyptians were hurrying up with a new army. What followed was a matter for much speculation in later times. "The angel of Yahweh," says the Hebrew historian, "went forth and smote in the camp of the Assyrians a hundred and fourscore and five thousand; and when men rose early in the morning, behold they were all dead bodies. So Sennacherib broke camp and departed." [1] Centuries after the Egyptians told Herodotus a curious story which in certain respects resembles the Hebrew. When Sanacharibos, king of the Arabians and Assyrians, advanced into Egypt, all the warrior caste refused to fight. Sethos, the Egyptian monarch, bewailed his fate before the god, then slept, and beheld a vision which bade him go forth boldly in reliance on the help the god would bring. The invaders were met at Pelusium, but before the two armies could come to blows, field-mice ate up the quivers, bowstrings, and shield straps. Unable longer to fight, the Assyrians were slaughtered in huge numbers.[2]

Angel and mice alike point to the pestilence, that bubonic plague which Assyria had already experienced in Syria. An eclipse, too, befell on the 6th of August, 700, and since it continued into the sunset, the effect must have been striking to a degree; ever a portent of evil in the east, the fear caused by the eclipse must have been a potent factor in persuading the Assyrians that the gods were opposed to further advance in the west.

Advance on this frontier was certainly abandoned. Negotiations were carried on with Egypt through Silli Ashur, the "Secretary for Egyptian Affairs." An actual treaty closed the war; the treaty itself, written on papyrus, has perished, but there still remains the lump of clay on which there was impressed the seal of Shabaka and the much smaller stamp seal of the Assyrian monarch. Nine years later a business document refers to Shushanqu, that is, an Egyptian Sheshonk, as the son-in-law of the king; international marriages therefore played their part in bringing about the peace.

All attempt to form provinces south of Samaria was abandoned. In the case of Ashdod, made a province by Sargon in 713, his successor went so far as to grant it once more autonomy under its own king. Pestilence, eclipse, or unsuccessful war, Sennacherib began a new policy, and the result was complete cessation of revolt in Palestine.

Arabia still continued to claim attention. In 694 Sennach-

[1] II Kings 19 : 35 ff.   [2] Herod. II, 141.

erib named a gate of Nineveh from a conquest of Sumuan and Teme. If he penetrated to the oasis of Tema, this was the farthest point reached by the Assyrian armies, but there is no reason to assume that this is so. At best, a gift from these cities is indicated. Sennacherib also claims the tribute of Karibi-ilu of Saba;[1] as little as in the case of Sargon and Itamra[2] can this be considered a sign of submission, but it does locate to a definite historical period another of the kings of Saba known from the native south Arabian inscriptions, Karabail. Near the end of the reign a promising situation developed among the northern Arabs. Power was equally divided between a certain Hazael and Telhunu, who was both queen and priestess of Atar-samain. The angry goddess surrendered Hazael to the Assyrians, and of her own free will took the road to their country, since she no longer wished to dwell among the Arabs. Telhunu abandoned her treasure city, Kapanu, in fear of the invader's power, leaving behind her gods and a thousand camels; she fled to Admutu, in the midst of the desert, a place of thirst, in whose midst is no provision or drinking-place.

Not until 698 did Sennacherib devote any attention to the affairs of Asia Minor and then because Kirua, the chief of Illubru, had induced a revolt of the Assyrian troops stationed in Hilaku. The inhabitants of Ingira, an Ancyra or Angora otherwise unknown to fame, unless it is the Greek Anchiale, and of Tarzi or Tarsus, supported him, seized the "Road of Que," which passed through the Cilician Gates, and closed it to traffic. The situation was too serious for the local levies to cope with and the royal army was ordered out.

The sculptures depict a broad river, surrounded by mountains and forests. Up the valley and frequently recrossing its windings are the marching Assyrians; here and there they must dismount and drag the chariots over the rocks. Ingira and Tarsus were pillaged and the Assyrians proceeded to shut up Kirua in Illubru, which lay on both sides the river and was guarded by long, low walls with equidistant towers, ornamented

---

[1] *Keilschrifttexte aus Assur*, II, 122.   [2] Cf. p. 211.

with cornices and angular battlements.   The houses were large
and square, and the windows high up under the roof were
decorated with Ionic pillars, the square doors were surmounted
by a plain cornice.   Across the river the suburb was less
crowded, there were numerous trees, and some of the residences
had open balustrades.

Passing over vineyards irrigated by the smaller streams, the
Assyrians cut down the trees to construct the "great flies of
the wall" which were to force the capture of the city.   It was
fired and the long line of warriors carried off the arms, chairs,
stools, couches, tables with heads and feet of animals, beds
with curved heads, high-backed chairs, and campstool-like
tables.   In artistic contrast to these scenes of terror, the sculptor has depicted directly under the walls a huge tree containing two nests and their bird parents.   One bird mother flies
about in alarm, fearing that the Assyrians will next hack down
her own tree; the other, with a worm in her mouth, is about
to present it to the hungry young in the nest.

Kirua was carried off to Nineveh, there to be flayed alive;
the Cilicians who had supported him were deported, and their
place filled with captives.   The weapons of Ashur were dedicated in Illubru, and before his image was set up a memorial
stele.   Three years later, an attempt was made to extend the
province to the north where a man named Hidi had united into
a more or less coherent kingdom the region known as Tabal,
with Til Garimmu as its capital.   This attempt at unification
was naturally taken by Assyria as a casus belli, and the siege
of the capital and the carrying off of its inhabitants as nat
urally followed.   Nothing is said about Hidi, and the expedition had no further consequences.

Strangely enough, this was one of the few events in Assyrian
history not in the Bible which was transmitted to the later
world.   The method of transmission is almost without parallel.   To-day we must consult a Latin or a German translation of an Armenian translation of the lost Greek of the Chronicle of Eusebius, who has given two parallel accounts without
realising their identity, one from Alexander Polyhistor, who

borrowed from Berossus direct, the other from Abydenus, who borrowed from Juba, who borrowed from Polyhistor, and so from Berossus, who borrowed from cuneiform originals! The account transmitted through Polyhistor is not inadequate. As the Ionian Greeks were making an invasion of Cilicia, Sennacherib marched against them, and after a severe hand-to-hand struggle, in which the Assyrians lost heavily, they ultimately secured the victory. As memorial, Sennacherib erected on the spot his figure, and in Chaldæan characters engraved an account of his heroism. Finally, he built Tarsus on the model of Babylon. This is a good paraphrase of the inscription just quoted; turning to Abydenus, we are scarcely surprised that Eusebius took them as separate accounts, for the battle took place on the Cilician coast and the Ionians were on ships. A battle on the seacoast, such as we find mentioned in Sargon's annals, has been transformed in the Greek mind into a battle on the sea, and this is the end of the oft-quoted seamanship of Sennacherib.

Haldia had been taught an effective lesson by Sargon and the Indo-European invasion had necessitated a struggle for very existence. In the Assyrian sources for the reign Haldia is never mentioned, for peace existed with Argishtish II. The buffer states between the two greater powers unconsciously slipped away from the effective control of either. No longer was the direct road between the two capitals safe for travellers, since Assyrian territory ceased before one had gone a hundred miles north of Nineveh. The facts were too bitter to be faced, and the writer insists that the tribes in the vicinity had never known a strong ruler among the predecessors of Sennacherib. This is deliberate falsehood, intended to blot from the memories of his readers the wonderful swing around the circle which his father had conducted in this very region, only to discover before his death that the cities had fallen into the hands of Urzana of Musasir.

Not content with virtual independence, the mountaineers from the spring and the River Tigris went even to the city of Ashur, deep down the river, since the gods had deserted them and made their paths not straight. This was invasion, so with his splendid body-guard and his men of battle who spare not, Sennacherib camped at the foot of Mount Nipur; like a mighty wild bull he took the road before them. Gullies, ravines, mountain slopes, and difficult spurs he crossed on his throne; places which were too steep for his throne he climbed up on foot, like an ibex to the lofty peaks above. Where his knees found a resting-place, he sat down on a rock of the mountain and drank cold waters from a skin for his thirst. Among the rocks of the wooded mountains, he pursued after his enemy and defeated them there among the stars.

A broad river, bordered on one side by reversed trees and formed by the union of a whole series of mountain torrents, is forded by the Assyrians. Although the country is rough, there are vineyards and orchards. The king rides in the midst of his forces; before him are spearmen and bowmen in their respective companies; after him is carried his second chariot on men's shoulders.

For these cities, which, like the nest of the eagle, the king of birds, lie on the peak of the difficult mountains, we are not confined to description and relief; we have the actual remains. The most important was located in the narrow gorge of Hasanah, now filled with flowers, as it was then with fruit-trees and vineyards. Guarding its entrance were two hills with strong forts. Alammu was washed by a small stream at whose level stood square isolated towers, sometimes with two stories. The single gate to the city was half-way up the hill, which was crowned by a small fort, crammed full of fighting men, while veritable "crow's nests" rose from the centre and afforded the archers a clean sweep. Where bows were not available, the defenders relied on slings or hurled down stones with their bare hands.

Across the valley lay another village with a suburb on the near bank. The cliff rose sheer from the water's edge. Access to the fort of unsquared stones at the very summit could be had only along a stoned road with frequent embankments. Our surprise at finding such a road among the wild Kurdish hills of to-day is increased when we identify it with the conspicuous road in the bas-reliefs up whose steep grade Assyrian fighting machines were being forced. A portion of the settlement was soon taken, but the remainder resisted strenuously. When a breach was made, spearmen hastened into the opening, but the less-picked soldiers were more interested in carrying off the captives and their gods. At the foot of the ascent Sennacherib incised one of his stelæ.

If we may judge from the number of stelæ erected in the vicinity of the modern Shakh, this was Tumurri, the chief town in the region, and the more modern walls, doubtless along earlier lines, point in the same direction. A high rock holds the citadel, the walls of the town run down the slopes, the two valleys which enter the mountain are likewise walled across. The six stelæ are on the hillside above and seem deliberately hidden to avoid mutilation at the hands of enemies.[1]

We may see Tumurri in another city on the reliefs, with isolated outworks, roof of a single step, and oblong doors. Double walls, with unusually low gates and of unusual height, were still more heightened by the boards which formed a fighting parapet above the towers. The defence was conducted by men armed with javelins having large points, and their most characteristic defensive armour was the oblong shield with the band across either end. Tumurri was taken by escalade, and down the slope wound the long procession of captives. There was much variety of dress; some wore robes coming down to their ankles or a knee-length tunic with sheepskin slung over it and with leggings laced up the front; others had a plain undershirt, an upper garment coming down to the knee, divided in front and buttoned at the neck; the tunics of some had a diagonal or even a sort of open-blouse effect. Their wives were clad in long dresses which reached to the feet, and over this a fringed cloak on the shoulders, with high round plaited turbans and a veil covering the head and neck. Richly decorated horses made up a large share of the spoil. Sennacherib then turned the direction of his weapons against Maniae, king of

[1] Bell, *Amurath*, 290 ff.; King, *PSBA.*, XXXV, 66 ff.

the city of Ukku in the land of Daie.   The land has already
attracted our attention since the period of the first Tiglath
Pileser, while the Ukkai often appear during the Armenian
wars at the close of Sargon's reign.   By paths which were not
open and by difficult trails opposite difficult mountains along
which none of the earlier kings had gone, he made his camp at
the foot of mighty mountains.   On his throne of state, with
much labour he penetrated into their strait passes, and in
trouble he scaled the peaks of the steep mountains.   Maniae
saw the dust-clouds from the feet of his approaching soldiers,
abandoned Ukku, and fled afar off.

The faithful reliefs again picture the sack of the mountain
city and the defeat of the defenders with their high crested
helmets, small round shields, and long spears.   The Haldian
trinity of gods had been adopted and the sculptor has celebrated this most unique of conquests, one a human figure with
outstretched arms, the second a lion-headed being with long
staff in hand, the third an image in a small frame.

Minor as these operations were, their chief interest is not
in their picturesque details.   They tell a story whose meaning
is clear.   The frontier is falling back and there is definite
threat for the future.

CHAPTER XXVI

SENNACHERIB THE CRAFTSMAN

IF there has never been presented a picture of the culture of Sennacherib's reign, this is in part due to his unfortunate reputation, in part to the position of that reign, between those of his father and of his grandson, with their still greater amount of cultural material. The perusal of the pages preceding should already have indicated that the period is important in the development of civilisation.

Nearly every corner of Ashur showed traces of his building activities. In the centre of the east front was a palace for his son, Ashur-ilu-mubalitsu. In the angle between the Ashur temple and the Tigris was an East House cutting into the city walls. The triangular court thus formed was named the "Parade Ground of the Heavenly Hosts," and various gates bore the picturesque titles of "Vari-coloured Gate," "Entrance for the Heavenly Host," "Gate of the Heavenly Wain," "Gate of the Fateful Chamber." The "Gate of the Heavenly Road of Enlil" led to the structure decorated with fishmen and scorpion men, while Ashur himself was presented with the new "King's Gate."

For the *kiretu* feast of the god Ashur, the invited dinner, when he collects the other gods to celebrate his conquest of the chaos monster Tiamat, Sennacherib constructed a "New Year's House" northwest of the city walls, but within the legal limits of the city. The approach was through a garden with trees planted in rows dug five feet deep in rock and watered from reservoirs by small connecting canals. A vestibule led through a court, likewise filled with trees and surrounded by pillars, into the cella. At the gate was a copper relief with a scene showing the gods.[1]

Sargon's palace at Dur Sharrukin was in considerable part

---

[1] *MDOG.*, 33, 24 ff.; 47, 39 f.

unfinished, but Sennacherib had no intention of living under the shadow of another's fame. Not many miles south, on a spur of a near-by mountain, lay a little town named Nineveh, with an exceedingly ancient sanctuary, Emashmash, belonging

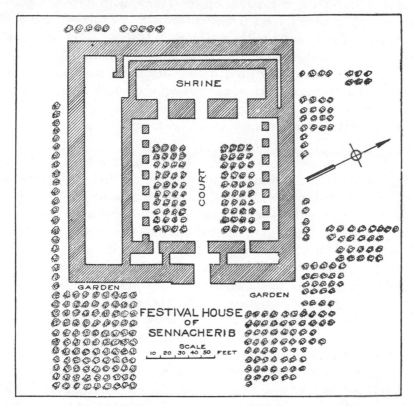

MAP 6. FESTIVAL HOUSE OF SENNACHERIB AT ASHUR.

to the most famous of Assyrian goddesses, Ishtar, who in one of her manifestations owed her title to the city. The Shumerian name of the shrine and the identity of that of the city with an older Nina of south Babylonia was sufficient proof of antiquity, and many kings, from Dungi and Hammurabi downwards, had honoured her temple.

But though these and many another had made dedications in Ishtar's fane, or had even rested under its shadow for the moment, last of all his own father, Sargon, there was no city of its size or sanctity in all Assyria which was so little associated with the fame of any previous monarch. In situation it was certainly superior to Dur Sharrukin; it shared with Kalhu and Ashur a location on the Tigris, with Arbela a position on the direct road from southeast to northwest and the prestige which went with a shrine of Ishtar. The best evidence for the wisdom of its choice is its survival. Ashur is a waste, Kalhu and Dur Sharrukin claim the tiniest of near-by villages, Arbela is a city of the second class, but Mosul, which has simply changed to the opposite shore, is far and beyond the largest and most important city in the ancient Assyrian territory.

Nineveh owes to Sennacherib its position as the capital par excellence of the Assyrian empire. The exalted city, beloved of Ishtar, wherein are all the shrines of gods and goddesses, the everlasting structure, whose design from of old with the writing of the heavens had been fashioned and whose structure shone brightly, the beautiful place, the abode of the oracle, where all manner of works of art, all shrines and treasures had been brought, the place where former kings had received the tribute of princes of the four world regions, thus Sennacherib sings the praise of the city he had chosen for his capital. Yet, with all these advantages, no one had realised the narrowness of its site or had pondered in his heart its enlarging or the making straight of its streets or the planting of its gardens.

Sennacherib it was who turned his ears and directed his liver to the command of the gods and set to forced labour and the making of bricks the population he had carried off. Reeds and rushes, the best of their kind, he brought from the Chaldæan land. The Tebiltu was a violent stream, which in its course had destroyed the ground within the city, and the cemeteries were burned and scorched in the sun. Since distant days it had come up to the very walls of the palace, so that in its mighty flood the foundations were destroyed and the substructure was weakened.

The former small palace was completely razed, the course

of the Tebiltu was changed, and its outlet was given direction. Within the enclosure of its walls, under which were
reeds and above mighty stones of the mountains, bitumen was
spread, and ground from the river was raised to be like a hill.
In the sculptures we see the king in his chariot, watching the
building of the two mounds. Between the two is the clay pit
and around crouch or kneel the men who make the bricks.
The captives wear short tunics and liberty-caps. They are
shackled at the ankles or with heavier bonds on the legs, with
a bar at the waist or with long rods attached to their girdle
rings. Thus encumbered, they lift to the top of the mound
huge stones, or have baskets filled with bricks or simple earth
roped to their backs. The new mound was to measure over a
thousand feet in length, while the breadth varied from about
two hundred and fifty feet at the south to almost six hundred
at the north. Its area actually comprises some hundred acres
and it has been estimated that the services of ten thousand
men for twelve years were required to raise the fifteen million
tons of the platform.

So that the foundations might not be weakened by lapse of
time or by the swelling flood, its earthwork was strengthened
with huge blocks of limestone. Written records were inserted
a hundred and sixty courses within the mound, a testimony
to later times. Afterwards Sennacherib determined to raise
the mound and added twenty more courses to the former
height.

In October, 702, Sennacherib could speak only in general
terms of palaces of gold, silver, and bronze, of malachite and
breccia, of cypress, pistachio, and pine, which for the abode
of his kingship he had made in the midst. Little progress is
reported for the next six years, though by November of 696
the mound had been carried yet ten courses higher. Outside
the main entrance, on the very edge of the mound, was placed
a gate-house after the model of a Hittite palace. On round
pedestals rested the columns which made the colonnaded hall
so pleasant an open structure in which to enjoy the mountain
breezes from the northeast.

The roofing of the palace was of beams of cedar and cypress, whose scent is good, the product of the Amanus and Sirara, snow-shining mountains. Doors of cedar, cypress, pine, and pistachio, with a plating of silver and copper he bound, and in the space within the building he opened light holes, so that the darkness from the roofing within the chambers he lightened, like the day he made them to shine. Thus is marked the introduction of the clear-story, which for so many centuries had beautified Egyptian temples; it is much to be regretted that the upper portion of the palace has not been preserved to show how the new idea was treated by the Assyrian architect. With clasps of silver and copper, their interior was enclosed, and the ramparts, cornices, and copings were decorated with brickwork, mouth stone, and lapis lazuli.

Because Ashur and Ishtar loved his priesthood and had pronounced his name, they disclosed the position of the great trees of cedar which had been growing since distant days and had become exceedingly great in the midst of Mount Sirara in which they stood concealed. As for alabaster, which in the days of his fathers had been considered so precious that it was used to decorate the handle of a sword, now they opened a store of marble in the depths of the Amanus, and breccia, for great stone vessels, which had never before been found, now revealed itself. When from of old the kings his fathers would set up an image of bronze in the palace, all the workmen groaned, through want of understanding and lack of knowledge for the work of their desire. Oil they poured out in divination, the fleece of sheep they sheared in their lands.

Sennacherib modestly admits that he was their superior in that he knew craftsmanship. Through the clever understanding with which the mighty Nin-igi-azag, that is, Ea, had endowed him, he took careful counsel with himself, and by the decision of his will and the prompting of his liver he made great lions of bronze, open at the knees, which none of his predecessors had fashioned. Castings of bronze he made and cunningly executed. With great beams and framework of meshre wood he constructed twelve shining lions, with twelve colossi, exalted, complete in form, and twenty-two female colossi, who were clothed in exuberant strength and abounded in life and vigour. According to the command of the god, he fashioned moulds of clay and poured the bronze as if he were casting half-shekel pieces. Here we have a direct reference to coined money, and we may compare the "Ishtar heads" of the Assyrian business documents which are the direct ancestors, in name as in fact, of the Greek coins called staters. Two colossi were gilded, female colossi were constructed of guanna metal, colonnades were formed with pillars of box, cypress, cedar, pine, pistachio, and were coated with pasalli metal and silver.

As support for the doors, bull colossi of white marble were quarried in Tastiate on the far bank of the Tigris. First, great trees were cut down to make rafts in the midst of the waters. In May, when the spring floods reach their height, they brought them across with difficulty to the other side on enormous rafts. In the crossing of the quay wall the great rafts sank deep, their crews groaned and were distressed in spirit, by main force and with tribulation they brought them. Following the command of the god, white limestone was discovered in abundance in the district of Balata, on the high hills back of the Assyrian Triangle, where to-day a half-dozen Kurdish huts force to the floor in vain escape from the smoke the traveller who seeks a refuge from the blizzard. Colossi and images were sculptured from alabaster and were constructed of one stone, of mighty proportions, standing high on their own bases, and female colossi whose appearance was glorious. Like the bright day their bodies shone, mighty slabs of breccia, cut free from their mountain on both sides, and for the construction of the palace they were dragged into Nineveh.

Vivid as is this description, we do still better when we turn to the sculptured slabs which encased the walls of the palace itself. We are in the mountains, with tall trees, vines, and the beehive huts constructed to-day only in north Syria. We first see the bull in the rough, a shapeless mass of stone extending over the low flat-bottomed scow on which it is being floated down the river. Upright beams wedged with wood hold the mass, and through two holes in the stone and a third knotted and fastened to a plug in the raft's fore, extend three cables. A hundred men to each, they drag the craft by means of smaller ropes fastened to their shoulders. By their dress they can be identified with the various captive nations—Chaldæans, Aramæans, Mannai, men of Que and Hilaku, Tyrians and Philistines. Some are stark naked, others have short checked tunics with girdle fringe, others again gather their hair in an embroidered turban and drape a fringed shawl so that their curls reach to the shoulder. A part work on the shore, a part in the water, a part push the boat. On the bull itself stands the master workman, who gives the signals with outstretched hands, while guards armed with sticks and swords drive on the hapless captives.

The bull, already carved, appears in process of removal to its permanent home. It now rests on a sledge with a rounded front. The motive power is again human, but the labour of the men is facilitated by the use of rollers and by the levers which give it the first start, though sometimes it takes the weight of men seated upon them or hanging from long ropes to move the enormous mass. On the front of the bull is a kneeling man, who beats time with his hands in that clapping cadence which rings so often in the ears of the Eastern traveller, that the men may work in unison. A second foreman gives orders with a trumpet and a third with a mace signals to those who use the levers. They are accompanied by men carrying ropes or saws, hatchets, pickaxes, or shovels, or dragging ropes and beams on carts with centred axles. Cork-like boats of reed or skin, rowed by wedge-shaped oars, follow along the bank, bringing down the huge stone door-sills. The inevitable genre is not forgotten, fishermen astride skins filled with air, patiently waiting a bite to hook and line. In studied contrast stands the king in his eunuch-drawn chariot, and holding in his hand a flower as he inspects the work. Again the contrast is presented, the wretched captives painfully dragging the sheer dead weight of the forty or fifty ton bulls up the steep slope of the newly built mound. Finally the bull is placed upright in a wooden framework, and is kept in place by guy-ropes and by forked poles. The whole process was almost exactly repeated when the bulls were once more removed by the nineteenth-century excavator.

"Palace that hath no rival" the completed structure was called, and for Assyria at least the name was true. The actual remains add little to the description and pictures already pre-

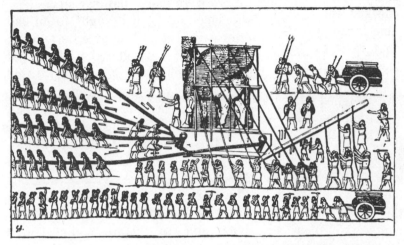

FIG. 129. TRANSPORTATION OF THE HUMAN-HEADED BULL.

sented. Since the corners faced the cardinal points, the visitor must approach it from the grand entrance at the northeast, beyond the Hittite colonnade. Across the front stood five pairs of bull colossi, twenty feet long and as many high, which formed the jambs. Unlike the bulls from the earlier periods, but four feet are shown. The beard, the body hair, the plaited tail, and the triple wings are made with the utmost attention to detail. Above the triple horns is a cap with rosettes and palm-leaves. Winged sphinxes with similar crowns formed the bases of the columns. The winged genius with spathe and basket appeared as in the earlier palaces. Along the whole front were lines of slabs depicting the Babylonian campaigns.

Passing inside, we find the usual three divisions, devoted respectively to the officials, the servants, and the women, but each was considerably larger in size than those at Dur Sharrukin, since the architects had grown more daring in their attempts to roof over larger rooms. The two great halls of audience, adorned with the reliefs which told the story of Merodach Baladan, were forty feet wide and no less than a hundred and fifty and a hundred and eight feet long respectively. Of lesser rooms there were more than seventy.

After the work on the palace had been brought to an end, all the Assyrian gods were assembled and great gifts and sacrifices were presented to them. At the dedication of the palace the heads of the Assyrian citizens were saturated with oil, their hearts were drenched with wine and mead. Led by mace-bearers, the servants appear carrying food for the banquet. In the place of honour is borne a pineapple, strange as it may appear to find it at this time and place. Ripe dates clinging to their branches and flat wicker baskets with pomegranates, apples, and dates come next. Assyria was no less blessed with flies in the days of Sennacherib than at present, the bearers must keep one hand free for the improvised fly-flapper of branches to drive them away. Hares and partridges contribute the meat, unless we are to include here the dried locusts strung on sticks, always a standard article of diet in the East, both before and since the days of John the Baptist. Dessert is marked by other strings of pomegranates, and the low tables, each carried by two men, on their shoulders, with heaps of dates, figs, and grapes, and baskets of sweetmeats. That the term "drenched" is no misnomer is proved by the fifteen jars, their mouths filled with flowers, which bend the shoulders of the bearers.

We turn to the official "Book of Ceremonies" for the banquet itself. On the appointed day of the festival the king enters first and a couch is placed opposite the main entrance. When the king has taken his seat, the official who is over the land, the master of ceremonies, comes in, kisses the earth before the king, makes his report, then brings in the ner of

the land and the great nagir of the land, and he, too, kisses
the earth before the king. After the ner of the land has likewise made his report, he conducts within the great messenger,
who does the same and withdraws. Only after them does the
crown prince enter and in obeisance bows the right knee. One

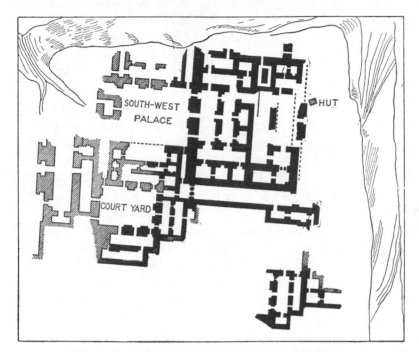

MAP 7. PALACE OF SENNACHERIB AT NINEVEH.

official brings in an iron contrivance, another takes his stand
with his staff of iron in his hand, places the charcoal in the
little brazier, and crouches over it. If the fire is ready, he
prepares it; if there is too little wood on the brazier, he goes
out and brings in wood and places it on the fire. If there is
too much fire, he goes out and brings in something to smother it.
Next they perform an incantation for the king, a sort of
grace before meat. The first palace guard takes his place of
duty opposite, he collects the soiled napkins and gives out
clean ones instead. He stands with the pitcher of water for

the hands, raises it on high, pours out the water and rinses the hands. The cereal foods and the meat are carried in, the commander-in-chief and the chief baker assume their position. Tables are brought in and on them they place all that is carried in and set them opposite the king.

Torches are lighted before the great Shamash and carried into the palace. The second palace official is by this time on guard; when they are prepared he has them lighted and brings them in. When the meal is entirely ended, they burn much incense between the king's sons and the nobles. Great drinking-vessels appear, the chief master of ceremonies takes his position, he recites the work of the musician. The deputy palace official places staffs in their hands and with another stands on guard. The chief baker declares "The feast is ended." The crown prince goes out, the nobles group themselves together in pairs, and rise. The dishes are removed, first those of the nobles, then those of the crown prince, finally those of the king himself, and the feast is ended.[1]

Thanks again to the care of Sennacherib for the future historian, we know the topography of the city proper to an unusual degree. The previous area of Nineveh had been but nine thousand and three hundred cubits; now twelve thousand five hundred and fifteen were added, so that the total was almost twenty-two hundred. This was no small city, fully two-thirds of Rome within the Aurelian wall, but as it was somewhat less closely settled, we may follow the analogy of modern oriental cities and estimate the total population at something like three hundred thousand. The inner wall was given a high-sounding Shumerian name meaning "The wall whose splendour overthrows the enemy." Its structure was limestone, laid up in courses and dug from the moat in front; its width was forty courses, its height a hundred and eighty, of which some seventy feet of height can still be observed. The whole face, up to the triply stepped battlements, was constructed of hewn stone.

Fourteen gates, changed the next year to fifteen, gave en-

---

[1] Klauber, *Beamtentum*, 16 ff.

trance to the city. Their names have interest for other than
topographical reasons. Beginning at the southwest corner,

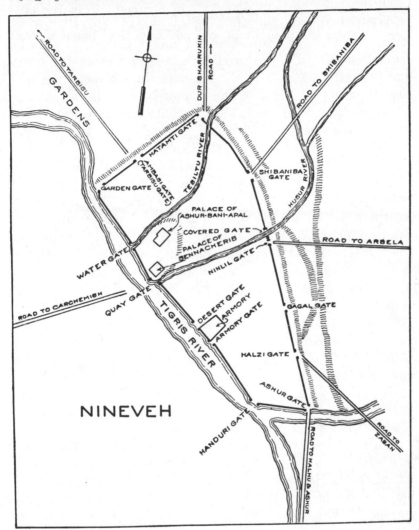

MAP 8. NINEVEH AS RESTORED BY SENNACHERIB.

they run as follows: The Handuri Gate, "Sharur who over-
comes the king's foes"; the Gate of the god Ashur of the city
of Ashur, "May the vicegerent of Ashur be strong," which

shows that the usual road to the older capital was down the east and not the west bank, and which also shows how sedulously Kalhu is ignored; the Gate of Sennacherib of the land of Halzi, "That overwhelms all foes," the direct route to Zaban; the Gate of Shamash of the land of Galgal, "Enlil who establishes my rule," covered by a huge tower to the north and fittingly dedicated to the sun-god, since it faced the sunrise; the Gate of Ninlil of the city of Kar Ninlil, an archaic name for the mother goddess and her city Arbela, earlier called "Ishtar, patroness of his land," later changed to "Of Sennacherib, establish his rule"; the Covered Gate, "That causes the flesh of the leprosy demon to go forth," that Leper's Gate which marred so many oriental cities; the Gate of the city of Shibaniba, "The choicest of grains and stores are in it ever," for the province of that name was noted for its fruitful soil; the Gate of the city of Hatamti, "That brings the product of the highlands," the mountains directly north, and though the direct road to Dur Sharrukin, this too was ignored; the Gate of the Adad of fertility, "Adad who bestows abundance on the land," the northeast corner where the ground was highest; the Gate of Nergal of the city of Tarbisu, "Urra who destroys my enemies," the road to the suburb so loved by Sennacherib; the Gate of the Gardens, "Igisigsig who has made orchards luxuriant," for the famous gardens were just north of the city in the angle made by the Tigris and the northwest line of the wall; later Igisigsig fell into disfavour and the gate was assigned to Sin and was named "Nannar who guards my lofty diadem."

The northwest corner of the walls touched the river, and just below, where the water was still comparatively free of pollution, the carriers came to the gate with the very appropriate name, Gate of the Watering Places, "Ea who directs my springs." When the great canal from the Gomel River was completed, an extension was conducted thither. Opposite the modern Mosul and not far from the bridge of boats and the eternal clatter of women pounding their clothes in the vain hope of making them clean, was the Gate of the Quay, where the Husur then flowed directly under the palace walls. "That brings the tribute of the nations" was its significant title, for the states which could be most easily plundered and with the best results lay to the west. The Gate of the Desert, "The gifts of the Sumuan and Teme peoples enter it," was not in existence in 696; the next year Sennacherib must have enjoyed some success over the Arabs. The last was the Gate of the Armoury, with the appropriate title, "That provides for all."

Six years later the armoury was complete. When Sennacherib began its construction, in close connection with the building of the inner wall, there was no foundation, the ground plan was too small, its form was not artistic. Its platform was weakened, its foundation had collapsed, its superstructure was in ruins. The palace was completely wrecked, a considerable portion of ground from the midst of the swamp and the neighbourhood of the city was added. The site of the former palace was abandoned, and on the swamp ground recovered from the bed of the river which flowed under the walls a terrace of two hundred courses enclosed some forty acres. In a favourable month, on an auspicious day, Sennacherib in the wisdom of his heart and by the co-operation of his clever architects, erected a palace of white limestone and cedar in the style of the Hittite land and a splendid palace in the Assyrian, which was greatly superior to the former in size and artistic effect. Great beams of cedar, the product of Mount Amanus, were used for the roofs, cedar doors were bound with strips of bright copper, and colossi from Balata were placed to right and left of them. In this were stored camp equipage, horses, mules, calves, asses, chariots, baggage-wagons, quivers, bows and arrows, weapons of war, harness for horses and mules whose strength is great when subjugated to the yoke, all that was needed for the rule of the black-headed folk.

The circuit of the inner walls was about eight miles, and the area within no less than eighteen hundred acres. Next this inner wall were the water defences. On the west the Tigris came close under the long, straight line of wall, the south side was very short and protected by a deep ravine. On the north and east and a hundred and fifty feet from the line of the wall was a moat of the same width and fifteen feet deep, cut from the living rock.   Lest these be filled too full with the backwash of the Tigris, massive dams at the northwest and southwest corners restrained the high waters.   Three successive dams likewise prevented the flooding of the city from the Husur. South of that stream a moon-shaped double line of walls projected forth, the central moat filled from a spring of living water, and beyond that was the double outer wall, "Wall that terrifies the enemy," also with a moat between.   The outer stone facing of mighty stones from the mountain has been carried away to build Nineveh's successor across the river, but the inner casing of burnt bricks and the core of mingled earth and stone still exemplify its huge bulk.

Sargon's visit to Haldia had familiarised the Assyrians with the splendid hydraulic works of the early Armenians; his son applied the knowledge to the watering of the Assyrian Triangle.   To increase the amount of land under cultivation, he dug a canal with axes over mountain and vale, from Kisiri to Nineveh.   One and a half double hours from the midst of the Husur, its ancient bed he lowered, and led the water by irrigation canals through the orchards.   High gardens, like Mount Amanus, of all choice and select trees, the glory of the mountains and of the Chaldæan land, within its grounds in rows he planted.   For the setting out of these trees, he divided plots in the neighbourhood above the city of Shapitan, and gave it to the sons of Nineveh and made them land dependents.

Waters were conducted from the foot of Mount Musri and were brought to rest in a swamp and a reed plantation specially made for the purpose.   The reed plantation was most successful.   The birds of the heavens, the igiru birds, whose home is far distant, built their nests, and the wild swine of the reeds and the deer of the forest brought forth their young in abundance.   The faithful reliefs picture the reeds far above the height of a man, and in their recesses a stag and two hinds, also a wild sow with her baby pigs.   Nothing in Assyrian art excels the latter for natural effect.   According to the command of the god, the king placed within the gardens all fruits,

vines, sirdu-trees, cypresses, miskanu, herbs, which all put
forth plentiful shoots and were more luxuriant than in their
native habitat.   Miskanu and cypress, the product of the
gardens and the reed beds, were cut down in the swamps and
used for the building of the palace.   In the hot weather, all
the orchards were irrigated; in the cold a thousand imers of
grain land above and below the city were watered every year.

With a true sense of dramatic fitness, Sennacherib has re-

Fig. 130. WILD SOW WITH YOUNG.

served to the last his most startling bit of information: "The
tree that bore wool they clipped and shredded for garments."
Surely this is our earliest reference to cotton, probably the low
shrub imported from India.   It is but a tiny seed, but from it
was to grow some of the mightiest trees in the industrial jun-
gle of the present.

Rarely in antiquity do we find common objects in the very
act of being transplanted from one country to another, but
here we learn the first introduction of the Egyptian well-sweep
in place of the old draw-well.   "That daily water in abundance for irrigation might flow, levers of bronze and buckets
of bronze I fashioned, and in the place of the draw-wells great
beams and wooden frameworks over the well-shafts I erected."
Sennacherib was amply justified in representing this prototype of the "Old Oaken Bucket" and the New England well-
sweep in his sculptures.   A labourer stands on a pier in the

river, separate from the stepped support of the weighted pole, and with the triangular buckets lifts the life-giving fluid to two higher levels.   The introduction of such a labour-saving device was compensation for many a barbarity inflicted in war.

The canals of Sennacherib were not constructed solely for the purpose of irrigation or for supplying water to fill the protecting moats.   Nineveh stood on the Tigris, and Sennacherib had earlier named one of his gates from the spot where the water-carriers drew their supplies from the current.   He regretted that its citizens were forced to drink its muddy water, carried in foul-smelling goatskins, or direct their eyes to the rain that comes down from heaven.   Their reservoirs were out of order and wells were not to be considered, for they could only furnish the brackish water which had percolated through the gypsum underlying the plain.   Through a canal Sennacherib brought a flood of sweet, never-failing water from Mount Tas, on the border of Urartu.   The earlier name was changed to "Sennacherib's Canal," after the water had been brought from right and left of the mountain and a stone bed had been constructed.   To the great gods he prayed and they heard his prayer, they directed the work of his hands.   By valves and a tunnel the sluices opened of themselves and permitted the rich water to flow down; it needed not the strength of the sluice people to open itself.   According to the wishes of the god's heart, he had dug the water, carried it from the stream, and directed its force.   The gods who aided in the work were rewarded with great sacrifices, the men who dug it were clothed in coloured garments and granted rings and bracelets of gold.   The completed work is assigned to the year and day that Sennacherib defeated Humbanimena, king of Elam (691).

Riding across the rolling plain and following up the line of that Gomel River which preserves the name of the Gau Gamela where Alexander won the world, we pass the raised stone track along which went the canal.   The plain gives way to a deep, narrow gorge, sheer into the heart of the limestone mountain, whose Misuri clan of Kurds preserves the name of

FIG. 131. ENTRANCE TO GORGE AT BAVIAN.
Snow-clad mountains of Urartu in distance.

FIG. 132. BULL FROM SENNACHERIB'S WATER WORKS AT BAVIAN.

Fig. 134. WARRIOR ON PAINTED BRICK.
(Esarhaddon.)

Fig. 133. "SQUEEZING" AN INSCRIPTION OF
SENNACHERIB AT BAVIAN.

the ancient Musri.   Myrtle and oleander make it gay in summer, and even in winter it is pleasant to linger in its sheltered recesses.   At the mouth lie the well-hewn stones of a small city, higher up the water flows from basin to basin, the lowest with two lions rampant.   The cliffs become precipitous, and on the left we see a sadly mutilated relief, the main figure of which is a huge horseman with pointed helmet and short square-cut beard, driving his lance at the enemy.   Before him stands Sennacherib, a deity with horned cap is behind, and above the gods stand on their appropriate animals.

The most impressive of these reliefs is the one which follows.   Two deities, Ashur twice repeated, face each other as they are borne by dogs.   They wear the high, square head-dress with horns locked in front, their left hands hold the winged disk, their right hands are extended in greeting.   Behind each is the royal figure, one hand raised in adoration, the other grasping the clubbed stick.   Above the frame, twenty-eight by thirty feet, and a sort of overhanging cornice, are two crouching sphinxes.   On either side of these are smaller rounded niches in which are to be seen figures of Sennacherib, and if their measurements are accurate, he was but five and a half feet in height.   On three are inscriptions, one easily accessible, the others under the crest of the cliff, where it is possible to copy them only with the aid of a rope let down from above.[1]

These are the inscriptions which furnished information as to the hydraulic operations and as to the final capture of Babylon.   In the edge of the water below are two massive fragments of rock which have fallen from the side of the cliff.   Two huge winged bulls, back to back, lead one in imagination to the gateway of the palace.   The illusion is still further heightened by the image of the lion slaying Gilgamesh which has been carved between them, and by the figures above, as if in a second story, the king worshipping two deities who stand on the dragons, with eagle heads, bodies and forefeet of lions, the hind legs with the talons of a beast of prey.   Such animals

[1] As was done by Professor Wrench at the time of our visit.

were the models from which the great Nebuchadnezzar copied the beasts with which he adorned the walls of Babylon.

So often have we considered the Romans as the first to develop the road system in a practicable manner that we can with difficulty believe that they had predecessors. Already the paved road and the uninscribed mile-stone from Dur Sharrukin have been brought to our notice. Sennacherib has left us two stelæ on which he appears with long, flowing robes, pointed helmet, and dagger. He tells us how he enlarged the site of Nineveh and extended its street, the track of the royal road. On a memorial stone he has placed this order: "Royal Road, let no man decrease it." Seventy-eight feet he has measured its breadth—the present-day Federal Aid road is generally thirty—and if in the future any citizen shall restore his old home or build it anew from its foundation and so encroach on the road, before his home on a pole they shall impale him. The stelæ were found southeast of the palace on the way to Arbela, and by their position prove that this paved road was the ancestor in line as it was doubtless in name of the better-known Royal Road of Persian times.

Sennacherib has been given the fame, in all probability never to be lost, of a savage warrior and nothing more. He won the hatred of the Babylonians and pro-Babylonians who compiled the later narratives, and he had the misfortune to attempt the subjugation of the Chosen People. Tradition said that no king, whatever his country, might hope for immortality unless he was a successful imperialist; Sennacherib was no more in advance of his age than have been the modern statesmen who held power in 1914 or 1919. We shudder at the thoroughness with which he destroyed Babylon, but we must not forget that cities have been destroyed in the twentieth century which had not betrayed the destroyer's eldest son.

If justice has not been done Sennacherib, it is because we have not read his own words. He repeatedly shows that he was more than a mere general. His statesmanship was vindicated when he refused to attempt the extension of provincial organisation on the Egyptian frontier and the reversal of both

Babylonian and Egyptian policies by his son only proved by the ruin they brought in their train how sound was his own. His one ideal was to be a true Assyrian. The misfortunes of his reign, above all, the loss of his first-born in Babylon, prevented overenthusiastic worship of the Babylonian civilisation, but it did not mean that he was opposed to the culture of other nations. He specifically asserts that his colonnade was made after the "Hittite," perhaps in reality Greek, model, his substitution of well-sweep for draw-well was the result of contact with Egypt, and the clear-story was equally borrowed from that country.

Normally we do not overemphasise the individual element in the public works attributed to the monarch, but Sennacherib asserts a personal interest. His boasts are almost pathetic when he assures posterity that he does know craftsmanship, that the god Nin-igi-azag did endow him with clever understanding, that the new process of bronze casting was discovered by his own wisdom and by taking counsel with himself. Other rulers claim all their works for themselves; Sennacherib stands alone in frank confession that he was aided by his architects, in recording the labours of his workmen and the rewards for those who constructed the palace and brought the watercourses to completion. Only a monarch who was known to have taken personal part in the work could have afforded to be so generous.

The library begun by his father was continued, and even volumes in ancient dialects of the Shumerian bore his library mark. His realism reappears in the reliefs which indeed mark an epoch in the history of Assyrian art. Again and again the knowledge of the site has shown that the scenery is reproduced with photographic exactness, so that, for example, we can take our position at the exact spot occupied by the artist when he drew the mound at Lachish. For the first time we have background, with full details of natural features, and we even have the first faint attempts at perspective. Species of animals and plants are as readily distinguished as are localities. Added to a strong feeling for the facts of nature is a positive enjoyment of every-day life—the lone fisherman, the peasant with the well-sweep, the weary warriors happy over their simple meal.

Sennacherib is the last ruler whose reputation would lead us to suspect possession of the more tender qualities. His sculptures show such horrors of warfare as can be cited for every struggle in the world's history, and wretched captives under the sticks of taskmasters, who are almost as savage as the men who chained men naked in the Christian galleys; they also show the birds in their nests and the little pigs following their mother, the tender scenes among the deported. His records tell of other horrors of war; it is the same Sennacherib who relates with sympathy how the crews of the rafts groaned and were distressed in spirit as they brought down the colossi, and he is positively jubilant as he tells how the workmen no longer groaned through want of understanding when they cast bronze and for that they might thank his own invention of a new process. Such sentimentality rarely has practical effect on the actual action of a ruler, whether called king or minister, yet it is worthy of more than passing notice when we find such sentiments in the mouth of an unusually practical monarch in such an iron age.

CHAPTER XXVII

ESARHADDON AND THE RESTORATION OF BABYLON

THE restoration of Babylon was due to a series of accidents. Sennacherib possessed at least two legal wives, the elder Tashmetum-sharrat, who lived for a time in the palace of Ashur-nasir-apal at Ashur, and the younger, Naqia, whose west Semitic name was translated by the Assyrians as Zakutu, the "Freed." Of the former queen would seem to have been born the eldest son, Ashur-nadin-shum, whose untimely fate we have already learned. His title of crown prince was transferred in October of the year of his brother's death, 694, to Arad Ninlil, but he too soon disappeared.[1]

Esarhaddon had spent his early life with no expectation of the throne. He had many enemies at court, and the scribes and seers, in particular one Kalbi, son of Nergal-etir, in tablet after tablet had reported to Sennacherib that Esarhaddon marched with an unfavourable and black sign. His father, however, made inquiry of Shamash and Adad, the lords of decision, and they returned favourable answer, saying: "He is thy associate." Their weighty decision he respected, and collected the men of Assyria, great and small, with all his other sons, and before the gods dwelling in heaven and earth he made them swear to defend the rule of his new colleague. At the beginning of the new year, Esarhaddon entered with joy the Succession House, the place of fear, wherein the fates of royalty are found.

His name, Ashur-ahi-iddina, "Ashur has added a brother," proved only too well that he was not the first-born, and he therefore received the more impressive Ashur-etil-ilani-mukin-apal, "Ashur, lord of the gods, has established an heir." An unusual honour was paid to the new prince. The year 687 had been especially honoured by receiving Sennacherib himself as

[1] For Babylonian relations, cf. *AJSL.*, XXXVIII, 83 ff.

eponym; he now transferred the honour to Esarhaddon as a sort of *consul suffectus,* and official texts were dated by the name of the new eponym.   Like his elder brother, Esarhaddon was made "governor of Babylon, holder of the reins over the black-headed folk."   However much his sympathies may have been with the repressive policies of his father, he was soon won over and became strongly pro-Babylonian.

But there were other children in the royal family: his sister Shaditu, for whom Shumai completed certain rites which "caused the mother to receive offspring";[1] Arad Malik; Ashur-shum-ushabshi, who received from his father a residence in the gardens of Nineveh; and the young Ashur-ilu-mubalitsu, who was installed in a house of limestone.   There were enough leaders in Assyria who suspected the effect of a residence in Babylonia and would support any member of the royal family who might challenge his right to the throne.   In the words of Esarhaddon: "An unloyal thought seized my brothers, the gods they abandoned, they plotted evil, a deed which was not according to the heart of the gods they planned behind my back.   In opposition to the gods, they wished to turn the heart of my father against me, the humble, but his heart loved me and his eyes were fixed upon my rule.   They revolted, and to secure the kingship Sennacherib they killed."

The revolt broke out in the beginning of 680, while Esarhaddon was living as crown prince in the city of Zaqqap. There was constant danger of assassination, his attendants were doubtful, even his mother hesitated to urge him upon an adventure which might end his life.   Then up rose the magician Bel-ushezib and prophesied to the magician Dada and then to the queen mother herself, declaring that her son was destined to obtain the kingship, rebuild Babylon, and restore its temple Esagila.

An important acquisition to the would-be king's party was Akkullanu.   He has taken the oath and the king shall see that he is devoted to his service.   From his heart he spoke when he declared: "Before the king I shall walk."   The king

[1] *H*. 57.

has asked him about an image which remained from the middle of July to the beginning of August in the city of Akkad; it should be made in the city and there take away his illness, and he asks: "Why are you and why the crown of Akkad?" They have told the king: "Thy father was in the midst of the house of their protection." The king will inquire why he has spoken of his image, in the midst of the eclipse of Nisan. He interprets the omen: When Jupiter meets with eclipse, it will be well with the king, the family of the nobility will be powerful, the decrepit will cease. It has come to his ear that before a month of days has passed, his opponent will be dead. Let the king perform the freeing incantation a second time, for why should he wait until the actual necessity be upon him? If he had not spoken to the king this day, would he not demand on the next why he had not filled the basin and shown wisdom? It has been nearly a month since he has heard from the king, but now he is rejoiced since the king is well.[1]

Adad-ahi-iddina too sent the king a word of cheer. Belit-abi-usur, the female magician, has brought the royal garments to Akkad. She prophesies return to Assyria and the securing of the royal throne. She brings an oracle from Ishtar: "The enemies of the king I shall conquer, those who take not the side of the king I shall not grant a throne." If the king give permission, let them take immediate action.[2]

Through her accredited representatives, Ishtar raised her voice. Sharply she takes Zakutu to task. The queen mother has begun legal action against her and has demanded: "Of the two sons thou hast placed to right and left in my bosom, where is the offspring of my heart whom thou hast left to fall on the plain?" Though his own mother forsake him, yet is the king no longer to fear; let him seize the kingship and the power. Esarhaddon was still fearful and Ishtar herself went out into the plain, whence she sent her greetings to her son in the city: "Fear not, O Esarhaddon, I am Ishtar of Arbela, with good have I filled thy lap. The former words which I spake to thee hast thou not trusted, now shalt thou trust the

[1] H. 48; 46.   [2] H. 149.

latter. The tattered garments from my palace take out, well prepared food shalt thou eat, well-mixed beverages shalt thou drink, in thy palace shalt thou be firmly fixed, thy son and thy son's son shall carry on the royal line on the lap of Urta."

Nor did Ishtar stand alone. Since the city of Ashur was in the hands of the rival party, it might be assumed that the titular god of the empire would be constrained to take their side, but Ishtar assured the doubting king that she had persuaded Ashur to be propitious; she had stood beside him in his youth, need he fear now? Nabu, lord of the writing pen, could ask: "Where is that foe who came forth against thee? Verily, I say unto thee, the future will be as the past." Bel Marduk, an unwilling captive in Ashur, likewise spoke through Ishtar's representative: "Fear not, O Esarhaddon, it is I, the Lord, who am speaking with thee, the beams of thy heart will I fortify, even as thy mother who gave thee birth. The sixty great gods who are with me will protect thee during thy life, Sin is on thy right hand, Shamash on thy left, the sixty great gods round about thee have taken their stand, thy line of battle they form. Put not thy trust in men, lift up thine eyes and look on me."

So Esarhaddon rent his clothes and wept; he was fierce as a lion and his liver cried out. To assume sovereignty in his father's house and to invest himself with the priesthood, he raised his hands to the gods who looked with favour on his petition, and in their eternal mercy they sent this oracle: "Go, delay not; at thy side we will march and will subjugate thy enemies." Thus encouraged, he waited neither one day nor two. The van of his army he did not inspect, the horses for the yoked teams he did not prepare, provisions for the campaign he did not issue. He feared not the snows and cold of February or the sharpness of the frost, like a flying swallow he extended his forces for the overthrow of his enemies. The road to Nineveh with haste and difficulty he went down.

Arrived in Arbela, he was hailed by Rimute, the seeress who counted her origin from the mountain fortress of Darahuia: "I will rejoice with Esarhaddon, my king; rejoice, O Arbela."

Then followed a whole series of oracles from Ishtar-bel-daini, the royal prophetess: "I am Ishtar of Arbela; O Esarhaddon, king of Assyria, in Ashur, Nineveh, Kalhu, and Arbela, distant days, eternal years, to Esarhaddon my king will I give. Thy great protector, thy kindly nurse am I." "For distant days and eternal years thy throne beneath the great heavens have I established; with nails of gold in the midst will I fix it. The gleam of the diamond before Esarhaddon, king of Assyria, will I make to shine. As the crown of my head have I fixed it." "Esarhaddon, true son of the Mistress, mighty sword, with my hands shall I annihilate thy enemies. Esarhaddon, king of Assyria, thou cup filled with gifts, thou mace with double axe, distant days and eternal years in Ashur do I give thee. Esarhaddon, thy good shield in Arbela am I. Esarhaddon, true son of the Mistress, thy understanding is sound, greatly do I love thee. On the earth is thy seed, in the great heavens thy family. On thy right will I burn incense, on thy left will I make fire to consume it." "The deceitful snares which they plan shall I cut off from before his feet. Thou, even thou, art king, O my king." [1]

In the capital, all was chaos. When the news was made public that Sennacherib was dead, the wife of the governor of Ashur hastily entered the palace to comfort him, but he sent her out. The inhabitants wept, a kid was sacrificed, the officials placed rings on their fingers and clothed themselves in red, the colour of death. They took their position before their chief and Qisa the singer, with his daughters, made music before them. They spoke to the prophet. The fastenings of the gate were opened, Danai brought forth the dead body, the other officials followed. The governor and his troops were covered with wrappings and the partisans of Esarhaddon frankly admit that at first they feared when they saw the drawn iron daggers of the governor of Ashur and his assassins.

After a time they plucked up courage and demanded of the messenger Hambi: "Why do we merely weep? The governor and his men are standing with drawn daggers at our heads,

---

[1] IV R., 61; Jastrow, *Religion*, II, 158 ff.; Langdon, *Tammuz*, 128 ff.

both in the palace and in the government house." Thus encouraged, Hambi went to the lock and gave order: "Open the door." While he was engaged in putting to death the sons of Zazaku, the writers had killed the governor, and the opposition to Esarhaddon collapsed.[1]

In more flowery, though hardly more exact language, Esarhaddon himself tells of this same failure of his enemies to retain possession of the capital: "The deeds of the miserable ones, which contrary to the hearts of the gods they did, they looked upon for evil, they took not their positions at their sides, their strength they made foolish, under me they laid them low. The men of Assyria who had taken the oath of the great gods by water and by oil to my rights to the succession and had then gone with them as helpers heard of the advance of my battle line, their troops they forsook, they fled and I captured them."

From Ashur the army marched north along the Tigris. Across the surging flood, now raised higher still by the access of water from the newly melted snow of the mountains, lay Nineveh. Appalled by the difficulties to be faced in the taking of the quay walls erected by his father, Esarhaddon again made trial of the oracle and was reassured: "Fear not, O king, it is I who am speaking with thee; I will not reject thee, I will give thee courage, I will not make thee ashamed. The river in safety I will make thee to cross." So, by order of Sin and Shamash, the gods of the quay, the troops reached the Tigris river wall and crossed the broad stream as if it had been a mere ditch. On the feast of Nabu, celebrated in the middle of March, Nineveh was entered, and Esarhaddon sat on the throne of his father in joy.

The final resistance of the rebels was still to be broken. The south wind, the wind of the god Ea, whose breath for the instituting of royalty is good, went with them. By favourable signs in heaven and earth, and by the words of the prophets, the gods regularly furnished him information and reassured his heart. In Hani Galbat all the mighty warriors attacked

[1] H. 473.

his advanced guard, but the fear of the great gods destroyed them. They saw the onrush of his weapons and panic seized upon them. Ishtar, mistress of conflict and battle, because she loved his priesthood, stood at his side and broke their bows. Their ordered line of battle she destroyed and in their assembly they said: "This is our king." By her illustrious command they took their position at his side and followed like young lambs, submissive and beseeching his lordship.[1]

The fleeing forces were followed as far as Carchemish, where an advance of oil for the king's household testifies to the royal presence. His two brothers, Adrammelech, who may be Arad Malik, and Sharezer, perhaps the Nabu-shar-usur who was chief eunuch and governor of Marqasi in 682, are said to have taken refuge in Ararat,[2] that is, Urartu. Esarhaddon returned home to devote his attention to the most pressing of the domestic problems. His followers must be rewarded. Bel-ushe-zib, for example, had prophesied his coming dominion when all in Babylonia were in fear of their lives. He feels that the king has now forgotten him, and for the third time he bewails his misfortune, since the king will not raise his head or do as he has been done by, and he modestly suggests that a talent of silver would be appropriate reward for his good deeds. Esarhaddon compromised by making him a royal astrologer.[3]

How serious had been the breakdown in administration is well indicated by the letters of another faithful follower, Akkullanu, who had been rewarded with the task of reorganising the city of Ashur. The stated dues of the god had fallen into arrears and the king had demanded the names of the officials who had not paid. The list is surprising: Barhalza, south of Nineveh; Rasappa, west of the capital; Kakzu, just south of Arbela; Tille, at the junction of the Tigris streams; Isana, west of Ashur; Arpad in the centre and Kullania in the west of north Syria. A still larger group had not turned in the barley and emmer. Included are again Barhalza, Rasappa, Isana, and

---

[1] Sources for reign, Budge, *History of Esarhaddon*, 1880; Abel-Winckler, *KB.*, II, 124 ff.; Harper, *Literature*, 80 ff.; cf. *Historiography*, 47; a badly needed new edition is in preparation by Hoschander.

[2] II Kings 19 : 37.   [3] *H*. 1216; Thompson, *Reports*, 90.

to them must be added Halzi Atbar, Urzuhina, and Diquqina on the road to Babylon, Birtum, Sharish, Parnunna, Rimusi, all to the north, Guzana in the fertile plain northwest of Nineveh, and, most disconcerting of all, Arbela herself, so busy producing oracles of encouragement that she had quite forgotten the more material recognition of the new monarch. Sixteen provinces are more or less remiss in the payment of their dues, and every part of the empire, from frontier post to religious capital, is represented.

Equally disturbing was the situation if one turned to the religious houses. A sort of visitation had been ordered for Ashur, and the report was sufficient to cause grave concern. The recorder of the bakehouse, a mere youth, had been removed by Sennacherib; he had been slandered by Ashur-zer-iddina, priest of Nineveh, and "in the troubles" being afraid, he received his turban, that is, had him beheaded, although he had not committed a serious crime. The recorder of the storekeeper lifted up the wooden dish of Ashur; therefore Sennacherib gave him charge of Ashur's dish. He is a turban-wearer's son and was not removed without reason. The food overseer also fell into the bad graces of Sennacherib, who received the son of his turban, another oriental euphemism meaning that he cut off his head. It is now eight years since he died, and his son stands in his office.[1]

The official who is over the house of the seers is dead, and Akkullanu sends on to the king his son, his brother's son, the cousin of the second priest, that the king may decide after a personal conference to whom the office should be given. As to the priest of the god Iminbi of the city of Nineveh, of whom he had already told the king "There is information in his mouth, question him," the king has ordered that he be brought to his presence, but no one has inquired of him.[2]

Formerly Ashur and his consort Ninlil went forth in peace and entered in quietness, and as many gods as went forth with Ashur entered in peace their abodes. Formerly they filled vessels with wine and placed them before the table of the

[1] H. 43.   [2] H. 577; 49.

king. Now, although it is already October, there is neither
wine nor vessels to fill before Ashur, there is neither chief cellarer nor deputy nor scribe. Foot by foot they have ceased
work, and although Akkullanu has reported the case to the
king, the king has not instituted an inquiry. A tablet of gold
has disappeared from the Ashur temple and has been seen in
the hands of the jeweller, Qurdi Nergal. At once Akkullanu
made inquiry of the scribe under whose charge it was, but the
king should conduct the investigation further. He need not
ask Tab-shar Sin, for he has eaten a gift from the thief. Let
him rather ask the men who in company and regularly eat the
gifts of the Ashur temple. Sin-naid was appointed an overseer of the city of Ashur by the king. He has inquired about
the gold, he has sent the name of the thief to the king. On
the 21st the gold was given to Tab-shar Sin, it was taken out
to be set before the king. Let Nabu-ahe-ushallim come, let
him continue the investigation. Nabu-belshunu orders Ashur-
mudammiq to give silver, whether two or three pounds, as
much as Akkullanu asks, for the breaks in the houses of Ashur
and Ninlil, let them examine it together, let them bring his
stylus before him, let one receive its return, let Nabu-belshunu
write it on his tablet.[1]

The king may ask what sort of work Akkullanu is doing for
the life and well-being of his lord. He is to carry the axe three
times before Dilbat. As to the appearance of Sin and Shamash
in conjunction and accompanied by a heavy wind on the 14th
of January, it signifies misfortune for Akkad as well as for
Elam and Amurru. Shall he come for the royal sacrifices of
burnt offerings or shall he remain where he is? Will the king
speak as is his wont: "Why have you not reminded me?"
When the sun rises, an eclipse two fingers broad will take place.
There is not in existence a freeing incantation against it; it is
not as if it were the moon. If the king gives orders, he will
write down the interpretation and send it to him. The planet
Mars has entered the road of Enlil, the constellation of the
Pleiades has been seen, it was faint, it was high. On the 26th

[1] *H*. 42; 429; 150; 185.

of May he watched until it rose higher and then sent its meaning: When Mars nears the Pleiades, a war will break out in Amurru, brother will kill brother in the palace, the prince, who is a wall of protection, will go to another land, through the wicked revolts of its king, its gods against the enemy will cause him to hasten. To-morrow, about evening, a libation will be offered in Tarbisu for the king. Shall he go or will he be told that he has not reminded the king? They shall not make this charge against him. The king has demanded why he inquired of the god; impatiently Akkullanu replies: "To whom are his eyes directed, from them should I inquire?" [1]

Akkullanu was not the only official who had complaints to make. Ashur-risua informs the king that in his father's time the housekeeper of Urta's temple took three fingers of gold from the golden beams at the head of the god, but reported it to Sennacherib. Later they cut off a strip a foot and a half wide by seventeen feet long and broke off some of the silver from the wall. Nabu-eriba, the kalu priest, and Galib, the guard in the god's house, were the lords of the breaking. Their companions, the men who were with them, they made come out. Ashur-risua and the overseer of Kalhu brought them to Shangu Ishtar, the ridu official of Ishtar, the chief doorkeeper. He has seen it, let the king ask him how much was broken off. However, he does not know how much was restored. Their profanation has come into the temple, to Sennacherib their profanation came. Some of them were trustworthy, but not one of them remains.[2]

A case at law still further illustrates the prevailing chaos. While Esarhaddon was yet crown prince, a certain Hani had been given charge of three hundred of his sheep. Taking advantage of the confusion, Hani sold the sheep and killed the shepherds, that they might not witness against him. In 679 he was brought before the chief judge of Assyria and was condemned to pay the cost of the sheep and additional blood-money to the extent of two talents of gold for each man murdered. Until these impossibly high sums had been paid or

[1] *H*. 45; 50; 470; 679; 47; 681. [2] *H*. 493.

until he was redeemed by his brother or his captain, he was to remain enslaved.[1]

The new régime, it was already clear, was to be under the ghostly control of the priestly advisers. Priestly influence was connected always with reverence for Babylon. Zakutu, mother of Esarhaddon, manifested a marked interest in Babylonia; here were her special cities, Lahiru and Shabbu; when ill, she felt the hand of Nana, goddess of Uruk, strongly upon her; to mitigate the wrath of the goddess, Esarhaddon reconstructed the chapel of Nana in the Eanna temple of that city. His wife was likewise a native of Babylonia. Adding force to all these family influences was the fact that his rebel brothers had found their support in Assyria; indeed, it is not beyond the bounds of probability that the support of the south was purchased only by the promise of restoration for the capital.

So, when Iddina-sharru and his son Zakir wrote to remind him of the manner in which the last Tiglath Pileser and his successors had guarded the chartered rights of Babylon and had firmly established the income of Esagila and Ezida, Esarhaddon was prepared to listen to their overtures. Very vividly does he place before us the sorrows of the stricken city, though none would suspect that the king he is so careful not to name is his own father.

Before his time, under the rule of a former king, hostile forces gained control in Shumer and Akkad. The men who dwelt in Babylon intrigued and planned insurrection. On Esagila, the temple of the gods, they laid their hands, and the gold and the precious stones they sent as a bribe to Elam. Marduk, lord of the gods, was enraged, and formed hostile plans for the overthrow of the land and the destruction of the men. Ashur swore an oath that was destined to bring ill luck and the heavens displayed signs of evil portent. The Arahtu Canal, a river of plenty, a mighty flood, was brought against the city like a deluge and the site was made like ploughland. The gods and goddesses who dwelt within like birds ascended to heaven.

[1] *J*. 164.

But the merciful lord Marduk had inscribed no more than ten years as the time of its ruin, for the compassionate Marduk was speedily appeased in his heart, he spoke peace and return to the lower country. Esarhaddon he chose from among his elder brethren and assigned him the rule of Assyria. In the beginning of his reign and in his first regnal year, when he had seated himself with might on the throne of his royalty, favourable signs appeared in heaven and on earth. Jupiter neared the sun, was seen, disappeared, changed himself, and reached the point where he was seen again and stood fast in his dwelling a long time. The stars of heaven went to their places, took the right way, abandoned the wrong; month by month the moon and the sun worked together to renew the gods, complete the temples, strengthen his rule, and establish the throne of his priesthood.

By the wisdom which Ashur and Marduk had granted him, Esarhaddon besought these two deities: "Kings of the great gods, creators of gods and goddesses, to a dark place and a difficult task have ye sent me, a work of renewal with men who are disobedient and lacking in understanding since ancient days. Ye who have created gods and goddesses with your hands, do ye yourselves act as builders, and the shrine of your exalted godhead shall be made according to your desire, without change of your orders. Grant to the learned experts, whom ye have called for this task, an exalted understanding like Ea, the creator, and may their wisdom and their understanding through your exalted word complete all the work of their hands through the word of Nin-igi-azag."

Before the judgment of Shamash and Adad he bowed down, and by their gracious order he caused the sons of the seers to enter the House of Wisdom. The requisite information as to Ashur, Babylon, and Nineveh was given in a dream sent to the king. They should enter the House of Wisdom which was in Ashur, the city of government, the abode of the god Ashur, father of the gods, and they gave the names of the skilled workmen who were to take part. On a favourable day of the favourable month of February, Esarhaddon himself entered the

House of Wisdom, the place of renewing whatever the heart
desires, and summoned the carpenters, the stone-masons, the
metal-workers, and the architects, the skilled workmen, and
set forth to them the building which Shamash and Adad had
shown in a dream. Ashur was bribed with a crown of red
gold and precious stones, so that he too looked now with favour
on the undertaking, and the other gods, those of the Babylonian rivals of Babylon especially, Borsippa, Der, Larsa, Sippar, were likewise conciliated. All the skilled workmen and
the men of the corvee were levied for the undertaking, they
were made to carry the yoke and on them was laid the corvee.

On an auspicious day and month gold and silver, food, spices,
honey, oil, cream, wine, sesame brandy, wine from the snow
mountains, were laid upon the foundation. The foundation-
stone was placed by the king on his head and carried to the
place where it was to be laid. With a mould of ivory, box,
ebony, and palm, bricks were formed. To the ground water
they went down and the terrace was made greater with bricks
held together with bitumen. The doors were of cypress whose
scent is good, overlaid with gold, silver, and bronze. Fifty
pounds of gold and silver went into utensils. All the various
grades of priests and attendants were reinstated, the images
of the captive gods were returned from Assyria and Elam and
were placed in their respective shrines. For an eternal prescription the fixed offerings which had fallen into disuse were
re-established.

The city likewise rose from its ruins. Imgur Bel, the inner
wall, and Nimitti Bel, the outer, were rebuilt from foundation
to coping. The sons of Babylon, who had gone into slavery
and had been given over to bond and band, were reassembled
and given peaceful habitations once more. Formerly they had
been "men with (definite) duties," "men of privilege," "men
under the protection of Anu and Bel," and they had enjoyed
"autonomy." Their "privilege," which had fallen into disuse, was returned to its place, and the "tablet of their freedom
from taxes" was written anew. To the four winds their way
was opened, and with the whole of the lands they might have

speech and carry on business.   So Babylon became once more a "city of privileges," an imperial free city, and similar rights were granted to Nippur, Borsippa, Sippar, and Der.

We should expect to find many traces of the building activities of Esarhaddon, but such is not the case.   In part this is due to the almost complete reconstruction undergone by Babylon at the hands of Nebuchadnezzar; it is also possible that the destruction was not so complete as Sennacherib and Esarhaddon would make it to have been.   Bricks of Esarhaddon have indeed been found, claiming the renewal of Esagila, and in particular of its pavement and temple tower.   Another relic of the honour he delighted to render Esagila is a bit of the treasure he dedicated at the shrine, a strip of lapis lazuli on which is depicted the god Adad brandishing the thunderbolt.

Shortly after his accession, Esarhaddon sent Ubaru as the new governor of Babylon.   He reports: "I entered Babylon, the Babylonians received me, and daily they bless the king: 'He it is who will bring back the captivity and the booty of Babylon.'   And from Sippar to the region of the Bitter River the chiefs of the Chaldæans bless the king: 'He it is who will make Babylon inhabited.'   All the lands take comfort before the face of the king my lord." [1]

The sad truth was that all the peoples and lands did not rejoice.   So far from the Chaldæans blessing the king in their homes about the Persian Gulf, the very first troubles of the reign, before even the rehabilitation of Babylon could begin, were with Nabu-zer-kitti-lishir, son of Merodach Baladan.   No long time after the battle of Halulina, he had submitted to Sennacherib, had been presented with rich clothes and a gold armlet, and had been nominated king of the Sealands.   His accession to the Assyrian cause may have had an important part in bringing about the fall of Babylon.   The same year in which Babylon was captured, the Elamite king Humbanimena suffered a stroke of paralysis, and after a year of speechlessness he was succeeded in March of 688 by Humbanhaltash I, who

[1] *H.* 418.

FIG. 135. A GUFA OR REED BOAT PITCHED WITH BITUMEN.

FIG. 136. RUINS OF THE TEMPLE OF EZIDA AT BORSIPPA.
The Temple Tower is one of the two traditional "Towers of Babel."

in all probability was the Elamite general Sennacherib claimed to have killed in the battle of Halulina.

When Sennacherib was murdered, so Esarhaddon informs us, Nabu-zer-kitti-lishir sent no embassy to express grief, neither did he indicate his joy at the accession of the legitimate ruler. The reason for this was that he had recognised the Irrigator, the title assumed by Esarhaddon's rival in Ashur. He informs the Irrigator, "The signs, whether of heaven or earth or underworld, I have written out in order, I have caused them to be said before Shamash. In sacrificial wine, in waters of cleansing, in anointing oil, I have boiled those birds entire, I have caused men to eat them. The image of the king of Akkad," this is Esarhaddon, "has brought before me visions, it spoke, saying: 'Why hast thou caused a restless spirit to dwell in the royal image?' A second time it spoke: 'Inform the Irrigator that Salla gave Nabu-usalli his servant for this purpose.' He inquired concerning Ningal-iddina, Shamash-ibni, and Naid Marduk, he spoke concerning the defection of the land. He said: 'Take the fortified cities in order, accursed is that one, he shall not stand before the Irrigator.' Let them inquire of Nabu-usalli, his servant, he will declare everything." [1]

Ningal-iddina, governor of Uruk, declared for Esarhaddon and Nabu-zer-kitti-lishir promptly besieged him in the Irrigator's service. Word was sent to Ningal-iddina, "Fear not, Esarhaddon sits on his throne," but the message was handed over to the Chaldæan, and he made himself still stronger.[2] But even while so engaged, he was sending to the king complaining that Abi-eriba, of the royal seed, had been commissioned to speak words of evil against him in the palace, and he reports certain news from his father's house.[3] Esarhaddon did not receive his excuses, levies from the near-by provinces surrounded him, and flight to Elam seemed his only recourse. Unfortunately for his hopes, the end of October of the preceding year had seen Humbanhaltash succeeded by another of the same name, and, strange to say, for the moment the new

[1] H. 223.   [2] H. 589.   [3] H. 511.

Humbanhaltash was pro-Assyrian. Nabu-zer-kitti-lishir was at once put to death and his brother Naid Marduk fled from Elam.

It was an unexpected reversal of the normal conditions when Elam could kill a son of Merodach Baladan; it was a still stranger situation when Assyria could grant another son the rule of the Chaldæan country. A letter from the Sealanders was largely responsible for his hospitable reception in Assyria: "There is no sin of our lord before the king. In the forest and the cold of the day he prays to Shamash and Bel for the life and welfare of the king his lord, and his heart is perfect with the king his lord. He trusts in the king his lord and he has returned to his allegiance and through the sceptre of the king his lord he holds sway. Thy father who terrorised all the non-kings and bore rule, by him he makes his affirmation. In the land of Akkad and in all lands there is no desire for any one but Naid Marduk. Behold, the king does not give answer. Naid Marduk is but one man; his men are a hundred thousand. Let the king send his decree." [1]

Not alone in south Babylonia was the accession of Esarhaddon not greeted with joy. When the restoration of Babylon was undertaken, he found the lands of the citizens occupied by the Dakkuru tribe, which had come to consider them theirs by prescription. At the first rumour of the new policy, they sent a formal protest through their chief, Shamash-ibni, though careful to speak of themselves as "the Babylonians, thy loving servants."

Esarhaddon's reply was short and caustic: "Word of the king to the non-Babylonians. I am at peace." Then, with intentional omission of the peace greeting to the recipients: "There is a saying current in men's mouths: 'Potter's dog sneaked into oven, potter makes hot fire within.' Behold, you who are no such thing have changed yourselves into Babylonians, and words which are no words, which you and your lords have made up, have you presented against my servants. There is another saying current: 'Lady of joy at judge's door,

[1] *H*. 958.

slop-jar for judge's wife.' The tablet of windy words and of howlings which you have written, I have placed in its seals and return to you." [1]

After such an expression of ill will, there was nothing left for the Dakkuru but revolt. Shamash-ibni was made prisoner and again Esarhaddon vents his spite in the stinging words he applies to the unfortunate: "A destructive scoundrel who feared not the renown of the lord of lords." Esarhaddon knew the fear of Bel and Nabu, therefore the fields were restored to their former cultivators. Nabu-ushallim, a "son" of that Balasu who had been their chief under Tiglath Pileser III, was appointed to succeed Shamash-ibni.

"During the disturbance and revolt of Akkad" a certain citizen of Borsippa named Mushezib Marduk had been deprived of his estate on the Euphrates, though it was "father's land, bought with money," and held under the protection of the king. The governor and ruler of the Chaldæans had granted it to one of his own partisans. Esarhaddon promised immediate restitution, but the course of justice was as slow as it is to-day, and before the royal seal could be affixed to protect its owner against later claims and to permit its transfer by inheritance, both Esarhaddon and Mushezib Marduk had passed away, and it was not until the ninth year of Shamash-shumukin that the heir, Adad-ibni, could bring the transaction to completion. Nabu-ushallim deposes under oath that the plot was from of old father's house, that it was bought with money, that no governor or ruler had rights in it. Thereupon the title to the estate was recorded in due form on the boundary stone, placed under the protection of the gods who were symbolised by the signs thereon, and the story preserved for future generations. [2]

Shortly after his appointment Nabu-ushallim wrote the king about the swamp people. In the days of Shamash-ibni, half of them fled to Amukkanu land and stirred up the enemy against Assyria. Let the king now send to Kudur of the Amukkanu that they bring out their camp and make them

---

[1] H. 403. [2] King, *Boundary Stones*, 70 ff.

dwell where the king desires. So long as they dwell with the Amukkanu, their brethren will not be submissive and will not do the king's task-work. Kudur, son of Shamash-ibni, calls himself the man whom the king has restored to life. He would perform the service of the king, may he not die like a dog from want and lack of food.[1]

Urta-ahi-iddina was in Nippur at this time, and the king made inquiry of him concerning the artisans, lesser officials, and fugitive serfs who formerly belonged to Shamash-ibni and were now with Nabu-ushallim. The Dakkuru chief flatly refused to surrender them unless he be shown the king's sealed order, and then only into the hands of a member of the royal body-guard. Nor does he approve the presence of agents of Nabu-ushallim, who have come with much money in their hands and desire to purchase horses.

He has also a report on Bel-iqisha, the son of Bunanu, the Gambulu chief, who had been implicated in the war with Nabu-zer-kitti-lishir. Bel-iqisha himself complains to the king: "From the time when first the king seized me, what was my sin against the king that the king should write: 'Thy heart has been perverse.' Where is my sin? Against the king I have not revolted, the feet of the king my lord I have kissed. Now all my powers are exhausted. Bel, Nabu, Sarpanitum, thy gods, surely know whether there is any sin of mine against the king. The king my lord has imprisoned me, I am dying of hunger. By thy gods, Bel and Nabu, I have eaten no food for nine days. As to the messages which the king my lord has sent since I was imprisoned, have I not replied thus to the king my lord: 'If in the wooded mountains of a surety I have gone, if as a messenger I have been courageous, judge whether there is any sin before the king my lord.'"[2] This is very different from the statement of the annals that he came with tribute of his own accord. But the annals does tell the truth when it adds that Esarhaddon strengthened his stronghold of Shapi Bel, made confident his heart, and recognised his archers as part of the Assyrian bowmen.

For Urta-ahi-iddina continued with the story of how Bel-

[1] H. 258; 756.   [2] H. 390; cf. 541.

iqisha went to Babylon, where he married one daughter to Bel-ahi-iddina, to Borsippa, where he secured a son of Nadinu for another, and to the Dakkuru, where the hand of the third was bestowed upon Zakir, the chief shepherd of Nabu. He also secured from Nabu-dini-amur the city of Bit Hussani on the Piti canal near Kutu, which contributed a hundred measures of dates and a similar amount of grain, though it was royal property belonging to the province of Babylon, and neither the father nor the grandfather of Bel-iqisha had ever enjoyed its possession.[1]

Just at this moment Assyrian officials seemed less necessary than Gambulu chiefs, and the king took Urta-ahi-iddina to task for his attitude. A very humble letter came in reply, with heaped-up salutations. The king has demanded why he had not sent back the personal troops loaned him by the king, and he promises so to do. There may be something sinister in the last statement, that Enlil-bani has arrived as king's servant and for the guard of Nippur,[2] for Urta-ahi-iddina may be identified with the *qadu* official of Nippur, and he, we know, was carried off to Assyria and killed before the first full year of Esarhaddon was ended.

The failure of Esarhaddon in his first attempt against Egypt offered an opportunity which Humbanhaltash was not slow to seize. He fell upon Sippar and made a great killing there, so that the ceremonial procession of the god Shamash could not move out that year. Kudur, the Dakkuru official who was responsible, had already reported that while he was in the enemy land, the Puqudu in a raid had destroyed the loyal Amukkanu, slaying the men, ravishing the women, and he has heard that they have marched against Zaba, the guardsman. Thereupon he sent troops to his aid and the captain Nabu-shar-usur seized them when he reached the Royal Canal. The king should know that Amukkanu is destroyed, that the Puqudu dwell in their land, and that the troops with him have not been ordered out. The Puqudu are the aggressors and "we abhor the sin of the land."[3]

After the capture of Sippar, while the king was encamped

[1] *H*. 336.   [2] *H*. 797.   [3] *H*. 275.

on the border of Egypt, an eclipse took place in July. None of his soldiers cared for the welfare of Assyria; right and left it smote. Now his messenger is with him, let the king question him. Kudur has performed the incantation for the eclipse, and sends a messenger to the king asking for many more. Nabu-shum-lishir, brother's son of Zakir, the magician of the bath-house, has cleansed the temple "Palace of the Mountain," and the binding and loosing for the governor, Bel-etir. Has not the king ordered him in the second year to come to see his face? Thus Kudur attempted to defend himself against responsibility for a mutiny of the soldiers which he attributed to the malign influence of an eclipse.[1]

The qadu of Nippur, perhaps Shum-iddina, the son of Gahul, and so a brother of the late king Nergal-ushezib (694–689), has the age-long excuse: "The king knows that I am exceedingly ill; if I were not ill, had I not been ill, I would have come myself to greet the king." In his place he has sent his brother Bel-usatu and ten well-born citizens of Nippur. "The king knows that all lands hate us because of Assyria, and we dare not set our feet in any of the lands where we might go. They would kill us, for they say: 'Why have you taken the yoke of Assyria?'" They have closed the city gates completely, they go not forth, for the watch of the king they keep. The messenger and the chiefs sent by the king have seen everything, let them make report to the king. "Let not the king surrender us to the hands of a substitute." There is no spring-water and the people committed to his care are dying of thirst. The king's father had given them permission to extend the Baniti canal to Nippur, and had promised that no prince should cut them off from it. Let the king send to Ubaru, governor of Babylon, who has charge of the canal. Otherwise, all the lands will say: "The men of Nippur, who have taken the yoke of Assyria, must in their thirst look to the skies for rain."[2]

Probably the last letter sent by the qadu reports that when the master of ceremonies and the minor officials went down to

[1] H. 276.　　　　　　　　　　　　　　　[2] H. 327.

the Chaldæans, the brothers of the Elamite king begged him
to go to their aid, but he refused, fearing to violate the oaths.
A son of Nabu-ahi-usur has entered Nippur, he has laid hands
upon Sippar, he has seized the nobles of Nippur. When the
qadu remonstrated with him, he mocked him in his native city
and cast him into prison in the sight of his own people. Pirki
also came into the city at the special request of the men of
Nippur. Let the king order an investigation of the city's
case and force the son of Nabu-ahi-usur to return to Nippur
as much as he carried off.[1]

Humbanhaltash "died in his palace without being sick,"
and his place was taken by his brother, the pro-Assyrian
Urtaku. The news seemed too good to be true, and Esarhaddon cannily took the precaution of inquiring of Shamash
whether Urtaku was to be trusted. When the god answered
in the affirmative, Esarhaddon sent a letter wishing peace for
his brother, his sons and his daughters, his nobles and his
land. The newly found brother was informed that Esarhaddon had accomplished all that the gods had ordered him.[2]
Eloquent testimony to the change which had come about in
international relations was the return of Ishtar and the other
gods from Elam. But neither Shum-iddina nor Kudur rejoiced at their return. Their enemies, Nabu-ushallim and Bel-
iqisha, had the ear of the king, and Kudur and Shum-iddina
were brought to Assyria for punishment.

Like that of his father, the reign of Esarhaddon is dominated
by his Babylonian policy. Like his predecessors, he took the
title "King of Shumer and Akkad," but never "King of Babylon." Instead, he contented himself with the title of "protector" of the city. The lists, however, count him as full king
of Babylon throughout his reign, and at Babylon itself business documents were dated by his regnal years. It was little
enough recognition of the good done by Esarhaddon for Babylon and of harm for Assyria.

[1] H. 328.   [2] H. 918.

CHAPTER XXVIII

SECRETS OF THE LIVER OMENS AND GREEK CONTRIBUTIONS TO A PALACE

No small space in the royal annals is devoted to the wars on the northeast frontier. The operations seem on a small scale, the individuals mentioned are quite unknown, and the casual reader might well pass the whole series by in the belief that here is only another example of Assyrian frightfulness.

The official optimism of the annals destined to posterity does not exceed the optimism of the oracular gods and goddesses. Ishtar asks where is the land of the enemy; since the answer expected is that there is none, the conclusion follows that Esarhaddon is to remain in Kalhu and in Nineveh as the shepherd of his people. The mighty men of the Elamites and the Mannai will be restrained, the Akkadian, the father of sin, will have his letter known, the plan of Mugallu of Asia Minor will be dissolved. Who is the man who has no friends, the man who is despised? Let him take courage under the shadow of Esarhaddon.[1]

Ashur was equally optimistic. The Cimmerians shall be given into his hands and fire shall be hurled into Elli, for Ashur has given Esarhaddon the four world quarters. In the house where he shines forth, in the house where he grew to maturity, he shall have no rival, he shall glow as the rising of the sun-god. The men of Harhar have plotted against the king, but he has declared "Unto Ashur I shall appeal," and his shame has been known. From within the gate of heaven Ashur will come quickly, he will hasten and make fire to consume them, and blazing stones will he rain upon them. His foes will he cut down, the river will be filled with their blood. This is the greeting rendered in the presence of the cult statue, let it be brought into the king's presence on a tablet. Let them pour

[1] Langdon, *Tammuz*, 139.

out oil and sacrifice lambs and burn incense, then let them read it to the king.[1]

Over against the official accounts, we may place a new source of information, the queries addressed to the sun-god Shamash and answered through the inspection of the liver of the sacrificial sheep. Intended as they were for the ear of the god alone, they confess the hopes and fears, and especially the latter, felt by the rulers. If we cannot with much assurance connect them with the events narrated in the annals, so much the worse for the formal history. Viewed in this newer and clearer light, the wars on the northeast frontier cease to be mere examples of Assyrian aggression and appear as they were in truth, a desperate struggle to hold the frontier against the foes who were in a bare half-century to break through and destroy the very name of Assyria. There is deep tragedy in these confidently phrased tales of victory.[2]

Much space is devoted to a certain Kashtaritu. Though called only a village chief of Karkashshi, this Iranian leader seems to have been the moving spirit of a great confederacy of Cimmerians, Mannai, and Medes, who were threatening the very existence of Assyria. "O Shamash, mighty lord," cries Esarhaddon, "that which I inquire of thee, do thou answer with sure promise. From this day, the 3d day of this month of May, to the 11th day of the month of August of this year, for these hundred days and nights, the determined period for the execution of the seer's office, in this determined time, shall Kashtaritu with his troops, shall the troops of the Cimmerians, shall the troops of the Medes, shall the troops of the Mannai, shall any enemy whatsoever, plan or consider, whether by assault, whether by might, whether by weapon, war, or conflict, whether by breach, whether by the battering-ram or the siege-engine, whether with one siege-engine or another siege-engine, whether by hunger, whether by oaths contrary to the gods and goddesses, whether by flattering words and an agreement, whether by any deceitful message, that the city should

---

[1] Strong, *BA.*, II, 637 ff.; Langdon, *Tammuz*, 134 ff.

[2] Knudtzon, *Assyr. Gebete an den Sonnengott*, 1893; Klauber, *Politische-religiöse Texte*, 1913; cf. Jastrow, *Religion*, II, 174 ff.

be taken, shall Kishassu be taken, into the midst of that city of Kishassu shall they go, that city of Kishassu shall their hands take, to their hands shall the property be measured out? Thy great godhead knows. The capture of that city of Kishassu by the hands of any enemy whatsoever, from this day to the day appointed by me, is it by the mandate, is it by the mouth of thy great godhead, O Shamash, great lord, appointed, shall they see it, shall they see it? Grant that after the time fixed by me, grant that against him their hearts shall plan evil, that they shall make revolt, grant that they shall inflict upon him a defeat and plunder his fields, grant that the decision of this day, whether it is for good or whether it is for evil, by a destructive rain shall not be destroyed, grant that something unclean or uncleanness shall not come to the place of the liver inspection, grant that the lamb of thy godhead which has been exposed for examination shall not be defective or faulty, grant that he who touches the head of the lamb shall not be clothed with unclean sacrificial garments, shall have eaten anything impure, shall have changed or mistaken the fixing of the hand, grant that in the mouth of the seer's son the incantation has not been hurried." Then follows the liver omen which was to tell whether the omen of the exposed liver was favourable or the reverse.

In the same laboured manner the troubled king inquired about many matters. Bartatua, the Scythian king, has demanded the daughter of Esarhaddon to wife. Far from resenting this suggested marriage with the barbarian, the only fear is that the sacrifice may be in vain. Will he speak with Esarhaddon true words of peace, will he truly say the "peace" which acknowledges his nominal submission, will he keep his oath to Esarhaddon, will he do that which is good for Esarhaddon? A second inquiry proves a successful marriage, for Bartatua is expected to march against Bit Kapsi and Saparda in the Median land, the enemies of Assyria.

Kashtaritu has attempted to excite Mamitiarshu, the Median village chief. Will he be successful? Esarhaddon has despatched a messenger to Kashtaritu. Will he be killed on the way by the Cimmerians or some of the other allies, and if he is fortunate enough to reach his destination, will he be put to death there? If he did win through, he made no impression on the barbarian, for the next tablet indicates that an army had been sent against him by the Assyrians. The allies had reached Uesi, once the much-contested outlet from Haldia; now Haldia had lost it, and the question is whether it will fall into enemy hands. Will the allies, now united with Dusanni, the Sapardian, capture in May the city they have attacked? Uesi fell, and the question is next whether the Scythian hordes which now occupy the Mannai provinces and have crossed the frontier into that country, will accomplish their purpose in July. Will they emerge from the pass of the city of Hubushkia and fall upon the cities of Harrania and Anisus? Will they ravage the Assyrian border and carry off much spoil? If an ambassador is sent to Hubushkia, will the Mannai slay him? Will the expedition against the Mannai be successful? Will the general enter the pass of the city of Sandu and aid the city of Kilman in May? Will they take the cities of Karibti and Suba in Saparda in the same month? The city of Dur Bel, the fortress of Esarhaddon, has been taken by the Mannai; will it be recovered? Will the expedition against the land of Sirish be fortunate? Will the Mannai or the Rimai fall upon it? Shall the general named upon the tablet go against the land of Kukkuma, the cities of Udpani and Ramadani, or will the Medes and the Mannai take them? Shall the commander-in-chief, Sha Nabu-shu, go against Amul and will he take it? What of Ahsheri, who has united with the Cimmerians? Will the city of Sharru-iqbi be taken by engines, hunger, or want, through fear or the defeat of the Assyrian troops?

In the case of Ahsheri, we need not regret the loss of the god's answer. Esarhaddon maintained publicly that he crushed the Mannai and the Scythians, but the answer of history is given by his son Ashur-bani-apal; the Mannai, he confesses, took it from his father, and Ahsheri continued a thorn in the flesh in his own reign.

Assyrian administration was not quite at an end, for we

have several references to the collection of "gifts" of horses, but there is ever danger from the confederates. Officials have gone for horses into Bit Kari of Media; will trouble arise from the Scythians? Will the party sent for horses to the cities of Antarpati, Karzita, and Bit Tad be a success, especially as Eparna must be taken into consideration? Esarhaddon claims in his annals the tribute of Shitirparna and Eparna, lords of the mighty cities of Patusharra, on the edge of the salt desert, in the midst of the distant Medes, on the border of Mount Bikni, a mountain of lapis lazuli. The comparison with the famous blue stone so desired in all antiquity is sufficient to prove its identity with the bluish, snow-clad Demavend, which towers over the present Persian capital of Teheran.

Again we are told of an inroad by which the natives were forced to take to the waters of their inland sea. Only those who were open of knees so much as reached the mountain top, and they were ultimately captured like birds. The nomads who dwelt far away in their tents were torn out by the roots like a flood, those who had entered the sea as a fortress and the mountain as a citadel did not escape the snare. The abode of the man of the mountain was changed to the sea and of the seaman to the mountain. From the midst of the sea the enemy said: "The fox is before the face of Shamash, whither shall he flee?" Thus they testified to their acquaintance with the ancient classic which told how the fox attempted to defend himself before the god when accused of theft. The literary style is excellent, but the inquiries to this same Shamash show the king fearfully begging to know whether his enemy will attack Bit Hamban, and this country is well on the way to Babylonia.

Little historical imagination is required to see behind the official inscriptions with the aid of these secret inquiries to the god. Details of dates, cities, individuals, may be unimportant; what is of supreme importance is the coming in of barbarians of our own Indo-European speech. To us of the north and west such an incoming cannot but be of the highest interest, even though we admit that kinship with us in speech need

not of necessity mean kinship in blood. Many of the names
of places and persons sound strangely familiar. For some
only slight phonetic changes are required to transfer their elements into similar meanings in our present-day speech. Shitirparna reminds us of another Chitrafarna of our schoolboy
days, though we knew him by the Greek corruption of Tissa-
phernes, the mortal enemy of the younger Cyrus. Many another is known to us from less-read Greek or Roman writings.
Madai, Gimirrai, Ishguzai play a large part in the pages of
the Father of History as Medes, Cimmerians, and Scythians;
Antarpati is the prototype of Atropatene, the classical name
of northwest Persia; Patusharra is the well-known land of
Pateischories; the men of Saparda are the Persian tribe of the
Sparda; Bartatua is that Protothyes, father of the Scyth Madyas, who overran the whole of the Assyrian Empire.

Sargon and Sennacherib had gained control of the Cilician
Gates. By the opportune alliance of the rebel Abdmelcart of
Sidon with Sanduarri of Kundi and Sisu, cities which as the
classical Cyinda and the mediæval Sis were to be famous as
treasure-city and as an Armenian political capital respectively,[1]
access was gained to the one competing pass across the Taurus.
At the end of this road lay the sacred city of Comana. The
first range of mountains was successfully crossed, and the
Assyrian general reached the province of Hubushna, the Ca-
bissus of Roman times, and but a short distance south of the
sacred city with its accumulated treasures.

Here they chanced upon one of the raiding Cimmerians,
whose name of Teushpa recalls that of the almost contemporary Teispes, ancestor of Cyrus. Ashur promised that they
would be delivered into Esarhaddon's hands and the Assyrians
claim that this promise was fulfilled. At any rate, the northward progress of the Assyrians was stopped and they turned
west across the mountains to the fertile plain where was the
earlier Cilicia and the Duuna land about the great city of
Tyana. The account ends at this point, and Esarhaddon goes

[1] Strab. xiv, 5, 10; Diod. xviii, 62; xix, 56; Plut. *Eumen.* 13; Suidas, *s. v.*; cf.
Ramsay, *Historical Geography*, 385.

out of his way to declare that he was the first to conquer this territory, although we know that it had been forced to pay tribute to his father and grandfather. In sober truth, he was chronicling the failure of the most ambitious attempt to subjugate Asia Minor.

More immediate menace was felt on the northern border, but the danger was no longer from Haldia. Argishtish II was succeeded by his son Rusash about the same time that Esarhaddon became king, but his kingdom was sadly shrunken. The line of fortresses from Erzerum to Echmiazin marked definite retreat of the frontier in the Caucasus-Black Sea region under Cimmerian attacks. The Mannai were now more aggressive than the Haldians, and the Urumia country was lost. Early in the reign of Sennacherib the direct line between the Assyrian and Haldian capitals had been cut, and in the inquiries through the liver omens we can actually see the Iranian confederates winning Uesi, the city in the pass which forms the most difficult portion of the route.

Farther west, where the first Tiglath Pileser and the last Ashur-nasir-apal made their most advertised conquests, the native Asianic peoples had organised a state to which they assigned the historic name of Shupria, which had not enjoyed an independent existence since Shalmaneser III, though a certain Shuprian played some part in the Armenian wars of Sargon. Quite as a matter of course, Esarhaddon calls its ruler a mere bandit; after reading the following letter from him, we may feel inclined to excuse the Assyrian king for his unkind feelings:

"Why has the king my lord sent days of want and privation and full of suffering? When thy father accepted slanders of this sort, which are not fit for remembrance, he did not send. And he who has sinned, front, back, right, left, above and below, the king of the gods, the exalted, will transfer all the dwellings to the hands of the man who fears him. As for the lapis lazuli, of which the king my lord wrote: 'Let them bring lapis lazuli,' the king my lord does not know that I went up after lapis lazuli, and as I was bringing the lapis lazuli the land revolted from me. If it please the king my lord, let a considerable force come to secure the lapis lazuli. When they come, food with them I shall not eat, water with them I shall not drink, with them I shall not go, before thy messenger I shall not stand, the royal peace of the king my lord I shall not ask." Not to ask the king's peace was flat rebellion, and yet he has the audacity to add: "Let not the king reckon it a sin!" [1]

Many Assyrian officials, up to the rank of governor, were fleeing the sinking Assyrian ship of state and were taking refuge in Shupria. Decaying Haldia suffered the same loss. Esarhaddon demanded that the fugitives be surrendered to the nagir he should send, and the demand was twice repeated, but the only reply was an attack on the Assyrian posts along the border.

Preparations for war followed. If we believe Esarhaddon, no longer did the king of Shupria say, "I fear not the great lordship of Esarhaddon," he fled in terror and rent his royal dress, like a slave he made his appearance, among slaves he counted himself. With prayer and beseeching and casting down of face, he ascended the wall of his city. He wept with piteous outcry, his fingers were opened in prayer, he besought Esarhaddon's lordship; because of the aid of Ashur and the fame of the king's bravery, he mourned for help. Thus he wrote to Esarhaddon: "Shupria, the land which has sinned against thee, to its whole extent shall it obey thee, thy governors over it establish, and it shall give thee obeisance. Tribute and tax, yearly, that cannot be measured, lay upon them. I am a thief, for the sin I have sinned fifty times will I repay; for one lost fugitive of Assyria, I will repay a hundredfold. Restore me to life, the fame of Ashur I will publish, I will praise thy might. Whoever sins against Ashur, king of the gods, to the command of Esarhaddon, king of the world, his lord, does not hearken, a fugitive from Assyria to his lord does not return, in my hands may I see, for the nobles who gave me counsel have planned with me rebellion which is not to my advantage, a great sin against Ashur have I sinned, to the

[1] H. 1240.

command of the king have I not hearkened. The sons of Ashur, thy servants, have I not returned, that which was for my own good have I not done. The oath of the great gods which I have transgressed, the command of thy royalty, which I have despised, has bested me. May the wrath of thy heart be appeased, may grace be granted me, loose my sin."

Esarhaddon replied: "Hast thou ever heard the word of a mighty king a second time? Yet have I, who am a very mighty king, sent to thee a third time and thou hast not hearkened to the word of my lips. The wrath of my heart hast thou not feared, and before my embassy hast thou not abased thy pride. War and battle hast thou raised against me, and the mighty weapons of Ashur hast thou destroyed in their abiding-place." So Esarhaddon heard not his prayer, received not his recantation, accepted not his petition, turned not his neck, his liver was not reconciled, the wrath of his heart was not appeased, grace he did not grant him, he did not say: "It is enough."

Uppume, the capital of Shupria, was situated on a mighty mountain, like a cloud. The Assyrians with difficulty and with pain built a great structure by piling up earth and stone and set it against the wall of the city. While Esarhaddon was engaged in marching about that region victoriously, on the 21st of December, a day which was not favourable for work, the children of the ashakku demons set fire to the mound by night. By the command of the king of the gods, Marduk, the north wind blew, the good lord of the gods took his position, he turned the tongue of the devouring flame against Uppume, so that it could not seize the mound but burned the city wall, which went up in smoke. The relieving force was put to rout and its members were hung around the city.

An image of the Shuprian king was therefore made, clothed with the dress of a suppliant, and fetters of iron were placed upon it. Products of stone, the work of his stone-mason, silver and red gold, he cut off and placed in the hands of his sons, Sheris and Kengi Teshub. To obtain grace and safety for his life, they brought it to the presence of the Assyrian king and begged him to lay the blame for ruin which could not be told on the body of the ashakku demons. Esarhaddon would hear nothing of such excuses. In vain did they offer sacrifices and pour out libations to the gods. "The word of the god will not be twice repeated, the days are complete, thy hour has come, thy time is near, from the god's mouth has gone forth the destruction of thy land, through his unchanging order has been spoken the captivity of thy men."

His mighty booty was brought to the presence of Esarhaddon and dedicated to his gods. Charioteers, body-guards, artisans, cavalry, officials of various varieties, axe-men, messengers, scouts, gardeners, are some of the groups which were recovered and added to the mighty forces of Ashur; the land of Assyria, like quivers, he filled throughout its whole extent. The remnant were divided like sheep among the nobles who served in the palaces; in the distribution the city of Ashur is conspicuous for its absence. The fugitives who had abandoned their lord and had escaped to Shupria were deprived of nose, eyes, and ears. There were likewise men who had fled from Haldia; Rusash, the Haldian king, had demanded their extradition but had not obtained it. Esarhaddon ordered an inquiry, and not a single fugitive was retained; they were all sent home to receive their punishment at the hands of their lord. The pressure of the confederated tribes, their own mutual decline, had compelled friendship between the two great powers of western Asia.

By order of the gods, the metropolis Uppume was rebuilt and the other towns had their names changed to such high-sounding sentences as "Ashur has brought back his land," "Who is equal to Ashur?" "The word of Ashur wavers not," "The word of the king wavers not," "Trample those who bow not down," "He who sees shall fear," "Destroying the enemy," "May its conqueror grow old," "He who took it shall be established," "May he grow old who has pacified the heart of Ashur," "Wall of Esarhaddon," "No enemy shall enter," "If thou fearest God, thou shalt possess thy land in peace," "Ashur hurls down my foe," "Ashur has increased its yoke."

In these cities were settled men of the upper and lower seas, for the second time that land was divided and two governors assigned. As for the casualties, Esarhaddon announces that they were one charioteer, two horsemen, and three sappers; he is simply quoting the inscription of his grandfather.[1]

The great attack on Uppume was in December of 673, but it was not until the end of 672 that its booty reached Uruk, where the king had taken up his residence. Just before the close of the reign comes an illuminating letter from Ashur-ukin. The king has written him in regard to the guards stationed above Urartu, the Mannai, the Medes, and Hubushkia, and once more we note how the Mannai and the Medes are directly athwart the main line of communication between Assyria and Haldia. He is to place between their eyes the necessity of watching and of turning their ears to the fugitives round about them. If a fugitive from these countries should flee to them, let him be sent to the crown prince. Let the scribe for the Mannai write a sealed letter. Ahu-dur-enshi, the captain attached to the crown prince, may they quickly send with soldiers. Just now two fugitives have fled from the Mannai, one an officer, and one bearded; he will bring them, for in their mouth is the desired information.[2]

At the beginning of his reign Esarhaddon took up his residence in Nineveh and developed a new suburb, the Kar Ashur-ahi-iddina, a large piece of land cut off from the field and used as a building site. Work had already been done there by Sennacherib, but the completion of the armoury was to the credit of his son. Captives tore down the smaller building, and in its place Esarhaddon erected a great limestone terrace. For the material needed in the construction of the building which crowned it, he turned to the seacoast and the midst of the sea. The contributors are mentioned by name, and a most impressive list it is. From Phœnicia came Baal of Tyre and Manasseh of Judah, Chemosh-gaber of Edom, Musuri, "the Egyptian," of Moab, Sil Bel of Ascalon, Achish of Ekron, Melechasaph of Byblus, Mattanbaal of Arvad, Abibaal of

[1] Winckler, *Forsch.*, II, 27 ff.   [2] *H.* 434.

Samsimuruna, Pudiel of the house of Ammon, Ahimelech of Ashdod—the only kings, be it noted, on the whole Syrian coast who still retained the shadow of independence. They presented great beams, tall columns, planks of cedar and cypress from the Sirara and Lebanon mountains, female bulls, slabs of many kinds of rare stones, including breccia.

On quite a different footing as regards their political status and of yet greater interest to the historian is the precious list of Greek rulers from Cyprus: Ekishtura of Edial, Pilagura of Kitrusi, Kisu of Sillua, Ituandar of Pappa, Eresu of Sillu, Damasu of Kuri, Atmezu of Tamesu, Damusi of Qartihadasti, Unusagusu of Lidir, Bunusu of Nurenu. The process of Hellenisation is virtually complete, for even the ruler of the Cypriote Carthage bears the same name as he of Curium.

The Greek names fall into two distinct classes. Peculiarly Cypriote are Onesagaras of Ledra and Eteandrus of Paphus, and of the second we actually possess armlets said to have been found at Curium, where in Cypriote script he is called Etevandoro of Papo. Pythagorus of Chytri likewise bears a typically Cypriote name and recalls the great Philosopher who was almost his contemporary. Distinctly Achæan and of the older type is the king of Idalium, Ægistheus, like in name to the knave who treacherously slew Agamemnon, lord of Argos; Cisus of Salamis, whose name is that of another Argive prince; Hereus of Soli, who reminds us that the greatest of all the shrines in the Argive plain was that of Hera; and Admetus of Tamassus, who at once brings to mind the husband of the devoted Alcestis. Only Damasus of Curium and Pytheas of Nure cannot be located in one of these groups.

That these kings sent tribute in the ordinary sense of the word is not for a moment to be believed. They sent gifts to the Assyrian king; in return they secured valuable commercial concessions, and the result is to be seen in the sudden burst of Assyrianisation which marks the art of the island. But seven Greek monarchs sent their gifts to Sargon; ten good Greeks appear as friends of Esarhaddon. The chief cities of Cyprus were now Greek, though in one case the change had come so late that the Phœnician name of Carthage was still in common use. The Greek was coming into his own.

Female bulls of shining bronze looked to both sides of the armoury, before and behind; the entrance was adorned with friezes of basalt and lapis lazuli. By the side of the building an Amanus park was laid out and canals brought water for the horses. In 673 the official completion was celebrated by a great feast in which all the high dignitaries participated. The bulls were still incomplete, the alabaster slabs were in similar shape, when Esarhaddon tired of his plan and construction ceased. The armoury fell into ruin, protected only by the fancy of a later generation that saw in its heaps the tomb of Jonah, buried on the spot where he had successfully preached repentance to the Ninevites.

Ashur had a new home and the near-by New Year's House was completed. The great northern wall was pushed out with a splendid limestone facing, with an entrance and with battlements. On the space secured an addition to the palace was prepared. Arbela was rewarded for her many favourable oracles by new constructions, and in Tarbisu he made an abode for the son of his heart, Ashur-bani-apal, where Akkullanu made libations for the king at evening.[1]

Esarhaddon's love was transferred in his later years to Kalhu. The earlier Tabiltu canal, which Ashur-nasir-apal had made to carry water from the Zab River to the capital, had become filled with débris and was no longer large enough to meet the new demands; the entrance restored by Esarhaddon still may be seen. If we have little record of the building, we have a fair number of letters and no small remains. Arad Nabu, for example, writes in to his master to state that the gold which arrived during the month of October has been inspected with the aid of the abarakku and the palace scribe; there are three talents of refined gold and four of unrefined in the palace, which have been deposited and sealed by the chief of the metal-workers. The gold for the statues of the kings and of the king's mother has not been given; let the king order

---

[1] *H.* 47; 628.

FIG. 137. "TOMB OF THE PROPHET JONAH," COVERING THE ARMOURY
BUILT BY SENNACHERIB AND ESARHADDON AT NINEVEH.

FIG. 138. "NINEVEH SHALL BECOME A WASTE."
Ploughed land where once were the houses of Nineveh. City walls in distance.

FIG. 139.   ALABASTER MODEL OF SPHINX.   (Esarhaddon.)

FIG. 140.   HUMAN–HEADED BULL.   (SARGON.)
(Louvre.)

the abarakku and the palace scribe to open the gold.   If the beginning of the month is favourable, let them give it to the skilled workmen that they may execute their work.[1]

The new palace was erected in the southwest corner of the city enclosure and faced north.   From the platform one passed through winged bulls into a great court, two hundred and eighty by one hundred feet in size, and surrounded on three sides by buildings.   From this one passed in turn through other bulls into the largest single room ever attempted by Assyrian architects, sixty-two feet wide and no less than one hundred and sixty-five feet long.   The proportions were imposing, and the result was over ten thousand feet of floor space, but the plan failed because the architect was unable to construct a roof to cover the hall.   He was therefore forced to run through the centre three piers of irregular shape and varying length, thereby blurring the original plan and making a series of smaller rooms.

Letters show the transfer to Kalhu and the various ceremonies which crowned the work.   Nabu-shum-iddina, overseer of Nabu, reports to the crown prince that the couch of Nabu is to be prepared in Kalhu on the 3d of May.   Nabu will enter into the couch house and the next day he will return. Since, as the crown prince knows, he is the overseer of Nabu's house, he will go to Kalhu.   The god is to proceed first to the palace enclosure and then to the park, where sacrifices are to be slain.   The charioteer of the gods will come from the divine stables and will take the divinity in procession and then bring him back.   He will advance in a stately manner.   Of the people who accompany him, each will offer his sacrifice, whatever it may be.   Whoever offers a qa of food may eat in Nabu's house.[2]

Arad Nabu likewise reports that on the 4th of May Nabu and Tashmetum entered the bedchamber.   He has given orders that the offerings of Ashur-bani-apal, the crown prince; of Shamash-shum-ukin, crown prince of Babylon; of the lady Sherua-eterat, of Ashur-mukin-palea, and of Shar-shame-

[1] *H*. 114.   [2] *H*. 65.

irsiti-ballitsu should be sacrificed before the divine pair in the bedchamber. He closes with the comforting assurance that they shall cause the king's sons to live a hundred years, shall make their sons and grandsons attain old age, and the king shall behold it all.[1]

Nergal-sharrani reports on the same happenings: To-morrow, the 4th, at evening, Nabu and Tashmetum are to enter the bedchamber. Let them eat food from the king on the 5th. The temple overseer shall lie down and they shall bring into the temple a lion's head and a torch. From the 5th to the 10th the gods shall remain in their bedchamber and the overseer shall do likewise. On the 11th Nabu shall set out, his feet he shall loosen, to his park he shall go, in his abode he shall then abide, the king he will bless.[2]

Cummin has been seen in the court which adjoins the temple of Nabu and fungus has appeared on the walls of the adjacent cribs. Incantations against them have been prepared, and the regular ceremonies are being carried on. Adad-shum-usur will do this on the morrow, let him do these extra ones also. As to what the queen mother, his lord, has made inquiry concerning the material required for the ceremonies, there is to be a mixture of good oil, water, honey, good spices, myrrh, hemp. One ox and two large lambs are to be sacrificed. Ninqai, servant of the queen mother, is not strong enough to carry out the ceremonies, she should not enter. Let the treasury be opened by the order of the queen mother, his lord, that the ceremonies may be performed. It is a month since he has been sick and the thorn has pricked him. From Dilbat is his sickness, through her good-will there is help, yet without the king he can do nothing. Let the king grant him escape from his illness.[3]

Inquiry has been made of Ishtar-shum-eresh about the images of the kings in Harurrum. They should be ready in March and the king wishes information as to when they can be brought in and where they shall stand. Ishtar-shum-eresh will place them the very day they are brought in. If it please

[1] H. 113.   [2] H. 366.   [3] H. 367 f.; 203.

the king, let the royal statues be placed right and left before the god, let the statues of the king's sons be placed before Sin. Then will Sin, the lord of the crown, monthly, without cessation, in their rising and their setting, be at the side of the king and will not take from him distant days, stability of throne, or gift of strength.[1]

The high dignitaries of Nineveh were forced to accompany the king to the "New House," as it was henceforth to be called. One of them writes from Nineveh: "I saw the inhabitants in Nineveh, they are all fools, none of the old families of Nineveh are any longer in Nineveh, those who stood before the king thy father are all in Kalhu." [2]

We cannot learn much from the ruins as to the art of the period. Only the hastily made bulls and lions of rough limestone represent genuine Assyrian art. The beautiful crouching sphinxes which supported the pillars are undoubtedly to be attributed to Egyptian influence and to this is due the delicate alabaster models from which they were enlarged. For the panelling of the walls Esarhaddon did not trouble himself to excavate new slabs; he went to the ruined palaces of Ashur-nasir-apal II and Tiglath Pileser III, nor did he spare those of his grandfather Sargon. Their beautifully carved reliefs he hacked off, sawed in two, or turned to the wall. He intended to carve in their place his sculptures, accompanied by the story of his own expeditions, but he never enjoyed the opportunity. The walls were still unadorned, the annals which were to cover them had been barely written down on tablets, the errors of the scribe were still uncorrected. Huge piles of slabs pillaged from earlier palaces were heaped up in the courts or in the great hall itself, awaiting the order to deface them. The order never came, for Esarhaddon was called away and never returned alive.

[1] H. 36.   [2] H. 1103.

CHAPTER XXIX

EGYPT AT LAST!

To an observant bystander it must have been obvious that the great danger to the future was to be found on the eastern frontier, where the resources of the empire were being drained in the effort to hold back the waves of barbarians dashing against its borders. It is difficult to understand why this was the moment chosen by Esarhaddon for the wildest of adventures, one which did for the instant bring much glory to Assyria but contributed no real strength, which rather hastened the inevitable day of reckoning.

Assyrian kings had long looked with desire upon Egypt, so rich and seemingly so defenceless. Tiglath Pileser III had reached the outermost limits, Sargon and Sennacherib had each defeated Egyptian rulers, but the boundary of the desert had never been crossed, and Sennacherib had wisely made his peace with the Ethiopian rulers of the Nile valley, and Syria had in consequence continued peacefully Assyrian.

Some time after the battle of Eltekeh, Shabataka (700–688) of Egypt was deposed by his cousin Taharka (688–663). The troubles at Esarhaddon's accession led to the revolt of Abdmelcart of Sidon; his only mentioned ally is Sanduarri of the Taurus region, but Egypt was doubtless in the background. His home on the reef where had been the earliest settlement of the Sidonians, and where are yet to be seen the remains of early buildings and of an aqueduct, fell an easy prey in 677, its dwellings were overthrown, its wall cast into the waters, and when Abdmelcart fled into the midst of the sea, he was drawn out like a fish.

The kings of the Hittite land and of the seashore had been gathered together to take part in the siege; they witnessed the formal transfer of the city to the mainland and its rechristening as Kar Ashur-ahi-iddina, "Esarhaddon's Fort," which was destined to be the seat of the governor. Colonists from mountain and seashore on the eastern border of the empire were settled with an increased tribute.

Among those present on this momentous occasion was Baal of Tyre. Esarhaddon tells us that in return for an increased tribute, he granted the cities of Marub and Zarephath, but a chance document from the Assyrian archives gives a slightly different aspect to the matter. This is the actual treaty which was struck between Esarhaddon and the more than half independent ruler of the island city. To be sure, it was somewhat one-sided, for Esarhaddon often speaks in the first person and enforces the penalties; notwithstanding, there is a very substantial *quid pro quo*. If Esarhaddon is able to insist that he may appoint a resident to watch over the Tyrian territory, that Baal is to obey any message sent by the king, that he is to appear when summoned by the resident, the commercial clauses are those of equals.

If the ships of Baal or the men of Arvad are shipwrecked in Palestine, neither men nor property are to be seized, but they are to be sped safely on their way, and the same is to hold true with ships belonging to Assyrian subjects. The routes open to the trade of Baal are carefully listed. He may enter Acco and Dor, in the land of Palestine, the seashore cities which are directly under Assyrian rule, Byblus, Mount Lebanon, and all the cities thereof; in short, all the cities in the possession of Esarhaddon, king of Assyria. In return Esarhaddon may enter the cities, villages, and strongholds of Baal, including the ruined cities which the Assyrian king had handed over to Baal as his share of the Sidonian booty. For this favoured position Baal is to pay no more than the tribute which had been agreed upon with Shalmaneser, son of Tiglath Pileser.

With the sanctions to the treaty, the Assyrian again appears as lord enforcing regulations upon his vassal. The Tyrian king is to be bound to his duty by the great oath of the gods. Gula is not to be to him a healing goddess, but is to instil bitter sickness into his body. The seven mighty gods are to strike him down with weapons. The Bethels and Akatiba are to leave him in the claws of a fierce lion. The great gods of heaven and earth, the gods of Assyria and Akkad, as well as the gods of Ebir-nari, the country west of the Euphrates,[1] are to send him a curse which cannot be turned. The Tyrian deities, the heavenly Baal, Baal, king of the city, the Baal of the north, are to inflict the punishments most feared by sea-faring folk, are to send evil winds against the ship, break the cables, smite down the mast, sink the ship in the mighty flood, and bring a hurricane against the sailors. Milgishu and Esh-mun are to destroy the land, lead its inhabitants into captivity, destroy the food for their mouths, the clothing for their bodies, and the oil for their anointing. Ishtar is to break their bows in battle, bring them to the feet of their foes, and make them captives. With such mighty oaths were client princes bound.[2]

While Baal was fortifying his position, his rival Abdmelcart was being decapitated. To show men the power of the lord Ashur, the severed heads of Abdmelcart and Sanduarri were hung on the necks of their noble followers, and with music and song they were marched into the Ribit Nina, where the author of the Genesis table of nations placed Rehoboth Ir,[3] and the present-day Mosul marks the ancient bridge-head across the Tigris from Nineveh. Long after, a beautifully polished vase of pale yellow and white stone, which had once been filled with holy oil, testified to the booty which the "great hand" of the king had carried homeward.

The seacoast thus made safe, Esarhaddon turned his attention to the other flank, for the single track across the desert was in constant danger from the nomads. In our day the Egyptian outposts were made safe through the bridge-head at Arish, on the Syrian side of the desert; in those of Esarhaddon the would-be invader of Egypt must first secure Arza-asapa, its predecessor at the Nahal Misri or "Brook of Egypt,"[4] under whose dry stream bed crept sufficient water to irrigate a last oasis before the full terrors of the desert were dared. The ruler of Arza-asapa, Asuhili, was led away to Nineveh, there

---

[1] The Abar Nahara of Ezra 4 : 10.   [2] Winckler, *Forsch.*, II, 10 ff.
[3] Gen. 10 : 11. [4] E. g., I Kings 8 : 65; II Kings 24 : 7; Isaiah 27 : 12.

to abide at the city gates with wild beasts, boars, and dogs for company. The desert bridge-head was safely Assyrian.

Other Arabs must be won over or tamed before the journey across the blazing sands to the border of Egypt might be undertaken. The north Syrian desert acknowledged the pre-eminence of the Qidri tribe, so much so that their chief was regularly entitled by the Assyrians "King of the Arabs." First of the chiefs to rule over 'the black goat's hair tents of Kedar[1] was Hazael, who had lost his gods to Sennacherib. Among the greatest was Atar-samain, the "Heavenly Athtar," whom the Assyrians identified with their own Dilbat or Venus. With a heavy gift he had come to Assyria, had kissed the royal feet, and had begged that his gods might be returned to him. Sennacherib, however, claims that he took him prisoner.[2] Esarhaddon continues the story by stating that *he* consulted the sun-god, *he* had compassion on him, repaired the broken portions of the gods, wrote on them the power of Ashur and the glory of his own name, and, thus adorned and renovated, handed them back to Hazael.

With them went a gift of more doubtful acceptance, the hand of Tabua, an Arab lady who had grown up in the woman's quarters of his own palace. The price paid for these royal favours was not high, merely an increase in his tribute of sixty-five camels. When Hazael was carried away by fate, his son Yatha was enthroned in his stead. As first-fruits from his new vassal, Esarhaddon imposed an increase of taxes by ten pounds of gold, a thousand precious stones, fifty camels, a thousand measures of spices. Wahab had no difficulty in per-suading these inveterate wanderers that they had no need of Assyrian protection. Treason to the Assyrian nominee could not be allowed to pass unchallenged; Esarhaddon sent his aid to Yatha and the rival chief was seized and brought to Nine-veh, there to take his place with the beasts and Asuhili in the city gate.

Toward the end of September, 676, the Assyrians undertook an expedition on a more extended scale into the Bazu, the

[1] Cant. 1 : 5.   [2] Cf. p. 310.

desert whither had fled Samsi from the wrath of Tiglath
Pileser.   The trace first ran through waste and alkali land, a
place of thirst, then through a hundred and forty hours of
desert proper, filled with thorn and gazelle mouth stone, twenty
hours of snakes and scorpions, which covered the land like
grasshoppers.   This brought them to the Bazu proper, a
mountain of some sort of stone, and through it the army
marched twenty hours more to a land where dwelt six kings
and two queens whose domain was spoiled and the gods and
other goods taken to Nineveh.   One of the fugitives, Lale of
Iadi, a desert Judah to be added to those in Palestine and
north Syria, heard that his gods had fallen into the hands of
the invaders, hastened to Nineveh and kissed the royal feet.
He was recognised as the new ruler of the Bazu, subject as
such to tribute and gift, and was permitted to carry back his
deities properly inscribed.

Taharka risked no chances of being attacked unawares.
Egyptian emissaries were found all through Syria, and they
enjoyed no little success.   Ikkilu of Arvad made no ado about
going over to the side of Egypt, though Baal at least was bound
by a treaty which possessed many advantages for him.   On
the Philistine plain Ascalon likewise hearkened to the Egyptian lure.

During his last years Hezekiah of Judah had been completely
under the influence of Isaiah, and so had been anti-Egyptian.
His death in 692 brought the twelve-year Manasseh to the
beginning of his long reign.[1]   The new-fangled innovations introduced by the régime of Isaiah, Micah, and their fellow intellectuals, found little favour in the more conservative countryside.   The accession of a young and pliable son of Hezekiah
began shortly a strong reaction towards the good old days before the reform.   For a time the conservatives contented themselves with restoring the cult to the conditions of the pre-
Isaianic days.   All the high places were restored, and in the
smaller villages around the capital, where the conservatives
were so well intrenched, the shaveling priests were allowed to

[1] Cf. L. E. Fuller, *Reign of Manasseh*, 1912.

burn incense. Since Ahaz had sacrificed his first-born in the vain attempt to persuade Yahweh to save Jerusalem from his enemies, the more humane had developed a story which proved that Yahweh himself would not accept the sacrifice of Isaac offered by his father Abraham.[1] The conservative reaction once more led men to pass their first-born through the fire in Topheth to Melech, the god-king.[2] In their minds, he was doubtless identified with Yahweh himself; the influence of an Assyrian monarch who was likewise god-king must also be considered. Divination of all kinds, even to the invoking of the spirits of the dead, was indulged in. The Baals were once more worshipped and Yahweh was called a Baal again.

Reaction is not quite the word to apply to the religious situation, since there were many innovations introduced from abroad. New altars were erected in the Yahweh temple and in its courts for the sun, moon, zodiacal signs, and all the host of heaven. The sun had his special chariots under the charge of the chamberlain, Nathan Melech, whose name celebrates the divine king. Altars were set up on the roof of the upper chamber of Ahaz.[3] In the cities of Judah and in the streets of Jerusalem the children gathered wood, the fathers kindled fire, the women kneaded the dough to make cakes for the Queen of Heaven and poured out libations for her.[4] This was certainly an importation of the Mother Ishtar of the Babylonians, and we find for the first time the cult of Tammuz, her son and lover, for whom the women of Jerusalem wept.[5]

Jeremiah protested against the foreign vanities in the spirit of the earlier prophets and cried indignantly: "Is not Yahweh in Zion, is not her king in her midst?" "Pass over to the isles of Cyprus and see; send to Kedar and consider diligently; see if there hath ever been such a thing. Hath a nation changed its gods? Yet my people have changed their Glory." "To what purpose cometh there frankincense from Sheba to me and calamus from a far country? Your burnt offerings are not acceptable to me nor are your sacrifices pleasing." "Ac-

[1] Gen. 22. [2] Cf. Jer. 7 : 31; 19 : 5. [3] II Kings 23.
[4] Jer. 7 : 17 ff.; 44 : 15 ff.; cf. II Kings 21 : 5. [5] Ezek. 8 : 14.

cording to the number of thy cities are thy gods, O Judah, and according to the number of the streets of Jerusalem have ye set up altars to the shameful thing." "Though Moses and Samuel stood before me, yet would not my mind be favorable to this people; cast them out of my sight and let them go forth into exile. I will cause them to be tossed to and fro, a terror to all the kingdoms of the earth, because of Manasseh, son of Hezekiah, king of Judah, for that which he has done in Jerusalem."[1]

For some years Manasseh was considered a loyal vassal of Esarhaddon, who numbers him among the seacoast kings who contributed to the new palace at Nineveh. As the reaction gained headway, it became more nationalistic, and Manasseh went over whole-heartedly to the Egyptians. In honour of the chief Egyptian deity, he named the son who was destined to succeed him Amon. In preparation for the revolt he constructed an outer wall to the city of David on the west side of Gihon in the valley, even to the entrance of the Fish Gate, compassed the sanctuary and Ophel round about, and raised it to a very great height, and put valiant captains in all the fortified cities of Judah. So Manasseh shed innocent blood very much, till he had filled Jerusalem from one end to the other, destroying alike the partisans of Assyria and the followers of Isaiah. "Like a destroying lion has your own sword destroyed your prophets" was the comment of the young Jeremiah.[2]

Esarhaddon called upon his gods and they registered their approval. On the road to the west he came to Harran, famous for its temple of the moon-god Sin. As Marduk-shum-usur tells Ashur-bani-apal: "When the father of the king my lord went to Egypt, he saw in the district of Harran a temple made of cedar. Sin was placed on a staff, two crowns were upon his head, Nusku stood before him. The father of the king went in, the crown he placed on his head, the oracle he heard: 'Go, conquer the countries in its midst.'"[3]

---

[1] Jer. 8 : 19; 2 : 10; 6 : 20; 11 : 13; 15 : 1, 4.
[2] II Kings 21; II Chron. 33; Jer. 2 : 30.   [3] H. 923.

FIG. 141. DRY BED OF THE "RIVER OF EGYPT" ON THE DESERT
ROAD FROM PALESTINE TO THE NILE VALLEY.

FIG. 142. CAMEL-DRIVERS ON THE DESERT ROAD FROM
PALESTINE TO EGYPT.

FIG. 143. ARABS DRAWING WATER IN THE DESERT COUNTRY
SOUTH OF PALESTINE.

FIG. 144. WATERWORKS AT NEGUB, BUILT BY ASHUR–NASIR–APAL
AND RESTORED BY ESARHADDON.

Adad-shum-usur quoted the incantation which casts down men and walls in the midst of battle.[1] The armies attempted to make these promises come true at the expense of the Egyptians, but with little success (675). Esarhaddon remained in Egypt the next year, but near the end of February, 673, the Assyrians suffered a serious reverse and the expedition came to a sudden end.

Failure in Egypt roused the Syrian states to new efforts and new states revolted. Nabu-shum-iddina must deplore that while certain of the officials of the house will be present, the men of Ebir-nari, that is, the region west of the Euphrates, will not come, and he attempts to avert the wrath of his master at such evil tidings by introducing his report with these humble words: "I am a dog, yet the king has remembered me." [2] Domestic troubles were added to foreign. His Babylonian wife was ill, and the king had taken up his residence in Uruk that she might go on pilgrimage to the shrine in search of healing. Although Esarhaddon had elaborately restored Ishtar's shrine, the goddess proved ungrateful, and in March of 671 the queen died, a portent of evil to the empire.

Once more Esarhaddon asks advice of his god. He is going to Egypt to fight with the Ethiopian Taharka. Will he get the better, will he return alive from this second campaign? Will he again walk in his palace of Nineveh? If he goes to Ascalon, so long as he remains in the Ascalonite territory, will the Egyptians and the others fight with him? If he goes to Ebir-nari, will he again return from Ascalon to his palace?[3] We cannot but believe that the great king already felt hanging over him the shadow of his fate. His physician, Arad Nabu, had no such foreboding; he was confident that the gods would grant long life to the king, especially as he himself would add his prayers day and night.[4]

Recruited by the troops which the commander-in-chief, Sha Nabu-shu, had withdrawn from the Elamite frontier, the army set forth from Ashur in the first month of the Assyrian year,

[1] H. 12.
[2] H. 67.
[3] Knudtzon, *Gebete*, 68 ff.; Klauber, *Texte*, 41.
[4] H. 113.

the April of 671. The Euphrates was crossed at its flood, the difficult mountains were climbed like a wild bull, and Tyre was reached. Baal sat tight on his island, and Esarhaddon could only say that he had cut him off from food and drink, the support of life. In despair of conquering the island part of the city, he broke camp and advanced towards the desert strip which shut him off from the Nile valley.

Ascalon was still held by Taharka's troops, but Esarhaddon had no hesitation in leaving so mighty a fortress in his rear. The stages of the journey are counted from Apqu in the territory of Samena, a datum not without its value to the Biblical student, for according to the Biblical topography, Aphek belongs to Judah and not to Simeon.[1] Thirty hours thence brought the Assyrians to Raphia, where his grandfather had defeated Sibu, and where until the Great War was the Turko-Egyptian boundary. Not far away they reached the stream bed of the so-called "Brook of Egypt," but there was no river here, we are told, and from this point onward the troops might drink only the nauseous water they had brought with them in buckets.

Although the army was now mounted on the camels secured from the neighbouring Arabs, the day's journey became ever shorter. To cover a space estimated at but twenty hours took no less than fifteen days, sufficient evidence of the difficulty of the way; next followed four hours over the gabe stones; four more, at the rate of two a day, brought the credulous Assyrians to the two-headed serpents, whose bite was certain death. Though they trampled upon these saurians, yet had they no rest, for the next four hours' march carried them through a land where the serpents were winged. The worst was yet to come, for the eight days consumed in passing through fifteen reckoned hours' distance brought the invaders into such difficulties that only the aid of Marduk, restoring life to the almost dead Assyrians, carried them through the next twenty days. Strange reading this for those who argue that the climate has changed for the worse in recent centuries! A rest in Magan fortified the spirits of the troops and enabled them to endure

[1] Joshua 12 : 18; 15 : 53.

the last forty hours which must be suffered ere they saw before them Ishhupri on the edge of the Nile valley.[1]

Egypt offered no rest for the wearied troops. Taharka's army was found at Ishhupri, and fifteen more days of unbroken marching, varied only by three great battles, on the 3d, 16th, and 18th of July, brought the force four days later under the walls of Memphis. Under the pitiless sun of mid-July, siege-engines were dragged up, and in a day and a half the capital of lower Egypt was theirs.

Taharka had already been five times wounded by spear-thrusts in the earlier battles, and now he slipped away to Thebes, but his brother, his wife, his palace women, his sons and daughters, his palace officials, the son of the former king, all the immense spoil of precious metals and of cattle, were led away to Assyria. The whole land of Ethiopia, such is the Assyrian boast, was torn away from Egypt. Over all Egypt were appointed kings, governors, fortress commanders, residents, and officials. Stated offerings were ordered for Ashur and the great gods, and the yearly tribute was to be six talents and nineteen pounds of gold; three hundred talents of silver; one thousand seven hundred and eighty-five seemingly of copper; one hundred and ninety-nine skins; one thousand one hundred and forty horses; thirty thousand four hundred and eighteen sheep; nineteen thousand three hundred and twenty-three asses, as well as ebony and boxwood. The names of the cities were changed and pompous Assyrian ones took their place. Fifty of the royal statues were inscribed with the deeds of the Assyrian king and were re-erected in the temples of Egypt.

None of these statues have survived, but one of the soldiers who took part in the expedition, Bel-shar-usur by name, has left us his figure, dedicated to some local deity. Bearded and long-robed, he appears in rose granite; on the back of the statue he has given his name, not in its Assyrian form, but as Bel-shazzer, and with it the banner of the detachment in which he served.[2]

[1] Rogers, *Haverford Studies*, II; *Parallels*, 357 ff.
[2] Lidzbarski, *Ephemeris für semit. Epigraphik*, III, 117 f.

Matters thus arranged in Egypt, Esarhaddon left his commander-in-chief, Sha Nabu-shu, as his representative, and began his triumphal march homeward. Ascalon at last recognised the futility of resistance, and Manasseh paid for his
treason by a term of imprisonment in Babylon.[1] Baal found
himself isolated on his island, his commerce falling into the
hands of the pro-Assyrian Greek kings of Cyprus. He made
his peace by bringing his daughter and all the tribute which
had fallen into arrears. The cities on the mainland were not
restored but were continued under Assyrian officials. Baal
might be thankful that the island had remained inviolate.

Lip-service it might be, but Esarhaddon was satisfied. On
the rocks of the Dog River, where the kings of Egypt and
Assyria before him had placed their effigies, he carved his figure, and with it an inscription which told of the capture of
Memphis, of Ascalon, and of Tyre. Farther north, in the
city gate of the Syrian Judah, his own stele represented Esarhaddon flanked by the two crown princes; he holds a rope by
which Taharka and Baal are ringed through the nose. In the
case of Taharka, we know that this is an unjustifiable boast;
perhaps he is also lying in the case of Baal. To say the least,
it is a curious commentary on his claim of Tyrian submission
that the later Greek chronologers give as the period of Phœnician naval supremacy the years 677--642, the very years when
Baal was free from Assyrian control.

Esarhaddon had no more than reached home when he received the news that Sharru-ludari, Necho, and Pakrur, three
of the kings he had installed in Egypt, had broken their oath
when there had been borne in upon them the obvious conclusion: "If Taharka is driven out of Egypt, how then can we
remain?" Messengers were sent him, suggesting: "Let us
make alliance one with another, and we will help each other;
we will divide the land between us and no foreigner shall rule
over us." Unfortunately for the patriots, the Assyrian generals got wind of the meditated treachery and the messengers
carrying the letters fell into their hands.

[1] II Chron. 33 : 10 ff.

FIG. 145. BAY OF ACCHO.

FIG. 146. RELIEF OF ESARHADDON SIDE BY SIDE WITH THAT OF
THE EGYPTIAN RAMSES II AT THE DOG RIVER.

For the last time Esarhaddon inquired of his god. The oracle was again favourable and his physician, Arad Nabu, assured him that Nabu and Tashmetum would cause the king to live to see his sons a hundred years old, their sons and grandsons attain old age.[1] The oracle was no more true than was the pious wish, for Esarhaddon never reached the Nile valley. In November of 669 death overtook him on the way.

[1] Klauber, *Texte*, 36; *H*. 113.

CHAPTER XXX

HAREM INTRIGUES FOR A THRONE

A SERIES of harem intrigues clouded the last days of Esar-haddon. His one legal wife had died before him, and the same fate had overtaken his first-born, Sin-iddin-apal, whose name, "Sin has given a son as heir," pointed to the priority which caused him to be inducted into the Succession House. The next in order, if age were to be considered, was Shamash-shum-ukin, "Shamash has established a name." A third bore that of Ashur-bani-apal, "Ashur has created a son as heir," to indicate that from birth he was destined to succeed to the throne. Any question of precedence must be argued between these two, for the other children, the lady Sherua-eterat, Ashur-mukin-palea, Shamash-meta-uballit, and Ashur-etil-shame-ersiti-uballitsu, scarcely merited attention.

The education of Ashur-bani-apal began early. At birth Marduk granted him a wide-open ear, an all-embracing under-standing; Nabu, scribe of the divine hierarchy, endowed him with his own wisdom; from Urta and Nergal he obtained viril-ity and unequalled strength. As he grew older he came to need teachers who were a little less divine. Among these, his father picked Nabu-ahe-eriba. He accepts the appointment: "May the great gods of heaven and earth grant long life to the king my lord. Since the king thinks on us, how many are there since that day—the king we have not seen, in the king's presence we would stand. Who has received such favour? Only a king could grant it. This is the goodness which the king has done me, since thou hast placed me before the crown prince, that I should be his teacher. I would speak with him. Such friendly words must have been given by a god."[1]

Thus Ashur-bani-apal secured the revelation of Adapa, the hidden treasure of the whole calligraphic art. In the houses

[1] *H*. 604.

of heaven and earth he was seen, and in the assemblies of the skilled artificers. Dreams and visions, however unclear, he learned to interpret. No tablet, whether in the learned Shumerian or the obscure Akkadian, was too difficult for him to master, and his chief joy was the reading of stone inscriptions which tradition said dated from before the flood.

Some of the subjects he studied with Nabu-ahe-eriba may be gathered from letters sent by his instructor to his father. The king had inquired about the flaming out of the sun; thus it is said: "When the gleam of the day is like smoke, in the beginning of the year, Adad will bring an inundation. When the day is dark and the north wind blows, it is the 'eating of Nergal,' the cattle will be small." "Day equals sun" interpolates Nabu-ahe-eriba. The rest of the words he received, he will send to the king. "Shamash in the way of Anu dissipates his brilliance, this means evil to Elam." "Thus it is written: 'Shamash goes in the way of Anu, and the extension of his brilliance ceases, this means fate for Elam. Through cold evil will come.' Four days at its rising the south wind blew, now the north wind blows." [1]

On the 22d of May Jupiter was seen close to one of the stars, on the 29th of April of the following year he disappeared from the heavens for twenty or thirty days. For one month and five days he remained out of the heavens; on the 6th of June he was seen in the region of Orion; he has exceeded his appointed time by five days. This is the interpretation: "If Jupiter is seen in June there will be evil for the land, grain will be dear. If Jupiter nears Orion, the god Nergal will eat. If Jupiter enters Orion, the gods will rage against the land. If Jupiter is seen in the way of Anu, the crown prince will kill his father and ascend the throne." Coming from the tutor of the crown prince to his pupil's father, such a statement was open to possible misconstruction. Nabu-ahe-eriba points out carefully that the Anu way denotes Elam, so that Jupiter is threatening Elam, not Assyria. His uneasiness persists, and even after this explanation he adds: "Nevertheless, as a pro-

[1] *H*. 405.

tection against mischance, let the king execute incantations of freeing from evil."

When he has completed the five excess days, Jupiter will round out a hundred days. . This is the interpretation: "If Nibiru rises, the gods will be angry, destruction will rule, peace will be broken, friendly relations will be destroyed, there will be floods and storms, a hurricane will rage, the lands will be destroyed; the gods will not hearken to prayers, will not accept beseeching, the seer shall not make incantations." This has been extracted for the king according to the tablet. The day of the eclipse is favourable, but he did not send it. The eclipse goes up from the mountain and turns to the west. Everything took place as was expected. Jupiter and Venus stood in the eclipse until it was free. To the king it is favourable. Whatever evil there is in it refers to Amurru, to-morrow the report of the moon's eclipse will be sent.[1]

Nor was the education of the crown prince merely learned. Daily he exercised himself in horsemanship and in chariot-driving, in holding the bow, in shooting the arrow, in hurling the heavy spear. Like a dealer in weapons he constructed the shields used by the squires of the bowmen and the spear-men, so that he was acknowledged the master of all the skilled artisans. At the same time he acquired such knowledge of ruling as behooved a king, and he walked in the path of royalty. He stood before his father the king, acting as intermediary for the nobles. Without him was no official named, no governor detailed to his province; his father recognised his ability and loved him above all his brethren.

More potent than the love which the gods had stirred in his father's heart was the fact that Ashur-bani-apal was the darling of the militarist party, which not even the Egyptian success could entirely conciliate, and which had never forgiven its monarch for the restoration of Babylon. When Esarhaddon set forth on his second trip to Egypt, Ashur-bani-apal was left in charge of affairs at home. Aided by the advice which the sun-god furnished through the liver omens, he carried on

[1] *H*. 407.

the imperial administration. His was the necessity of deciding whether the rab mug Nabu-shar-usur should be sent against Ikkilu of Arvad or against Egypt; whether Sha Nabu-shu, the commander-in-chief, would have trouble with the men of Elli, the Medes, or the Cimmerians; whether Assyria would suffer from the Shuprians, the Ahlame, the Ethiopians, or the Egyptians.[1]

The disastrous defeat of 673 proved that all the Assyrian resources would be called upon to conquer Egypt; Esarhaddon came to the conclusion that Ashur-bani-apal should be left behind with full powers. All the great gods, beginning with Ashur, their father, were besought for permission to grant him this favour. Balasi was asked about the best days for the appearance of Ashur-bani-apal before his father. He replies that the fourth day is a good day, when the beginning of the month arrives it will be favourable for action. They have told the king: "On the first let not the king's son go out of the gate." The king may go out of the shrine and order that his son be brought before his face. The king has inquired about Ashur-mukin-palea. Let him also come on the fourth, it is a favourable day.[2]

The star Mars is dominant for the crown prince, its brilliance is increasing. It will be dominant until the middle of May, and if the crown prince should come before the king while Mars was so dominant and harm should befall him, would not Balasi and his friends be responsible? He should not return to the land of Subarti (Assyria), into the shrine he should not go. No one should enter the palace before the king, since that would be sin. If it is not agreeable to the king to do it this month, then let him enter in April, the beginning of the year, when Sin has finished the day.[3]

Despite this warning, the ceremonies were gone through with on the 12th of Airu (May), while the feast of the goddess Gula was being celebrated. Men of Assyria, great and small, from the lower and the upper seas, were collected and ordered to swear by the great gods that they would protect the position

[1] Knudtzon, *Gebete*, 66 f.; Klauber, *Texte*, 44.   [2] *H*. 354.   [3] *H*. 356.

of Ashur-bani-apal as crown prince and afterwards as ruler of Assyria. Accompanied by the rejoicing of the whole army in camp, Ashur-bani-apal entered into the Succession House and was exalted above his brethren.

On the next day, the 13th, the ceremonies of "shepherdship" were to be carried out. Adad-shum-usur gives the directions. When the crown prince shall come to the court of the temple, he shall enter the reed hut. He shall seat himself and pray, then shall turn and come from the shrine. The Shearer shall enter that he may eat bitter herbs, and they shall make him drink out of a vessel made from a skull. The gate of the enemy's domain shall be in gloom. Actually, the ceremonies of shepherdship were carried out by Nabu-nadin-shum, who sealed the message from his lips and sent it to the king by special messenger. Esarhaddon writes Adad-shum-usur about the use of the royal image. It is suggested that the rites be performed on the 16th, since that is a good day, though the 17th is not. Let the ceremonies be performed as their fathers did it for their lord, and as the Irrigator did it the last time. Bel and Nabu have established justice, why should there be delay? [1]

Basi, however, has been approached by Nabu-nadin-shum at the request of the king, and he advises that he sit down on the 15th and rise up on the 22d, and on the 24th go out to the river to complete the ritual. Further instructions can be furnished when they appear before the king. In its freeing incantation, it is said: "On the seventh day he shall abide in the hut, cleansing rites shall be performed over him, the ceremony used for a sick man shall be carried out." For seven days they have made the lifting up of the hand prayers before the gods of the night and the incantation destroying all evil at the same time has been repeated. The seven days he remains in the hut he shall show himself to the gods of the night and reverence his god and goddess. If the king wishes this done at once, the eighth is a favourable time.[2]

As to the freeing incantation from all evil, which the king

[1] H. 4; 369; 362.   [2] H. 53; 370.

has decided should be performed the next day, that day is
not favourable; they will make preparations on the 25th, on
the 26th they will bring it about. Let not the king speak of
the content of those signs; Bel and Nabu are quite capable
of bringing sufficient help and they will cause it to come to
the king. Esarhaddon has asked Bani, deputy of the chief
physician, why he makes libations for Nabu-nadin-shum; the
answer is that it is really for the king, since Bel and Nabu, the
same gods who protect the king, have restored his life. The
Mistress of Life, the king's gracious divinity, who bestows
length of days, old age, offspring, fulness of life to the king,
has also taken his hand. Through the agency of the god and
the protecting genius of the king he lives.[1]

The happy event left its natural impress upon the next
generation. We find such names as Mar-sharri-bel-ahe, "The
king's son is the lord of the brethren," Nabu-mar-sharri-usur,
or Sin-mar-sharri-usur, where Nabu or Sin is invoked to protect the crown prince. Flattery went so far in one case that
a certain youth was known through life as Mar-sharri-ilia,
"The crown prince is my god!" Flattery could go no further.

According to Ashur-bani-apal himself, this was a time of
almost millennial felicity. The gods looked with pleasure on
his good works, for it was their order which had placed him
on the throne of his father. The nobles and high officials
loved his rule, for he secured them favours from his father.
Because of the naming of his mighty name, the four world
regions rejoiced and the subject kings from the upper and
lower seas sent embassies to express their joy at his accession.
The weapons of the rebellious enemy were left in their camp,
the charioteer loosed his span of horses; their lances lost their
sharpness, the filled bows took their rest. Evil-doers were
kept down so that they planned no warfare. In city or in
house, no man took away the goods of his neighbour by force;
in the territory of the whole land no man provoked to evil.
One might traverse alone and in safety the most distant
streets. No robber poured out blood nor was an evil deed

[1] *H.* 51; 204.

perpetrated. The lands occupied a peaceful abode, the four world regions were happy as fine oil.

Very different was the reality. Around a hard-working crown prince was a large staff—an abarakku, a rein-holder, a guardsman, a recorder, a charioteer, a captain, a head baker, a chamberlain, an Aramaic scribe, not to speak of the several deputies and privates of the guard. Through them he carried on his administration.

Best wishes are sent by Marduk-shakin-shum to Ashur-bani-apal and his brothers. He has written all the words on a tablet as the king's mouth has spoken. The king has ordered him, if he should go to Kalhu, to send to Ahuni. He has already collected thirty or forty good tablets. At first he misunderstood the king's letter, now he realises what was desired. It is true that the space assigned was too small for an orderly arrangement. He is regularly performing the ceremonies and has brought a burnt offering. The women are collected together in the treasure-house. The king has inquired the reason; they are therein for the food and for pouring out water on the head in abundance. Since they are so many and abide in it together, if it please the king may they abide in the open. When they have prepared the rites to the 14th, may he go to the river. Let the king send orders how the ceremonies are to be completed. As to the maid who is with them, how does the king mean? When he says that they should perform the ceremonies over her, is this to be done by them? Let the king wear for a sufficient time the white garments he has written about. Two days, the 20th and the 21st, are enough; on the 22d let the king gird up his loins and act as usual. When Kinu-naid sees the royal edict, he will die of bitterness of soul. Yesterday the observation failed and Marduk-shakin-shum is sadly disturbed.[1]

It is quite impossible to perform the rites on the 24th as the king desired, for the tablets are too many. Whenever they bring the images seen by the king into the midst, then within five or six days they shall take up the first. The month of

[1] *H*. 453; 17; 378 f.

January is a propitious time for the performance of the free-ing incantation. During that month let the crown prince per-form them, and let also the people whom the king has indi-cated. As to the Shumerian originals of the freeing incanta-tions which the king has ordered sent by messenger to Nine-veh, Nabu-nadin-ahe shall bring them and the tablets of another series as well. Let the king perform the ceremonies on the 2d of January, then let the crown prince perform them on the 4th, and the people may perform them on the 6th, un-less the king should desire to have them gone through at once. Some rites have been omitted, and Marduk-shakin-shum had written that they would be given the next day. Then it came from his heart that there was a sign of opposition on that day, and therefore it was unfavourable. Let the ceremony be postponed until the 7th, when they will arrive in person and execute them.[1]

There is no indication that he is crown prince when Ashur-bani-apal addresses his father. The king his lord has bidden him to order Rahis-sharri to come to be questioned; he claims he has acted by order of the king and suggests that his ques-tioner ask Iaze about the Cimmerians. To the further ques-tion, "Why are the Cimmerians?" he replies that the enemy are destroying.[2]

A whole group of letters are directed to Ashur-bani-apal as crown prince. He must write his subordinates about this Rahis-sharri, to the deputy and Nabu-dini-amur about the thirteen men Ae-ibni carried off with him when he fled from Der. His father orders Ashur-ukin, who was stationed on the Haldian boundary, to send deserters from the country round about to the crown prince. Shumai writes to tell him that he has expended four hundred of the thousand measures of grain given his father, the remaining six hundred are still in his pos-session. As the chiefs of all the world entered before the father, may they enter before the face of the crown prince.[3]

The nobles of Arbela have business with the crown prince, and an unknown writer announces that he has learned from

<hr>

[1] *H.* 18; 20.   [2] *H.* 1026.   [3] *H.* 430; 434; 948.

Nabu-nasir, the staff-bearer, that Sin-balatsu-iqbi, son of Nin-gal-iddina, has sent a pound of gold by the rein-holder to Saba, the steward of the crown prince. Another correspondent reports that the limestone foundation is ready to have the royal name inscribed upon it. Nabu-shum-iddina, priest of Nabu at Kalhu, writes about the placing of the new bed in the "Couch House." Nani tells of a shepherd who came to him in Kalhu. Ibashshi-ilu, astrologer and priest of Bel in Babylon, complains bitterly of Ashur-natkil, the captain of Adinni.[1]

Sharru-naid, son of Bel-rimanni, the priest of Bit Kidmuri, reports that the chief butler who holds the weapon of Marduk has without authority of the king or the crown prince seized and imprisoned him, the house of his father he has plundered, as much as his father acquired under the protection of the king he has taken away. One talent and one pound of fine silver, the vessels of the treasure-house and the house of the queen mother at the same time he carried off. Is he to rescue his father's estates? He has been to the house of records. May the crown prince give heed, without the authority of the king or the king's son, nothing can even be spoken.[2]

The scribe of the "New House," Ishdi Nabu, writes the crown prince about Ashur-shezibanni, and informs him that he is bringing the dues of Nabu. Nadin-shum-ilu, son of Aramish-shar-ilani, the musharkis of the king's order, has made memorial before his face, saying: "My father has died in the enemy's land. Fifty of his personal guard have taken twelve horses and have located in the vicinity of Nineveh. I spoke to them as follows: 'My father is dead, why do you neglect the watch of the king?'" He is being sent on to the king to give further information. As for that Carchemish merchant, his servants killed him, but Ishdi Nabu has permitted no guilty man to escape, they have been made "protected" servants of Ninlil and the Queen of Kidmuri, to whom mothers pour out libations. They have been brought to the king. As for Sippar, let the king be patient, they have no anxiety.[3]

[1] H. 445; 65; 950; 189; 500.   [2] H. 152.   [3] H. 186 ff.

The task work of the city of Tarbisu instituted by the father of the crown prince has been seen, accepted, and performed by Shupa, who said: "May my name be acceptable before my lord." His father's scribe, for the reckoning of the work, committed it to the hands of drunken men. His father's messenger, whom he appointed over it as his jurisdiction, heard as follows: "The scribe directing the work has gone, he has broken out and has fled with the money." That which should have completed the remainder of the work has not been given. Now let them assign the tax which the king receives from his father to the crown prince, let him direct the work, let Shupa perform the work which is in Kalhu, which was committed to his father, that Shupa may render an account to the crown prince. There is no one who will listen to him and come, unless it be a man from before the crown prince. If the crown prince turns his face away, he will return and die. Has he not already rendered to the crown prince the service he should do? He, his brother, and his mother, reverence the crown prince his lord. Let the crown prince inquire about his grandfather, Ashur-bel-ukin; did he not stand at his side as leader when Sennacherib gave him a position, did he not appoint him among the scribes? Let not the crown prince permit him to be cast down, let not the name of his grandfather and the official position of his father perish from the crown prince's house, for in that house stood his father and his grandfather. The king, the father of the crown prince, loved the son of a master-workman, his face was towards the son of the lord of his work. What are Shupa's sins? He is the dog of the crown prince beside the threshold of his house.[1]

If we turn to the oracles, we find how little truth there was in the millennial picture drawn by the young prince. So far from the world quarters rejoicing like fine oil, he must inquire about combinations of enemies: the Ituai, no longer a part of the Assyrian army, the Elamites, Ahlame, and Cimmerians, the men of Acco and Egypt; again it is one of the Mannai, Medes, Cimmerians, Sidonians, and Egyptians; a third adds

[1] H. 885.

Shuprians, Pilpatai, Ethiopians, and Shabuqai to the Ahlame and Egyptians.

Nor was it this encircling ring of enemies which alone was to be feared; the last inquiry asks also whether there is danger to be anticipated from the bearded chiefs, the king's Companions, his own brother or the brothers of his father, the members of the royal family. He doubts the loyalty of his charioteer and of his chariot attendant, of the night-watch, of his royal messengers and of his body-guard, of the officers in the palace and those on the frontier, of his cellarer and baker. He fears for what he eats and what he drinks, he fears by day and by night; in the city and without there is danger that a revolt against him will be undertaken.[1]

That his fear for what he drank was not without foundation is shown by an episode in one of the letters. Esarhaddon had ordered a potion to be prepared for the sickly Ashur-bani-apal; Adad-shum-usur, always a good friend of the crown prince, did not quite dare to accuse his rivals of an attempt to poison their patient, but he broadly hints it. As for the potion of which the king has sent, it is very good, since the king has chosen the persons who have made it. He and his colleagues will hasten to make them drink first, then afterwards the crown prince shall drink it. Then he loses courage: "But what am I saying! I am an old man who has lost his reason. That which the king has spoken is as final as the word of God." [2]

After his return from his successful Egyptian expedition of 671, Esarhaddon was persuaded to grant this same title of King's Son to Shamash-shum-ukin, localising it in Babylon as the first was connected with Assyria. Partisans of the elder son no doubt felt that this was an attempt to console him for deprivation of undoubted rights by a position of inferior honour. Thinking patriots must realise that to overturn the existing settlement, however strong the appeal of Shamash-shum-ukin's seniority, was to invite trouble at no distant date.

Adad-shum-ukin, wise old courtier that he was, protested

[1] Klauber, *Texte*, 44. [2] *H*. 3.

against such division of authority: "That which cannot be done in heaven, the king my lord is doing on earth and is showing us. Thou didst clothe thy son in royal robes, thou didst order Assyria to obey him, now thou hast set up thy eldest son in Babylon. What the king my lord has done for the kings his sons is not good for Assyria. Now Ashur has granted thee, O king my lord, to rule from the rising to the setting of the sun; look on these thy gracious sons and rejoice thy heart. The king my lord has caused to arise from his heart a word which is not good and by it thou art made weak." [1]

Such plain speaking was not to the taste of Esarhaddon, and the ban was placed on Adad-shum-usur. Letters came from the sinner and his friends declaring that he did not say what was charged against him, that he and his son Arad Gula would share in the installation ceremony and would support the new arrangements. Ishtar-shum-eresh, colleague and close friend of Adad-shum-usur, assured his lord "from his heart he did not speak it." [2]

By the 1st of May, 670, we find the title "crown prince of Babylon" assigned to Shamash-shum-ukin, although the formal installation was delayed until later in the month. Marduk-shakin-shum has on the day of writing recited twenty-one tablets by the riverside, including one, two, or three hand-raisings to the moon and sun gods, the stars Mars and Tartahu, and various freeing incantations. At evening Arad Ea will perform the rites and ceremonies on the roof of the palace. The king should realise that a magician cannot offer up prayers on an evil, unpropitious day. On the following evening, the 15th, Marduk-shakin-shum will himself perform the incantations. The next two he will carry out the rites before the various goddesses, Dilbat, Belit, Sarpanitum, Gula, and Nana. He has spread forth his hands and besought the god, and the gods have blessed the king and his sons. If it please the king, let them send to Kalhu and there recite prayers to Sin, and at the same time freeing incantations for the crown prince of Babylon, whatever sin may need expiation. [3]

[1] H. 870.   [2] H. 594; 117 f.; 656; 34.   [3] H. 23.

Ceremonial visits in company with the king's sons were made by Adad-shum-usur, Ashur-nasir, Sasi, and Arad Ea to Kalhu on the twelfth day, to Nineveh on the fifteenth. Arad Gula expresses the pious hope that the gods, as many as this day preserve all things, may stand among the protectors of the king, of Ashur-bani-apal, and of Shamash-shum-ukin, very greatly. The whole ceremony has been completed on the twenty-second day. They have taken charge of everything and have written the tablets together. How shall the rents in the garments be mended?[1]

All present took the oath. Esarhaddon ordered: "Make Adad-shum-usur swear; why does he declare 'The king's son should not go with Shamash-shum-ukin to the installation service before the 22d of October'?" He has already taken the oath in the city of Akkad, by the gods of the king he swore. Let them fill a hundred days. In gratitude for his deliverance, his letters heap up the titles, Great King's Son, Son of the King of All Lands, Son of the King of the Lands. One contains an instructive slip. He begins "To the King's Son of Ashur," then remembers that there is now more than one King's Son, and adds after "Ashur" the word "great."[2]

Mardi was another of those who found it wise to make a sudden about-face. "To Bel, Nabu, and Shamash constantly I pray for the king my lord, saying: May the crown prince my lord receive the royalty of his father's house. I am his servant, his dog, and his staff. In his shadow may I see light. Bel, Nabu, and Shamash, when they hear my prayer, will grant everlasting dominion, an enduring reign, and like the going forth of the sun all the lands in thy course shall be bright. But I am in the midst of darkness, no one brings me near the court of the king. My misdeeds against the crown prince they accepted, the king my lord has sent concerning me, saying: 'Pardon his misdeeds, grant it.'" His brother was seized in prison with hunger, before he could escape; he fled to the city of Ashur, for mercy he laid hold of the king. The messenger of the crown prince he sent with Mardi, for the return of the

[1] H. 1004; 117.   [2] H. 594; 1004; 654; 10.

property destroyed by the governor of Barhalza. But Sirapa refuses submission, he will not surrender it, for he says that the king knows how this man of Barhalza hates him and the orchards he will not permit to be returned.[1]

With affairs arranged to all seeming in a satisfactory manner, Esarhaddon took the road to Egypt. On the stele which he erected in the outer gate of the northern Judah appear the two crown princes, Ashur-bani-apal to his right, Shamash-shum-ukin to left. Each folds his hands in the attitude of respect usual in the presence of a superior, but each bears a smaller edition of the tiara. Ashur-bani-apal is clothed in the same royal dress as his father, but his brother wears the Babylonian robe, looped fold above fold as did his predecessors on the throne of the south.[2]

Erection of the stele is the last event we can assign to Esarhaddon's reign, for in November of 669 he died on the road to Egypt. Again we have from Ashur-bani-apal a picture of millennial bliss: "When I assumed my seat on the throne of my father, Adad poured out his rain-storms, Ea opened his springs, the grain grew fifteen inches long, it increased, the cypresses were always green, the orchards bore their fruit in rank profusion, the cattle brought forth their young with ease. During my period of rule, fulness rained down; during my years, abundance was heaped up." [3]

By order of the gods Adad brought back the rains, Ea opened his springs and made richness, blessing, and overflow in the land. Ashur-bani-apal gives us the prices which prevailed at his accession; if we may accept his statistics, the shekel did have unusual purchasing power, for with it one might secure two hundred and thirty-four qa of grain, two hundred and seventy qa of dates, sixty-six qa of sesame, eighteen qa of oil, ten pounds of wool, while as for wine, which was produced on the mountain tops and did not exist in Assyria,

---

[1] *H*. 916. [2] E. Unger, *ZA*., XXXI, 236.
[3] Transliteration and translation of all official sources for the reign in **M.** Streck, *Assurbanipal*, with full bibliography, introduction, and indexes; the cuneiform sources are widely scattered, but the most important are in George Smith, *History of Assurbanipal;* S. A. Smith, *Keilschrifttexte Asurbanipals*.

eighteen qa also sold for the shekel. Comparison with the
average range of prices makes it clear that this was indeed
low; unfortunately, those same business documents prove that
prices soon went back to normal.[1]

Nabu-shar-usur, just promoted to that position of commander-in-chief, which he was to hold for thirteen years, and
blessed with a grant of land as well, rehearses sentiments typical of those who had gained by the change: "On thy throne
thou art seated, thine enemies thou shalt take captive, thy
foes thou shalt conquer, the enemy lands thou shalt despoil."
He must admit that there are enemies, and the shadows deepen
as he confesses that the whole land is hostile to the rule of his
master.

In truth, the official optimism was far from correct. The
death of a ruler away from the capital has always been the signal for trouble in the Orient, and this was no exception. The
sons of Esarhaddon were young their position was anomalous,
revolt was threatening.

One rebellion seems to have been nipped in the bud. A certain Sasi was the "official over the city," perhaps of Harran.
Supporting him was another "official over the city," Auiani,
Bel-ahi-usur of Harran, Ishtar-nadinat-apal, the scribe, Arda,
and Nabu-etir. Nusku of Harran was appealed to for an
oracle, and the conspirators were informed: "Royalty is for
Sasi, name and seed of Sennacherib is destroyed." News of
this oracle came to Ashur, and the king was much disturbed.
An appeal to Ningal was equally disconcerting: "Evil for thy
soul and the souls of thy people, from father to mother, all
of them evil." Nabu-rihtu-usur encourages the young king.
Bel and Nabu, the Ishtars of Nineveh and Arbela, shall grant
him long days, the rebels have sinned against their oath to
him, it is their name and their seed which should be destroyed
from his palace; he may expect the punishment of those who
have conspired with Sasi, his soul shall not be destroyed, royalty shall not be taken from his hands. Let there be an investigation. The shetu official has brought out the slave girl

[1] Meissner, *OLZ.*, XXI, 119 ff.

of Bel-ahi-usur, from the house of Sasi; let her be put to the ordeal, let Bel-ahi-usur be brought from Harran, let the rab mug interrogate his family under the gate of the Nabu temple. Let the paternal uncles of the king be on guard, let the king himself remain in his palace and save his life.[1]

It was indeed fortunate that there was one strong hand at the helm, woman though she was. Sammuramat gained eternal fame as Semiramis, but Zakutu, wife of Sennacherib, mother of Esarhaddon, grandmother of the young princes, and at all times a power, was in actual history the greatest of Assyrian queens. In the emergency she came forward with an oath for the Assyrians, for Shamash-shum-ukin, distinguished from his brothers only by his first place, for Shamash-meta-uballit and his younger brothers, for the seed royal, the governors, the high officials, the deputies, the magistrates, the officials of the whole land, the Assyrian people, every man and woman. Straight to the point she comes: "You who in your heart are hostile to me, you who counsel and discuss a wicked scheme, a treasonable counsel, you who speak concerning the raising up of a revolt against Ashur-bani-apal, the second day concerning the murder of Ashur-bani-apal, you are to tell me, his mother, and likewise Ashur-bani-apal, whether you hear it among the soldiers, the leading fighting men of your midst, or among the captains, or even among his brethren." [2]

Part of the actual oath is preserved: "The watch of Ashur-bani-apal, king of Assyria, our lord, shall we watch, the watch he commands we shall watch, whoever speaks evil words against Ashur-bani-apal, king of Assyria, or against one of his officials, and we hear it, we shall place him in fetters and Ashur-bani-apal, from this day, so long as we live, will we love. We will not make war against his land, we will not speak evil, the enemy of Ashur-bani-apal shall not be our lord. Whatever he tells us, according to the word of our oath we shall bring our bows, with him will we take our stand, his enemy with willingness of heart we will cast down. Even a son will we seize and to the king we will send him. Ashur-bani-apal, king of As-

[1] *H*. 1217.   [2] *H*. 1239.

syria, will we love, his enemies will we hate, from this day, so long as we live, another king or another lord opposed to him we shall not seek, a letter to his enemy we shall not send, a messenger from another land we shall not receive. The road for his feet we will establish, the kingdom of Ashur and of Akkad we will support by the oath of the gods." [1]

The scribes of Nineveh, Kakzu, and Arbela, so Ishtar-shum-eresh sends word, have come to take the oath, the men of Ashur have neglected to do so. If it please the king, let those who are already there take it at once, since the men of Nineveh and Kalhu are kept away from home. Bel and Nabu will enter on the eighth day. Or will the king rather say: "Let them come, do their devoirs, and depart"? Let them set out on the fifteenth day, for in the prayers for April it is written: "On the fifteenth, early in the morning, let them take the oath, on the night of the fifteenth under the stars let it be established." On the sixteenth the scribes, seers, magicians, physicians, augurs, the companions of the palace and the dwellers in the city will take the oath. The twentieth, twenty-second, and twenty-fifth are suitable for establishing the oath, whenever the king gives orders, they will be made to take the oath. From the twenty-seventh to the twenty-eighth, according to the king's orders, they are to reveal the order in Arbela. Esarhaddon had met his death in November; allowing a month for the news to reach Assyria, three months of unrest had elapsed before it was safe to impose the oaths. [2]

A peculiar situation is revealed by a letter of Kabtia: "As to the oath of Babylon, as to which the king has sent, I did not receive the sealed letter from the king which Ashur-ramin-sharri brought for me. Since I and my brothers had gone into the land of Arashu, we kept the guard with him. At the time fixed for the oath at Babylon, I could not reach it. On the road the representative of the palace met me, and when he brought me into Nippur and Uruk, I found myself in the midst of thy gods and the ceremonies of taking the oath to the king

[1] *H.* 1105.   [2] *H.* 386; 33; 384; 35.

my lord. But I was not content to take the oath to the king there, for I said: Let these peoples, their sons and their wives, take the oath of the king, I shall not take it; according to the orders of the king I shall take it when the elders take the oath in Babylon." His excuse was accepted and Kabtia continued in the royal service.[1]

One letter furnishes a list of the men who could be trusted in the crisis, servants who would not revolt against their lords, such as Balasu, Bel-shar-usur, Nabu-rimanni, Adunu-milki, Pan Nabu-lamur. Ishtar of Arbela came to the aid of the youthful Ashur-bani-apal, as she had done to his father before him: "This is the royal order of the Mistress: Fear thou not, O Ashur-bani-apal, for that which I have promised will I do and give thee. Surely over the sons of the four tongues, over the protection of the officials shalt thou exercise kingship. Thy royalty in the Succession House have I established, the installation dress have I girded on thee." The promised aid was not forgotten and throughout the reign Ishtar of Arbela was of even higher repute than in the days of Esarhaddon.[2]

While Ashur-bani-apal prayed to Nabu, Zakutu made her vows to his wife Tashmetum and dedicated to her a breast of gleaming red gold for the life of her beloved Ashur-bani-apal, for the enduring of his throne, and for herself, her own life, the length of her days, for the establishment of *her* reign, that she might make the king her husband (!) fortunate by her words, so that the goddess might make them grow old together.[3]

The true wife of Ashur-bani-apal was likewise a lady of strength. Ashur-sharrat, "the city of Ashur is queen," appears twice in the pictorial record. Once she is represented on a stele at Ashur, seated on a throne, her right hand extended, in her left a flower, a battlemented crown on her head, and wearing armlets and decorated earrings.[4] The other is the famous drinking scene. In both she is not unattractive according to Eastern notions—curly hair, ample figure, generous nose over slightly overhanging upper lip, arched eyebrows,

[1] *H*. 202.   [2] *H*. 875; Strong, *BA*., II, 633; Jastrow, *Religion*, II, 171.
[3] *J*. 644 f.   [4] Andrae, *Stelenreihen in Assur*, No. 1.

smiling mouth. But she smiled while above her hung the bleeding head of an Elamite king!

She too had known trouble. A letter written just before her husband's accession affords a peep into the intrigues and hatreds of the women's quarters. The authoress is Sherua-eterat, daughter of Esarhaddon, and she sends a curt "word of the king's daughter," as if she were herself a monarch. She gives Ashur-sharrat no title, and the peace greeting is conspicuously absent. "Why have you not written your tablet or dictated your letter? Or shall men say: 'Is this one the mistress of Sherua-eterat, the eldest daughter of the Succession House of Ashur-etil-ilani-ukinni, the great king, the mighty king, the king of the world, the king of Assyria'? But you are only a daughter-in-law, the house mistress of Ashur-bani-apal, the crown prince of the Succession House, son of Esarhaddon, king of Assyria."[1]

Sherua-eterat is own daughter to the reigning king, whom she refers to by his new name, the name which made him rightful successor to his father; the mere daughter-in-law is connected with that earlier name which confessed that he was not the first-born. We know that Ashur-sharrat emerged triumphant from the contest; what was the fate of her opponent?

[1] *H*. 308.

CHAPTER XXXI

BROTHERLY SETTLEMENTS

THE energy of the queen mother quelled all opposition, and Ashur-bani-apal was safely seated on his throne. The commands of his father, by whose oath that could not be broken he was bound, might now be carried out for the other brothers. Esarhaddon had rebuilt Babylon, but the cult statue of its divine king Marduk still languished in captivity. Once indeed he had thought of sending it back, and had gone so far as to inquire of Shamash whether the officer whose name was written on the tablet should be sent to Babylon to Marduk, and concerning the trip from Ashur down the river and then across to the city.[1]

Marduk was still a captive in Ashur at the death of Esarhaddon. Ashur-bani-apal appeared before him, Marduk filled his hand, and the king solemnly seized the girdle of the god and spoke as follows: "Think on Babylon, which in the wrath of thy heart thou didst destroy, to Esagila, the temple of thy lordship, turn thy neck and direct thy countenance. Long enough hast thou abandoned thy city, a place which is not fitting hast thou taken as thy residence. O thou Enlil of the gods, do thou, O Marduk, order the march to Babylon; through thy illustrious word, without rival, establish the entering into Esagila."

Not content with this, Shamash was asked whether Shamash-shum-ukin might go through the ceremony of taking the hands of Bel before the statue was returned, and in this manner secure the legal right to rule Babylonia. Does it please the sun-god and Marduk that Shamash-shum-ukin seize the hands of Bel in the city of Ashur, and then go before the face of Bel to Babylon?[2] Vassalage to Marduk while he himself was a vassal to Ashur and a captive of twenty-one long years in the

[1] Knudtzon, *Gebete*, 104, 106.   [2] *Ibid.*, 149.

enemy's country was a strange travesty of the ancient custom, but the desires of princes prevail with the gods, Shamash-shum-ukin took the hands of Marduk in Ashur, and thus counted his first official year from the March of 668.

Two months later Marduk began his journey by water from the city of Ashur. Along the route cattle and lambs were slaughtered, spices were scattered, heaps of wood were fired which gave light for an hour's distance. The whole body of Assyrian troops surrounded the god like a rainbow; day and night there was music.

Arrived in Babylon, the Abode of Life, Marduk found await-ing him on the shore his wife, the Mistress of Akkad, Nana, Usur-amatsu, Hanibia, and Adanissi. Nergal came from his temple of Eshitlam in Kutu, Nabu followed the continuation of the sacred way from Borsippa to meet his father, Shamash approached from his gleaming home in Sippar. All the gods of Shumer and Akkad bowed before him in humility, like whimpering puppies. The ceremonies of the mouth-washing were completed, and sheep, oxen, and fish, the abundance of the sea, were offered.

His other brothers next received attention. After Ashur-bani-apal came Ashur-mukin-palea, "Ashur has established my rule." Already Esarhaddon had been troubled by his health, he had said to the physician Arad Nana, "He is in your hands," he was disturbed whenever the face of his son became pale. Arad Nana is with him and takes care of him, but the beginning of the month is unpropitious for performing rites, and the physician plaintively demands of his master whether he should die in performing them. The king need not be anxious about the health of his tooth; Arad Nana has much improved it.[1]

It is exceedingly well with Ashur-mukin-palea and Ashur-sharrani. The ceremonies about which the king made in-quiry were carried out in December, they recited the series "Sickness and death shall not come to the palace," also the series "Sickness and pestilence shall not come to the house of

[1] *H.* 109.

a man," as well as many freeing incantations. In February there will be lifting up of the hand, prayers and incantations against evil, witchcraft, pestilence, and sorcery. The ceremonies carried out in March include the images of Anu, of Namtar, of Latarak, of death, the image of a man in clay, the image of a man in mud from the garden canal, seven loaves of barley, fifteen blades of silver, before Gula, mistress of the waste fields, seven barleycorns of silver, and seven of gold, of bronze, of lead, and of iron from the city to the river, seven staffs of tamarisk, of palm, seven jars of wine, seven jars of beer, seven jars of milk, seven jars of honey.[1]

An altar will be placed on the 16th of September, before the god Sin they will make ready, incense and cypress for Zaqar, the god of dreams, will be placed at the head of his bed. With kidrusha and qulqulani plants his hands and feet will be washed. A lump of salt, qulqulani plants, cypress, earth, before the door in his belt shall be placed, his head will be lifted up. Since he is not weak, as long as Ashur and Nabu, the king's gods, reckon him with living men, they will not cease to carry out the ritual for his welfare.[2]

Orders are transmitted to Nabu-ahe-eriba that Ashur-mukin-palea should enter the royal presence on the 1st of the month. He will come when Venus shines forth; just now it appeared at sunset and remains fixed. He quotes the omen: "The hired servant will increase, he will be perfected, he will arrive." The king has inquired of Adad-shum-usur as to the welfare of Ashur-mukin-palea and has ordered that he come quickly with him and with twenty men appear before his face. The month of August is favourable, its favourable days are many. He lifts up his feet on high, he dances with joy. It is exceedingly favourable to enter the royal presence. Favourable for the journey is the 2d, the 4th is very propitious. Shortly after, Ashur-mukin-palea was on his way to the ancient city of Ashur, where he was to be "marked" as an urigallu priest. Serving thus his "father," he survived for at least twenty years when his property is found listed.[3]

[1] H. 977. [2] H. 450. [3] H. 82; 652; 77.

Another brother, a sickly youth of five years with the un-
wieldy name of Ashur-etil-shame-ersiti-uballitsu, "Ashur, lord
of heaven and earth, keep him alive," was given the same
priestly position before the Sin who dwells in Harran. An
older brother, also sickly if we may trust the evidence of his
name, Shamash-meta-uballit, "Shamash causes the dead to
live," appears in two earlier letters. In one he writes that
the royal maid servant, Bau-gamelat, is very sick, she eats no
food, may the king order that a physician come and examine
her. He has gone into the district of Nineveh, the bricks are
in place in the royal guard-house, the chariot of cypress is
broken and ruined, let the king send word that it be repaired.
He appears no more in history, and the reference to him by
Zakutu makes it not improbable that he was unwilling to
accept the lowly position of his brothers and paid for his refusal with his life.[1]

His brothers settled, Ashur-bani-apal turned his attention
to the case of the higher officials. The danger incurred by
Adad-shum-usur in his protests against the division of the
kingdom might now hope for reward. He hastened to greet
his new monarch in language which closely followed the phrase-
ology of the claims of millennial bliss formulated by Ashur-
bani-apal himself.

"The king of the gods has proclaimed the name of the king
my lord for the dominion of the Assyrian land. Shamash and
Adad, because of their steadfast regard for the dominion of
the lands of the king my lord, have established a gracious
reign, ordered days, years of righteousness, abundant rains,
copious inundations, fair prices. The gods are revered, the
fear of God is strong, the temples flourish. The great gods of
heaven and earth are kindly disposed towards the king my
lord. The old men dance, the young men sing, the maids and
matrons are gaily decked. They take in marriage the women
and embrace them; reproduction is blessed. To those who have
sinned and looked for death, the king has given new life; those
who were long captive, thou hast set free. Those who were

[1] *H*. 228; 658; 341; 766.

many days ill have been restored to health. The hungry are satisfied, the lean grow fat, the naked are covered with clothing.

"But in all this rejoicing, only I and my son Arad Gula are downcast in heart and disturbed in soul. Since of late the king has shown his love for Nineveh and his people, in that he has given orders to his nobles: 'Bring your sons, let them stand before me,' permit also that my son Arad Gula stand with them before my lord the king. Then, with the rest of the people, we too shall rejoice and dance for joy. My eyes are fixed on the king my lord, for there is not a man among those in the palace who loves me; there is not even a friend to whom I might give a 'gift' and who would receive it and take up my cause. So let the king have pity on his servant and may none of my slanderers among all the people see the desire of his heart upon me." [1]

As for Arad Gula, no one has considered him, he is dying of a broken heart. To lay hold of the king's hand was his hope, since the king has been to many people a restorer of life. May he himself see the king's face among those who are acceptable. Alas, he is dying for lack of food, he begs like a dog, hitherto he has not been negligent. There is not a maid servant nor a man servant with him, he is submissive.[2]

Ashur-bani-apal replied most graciously: "May Ashur, Shamash, and all my gods hearken to this message, including all that you have written. I have heard from the mouth of my family that ye are a trustworthy family, but now I know it for myself and I have seen it." Adad-shum-usur was now an old man and the king provided an assistant in the person of Marduk-shakin-shum, softening the blow by "look upon this as a mark of kindness, since I myself consider it a mark of grace." Adad-shum-usur cannot restrain his enthusiasm: "The father of my lord king was the very image of Bel, and my lord king is the very image of Bel also. By the word of two such lords of peoples, whoever established or altered or will attain such favour? Since the king has collected us and made us to stand in his presence, may all the great gods of

[1] H. 2. [2] H. 657; 659.

heaven and earth make them to come to the king my lord together with his seed, his name, and his offspring. In their families may they cause them to enter as long as Sin and Shamash are established in the heavens. With us may thy heirs rule the land of Assyria forever, and as for us, as long as our family exists, we shall continue to pray for the life and welfare of the king, and may his old age endure unto the days of our grandchildren." He has no feeling of injury because Marduk-shakin-shum has been made his assistant, rather "may god and man requite the kindness of the king a thousandfold. Let him assist me this very day, I shall regard him as a helper in this kindness which I have received from the king my lord." [1]

The enthusiasm of Adad-shum-usur for his new lord showed no sign of abatement, and the succeeding letters present the acme of courtly letter-writing. "Like the Sun God and the Moon God in the heavens, the dominion of the king my lord is established, may his offspring be established over all the lands. May they bring the riches of the land of Assyria and of the land of Akkad and of all their lands to the king my lord. May they assure him health of mind and body, cheerfulness of spirit, an old age of distant days, age-long perpetuation of reign, extensive increase of descendants, and firm establishment of offspring.[2]

"May the great gods whose names the king has written down permit the king my lord to behold the fruits of his labour, because of that word and that commendation which the king pronounced and sent to his dog, his slave, the ancient servitor of his house." He will pray that mighty lands may be a gift to the king, and it will be his task, morning and evening, to beseech the gods for the welfare of the king and of his sons, for perpetuation of his name, that a thousand times a thousand years' health of mind and of body shall be their gift to the king. For now he knows that the wisdom of Ea and Marduk and the work of his servant's hands shall prosper because of the commendation which the king sent to his servant.[3]

[1] H. 6. [2] H. 7. [3] H. 9.

He has received word from the king: "May thy heart be good, may thy gums not be shortened with hunger." For this good deed, which before gods and men is pleasing, Adad-shum-usur will satisfy his appetite, he will summon his courage, since the king has acted towards his servants as a father to his children. "Since men lived, what king has shown such grace to his servants and where is there a friend who has returned good to his friend like this? May the great gods of heaven and earth requite this generous act to his descendants as long as heaven and earth endure. When I heard and saw this good word, this deed of grace, which the king did, my heart was joyous, it lived again. Many cattle are in my possession, for sacrifices I have vowed them. Through the long life of the king my lord, as I grow old in the service of the king and as I am true to the king, may I die the appointed death, may the king heap up my funeral pile and place me in the mound, may he set it up. To my sons in like fashion may the king give orders, may he outlive their grandchildren.

"As to what the king has declared: 'Thou, the sons of thy brothers, the sons of the brothers of thy fathers have I collected, before me shall they stand,' so may Ashur and his family, Bel and Nabu with their families, the great gods of heaven and earth, every one of them, may they collect name, seed, descendant, sprout, seed of the womb, of the king, before their eyes may they make them to stand, so long as heaven and earth endure, may they be rulers of all lands, as gracious, as good, as dignified, as orderly, as faithful. Because of what the king has done, may the king my lord prepare and execute a decorated monument in the form of a sealed document for preserving it in its completeness." [1]

The royal family had by now reached that period in its decline where physical degeneracy had set in. The younger sons showed by their very names their sickly physique. We find Ashur-bani-apal before his accession praying aid for his father and for himself, that the disease causing hand of god or goddess be removed, that health return to himself, and so frail

[1] *H.* 358.

did he remain that after he became king he must again inquire whether he would recover from his sore sickness.[1]

A sick-room atmosphere fills the letters. The crown prince, Ashur-bani-apal, has the fever, the god is angry because of the king's sin, let the king make his prayers of supplication in that day. The physician will make a substitute image in human form for the crown prince, with a view of thus deceiving Eresh-kigal, the goddess of the dead. Shamash-shum-ukin, however, is well, he is in no need of medical attention.[2]

Ikkaru has sent the king ointment, tarpa wood, and a third of a hundred vessels of drink. Whether they brought them to the king he does not know, he has seen no reply to his letter, nor has he heard of the welfare of the king. Shamash-shum-ukin is well. From the 22d day he shall give the blood of drinking, three days shall he drink it, and three are also the days he prescribes for the palace. Bel, Nabu, and the Mistress of Life care for the life of Shamash-shum-ukin.[3]

Arad Nana reports that it is very well with the crown prince. The day he came, he tarried, he gained strength, he remained until he had completed the month. The service performed for him is worth five-sixths of a shekel of silver, an inexpensive enough treatment for one who was almost king. It is not so well with another patient who had a bad nose-bleed. Yesterday, before evening, so the rab mug reported, there was a severe hemorrhage. Arad Nana insists that the dressings are not properly applied, since they are placed over the nostrils; they thus obstruct the breathing and come off when the bleeding begins. They should be placed within the nostril; then the air will be kept out and the bleeding will cease. To-morrow he will come in person and give further instructions; in the meantime, he begs word of the patient's condition.[4]

The queen mother Zakutu is well, but there is question of the food being properly boiled. Another unfortunate suffered from the same diseased eyes which are such an infliction in the modern Orient. Arad Nana removed the bandage yes-

---

[1] Knudtzon, *Gebete*, 116 f.; 108 f.; 143 f.; 147 f.; Klauber, *Texte*, 49.
[2] *H*. 439.   [3] *H*. 740.   [4] *H*. 108.

terday towards evening; there was pus upon it the size of the tip of the little finger. Whoever of the gods put his hand to the case has surely given his orders; in seven or eight days he should be well.[1]

Continually the king has been asking why Arad Nana has not made clear his disease and cured him. Now he has sent a sealed letter which he hopes they will read before the king. He will make prescription: let the ceremonies be carried out by a seer, let them bathe the king and straightway the fever will depart from the face of the king; let them apply to him oil two or three times. There is infection in the pus, let them bring licorice before the king, as they have done twice already, let them rub it in vigorously, then he will come and give further instructions. At once the strength of the king will revive, in the midst of the full tide to the king he will bring. The king shall place on his neck the salve he will send, on the appointed day let the king be anointed. He will speak the truth with the king as the king demanded; the pain in his head, his sides, and his feet has come from his teeth, they must be extracted. Many a present-day physician has made the diagnosis! The prescription for another malady is equally modern—complete rest. Let the king also anoint himself on account of the wind, let him make incantation over the pure waters in the bowl in which he washes his hands, let him not pour it out, then the sickness will quickly pass away. Hygiene for the disease, bread pills for the imagination have been anticipated.[2]

After he became king, Ashur-bani-apal anxiously asks Marduk-shakin-shum about the incantations beginning "Art thou the evil spirit?"—for he desires to drive out the evil spirit and the "one who falls from heaven." The magicians are to perform the rites according to whatever has attacked him. The magician shall approach the path, he shall hang a cuckoo on the door-post. He shall put on red garments, the emblem of death, a red bird he shall carry, a raven on his right shall stand, a falcon on his left; the bars of the seven gates of the under-

[1] *H*. 719; 392.   [2] *H*. 391; 586; 110.

world he shall lay upon them. He shall smite the patient with the lash, he shall recite the incantation: "Art thou the evil spirit?" He shall cause his deputy to go around the bed of the patient with censer and torch. He shall recite the incantation "Go forth!" as far as the gate; the gate itself he shall bewitch. Morning and evening he shall perform the rites until the demons have been driven forth.[1]

Inquiry is made about a fever. Marduk-shakin-shum replies that he is the one who loosens, let him come to the king and he will make the proper incantations. Bel and Nabu will lay life-giving hands upon him. Then comes the cold period of the fever and the king again makes inquiry. He is reassured; there is no guilt and the gods will soon loosen the curse.[2]

Ashur-bani-apal now found time to restore the customary sacrifices for the dead, and especially for the spirits of former kings, which had been allowed to fall into disuse. Thus he had done good for God and man, for dead and for living, yet is this cry forced from his lips: "Why has sickness, woe of heart, misery and destruction bound me? In the land is battle, in the house is intrigue; they are never taken from my side. Destruction and an evil word are lined up against me; ill of heart and ill of body have bowed down my form. With 'Alack' and 'Alas' I end my day; on the day of the city god, the feast-day, I am destroyed. Death is bringing upon me my end, I am oppressed; in want and sorrow I grieve day and night. I wail: 'O God, give this to those who do not fear the gods; may I see thy light! How long, O God, wilt thou do this unto me? As one who fears not god or goddess have I been afflicted.'" Far indeed is this from the hero, mighty in strength through Urta and Nergal, who brought in the millennial dawn!

[1] H. 24.   [2] H. 664; 663.

CHAPTER XXXII

THE LOSS OF EGYPT AND LYDIA

EGYPT and its problems remained as a legacy from his father. "The kings of the lands spake one with another: 'Come, let us go against Ashur-bani-apal; he brought their fate upon our fathers and our fathers' fathers, let not his might restrain us also.'" To this threat Ishtar of Arbela made answer: "The kings of the lands will I overthrow, will place under the yoke, will bind their feet with strong fetters. A second time do I tell you. As with the Elamites and the Cimmerians, I will arise, the thorns I will break, the thorny plants will I open a way through. I will fill the land with blood, will turn it into a desert with weeping and wailing. Dost thou ask: 'Where shall be weeping and wailing?' Weeping has entered Egypt, wailing has come out therefrom. The Mistress is thy mother, fear thou not; the Lady of Arbela is she that bare thee, fear thou not. As she that beareth cares for her child, so care I for thee; as an amulet in the form of a hand, carry I thee between my breasts. In the night stretch I a covering over thee; all day long care I for thy covering. In the morning I care for thy prayer, I care for thy deed. Fear thou not, my little son, whom I have made great." [1]

A whole group of gods lends encouragement through Marduk-shum-usur. Sin and Shamash will grant the new king health, Nabu and Marduk will bestow fame and offspring, the Mistress of Nineveh and Ishtar of Arbela will protect him like a mother or sister. He reminds Ashur-bani-apal how Ashur spoke in a dream to his grandfather, Sennacherib the wise: "O king, lord of kings, offspring of the wise and of Adapa, thou hast surpassed the wisdom of Apsu and of all the wise men." He adds for full measure the story of how Esarhaddon was promised conquest of Egypt by Sin of Harran, and of how he marched forth in the confidence of this prediction and did

[1] Strong, *BA.*, II, 633; Jastrow, *Religion*, II, 171.

indeed conquer Egypt. The other lands which have not yet submitted to Ashur and Sin will likewise be reduced by the king, the lord of kings. With the help of the twelve gods he shall reign a thousand years, till he stand an old man.[1]

Soon after, the troops in Egypt did succeed in defeating the rebels, and two out of the three leaders were taken alive. Brought in chains to the court, Sharru-ludari promptly disappeared, but Necho was forgiven. The treaty concluded with him was on much stiffer terms than before, but he was presented with coloured dresses, golden necklaces, bracelets, an iron sword with the royal name inlaid in gold, chariots and horses and mules. He was returned to Kar-bel-matati, "the Fort of the Lord of Lands," the Assyrian name for Sais, and with him went an Assyrian governor, "for a support to him," ironically remarks Ashur-bani-apal. His son Psammetichus was likewise given an Assyrian name, Nabu-shezibanni, and was granted a position of equality with his father as ruler of Athribis, now called by the clumsy name of Limir-ishakku Ashur, "may the patesi of Ashur be illustrious."

Taharka died in 663, shortly after associating his nephew Tanutamon, the son of Shabaka. Informed by a dream that he was to rule both north and south Egypt, Tanutamon advanced to Memphis, drove out the Assyrians, and forced their supporters to sue for peace. Necho died, and his son took refuge within the Assyrian lines in Syria. Assyrian rule was confined to the Delta, and even here a raid by the Ethiopian brought in a certain number of princes ready to place themselves on what they thought the winning side.[2]

As soon as the troubles with the Elamite Urtaku were composed, the Assyrians returned. Memphis was retaken, and then, after a march of a month and ten days, Thebes as well. Great was the plunder, gold and silver, the "dirt of his land," precious stones, cloths, great horses, apes of various kinds, the products of the Egyptian highlands. The later editions of the official history add two high obelisks of gleaming electron of a weight of 2,500 talents, which once formed the door-posts of the temple entrance.

[1] H. 923.   [2] Breasted, *Records*, IV, 467 ff.

Fig. 147. THE ACROPOLIS AT SARDIS.
(The Pactolus, "River of Gold," in foreground.)

Fig. 148. VIEW FROM THE ACROPOLIS OF SARDIS.
(The burial mounds of the Lydian kings in the distance.)

The sack of Thebes produced utter stupefaction. Immortal form to this feeling was given by the Jewish prophet Nahum when fell "No Ammon, that was situate among the rivers, that had the waves about her, whose rampart was the Water, and her wall was the Sea. Ethiopia was her strength and Egypt also, it had no limit; Punt and the Libyans were her helpers. Yet she was carried away, she went into captivity; her young children were dashed in pieces at the head of all her streets, for her honorable men they cast lots, and all her nobles were bound in chains." [1]

The fall of Thebes marked the end of the Ethiopian domination of Egypt, but the Assyrians enjoyed small reward for their toil. Psammetichus returned and began to consolidate his position. Signs of what was coming were not infrequent. Thus, for example, Ashipa, the Assyrian officer in charge of the Arabs on the Syrian frontier, complained to the king about Nabu-shezibanni, as Psammetichus was still called; Ashur-bani-apal was powerless to take action, and could only assert that he was the dog of the king.[2] Later Ashur-bani-apal tells us how Gyges of Lydia sinned in sending aid to the Egyptian ruler, but no casual reader would dream that the Pishamilki of this passage is the Nabu-shezibanni who is listed not many lines before as an Egyptian subject king. A third time he appears, as a supporter of the revolted Shamash-shum-ukin, but again he is disguised, for his title is "King of Meluhha," which by this time had come to be equivalent for Ethiopia. Psammetichus, however, was now king of all Egypt, and counted the beginning of his reign from 663, the date of Taharka's death.

Our royal historian inserts a passage about 667 which tells how Ikkilu, king of Arvad, who had dwelt safe in his island in the midst of the sea, like an immense fish, and had gone up to the great sea, refusing to accept the Assyrian yoke, suddenly became submissive and promised to pay the yearly tribute of gold, purple, fish, and birds his suzerain demanded.

Decidedly different is the picture drawn by the Assyrian fiscal agent, Itti Shamash-balatu, whose troubles are described

[1] Nahum 3 : 8 ff.   [2] H. 298.

in a confidential despatch. His station was at the "Assyrian Harbour," known as Amurru when it gave its name to all Syria and Mesopotamia, for the island was forbidden ground to him. "The king my lord knows that Ikkilu will not let go the ships, that they cannot come to anchor at the wharf of the king my lord. Every wharf he takes for himself. Whoever comes to him, he establishes his feet; whoever comes to the wharf of the land of Assyria he kills, his ship he destroys, for he says: 'They have sent from the palace.'" Some official is now in Simirra, he will go to Assyria, whatever the obstacles he will investigate the report and have speech with him. The king will at once ask: "Why did you not seize him?" He fears because of the king's father and cannot seize him. The king should know that there are many, even of the King's Companions, who gave money to this house; they fear as do the merchants, but he trusts only the king. Not a shekel, not a half-shekel, has he given to any one, to the king he has given it, for the king restored him to life from a thousand deaths when he was a dead dog; therefore, the king is his god.[1]

From this secret despatch we realise how small was the authority of the Assyrians over these Phœnician cities, when the highest nobles from the court must condescend to pay blackmail, and when discrimination could be safely employed against Assyrian merchants. This favoured position was lost when, a few years later, Ikkilu died, and his sons in their rivalry called in their suzerain to decide their claims to the throne. The royal approval fell upon Azibaal, the other claimants were granted the court dress of varicoloured stuffs and the royal ring, but were prudently detained in the capital, that Azibaal might find a rival should he at any time in the future attempt the independent rôle of his father. Near by has been found a copy of Ashur-bani-apal's Niniil inscription, in the Babylonian character, but with mistakes which prove that it was engraved by a native Syrian.[2]

Final mention of Syria in an Assyrian inscription comes in the latest part of the reign, when the citizens of Ushu, at the

[1] H. 992.   [2] Löytved-Sayce, ZA., VII, 141.

foot of Mount Carmel, where is now the flourishing port of Haifa, refused to pay tribute to the Assyrian governor; the hand of Psammetichus, now embarked upon an aggressive Syrian policy, is doubtless to be recognised. For the last time the Assyrians were successful in Palestine; the citizens were executed or deported. Punishment was also meted out to the men of Acco across the bay; their leaders were impaled about the city; the remainder were taken to Assyria and formed into a company for the army.

In the last days of his father, a certain Mugallu had appeared with his army before Melidia. Loss of such a city, a great Hittite centre which still presents a large mound and numerous sculptures and inscriptions, was much to be dreaded, since it controlled the one adequate route which ran east from Mazaka to the Euphrates crossing, and then by a corner of Haldia to Amedi and to Nineveh. Esarhaddon hastened to his god, told how Mugallu with his camp was before the city, how the commander-in-chief with the royal troops and the local levies had gone against him, and inquired whether he would be successful in driving Mugallu from the walls of the beleaguered town.

An eclipse in January, which had of old been supposed to mean that the king of Amurru would be decreased and become a fugitive, was assumed to apply either to Ethiopia or to Mugallu. It certainly did not apply to Mugallu, for in the next inquiry we find Mugallu given the title of Melidian, quite as a matter of course. Now he has united with Ishkallu of Tabal against the city of Ishtiaru, and the question is whether during the month of May they will have any success against the army of the commander-in-chief, Sha Nabu-shu. If he breaks camp, with either Mugallu or Ishkallu or any other enemy, will he fall upon them in broad daylight or in the dark night, will he defeat and plunder them, or make ill the heart of Esarhaddon, king of Assyria?[1]

About the time Ashur-bani-apal took the place of his father, Mugallu decided to make his peace with the empire. In the

[1] Knudtzon, *Gebete*, 55 ff.; Klauber, *Texte*, 27; *H*. 629.

royal inscriptions, to be read far from the frontier, Ashur-bani-
apal attributes to the fear of his royalty the submission of this
prince, who had raised his weapons against the kings his
fathers; Mugallu did send an embassy without war or battle,
but it was not received with the complacency which the king
publicly assumed. Again he had recourse to the oracle and
begged Shamash to answer him truly, whether he should receive the embassy which Mugallu had sent to make submission, and whether the Melidian would keep his plighted word.[1]
The answer was favourable, and a tribute of great horses was
accepted from him. Horses are quite what we should expect,
for Cappadocia has always been famous for her roadsters, but
the actual beasts were hardly larger than ponies, and their
great size existed only in the scribe's imagination.

In the same inquiry mention was made of Ishkallu, king of
Tabal, and a companion who can only be the king of the
Hilaku. The latter were just on the point of leaving the fertile plains of southern Cappadocia, where they had been settled something more than a century, en route to the still more
fertile plain of Cilicia, which was henceforth to carry their
name. Another inquiry dated in August shows them on their
way. Will they go down from the place they now occupy to
Que, will the men of the Kuzzurakkai do anything?[2] Like
Mugallu, the Hilaku secured their objective, and then, settled
in their new domain, made their peace with the empire. A
generation later, after the fall of Babylon, Sanda-sarme appeared in person with his gifts, presented his daughter, and
kissed the royal feet.

In October of 668 the youthful king asks for the last time
of the fate of Asia Minor. He would know of the allies of the
Hilaku, of a ruler whose name ends in shattu, and of a son of
Kanda. Now Kandaules is known to mean "Kanda's son,"
so we may see in this individual that Kandaules who was deposed by Gyges in Lydia. We are hearing of the beginnings
of the Lydian Empire.

---

[1] Knudtzon, *Gebete*, 54.
[2] Knudtzon, *Gebete*, 60, 62; Klauber, *Texte*, 43.

On their confession to the gods, the Lydians were no strangers to the Assyrians. Not a hint of the fears engendered appears in the official records, and when Kandaules was supplanted by Gyges, who reversed his predecessor's policy towards the empire, the official scribes worked up a story which was as notable for its purple patches as for its lack of historicity.

Lydia, according to this story, was a far-away district at the crossing of the sea, and of which the kings, his fathers, had not so much as heard. Ashur appeared in a dream to Gyges and thus addressed him: "The exalted feet of Ashur-bani-apal, king of Assyria, the desire of Ashur, king of the gods, the lord of all, do thou seize, fear his royalty and beseech his lordship. As one who makes vassalage and furnishes tribute, may thy supplication approach him." The very day the dream appeared, a messenger was started towards Assyria.

A still later version narrated the approach to the Assyrian frontier. "Who art thou, stranger," the guards are represented as saying, "to whose land has never any messenger directed the way?" They brought him to Nineveh, and men who spoke all tongues, from the rising of the sun to the setting thereof, all with which Ashur had filled the royal hand, attempted speech with him, but a possessor of his tongue was not found.

This version breaks off at this point, and we are unable to conjecture how Ashur-bani-apal finally discovered that the messenger had come for the purpose of promising submission. The original story, however, is sure that from the very day his ambassadors set out, Gyges was able victoriously to combat the Cimmerians who were oppressing his land, and in gratitude thereof sent the captured chiefs as the first-fruits of his submission. Suddenly his messengers ceased to appear; he trusted to his own strength and sent troops to the support of Psammetichus of Egypt. When the news of the aid given to the rebel was brought to Ashur-bani-apal, he raised his hands to Ashur and Ishtar: "Before his enemies may his corpse be thrown, may they carry off his bones." As he had prayed, so it came to pass. His corpse was thrown before his enemies, his bones they carried away. The Cimmerians, whom he had formerly conquered through the name of Ashur-bani-apal, became masters of his land. After him his son sat on his throne; he recognised the evil deeds done by his father, and sent once more his embassy to court with the humble prayer: "Thou art the king whom God hath recognised. Thou didst curse my father and evil came upon him; towards me thy servant who feareth thee be gracious, and I will bear thy yoke."

The recital is not without its charm as a literary composition, for the purpose of the historian it is obviously inadequate. With the aid of the Greek writers and with some knowledge of the general background, it is possible to come somewhat nearer the truth. Gyges had gained an uneasy throne by the deposition of Kandaules, the last of the Heraclidæ.[1] He had sensed the threat of the Cimmerians, who had destroyed the Phrygian kingdom about 680 and had forced the death of the last Midas by his own hand. The fame of the Assyrians had reached him, and he hoped that the two civilised empires might come to some agreement to crush the common foe between.

When he realised the hollowness of the imposing imperial structure and the hopelessness of securing substantial aid for an enterprise so far beyond the bounds of their particular interests, he looked about for other helpers. Psammetichus had just thrown off the Assyrian yoke, and it seemed that a new period of prosperity was dawning for Egypt. Aid given to Egypt might be doubled a little later, so Gyges had no hesitation in sending him those mercenaries whose scribblings are to be seen in the temple of Thutmose III at Wadi Halfa.[2]

Aided by the Treres and the Lycians, the Cimmerians fell upon Lydia in 652, and Gyges met his death in battle. Sardis was sacked and Ionia felt the attack of Dygdamis's hordes. The joy of Ashur-bani-apal at the death of Gyges was not quite so great as he pretends; when the Cimmerians swung away again to the east and approached the Assyrian frontier

[1] Herod., i, 7 ff.
[2] Sayce, *PSBA.*, XVII, 42.

in Cilicia, they presented a danger of the first magnitude.[1]
To increase his terror, an eclipse of the moon showed the light
portion of the disk in a form which the court scholars recognised as a kidney.   On investigating their store of tablets, they
came upon this terrifying statement: "When the moon in its
appearing is spread out like a kidney, Enlil will go against the
land for evil, there will be an attack on the land by the Guti,
and that land will be destroyed."   Substituting only Umman
Manda for Guti, they sent word to the king, who in frantic
terror rushed to the oracle of Marduk to inquire of this Tug-
dame and his son Sandakshatru, of this Umman Manda king
who was the creation of Tiamat, the primeval chaotic monster, and the model of an evil demon.   Ashur-bani-apal furnishes no details of the danger or of the manner in which it
was averted, but his abject terror and the equally pronounced
joy with which the outcome was greeted testifies to its serious-
ness.

Doubtless there would be much to tell of the relations between Haldia and the northern barbarians were the record
preserved; as it is, we know only Haldian relations with
Assyria.   These relations were friendly so long as Esarhaddon
lived, but the accession of a new and youthful ruler and the
troubles which marked his first year proved too great a temp-
tation to Rusash II.   He had gladly received back the Haldian fugitives from Shupria, but now he desired to wean that
same country from the Assyrian alliance.   In his extremity
Ashur-bani-apal again went to Shamash.   Will Rusash the
Urartian, alone or with his troops, or with the Cimmerians or
with his other allies make plans, will he leave the place where
he is encamped, to kill, plunder, take prisoner Shupria, the
cities of Uppume or Kullameri or the other forts of Shupria,
will he rob much or little, or appropriate for himself?[2]   For
a moment there was danger of open war, when one of the Haldian officials, Andaria, made an unexpected night raid against
those two cities.   Fortunately the Assyrians were awake to

---

[1] Herod., i, 15; Strab., i, 3, 21; xiii, 4, 8; xiv, 1, 40.
[2] Knudtzon, *Gebete*, 48.

the situation; in spite of the darkness they promptly fell upon
him, cut off his head, and sent it to Nineveh. Actual warfare
between the principals was avoided, and in all but one version
of the incident this international breach of the peace was cleverly camouflaged by calling Andaria the village chief of Lubdu,
an ancient place name the scribe had resurrected for the purpose.

Never again do we have war between Haldia and Assyria.
The common danger from the north brought the two countries
together in ever closer alliance, though the pride of Ashur-
bani-apal would not make the admission in writing. About
the year 648 a third Rusash, the son of Erimenash, sent an
embassy to Arbela. Action against their mutual enemies was
doubtless the reason, but Ashur-bani-apal pretended that it
was through fear of his majesty and that its purpose was to
ask his peace, the technical expression for recognition of lordship. He even went so far as to fashion a relief, showing the
king in his chariot receiving the ambassadors.

Yet more humble was another embassy, which is the last
event commemorated in the annals. While his predecessors
had sent concerning brotherhood, that is, had claimed equality,
Sardurish III heard of the mighty deeds of the Assyrians, and
like a son to a father, he forwarded his heavy tribute, and
wrote: "Verily may there be peace to the king my lord."
Once more we may question whether it was not the report of
Cimmerian victories rather than of Assyrian which caused the
embassy.

The hitherto faithful Mannai had attempted to free themselves from Assyrian overlordship by the aid of the Scyths;
the clever diplomacy of Esarhaddon married Bartatua to his
daughter, and thus the Scyth chief became brother-in-law to
Ashur-bani-apal. Ahsheri was forced to stand alone, but this
did not prevent the Mannai from seizing the forts near Paddiri. Nabu-shar-usur, the new commander-in-chief, took personal charge of the forces designed to recover them, and his
king inquired through the liver omens whether he would win
them back and return alive. Nabu-iqbi, the royal astrono-

mer at Kutu, predicts that as the gods have given Egypt and Ethiopia into the hands of the kings, so will they grant success against the Cimmerians and the Mannai.[1]

A third omen is found in a letter from Nabu-shar-usur himself: "When the constellation of the Virgin shines forth from the sunrise like a torch and in the sunset fades away, the troops of the enemy will be severely smitten. When the south wind blows all night, and having blown all night continues, and as it continues becomes a gale, and from a gale increases to a tempest, and as a tempest does sweeping damage, on whatsoever expedition the prince goes he will obtain wealth."

Discussion of the proposed expedition follows: "Whereas the king has ordered his army: 'Enter into the midst of the Mannai,' the whole army should not enter. Let the cavalry and the Dakku invade the Cimmerian land, who made the declaration: 'The Mannai pertain to you, we shall not interfere.' This is an obvious lie. The offspring of their fugitives reverence neither an oath by a god nor a formal treaty. Let the chariots and baggage-wagons take their position on either side of the entrance. With the horses and the Dakku let them plunder the produce of the Mannai, let them return and bivouac at the entrance. Once and twice they entered. On the 15th the full moon appeared with the sun; this is an omen against them. Wilt thou be hindered by the Cimmerians? If they do approach, their comings and their goings I do not know. I have sent a messenger to the king, may the lord of kings inquire of a man acquainted with the country, may the king at his pleasure reinforce his army with raiders in addition to the other fighting men. Do thou provision for thyself a fortress in the enemy's midst, let the whole army enter it. Let the Gududanu go forth and let their soldiers seize the produce; let them inquire whether the Indaruai have departed. Let the army enter into their cities, let them overthrow them."[2]

As Nabu-shar-usur had evidently feared, Ahsheri made a night attack upon the Assyrians, but was repulsed and pur-

[1] Knudtzon, *Gebete*, 150 f.; Thompson, *Reports*, No. 22.   [2] *H*. 1237.

sued for three double hours' distance. Izirtu was abandoned
for his stronghold Atrana, and for a stretch of fifteen days the
Assyrians systematically harried the country. Paddiri, the
centre of the former Assyrian province, was restored to the
empire. Ashur and Ishtar handed over Ahsheri to his subjects; they revolted against him, and threw his dead body into
the street. His son Ualli at once made his peace with the
Assyrians, sent his eldest son, Erisinni, to pay his devoirs in
Nineveh, his daughter entered the Assyrian harem, but the
increased tribute of thirty horses was a scanty return from
the oracle which declared that the prince on his expedition
would obtain wealth.

Nor were the Assyrians more successful with the Medes farther south. A despatch from Adad-ittia tells how two captains of cavalry were sent to Sanha and Ulushia, to the loyal
servants of the king in those localities. Grain and water are
there according to their tablet of instructions, their watch is
strong. The king knows that Ishtar-babilia is a double-
tongued man; he has been sent into Tikrish and reports that
the son of Ahsheri remained in his frontier camp as long as
they were on the Mannai border. After Nergal-bel-usur arrived, Adad-ittia broke camp and entered the Mannai land.
He sent his third deputy to him, saying: "Come out." He
replied: "I am sick." Adad-ittia then urged him: "Let your
son come." He answered: "He too is sick, but I will send my
brother with the soldiers." Adad-ittia's messenger made still
another trip, but has not yet returned. All the other contingents of the village chiefs are in his presence.[1]

We last saw Yatha, lord of the desert Arabs, holding his
throne against his rival Wahab by the aid of the Assyrians;
after a time he wearied of the yoke and lost his gods. The
arrival of a new king seemed an auspicious occasion to rein-
state himself; he appeared in Nineveh, took the oath, and received back his deities. As time passed, and memories of
Nineveh became dim, he forgot his oaths and began to plunder
Syria. The troops stationed on the southern frontier were or-

[1] H. 342.

dered out, and there ensued a series of minor actions in Hezron, Edom, Iabroda, Ammon, the Hauran, Moab, Seir, and Zobah.

The nomads were easily dispersed, their tents burned, their flocks and herds carried off. So great was the booty that camels were reckoned as sheep, and their price was but half a shekel apiece in the Gate of the Merchant, though the normal rate was a mana and two-thirds. To such straits were the fugitives reduced that they were forced to eat the flesh of their children. Yatha fled to the Nabatæans, and his place was taken by Abiyatha, who had purchased his position in Assyria by promising a yearly tribute—gold, eye and mouth stones, kohl for painting the eyes of the palace ladies, camels and asses for them to ride. Another of these Cedarene kings who had attacked Syria was Amuladi; there was no need of a call for Assyrian troops, since Chemoshhalteh of Moab seized him and sent him to Nineveh. Nadnu, too, the king of the Nabatæans, whose far-away people had never sent tribute to the earlier rulers, besought the king's peace and promised an annual contribution.

Nabu-shum-lishir reports his war with the Cedarenes. According to royal instructions, he came to their land, and through the Fortune of the king he completed their defeat. Those who escaped the iron dagger were yet reached by the outraged royal oath against which they had sinned, and now they are dying of hunger. When a small Assyrian force set out from the Nabatæan country, they were attacked by Aiakamaru of Mash; all were slain but one man; later he escaped to the royal city, and is now being sent on to the king. Other Assyrians, servants of the king, refused to revolt in the city of the Bibarbar tongue, and were attacked by the Arabs. Fifty Assyrian colonists of Haluli and twenty Birtai were wounded. One of them escaped, and Nabu-shum-lishir made a slaughter of the Arabs; for the sake of the district's inhabitants he established the king's servants in the midst. There has been no breakdown of administration, he has restored order, and seven of their language, including the friend of

Itailu and an official of Shamash, he is sending on to the king.[1]

Bel-liqbi is in Zobah in middle Syria, which had been made a province as early as 683. He has found that Hesa is a cara-vansary, but is uninhabited, nor do rab kalle nor rab raksi function in it. This is a striking illustration of the void which was being created in central Syria by the civil wars and the deportations, for Zobah was a great Aramæan centre in the days of David and again in the early years of Roman rule as Chalcis it played no small part. Now Bel-liqbi would con-struct thirty houses in Hesa, since there have been none since the governorship of Nabu-salla. The captain's heavy armed bowmen are at present settled in Hesa; he would transfer them to Argite, where fields and gardens could be assigned them. Let the king send a letter to the governor Nabu-salla, that he may appoint his deputy Iairu to be chief over the city of Mete. He will appoint Sin-iddina, the majordomo of Uhati, over Sazana, quickly they will cultivate this fertile place and will fear the king. Yesterday and the day before the Arabs came in and went out, there is complete peace. Amiliti, son of Ameri, has arrived in Zobah and he asserts that all is at peace. Uhati, too, sends two letters to report that all is well with the forts and with the whole desert of Hamath. Ashipa has asked about the Nabatæans, the king advises him that they are before his face, that is, he may do as he pleases.[2]

On the revolt of Shamash-shum-ukin, Abiyatha and his brother Aimu came to his aid and succeeded in breaking through the besieging lines. As food began to run short, they sallied forth and again broke through the cordon. In some manner, Abiyatha placated Ashur-bani-apal, but the desert had its usual effect; once safe in its expanse, he gave up all pretense of respect for the empire and allied himself with the Nabatæans who already regretted their promise of a yearly contribution.

A regular expedition was therefore planned. Leaving Nineveh when summer was already upon them, they plunged

[1] H. 350; 260; 262; 953. [2] H. 414; 224 f.; 305; 298.

into the desert. Beyond the Euphrates, they first crossed high mountains where trees cast a welcome shade. A region of thorns proved introduction to the desert proper, a land of thirst and fatigue, in whose midst was no bird of heaven, where even the wild asses and gazelles could find no pasture. For some hundred double hours, nearly five hundred miles, the weary track was followed. In the middle of June, they left Hadatta and came to Laribda, a fort of "seal" stone, and camped at the water-holes. Another region of thirst carried them to Hurarina, whence they proceeded between Iarki and Azalla into another desert strip where was no beast of the field and where no bird established her nest. The Nabatæans and the Isamme, whose eponymous ancestor was Mishma, the son of Ishmael,[1] and the sept of the god Atar-samain, were pursued for eight double hours. Returning to Azalla, where the exhausted troops drank the water of satisfaction, they followed the fleeing Arabs through another region of thirst and fatigue to Qurasiti. The sept of Atar-samain and the Cedarenes under another Yatha, the nephew of the former, were defeated; his gods, his mother, his sister, and his wife— the order is interesting—were made prisoners, and the way was taken back to Damascus.

Once more the terrors of the desert were braved. Near the end of July the heat was at its maximum, and the army was able to make six double hours only by marching the whole night through. From Hulhuliti, still counted twelve hours south of Damascus, they reached the impassable mountain of Hukkurina, where they fell upon the personal sept of Abiyatha and carried the two leaders to Assyria. Guards were placed at all the wells and water-holes, and the Bedawin, shut off from the priceless fluid, were forced to slay their camels and to drink the bloody fluid enclosed in their humps. When they asked themselves, "Why has this evil fallen upon the Arab land," only one answer was possible: "Because we have not observed the great oath of Ashur, we have sinned against the goodness of Ashur-bani-apal, the king whom Enlil loves."

[1] Gen. 25 : 14; I Chron. 1 : 30.

The dependents of Yatha began to mutter revolt and his only hope lay in flight to the Assyrians. He received no welcome but was sent bound to court, where his cheeks and jaw-bone were pierced, a rope was inserted, he was chained with a dog-chain and set to guard the gate of Nineveh. The very last picture we have of Ashur-bani-apal shows him in a chariot drawn by four kings and one is the wretched Yatha. Aimu was less fortunate, for his punishment was flaying alive.[1]

Permanent results of these campaigns there were none. At best, the Assyrians had penetrated a few hundred miles into the north Syrian desert southeast of Damascus, perhaps as far as the region directly east of the Dead Sea, for the still general belief that the armies went deep into the heart of the peninsula fades when the distances are plotted on the map. The soldiers had endured great hardships and had brought home picturesque accounts of what they had seen and suffered. It was fitting that one of the rooms in the palace at Nineveh should be decorated with reliefs showing the progress of the Arabian expeditions.[2]

[1] Note that Yatha and Abiyatha are royal names in south Arabian Main.
[2] *Bulletin Amer. Geog. Soc.*, XLIV, 433.

CHAPTER XXXIII

THE INTRIGUES OF ELAM

INTERESTING as these various phases of foreign relations have been, they yield in importance to the question of Babylonia and Elam which dominates the reign and forms almost a dramatic unity. From the very enthronement of the two princes, the problem of Elam was a vital one. Elamite intrigue was felt in the beginning year of the double reign, when the village chief of Kirbit, Tanda, was moved to plunder Iamutbal, the eastern border of Babylonia. This affected the territory occupied by the citizens of Der, who appealed to Ashur-bani-apal for protection against the marauder. The near-by Assyrian governor, Nur-ekalli-umu, was ordered out against him, and in due time the leading rebels were impaled about the city and the others were deported into Egypt.

A private quarrel in Babylon seemed about to plunge the country into disorder. The house chief Sillai and the scribe Marduk-eresh complained to the king: "The house of our lords, our governors, is new. The king does not realise that the governor of Arrapha has taken the gift which the king presented to our lords. Let me make known that the house of our lords is reduced. The king knows that our lord had no legal contest with his opponent, and when we plead our case he is suspicious of us. Let the king appoint one of his Companions over us that he may bring information about us to the king and let him appoint a guardsman over the house of his servant, let him give judgment concerning his house." [1]

His chief opponent was Zakir, the head shepherd of Nabu, who had already earned the respect of Esarhaddon by his request that the sanctuaries of Babylon should be treated as they had been by Tiglath Pileser III, and who had further won his regard by prophesying harm to Amurru as the result

[1] *H.* 415.

of an eclipse. His reply to Sillai was ready: "When the sky is smitten with darkness, abundance will be in the land. Sillai has written by the hand of Shakin-shum: 'To death will I consign thee, for why hast thou written: "Sillai has taken my goods"? 'Munnabittum is your witness and Bel . . . is in charge of my case. As for a witness, what has he taken from my goods and how much?' When he learns that I have written to the king—and there is still more that I have not told the king—he will take all. I have prayed in my father's house, but he has always intrigued, he has plotted constantly against me, let not the king abandon me." [1]

Munnabittum does indeed write to the king in response to an inquiry about Ashur-etir, the son of Sillai. Nabu-apal-iddina has killed his servants, although the king has decided the case, no one gives them a thought, they plead for their lives. He and his brethren have pleaded their case before the king, whatever the king wishes, let it be decreed. [2]

As a result of this series of complaints and counter-complaints, Bel-etir was killed by Shuzub of the Gahul family; so notable was this atrocity that the fact was inserted in the general history we call the Babylonian Chronicle under the date of January, 667. Through Bel-uballit, the citizens of Babylon sent a protest to the two monarchs: "The kings our lords, from the time they ascended the throne, set their faces to protect our chartered rights and for our welfare. The kings our lords have ordained that those who occupy our fields, whether a woman of Elam, of Tabal, or of the Ahlame, should have protection, as they have declared: 'The gods have given you open ears and an open heart. For all the lands is Babylon the bond of the lands; whoever enters there, his protection is guaranteed.' 'One breaking through of the house of Babylon' is the name given to the charter. 'A dog which enters shall not be killed.' " Eteru, as he is here called, had with his sons taken the feet of the king's father, the watch of their lord they kept; in spite of this protection he has been killed and the women folk of his sons carried off. The citizens beg for

[1] H. 137; 416.   [2] H. 928.

aid, "since in the name of Babylon are women who are there married secure in their right through us." [1]

Zakir replies to this as follows: "They seized the sons of Eteru, the Sealander whom the king appointed, but declared it was by order of the king. They gave blame to the sons in the sight of the king, but Ubaru, governor of Babylon, says it is not a royal order. Earlier, in Kalhu, the king accepted what was for the peace of Babylon, he has lifted up his heart in their behalf, he has established affairs in Babylon." He says: "The city was ruined, I reduced it to order, its independence I established." This is the word received from the mouth of the king of lands, these the king had admitted. But the Babylonians have been given a bribe, the wages have been held back, the king released men for money; let him set free a hundred from Elam and the Hittite land, for the sake of Bel and Sarpanitum may they be free from death. They will give money for those whom the king permits to live, the good word which the king withholds can avail nothing without the power of the king. Sillai, the Babylonian, does not wish this; the king is well acquainted with the matter, let him do as he wishes. [2]

Sillai seems to have gotten the worst of the bargain, for Belusatu, the royal shepherd, writes his master that Sillai is in prison, without the king's aid he will die. His opponents do what they please and bring the affairs of the king into confusion. Sillai begs "May the king hear me." [3]

Elam had been on good terms with Assyria since the accession of Urtaku in 675. When a great famine held Elam in its grasp and the people were in sore need, Esarhaddon sent grain to his royal friend and allowed his subjects to remain in Assyria until there should be harvest and rain. The youth of the new rulers and the division of the empire quite counterbalanced any pro-Assyrian leanings cherished by Urtaku. [4]

One of the most important of the Aramæan tribes of Babylonia, the Gambulu, was ruled by Bel-iqisha, who had been recognised by the Assyrians as a shatam official. His relations

---

[1] H. 878.   [2] H. 702.   [3] H. 1111.   [4] H. 295.

with the Assyrians deputed to Babylonia were not happy, and he had frequent complaints to make to the king. He has had trouble over two mares and he has been slandered before the abarakku. He has been mocked by a scribe who declared: "I shall remove thee from this house." Since the time when the king appointed Bel-iqisha in the house of his lords, he has had no power over anything in the house of his lords. He has spoken to his own private secretary and has been told: "He has boasted that he has subjugated the whole house of my lords to himself." He has distributed gifts and in this manner he has destroyed Bel-iqisha. At last he has even given bribes to his private scribe and has alienated him. These five months Bel-iqisha has been waiting orders from the king while his sons have gone to Kalhu. All the sons of the other chiefs have been exalted, but his sons tarry and the king has closed the way.[1]

Matters were reaching the breaking point, and Bel-iqisha may be already picking a quarrel with the king when he writes rather insolently: "The servants of the house of my lords whom the king this day has distinguished by promotion, Taba-lai, the son of Bel Harran-aha-usur, whom he has made captain, Nabu-sakip, whom he has made shalshu of the standing army, and Emur Marduk, whom he has made a guardsman, these three men are hard drinkers. When they become drunken, not one of them will turn away the iron dagger from those who meet them." Bel-iqisha has sent the report that he knows, let the king do as he will.[2]

The Elamite governor, Marduk-shum-ibni, was eager to begin an offensive against Babylonia, and persuaded Bel-iqisha and Nabu-shum-eresh, the qadu, to desert their master. Messengers reported that the Elamites were advancing against Babylon, and that they covered the ground like grasshoppers. Great was the alarm in Assyria, where the command devolved upon Nabu-shar-usur. Ashur-bani-apal demanded of Shamash whether the Gambulu would fight for or against the Assyrians and whether his general would return alive.[3]

---

[1] H. 84; 698. [2] H. 85. [3] Knudtzon, *Gebete*, 153.

Soon it was learned that Bel-iqisha had indeed revolted and Nabu-ushabshi, governor of the city of Uruk, was ordered to lead his levies against the chief city of the Gambulu. Nabu-ushabshi was nothing loath, for, as he answers, "The gods of the king my lord surely know that since Bel-iqisha revolted from the hands of the king and went over to Elam, he has plundered my father's house, and has gone about seeking to kill my brother." He is frankly sceptical about the success of the king's plan; if it does not force submission of the Gambulu, let all Akkad be collected and the land will be returned. Sharru-emuranni was much troubled about Bel-iqisha and the king's gold. His men went to the Puqudu, Uruk, and Sapea, fifty of them build their house according to his orders; following his master's instructions, he has despatched cavalry under a captain.[1]

Shortly after, Urtaku died by the death-dealing stroke of Nergal, that is, by the pestilence, and his place was taken by Tep Humban, the former chief of his bowmen. An anti-Assyrian policy was continued and Massi was sent to aid the Gambulu where Bel-iqisha had met his death by the bite of a wild boar and had been followed by his son Dunnanu. Dunnanu and Massi were soon Assyrian prisoners and the men of Nippur were praised for having arrested Rimutu. Rimutu now promised Nabu-dur-usur that he would pay tribute to the king and when the Gambulu asked for him in the place of the deposed Dunnanu, Ashur-bani-apal graciously replied: "Let him come and see my face; I will clothe him with the ceremonial robe and will cheer his heart. Over you do I appoint him." Happily the Gambulu admit that they are dead dogs, let Rimutu come in the joy of their lord, let him bind the land.[2]

In his efforts to destroy rival claimants to the throne, Tep Humban forced out of the country over sixty of the royal family, including Humbanigash, Humbanappa, and Tammaritu, sons of the late king, Kudur and Paru of Hilmu, sons of his brother Humbanhaltash, and free-born citizens without

[1] *H.* 269; 313 ff.; cf. 914.   [2] *H.* 228; 910; 293; 915.

number. They found in Assyria a royal welcome, for in them was the nucleus of a pro-Assyrian party in their native land.

The reception extended by the Assyrian government to these exiles called for protest, and month after month Tep Humban sent to demand their surrender. Ashur-bani-apal refused to listen and detained the legates, Nabu-damiq and Humbandara. They are represented, a fat old eunuch and a young official, with the tablet which contained their rash demands and with their whips of office in their girdles, in the relief which commemorated the embassy of the Haldian Rusash.

To the consternation of the Assyrian, war was renewed by this "form of an evil demon," but the gods gave encouragement. The moon-god rested from dawn to full morning light, the sun was darkened and rested for three long July days. This portended the end of Tep Humban's rule; soon after he was stricken, "his lips slavered, his eye rolled, wildness was imparted to it." Despite this epileptic attack, preparations were continued by the Elamites, and the alarm increased the next month when it was learned that the Elamite had reached Bit Imbi and was threatening Der.

Ashur-bani-apal was in Arbela and promptly sought out the local Ishtar. With tears streaming down his face, he begged her aid in return for the many shrines he had rebuilt and for the many services he had rendered her. The answer came through the seer. In a dream of the night, he saw Ishtar appear to the praying king, quivers to right and to left of her, bow and sharp battle-sword in her hand. Like a mother she spoke to him and protected him in her bosom. Ashur-bani-apal impulsively declared that he would go whither so ever she went, but the goddess knew his character too well to take him at his word. While she marched against his enemies, flames going before her, he was to remain at Arbela in the shrine of Nabu, eating food and drinking sesame wine, making music, and praising her godship. His face was not to be pale, his feet incapable of motion, his strength wasted in battle. The seer gave the answer he knew would please his master and in inscription and sculpture Ashur-bani-apal admitted his lack of bravery. As he grew older, he became somewhat ashamed of this record and claimed the war for himself, though the very pictures on the wall of his palace gave this statement the lie.

So interested was Ashur-bani-apal in relating the interposition of Ishtar that he had little space to spare for details of the war. Fortunately, we may have recourse to the sculptures and to the inscriptions which were drafted to be placed upon them. By September the Assyrian armies were ready to march out from their base in Der, accompanied by the pretender Humbanigash. Tep Humban fell back from Bit Imbi to Susa, collected his gold and silver, and took up his position at Til Tuba, not far from Tulliz. One flank rested on the Ulai River, the other on a hill, and between were date-orchards. In the rear was Mataktu, its battlemented towers behind the protection of a stream junction.

After another convenient vision had appeared to the seer and the troops had been properly encouraged, the army moved to the attack. Early in the action Simburu, the Elamite nagir, deserted to the Assyrians. Ituni, a eunuch general of Tep Humban, was seized by the hair and was decapitated before he could destroy his bow with his own sword. Urtaku, son-in-law of Tep Humban, was wounded by a javelin; as he lay on the ground, he implored his captor to cut off his head and present it to Ashur-bani-apal, who would perchance take it as a good omen. The pole of the chariot which conveyed Tep Humban broke and the horses ran away. His eldest son, Tammaritu, was acting as driver; he seized his father by the hand and begged him to pour out a libation and flee. A javelin wound in the right side brought Tep Humban to his knee, but he still urged his son to shoot with the bow. When he saw that the day was lost, he tore his beard and fled to the woods with his still faithful son. Here they were overtaken, the son brained with the mace, the father decapitated, and his head, javelin, and bow forwarded to Assyria.

The Assyrian general, likewise a eunuch, led forward Humbanigash to receive the acclamations of the multitude; to many it must have seemed an omen of ill that it was the left hand of the officer which led him. His new subjects went down on their knees and kissed the ground when Humbanigash raised his hand in blessing while from near by Mataktu came forth singers and musicians to celebrate his home-coming. Assyrian soldiers in the procession were a less welcome element, and there were those who could not forget that for three days the Ulai had been dammed by the slain. Tep Humban's severed head was received in Arbela, and the fallen monarch's bow was dedicated to the goddess whose was the glory.

With Elam in the friendly hands of the second Humbanigash, Ashur-bani-apal could attend to the petty princes who had aided Tep Humban. Humbankidinni, the nagir of Hidalu, brought in the head of his former master Ishtar-nandi and the Hidalu were made safe by the kingship of a younger brother of Humbanigash, another Tammaritu. Of the other rebels, Marduk-shum-ibni was dead and Nabu-shum-eresh had succumbed to dropsy.

Ashur-bani-apal was about to leave Arbela for Nineveh and the severed head of Tep Humban was intrusted to Dunnanu's neck for transport. As the musicians led the ghastly procession into Nineveh, the terrible sight crazed Humbandara and Nabu-damiq, the ambassadors who had received their commissions from the dead monarch. One tore his beard, the other thrust his girdle sword into his bosom. Aplia, son of Nabu-ushallim and grandson of the famous Merodach Baladan, was extradited from Elam; Mannu-ki-ahe, Dunnanu, and Nabu-ushallim, the Gambulu chieftains, had spoken blasphemy against the Assyrian gods, and for this crime they had their tongues pulled out by the roots and were flayed alive.

The horrible scene is represented on one of the bas-reliefs, although, strangely enough, the names have never been filled in the blanks left for the purpose. Dunnanu was placed on the rack and slaughtered like a lamb, his brother Samgunu and Aplia were slain and their flesh distributed among the surrounding lands. Nabu-naid and Bel-etir, sons of Nabu-shum-eresh, were forced to crush the bones of their father, and the head of Tep Humban found its final resting-place over the gate which led to Ashur. Like many a weakling, Ashurbani-apal combined artistic tastes with a cruelty which augured ill for the future of Assyria.

CHAPTER XXXIV

THE FAILURE OF THE DUAL MONARCHY

SEVENTEEN long years Shamash-shum-ukin had remained loyal to his brother. During this whole period, there had been a difference in the theory of the state which was fraught with danger. To the partisans of the southern monarch, there was only an Assyrian empire, one and indivisible, where by the accident of circumstances there ruled two kings who for convenience had divided the world between them. Shamash-shum-ukin always called Ashur-bani-apal "brother," and his followers regularly refer to the "kings our lords." Ashur-bani-apal does indeed give Shamash-shum-ukin this title of "brother," and even uses in his official documents that of "equal brother," which he likewise gives to Marduk as the peer of Ashur, but no servant of his ever recognises more than one "lord king."

Cold facts did not agree with the theory of equality. Shamash-shum-ukin did indeed possess Babylon, once the capital of the alluvium, but not even all of north Babylonia was under his control. He is invoked in business documents from Borsippa, Dilbat, Sippar, Dakkuru, and Nagitu only; in other words, in the territory immediately surrounding the city of Babylon. The governor of Uruk, for example, reported direct to Ashur-bani-apal and spoke of Shamash-shum-ukin as a private individual. When Ashur-bani-apal restored the temple tower in Nippur, the ancestor of all Ekurs, "mountain houses," his Shumerian recital omitted all reference to his brother. We even find a certain Nabu-bel-usur who is shaknu or governor of Babylon; he too must represent another check on Shamash-shum-ukin.

While Shamash-shum-ukin is never mentioned in the building records from outside his territory, Ashur-bani-apal was very careful that proper credit should be given himself in Babylon. There was indeed much of building in Babylon in this period. Esagila was adorned with gold, silver, and precious stones, with beams of cedar and cypress from Amanus and Lebanon, with gates of box, palm, fir, and cedar. Arad-aheshu, the official in charge, reports direct to Ashur-bani-apal and merely refers to the "king of Babylon." They have built the house of Esagila and its upper court where the Lord and the Lady dwell, together with its temples, the house of the shrine of Tashmetum, the lower court with its temple. A protecting wall of prayer has been constructed, the god Nabu will have his abode, the whole structure will be covered with bitumen. The king of Babylon has spoken thus: "Make a continuous wall for Esagila; make also the house of the Lady of Babylon. Let them tear down the courts of Esagila." It is implied by Arad-aheshu that he will not execute these orders until he has authorisation from his own master.[1] Ekarzagina, the house of Ea in Esagila, was rebuilt, Ebabbara of Sippar was restored through the labour of the brick-god and was raised mountain high, Ezida of Borsippa was renewed, and Imgur Bel and Nimitti Bel, the walls of Babylon, were made anew with their gates and towers.

The attitude of Ashur-bani-apal is best shown by the installation record worked into almost all the inscriptions which celebrated Assyrian building in Babylonia: "In the days of *my* reign, Marduk entered Babylon, the appointed temple offerings for Esagila and the gods of Babylon *I* established, the chartered privileges of Babylon *I* bound fast. 'So that the strong should not injure the weak' "—he is quoting the Code of Hammurabi and the quotation sounds strange in the mouth of an Assyrian—"*I* established my brother on an equality as king over Babylon. Esagila, which my father had not completed, *I* finished." Ashur-bani-apal would gladly have assimilated Shamash-shum-ukin to the position held by his younger brothers, who were to be purely ornamental means of keeping within the family the control of the most sacred city states.

[1] *H*. 119 f.; cf. 1066.

Granted that Ashur-bani-apal is telling the truth when he speaks of soldiers, horses, chariots, cities, fields, vineyards, peoples, with which he filled the hand of his brother to a degree greater than his father had given order, patriotic Babylonians could not forget the fact of dependence. Nor are we without further evidence that the Assyrian overlords treated the Babylonians as a conquered people. We have a complaint that Hulala, the housekeeper of Shamash, has carried off the sky or ceiling from Esagila and has killed the priests of Bel. The people are angered at the robbery of Babylon's most honoured shrine, and declare that they are no longer safe, they will be made like the city of Gana.[1]

So in May, 652, the revolt flamed forth. In token of formal break with the old era, sacrifices were no longer offered for Ashur-bani-apal before Marduk and his fellows. A bid was made for Uruk and the south by a bilingual inscription in which the Shumerian was constructed without much accuracy from fragments of earlier writings and by the assumption of the title "King of Amnanu," sanctified by Sin-gashid of Uruk a thousand years before. All Babylonia, from Aqaba near the north line of the alluvium to Bab Salimeti at the mouth of the Euphrates, planned revolt and all the elements disaffected against Assyria, the Amukkanu, Dakkuru, Puqudu, Gurasimmu, were included. To the Elamites the scribe adds other foreign peoples, the Guti, Amurru, and Meluhha; we are to see in these the tribes on the Median border, the men of Syria, and of Egypt, not long since free from the Assyrian yoke.

Ashur-bani-apal acted at once—in writing. Hostilities were begun on the 23d of May with a letter by the hand of Shamash-balatsu-iqbi to the citizens of Babylon: "As for the words my not-brother has spoken, I have heard all that he told you. They are naught but wind, do not believe him. By Ashur and Marduk, my gods, I swear that they are shameful words which he has spoken against me. In my heart I consider and with my mouth I declare: More than craft doth he practise when he says: 'I will make the reputations of the Babylonians

[1] H. 468.

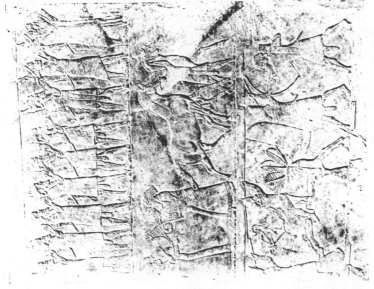

FIG. 150. MUSICIANS AND SOLDIERS OF ASHUR-BANI-APAL. (Louvre.)

FIG. 149. ASHUR-BANI-APAL IN HIS CHARIOT. (Louvre.)

who love Ashur-bani-apal as shameful as his own.' I, for my part, do not hearken to it. Your brotherhood with the sons of Ashur and your chartered privileges have I protected; hearken not a moment to his lies. Destroy not your good name, thus far unsullied before me and before all lands, make not yourselves sinners against God. There is another matter which, as well I know, you ponder in your minds: 'Since we became attached to him, our taxes are excessive.' No tax exists, for the offering was naught but a name; now, however, since you have taken your stand with my adversary, let it be regarded as an imposition of taxes upon you and a sin against the oath before God. Behold, I have written you at this time that in these matters you should not pollute yourself with him. Speedily let there be a reply to my letter; the apportionment which I have set apart for Bel shall not this wretch, forsaken of Marduk, take from my hand and destroy." [1]

The verbal attack produced no results and the alarm in Assyria increased. Zakutu, the aged grandmother to whose devotion the royal brothers had owed their throne, took refuge in prayer. "O God," so runs her supplication, "I beseech thee concerning that matter of the revolt which they have reported to Ashur-bani-apal: 'They are stirring up revolt against the city.' Is it decreed, is it established, will it come to pass, will they take the offensive, will they conquer, shall I die, shall they take possession? Heed not that a woman has written this and placed it before thee." [2]

Two months after the last attempt to win over the Babylonians, on the 27th of July, Ashur-bani-apal inquired of Shamash whether his troops could cross the Euphrates, enter Babylon, and secure Shamash-shum-ukin. The reply was unfavourable. Ishtar of Arbela, on the other hand, lived up to her past reputation. His bow is to be mighty, his weapon exalted over all foes. The people of Akkad shall in their hunger gnaw bones; the rebels who plot in assemblies and fear not her divinity shall be given into his hand. It is Ashur-bani-apal, reverencing her divinity, who shall complete the

[1] H. 301.   [2] H. 1367 f.; Waterman, *AJSL.*, XXIX, 6; 24 ff.

shrines of the gods and restore the sacrifices; as for Shamash-shum-ukin, who has not observed her treaties and has sinned against the grace of his brother, the king beloved of the goddess's heart, with mighty restraint has she restrained him and will bind him, in the noses of his chiefs will she insert cords. By her order shall Ashur-bani-apal plunder their cities and carry home to Assyria their vast wealth.[1]

South Babylonia was still under Assyrian control, but it was hard pressed by the troops of Shamash-shum-ukin. Taking the treasures from the temples, he sent them to Humbanigash, who had lost his enthusiasm for Assyria when Ashurbani-apal had demanded the return of the goddess Nana from Susa. A son of the late Tep Humban, Undasu by name, was commanded: "Go, take vengeance from Assyria for thy father, thy begetter." The Pillatu and the Hilmu accompanied him.

A letter from Humbanigash to his brother Amagunu was captured by the Assyrians. Aisaggi and Bel Harranishu, the two men sent to him, did not enter the city. When they capture Esiggi, they will set him before Humbanigash. Formerly, so the messenger asserts, he sent him a message, but none has arrived. Humbanigash made an end of the discussion by saying: "The command of thy messenger I perceive, behold I have sent thee command by the hand of thy messenger." They replied: "I will not hearken to him, he will not yield, hither they shall not come." When he comes, let him take the message. The two kings are restored together. As many as dwell in the house of his father, now Umbartashu, qepu of Hamu, has opened it, he dwells in that city. To him the king will hearken.[2]

Accompanied by Nabu-bel-shumate, Humbanigash descended upon Uruk and with lack of respect trod down the Assyrian land. One of the officials stationed at Uruk relates how Humbanigash entered the Hidalu city and one of his sons came with him into the land of Parsua; with them went Nabu-qata-sabat, ambassador of Shamash-shum-ukin, and a mes-

[1] Klauber, *Texte*, 102; Langdon, *Tammuz*, 146.   [2] *H*. 214.

senger from Rashu. Ten thousand of the writer's clan they killed, and now he is in Shama.[1]

Ningal-shum-iddina was no longer governor of Ur; his place had been taken by his son Sin-tabni-usur. Ashur-bani-apal was not without suspicions as to his fidelity, for he inquired whether, if he should be placed in Ur, he would remain faithful, or whether he would go over mouth and heart to Shamash-shum-ukin. The liver omens confirmed his choice.[2]

Soon after he appeared in Ur, Sin-tabni-usur wrote Aplia, governor of Arrapha, and Nabu-ushabshi, governor of Uruk, that a messenger of Shamash-shum-ukin had arrived and was stirring up rebellion against him. The Gurasimmu had revolted from his hands and if he were not quickly reinforced he would succumb. Nabu-ushabshi collected a body of five or six hundred bowmen from among the citizens of Uruk and with Aplia and Nurea, governor of Zame or Mazamua, went to his aid. Nabu-ushabshi's son, Nabu-zer-iddina, was sent against the Gurasimmu and delivered Sin-tabni-usur from their hands; five or six of their chief warriors were seized and delivered to Aplia. Bel-ibni was also aiding but there was danger from the Puqudu; however, Kudur and the people of Uruk were now safe and Nabu-ushczib the bowman was in charge.[3]

Plunder of the Sealands is reported by Sin-tabni-usur. The Ekushai are ancient subjects of his father's house, under the protection of the kings, the fathers of his lord; they feared his father Ningal-shum-iddina. Now some of them have sent to their kinsmen, let the king send to the governor that their tribesmen may be established under the king's protection. As to Bel-uballit, he is the son of his nurse, together they nursed one breast.[4]

Then Nabu-ushabshi and the elders of Uruk complain that Sin-tabni-usur is attacking the people of Uruk and is carrying off the plunder; the king ought not to forsake the blood of his servants. When he slays any one, Sin-tabni-usur does not allow the report of it to reach the king, and behold, he does

[1] H. 1309.   [2] Klauber, Texte, 135.   [3] H. 754.   [4] H. 920.

slay the men of Uruk. Let the king act, faithfully establishing the feet of his servants.[1]

When the Puqudu came into the suburbs of Uruk, they carried off ten men. Nabu-ushabshi went out against them and made a slaughter among them. He questioned their commander "Who sent you?" and received the reply "Sahdu, brother of Nabu-ushezib, sent us and said: 'Go, capture a man from the vicinity of Uruk and let me inquire from him why they have assembled so large a number of Assyrian troops at Uruk and whither is their journey.'" He has had disturbing messages from the Gurasimmu and the Puqudu bowmen have gone against Bit Ihtir. Through a confederate of Sin-tabni-usur, two or three thousand made the attack, but he has raided their land and restored some of the booty. He has seen Sin-tabni-usur, he writes in another letter; he has sent to his brother Sin-bel-aheshu, saying: "Why do you hurl men against me? Cut a covenant." He will force the brothers of Sin-shar-usur to enter the royal presence.[2]

This Sin-shar-usur was governor of Hindanu and brother to Sin-tabni-usur; in spite of his relationship, he did not hesitate to accuse his brother to his king. Already a third brother, Sin-balatsu-iqbi, had been reported to Ashur-bani-apal and Shamash-shum-ukin had warmly taken his part. Sin-tabni-usur quite naturally protested that these reports were false and Ashur-bani-apal sought a second time the advice of the sun-god, in July, 651.[3]

Shamash again made favourable answer and the king replied to his governor's complaints: "How could Sin-shar-usur speak evil words against thee and I listen to them? Since Shamash deranged his mind, and Humbanigash has slandered thee before me, they have marked thee for destruction, but Ashur my god keeps me far from it. I would not willingly kill my servant and the foundation of my father's house. Is it not in their mind that thou shouldst perish with the house of thy lord? Would I wish to see that? He and Humbani-

[1] H. 753.   [2] H. 1028; 974.
[3] H. 426; 445; 1207; 1248; Klauber, *Texte*, 129.

gash have plotted thy death but because I know thy loyalty I have conferred upon thee more favour than before. These two years thou hast withstood the enemy and famine for the sake of thy lord's house; what could they say against the servant who loves his master's house and I believe it? As to the services which thou and thy brothers, the Assyrians, have rendered, about which thou hast written, that which thou hast done is well, the guard hast thou kept. This thy path before me is good, and favours with which I shall requite thee shall be unto children's children." [1]

Barely had Ashur-bani-apal told one of his correspondents flatly that Sin-shar-usur was not a lover of Assyria, "my affairs are brought to overthrow," when Sin-shar-usur was proved the true friend of the king and Sin-tabni-usur went over to Shamash-shum-ukin. The citizens of Ur were more loyal, but they were hard-pressed and in sad need of aid. "Daily have we prayed for the king and kept his watch; for my hunger wilt thou make me eat the flesh of our sons and daughters?" They have still a kindly feeling for their former governor and are inclined to find excuses for him. "Sin-tabni-usur was in the service of the king with us, but distress and hunger have caused him to revolt and to take the feet of Shamash-shum-ukin. Before the king our lord he did not come. As regards Sin-tabni-usur, the servant of the judge of whom the king has spoken, the king will surely know." [2]

No effective answer could be made to this appeal and soon we have a series of letters, from those who still remained loyal to the king in south Babylonia, which presents the results of this inactivity. The men of Shattena tell how these many years they have kept the watch of the king. The cities of the Gurasimmu, the Puqudu, and the Sealands are plundered, there is not an inhabited city left there except Ur, Nippur, Eridu, and Shattena. [3]

Protests of loyalty still come from the Gurasimmu: "A sin against the king our lord have we not committed; let him inquire when there was any one who devastated the Sealands

[1] H. 290.   [2] *H*. 1002; 1274; cf. 1236.   [3] *H*. 942.

and the Puqudu and gave tribute to thy father more than the Gurasimmu. Quickly we shall behold Sin-shar-usur." [1]

The lie to this claim is given in the next report of the nobles of Shattena: "We who are in the midst of Akkad have the Puqudu opposed to us. Unto the king our lord have we written, troops for our assistance let him send. The Gurasimmu were loyal, but the enemy came against them; because they had seen this and because news from Assyria is lacking and because none of the governors has come to their assistance, they have gone over to the enemy. Eridu and Ur, which were left to Assyria, have chosen to go over to the enemy. Now all the Gurasimmu are hostile; there is not a city among them which has remained loyal to Assyria except Ur and Kissik and Shattena, and the king my lord knows that Ur is in the midst of Akkad. Because of its pre-eminence with its temples we are ruined. The Puqudu and the Sealands hate us and they plan evil against thy temples. With slaughter and raids they are making an end of us, everything is destroyed, we shall fall into their hands. Now the Puqudu, the Sealands, and the Gurasimmu are mustering, they have risen against us. Let the king our lord send troops for the protection of his temples. The treasures which the kings thy fathers gave to Sin will the enemy capture and the land will slip away from the hand of the king and the land of Assyria before them. The officials of the king lift up their eyes towards the fortresses." [2]

"As we entered into the oaths of thy father, so we have entered into the oath of our lord. Since the king has ordered us to send whatever we see or hear, the troops who are in Uruk have sinned a sin against the king. When the men of Uruk saw it, they told us, and we according to their report send to the king. Behold, we are sending the rebels and witnesses to the king, and when they are before the king, let him ask them. The complaints of the king I have heard, let a messenger of the king come, let him ask me. Zer-ukin, son of Labashi, speaks thus: 'That which I have heard when the

[1] H. 947.   [2] H. 1241.

king made me hear, the lands sinned.' Behold, the son of Ishi-etir has come, before he escapes; lest he flee, let the king raise his head and ask him." [1]

About this time we have a letter to the queen mother from Naid Marduk, king of the Sealands, giving the news of Elam. The enemy has seized the bridge—at least, that is what a messenger states, though he has not yet sent out his own scouts. Let the bridge be restored and the bolts strengthened. Sin-tabni-usur has taken the side of Humbanigash. At the end of July, his messenger reached Naid Marduk on the border; he will forward him to the palace. Let his lord know that his heart is perfect with the house of his lord.[2]

This letter was the last from the aged ruler, for soon after we read another from old and young of the country. Once and twice the messengers of Tep Humban, brother of the king of Elam, the nagir official, and Zineni, have come to them and say: "Come, receive Nabu-ushallim, the son of your lord, to you may he come." They refused to receive this brother of Naid Marduk and son of Merodach Baladan, but declared: "Naid Marduk, our lord, is alive, and servants of the king of Assyria are we. Would you make him noble in the land, send him to the king of Assyria; if it please him, let the king make him great, do you send him into the house. We shall not sin; over us shall he not be prince." They were sending him with bound hands to the Assyrian king when the Targibatu, the men of the stream, the Dutai and the Banu, seized a field belonging to them and gave it to him. Now his messengers have come before the elders of the Sealands, saying: "Come up to my face, send down troops to the Sealands; if you do not come up to my face and do not speak, I will come to your land and will destroy your homes. Of a truth shall ye say: 'The face of the king of Assyria we fear.' " [3]

Messengers have come from the king of Elam, requesting that they make Nabu-ushallim their king. He adds: "I have news of Naid Marduk, he is dead; you are my men and not the men of the king of Assyria; over you he shall not reign."

[1] *H*. 472.   [2] *H*. 917.   [3] *H*. 576.

When Nabu-ushallim conquered the Targibatu people, one of their men was on guard among the men on the Inazaru River. Nabu-ushallim discovered him and despatched him to the king of Elam, who talked with him and returned him to the Sealands; since they were loyal servants of the Assyrian king, they forwarded the messenger to him. Their conclusion is a complaint: "Why must we send once and twice to the king our lord?" The sequel to this neglect is found in a third letter giving news of Iakin; Nabu-ushallim has crossed to that region and the cities are being taken by him. Sillai also reports that he is on his way with an Elamite army.[1]

Meanwhile, Ashur-bani-apal had been attempting to hold Nabu-ushallim and that gentleman had been playing a double game. The king has complained about the Aramæans on the Harri River near Uruk and Nabu-ushallim attempts to throw the blame on some one else. "O ye gods of the king, in spite of the many men of good-will whom the son of Iakin oppresses, we shall hear peace at his mouth. Let the king send to them, let him not send the servants of the king, they are not trustworthy." The messengers of the sons of Zeruai have come for reports of the king and spoke to the land; let a king's messenger come to offset their intrigue with the Mamai. He has collected much straw.[2]

After all, Nabu-ushallim did not secure the Sealands; when next we catch a glimpse of them, they are ruled by Nabu-bel-shumate, the nephew of Naid Marduk, and so grandson of Merodach Baladan. He is continuously sending his messenger to ask the welfare of the king. The kindness of a father to a son, is it not true that thus the king has done for him and for his people? He loads his letters with the most fulsome wishes for cheer of heart, health of body, and length of days from the gods. He has heard that the king of Elam is oppressive, that many of the cities have abandoned his cause, saying: "We will not come into thy hands." The robbers and fugitives, who came to the Gurasimmu, five hundred in number, were captured by Sin-balatsu-iqbi, still another

[1] H. 1114; 1131.   [2] H. 747 ff.; 527; 1011.

brother of Sin-tabni-usur, and were handed over to Natan, whom the Assyrians had made king of the Utta tribe. Hitherto the king has not believed what he wrote, now Lala, king of the Bazu tribe, is before the king, let him be asked, let the crown prince bring his servants.[1]

Nabu-bel-shumate did not long keep up the pretence. Messengers were sent by him to Shamash-shum-ukin, he went down to the Gurasimmu, persuaded them to change their king, and led them to revolt.[2] Near the end of March, 651, Ashur-bani-apal sent to his faithful "reporters," Ashur-danin-sharri and Danai, who had taken up their official abode in the "New Palace." "Nabu-bel-shumate, who has not guarded the welfare of Ashur-bani-apal, king of Assyria, the creature of thy hands, his lord, who has spoken contemptuously of thy great name and has despised it in his haughtiness, now has Ashur-bani-apal, king of Assyria, heard as follows: 'He has collected his archers in Elam.' Will he advance, will he fight with the troops, the warriors of Ashur-bani-apal, king of Assyria, either with the Assyrians or the Akkadians or the Chaldæans or the Ahlame who have taken the feet of Ashur-bani-apal, the creation of thy hands? Will he make battle and defeat them? Grant that he may not set forth or make a stop in Elam or in his own land, either to fright them or to assist them, and into the territory may they not enter."

The sheep's liver was inspected with the discouraging result: "If there is a station, the path double, and the left path lies on the right path, the enemy will cause his weapons to rage over the weapons of the prince; if a finger lies on the right side of the station, there will be a downfall of the army, or of the temple; if the left side of the gall-bladder has grown fast, thy foot shall tread down the enemy; if the finger is normal, if the back part of the liver is damaged to the right, there shall be damage to the head and a change of allegiance in the army; if the lower part goes, if something is on the crown and the middle finger of the liver is loose in its foundation, when something is bright, the inside of the sheep normal; here are five

---

[1] *H.* 832 ff.   [2] *H.* 1326; 1236.

unfavourable signs, not a single good one has been preserved; as a whole, the report is unfavourable."

An inquiry as to the king's health continued the series on the 26th of the next month. The reply was overwhelming: "If the station is preserved, the path doubled, the arms lie, there shall be a change of orders, derangement of mind, the journey you plan will be a failure, another time you shall set forth, the command of the king will be without effect in the assembly, a second time they will abstain; if it is concerning the exercise of the healing craft, the physician shall not so much as lay his hand on the sick, the seer shall not undertake an incantation." When such disheartening omens were received, we can understand why the situation was not handled with greater firmness.[1]

[1] Klauber, *Texte*, 105 f.

CHAPTER XXXV

BEL–IBNI, THE VICEROY

BEL-IBNI, the Chaldæan, was a descendant of that Merodach Baladan who had gathered in his own person all those earlier claims to the rule of Babylon inherent in the Iakin tribe. His own name he probably received from the Bel-ibni who had been Sennacherib's puppet king. His father was Nabu-kudurri-usur, and it is all but certain that the greater Nebuchadnezzar, to use his Biblical name, was his grandson. The family seems to have been settled in Borsippa, for it is from thence that Nabu-kudurri-usur indites a letter to the effect that on the morrow Tashmetum, the warrior of the gods, will go out in procession and will take up her residence in the New Year's House, where sacrifices will be offered to her. After she has loosened her girdle, at evening she will return to her own dwelling again and will give blessing to the king.[1]

A similar peaceful appearance brings Bel-ibni for the first time on the scene. In the fifteenth year of Shamash-shum-ukin, Bel-ibni's son Shamash-iddina acts as witness to a loan made at Nagitu near Babylon by Nabu-bel-shumate, with whom Bel-ibni was to wage unending feud. Nabu-kudurri-usur likewise has a good word for Nabu-bel-shumate.

When next Bel-ibni appears, he is sadly in disgrace. He sends duplicate letters to the king to beg pardon and to the commander-in-chief to intercede for him; the hands of the commander-in-chief he has seized, let him not be put to shame. "Since at the first, I did not appear before the face of the king, it was because those who arrived from Elam to secure pardon for themselves slandered me in the palace; every one of my enemies from Elam prepared evil words against me and wrote to the court. When I heard of this, I was afraid and did not come. Now I desire the royal service. As many as formerly

---

[1] *H*. 858 f.

sinned, the king thy father forgave their sins; however much they have slandered me in the palace, I have in no manner committed sin. From the hands of the king may they not take me; by the mouth of the king my lord may it be said that I should not fear before the face of the king my lord and may the king count me among his servants. May the signs of the service of the king my lord be extended to me, may I not be made ashamed before the Babylonians, my brothers, may not my head be laid low. The sign of signs from the king my lord may I see. In this shall we trust; I and my brothers, my sons, and my dependants will come; the feet of the king our lord we will kiss, the service of the king our lord we will assume. May I hear a reliable word from the king?" [1]

One of his chief enemies was Kudur. Iqisha, the physician whom the king sent to heal him, has restored him to life. He was about to go and see the face of the king that he might add to his life and live, but the chief baker met him on the journey, and forced him to return to Uruk to receive a sealed order from the palace. He forwards the complaint of the gate official to the effect that Bel-ibni's family are not lovers of the king's house, it is not good that they should pass over to Uruk. Another official is even more emphatic: "Bel-ibni is a liar and the king my lord knows it; from the time the king gave the Sealands to Nabu-kudurri-usur, his son Bel-ibni has not presented himself. For this he hates us, maligning words he speaks, let not the king trust the words of his mouth."[2]

Despite such strong opposition, the king did listen to the words of his mouth. Bel-ibni and his family were too powerful to be punished on mere suspicion. His father's government was confirmed to him, and near the end of April, 650, the Assyrian monarch issued his proclamation to the people of the Sealands, old and young, announcing that Bel-ibni, the King's Companion, had been appointed to the rule of their country. Let them do at once what is in the sealed order to the Sealanders. He is by no means sure of Bel-ibni's reception, for he adds: "Behold, now, the pupil of my eye is upon you.

[1] *H*. 283; 793.   [2] *H*. 274; 277; 1106.

I have separated you from the sin of Nabu-bel-shumate and the courtesan of Menanu. You shall see the fate of servants who steal the possessions of their masters, for is it not right that I should take them away and send my army, that they may make a reckoning? Your land and your devotedness is before me." [1]

The first task of Bel-ibni was the securing of Nabu-bel-shumate. Originally, so he reports, he came with his father and son from Urtaku and killed his brother Bel-li; when Humbanigash attacked Uruk, Nabu-bel-shumate followed after him, he trod down the Assyrian land with lack of respect, and carried off to Elam all the possessions of Bel-ibni's family. After his father, a sinner against the oath of loyalty to the Assyrian king, had died in Elam, Nabu-bel-shumate forsook the place of sin where he had sinned, but otherwise he took no action. Ashur-bani-apal sent a sealed letter to Bel-ibni and Aplia to order that the people of the land should collect; the letter was stolen and the thief gave it to Nabu-bel-shumate, who has not even taken the trouble to declare that he is a lover of the Assyrian land. Since he is an enemy of Assyria, Bel-ibni has not sent to him; let him rather make declaration before Ashur: "I am an enemy of Assyria." They have not summoned the men from Kudur, they are assembling them to Bel-ibni and make them take the oath. [2]

As a result, Ashur-bani-apal followed up his proclamation to the Sealanders with another to Bel-ibni and the citizens of Nippur and for good measure forwarded a duplicate to Nabu-ushabshi and the men of Uruk. He reminds them how with the iron dagger of Ashur his lord he has destroyed the land with fire, and how when they had gone forth and trampled down the land, it turned its face towards the king. They are to keep watch for Nabu-bel-shumate and to seize all his followers; like a winnower at the gate they are to sift them. He may change his scheme of escape, so every one should be questioned. Whoever allows him to escape shall be deprived of descendants; if he is taken, dead or alive, his captor will be

[1] H. 289. [2] H. 998.

laid on a balance and his weight given in gold, even as Sennacherib gave Adad-baraka his weight in silver for the capture of Shuzub.[1] Why do they hesitate? He has written them, they are commissioned, let them see that they bind him ere he escape.[2]

No one was to receive this royal reward; Nabu-bel-shumate made good his escape and tooκ with him many an Assyrian noble as prisoner, among them Bel-shunu, brother of Belibni. The king inquired his fate of Enlil-bani in Nippur, but the messenger could not reach Bel-shunu or speak to him. Rumour, however, states that Nabu-bel-shumate put him in prison. Shum-iddina, whom the king had commissioned governor of Marad, is now with Enlil-bani. There are many tongues in Nippur under the protection of the king; Enlil-bani fulfils the orders of the king and confers with them. Ashur-bel-taqqin, the governor of Nippur, has been intrusted with the forwarding of the sealed orders and the messenger of the king, but when they arrive he sits idle three and four days and pays no attention to them. When Enlil-bani taxed him with this, "The men of Nippur and of the entire land ridicule us," he only turned his hand against the writer.[3]

Men of Tabal are in the fort. Ashur-bel-taqqin gave the writer what news he had heard. The Gurasimmu who were with him set their face to the harvest, and when he fled, he entered Babylon. The other Ashur-bel-taqqin was at the ford of the river to meet him when he heard of his coming; the first Ashur-bel-taqqin heard of this, after he had sent his tribute, he did not approach him until Ashur-bel-taqqin died, he did not enter the Gurasimmu, then he destroyed the house of the sender. According to Urta-ahi-iddina, Enlil-bani and the bowmen of Nippur stand in the watch where the king appointed him, and he himself keeps the watch in his rear in the city of Bit Sheri.[4]

For the present, the escape of Nabu-bel-shumate seemed more than compensated by the freeing of south Babylonia.

---

[1] Cf. p. 292.　　　　　　　　　[2] H. 292; 297.
[3] H. 238.　　　　　　　　　　　[4] H. 967; 797.

Bel-ibni received a rescript: "Go as turtanu over the troops, to the Sealands go down."[1] Soon there came a hymn of rejoicing from the fortunate governor: "The many good things which from the beginning the king my lord has done me and has caused to be given me, who am a dead dog, the son of a nobody, the king has made to live. All their fulness I cannot find out. And behold these great kindnesses, which the king my lord has given me and done, the setting up of the house of Merodach Baladan, the king my lord has given. What requital could I make to the king my lord, even if I were to die, than to pray the great gods of heaven and earth for life and length of days for the king my lord, and the blood of my lambs for the guard of the king my lord will I give. Now will the king my lord see the loyalty of his servant to the house of his master. What am I when I keep the watch of the king my lord? A slave subduing sin, a lance head in the hand of the king my lord am I. The king my lord has placed me in heaven."

This ebullition over, he returns to business and states that on the 16th of the month he came with the official who is over the palace to the city of Kissik, where there assembled to him many of the Sealanders who professed to be the king's servants. On the next day he made them take the oath and on the third he went to the Sealands themselves, which are now entirely won back to the service of the king.[2]

The citizens of Kissik felt quite differently. They had been assured by the king that when they were set free before his gods, the skilled workmen who were with them were also freed. When he learned that the enemy were encamped against them, he gave additional command: "Whoever deserts to you, receive and send on to me." When, therefore, the Nuhanua deserted to them, they were received and they made report: "The Puqudu are divided." They were forwarded to the king. Since the time when Sin and Nergal, the king's gods, completely delivered his enemy into his hands, his hands shall take them all, as many as there are, and the bow of the king

[1] *H*. 795.   [2] *H*. 521.

they have not let go. All the Chaldæans tremble. The men
of Kissik are the king's dogs, no one can turn them away
through the word of an enemy. The enemy went down to the
Sealands and the post of Bel-ibni, who is at the head of the
boundary of the Sealands, but Bel-ibni restrains the men of
Kissik from advancing against the invaders.[1]

Again they invoke Sin and Nergal as they relate the sad
fate of their brethren at the hands of Bel-ibni. When they
escaped from their prison-house in Elam, whither Nabu-bel-
shumate had carried them, they returned to the Sealand and
felt at ease, for they thought: "This is the king's domain."
But Bel-ibni seized them and drove them out, though the king
of Elam had not descended; let Darri-sharru, who brought
them forth from the prison-house, be witness. The king should
realise that all men hate the citizens of Kissik, they reproach
them: "You hear a stupid report and send it on to the king."
They have sent their brethren of Kissik to the king to ask for
justice.[2]

Nabu-ushabshi puts a different aspect on the matter. Ten
years before, Bel-etir and his son Pir Amurru went to Elam.
Shortly after, they returned and whatever was evil for Assyria they practised in Uruk. They were forced to retire to
Elam, where Bel-etir died, but Pir Amurru reappeared in Uruk
in November with letters for himself and Aplia. He may be
expected to say that he has come direct from Elam; let not
the king believe him, he has not been back since November
when Nabu-ushabshi forwarded to his master the letters he
brought. If the king desires confirmation in this matter, let
him ask Idua, the servant of Kudur; since he has been in Uruk
and this matter happened at his side and before his face, he
shall inform the king how full of lies are these letters. If the
king does not yet understand the letters sent by the guardsman Darri-sharru in November, let him ask him.[3]

A revolt in Elam supplanted Humbanigash by Tammaritu;
the Assyrian relief professed to show the head of Humbanigash, cut off by Tammaritu in the midst of the battle, but it

[1] H. 210.   [2] H. 736.   [3] H. 266.

was not in the Assyrian interest, for he said: "Shall they cut off the head of a king of Elam in the midst of his troops? Why should Humbanigash kiss the ground before the ambassadors of the king of Assyria?"

A letter has arrived from Kudur; it states that Tammaritu is about to lead his troops against Assyria. Is the report true and worthy of dependence? From the 1st of March to the 1st of the next month shall the troops of Tammaritu make war against the border of Assyria, shall they come to Nippur? When the Puqudu hear this report, will they revolt?[1]

How low Assyrian influence fell is shown by two letters, partial duplicates, which Ashur-bani-apal wrote to the south Babylonian tribe of the Rashi. In an almost imploring tone he asks: "How have I fared in my love for Elam? I have loved my true friend, even my enemy have I not defamed. I have shown kindness to every one, yet they have done evil to me. In the days of Urtaku, there was a famine in Elam," and he granted them aid. "Then there were the fugitives, both kings and nobles, whom I received; I gave them food and drink, I brought them back to their land. They, however, have put in chains my messengers whom I sent to greet them, they have made alliance with my revolted servants." "My advocate has spoken judgment, through the mouth of the gods, his ears have caught a true word from the god: 'Let him come and with Tammaritu seize the river.' Is it not true that as I pray to Ashur and Marduk, so it will be done, that my wrath may be satisfied?"[2]

Marduk-shar-usur was in command of the troops operating in central Babylonia. Through fear, he collected a force sufficient to bring to an end the sway of Tammaritu, but he left behind a series of complaints of oppression. Hidalu and Iahdik were occupied by the Elamite but Bel-etir and the qadu officials fell into the hands of the Assyrian general. The Parsua were in Elamite employ and the rebels begged that they be sent quickly thither.[3]

Nabu-ushabshi, governor of Uruk, regularly begins his letters

[1] H. 1195.　　　[2] H. 295; 1260.　　　[3] H. 960 ff.

with the pious hope that the deified Uruk and its temple Eanna may be gracious to his lord. Daily to Ishtar of Uruk and to Nana he will pray. He sends letters in duplicate about the sheep of the temple and of the Puqudu city; he has learned from the shepherds that they are detained in the city of the Rua. In memory of the horse once beloved by the passionate goddess, three white horses with silver trappings and copper fittings have been brought into her sanctuary; on the trappings was written: "From Tammaritu; sent by the king of Elam to Ishtar of Uruk." Nabu-ushabshi feared before the face of his lord; he retained the horses but forwarded to Assyria the shepherds and the fittings.[1]

A deep impression was made on the king's mind by the wonder of these white horses, for we find him complaining that they had not yet arrived. The letter continued with matters of more moment than white horses. He has learned that his orders have not been carried out and Nabu-ushabshi has sent no explanation, he has merely asked: "What is my sin?" Ashur-bani-apal is very careful to point out that there has been no sin on the part of Nabu-ushabshi, it is the sin of his clan; the governors and prefects did not go or take their stand with him, and so the work was left undone. Nabu-ushabshi had hinted that the king had no love for Uruk and reported that the Gurasimmu had revolted from the hands of the king. When he saw the guard was without strength and was as one dead, the king ordered its removal. The king has no fear for Nabu-ushabshi, since the governors of Arrapha and of Lahiru are with him. Whatever is good to do, that let him do, whether it is to dam the Harri River or to trample down the men. In answer to a second letter, the two captains Bel-etir and Arbaia are sent with two hundred men; let them take their position by his side and with him carry on the work.[2]

The men fear, the waters are high, the people drink from the waters. Nabu-ushabshi will see Sabda. Let the king inquire of Bel-ibni, the Sealander, for news of the lower city of the Puqudu; he has gone out, he was stationed with Nabu-

[1] H. 268; 751.   [2] H. 1108; 543; 273; 1244.

ushabshi for several months.   As to the brother of Shum-ukin and Aheshai, about whom the king sent, the guard has brought them according to the royal order.   In large measure, those who are over their men as well as Aheshai do not love the Assyrian land.   They resisted Esarhaddon, the king's father.[1]

Arad Nana, the guardsman, by whose hands the king had sent a sealed order about Der, was on the road to Nippur, but when his servants heard that he was ill, they forsook him and went to Uruk.   Nabu-ushabshi cast down and seized the servants and the men of Nippur who forsook him and despatched them to the king.[2]

"I am a dead dog and am anxious to behold the face of the king, for when I see the face of the king I shall live again, and I who am in want shall prosper.   When I stood before the king, since I was fearful, my words did not come at once and I did not speak with the king.   As for Kudur, son of Nabu-nasir, I and he and all our brethren have kept the watch of the king; our houses on account of the service of the king of lands our lord are in ruins." [3]

Perhaps it is Kudur who writes the delegate that the Puqudu who dwell on the Kadannu River send their messengers daily to the son of Iakin.   Let the delegate send to the governor and let Tugibi-ilu of the Amukkanu, who dwell in the house of the shepherd, go down to them.   If he gives them into the hand of the delegate, then is he the delegate's servant; if he does not so deliver them, then let the delegate know that his heart is not with the delegate.   When the delegate sent Salamu to Nabu-ushabshi, Nabu-ushabshi was taken and sent to the delegate.   He is his true servant.[4]

The queen mother is assured by Aplia that he prays day and night to Nabu and Nana for life and length of days.   May the queen mother see it.   A messenger reporting grace from Bel and Nabu has come to the king of lands.   The grain of the harvest and the beasts of burden are prepared.   Fugitives have escaped to Elam and refuse to return.   The king will surely ask why he has not previously reported the loss; he

[1] H. 752.   [2] H. 866.   [3] H. 880.   [4] H. 1052.

feared the wrath of the king's heart, for he said: "Behold, he will slay me." [1]

The sons of Bel-iddina, the sons of the deceiver, the sons of the murderer, have been seized on the road to Babylon and are being sent to the king. To him they pretended to be fugitives, but Aplia very solemnly assures his master: "Very great are their misdeeds before the king." Shula, the governor of Dilbat appointed by Shamash-shum-ukin, is the son of their sister, and the men of Dilbat are in rebellion. When Shamash-shum-ukin went out against the city of Kar Nergal, one of the king's forts, Aplia was in the royal camp. When Zamama-eriba went out with Shamash-shum-ukin, he killed Rimanni-ilu, the musharkis official, and took his robes. When he broke out of Babylon and fled to the king's camp, he declared: "The turban which is on my head is that of Rimanni-ilu, the musharkis." The turban on his head came to the king; it is that of Rimanni-ilu. These men are not friends of Assyria, they are enemies. When they do such things, whether good or evil, Aplia sends them on to the king and he will face death to establish their truth. Let the king send orders to his servants to cut off the road between Babylon and Borsippa. [2]

About this time, Pir Amurru, or, rather, Pirawurr, as he writes himself, sent a long letter to his brother Bel-etir. Its extraordinary interest lies in the fact that it is not written in cuneiform and on a tablet but in Aramaic on a fragment of a potsherd. Sometimes our old friends appear strangely in Aramaic dress. His brother is in the land of Akkad while he is with Arbaia, he went out from Uruk with Ger Saphon and Ugammir. Four friends are in Beth Awukkan (Bit Amukkanu), a messenger of the king of Babel has come with a letter from him in his hand. Pirawurr has been detained in Hafiru in the desert. He went to the Madai, the Medes, and again he was detained. Then he came before the king as one among the dogs, but the king gave him oil and bade him grind for him that he might have olive-oil. Then he wrote and established the fact that the enemy was in Beth Awukkan. The

[1] *H*. 324 f.; 764.   [2] *H*. 326.

king asked his father about various well-known officials and his father replied that Upaq-ana-Arbail, astrologer at Uruk, would come to Ashur. He asked if they tore the women. Pira-wurr declares they are his servants, yet have they made destruction, although they were · from Beth Awukkan. His brother sent Naid Marduk, who aided them. Zaban-iddina and Nabu-ushallim of Beth Eden (Bit Adini) did something, and this recalls to his mind that Tiglath Pileser carried off prisoners from Beth Awukkan, Ululai from Beth Eden, Sargon from Dur Sin, and Sanherib from Kish. In each case, we have the name of the king, Tiglath Pileser III, Sargon, Sennacherib, exactly as it is found in the Hebrew Bible.[1]

Bel-ibni reports that the king's sceptre is now established upon the Bitter Waters, the Persian Gulf, yet not so firmly but that he suggests the coming of a score of Sidonians to build ships to sail upon it. Furthermore, he has important news from Elam. The nagir official has begun a revolt and has killed the king's brother, but the Elamite ruler is about to attack him. Nabu-bel-shumate, smitten of Bel and cursed by the gods, has carried off all his goods to Elam and through breakdown of heart has entered the city of Pakkimiri. This is a contemporary account of the beginning of the revolt against Tammaritu. Early in 649, there was a battle in which the king was not present, and Intapigash supplanted him.[2]

The deposed monarch fled by the way of the sea and the sculptures show the ship on which he escaped, his brothers and his seventeen relatives, the eighty-five princes who filled it, how it was caught in the mud and Tammaritu was borne on the back of a retainer over the rough ground and through the reeds until he came to Marduk-shar-usur. At this point, the fugitives fell into the hands of Bel-ibni, who at once hurried the news to Ashur-bani-apal. A kindly letter informed the fallen monarch that Bel-ibni had written about him and very humbly Tammaritu replies to "the king my lord," from whom he had heard good words; by the heart of the god and the protecting genius of the king he lives. Ashur-bani-apal was care-

---

[1] Lidzbarski, ZA., XXXI, 193 ff.　　　　[2] H. 795; 521.

ful to address him still as king. On the 16th of September,
he draws attention to the Rashu tribe who are in Tammaritu's
rear, and speaks of the treading down of the land by the new
king who is now directing the warfare against Assyria. But
Tammaritu need not fear, for many good deeds will be done
him. Complaint is made against Nabu-bel-shumate. Ashur-
bani-apal has settled thirty or forty sons of the former king
and one thousand six hundred and fifty other souls, they enter
before him. Soon there will be a feast for his people. It is
Tammaritu's watch they keep. Ashur-bani-apal will do for
Tammaritu things no father would do for a son.[1]

Shuma, sister's son of the deposed monarch, has fled from
Elam to the Dahha tribe, and has been taken under Bel-ibni's
protection. He is sick at present, later he will be forwarded
to the king. A messenger has informed him that Natan and
the Puqudu folk who live in Tilqa went to Nabu-bel-shumate
to the city of Targibatu and each of them has called upon the
name of the god as follows: "According to the agreement we
will send you all the news we hear." They have sold him three
thousand cattle for silver and they spoke to him thus: "May
our sheep come and pasture in the field of the Ubanat tribe?
You may trust us in it." Bel-ibni prays that a messenger
may come from the king to open wide the eyes of Natan, and
to give him this order: "If you send into Elam anything for
sale, if a single sheep crosses the border into the pastureland
of Elam, I will no longer permit you to live." [2]

He is taken severely to task by his royal master: "You
have opposed Kisir Ashur and you have written about the
Puqudu on the Harru River; a man who loved his master's
house would have immediately written his lord what he saw
and heard." [3] Following this came a letter sharper in tone.
"As to that boundary of the Gurasimmu of which you have
asked me, I did not give you authority to do according to your
own wish; what I told you, that do and give. What is now thy
command? Why have you not done according to my order?
You, who are my Companion, and know my fear! One who

----

[1] H. 284; 1040; 1022.   [2] H. 282.   [3] H. 402.

knew it not, how would he do? Behold, if you wish a word of grace, collect thy bowmen as thou wilt. How shall I desire the return of my good-will towards thee? What Sin-dini-epush does have I seen; whatever is good for him, that do, and in the proper time thou shalt see thy reward." [1]

Nor did the king confine the blame of Bel-ibni to the private ear of that unfortunate official. When the citizens of Nippur sent a delegation of fifteen elders to bring peace-greetings to their king, but a part of them were admitted into the royal presence. Ashur-bani-apal tartly answers their complaints: "It is the sin of your governor, for he is your governor; in the second place, it is the sin of the master of ceremonies who did not bring you in. I swear by Ashur my god that I did not know that half of you came into my presence and the other half did not. As for this one," that is, Bel-ibni, "I know who he is, but the devotedness of you all is as one to me." As to Hanana, Rimutu, and Aiau, the men of the Rua, let them not be negligent in guarding them. [2]

While Ashur-bani-apal freely defended Kisir Ashur to Bel-ibni, since he was the governor of the Babylonian Dur Shar-rukin and commander of the crown prince's body-guard, he spoke sternly enough to Kisir Ashur himself: "The houses of the musharkis officials are complete, you have rebelled against me, quickly give them to your servants." Kisir Ashur could only protest that his opponents had not spoken the truth; let a direct representative of the king be sent who should tell the king the truth. Let him see whether those houses are built and if they are, then let the king punish him for his sin and say: "Why do you not speak truth with me?" The king has likewise demanded why he has taken the houses of Shepe Ashur and given them to his own men. When Shepe Ashur went to Simiri, his servants went with him, and so Kisir Ashur took their houses and gave them to the men of Marhasai. Let Shepe Ashur have the governor build houses there with his own servants. [3]

With Tammaritu brushing the ground with his beard and

[1] *H*. 291.   [2] *H*. 287.   [3] *H*. 190.

following the royal chariot as a vassal, Ashur-bani-apal could adopt a firm attitude towards his successor Intapigash. He first wrote him a friendly letter (649). This produced no result and a sharper message was sent: "Since thou wilt not surrender the Assyrians carried off by Nabu-bel-shumate, I will march against thee; thy cities I will destroy, the citizens of Susa, Mataktu, and Hidalu I will carry off as spoil, from thy royal throne I will cast thee down, another on thy throne I will cause to sit, the fate of Tep Humban I will bring upon thee."[1]

This was answered by another invasion of the alluvium. Marduk-shar-usur, the Assyrian commander-in-chief, was seized and a great slaughter made in the land. Sin-iddina and Shuma, the son of Nabu-ahe-iddina, raised the land against Assyrian rule and carried off a part of their colleagues who were with Bel-ibni, and presented them to Nabu-bel-shumate.[2] Again the king was implored to send aid, five hundred horses for Nippur and a hundred for Uruk; let the king send the prince Natan.[3]

One official account states that Intapigash did set the Assyrians free, and that he made alliance with Ashur-bani-apal; an alternate says that when the Assyrian ambassador reached Der, the Elamites heard of it and revolted. The story is more truly told in the despatches of Bel-ibni.

Humbanshibar, the Elamite nagir, and his nobles have collected in Taidi, they have prepared revolt and have provided for their plunder. When the Assyrians reach Der, then will that smitten of Bel, accursed of the gods, Nabu-bel-shumate, and the sinners who are with him, be captured and the prisoners released. Already Bel-ibni has won a victory which has had pleasant personal results. His brother Bel-shunu, four years a captive of that smitten of the gods, Nabu-bel-shumate, who had carried him off and had made him see the darkness of all lands, has been freed from his bonds. Shortly he will be sent to court.[4] Here he was well received

---

[1] H. 1151; cf. 1125; 1167; 1323.   [2] H. 963.
[3] H. 622.   [4] H. 460.

and as reward for his sufferings was made governor of Hindanu and gave his name to the year 648.

Bel-ibni's troops surrounded a hostile Elamite city, cattle and spoil they carried off, they retreated again to Der, which they entered on the 14th of December (649). The riding horses he sent to Maliku, whose troops have come to Bel-ibni and have been ordered to Der. They report that when Zer-iddina arrived, the nagir assembled the people of the Elamite land, he made them enter the temple and there they keep watch. The king will ask: "Where is the king of Elam?" He is in Bit Imbi.[1]

[1] *H.* 1063.

CHAPTER XXXVI

THE DECISION OF THE GODS; THE DEATH OF SHAMASH–SHUM–UKIN

WHILE south Babylonia was being lost and won again for Ashur-bani-apal, the north was completely abandoned to Shamash-shum-ukin. The only Assyrian campaign was that to win the ear of the gods; in this Ashur-bani-apal excelled. On the 8th of August, 651, the seers are inquiring whether the Elamites will collect and make battle. On the 15th of October, we find him asking about his "faithless brother," as Shamash-shum-ukin is henceforth to be officially designated. It has been reported that he has fled to Elam; is this true? The reply is in the negative. To his request the seers add their own prayer, that the great gods, the lords of decision, send daily grace to their lord. The 16th of the next month, the great battle with Shamash-shum-ukin was about to begin and the distracted king begged the heavenly powers to inform him whether his troops would be fortunate in the encounter. This time the reply was favourable. He is asking on the 11th of February, 650: "Will Shamash-shum-ukin leave Babylon, will he flee to Elam?" About the same time is the query: "Shall they cross the four rivers, will they camp in Bab Same, will they engage with the troops of Shamash-shum-ukin in battle, what will be the outcome?" [1]

This is the forecast of the skirmish which took place at the camp of Bab Same. In another document we have the list of the persons taken prisoners after the conflict, including the woman of Iddua, the chief builder of Bab Same, and a son of Aplia, the governor of Arrapha. Babylonia was beginning to be won back for Assyria.[2]

Through Bel and Nabu, who have given power to the king of lands, his lord, Marduk begs that his servants may speak

---

[1] Klauber, *Texte*, 128; 109; 107; 113; 118.   [2] *J.* 891.

468

their thoughts to Ashur-bani-apal. The assigned work is not done, it will be complete in two months. People say that Sippar is a door before them, it will turn the people to the hands of the king. The officers suggest that a camp be established in Dilbat, then men will pass over and a caravan may not go around them, their troops will go forth and plunder the caravan. Let them make a wall as of a camp of Babylon, let them provide wooden shelters and drinking-vessels. Let there be five hundred and twenty horses of the king of lands in Kutu, let them be in quietness, let men who wish for their life flee from Babylon.[1]

Sippar fell into Assyrian hands. Ashur-bani-apal was encouraged to ask whether on the day when the troops move into Sippar and Shamash-shum-ukin hears it, he will go out of Babylon and flee in the direction his eyes turn. The answer was a negative. Then he asks whether the man whose name is on the tablet should be appointed over the Amukkanu, and whether, if he is so placed, he will come to an understanding with Shamash-shum-ukin or with Nabu-bel-shumate or with any other monarch. In the past, Ashur-bani-apal had done much for Zakir. He could not believe that all these past benefits had been forgotten and in October of 650 he sent a letter to Zakir and Kabtia, protesting against the reports from Kutu that the son of Zakir would be no longer one of the king's servants. Let them not fear and desert the cause of the king.[2]

The royal troops stationed at Birat have been sent, in accordance with the royal order, into the swamps of Birat by Nabu-shum-lishir. There they were attacked by the troops of the Babylonian king. He claims the victory with a loss to the enemy of four killed and nine captives, who are sent as proof to the king. Birat is a ruin, its gods have been carried off. If he might only see the king's signet-ring, he would be restored to life; when he sent his messenger, he had not seen the royal seal, he lives not, he is dead; let not the king abandon him.[3]

With Aqar-bel-lumur, he states that he has news of the

[1] H. 804.   [2] Klauber, *Texte*, 139; H. 944.   [3] H. 259.

son of Iadu, in whom with a little good-will we might find a Judæan. He is in Babylon; the month April he observes because the month April brought him forward. Seven hundred soldiers have they supplied to the king, now he is going against the city of Patnu. Aqar-bel-lumur himself describes the manner in which the son of Dakkuru sinned against his family, killing his mother and brothers with hunger, but the king has returned no answer to his complaints. He is in fear. The king knows he cannot retain his house or his servants, his property in Babylon has been seized by the son of Dakkuru. Lugal Maradda, the god of Marad, is the brother of Nabu, also the brother of Nergal is he. The king's father saved Marad, when he wrote, "In Ezida before Nabu have I placed the governor of Marad," he brought tribute voluntarily to the king's father, but now the son of Dakkuru has brought Marad to himself.[1]

More than all lands has the king spoken kindness with Bada, in the protection of the king he has planned kindness and executed it. Let him bind the bonds of the loins of Aqar-bel-lumur, let him bring his servants and come, let the king fear. No one will bring a word of the king, when there is one, quicker than Aqar-bel-lumur. He considers everything pertaining to the king as a sacred offering and to the king he presents it. When there has been terror, as many as seven times has Bada sent to the king. The men, as many as were their fathers, are dead, their houses the king has assigned to their sons. Behold these servants are the offspring of mercy, who, if the heart of the king does not forsake his servants, will not destroy the house of the king's servant.[2]

Ashur-bani-apal began to be encouraged and encouraged his Babylonian supporters: "Do not fear, keep the watch of the temples; Shamash-shum-ukin and all his men are shut up in the city, my army has surrounded them. Now, whenever you see any of his messengers, kill him or take him prisoner."[3]

While all these operations, each intended to weaken the allies of the rebel brother, were being carried on, that unfor-

[1] H. 261; 852 f.　　　　[2] H. 892.　　　　[3] H. 1186.

tunate remained shut up in Babylon. The business records in particular reveal the misery caused by the Assyrian blockade. Already in November of the eighteenth year of Shamash-shum-ukin, we hear that "in those days want and misery were laid upon the land and a mother would not open the door to a daughter." A year later, we have a loan of money to be paid without interest on the day when the face of the country is opened, and we learn that men are dying for lack of food. In May of the twentieth, another document says: "In those days, the enemy was encamped against the city, want was laid upon the land, the price of three qa of grain was named as one shekel of silver when it could be secured in secret." When we realise that this was more than sixty times the normal price, we understand how severe was the famine in the beleaguered city.

Rarely indeed are we able to behold the innermost feelings of the men of the empire. A happy chance, almost without parallel in antiquity, has permitted us to read the changing thoughts of the two protagonists as they besought from the depths of their hearts the deities they believed they had offended.

Ashur-bani-apal directs his appeal to Nabu: "I declare thy exalted state in the assembly of the great gods; among the assembly of those who sin against me, may my life not be spent. In the house of the queen of Nineveh, I pray to thee, hero among the gods his brethren; thou art the help of Ashur-bani-apal, forever and ever. Thy servant am I, I cast myself at the feet of Nabu; leave me not, O Nabu, in the assembly of mine enemies."

Nabu was the god of wisdom, he was also the god of Borsippa which had been eclipsed by the fame of Babylon as Nabu had been eclipsed by Marduk; he was pleased to be gracious to the enemy of those who had surpassed him and his city: "With thee, O Ashur-bani-apal, am I Nabu to the end of time; thy feet shall not be lame, thy hands shall not be weak. Let these thy lips not tire to beseech me; thy tongue shall not be shut within thy lips since I give thee good words. Lift up thy head, let thy body enter the temple Emashmash; thy mouth is a speaker of good, since it prays to the goddess Ur-kittu. With thy body which I have created, pray to me in thy going out to Emashmash; with thy fate, which I have determined, pray me: 'Grant long life to Ashur-bani-apal.'"

Lowly kneeling, Ashur-bani-apal besought Nabu his lord: "To thee, O Nabu, I give myself, leave me not; my life is written down before thee, my soul is sheltered in the bosom of Ninlil. To thee, O hero Nabu, I give myself; leave me not among them that sin against me."

There answered a priest who gave omens from the dead, standing before his lord Nabu: "Fear thou not, O Ashur-bani-apal, long life will I grant thee. To favouring winds will I intrust thy soul, my mouth speaking good things will bless thee in the assembly of the great gods."

Ashur-bani-apal opened his hands, he prayed to Nabu his lord: "He who taketh his stand with the Queen of Nineveh is not contemned in the assembly of the great gods; he who is bound to the girdle of Urkittu is not contemned in the assembly of those that hate him. In the assembly of mine enemies, leave me not, O Nabu; in the assembly of those that oppose me, leave not my soul."

"Little wast thou, O Ashur-bani-apal, when I committed thee to the Queen of Nineveh; weak wast thou, O Ashur-bani-apal, when thou sattest on her knee. Four nipples were placed in thy mouth; two thou didst suck and with two didst thou cover thy face. Thy enemies, O Ashur-bani-apal, shall be like grain scattered by the waters, like cress with which the spring is filled, shall they be struck down by lightning before thy feet, whilst thou, O Ashur-bani-apal, standest opposite the great gods and dost praise Nabu." [1]

Shamash-shum-ukin made his confessions to Shamash, the oracle god from whom he had received his name. For his prayers, he selected various extracts from the standard literature of the time, but he did not hesitate to make any changes necessary to fit his own case. When first the revolt breaks

---

[1] Craig, *Texts*, I, pl.Vf.; Streck, *Assurbanipal*, 342 ff.

out, we find him confidently approaching the deity: "Mighty lord, mountain of the Igigi, prince of the Anunnaki, deciding chieftain; my lord, I trust thee, I look to thee, my ears are inclined to thee. My posterity, as many as I have, do thou order; the building of my name do thou command. Loosen the sin, loosen the distress; do thou lay upon me thy great power of life. May they write me down as king, O excellent lord, prince; that which they talk may they bring to completion. Among the people he has proclaimed my command; may thy servant live and be at peace."

Then things do not go as successfully as he might wish and we detect the note of doubt: "A mighty one as a partner thou grantest me; to him who is not worthy thou dost give a son. The door and the bolt of heaven thou openest; for him who seest not, thou makest light. The unopened documents of my glory thou dost proclaim; among the lambs thou makest plenteous the meat. Do thou grant mercy; may I drink wisdom; in dreams where am I? O turn the black dream to favourable meaning. Righteously may I walk, my partner may I overcome; in thy days may I prolong thy favour." "Shamash, turn back the hostile one, bound in evil case on my left hand; the god Siris, pardoner of gods and men, on my right hand have I exalted. Verily, I shall consult the dog; verily I shall consult the swine; verily I shall consult the bird; verily I shall consult the fish. Unto the City (Babylon) he has given it; upon the earth he has approached, into the brick verily he has entered."

He becomes ill and the incantation for the hand-raising prayer to Sin is performed. A cypress censer is placed before Sin, and twelve cakes of thyme and of sesame are prepared. Must, honey, and butter are also made ready. An image of Zaqar, the dream-god, is placed at the head of his bed, that the message of the moon-god may be brought. The wrapping of hands and feet are removed and the appropriate incantation is recited. A clod of earth from the outer gate is bound in his cloak.

"O Sin, brightly shining Nannar, god both pure and radiant,

new-born Sin, lighting the darkness, fixing the brightness for far-distant peoples, granting good fortune at thy hand for the black-headed people, brilliant thy rising in far-distant heaven, bright is thy light like the Fire in his blazing, filled with thy brilliance is the earth far extending, glad are the nations, they revive when they see thee, god of the bright light, in might without equal, whose purpose is learned by none among mortals."

At this point comes an insertion: "I am thy servant Shamash-shum-ukin, I have presented thee a pure evening oblation, I have poured out before thee the best beer and honey. I bow down, I take my stand, I seek thee; favouring thoughts and righteousness establish for me. My god and goddess, since many days angry against me, with justice and righteousness grace me, may my path be favouring, my way be upright. He will send Zaqar, god of dreams, in the night may I hear absolution for my sin; my sin do thou pardon and forever will I sing thy praise."

Ashur-bani-apal and his armies are approaching and the last prayer of the series marks the black despair of the days when Shamash-shum-ukin was shut up in his capital, awaiting his fate: "Ea, Shamash, and Marduk, what is my transgression? Affliction hath overtaken me, evil looks down upon me. In my citadel am I beleaguered, they plan against me as a soul in burning; verily already a soul in burning am I. From the midst of the darkness have I seen thee going forth, O thou great bull; on my right hand lie overthrown my house beams, the mighty flood over my head has passed. Like a bird are my pinions clipped, broken is he who is no longer mighty; to supplication are turned my hands, my weakness is more than my loftiness. Like a dove moan I day and night, I wail and weep bitterly; tears are forced from my eyes. Shamash, in thy lofty eye is appeasement; loosen and remove the sin of my father and my mother, take away the curse of wrath. Ea, king of the abyss, Marduk, lord of those who dwell on earth, who changest the way, may my sin be made good by him, my look may he receive, favour may his innermost heart seek for me. Ea, Shamash, and Marduk help me, to you I look;

may I be pure and clean, O Nusku. My god whom I know not, consider how I exalt thy mighty name loudly, yet hast thou ravaged my people. Thy words have I disregarded, fully I admit it; my god, whiten, loosen, free my heart from the words of my blasphemies, accept my supplications, grant my gifts to thee, turn it into a favourable omen." [1]

The despairing cry to the gods was of no avail and by the middle of July, 648, the inhabitants were eating the flesh of their sons and daughters and gnawing their leather trappings. Shamash-shum-ukin could expect no mercy; in despair he cast himself into the fire and perished. The funeral arrangements were confided to the astrologer Mar Ishtar. With the aid of Dumuqu, the son of the shatam official, the grave vault was constructed, Shamash-shum-ukin and his palace lady were laid to rest in peace, their grave chamber was prepared, the grave they bewailed, they made a burning, all their salves they salved, many freeing incantations were recited, a house of washing and a house of offerings were completed, the appeasing incantations contained in the tablets were gone through. May the king's heart rejoice, the men of Akkad fear, but their hearts have been established and the right way they have taken.[2]

The fate of the citizens was terrible enough, and even those who had attempted to abandon the Babylonian prince in his last days were not received. They were carried off to Ashur to meet Ashur-bani-apal, and by the same sculptured bulls which had witnessed the assassination of Sennacherib, their tongues which had blasphemed the gods were cut out and they were deprived of life. The streets and public squares were choked by the bodies of those who had died of hunger and pestilence during the siege, and to them were added the slain in the sack of the city. There was great feasting for the wolves, vultures, and fish, for the dogs and swine which roamed the streets.

---

[1] Myhrman, *Babylonian Hymns and Prayers*, 22 ff.; Prince, *AJSL.*, XXXI, 256 ff.; Langdon, *PSBA.*, XL, 104 ff.

[2] *H.* 437.

CHAPTER XXXVII

LAYING THE FOUNDATIONS OF CHALDÆAN EMPIRE

BABYLON lay prostrate, her king was dead, her citizens slain or scattered in flight. Yet even in her degradation, the spell of Marduk was potent. Shortly Ashur-bani-apal issued his proclamation to the Babylonians and began by calling them "men under my protection," that is, they were still to be recognised as citizens of an imperial free city. "It is well with me, my palace, and my sons, may it be well with you and your sons. From this day may your heart be of good cheer and at the appointed time of Marduk I shall see the lofty power of the god, the decision of his great divinity, first may I see. Neither father nor mother made me great, they granted me truth and righteousness, a good destiny they fixed for me. In my reign, there was abundance in season, good things in my palace I established." [1]

Ashur-bani-apal likewise gave orders that the citizens be assembled, and permitted the noble families of Babylon and Borsippa to seek the king's peace, that is, give in their formal submission. They declared "it is the feast of Babylon" when they heard that the Assyrian king had ordered sacrifices. The men appointed by the king drew near and entered, they offered once more the sacrifices before Bel. Zer-ibni, son of Eteru, who was well known to the king, entered the temple as housekeeper that the regular offerings might be established once more. [2]

The re-establishment of the temples in Borsippa was intrusted to the kalu priest Pulu. He removed certain objects from the festival houses of Nabu and Tashmetum, the team he cut off, and the vessels of gold which Sargon had made for the temples. The goldsmith placed gold upon it, the old work he removed, he made it new, and the mighty ruler of Nabu

[1] H. 926.   [2] H. 971.

476

stands upon it. The housekeeper saw it, he caused him to return, he placed no one in Eshallit. He made him appoint the chief officials of Emineshu in the midst of the temple and images of the kings he had placed before that of his father, one before Bel and one before Nabu. The wine-offerings they increased, the grain of the tribute has been gathered. In the libation house of Bel and Anu he enters, twice during the year the sacrifice of its god is to be offered. Six men, who were all hidden before him, he did not show to any one who was with him and a woman who made an appearance for Tash-metum. This is the ceremony he is to perform, no one with him shall see it, neither a second-class priest nor any official, not even the chief officer of the king. Before Nabu he will establish it, may it endure forever. That which is done in the house of Marduk, whether it has ceased for one month or for two, may it be done forever.[1]

Bel-shunu, back from his captivity in Elam, assures the delegate that the nobility of Babylon are devoted friends of the king. They have requested that some one be sent to their land and Nabu-ahe-eriba has been ordered to advance to the bridge. Another son of Iakin has spoken with the Babylonians about the king's entrance into the city; he reports: "Certainly Bel will take action and when the king completes the ritual the god will hearken to him." Let the troops come and the king will attain his desire.[2]

The city streets were at length cleansed, the corpses were cast outside the walls, and with lamentation and prayer the city was made pure in the sight of the gods. Whether Ashur-bani-apal actually did visit the rebel city is unknown and the question as to whether he ruled there as king has been hotly debated. During the remaining twenty-two years of Ashur-bani-apal's reign, the business documents are dated by the years of Kandalanu. Since this dating is not continued beyond the death of the Assyrian king, there seems at first sight reason to assume that Ashur-bani-apal took this title in Babylonia as Tiglath Pileser III had been known as Pulu and Shal-

[1] *H.* 951; 975. [2] *H.* 844.

maneser V as Ululai, yet it must be admitted there are passages which seem to imply that the two were not identical. At any rate, the actual administration was intrusted to Shamash-daninanni, who appears as eponym in 644, sometimes as governor of Akkad, sometimes of Babylon.

Beginning with Nippur, the south honoured Ashur-bani-apal in his own name. Here too there were serious problems of reconstruction. Not all the local chiefs were of proved loyalty and the defeat of Shamash-shum-ukin had left them much troubled. For instance, we have a rather pathetic letter from Ea-zer-iqisha to his mother Humbushti. He has been slandered before the king, for they declare that he and Nabu-shezib have been friends of the king of Babylon. Ea-zer-iqisha replied that this accusation had been first learned from the king of Babylon himself. When the king inquired of him, he answered: "Urta destroy the lie, his mouth lets loose overflowing wickedness." He has heard that the Puqudu have violently taken away his home and his family from Nabu-shezib, whom the king of Babylon appointed, so that he must escape to the Amukkanu. This he has reported to the king, reminding him that he is closely bound to the king; let the king be wise of heart, since he is faithful to the king. If it please the king, let him send four men to the Amukkanu; if Nabu-shezib is there, he is the lord of his people, the hands of his king, the lock of hair from his head; if Nabu-shezib is not there, and the people who are like the House of Amukkanu put it in the hand of the king, let the king be wise when he comes with him and the Amukkanu declare: "No one has entered here and the servants of the king are untouched." He begs of his mother that she quickly send a message proving that Amukkanu is loyal, and asks: "Am I a fugitive who can escape from thy hand?" [1]

We hear no more of Ea-zer-iqisha, but his son is the topic of a report from Bel-ushallim, forwarded through Nabu-ushab-shi, on the 19th of May, 648. The king replies that a good deed has been done by him. Nabu-ushabshi has also sent

[1] *H.* 896.

about the matter of Humbushti, urging that it ought not be settled until Bel-ushallim arrive; the king answers: "Come, see the friendly face of the king, give counsel for the path of thy lord, may he hear thee." [1]

No revolt need be feared in north Babylonia; the capital lay prostrate, the lesson had been learned. Quite different was the situation in the south and east, where the actual ruler was Bel-ibni, the Chaldæan. His letters are full of wars and rumours of wars, the same as before the death of Shamash-shum-ukin. Through all the difficulties which could be devised by a royal master almost as hostile to him as to the Elamites, Bel-ibni held his steadfast way; thus were laid the sure foundations of that empire which his son Nabopolassar was in such seeming suddenness to bring into being.

No sooner was Intapigash enthroned in 649 than Humbanshibar, the Elamite nagir, was in revolt against him. By July of 648, Humbanshibar was in friendly communication with Bel-ibni and with Ashur-bani-apal, and he received a kindly reply from the Assyrian king.[2] Some time after, a third Humbanhaltash appears to have supplanted Intapigash, but the war continued unabated. Various tribes, so Bel-ibni reports, such as the Hilmu, the Pillatu, and the Iashian, are in sad straits; they are making meal of bitter herbs and of plants which only the wild asses eat. They rub it with their hands, they mix it, they eat it, on it they live. Nabu-bel-shumate, whose skin may Nabu give to be taken, has hired their troops to go against Bel-ibni for ten gur of dates and two slaves. Two hundred and fifty Gurasimmu who were on his side crossed over on rafts, plundered two of the pro-Assyrian clans, stripped the dead before the face of Bel-ibni, and made good their escape. Since the gods of the king stood by him, Bel-ibni embarked four hundred soldiers on ships, they crossed the Bitter River to Elam, under the protection of the king they made a destruction among the Hilmu and the Pillatu. When they had slaughtered five or six hundred of their cattle, they decamped; a hundred and fifty of the carcasses were brought

[1] *H.* 517.　　　　　　　　　　　[2] *H.* 1170.

back. But Nabu-bel-shumate, cursed and cast off by the gods, settled the Assyrian captives in Hupapanu.[1]

Bel-ibni has taken the treasures of Admanu, prince of the Mannu land, and of the Assyrians who were with him in the Nahal land, and has forwarded it all to his master. A hundred and fifty soldiers were despatched to the Akban and the Ale lands, on the other side of the Takkatap River, and there they slew many warriors. They made a hundred and thirty prisoners and burned their villages with fire. Amurru-zer-ibni and his companions gathered a "bow" of three hundred men, and when they saw the advance of the king's servants, they planned an ambush on the Nahal River. The Assyrians, however, changed their line of march, and seized a ford three thousand furlongs above them. When they saw that their opponents were many, they rose up, they drew up in line of battle, as many as they could they killed. To one another they said: "We are fourteen double hours distant from the Sealands; if we must die, let us die with an illustrious name." The gods of the king stood by his servants, they killed seventeen of the enemy's warriors and sixty or seventy they wounded. Of the king's servants, twenty received wounds. Bel-ibni collected the remainder of his bowmen, six hundred in number, with fifty horsemen, and took up his position in Bab Marrat. He sent a party on rafts to Mahmiti, they captured fifteen hundred cattle belonging to the king of Elam and the prince of the Pillatu. Five hundred they brought back on rafts, the remainder are still there. After deducting those who have been slaughtered and those sunk in the Bitter Waters, there still remain a hundred of the first-class cattle and forty herders to be sent on to the palace.[2]

On their last expedition, when the Assyrians entered his land and made a destruction, all the Elamites rose against their lord. In fear of both his new and his old enemies, Humbanhaltash abandoned Mataktu, crossed the Ulai with all his clansmen, and took refuge in Dalah among the mountains. When Bel-ibni saw that their troops were few while the As-

[1] H. 1000.   [2] H. 520.

syrians were many, he crossed over and took up his position at Bab Marrat, to the gods of the king they prayed. The abandoned settlements, including Mataktu, were burned; Ashur-bani-apal was very anxious for further news of these burned cities, fearing that their treasures might not have been rescued. Bel-ibni reassures him and tells of treasure safely carried off from Mataktu. But he must pause to complain: "Once and twice have I sent captives and three hundred horses to the lord of kings, my lord, and the king my lord has vouchsafed no reply. I have done him a great service and to the lord of kings, my lord, have I given them, but the heart of the lord of kings, my lord, is angry, though except for a horse for my watch and two or three that were sent away, I have forwarded all to the lord of kings, my lord." [1]

This is a propitious time to send an embassy: "If you do not quickly seize Nabu-bel-shumate and the ambassadors of Shamash-shum-ukin and hand them over, I will destroy you all." Ashur-bani-apal accepted the suggestion and the embassy was sent. In July of 645 Humbanhaltash promised to comply with the demands of his "brother." From the beginning the Sealanders have been sinners against Assyria and it was from there that Nabu-bel-shumate came. Nabu-bel-shumate and the Sealanders who broke into Lahiru have sinned against both kings: "If they are in my land, I will send them by their hands; if they have crossed the river, do thou take them." [2]

This is evidently the true account of the "seventh" expedition which Ashur-bani-apal narrates against Elam. It began in June and Ashur-bani-apal, who commanded in person, carried Tammaritu with him. Men of the cities of Hilmu, Pillatu, Dumuqu, Sula, Lahiru, Dibirina, places with which we have in part already become familiar, heard of the royal approach, and with flocks and herds hastened to Assyria. Bit Imbi, which had formerly been the royal city and which like a great wall blocked the way to Elam, had been taken by Sennacherib, but the Elamites built a new Bit Imbi in front

[1] H. 462; 794.   [2] H. 462; 879.

of the earlier. The new Bit Imbi suffered the same fate as
the old, the defenders who had refused surrender were decapitated or had their lips cut off, they were carried for ex-
hibition to Assyria. Imbappi, the resident, or, according to
another account, the commander of the bowmen of Bit Imbi,
a son-in-law of Humbanhaltash, was made captive and with
him the wife and children of Tep Humban. Humbanhaltash
heard of the approach of the Assyrian king and fled from Mataktu to a mountain. This flight, at least, we have heard of
before, but it was from Bel-ibni and not from Ashur-bani-apal.
Humbanhaltash, who had fled to the city of Bubilu, after Elam
had revolted, and had established himself on the throne of
Elam, left Bubilu and like a fish fled to the bottom of distant
waters. Tammaritu was reinstated in Susa by the Assyrians,
but he plotted against them, saying: "The people of Elam,
in whatever direction they turn, are subject to Elam; they
will enter and take the booty of Elam." The gods therefore
deposed Tammaritu and the Assyrians marched victoriously
through all Elam. The campaign is ended with a long list of
cities made captive and of spoil of wagons, horses, and mules.

Bel-ibni knows nothing of Tammaritu; according to him it
was Intapigash who must be driven out when Humbanhaltash
returned. Humbanshibar, the Elamite nagir, has deserted,
for they say: "We will settle among the Huhan tribe or in
Hidalu." They are all in fear of the royal troops, they have
seen misfortune, fear has entered them. Hunger has broken
out among them, the whole land has fallen away from them.
The Dahhasharua and the Shallukea have all revolted against
them, saying: "Why have you killed Umhuluma?"

On the day when Humbanhaltash entered into Mataktu,
he collected all his confidants, he spoke judgment with them:
"Did I not tell you before I fled that I would seize Nabu-bel-
shumate and surrender him to the Assyrian king, so that he
might not send his troops against us? You did not obey me,
you are witness of my word." Bel-ibni still has advice to offer:
"Behold, if it is right in the eyes of the lord of kings, my lord,
let them bring me a sealed order that Humbanhaltash should

seize Nabu-bel-shumate and I will as secretly send it to the king of Elam. Perhaps my lord will say: 'The idea is good but I will send a secret letter direct to them.' Now when the ambassador of the king my lord goes with an escort to Humban-haltash, then will that smitten of Bel, Nabu-bel-shumate, hear of it, he will pay a ransom to his nobles and will save himself. Perchance the gods of the lord of kings, my lord, will so bring it about that they will take him with unstrung bow and will send him to the lord of kings, my lord."

They are collecting all the grain levied as impost in Elam; they distribute it through the sharnuppu officials, and thus these officials secure their living. They distribute it from Dalah to Rade, and the Shallukea tribe give it to them. As long as Umhuluma lived, when he knocked at the door, Nabu-bel-shumate was in fear for his confederates. Now Nabu-bel-shumate and his majordomo Nishhur Bel seize every shar-nuppu they can find and they say: "If you demand it for Umhuluma, you are depriving us of our means of support, you are destroying the men of our house with hunger; behold, to the very last qa and a half, you must restore the grain which you have stolen." Report of this has been made to Humban-haltash; he has made demand two and three times, he has not yet secured it from their hands.[1]

Near the end of January, 642, there arrived before Bel-ibni a certain Bel-upahhir, the son of Marduk-shum-ibni, the shupparshaq official, who had been sent with a message from Humbanshibar. He begs that an embassy go to the king of Elam and asks: "What is the sin we have sinned against thee? Wilt thou not enlighten us concerning the whole matter? Elam will deliver up Nabu-bel-shumate rather than live in shame." Before this message could be forwarded to the Assyrian king, a second embassy arrived with the news that Nabu-bel-shumate was no more. When he learned that Humbanhaltash had at last determined to surrender him, he despaired and ordered his faithful squire to kill him, so they fell upon each other and they died.

[1] *H.* 281; cf. 1286.

Preserved in salt, the corpse was sent on with the head of the shield-bearer to Bel-ibni, who promised to bring it in person to the Assyrian monarch, "ere the days become hot." In March he will come to Assyria to view the king's face, he will bring a thousand captives with him. Since provisions are scant in the land, he must buy grain and dates from the Puqudu, giving silver in exchange. Let the king send one of of his body-guard to bring food for the captives on the way.[1] The last act of the sordid tragedy was staged in Assyria, where Ashur-bani-apal cut off the head from the corpse of Nabu-bel-shumate and hung it around the neck of Nabu-qata-sabat of Bit Sin-magir, an official of the dead Shamash-shum-ukin.

On the day that he set forth from the Sealands, Bel-ibni sent five hundred of the royal troops to Zabdanu with the orders: "Establish a garrison in Zabdanu, make raids into Elam; make a slaughter and carry off captives to the city of Irgidu." Evidently, even the surrender of Nabu-bel-shumate had not sufficed to keep permanent peace between Elam and Assyria. When they reached the city of Irgidu, distant only two double hours from Susa, they killed Ammaladin, prince of Iashian, Dala-ilu, son of Abiate, and two hundred nobles of the city. The journey was long, but a hundred and fifty prisoners rewarded it. When the princes of Lahiru and of the Nuga tribe saw that the Assyrians were upon them, they feared and gave themselves up, they made a treaty with his sister's son, Mushezib Marduk, whom Bel-ibni had placed over the garrison. They made their solemn declaration, "Servants of the king of Assyria are we," collected their bowmen, and proceeded with Mushezib Marduk to Elam. News sent back by Mushezib Marduk asserts that Humbanigash, son of Amedirra, has revolted against Humbanhaltash, from the River Hudhud to the city of Hindanu they have taken their stand by him; Humbanhaltash has brought together his forces and now they face each other on the river banks. Iqisha-apal has been sent to the palace to present the latest news from Elam.[2]

[1] H. 792; 1284.   [2] H. 280.

This is the latest and the last authentic news from Elam. These letters must belong to the first portion of the events which the official historian has taken as the basis for the "eighth" campaign of the king. For a second time, we are told, Ashur-bani-apal captured Bit Imbi, Rashi, and Hamanu. When this news came to Humbanhaltash, he again fled from Mataktu and took refuge in Dur Undasu, which the scribe has forgotten was made Assyrian in the previous expedition. Ashur-bani-apal crossed the Idide and behind its protection prepared for battle. Again cities were taken, seven of which had been secured on the preceding trip. As it was in flood, the Assyrians feared to ford the Idide, and only a dream from Ishtar of Arbela, rather far from home to be sure, induced them to cross. Fourteen royal cities and twelve regions fell to the invaders, and Humbanhaltash fled to his always-ready mountain. The Assyrians captured Bununu and the other cities on the border of Hidalu, the men were slain, the gods were spoiled to appease the spirit of the lord of lords.

We have no check from the letters for the statements which follow. After penetrating sixty double hours into Elam, we learn, the expedition returned to Susa, the great city, the seat of their gods, the place of their oracles; first of all Assyrian kings, Ashur-bani-apal entered the palace of the kings of Elam and opened their treasure-house. All the spoil carried off in former times or given in payment by Shamash-shum-ukin, precious stones and metals, clothing and weapons, palace furniture, chariots, horses and mules with trappings of silver and gold, for the last time the reader will be troubled with such a list. The palace furniture in particular, that on which the king sat, lay, ate, drank, washed, anointed himself, became Assyrian prey.

Encased with lapis lazuli and shining with bronze horns, the temple tower of the chief shrine was torn down. Shushi-nak, the god of their oracles, who dwelt in hidden places, whose divine authority none saw, and many of his attendant gods and goddesses, with all their belongings, priests, and temple servants, were carried off to Assyria. Thirty-two statues of their kings, of silver and gold, of bronze and white marble, were taken from Susa, Mataktu, and Huradi. Included among them were statues of Humbanigash I, son of Humbandara, of Shutruk Nahhunte II, of the later Tammaritu, of Hallutush. The latter, though he had fought only with the grandfather of Ashur-bani-apal, suffered especially evil treatment in effigy, for the mouth of the statue was cut off, its lips torn out, and the hand which held the bow was amputated. The winged lions and bulls, the guardian gods who watched over the temples, were dragged away, the temples were razed, the secret forests which no stranger had ever entered were burned by the Assyrian troops. The burial-places of the kings were all destroyed, their bones were conveyed to Assyria, where, in a foreign land, their shades were deprived of food and drink, and no repose was allowed them. So terrible a fate for long-dead enemies is fortunately rare in the Assyrian annals.

For almost two months, Elam was wasted. The dust of their cities was brought to the Assyrian land. The voice of men, the movement of flocks and of herds, the sound of music was no longer heard in its fields. Wild asses, gazelles, the beasts of the open fields, were permitted to lie down in its midst. One thousand five hundred and thirty-five years before Kutir Nahhunte had carried off the goddess Nana from her Eanna temple in Uruk;[1] Ashur-bani-apal had demanded her return from Humbanhaltash but in vain, now she took the straight road to her home, which she reached near the end of November. Of the captives, some were devoted to the gods and sacrificed, the soldiers were added to the army, the remainder was distributed among the nobles.

And then comes the anticlimax. Humbanhaltash returns for the third time from his mountain, for the third time he reoccupies his plundered city of Mataktu. It is a sad slip of the scribe, for it leaves no doubt that we are dealing with another raid such as Bel-ibni was wont to report to his master in Assyria.

[1] In reality, this took place in 1173; cf. p. 58; a thousand years should be deducted!

As the story continues, the narrative is not free from difficulties. The place of the much-driven-out Humbanhaltash is taken by Pae, who appears in the letters only as the resident of the Aramæan land whose messenger came to Nippur to report that the kings came to an agreement, one with another.[1] According to Ashur-bani-apal, Pae soon fled from Elam and embraced his feet. Then we learn of the rebels in the various cities who had retreated before his former expeditions to Saladri, a difficult mountain, but who finally descended, surrendered, and were added to his bowmen. Two columns later, after the recital of the Arabian wars, we hear of the fourth flight of Humbanhaltash from his revolted servants, for the fourth and last time he escapes to his by now most familiar mountain. Brought down like a falcon, he was carried alive to Assyria; together with Tammaritu, Pae, and the Arab Yatha, he dragged the king's chariot to Emashmash, the Ishtar temple in Nineveh.

Thus ends the last of the Assyrian historical writings. Without doubt, much of the account is untrue, for the successive editions issued for Ashur-bani-apal successively degenerate in historical value. Yet a capture and destruction of Susa is proved by the completely splintered native monuments found by the excavators. A certain Mannu-ki Ashur is listed as governor of Susa, a Pudiu as that of Elam, another has lost his name. The author of one of the Aramaic letters intercallated in the Book of Ezra lists men of Susa, the Dahha, and the Elamites as part of the nations settled in Samaria by the great and noble Osnappar, in whom scholars are agreed that we should recognise Ashur-bani-apal.[2]

At the same time, the letters come to a sudden stop. Where a moment before we have been listening to the very words of the chief participants, now we have a dead silence. We ask the fate of our old friends of the letters, in particular we would know what was happening to Bel-ibni and the little empire he was building up; only his presumed relationship to Nabopolassar makes it possible to conjecture that much was hap-

[1] *H.* 1115.   [2] Ezra 4 : 9.

pening and in his favour in this period of darkness. The events
last discussed took place about 640; from this to the end of
the reign in 626, we have only the business documents.

An uneasy consciousness of impending disaster overhung
the court, and not all the claims of a less and less honest history could conceal the danger on every side. No longer were
the gods to be found in their accustomed shrines, they were
angered at their worshippers. In May of 645, for example,
the king appointed a solemn day of lamentation which, as he
informed Kudur, should be observed by the leaders in Akkad
in the following month. Lamentation and the putting on of
mourning garments is ordered and wine is to be poured out
before the deities. Nana, Usur-amatsu, Arkaitu, the goddesses of Uruk, are to be especially besought. After they have
forgiven the sins committed by their devotees, after they have
changed the weeping into joy, then it may be hoped that they
will restore the temporal power into the hands of the king.[1]

[1] *H*. 518.

CHAPTER XXXVIII

A ROYAL SCHOLAR

DEGENERATE and a monster of cruelty Ashur-bani-apal might be called by his enemies, there was a more amiable side to his character. In that puzzling contradiction so often found in certain personalities of history, he owned a very genuine interest in culture of every sort. Above all other periods, his reign marks the golden age of Assyrian art and Assyrian literature and for its glories he deserves no small credit.

Alone of Assyrian kings, he gives us his autobiography, and the greater portion of it is devoted to his education. He learned to read the learned Shumerian or the obscure Akkadian. Present-day scholars who have passed beyond the conventional first year's course in Assyrian, who have attacked the Babylonian of a dozen or fifteen centuries before with its wilderness of variant sign forms and its differences in phonetics and vocabulary, and have then attempted the agglutinative Shumerian, the very reverse of all inflected languages hitherto learned, unless one has perchance travelled in the Turkish-speaking portions of the Near East, will sympathise with the young prince. He was fortunate in having a learned instructor, Nabu-ahe-eriba, and there was at his disposal the whole apparatus by whose aid generations of students had mastered a language so utterly apart from their own. To this day we possess a dictionary of Shumerian prepared by one of his scribes while Ashur-bani-apal was still crown prince.[1]

This interest he retained throughout his reign and it ultimately resulted in the formation of a great royal library. Such a library was not, as has been generally supposed, a novelty in an Assyrian palace. His great grandfather Sargon has left his library mark on a number of tablets and a somewhat larger number were copied by individuals whose activity extended

---

[1] Delitzsch, *Lesestücke*, 3 ed., 86; Johns, *AJSL.*, XXXIV, 60 ff.

through his reign and into that of his successor. Letters from
the close of Esarhaddon's reign speak of the preparation and
copying of tablets, many of which were in Shumerian. These,
however, were not copied primarily for preservation in the
library but for special and very practical occasions, such as
the installation of the crown princes. To judge from the extant remains, these collections were comparatively small.

It is indeed to the honour of Ashur-bani-apal that through
his personal interest there was brought to the libraries of Nineveh almost en masse the wisdom of the Babylonian past. A
"word of the king" to Shadunu illustrates the instructions to
the subordinates who were to collect the material. The day
he sees the tablet, he is to take Shuma, son of Shum-ukin, his
brother Bel-etir, and Aplia, son of Arkat-ilani, together with
the men of Borsippa with whom he is acquainted. He is to
search out all their tablets, whether they are in their houses
or deposited in Ezida. Ashur-bani-apal particularly desires
certain series, such as those dealing with the river ceremonies
of the months of April and October, with the royal bed, or
the incantation beginning "Ea and Marduk have completed
wisdom and its securing." Incantations dealing with warfare, such as "In the battle no spear shall come near the man,"
"Going into the field or entering the palace," as well as ritual
texts and prayers, the "lifting up of the hands," should be
included. Whatever is written on stones, "such as are of advantage for my royalty," is not to be neglected; Ashur-bani-
apal desired models for his own historical efforts. "The purification of the city," "The view of the eye," "For the agony
and every need" form another category. Let every tablet
in their own apartments, in so far as they are not in the Assyrian, be sought out and forwarded. Instructions have been
sent the shatam and shaku officials, no one shall refuse him a
tablet. If any tablet or ritual text not specifically listed be
thought of advantage to the palace, let that too be sent.[1]

Once we stumble upon a reference to earlier history.
Asharidu is writing from Kutu: "The tablet which the king

[1] Thompson, *Letters*, No. 1; Martin, *Lettres*, 18 ff.; Klauber, *Alte Orient*, XII, 22.

is following is small and incorrect. Now the original tablet which Hammurabi the king prepared contained an inscription dealing with Hammurabi the king, as I have written. From Babylon I have brought it." We might thus far conjecture mere antiquarian interest in a mighty king who had ruled Babylon fourteen centuries before himself, but Asharidu continues: "Let the king perform the ceremonies at once." There is a practical reason for the copy.[1]

What were the contents of this library and what was the native classification of its books? We can in part answer these questions by noting the various types of labels which were suffixed to the tablets. A few follow the earlier custom and are merely marked: "Palace of Ashur-bani-apal, king of the world, king of Assyria." As the number of tablets grew, stamps were prepared which printed the whole phrase at once and in large characters. More colophons form a regular paragraph in themselves, beginning with an elaborate genealogy and ending with emphatic curses on those who would destroy the work of his hand. A common form declared that "in agreement with the original tablets and documents I caused copies of the Assyrian, Shumerian, and Akkadian to be written, compiled, and revised in the chancellery of the experts, and as precious possessions of my royalty I made them to be laid up."

For the bilingual and grammatical texts, a fuller paragraph testified to their value in his own learned education: "Palace of Ashur-bani-apal, king of the world, king of Assyria, who trusts Ashur and Ninlil, to whom Nabu and Tashmetum have granted a wide-open ear, and have endowed me with clear insight into the noble art of writing; whereas none of the kings who had preceded me had acquired that art, the wisdom of Nabu, the grouping of all extant collections on tablets I wrote, compiled, and revised, and placed them to be seen and revised in my palace." Whether we are to accept as exact truth the rather startling statement as to the illiteracy of the earlier Sargonid monarchs, Ashur-bani-apal is certainly making claims

[1] H. 255.

to unusual learning. The contrast with his grandfather is especially instructive; Sennacherib boasts of his personal ability as shown in the introduction of new mechanical devices, Ashur-bani-apal is chiefly interested in the knowledge of the past.

We should nevertheless be mistaken did we assume that he was less practical than his predecessor, that he was more imbued with the modern ideal of knowledge for knowledge's sake. He is the "darling of the great god, to whom Shamash and Adad have given a wide-open ear and the science of the seer, the mystery of heaven and earth, the wisdom of Shamash and Adad has he learned, with it his breast has been filled," but it is only that he might the better utilise the portents furnished by these gods, for this colophon appears on the omen tablets by whose means Shamash and Adad gave advice as to the conduct of the empire. A practical purpose appears again in the notes to the medical texts, where he speaks of "healing and the work of the lancet's lord, the placing in order of the sorcerer's task, the complete knowledge of the great medical art of Urta and Gula," which he prepared for his collection. Nabu, the patron saint of writing, is besought in a formal prayer to look in future days with approval on the library and to grant grace to Ashur-bani-apal.[1]

Every phase of Babylonian literature was represented in the library. By scholars of the last generation, this collection was studied for a knowledge of Babylonian rather than of Assyrian thought. Within our own generation, its value in this respect has been much decreased. We now possess a wealth of documents from the first dynasty of Babylon, and we can see that the library copies were derived from the recensions prepared at this date and systematically redacted to increase the prestige of Marduk. For earlier centuries, we can use their data only with the utmost caution, a caution which is shown to be amply justified when we compare these Marduk crammed editions with those from the dynasty of Ur, four hundred years before, when Marduk was unknown to divine society. Internal evidence, supported by a few ac-

[1] Colophons collected, Streck, *Assurbaniapal*, 354 ff.

tual examples from still earlier periods, shows that the origins must often be sought in times almost prehistoric, when Enlil of Nippur, or even Ea of Eridu, was the dominant god in the pantheon.

As the value of the documents in the library of Ashur-bani-apal has progressively lessened for the study of Babylonian literature, religion, and customs, there should have been a renewed interest in another question, the degree to which they are Assyrian and not Babylonian. Our letters show the actual process of transportation from the alluvium, and we might expect them to be exact reproductions of their exemplars. But Ashur-bani-apal specifically and repeatedly asserts that they were not merely copied from their originals, they were compiled and revised. Investigation in detail would surprise the investigator by the large number of cases in which this Assyrian revision has resulted in essential change.

An already quoted prayer used by Shamash-shum-ukin in his moment of ultimate woe is a striking illustration. A prayer to the moon-god, it can be traced back to an origin at least as early as the first dynasty of Babylon. Transported to Assyria, its whole character was changed by an interpolation of ten lines which made it now an appeal by the king in the ominous period at the end of the month when the moon-god temporarily withdrew his light.[1] A careful collection of all the interpolations made by the Assyrian scribes to their Babylonian originals would throw as valuable a light on the characteristics of Assyrian literature and religion as do the insertions made by the Hebrew scribes after the Greek translation of the Bible had been executed.

By no means all the tablets shelved in the library of Ashur-bani-apal were copied from Babylonia. Nearly a thousand business documents, fifteen hundred letters, a large group of omen texts, are firmly dated to the last Assyrian century. To-day we call them archival material, but the Assyrians saw no reason why they should not be placed side by side with the other writings. Many of the letters, those of Adad-shum-usur

[1] Langdon, *PSBA.*, XXXIV, 152 ff.; XL, 106 f.

in particular, are deliberate literary productions. The mass of the literary compositions, properly so called, shares the anonymity which shrouds so much of oriental writing, but a more careful examination will doubtless prove that many can be dated to the reign.

For no reign do we possess so large an amount of literary material which may be exactly dated because of its association with the reigning monarch. Edition after edition of the historical chronicles was issued, and each marked an improvement in the eyes of a literary king, if not in the eyes of the modern historian who must sift the facts from the rhetoric or the deliberate misrepresentation. Scattered through them are passages which represent the highest flights of the Assyrian literary art, and if some of them sound a little too rhetorical to suit the present-day taste for realism, others, such as the messianic sections, will compare with the messianic chapters of the Old Testament, which doubtless they helped to suggest. To what extent this Renaissance in the writing art is directly due to its royal patron may be a question; in view of the marked individuality of some of the passages, such as the autobiography, in view also of his specific claims to literary excellence, it would be rash to deny that some at least embody the actual words of the scholar king.

In no respect was Ashur-bani-apal behind his predecessors in his building. All Babylonia rejoiced in his constructions; in Nippur and the south they were in his own right, in Babylon and its vicinity Shamash-shum-ukin was associated, but the letters show the claim of the northern brother to the greater part was no idle boast. Structures erected in Assyria could be assigned to no other person. As crown prince, Ashur-bani-apal had enjoyed a palace his father erected for him in Tarbisu. The standard of Nabu, housed in a northern Eshitlam, had fallen into decay, but was restored by the filial love of the king. Ashur's temple in his namesake city had not been brought to completion; Esarhaddon's son covered the walls with gold and silver, plated high columns with the less-precious metal, and set them up in the gate "Fulness of the Lands."

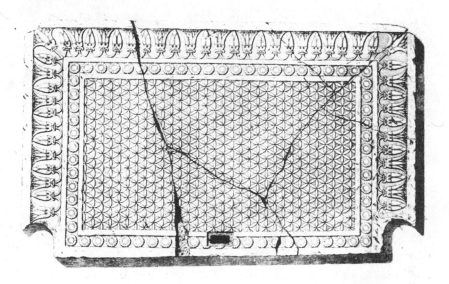

Fig. 151. DOOR-SILL IN THE PALACE OF ASHUR-BANI-APAL.

Fig. 152. NETTING THE DEER

Fig. 153. LION ESCAP-
ING FROM CAGE.

Ashur entered his chamber of eternity and his consort abode in a renovated Esharra.

Aid given through dreams by Ishtar had been the special reliance of Esarhaddon and was likewise of his son. The accession of that son found the Arbela temple in ruins, the inner wall could be no longer traced, the outer wall was incomplete. Both were ended, the feast-house of the goddess was made to shine like the day with his gifts of metals, the standard at its entrance was covered with gold and silver. Ishtar's temple at Milkia, Egal-edin, "the palace of the open field," was in more serious state, for some enemy had completely destroyed the city; the foundations of the New Year's House were laid with ceremonial mourning and completed with ceremonial joy.

Esarhaddon had been a devoted worshipper of the Sin of Harran; before his first full year, Ashur-bani-apal began to clear away the débris of the ancient temple erected by Shalmaneser III. It was to be thirty courses high, three hundred and fifty long, seventy-two broad for the eastern portion and a hundred and thirty from the back of the city to its centre. Its foundation was of stone from the mighty mountains, its roof was of cedar and cypress felled by the seacoast kings, and with hardship brought from their difficult recesses. Ehulhul at last rightly merited its name, the "House of Joy."

Great doors of cypress were covered with silver-plating and the dwelling of Sin with seventy talents of gleaming zahalu. Two mighty wild bulls were formed in the same manner in silver and their bodies were fashioned from twenty talents of hammered bronze. To hurl back his enemies and to trample down his foes, he placed in the gate two silver figures like Lahmu, the chaos monster; they appeared as if they had sprung from the deep, they protected the path of his royalty, they brought in the fulness of mountain and sea. Nusku, the exalted messenger of the gods, found his Harran shrine Emelamanna restored within the great temple.

A temple estate, granted by Sargon and then taken away, was returned. Ashur-bani-apal had not forgotten that Harran was once the metropolis of Mitanni, and that its deity still had power to grant sovereignty. His youngest brother, Ashur-etil-shame-ersiti-uballitsu, was marked as an urigallu priest for the service of Sin in Harran; he was to be but the viceroy of his brother who formally took the hands of Sin and Nusku, and was thus recognised as king of the old Mitanni.

Babylon, Ashur, Harran, all these might be highly honoured, but the true capital of Assyria was Nineveh. Sennacherib had erected mighty walls, but through "the pouring rains and the heavy storms which Adad had caused to pour down every year of my reign," they had fallen into disrepair. This might be permitted so long as the foes of Assyria were far away, but when Shamash-shum-ukin revolted, the walls were hurriedly put into shape. Ishtar, lady of the lands, had in the wrath of her heart deserted her temple of Emashmash, she had seated herself in a spot not worthy her exalted nature. Restored with gold and silver, Emashmash gleamed like the stars, the writing of heaven. Nabu was granted in the capital an Ezida such as he already possessed in Kalhu, and here was preserved a part of the palace library.

The larger portion of the library was conserved in Sennacherib's palace, the residence of Ashur-bani-apal in his earlier years. One of the unsculptured rooms was covered with representations of the defeat of Tep Humban. By the time the revolt of his brother had been put down, the palace was too ruinous for repair. The tender-hearted Ashur-bani-apal could not endure to behold its downfall, for it was connected by too many sentimental ties with his past. Within its walls he had grown up to maturity, while crown prince he had lived under the protection of its gods, after he had seated himself on his father's throne they had sent him many truthful reports promising the defeat of his enemies. On his bed of night, they had granted him many dreams so favourable in character that he had rejoiced at their memory in the morning. The site, he felt, had without doubt been established by the gods for good fortune, it brought luck for its lord.

Hard by the newly cleared ruins, only fifty courses distance away, the foundations were laid, with scrupulous regard to

the rights of the gods and without encroaching on their area.
On an auspicious day and month, the walls were sprinkled
with wine, the inhabitants of the land brought up the bricks
on the heavy Elamite wagons. Yoke and corvee were borne
by the captive Arab kings, they carried the corner-stone.
Cedar beams from Sirara and Lebanon formed the roof, the

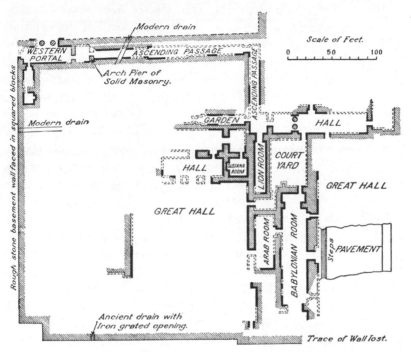

MAP 9. PALACE OF ASHUR-BANI-APAL AT NINEVEH.

bronze-covered doors were of sweet-smelling líaru cedar.
Gleaming bronze sheathed the high pillars, which were placed
upon the architrave of the gate to the Hittite colonnade. A
great park, with all sorts of trees and fruits, was planted near
by, the predecessor of the more famous hanging gardens of
Nebuchadnezzar to judge by the representations on the slabs.
With elaborate ceremony, the palace was dedicated to the
gods and Ashur-bani-apal entered under a canopy.

The palace seems to have been well preserved down to

the middle of the nineteenth century. The plundering methods of so-called excavation then in vogue were applied with
unusual thoroughness to this ruin. A wonderful booty of
sculptured slabs was won, but neither adequate plan nor description was ever attempted.

Roughly quadrangular in shape and with the corners directed to the cardinal points, the new palace was to occupy
the northern angle of the mound. A great wall of uncut stone
with facing of squared blocks enclosed the whole area and
iron gratings covered the drain exits. The only entrance now
in existence is at the northwest corner. The visitor passed
between two columns, turned sharply at right angles, and
found himself in a guard-room whose arched inner gate was
set in a pier of solid masonry. This formidable barrier safely
negotiated, he slowly ascended a long covered passageway
along the northwest wall for nearly two hundred feet, which
was lined with reliefs showing the royal stud and scenes from
the hunt.

Still ascending, the road turned to the southeast and was
carried to the centre of the structure, where a rude cross was
formed. A single door led to the western arm of the cross, a
long narrow room which apparently was the approach to the
women's quarters. Its sculptures represented the park, with
vines trained on fir-trees, with lilies and other flowers, with
musicians and tame lions. Particularly worthy of notice are
the arched doorways, one with a double row of rosettes above
the arch proper, and above that flat lines containing other
double rows of rosettes and the lotus flower and bud. Near
by a room illustrated the Elamite campaigns.

Beyond the axis of the cross, the ascending passageway
opened out into a long narrow room whose walls were completely covered by the lion-hunt, the supreme achievement
of the Assyrian artist. When discovered, it was filled completely with tablets. The eastern arm of the cross led through
an entrance-hall twenty-four feet square and between two
columns into a main hall eighty feet in depth. Four irreg-
ularly placed exits break the monotony of the unsculptured

Figs. 155–156. LION HUNT, ON HORSEBACK.
(Cast in Metropolitan Museum.)

FIG. 157. HUNTING WILD ASSES.
(Cast in Metropolitan Museum.)

walls. The ground plan is very strange for an Assyrian palace, it seems rather an anticipation of the basilicar type.

If the visitor passed through the door just to the right of the columns, he traversed a small court and was then in a huge hall, one hundred and forty-five by twenty-eight feet, the audience-chamber. As was fitting, the sculptures dealt with the most important events of the reign, the Babylonian troubles, while in the room to the right the latest of all conquests, that of the Arabs, was depicted.

An unusually broad opening in the middle of the left side of the audience-chamber led down a flight of steps to a great court, paved with sculptured slabs. Their border was of conventionalised lotus flowers and buds, a motive imported straight from Egypt, next came a row of rosettes, and with them a line of what appears exactly like the Greek acanthus. In the centre were rosette-ringed squares with the rosette-centred quatrefoil and with the more conventionalised lotus flowers between. The gate to which this led has disappeared with the crumbling away of the mound edge.[1]

Artists unanimously admit that the reliefs found in the palace of Ashur-bani-apal represent the climax of Assyrian art. The slabs of a historical nature follow essentially the types of their predecessors, from which they are chiefly distinguished by greater attention to detail and by finer finish. The peculiar beauties of the art are rather to be found in the reliefs which deal with nature, for from the day of their discovery they have sufficed to give Assyrian art a unique reputation.

We may well begin with the most famous of all, the slabs in the room which contains the lion-hunt. The oft-repeated reproach that the Assyrian artist did not understand composition must be waived in at least this instance, for even with the too numerous gaps in the recovered series, the whole forms an artistic unity.

The hunt is staged in an open part of the park, and is marked by a hunting-lodge on a small ruined mound. The lions are

[1] Plan, Rassam, *TSBA.*, VII, op. p. 41; cf. Rawlinson, *Monarchies*, II, 213 ff.

forced out into the open by soldiers who lock their round shields into a solid wall while they threaten the beasts with their spears; archers behind them render still more unlikely their escape.   Into the enclosure formed by the spearmen the horses are led that the master of the hunt may choose the two who are to be yoked to the royal chariot.   Lest they be affrighted by the roaring lions, eunuchs hold before them screens seven feet high, but in spite of this precaution the master of the hunt has difficulty in harnessing the animals.   One is just having his last strap buckled, the other is trembling at the sound, his mouth is open, his ears laid back, while a groom pulls down his lifted head by the halter and attempts to back him into place.   The charioteer calmly takes the reins, the king reaches for the bow, one attendant grasps a spear, the other closes the tail-board of the chariot.

Before the wall of soldiers is a square cage of logs pegged to the ground, and upon it stands a smaller cage in which the attendant cowers as he lifts the bar and permits the lion to spring forth.   Our next scene shows the king in full pursuit of the maddened beasts.   Behind him is a long trail of dead and dying lions, while those more slightly wounded dash against the enclosing line of soldiers.   On the edge of the forest stand hunters with huge mastiffs straining at the leash.   Not all the men are so brave; the eunuchs and unarmed servants are in full flight.   Some attain the safety of the artificial mound, some seem determined not to cease their mad rush before reaching the palace.   Ashur-bani-apal thinks only of pursuit, and the lion which has sprung upon the rear of the chariot is left to the companion spearmen to despatch.

Another scene shows the king followed by his companions on horseback.   In utmost fury, a wounded lion has seized the chariot-wheel in his jaws; the king coolly hands over his bow to a eunuch and pierces the beast with his spear.   Before him is a lion, shot through the brain and in his last agonies.   A terrible danger appears, a lion is actually in the chariot; before the fearful spearman can strike him, the king has driven his short sword through his neck.

Alongside a group of servants going out to the hunt with all the paraphernalia needed, some packed on muleback, others carried over the shoulders, and including nets, ropes, and stakes, we see the return from the hunt. Before struts the master, carrying his bow; six sturdy eunuchs follow, the dead lion raised high in their arms. Two eunuchs come after, carrying birds' nests filled with the young, a grown bird, and a hare. Armed guards close the procession.

The lion-hunt from the chariot forms a single huge picture developed over an entire hall; smaller isolated scenes present the lion-hunt on horseback or on foot. Ashur-bani-apal appears in the saddle and leading a second horse. A lion bristling with arrows has seized the flank of the horse, who lashes out with a mighty kick. The whole effect reminds us immediately of those primitive Greek sculptures of the lion seizing the bull, such as occurs in the earliest pedimental relief from Athens. Another lion attacks the king himself; without swerving his mount, he drives the long spear directly into the gaping mouth and the tip appears below the mane.

Behind the protection of a long shield held by the trembling squire, the dismounted monarch watches three lions. One has just been permitted to leave his cage, the second is about to leap at the royal throat, the third is already in the air and is being threatened by the spear-armed attendant while the king fits an arrow to the bow. Or the king seizes a rearing lion by the tail, and his chariot and its occupants await his pleasure at a safe distance. He abandons his bow and arrows to his eunuch while he grasps the rampant lion by the throat and drives his short sword straight through his body or brains the beast with his mace. Final scene in this group is the libation over the dead animals, four already collected at the monarch's feet, a fifth in the act of being carried in by eunuchs. Again in evidence are the musicians, the servants with fly-flappers, and the soldiers.

Whatever his dislike of the stricken field, Ashur-bani-apal cannot be denied credit for personal courage, if we admit the testimony of the sculptures, and it is significant that the greater part of the reliefs is devoted to struggles with the king of beasts. Less spectacular methods of hunting were not neglected. Next to the lion, he most willingly hunted the wild ass of the desert. Mounted on his swiftest Arab steed, he shot down the asses as they galloped at full speed, coursed by dogs, or lassoed by the hunters. The still swifter gazelles were also pursued; to reach bow-shot distance of them, it was necessary for the king and his lone companion to hide in a shallow pit. Occasionally he descended to trapping, and a scene presents a number of fallow deer rushing blindly into the high-netted enclosure; one is already caught and is being untangled by the huntsman, another hunter is strengthening the ropes.

Our final scene is the banquet. In a vine-clad arbour surrounded by date-palms, Ashur-bani-apal reclines on a high-cushioned couch with richly carved supports. His body is half covered by a spread, his hair is crowned with a chaplet of flowers, in his left hand he grasps a huge lily, with his right he is lifting to his lips a richly chased bowl of wine. Ashur-sharrat, his queen, sits bolt upright on a high-backed chair with curving arms, richly decorated supports, and footstool. A tiara crowns her head, her short hair curls on her shoulder, a necklace of huge stones encircles such neck as is possible between solid head and ample body, bracelets adorn her chubby wrists. A rich underjacket is all but lost under the long fringed robe which is swathed about her body, its lowest fold coming down to the jewelled shoes, its last thrown carelessly over the arm and hanging down the side. Between the two stands a small table, supported first by reversed and truncated cones and then by lions' feet, while the central support is a column with three Ionic volutes strung along it. On its surface is food and a casket of ivory such as has been preserved in the original. By the side of each is a censer with acorn-shaped top, and behind each are servants with fly-flappers. Musicians entertain the royal pair, and food is being served by attendants, who have some difficulty in keeping off the flies. Birds and grasshoppers furnish a pleasant touch of nature, until we catch a

FIG. 158. BANQUET OF ASHUR-BANI-APAL AND HIS QUEEN, ASHUR-SHARRAT.

(Cast in Metropolitan Museum.)

glimpse of a grasshopper disappearing down a bird's throat, and until we observe the direction of the king's glance, for there hangs the bleeding head of Tep Humban from the branch with the less-ghastly fruit.

With these bas-reliefs, Assyrian art reached the highest point to which it seemed possible to aspire. They show their superiority to those which had gone before in fineness of finish and minuteness of detail. If the innate modesty of the Oriental prevented the artist from studying the nude human form of the athlete, the lack was made good in the case of wild animals, for the frequent royal hunts permitted him to study the hunted animals in their every movement of life or in their distortion when wounded or dead.

Few artists, ancient or modern, enjoyed such facilities for studying lions in the life. The lions of the greatest artists of history are generally the result of convention; some never saw a living animal, others have observed them only in captivity. Complaint that sculptured lions are grotesque is a commonplace of present-day art criticism. One can have no doubt that they were copied from live models when we inspect the productions of the nameless Assyrian master.

The lion with fangs set in the chariot-wheel, the wounded lion coughing up his life-blood, the lioness paralysed by the arrows in her spine yet gamely dragging herself along on her fore paws, the wild ass glancing back over his shoulder as he rushes at full speed, the stag dashing through the reeds to the safety of the lake, the shy, graceful gazelles, the mastiffs straining at the leash, the horses in terror of the king of beasts, we might literally pass from one relief to the next in regular order when we enumerate the scenes which are true to life. In the words of one of the greatest authorities on Greek art, "the magnificent rendering of lions, horses, and dogs in these reliefs has never been surpassed, if equalled, in any sculpture ancient or modern." [1]

[1] Ernest Gardner, *Handbook of Greek Sculpture*, 49. The reliefs, Layard, *Monuments of Nineveh*, II; cf. for descriptions especially Bonomi, *Nineveh and Its Palaces*, 386 ff.

CHAPTER XXXIX

HEIRS OF THE AGES

In Assyrian culture we meet for the first time in history a civilisation whose possessors may rightly be called "Heirs of the Ages." Not that the earlier civilisations were not complex, for Egypt and Babylonia were inhabited by mingled races with individual cultures, and each admitted influences from the other; compared with Assyria, their culture was simplicity itself.

Current practice treats Assyrian civilisation as a mere extension of the Babylonian, and there is a certain justification for this view. Yet, even if we thus narrow the influences exerted upon the Assyrians, the heritage from the south was far from simple, for the Babylonian culture which influenced the historical Assyrians was itself a complex of Shumerian and Akkadian, of Amorite and Elamite and Kashshite, strengthened and vulgarised in the later centuries by the invasion of the Aramæans.

Such complexity as was found in the Babylonian civilisation was due primarily to the settlement within the alluvium of foreign peoples. This was in part true of Assyria. To judge from the place names, an earlier stratum of the population was of that race which had overspread all western Asia in Neolithic times, and how many more layers of peoples had preceded the historical Assyrians it is not easy to decide. Before the true Assyrians came in, Assyria was a confused medley of Semites and non-Semites.

The true Assyrians were Semites and close to the desert; thus they brought with them, almost undiluted, the truly desert, that is, Semitic point of view. Comparative assimilation of the various elements had been completed by the time that Assyria became a world-power, but the fusion was in many respects imperfect. The lower classes were in a state of inferiority amounting to serfdom, and the different dress of nobles and commons, as we see them, for example, in the gate sculptures of Shalmaneser III, points in the same direction. All now spoke the Assyrian language and appeared to have left behind their peculiar, non-Semitic characteristics.

It was not from these lower classes that the complexity of Assyrian culture was to develop. A period of Shumerian control is indicated by the names of the sanctuaries and by early examples of art, and this cultural element was emphasised when Ashur fell under the physical control of the Babylonia of the Ur dynasty. The Amorite dynasty of Babylon was likewise under considerable indebtedness to the Shumerian civilisation, but in race they were close to the Assyrians, and their lordship over Ashur strengthened the Semitic features.

More mature consideration indicates that the unlikenesses between the two civilisations are as great as the similarities. The chief cause, it will soon be recognised, is the fact that while the culture of Babylonia was always local and somewhat nationalistic, that of the Assyrians was almost from the beginning imperial in that it rested on the subjugation and incorporation of peoples of different languages, races, and cultures, not to speak of a difference in political organisation far greater than was to be detected between the city-states of the alluvium. Thus the Assyrian empire rested upon a far more complex grouping of peoples than had ever before been seen. A glance at the ancient ethnographic map will confirm this to the fullest satisfaction.

Earlier political obedience, close similarity of language, common deities and methods of worship, a general likeness in civilisation, all contributed to unite Assyria to Babylonia from an early period, and as it came more and more to be accepted as matter of fact that Babylonia should be a political dependency of Assyria, the cultural bonds became ever closer, until there was no little danger that the spontaneous northern civilisation might be ruined by the effete culture of the south. That this was not entirely accomplished, that Assyria retained something of its native habits in living, was due in considerable degree to the ever-close contact with the desert tribes, in part to relations with other peoples who in many respects were superior to the men of the alluvium.

We can hardly overestimate the part played by the Aramæans in the development of Assyria. As early as the fourteenth century, the pressure of the true Arabs had forced the Aramæans into the Assyrian world. They first collected into little city-states, each surrounded by villages of farmers, but when Ashur-nasir-apal II and Shalmaneser III destroyed their city-states, the inhabitants abandoned their farms as easily as they had taken them up and began to turn their attention to the trade opportunities presented by the Assyrian conquests, and for the proper exploitation of which the Assyrians were temperamentally unfitted. Gradually, the whole internal trade of the empire fell into their hands, and by the time of Sargon a large proportion of the trader names is Aramaic. An index of the rapidity with which Aramaic influence increased is furnished by the weights employed in the course of trade. Under Tiglath Pileser III, only Assyrian characters were used to give their value, Aramaic appears side by side with the cuneiform under Shalmaneser V, after Sennacherib Assyrian never occurs and its place is taken by the Aramaic alone. Cuneiform was used in business documents to the end of the empire, but Aramaic dockets permitted a hasty inspection.

Rival to the Aramæans were the Phœnicians, yet they seem to have agreed tacitly upon a delimitation of territory. The former possessed a monopoly of the land, the other of the sea, and not all the might of the empire could force to its knees the island city of Tyre. Accommodation was fortunately easy. Assyrians cared little for trade, Phœnicians cared even less for empty liberty when a reasonable sum might secure for them the external trade of the empire. Rich gifts now and then passed up to the Assyrian capital or met the monarch on his infrequent trips to the Mediterranean, but the letter from the Assyrian financial agent at Arvad or the treaty with Baal of Tyre indicates the degree to which the sea-borne trade of the Syrian coastland had become a Phœnician monopoly.

These were the most important cultural elements within the empire. The reader naturally expects mention of another, the Hebrew. Within the Assyrian period, they produced nothing new in material development, and gave little or nothing to the surrounding peoples. Now and then they illustrate certain movements for which we have less evidence elsewhere. On the other hand, this was the period in which the Hebrew religious thought ceased to be like that of the other Semitic peoples and began that evolution which was to result in the later Judaism, in Christianity, and in Islam. The effect of the Assyrian culture on the Hebrews in this formative period is one of the most important questions to be considered by the historian.

Scarcely less to demand consideration are the peoples across the boundary. Portions of their territory were for longer or shorter stretches of time under the Assyrian standards, slaves and captives bearing their outlandish names and speaking their "women's languages" were included in the Assyrian families or were settled on the abandoned farms. This means of introducing fresh blood is often concealed by the good Assyrian names which the captives or their descendants assumed, but sufficient evidence remains to indicate how large was the foreign element in the later empire.

Egypt was under the direct Assyrian rule for less than a generation, but Egyptian influence can be scarcely measured by this brief length of time. All relations with her were not hostile, as we might assume from the annals. Treaties of peace were made through an Egyptian scribe, the most picturesque of the Assyrian war recitals was prepared by a historian with an Egyptian father, common men were called Musurai, the "Egyptian," Sennacherib had an Egyptian son-in-law and introduced from the Nile valley the well-sweep and the clearstory, Egyptian motives appear in the ivory or bronze work, many of the horses in the royal stables came from Egypt or Ethiopia. These are definite connections with Egypt; the more we study the general civilisation of Assyria, the more probable seem other contributions from the Nile.

Another people whose influence must not be underestimated is the Haldian. Their specialty was hydraulic works, with metallurgy a close second, and in regard to each their influence on Assyria is marked. Haldian nationals appear in Assyrian contracts as early as the reign of Sargon, and Haldia is often invoked in names otherwise good Assyrian.

In architecture we have frequent references to the *"bit hilani,"* admittedly "Hittite," but we have seen some reason to suspect that it may really be something like a Greek temple. Greek wares appear within the limits of the empire, especially on the Philistine plain, the Greeks of Cyprus were in close touch with the kings, at times they successfully contended with the Phœnicians for the foreign trade of Assyria, their metalwork and ceramics show pronounced traces of Assyrian influences. A Greek Ionian adventurer appeared in Philistia as leader of the anti-Assyrian party.

Early warfare brought the Assyrians into contact with the peoples of Asia Minor, a small part of the peninsula was nearly always Assyrian. A considerable number of the "Hittite" states which had survived the fall of the great Hittite empire still retained much of that peculiar culture in north Syria and northwest Mesopotamia; how this mixed with the Assyrian may be seen in the remains from Carchemish. Reports of warlike and diplomatic relations with the more-distant states of Asia Minor, Phrygia and Lydia, are stressed by the discovery of similarities in the archæological finds.

Mention should be certainly made of the influence of the incoming Iranians on the northeast border. Many of their peoples were found within the Assyrian frontiers, some as subjects, others as slaves; towards the end they became valued allies, worthy of intermarriage with the royal family. Like the Hebrews, in this period they gave little to international culture, but they were showing themselves admirable students of what they saw.

Brief though this survey be, it should suffice to refute the suggestion that Assyrian culture was the immediate and unchanged successor of the Babylonian. The truth is that it was highly complex in origin, to a degree greater than any-thing previously met in the world's history. To the peaceful interchange of commodities in trade, of new processes in tech-nology or new animals and plants for the agriculturist, there was added the mingling of objects taken in war or brought in as tribute, until the palaces of the Assyrian capitals became veritable technological museums. Predatory nobles might scorn the lessons to be learned, there were many artisans at-tracted to the centres who would be less inclined to pass them by. The one-sided nature of our sources does not permit us to speak with equal certainty of the mingling of thought, but we may be sure that the Hebrews did not stand alone in this respect. While the court borrowed more and more of Baby-lonian magic, and the intellect seemed to be ever more Baby-lonianised, great circles of thought outside Nineveh were de-veloping along more eclectic lines.

The final touch was given by the system of deportation practised by the government. Political effects aside, the social consequences were far-reaching, and endured long after the memory of the Assyrians had become legendary. When ruling class and commercial leaders, when prophets and intellectuals were violently removed to what seemed the opposite ends of the earth, nationalism was effectively blotted out, and with it went the chief support of a narrowly local culture. Old customs, even to the older languages, might remain in the ob-scure instincts of the silent masses; in spite of themselves the intelligent classes were welded into one international society. It was the revenge of history that other languages, Aramaic and Arabic, other civilisations, Persian, Hellenistic, Muslim, were to be the heirs of this cosmopolitan culture.

CHAPTER XL

THE ASSYRIAN MANOR

AGRICULTURE was the basal Assyrian industry. As with the Romans, there was always a certain taint associated with business, which, as a consequence, was generally abandoned to foreigners; agriculture shared with war and administration the roster of activities fit for the world masters. To a degree quite unusual in most periods of history, the Assyrians recognised the vital relation which exists between the land and civilisation, the need of food and of other agricultural products for the successful extension of empire, the importance of a reservoir of seasoned farm laborers who might be inducted into the army. While, therefore, the business records preserved in the royal archives are of a highly specialised character and whole categories of business activity are lacking, agriculture is well represented.

Behind the Assyrian, and not far behind, was his nomad life. How deeply he was influenced by this phase of his past we have had repeated opportunity to realise from his detailed history. His earliest settled home was on the edge of the steppe, and ancestry and environment alike tended to make much of his wealth lie in his flocks and herds. At his doors were broad expanses of grasslands whose lack of water prohibited a regular agriculture but invited grazing. The prairies were dotted by his big, heavy-fleeced, fat-tailed sheep, or his equally large and well-covered goats, who were guarded by half-savage shepherds clad in sheepskins against the blazing sun of summer when all the landscape was a mist of finely blowing silt or against the chilling wind of winter which swept the level expanses from the snow mountains of the not-far-distant north. They were assisted by their faithful dogs, half mastiff in breed, and scarcely less savage than their masters, who did not hesitate, if the occasion appeared propitious, to murder those who might testify to their thefts. From these flocks, the nobles obtained their rare meat meal, mutton, and the material for their woollen clothes. Each of the high officials had his individual flock; one in particular belonged to Esarhaddon while crown prince. Sheep are numerous in the Harran census, with as many as one hundred and eighty-eight to one shepherd, but goats are rare.

Ashur was not all rough hill or arid steppe. Before the city lay a small but fertile plain which was continued by the narrow bottomlands along each side of the Tigris. The agriculturist soon moved to the west, to the fertile stretch of country south of the Singara hills; east of the Tigris the rolling Assyrian Triangle afforded a more diversified cultivation, Mesopotamia and its extension in north Syria furnished broad prairies where great estates might develop.

Fortunately for Assyria, its land system was not modelled on that of Egypt, with its almost total absence of property held in freehold, but on that of Babylonia. Whether the Shumerians recognised any farm land which was not controlled by the god, either through his vicegerent on earth, the patesi, or through the temple, is not clear, but with the first appearance of a Semitic kingdom we find freehold in full use; Manishtusu, king of the great Sargonid dynasty as he was, might not challenge the right of the common people to their lands but must pay in full their value or substitute other lands in exchange.

Much the same feeling is found in Assyria, and the later Sargon could secure the site for his projected city only by these same means, purchase or exchange. We are not dealing with the subjects of an all-embracing state who have no personal rights save as they receive them from an all-powerful sovereign, but with a definite farming group which can in a sense be called middle class, however closely it may have been limited to the members of the ruling race.

There was indeed a theory, still common in the Near East, that the land was the personal property of the monarch and that those who tilled it were likewise his possession. In actual practice, a very considerable part of the arable land consisted of crown land, "king's estate." Land was also attached to the various offices in the imperial administration; for instance, the Harran census shows land belonging to four provincial governors, to the commander-in-chief, the chief judge, the ner of the land, and the abarakkus of the crown prince and of the Ashur temple. Such estates belonged to the office and not to the individual who at the moment happened to hold the office in question.

On the other hand, a very considerable portion of the land was less subject to the state than is ordinary freehold property to-day. During the chaos in Babylonia which resulted from the coming in of the Kashshites, there had developed a condition which can only be called feudal in the narrower sense of the word. To retain the support of the great chiefs who accompanied them into the alluvium, the weak Kashshite kings granted huge tracts of land and fortified those grants with immunities from taxation and from public service which made each feudal domain almost an independent state. To protect rights often taken by force from the older inhabitants and always subject to encroachment when a given monarch was a little stronger and anxious to reassert the central power, the nobles prepared boundary stones, containing the texts of the charters inscribed upon them, and under the symbols of the gods who were invoked in the elaborate curses which ended the document. Their primary value in the present investigation is in the long lists of exemptions that show the dues ordinarily inflicted upon the land.

The charter was borrowed by the Assyrians, and we have a considerable number dating from 793 to the end of the empire. In external appearance they differ from those of Babylonia, in that they are never written on stones nor do they contain the symbols of the gods under whose protection the deed is placed. Royal self-praise equally begins them, and the conclusion with its appeal to the gods has some likeness to the much more elaborate cursing of the Babylonian models.

It is significant that the first Assyrian imitations of the

Kashshite charter date from the period when a breakdown of the central power was already under way. The closest approach is to be found in the stele of Bel Harran-bel-usur, but his demotion at the hands of Tiglath Pileser III showed that the style was not to be repeated;[1] the best known is the one dealing with the expropriation by Sargon of the lands which were to become Dur Sharrukin.

More typical would be the charter granted by Ashur-bani-apal to Baltaia: "The fields, gardens, and serfs, which he has secured under my protection, and has made his own estate, have I freed and written down, with my royal seal have I sealed it, and to Baltaia have I given it. As to those fields and gardens, no grain tax shall be collected, no straw tax shall be required, seizure of herds and flocks shall not be made, dues, corvee, levy, shall not be made on those fields. From dock and ferry tolls it shall be free, no hides shall be given."[2]

Occasionally, the letters afford a glimpse of the operation. Amel Nabu, for example, reminds the king that he has said: "Come, plant a harvest, gather for thyself fulness and in my protection enjoy it." Let a king's messenger come and view his father's land which the king returned to him; how Mannu-ki Raman has made it to go to ruin! He has refused to give the grain and straw, he even asserts: "For thy seed there is no grain." Sharru-naid wishes to rescue his paternal estates from the chief butler who has seized them; he has been to the "house of the records," but only the king or the crown prince has authority to order their return. Such letters illustrate the back flow to the king through change of dynasty, confiscation, lapse of time, lack of issue, or usurpation by officials.[3]

No mention is made of tilled land in central or southern Syria, Asia Minor, Armenia, or Babylonia. The absence of the last from the royal archives is naturally to be explained by the preservation of these records in Babylonian cities; the other territories were on the borders where the Assyrian land system had not subverted the ones in local use.

Worthy of special notice is the large amount of land in Meso-

[1] Cf. pp. 168 ff., 203.   [2] J. 647.   [3] H. 925; 152.

potamia with its Aramaic population.   The Harran census
confirms what we observe from the many sanctions in the
documents by the Sin of Harran, that there were many more
fertile fields in this region than there are to-day.   In addition
to Harran itself, we hear of three centres which had possessed
kings in the days of Shalmaneser III, Sarugi, the Biblical Serug,
Balihi on the river of that name, and Til Abni, in the west
Mesopotamian steppe.

A whole group of private records come from Kannu, which
some have thought a transplanted Canaan, since Israelites were
settled in this portion of Mesopotamia.   The god of these
settlers is Apil Addi, the son of the west Semitic Adad, and
not Yahweh; since other documents in the group assign the
penalty for breach of contract to Sin of Harran, they must
belong to the same population as that dealt with by the Harran census.

North Syria was in many respects the continuation of the
Mesopotamian plain and here too we have the evidence for
the great estates.   Once grain paid for in Nineveh is to follow
the standard of Iaudi land, that north Syrian Judah whose
king Azariah was once confused with the Biblical Judæan.[1]
A whole "city" in the province of Arpad is sold, and it was
bounded by Neribi or Nerab, from which has come an important Aramaic stele.   Included were fifteen hundred fruit-trees,
a vegetable garden, and six souls.

Lands dedicated to the service of religion formed the most
important single category.   They never ceased to grow in
amount and no deduction might be rightfully made from them.
Yet the temples never had the position in Assyria that they
held in Babylonia, for Assyrian kings never permitted the
priesthood to assume too much power; indeed, our fullest
knowledge of the grants made to religious houses comes from
the royal annals.

As early as the first Shalmaneser, the king is found restoring the cult and the free-will offerings, increasing the slaughtered sacrifices, and the showbread for all the gods.   Otherwise

[1] Cf. pp. 184 ff.

expressed, this means the possession of the lands to furnish the needful supplies. Tukulti Urta I established the daily offerings in kind for his new city. On his visit to Babylon, Shalmaneser III granted sacrifices and free-will offerings in Esagila, its chief temple. When Sargon conquered the chiefs of the Uknu region, the "seizure" of the cattle and sheep went to Bel Marduk, lord of Babylon, and to his son, Nabu of Borsippa. Sennacherib ordered the Hirimme to pay their first-fruits of sheep, wine, and dates to the gods of Assyria eternally.[1]

Property held by the temples was, as a rule, freed from other burdens. Manifestly, its occupants were able to make an added profit, since prices would be set by those lands which paid the heaviest taxes and still remained in cultivation. But while the economic supremacy of the temple was secured by the religious fear and reverence of the commons, the king and his officials did not suffer from the same scruples. Even though there was not felt the need of quite so elaborate a curse as was demanded in Babylonia, every charter closes with the words: "If a king or a prince shall change the contents of this docu-ments, may Ashur" and the usual list of gods "curse him." The royal inscriptions are full of the restorations of the vari-ous temple dues and offerings, but they are eloquently silent when their royal authors take them away. No man appears more religious than Sargon. For the good of his soul he granted an estate to Sin of Harran; it is only through his great-grandson that we discover how he revoked the grant and great suffering was brought upon his people.[2]

Nor did king and high official hesitate to extort forced loans from these ever-wealthy subjects. Ningal-iddina, for instance, "borrowed" a silver vessel of fifteen pounds weight from the Nana temple in Agade when there was sudden need of money to drive back a threatened Elamite invasion. When Akkul-lanu was beginning to reorganise Ashur after the troubles incident to the accession of Esarhaddon, he found that a goodly proportion of the most important provinces had neglected to

[1] Cf. pp. 122, 252, 288.   [2] Cf. pp. 289, 495.

send in the "perpetual ordinances of customary dues" belonging to the god Ashur.[1]

Our first reference to regular taxes comes from the reign of Tukulti Urta I, who inflicted upon the conquered peoples tribute and present. With Tiglath Pileser I, we have tribute and gift, the regular terms for the remainder of the history; it included vessels and slaves, flocks and herds, and was to be yearly carried to the city of Ashur and into the royal presence. Ashur-nasir-apal established governors and vassalage in the conquered lands, service and forced labour he laid upon them, and overseers, that is, subgovernors, were appointed to collect taxes. As equivalent for regular taxes, we have horses, silver, gold, grain, and straw. What is meant by forced labour is shown in the construction of his city of Kalhu, which was built, not by captive slaves, but by the work of the lower classes in the countries conquered. Forced labour of this type does not appear in the royal annals after 880, and there is no mention of it in the detailed tribute list of Syria furnished by Shalmaneser III.[2]

Thus far we have been given information only as to what was enforced upon the conquered peoples. That the Assyrians were no better off is proved by the passage where Tiglath Pileser III, in speaking of the Median tribes settled in Syria, informs us that the dues and corvee were imposed upon them as if they were Assyrian, and by a similar statement of Sargon as to tribute and tax. We actually have the "Assyrian corvee" placed upon the captives settled in Hilaku when it was made a province. The Uknu chiefs were to pay a yearly gift, silver and five per cent of their cattle and sheep; this appears to be identical with the "seizure" of cattle and sheep which was to go to Marduk and Nabu.[3]

Various agricultural taxes—grain, straw, seizure of herds and flocks, dues, corvee, levy or palace levy, dock, ferry, ship, door, gate dues—are briefly listed in the charters; we have the impression that the Assyrians at home were sufficiently taxed. Added details come from the business records. Since we are

[1] J. 930; H. 43; cf. p. 343.   [2] Cf. pp. 66 ff., 97.   [3] Cf. pp. 172, 252.

largely dealing with lands belonging to the inner circle at court, we frequently hear of estates which are free, "the grain tax he shall not collect, the dues shall not go to his city," "it is free, without straw requisition." These are the two chief taxes, the former on that which can be plucked, the latter on what can be trodden down. The two taxes did not go together, for in one example a tenth of the property came under the first and a fourth under the second. In case the lands are not free, these taxes are regularly paid according to those imposed upon the nearby city.

Like the Romans, the Assyrians realised that the only sound basis for taxation is a census, and we have much evidence that the rulers made a careful check on both men and their products. One letter shows the king ordering an official to set down in writing the names of the free-born citizens, doubtless for the purpose of exemption. Ina-sharri-bel-allak has to report that he went out from Shabrishu to meet the men and the large cattle they were bringing from the city of Guzana. He was fortunate and met them, he made them take shelter and inspected them on the spot. The kalak boatman lacked three souls, the gardener three, another four, a total of fifteen was lacking according to his tablet. He therefore sent one of the guardsmen for the remainder.[1]

Many tablets from an actual census taken of the cultivators of the rich lands around Harran have come down to us.[2] The tablets are in sections, each of which deals with one family group. Usually the father is named, so that it would appear that the holding is hereditary. Then follows the status of this head of the family, whether irrigator, husbandman, vigniard, shepherd; his sons are listed by name, his daughters are counted, generally there is but one wife. The number of slaves is given and then his holdings in *imers*, that is, the amount of soil which can be sown with an ass load of seed. The average holding is something over twenty *imers*, with an extreme range from twelve to a hundred. Part of the census covers a town,

---

[1] *H.* 900; 167.
[2] Johns, *Assyrian Doomsday Book.*

as copper and iron smiths occur who possess houses but no fields.

Serfs are regularly mentioned by name in the sale of the lands and in the same sentence with the flocks and herds. No special word is used to distinguish them from slaves, though their father's name is generally added, that of the slave almost never. Elsewhere they are called *mushkenu*. Like the serf of mediæval Europe, they could not leave the land or change their master, but they could and often did buy additional land, stock, or equipment. They probably paid a third of their income to their master.

Government's hand lay heavily on the serf. Aside from the payments in kind, there were certain specific and rather onerous duties to perform. The military basis for the whole organisation comes out most clearly; many of the settlements may be compared to those of the Roman coloni. A town of the Gambulu, "booty" of that land, "all whom I settled there," appears in the Harran census, and a considerable percentage of the men enumerated are still "empty," that is, unassigned to lands. We have also individuals from the fugitives whom Nabu-ahe-shallim brought. Once, when the Mannai were hostile, a Mannai town was settled. The Ituai, originally an Aramæan tribe south of Ashur, after their conquest were formed into a fighting unit. Four of these Ituai, two with Babylonian, two with Assyrian names, sell a field in the Goldsmith's City in 744; the land is "under guard," that is, it owes military service. Lushakin has a perfectly Assyrian name, but his father was the Egyptian Absheshu, and the land he holds must have been assigned him when he was taken from Egypt in the days of Esarhaddon.

By the time our documents become available, the military unit was the pair made up of the bowman and the shield-bearer. The unit of land for those to whom it was assigned on military tenure was the "bow," for which a military unit was to be furnished. For example, the Sute tribe settled in Til Garimmu in Asia Minor by Sargon were not merely to pay the dues and the corvee as the natives among whom they were settled, they were to be "men of the bow" under the supervision of the provincial governor.[1]

A peculiar feature of this military service seems to be its almost exclusively agrarian character. Imperial free cities were freed from all military service; it looks as if the Assyrian rulers contemptuously excluded shopkeepers as unfit for the arduous service of the army. The force thus secured, the "people," corresponded somewhat closely to the fird of Anglo-Saxon times. The process was entitled "calling out the fird," or "calling out the land fird." Slave and peasant alike bore the obligation; slave sales regularly note that the slave has served his time for government.

Serf and slave must in addition serve the state in an economic way. Peasants must work the crown lands, and one of the most serious complaints lodged against Shalmaneser V by Sargon is that he forced the citizens of the free city of Ashur to labour as peasants.[2] Canal up-keep was through the corvee and fell upon the abutting owners. References to "task-work" fill the letters, though the term is likewise used for religious ceremonies. In the provinces, at least, it seems to have consisted of almost anything that the official in charge might demand; some letters inform the monarch that the "task-work" is being properly carried on, others indicate the reverse, and the labourers themselves declare "the task-work is heavy, heavy upon us."

Daughters of the peasant's family and female slaves were subject likewise to a service, "king's maidship." There is reason to assume that this time was spent in the great weaving establishments, for one group of documents deals with the amount of wool assigned to the various cities for working up.

As a rule, the serfs must have been extremely poor, not far from the limits of subsistence. Many were "empty" men, without even a plot of soil to cultivate, dependent on the need for seasonal labour as at the harvest. A distinct tendency to check population may be noted; the Harran census shows small families, the largest of eight, and as against one hundred and

[1] Cf. p. 225.   [2] Cf. p. 206.

sixty-six adults in the entire list preserved, there are but one hundred and three children. Such a proportion was too small even to keep the population to its present number.

Constant need of assistance from the landlord resulted in a system something like our working of the farm on shares. Among the documents in the royal archives, the largest single group consists of the so-called "loans." The first party to the transaction is the owner of the estate, who advances to his tenant silver or bronze, that is, money, or grain, oil, wine, or cattle. In general, the advance is made until after the harvest, or, rather, it is intended to finance harvesting, furnish food for the day-labourers, secure animals for the work.

In all ages and throughout all countries, not excepting our own, the greatest problem of the farmer has been the securing of loans for his seasonal necessities without recourse to the usurer. With strangely enlightened self-interest, the Assyrian landlord saved his tenant from this fate. Nor was this action taken to enslave the peasant to himself, for he went so far that he refused to accept interest at all if the loan was paid at maturity. Only the negligent and slothful, who did not pay when the harvest was first in, were charged interest; then it was generally twenty-five per cent for money loaned and fifty for grain. This appears most oppressive to us, but it was simply the ordinary rate of interest in the open money market, and indeed some of the loans expressly state that if it is not repaid by harvest the interest shall be the current rate in Nineveh. In the case of the grain, at least, the landlord actually lost money, for he made his loan when grain was dear and received it back when it was at its cheapest.

"Den of lions" as hostile contemporaries called Assyria, its fall worked unmitigated harm to the poor peasant. Although Babylonia was exceptionally an agricultural country, the "business men" of the alluvium were far less in sympathetic touch with the peasant than the Assyrian nobles. Blind to the fundamental nature of agriculture and to the necessity of a prosperous farmer class as the basis of a state's prosperity, they demanded interest on all loans, and the usurer ruled the peasantry. The serf disappears as a separate class in the late Babylonian documents; the enslaved farmer might recall with regret the days when Assyrian nobles were more kind than merchants.

In the terminology of these documents, a "house" means an estate, while a house in our sense of the word is a "built house." Beams and doors are given special mention in the sale of a house; in Babylonia the door did not go with the house and was regularly provided by the lessee. Connected with the "house" were the sheepfolds, the bath-house, the store-room, the upper house, the breezy upper room of the Bible and of modern travel, and last, but still worthy of mention, the cemetery.

Wells are frequently referred to and are sometimes sold by themselves, but springs are never found in the region devoted to the great estates. Something like half the land of the Harran census was under irrigation. The larger machines were operated by two, four, six, or even eight oxen, and must have been much like those in use in Babylonia to-day. There was also a hand-machine with pole and leather buckets; this can only be the Egyptian shaduf, or well-sweep, introduced by Sennacherib and shown in his sculptures.[1] Distinction was made between the different grades of land, waste land, land cultivated but not enclosed, grain land, and irrigated land. The two-crop system was regularly followed, with the land cultivated one year and the next fallow to allow the return of fertility.

Already in the earliest Babylonian centuries, the plough is known; by the Assyrian period, it had become large and complicated, such as it appears in the tile-work at Dur Sharrukin or on a monument of Esarhaddon. It was regularly drawn by one or more oxen; both longhorns and shorthorns were known, but each had the hump which relates them to the sacred zebu of India. While in Egypt the hoe and plough were still evidently connected, the Assyrian hoe had become rather a pick. A sickle such as Ashur-nasir-apal carries was used to cut the grain, the straw was later gathered up, the

[1] Cf. p. 331.

threshing took place on the floor just outside the village. Animals usually trod out the grain, at times the spiked sled was employed, the chaff was winnowed away by throwing it upward into the breeze. Then, as now, barley was the chief cereal, so much so that it was called "grain" for short; split wheat, such as is broken up to-day for starch, was more valuable; at the top of the list stood real wheat. Durra was common and was actually found in a tomb at Ashur. Sesame was the usual oil, though it was not so much in evidence as in Babylonia; the olive of the Assyrian Triangle might not be of first-class quality—the mountains roundabout were well adapted to its culture.

These great estates did not stand alone, their relative importance is somewhat exaggerated by the fact that what we have preserved is the royal archive. References to gardens are not infrequent; sometimes they are sold with the great estates, sometimes separately. In Babylonia, the typical garden product is the date; while the fertilisation of the date-palm plays a large part on the palace reliefs, Assyria was too far north to bring the fruit to ripening and the vine took its place. Nearly all the gardens in the Harran census are planted with the vines, whose numbers on the various farms range from two thousand to twenty-nine thousand. One district has a total of two hundred and eighty-two thousand, another forty-one thousand.

A vegetable-garden in Nineveh is located before the old bridge, bordered by the Royal Road and the river and by the garden belonging to the god Nergal. The fertile strip of country south of the Singara range and watered by the little streams which run a short distance into the prairie is to-day dotted by tiny mounds where once stood a collection of farm dwellings. Two documents have survived to testify to their earlier life. One tells of a garden in the land of Singara with twenty-four hundred fruit-trees; in the other a garden in the land of Singara, in the "house" of the goddess Ishtar, is sold with a thousand fruit-trees, two *imers* in the midst have terebinths, six *imers* of low-lying ground are in grain, there is a garden of herbs, and all the boundaries consist of other gardens. The largest estate of this sort we find is of fifty *imers* with ten thousand fruit-trees, a canal of standing water, and with it goes a serf expert in the use of the watering-machine.

Riparian rights were of the utmost importance. In general, they seem to have been exercised by cities, for one landlord is informed: "Water from below his city he shall drink, yet the dues shall not be owed to his city." Yet a letter tells us that the banks of a river of water belong to the king, they flow only for himself, they are not free.[1]

What might be expected in these gardens is shown by a tablet which gives a list of the plants grown in the garden of Merodach Baladan. Not all the names can be identified and doubtless some of the plants were rarities at that time, as was the cotton cultivated by Sennacherib. Garlic naturally heads the list, for it has always contributed largely to the peculiar odor of an oriental city, and onions and the shallot are a close second. Lettuce, cress, dill, cardamon, the precious saffron, hyssop, coriander, thyme, assafœtida furnish the typical oriental garden. Beets, turnips, radishes, cucumbers are familiar to us of to-day. Alfalfa is a great surprise; it appears as *aspastu*, a good Iranian word meaning "horse fodder," and shows that their chief food on the Iranian plateau had followed the horses into the Fertile Crescent.[2] Licorice, now exported to adulterate American tobacco, chicory, also well known as an adulterant, poppies, standing for the idea of fruitfulness rather than for sleep, cummin and cassia, these are some of the additional plants we might mention.

Some of these gardens belong to small owners, and freeholds of a purely agricultural character seem likewise to have existed. These last, however, can be traced only in the vicinity of cities which have been granted special rights; in fact, it is extremely doubtful whether any but citizens of an imperial free city possessed actual freehold.

[1] *H.* 154.
[2] List, Meissner, *ZA.*, VI, 291 ff.; latest discussion of plant migration, B. Laufer, *Sino-Iranica*, 1919.

As the Assyrian empire extended, it took in the foot-hills of the mountains, the chains to the east along the present Persian border, those on the slopes of the Armenian barrier, or the fertile western hillsides of Syria and Palestine. The mountains bred a hardy race, little fitted to be serfs, while the narrow valleys did not encourage the formation of extensive estates. A single reference in the documents is to a garden with a thousand fruit-trees and a stone wall. On these sunny slopes flourished the vine, such as furnished the drinks for the famous wine-card of Nebuchadnezzar. Syria and Palestine cultivated the fig, and above all the olive; so much so that the agriculture of those lands has been called an olive culture.

Even in the hills of distant Palestine, the advance of civilisation was producing its inevitable effect, that adding field to field which the Hebrew Amos so strongly condemned.[1] In so far as it was successful, it tended to break down the sturdy population of the country and to send them to the city slums. But the Assyrian empire never was urban in the sense that later civilisations have become. Assyria always provided her own food, and for many centuries her best soldiers came from these same farms.

[1] Cf. p. 170.

CHAPTER XLI

THE IMPERIAL FREE CITY

"POLITICAL freedom first appears with the Greek city-state," is a dictum repeated in all the manuals of government. The truth is that in many respects the typical Greek city-state was only a small and late approximation to the mighty cities which had set the pace in the preceding centuries in the mighty Assyrian empire. While the mass of the Assyrians—natives, conquered provincials, or deported settlers—were serfs and suffered all the disadvantages of serfdom, the cities were the centres of a very respectable freedom which was of a respectable antiquity.

City-states appear in the earliest Babylonian history and continue to be the units of organisation to the end. Ashur likewise began its career as a city-state, and this form of government left its traces throughout the whole history of the imperial organisation. So long as the only town of first-class importance was that which gave its name to the state, there was no need of special privilege to the city as such, and after more than one city had been conquered, the king-god and his deputy on earth might still be considered as separate monarch of each. With closer centralisation and co-ordination, the cities came to be considered separate identities, and there arose the problem of handling them to the best advantage of the state. It was then there developed that distinction between citizens of the state as a whole and the citizens of one particular municipality; for the first time the townsmen began to be granted charters with clearly defined special privileges. From the local nobility was chosen a council of elders who possessed very wide administrative and judicial powers; the merchants under a chief also played a large part in state affairs.

Imperial free cities in Assyria represent the attempt to meet the problem of handling the Babylonian cities, with their long histories, their local jealousies, their high cultures, their more developed economic life. Such cities of a privileged character are first referred to in connection with the expedition of Shalmaneser III to Babylon, which is called by the king the "Bond of Heaven and Earth, the Abode of Life." Sacrifices and freewill offerings are assigned its temple Esagila—that is nothing new—but gifts are likewise dedicated to the men of Babylon and Borsippa, who are called "men of privilege," "protégés of the great gods." The term "privilege," in its different forms, is the distinguishing appellation of the imperial free city.[1]

Tiglath Pileser III equally guarded the "privileges" of Babylon and established the income of Esagila and Ezida, but his son Shalmaneser V was of a different mind. Sargon is the first to speak of similar rights in Assyria, but he implies that they had long been recognised. Although it was a city under protection, an ancient and exalted city, which Ashur had made famous among the world regions, the "Bond of the Lands," the old title of Babylon, it had no rival; from of old its citizens had known neither due nor corvee; Shalmaneser had harshly treated Ashur and had forced its citizens to execute the corvee as if they had been peasants. When Sargon took his place, he extended their freedom from taxation, from the land levy, from the summons of the recruiting officer, from quay and bridge dues. All the temples of the land were freed. A silver tablet was inscribed with the "privileges" granted to the city and placed before the cult image of Ashur. The "freedom" of Ashur and Harran, which from distant days had fallen into desuetude, was restored and the neglected "privileges" were collected and returned to their places. Sargon extended his protection over Harran and as the "man," in the strictly feudal sense, of the gods Anu and Dagan, wrote their "freedom."[2]

After the recovery of Babylonia, Sargon restored the fields

[1] Cf. p. 122. [2] Cf. p. 206.

occupied by the nomads to the citizens of the alluvium cities, established Ur, Uruk, Eridu, Larsa, Kissik, and Nimid Laguda, returned the captive gods, renewed their "autonomy," and restored the fixed offerings which had fallen into disuse. He seems to have divided the cities into classes. For Sippar, Nippur, Babylon, and Borsippa, he made restoration, to the "men of privilege" he made good their losses, established their position as "protégés," protected their weakness. Der, Ur, Uruk, Eridu, Larsa, Kissik, Zarilab, Nimid Laguda were given back the fields taken by the Sute, their disused fixed offerings were restored, their "autonomy" was established, they were freed from dues, their men were reconciled.[1]

What this "freedom" consisted in best appears in one of the building inscriptions of Esarhaddon. Citizens of Babylon are "men with definite duties," as compared with serfs whose duties were not definitely defined and so were liable to all. They are "men under protection" and "protégés" of the gods Anu and Bel, they possess "autonomy." Esarhaddon restored their "privileges" and rewrote the "tablet of their freedom." The economic consequences of this "freedom" are especially indicated. To the four winds, that is, to all corners of the empire, he opened their trade routes, they might carry on business with lands of every speech.[2]

Most illuminating is the letter from the citizens of Babylon which protests the murder of one of their number to the brother kings. It is true that from their accession, their lords have protected their chartered rights, and have guaranteed protection to all the foreigners who enter to till their fields. Especially have the present rulers increased their chartered rights so that even the women of Babylon have protection.[3]

Best proof of the importance of these imperial free cities is the effort of the various monarchs to conciliate and win over their inhabitants. Grants of rights to Ashur and Harran, pavement of a new street in Babylon by Sennacherib, the rebuilding of Babylon by Esarhaddon, many a case where we see only a religious dedication, a renewed temple, is in

[1] Cf. p. 256.   [2] Cf. p. 349.   [3] H. 878; cf. p. 432.

reality a concession to citizen pride, for no mediæval city looked more proudly and more jealously after its miracle-working shrine or its cathedral than did these Babylonian and Assyrian burghers.

We instinctively seek to compare these free cities with the city-states of Greece, for they were nearly contemporary. Urban economics were as highly developed in Babylonia or in Phœnicia as they were in the earlier Greece. Such a city would be at least as populous as the average Greek city and its trade relations far more complex. The Greek city, then, is no isolated phenomenon; it must be considered in the light of its environment and of its rivals.

Nor should we stress the matter of political freedom in the comparison. Babylon had slaves, it is true, but not all the apologists for Greek democracy can conceal the fact that Athens rested largely on a servile foundation. Serfs tilled the fields around the urban centres; the evidence does not show their lot to have been as bad as that of the serf population in some portions of Greece. If the Babylonian term *mushkenu* is the ancestor of the French *mesquin*, the word helot has a still uglier meaning. Democracy, even in the days of Cleon, gave political rights to barely a tenth of the population actually settled in Attica, nor did this political liberty much improve the economic position of the day-labourer; the majority of Greek states had in every century much the same aristocratic constitution based on wealth that was to be found in the merchant cities of Babylon, Nineveh, or Tyre. The metic was no new fact in Greece; in Babylon the resident alien was admitted by special charter and his rights were carefully guarded. Not alone the fact that the checker-board system of street planning was usual fifteen hundred years before it was introduced into the Piræus proves Babylon first in city development.

Perhaps the comparison is not entirely to the point. Babylon and Nineveh and Tyre have less in common with the rather lawless Greek or mediæval Italian city-state; closer analogies will be found with the more sober free states of the north, themselves an admitted part of a great empire which claimed universal dominion.

A surprisingly large amount of self-rule for the cities is indicated by the letters. Often the governor sent from Assyria turns out to be a local notable, decorated by an Assyrian title. The real ruler is the council of elders. Often they write in complaint of their nominal ruler, and their complaint is always treated with respect; not infrequently the monarch takes their side as against his own representative. In case of rebellion, appeal is made to the citizens, they are held responsible for the escape of a rebel, they remain loyal to the Assyrians even after their Assyrian governor has fallen away.[1]

A striking difference between the free town of antiquity and the modern municipality is that citizen territory did not end with the walls. Legally within the municipality was a large amount of arable land, and some of the most highly prized rights of the burghers consisted of this freedom from the ordinary land taxes. Thus the citizens were landholders, if not land-tillers, as well as traders and artisans.

In the case of the typical Greek city, there was a constant tendency for the farming population to move to the urban centre, and soon the citizens found it necessary to import food from abroad. Thus the typical Greek state was ill balanced, at the mercy of foes who controlled the sea, and the food problem often furnished the chief matter for dispute in local politics. The Assyrian city possessed land in sufficient quantity to make for safety in war and balanced development in peace; those of Babylonia lay under the constant menace of the Aramæans. Assyrian control of the alluvium was intermittent, and whenever there came a lapse, the nomads had the habit of occupying citizen fields. The annals are therefore full of the restoration of fields to citizen owners whenever Assyrian control was assured. It need hardly be added that the generality of citizens were pro-Assyrian, the Aramæans as a rule in opposition.[2]

Alexander the Great was not the first ruler to found cities bearing his name. The first Shalmaneser wears with special

[1] Cf. pp. 442, 445, 447, 455, 465.   [2] Cf. pp. 122, 175, 251.

pride the title "Founder of Cities," and every ruler of importance followed in his footsteps. Foundation of a city already in existence sometimes had no special significance, as when Til Barsip ceased to be the capital of the independent state of Adini and as "Shalmaneser's Town" became the capital of the same territory, formed now into an Assyrian province.[1]

Foundations among the barbarians told a different story. In particular the provincial capital saw a much more complex life than the mountaineers had realised could exist, and the demands of the governors for something more of the comforts of life enjoyed at home raised the ideals of the local magnates. Doubtless the mountaineers were far less happy than in the days of wild independence, when they could rob and kill each other according to all the rules of the game, but however we may sympathise at heart with these picturesque bandits, reason assures us that it was much better that they should be within the domain of the Assyrian peace.

In exchange for their liberty, they now suffered taxation and forced labour; they also had improved methods of agriculture, better food, even for the poorest. For the higher classes, there were luxuries and the introduction of better technical methods or at least use of products thus manufactured. The wants of the governor, of his staff, of his resident troops, led to the flocking in of traders who in turn demanded the service of natives to care for them in various ways. Thus there rapidly grew up towns of some size, and more than one important city of later fame began its civilised career in just this manner.

Tarsus, the city of St. Paul, seems actually to owe its victory over its predecessor Mallus to its foundation by Shalmaneser III. Nisibis, for years the rail-head of the Baghdad Railroad, prepared for its refoundation as an Antioch and for its temple of the Roman Severus as a chief Assyrian provincial capital. The "Wall of Ashur-nasir-apal" and the "Watch of Ashur" at the narrows of the Euphrates paved the way

[1] Cf. p. 119.

for the Palmyrene outpost which immortalised the name of Zenobia, where the Arab middle ages knew the magnificent fortresses of Halebieh and Zelebieh.[1]

In the foundation of the various Alexandrias, Antiochs, Seleucias, and the like, we are told that Alexander and his successors set up the ideal of the city as opposed to the typical village life of the Orient. Village life is not exactly the term we should employ when dealing with an empire containing such cities as Nineveh and Babylon, and it is doubtful if, for example, the Antioch in Mygdonia was larger than its predecessor a few miles away, Nasibina. Study of the map of the provincial organisation with its dozens of provincial capitals, the casual references in letter and business document, point to an urban population as great as we may assume for the Hellenistic period. Seleucia, we may be sure, had little to improve on its predecessor Babylon, and its aristocratic constitution and its council of elders find their analogy more closely in Babylon than in Athens.

The term "economically free" can be truly applied to cities which possessed charters such as we have studied, and indeed the economic life of the empire centred in her free cities. Assyria was in truth no "nation of shopkeepers," and her ruling class cared as little for "business" as did the Roman. It is not entirely an accident that while tablets recording business transactions have been found in Babylonia, literally by the hundreds of thousands, Nineveh has furnished less than a thousand which are narrowly devoted to business, and, at that, half are concerned with agriculture. Doubtless the few private documents hitherto found will be largely increased, especially when the material from Ashur is published, but we can predict that the difference will remain. The categories of business transactions not represented by a single example from the palace archives are the most eloquent witnesses to the limitations of purely Assyrian economics.

Little though the Assyrians were interested in such matters as production, trade, commerce, as warriors and administrators

[1] Cf. pp. 144, 80, 93.

they could not ignore them. War had a decidedly economic basis; successful war paid, through the collection of tribute and spoil, especially if no account were taken of the lives lost in the fighting. In the same way, it paid to administer provinces which gave a large portion of their income to support the palace. We should not be oversevere on the Assyrian imperialist, for his rule meant peace, and the provinces within the borders of the empire might well feel that complete cessation of war, and the fact that there was but one distant court to support was compensation for taxes and loss of independence. Patriots might talk rebellion, business men were warmly pro-Assyrian.

The Assyrians themselves might despise trade and industry, there were others within the empire who did not. Their rulers might think of the empire as a political organism only, the subject nations soon learned to conceive of it as an economic unity, to realise how advantageous it was to live within a single frontier and under the protection of its armies. All the routes traversed by Assyrian armies had already been followed by caravans, and when they were protected by Assyrian patrols, more caravans might be expected.

Babylonian merchants had long since ceased to be content with a commerce which was confined to the alluvium, and already the great lawgiver Hammurabi had made special provisions for the case where the capitalist sent his agent to deal with less-civilised tribes, where robbery was in most matter-of-course fashion assumed as part of the risk. This trading instinct had been strongly reinforced by the Aramæans, who took none too kindly to the settled life of the village, and soon translated their desert nomadism into the scarcely less-nomadic life of the wandering peddler. By the end of our period, trade in the interior had largely fallen into their hands.

Babylonians, Assyrians, Aramæans, none of these cared for the sea. While there was no little river-borne commerce within the empire, no trading fleets, so far as we have evidence, were to be found on the Persian Gulf. If there was intercourse with India and the Far East at this early date, it must have been overland and not by the sea.

With the Mediterranean, the case was different. From the earliest recorded history, Egyptian and Cretan ships had moved from port to port of the tideless sea. The Old Empire in Egypt already knew of "Byblus ships," so called from the earliest coast city in Phœnicia, and when these maritime states declined, somewhat before the beginning of the first pre-Christian millennium, the Phœnicians took their place. By the time the Assyrian armies brought the Syrian seaboard within the Assyrian sphere, Phœnicia had secured the definite control of the sea.

The Phœnicians have been called craven because they regularly paid tribute instead of fighting. It all lies in the point of view. An accusation of cowardice can hardly be levelled at the sailors who explored the boundless Atlantic in mere skiffs, and more than one Assyrian king of kings could testify that the merchant princes of Tyre could put up a sufficiently stout resistance when they deemed it necessary. Such armed refusals were intended as a very specific warning that there was a definite financial limit beyond which the Phœnicians could not be coerced into paying more. Each time the lesson was enforced upon a new monarch and successfully.

A case in point is the treaty with Baal of Tyre. Evidently Esarhaddon had attempted to increase the tribute, for in the treaty Assyria expressly renounces any increase above that paid in the days of the last Shalmaneser, and that meant an actual loss, with the drop in the purchasing power of money. Never did the Phœnician look upon this payment as "tribute"—it was payment for value received, and in not a few cases, as the letter from the financial agent at Arvad shows, the clever traders gave the Assyrian officials decidedly the little end of the bargain.[1]

No argument would have been needed to convert the business men of the ancient Orient to the mercantile theory; to them the basis of all wealth was to be found in the precious metals. No ore deposits existed within the limits of the original Assyria, still less did they in Babylonia, and a very real motive for the struggles in which the Assyrians were engaged

[1] Cf. pp. 375, 417 f.

was the securing of such territory. Possibly a little gold was found in the edge of the Armenian mountains, though there is no proof that any was recovered in antiquity. No territory bearing gold on a large scale ever passed into Assyrian hands, and the nearest they came was in the brief interval they possessed the Nile valley, and thus the key to the upper Nile gold-fields.

Silver was another matter. Just north of the Cilician Gates were the silver-mines now called Bulghar Maden, the "Bulgarian Mines." Prehistoric implements in the most beautifully smoothed of greenstone indicate that they have been worked from almost unbelievably early times; a huge Hittite inscription where once the valley entrance was guarded by a high-set fortress shows that it was utilised in their days; the shipments from these mines made the glories of Mallus and of the Aleian plain when Homer wrote, and when their port was transferred to Tarsus, the ships of Tarshish became famed throughout the Mediterranean.

Shalmaneser III secured the outlet to this silver production when he brought Que under his rule, but it was soon lost. Tiglath Pileser III recovered it and penetrated within the Gates to the mines. With varying success, Sargon, Sennacherib, and Esarhaddon attempted to retain this wealth, but the invasions of fresh tribes from the north ended their efforts.[1] Elsewhere along the Armenian rim, silver might be mined but the veins were small and the returns meagre.

Copper was nearer home. Near the crest of the Armenian barrier range, not far beyond the sacred grottos of the west Tigris, were those mines of Arghana Maden which were so valuable a recourse to the Germans during the World War. They made the wealth of Alshe and Mitanni; Shalmaneser I founded a settlement to control this region, and thereafter every strong Assyrian monarch followed his example, but rarely with more than temporary success, for the Haldians knew their value quite as well and added a greater mountain valour to a higher metallurgical technic. Less-important cen-

[1] Cf. pp. 144, 189, 225, 311, 363.

tres of copper-mining were almost without exception too far within the Haldian border to allow even raiding.

After the stalemate between Sargon and Rusash, the Assyrians turned their attention to a second great source of supply, that island of Cyprus which has given its name to the metal among the western nations. Sargon, Esarhaddon, Ashur-bani-apal claim the vassalage of the chiefs of the island, and the first sent them his carved figure; at the best, he was able to secure a limited supply of the coveted copper at the price of trade privileges to the wide-awake Greeks. We may note the nest of copper implements found at the Gate of the Metal Worker in Ashur.[1]

Copper in its simple form is hard and intractable. We do not know when or where this was remedied by the use of a tenth part of tin, but the resulting artificial metal, bronze, marked a great advance in the use of the metals. It was comparatively easy to work, and the amount of metal in ordinary life increased apace. It was first being utilised on a large scale when Assyria made her first bid for empire, and the bronze sword of Adad-nirari I is one of our earliest examples. The old belief that the tin for the mixture was transported by the Phœnicians from the Cassiterides near Britain can hardly be accepted when we realise that tin is found along a band running diagonally from northwest to southeast through Persia and that this belt was, at the point north of Lake Urumia, within striking distance of Assyrian armies.

More than any other material factor, the use of iron by the Assyrians contributed to their conquest of the world. Iron was known, we can hardly say used, in very early times in Egypt, and the same seems proved true by the business documents of the Babylonians. It was first mined on a large scale by the peoples of Asia Minor, and it is with Hittite ascendancy that iron begins to be widely distributed. The rise of Assyria coincided with the development of the new metal, and the Assyrians were quick to see the advantage offered by its utilisation both in war and in peace. To what a degree the Assyrians

[1] Cf. pp. 226, 369.

had entered the iron age, the finds in Sargon's palace prove. Of iron alone can we say that a considerable territory belonged permanently within her limits. To the northeast of the Assyrian Triangle, in the mountain provinces which were formed in the ninth century, are numerous sites where the presence of iron has been detected. However, there is little proof that they were worked to any degree, and it remains probable that the chief source of iron was the southern shore of the Black Sea.

Other metals were little used by the Assyrians. Lead objects occur occasionally, but zinc and the mineral products more prized by the moderns—platinum, antimony, nickel, mercury, manganese, cobalt—were little regarded, and it goes without saying that the importance of the deposits which have turned the attention of present-day business men to the region, coal and above all petroleum, was not realised in antiquity.[1]

Much has been written, and truly enough, on the tremendous change which takes place in the life of a country when it transfers from the régime of natural commodities to one where money is in current use. As applied to the ancient Orient, it is essential fallacy to speak of a régime of natural economy because the economist does not find neatly rounded and milled bits of the precious metals like the coins of the present day. The moment, for instance, that the gur of barley was accepted as the standard of value, the merchant of earliest Babylonia could reckon in such terms and an artificial standard of accounting was established with the full set of ensuing consequences which produce a money economy as distinct from crude barter. This transition to a single standard was the easier because in early times barley was the single staple crop of Babylonia; the situation was exactly paralleled in colonial Virginia when the staple crop of tobacco became legal tender.

By the side of the barley standard, from the earliest cen-

---

[1] Cf. for brief discussion and complete further bibliography, *Geology of Mesopotamia and its Borderlands*, compiled by the Geographical Section of the Naval Intelligence Division, Naval Staff, Admiralty.

turies the precious metals and especially silver were used in weights. This habit in all probability runs back into Neolithic times when the glittering and very rare metals were first isolated. Their extreme scarcity made the precious metals a rather poor circulating medium; as in Virginia the staple crop formed the better standard for accounting.

Increased contact with the men of the mountains gradually increased the scanty store of silver in the alluvium until it was possible to weigh out small amounts in business exchanges where barley would have been too clumsy. Some fifteen hundred years before the supposed invention of coined money by the Lydians, bits of refined silver were stamped with the image or superscription of the god whose temple guaranteed their fineness. Some were in the form of bars or slivers of metal, the ancestors of the Greek obeliskoi or spits, in turn the ancestor of the tiny obol the Greek buyer carried in his mouth to market. Others were round, and so the ancestors of our coins of to-day.

These coins were of the same weights as had been dealt from the scale-pan, and the chief of them, the shekel, the "weight" par excellence, a sixtieth part of the pound, was carried over to the Greeks as the siglos. With the advance of these coins to the west went the weights of whose system they were a part. It is impossible here to cover the complicated story of how the Babylonian weights conquered Greece and the west; as a single illustration may be cited the evolution by which the mina became the Greek mna and the English pound.

Early Assyrians seem to have used lead for a cheaper money and copper is mentioned fairly often to the last century. Assyrian contracts frequently substitute for a given weight of silver what are called "Ishtar heads." They differ from the "Shamash heads" of the first dynasty of Babylon only in the name of the deity whose face or symbol appeared on the coins; they interest us more because in name they are the prototype of the Persian and Greek stater. The most striking testimony to the common use of coined money, because so casual, is where Sennacherib explains a new process of casting huge figures by saying that it was done as easily as if he were casting half-shekel pieces.[1]

We should expect to discover examples of coined money. A treasure-trove from Ashur, where it had been hidden in a jug, is what we have been expecting. Pieces of silver were cast and then cut roughly into bars, rings, and the like; there have also been found moulds for the precious metals in the form of stars, crescents, and various animals. None of these are inscribed, but we can imagine something of how they must have looked from a find at the northern Judah, bars of silver with the inscription in Aramaic "Bar Rekub, son of Panammu."

The most rigidly theoretical economist must admit, then, that coined money was in existence, and that the money régime was in full progress. Immature as compared with the condition of the world since the Industrial Revolution, perhaps even as compared with the age of handicraft which preceded the revolution, it is still a phase, if an early phase, in the evolution of the money system.

The nobility, "men of birth," and the merchants comprised a middle class in the Babylonian cities, quite in the European sense of the word. In addition, the cities included a considerable number of artisans who were not slaves or serfs, and yet not members of the nobility. Very little is known of their activities in Assyria, but it would appear as if they followed a hereditary trade; they passed through an apprenticeship in Babylonia; it is possible that the "Houses of Wisdom" found in the various cities were craft guilds. Certainly, their social status was not low, for a very definite respect is felt towards them.

However, in city as in country, the basis of ancient society was the unfree man. Corresponding to the country serf was the city slave. Perhaps the associations implied by the term "slave" are too unpleasant, for, in the words of the man who best knew the economic life of Assyria, he "probably had more real freedom than any other who ever bore the name of slave."[2]

---

[1] Cf. p. 321.   [2] Johns, *Deeds*, III, 373.

From the strict legal standpoint, he was indeed a thing, mere property, as have been all slaves in all ages, but he was also recognised as a human being.

Domestic slaves were comparatively few in numbers. In the less wealthy families they were almost exclusively women, engaged in domestic manufacture, such as weaving, and sometimes with the status of a wife of an inferior grade. This situation is reflected in the price of the female slave, which is regularly as high as the male. Only the few great houses possessed any large number of male slaves, and in all probability they were mostly eunuchs. The largest number of slaves in the possession of a private individual is thirty, and that is near the end of the empire.

In great part, the slaves were married, lived in their own houses, carried on their own business, and only paid their yearly "tribute" to their master according to the fixed custom. Nearly all the industry and a considerable part of the business carried on in the empire was in their hands. They regularly bought and sold property and it is not unusual to find one slave owning another! Aside from their annual tribute to their masters, certainly no greater than the average Oriental of the lower classes pays to the usurer to-day, their only disqualification seems to have been their inability to choose their own masters and the necessity of remaining more or less closely under that master's oversight. Thus the slave was merely a source of assured income to his master, and, like the serf, it was rather his service than his body which was transferred.

Such slaves lived a not unhappy life, yet now and then the signs of slavery, the shorn hair, the marked ear or hand, proved too much and the slave became a fugitive, or pretended to be free. Quite different was the fate of the unfortunates who had been enslaved in war from that of the "house slave," or the slave by purchase or debt. Heavily shackled and whipped on by the overseer, he laboured at building palace platforms or other varieties of rude work until he perished.

How closely the position of the slave was assimilated to that of the conquered provincial may be realised when we remember that the word for his rebellion against his master is the same as the refusal to pay the provincial dues. It is not surprising that he formed a large part of the army and that the various officials, especially the governor of the province or the mayor of the city, were able to demand his service for the army or the corvee.

Family groups form a considerable proportion of the slave sales, and it has even been suggested that the slave was never sold without his family. Sometimes, no doubt, slaves were recruited from captives taken in war, though this does not of necessity follow from the possession of a foreign name; the slave might have been acquired in the ordinary course of commerce. Nor does the fact that half the slaves bear Assyrian names prove that each represents the case of a free person who has lost his liberty for debt, though such instances are not unknown; in many cases, the father has a foreign name, which shows that the dependents had changed to those common among their masters.

A large portion of the increase must have come from the births in slave families, as we discover from the number of children sold. Where we find a master buying a slave as wife for his slave, we may be sure it was desire for increase of a profitable property and not sentiment which urged him to the purchase. On the other hand, we have a considerable number of cases where girls are bought by parents as the cheapest and most satisfactory method of providing wives for their sons. We have a fair amount of evidence for manumission. Doubtless the slave might buy his freedom from the profits of his business, he might be redeemed by his clan or by a superior officer if he had been sold for debt or had been enslaved for crime, he might be adopted by his master, the slave woman and her children were free if her master married her. In the slave sales, there is always recognised danger that the seller might later declare that he had manumitted the slave.

Such slaves as we meet in our documents were generally bought for the use of the palace and from private individuals, a few at a time. The greater number were secured by two men who held the title of "rein-holder," a sort of "director of domestics." Beginning with 710, Shuma-ilani has a career of over fifty years, in which he buys fifty-four slaves as well as makes loans. As he grew old, he was assisted by Rimani Adad, who begins his career in 676 and five years later was "great royal rein-holder." In the next sixteen years, no less than seventy slaves passed through his hands.[1]

[1] Johns, *Deeds*, III, 83 ff.

CHAPTER XLII

BUSINESS ARCHIVES

Assyrian business life is known to a much less degree than in the case of Babylonia. Private documents are almost entirely lacking and the court archives contain but few categories. Considering the Assyrian character, this is not surprising, but it does blur the picture and we cannot always be sure that we may fill up the details from Babylonia.

The typical Assyrian business document falls into three sections, the introduction, the business transacted, the attestation and date. In the first, we have mention of the seal of the party, seller, borrower, or the like, against whom the document furnished protection. Thereafter followed a blank space in which was affixed the seal. The old-style cylinder was still in use, but the newer seal stamp was already coming in. Some borrowers were too poor to afford the elaborately carved seal in semiprecious stone; in such cases we read "Instead of his seal, he has affixed his thumb-mark," for the discovery that lines of the thumb are never the same for any two individuals was not first made in a modern detective agency. The third section gives a long list of witnesses, each preceded by the word "before," and the various titles here collected have already been utilised in the study of the Assyrian administrative system. The name of the scribe regularly appears in this section, and sometimes he is said to be the holder of the original tablet, in which case we have only the duplicate without the seal. All documents are exactly dated by day, month, and year, the eponymy of the official from whom it was named.[1]

In our classification of these documents, we should follow

[1] The whole of the Nineveh archives in C. H. W. Johns, *Assyrian Deeds and Documents*, 1898 ff.; with elaborate commentary and partial translation; the business documents only are transliterated and translated, with brief presentation of the legal facts, Kohler-Ungnad, *Rechtsurkunden*, 1913.

the Assyrian logic and not our own. We shall therefore begin
with the simplest form, which runs as follows: "Sixteen shekels
of silver, the property of Kisir Ashur, for the use of Ahdi
Shamshi. For return he has taken it. On the 1st of July he
shall return the silver. If he does not return it, it shall increase by a quarter. April 11, year Bel-ludari was eponym.
Before Girittu, before Nargi, before Ardi Banitu."[1]

This is simply the record of an advance of funds to a tenant
to carry him over the harvest, which would be certainly ended
by the 1st of July; it is of the utmost significance that the
typical form of business document is connected with agriculture. The next development, again following the Assyrian
logic, is the following: "Two pounds of silver, the principal,
according to the pound of Carchemish, belonging to Addati,
the 'governess,' for the use of . . . ia, the deputy of the chief
of the city." Thus far, the first type has been followed. Now
comes a paragraph which according to our sense of order would
belong to quite a different category: "Instead of the two
pounds, he has placed an estate of twelve imers, a field in the
desert of the city of Ashur, (with the serfs) Qurdi Adad, his
wife, and his three sons, Kandilanu and his wife, in all seven
souls and twelve imers, as pledge for the use of Addati. On
the day he gives the silver, he shall bring back the people and
the field."[2]

What we have here is a true loan, with the fields and slaves
as security, to be returned when the loan is paid; meanwhile,
the lender has the use of the field and of the accompanying
serfs to repay her for the interest lost. Exactly the same loan
form is also used for leases, terminable at will.

First developed for agricultural purposes, it was carried over
into other business forms. Thus we have it used where six
workmen secure an advance of bronze, grain, and drink, and
are in return to repair a ruined house, make firm the beams,
fix the woodwork, set up the roof; if the brickwork and the
fastening are not complete by the end of October, they are
to continue until they finish. More deplorable is the case of

[1] *J*. 1.   [2] *J*. 58.

Ishdi Ashur who must give his daughter Ahat-abisha to Zabdi in lieu of interest on thirty shekels of silver, so that the girl is considered sold, and must still manage to repay the principal.[1]

Again following the Assyrian way of thinking, we must make a totally separate class of the advances of barley. While the tablets we have been previously considering are written the long direction and with clay covers containing a duplicate, the barley loans are on heart-shaped tablets through which has been run a string. The greater part deal with the activity of one man, the royal steward Bahianu, who makes these loans to the peasants on the royal estates. As illustration of his activities, we may quote: "Two ass loads of barley to Nabu-nur-nammir, one to Latubashani-ili, one to Sabtanu, belonging to Bahianu, for their use, for return they have taken it." The next month we read: "One ass load from Sabtanu, one ditto from Latubashani-ili, in all two ditto barley they have paid in full to Bahianu; Nabu-nur-nammir has not paid." We may be sure he paid later and with penalty.[2]

The abode of Bahianu was in Maganisi, in the midst of the great grain-fields of central Mesopotamia, and that his relations were mostly with Aramaic-speaking individuals is shown by the relatively large number of tablets which have Aramaic indorsements on them. One is entirely in Aramaic: "Barley of the king's son to Nabu-eribani from (the city) Airan, five (homers) for seven (months) and five reapers. Eponymy of Sharru-nuri (674)." Another says merely: "To Menahem." Menahem is a purely Hebrew name and just here the Israelites were settled.[3]

After a service of at least forty years, Bahianu died in full prosperity, but his heirs did not share it. His property, which included three pounds of gold, two talents of silver, five mules, and ten camels, was plundered.[4]

A third type of business document, the record of sales, was

---

[1] J. 90; 86.   [2] J. 134 f.

[3] Johns, Deeds, III, 226; J. 245; cf. J. H. Stevenson, Assyrian and Babylonian Contracts with Aramaic Reference Notes, 1902.

[4] Johns, Deeds, III, 217 ff.

differentiated by being placed on a long narrow tablet. Whether of slaves or of lands, the general formulas were about the same, and the following may be taken as sample: "Seal of Mushezib Marduk, governor of the horses of the New Palace, lord of the person transferred, Ahushina, a weaver of embroidered cloth, the slave of Mushezib Marduk, has Rimani Adad, the rein-holder of the king, from Mushezib Marduk for one and a half royal pounds bought and taken. The silver is complete and given, that person is bought and received. Return, suit, complaint, shall not be. Whoever in future shall rise up, shall act contrary to law, whether Mushezib Marduk or his sons or his brothers or his brother's sons, or shall institute suit or complaint against Rimani Adad or his sons or his son's sons, five pounds of pure silver and one of fine gold shall he place in the lap of the god who inhabits Nineveh. In his suit he shall plead and shall not recover. The silver tenfold to its owners shall he return. (Recourse for) seizure by epilepsy (shall be permitted) within a hundred days, a defect for all time." [1]

By the first clause, title was transferred; then followed the seal. In addition to the danger from the heirs of the seller, there was also the possibility that various officers, especially the governor of the district or the mayor of the town, might demand further service, and on the seller was specifically imposed the duty of seeing that the buyer was not held responsible. Even Shaditu, daughter of Sennacherib, was not safe from this danger of reclamation by reason of her royal rank.[2]

Oath by the gods, so common in early Babylonia, survived in Assyria only in the royal charters and then they were merely guarantors. Instead, we learn that Shamash, or perhaps Ashur or Bel or Marduk, is "lord," that is, advocate, "of his case." Heavy penalties, so great as to be prohibitive, are to be paid to the various deities, who are carefully defined as to place, to Ashur and his Lady who live in Esharra, to the Lady of Nineveh or Ishtar the Assyrian who dwells in Emashmash, to Ishtar of Arbela, to the Lady of the Waste Places, who may

[1] J. 172.   [2] J. 441; 560; 582; 804.

be Ashratu, to Sin of Harran or the lesser Sin of Dur Sharrukin, to the Adad of Dur Bel, of Kakzu, of Anat on the Euphrates.

Such a list of gods cannot be accidental. Ashur and the various Ishtars are thoroughly Assyrian, Adad and Sin are west Semitic. Babylonian deities are conspicuously absent. One curious penalty was the dedication of white horses, presumably for the divine chariot, at the feet of some god, notably Sin of Harran. Urta of Kalhu has some hope of receiving a great bronze bow if the sale is contested. A trace of earlier savagery survives in another where the Lady of the Waste, Sin, or Adad, await the burning alive of the eldest son or daughter of the offender. The penalty points to human sacrifice in the more or less distant past, perhaps it is not quite safe to assume on the basis of these threats that it was a regular part of the ritual.

More innocent, grotesque indeed to our minds, though terrible enough to the Assyrian, was the ordeal. The offender is to eat a pound of some magical food, he is to drink the contents of a written bowl. None of these written bowls has come down to us from Assyrian times, but the custom survived and a few generations later Mandæans, Syrians, and Jews wrote in their respective languages, or even in Pehlevi and Arabic, on similar bowls and believed in the efficacy of their charms.[1]

Other penalties are pulling out the tongue, presentation of a talent of lead to the chief, or a talent of lapis lazuli. That these threats were not always in vain is proved by the list of temple lands where are included the fields presented by the governor of Sime in the days of Tiglath Pileser as blood-money. The sales clauses of these contracts closely parallel the charter of the Babylonian Marduk-nadin-ahe, and there is some likelihood that we should find there the original of these phrases.[2]

Sales for land follow much the same form as the slave sales. There was no separate form for mortgages, for a mortgage

---

[1] J. 481; for the later bowls, cf. J. A. Montgomery, *Aramaic Incantation Texts*, 1913. The three bowls found at Ashur, *MDOG.*, XLIII, 13, as well as the one shown me at Mosul, are later than Assyrian times.

[2] J. 806; Johns, *Deeds*, III, 338; 366.

meant a quasi-sale and it was the regular custom to hand over the article mortgaged for use in the place of interest. Thus the "governess," though of royal blood, mortgaged a field to Inibi Ashur who "ate" it, that is, enjoyed its usufruct, until a messenger should come from the house of its lords, when he freed the field from the mortgage for the benefit of its lords.[1]

By the sales formulas, Milkia, governor of Rimusi, who was in Nineveh in 681, raises twenty pounds on an estate at Shadi Samalla in Rimusi, with twenty-seven serfs, their fields, houses, gardens, cattle, sheep, and family possessions as security. His need must have been pressing, perhaps he was already anticipating the rough times which were coming with the assassination of Sennacherib a few months later, for he received but a fraction of what the estate was worth.[2]

A fourth group consisted of the "judgments." In Babylonia there was a bank of judges, in Assyria a single judge was deemed sufficient. The majority of the judgments which have come down to us were decided by the sartenu or chief justice, though other cases were tried before the mayor, his deputy, the delegate, or the inspector. A typical case would run as follows: "Judgment in favour of Nabu-shar-usur, the scribe, against Ahu-lamashshi, the son of Dilil Ishtar, of Shabireshu, an irrigator, at the hand of Ahu-unqur, son of Akkullanu, the harvest overseer of the chief cellarer, in regard to the restoration of a bull which Ahu-lamashshi stole from the house of Nabu-shar-usur. Before the deputy mayor of Nineveh they came, one bull, the equivalent of the bull he stole, he imposed upon Ahu-lamashshi. In lack of his fine, he was held; the day he brings the bull, he is free."[3]

"Seal of Nabu-taris, slave of Sapanu. Four souls, slaves of Shangu Ishtar, he stole. Before the delegate he was brought, two hundred and ten pounds of bronze were imposed upon him. In lack of the bronze, he is detained. Whoever shall give Shangu Ishtar the two hundred and ten pounds may release his slave." Regular sale formulas follow.[4]

[1] J. 62.
[2] J. 59.
[3] J. 160.
[4] J. 161.

While Adad-risua was away and only his woman Shulmu-naid was in charge, Kanunu took the opportunity to claim her as a slave. The mayor, Nabu-ahe-iddina, decided that Adad-risua must be given full opportunity to appear; if he does not appear at the set time, the guarantor, a certain Nabu-ahi-iddina, shall give Kanunu slave for slave.[1]

One case may be considered to represent equity proceedings: "Seal of Bel-shar-usur, the footman. Judgment which Ninua contested with Bel-shar-usur concerning his slaves. If on the new moon of June Bel-shar-usur has not brought his arrears to Ahu-eriba and Adad-shum-iddina, in the hands of Ninua has not laid it, the silver is lost. If he brings his arrears and places it in the hand of Ninua, Ninua shall give thirty shekels of silver to Bel-shar-usur. Also, when Lategi-ana-Ashur is seen, his compensation he shall give." [2]

Shamash-nasir brings suit against Arbailu-hamat, wife of Sananu, and her son Nabu-eriba, two souls from the city of the king's daughter, concerning his income and his pledge, as follows: "One pound of silver have I given you, from the house of the king's official have I brought you forth, your property, fifty ass loads of grain, a watering-machine, and one ox, worth twelve and a half pounds of silver, have I taken." Arbailu-hamat and Nabu-eriba replied: "For the objects pledged we will serve you." Arbailu-hamat, Nabu-eriba, and three others shall serve Shamash-nasir. Whoever to-morrow or the next day brings suit, whether her brother or her governor, shall give pledges to Shamash-nasir, he shall take them out, they shall be free.[3]

Salmu-sharra-iqbi appears in the rôle of a doubtful benefactor. He has redeemed Mannu-ki Urta, his wife Arbailu-sharrat, and his daughter from the merchant, perhaps a foreigner, and has secured for them technical freedom. But since good money has been invested, they are to work for him to pay the interest on his investment until the governor or some one else pays the money and redeems them.[4]

[1] J. 166.
[2] J. 105.
[3] VS., I, 96; KU., 655.
[4] J. 85.

We have also cases of self-pledge, as where Nargi promises to serve Bel-duri, the subgovernor of the crown prince, for grain and a bull loaned him from the crown prince's stores, and he will serve until return can be made. In place of silver will Belit-ittia, the slave of the governess, serve Sinqi Ishtar as long as she lives. How a woman who is already once enslaved can be again enslaved because she has not lived up to her contract is one of the mysteries of the very peculiar Assyrian slave system.[1]

Two cases of murder are cited. Silim-ili has killed a slave of Siri. As substitute for the slave, he is to give his wife, his brother, or one of the others who seal the tablet. If this is quite alien to our thought, the other is still more so. Samaku has been killed by Atar-qamu, the scribe. Sahish, daughter of Atar-qamu, with her family, is to be given to Shamash-mukin-ahi, Samaku's son, "in the place of the blood, the blood will be washed out. If he does not give the girl, they shall kill him upon the grave of Samaku." The case must have been of unusual interest, for Ashur-bani-apal was himself concerned and the witnesses are headed by his turtanu, Adalal, and by Adad-babau, turtanu of the crown prince.[2]

Dedications to the gods appear. Mannu-diq, shield-bearer and minor official, dedicates his son Nabu-sharik-napishti to Urta of Kalhu for the life of Ashur-bani-apal, king of Assyria. Strangely enough, even with this pious object in view, there was danger of the son being reclaimed, if not by his relatives, then by his governor and his captain of fifty.[3]

Placing side by side two tablets from different sources, we may trace a little tragedy. This same Urta of Kalhu had been served by the lady Raimtu as a sacred prostitute. A son born during this period, Dur-maki Ishtar, had been handed over to his uncles Bel-naid and Nabu-naid and to his cousin Ardi Ishtar. Not entirely proud of his birth, they quietly put him out of the way and at the same time secured cheap credit for themselves by dedicating him to the Urta of Kalhu in whose service he had been born. Here he should await tax and forced

[1] J. 152; 76.   [2] J. 618; 321.   [3] J. 641.

labour. Quite grandiloquently they close with the blessing and curse especially dedicated to royal charters: "You who hereafter against this document do no injury, Nabu will hear your prayers; but whoever does damage, may Urta, whom in his prayers he names, forever be hostile." [1]

After a time, Raimtu retired from the service of the god and married a respectable husband, Sinqi Ishtar. Her life in the temple had made the probability of her bearing more children remote if not impossible, her own son, Dur-maki Ishtar, was lost to her in the service of Urta, and the pair decided to adopt Ashur-sabatsu-iqbi, the son of her brother Nabu-naid. His true father carefully protected his position, "Even though seven heirs be born to Sinqi Ishtar and Raimtu, Ashur-sabatsu-iqbi is their eldest son and heir," but he has lost all control over his son; if Nabu-naid attempts to reclaim his son, "his eldest son and heir he shall burn in the offering house of Adad." Another son had been torn from his parent.[2]

And now we have fragments of an Assyrian code. Since copies of the great code associated with the name of Hammurabi had been found in Nineveh, it was naturally assumed that it or a modification was used by the Assyrians, though important differences had been found in their business records. Similarities to the older code are indeed found, but it is doubtful if there was any direct relation.

Our code is to be dated about the middle of the second millennium, when the city of Ashur was still the one urban centre in the little kingdom. It is therefore much later than the Hammurabi code, but this is early in the Assyrian development and it may have been modified in the millennium which followed. For good and for evil, it represents a different stage in social evolution, but it also represents differences in temperament. The part best preserved is seemingly the last tablet. It deals largely with crimes and with the position of women; the number of punishments mentioned in the sections preserved and the large amount of social vice indicated make

[1] J. 640.
[2] Peiser, *OLZ.*, VI, 198 ff.; *KU.*, 41.

an unfortunate impression which would have not appeared so strongly if we possessed the whole of the laws.

Drastic as are the punishments, one characteristic feature of primitive codes, the law of talio or like for like, is almost entirely missing; another characteristic of early law, payment instead of personal punishment for crimes, is likewise absent. There is no evidence for those variations of punishment, according as the sinner or the sinned against is an aristocrat, a freeman, or a serf; it deals with Assyrians, and we have had frequent opportunity to observe that even the deported were reckoned as Assyrians when tribute, tax, and corvee were inflicted upon them. We may therefore say that all Assyrians were equal before the law. In each of these cases, the Assyrian code is the more modern!

Punishments are much the same as we find in the Hebrew codes, lashes, mutilation of members, boring the ear. More horrible punishments, such as impalement or castration, are reserved for crimes which public opinion has always considered peculiarly abhorrent, abortion or unnatural vice. Misdemeanours may be compounded by a fine, payable in lead, as in our modern courts. The frequency of a month in the king's service points to the larger part played by the power of the state. Self-help is legally confined to violations of family honour, just as our modern jury so regularly administers the "unwritten law." Assyria was our superior in one respect; the man in the case suffered the same punishment as the sinning woman.

Less pleasant is the realisation that wives are the property of their husbands and are treated as such. Marriage has as little sentiment connected with it as in Babylonia, and the wife is a less equal partner. Preliminary negotiations are conducted by the parents and a large portion of the extant code carefully enumerates the rights of the different parties at each stage of the performance. The bridegroom's father must present the father of the prospective bride with certain gifts, but this is not absolute pledge; if the betrothed girl dies before actual consummation of the marriage, the money may be restored, or the bargain may be met by another daughter. This is quite in line with the mercantile attitude of the Babylonians.

At the time of marriage, the husband must present his wife with a bride-gift, the bride brings a dowry. While a wife she has no control over her husband's property, and if she sells or even pawns his possessions, she is treated as a thief and the one who takes it from her is prosecuted as the receiver of stolen property. If his wife steals from others, her husband may ransom her or leave her to the punishment of cutting off her nose. Much space is devoted to crimes against women; a wife or daughter is thought of as property which has been damaged; the husband may take back his damaged goods and inflict such punishment as he desires or he may ask the authorities to inflict it, but in either case the man receives the same penalty.

Divorce is entirely in the hands of the husband and if he wishes he may give his cast-off wife something, or he may send her away empty-handed; when she returns to the house of her father, now her sole refuge, he may follow her up and deprive her of her bride-gift. Her dowry remains for her sons, though even here the father may distribute it as he wishes. On his death, what her husband specifically gave her remains hers, even though she has no son, but if she has children, it belongs to them. A widow without children was married by custom to another brother of her husband or even to her father-in-law, quite in the fashion of the Biblical levirate. If none of these survive, she is a widow with a tablet to testify to her abnormal status.

"Widows" with such a tablet formed the one group of women which was virtually the equal of man. If she married a man and lived in his house, she lost control of her possessions, but if he entered her house, all his property was transferred to the heiress. The one exception to the rule that every marriage is a contract, and therefore must have a written witness, is in the case of the widow. If for two years she lives in a man's house, a common-law marriage is presumed.

A wife abandoned by her husband must remain unmarried for five years, the sixth she is free. But if she does break the marriage contract by remarrying, the only penalty is that she must return to her first husband, leaving the children of the second marriage to her second husband. If, however, it is a mere case of betrothal and her husband has been taken captive by the enemy, two years is all she need wait. If she has neither father-in-law nor son to provide for her, she may make oath that she has no means of support and become a dependent of the palace. On request of the judges, the officials grant her for two years the estate formerly cultivated by her husband; at the end of that time she is free to marry the man of her heart, she is given a certificate of widowhood. If her husband was in the king's service, he recovers his property at his return without more ado; if he was not, he must pay the state for her support before he can recover. If he does not return at the end of the two years, the property escheats to the king.

If an abandoned wife has a son but no special gift from her husband, she may dwell with whatsoever son she desires. As a bride whom one loves, they shall bind themselves to her, even though she be but a stepmother. In return, she shall do their labour.

The lawgiver quite agreed with St. Paul as to the lack of propriety in women appearing in public with uncovered heads. Only women of the lowest moral character might walk the streets with bare heads and on them it was obligatory. Slave women were in an intermediate class, for their heads were covered but their faces were unveiled. Any sort of marital relation, full wife, concubine, captive, even women whose past had been notorious, if now they were legally married and so the property of their husbands, were veiled and covered. Veiling or head-covering out of one's class was severely punished. We have here the beginning of Oriental seclusion.

Quite in the spirit of Deuteronomy is the provision for the legal marriage of the captive woman; her possessor need only place her veiled among a half-dozen of his comrades and declare her his wife. Even though he had not done this, her children inherited if there were no children by the "veiled wife."

Aside from crimes connected with women, the only crime mentioned in the extant portions is sorcery, whose punishment was death. Report on this crime was to be made direct to the king. Sorcery, we may suspect, was feared in Assyria as in the later Roman Empire, because it was so frequently connected with conspiracy against the state. When the sorcerer is seized, he is reminded of his oath of loyalty to the king and the crown prince.

Property laws are preserved to a much less degree. Property is considered to belong primarily to the family, the eldest son has a double portion, the younger sons work for him on an undivided estate. Crimes against property were severely treated. Encroachment of boundaries meant a triple restitution, blows, and a month of the king's service. Utilisation of a field against the wishes of the owner was not condoned, the cultivator lost his produce and was punished. Irrigation was carefully regulated, and in case of dispute each lost common rights and was confined to his own.

In the business documents, we frequently find the statement that no reclamation is to be made by any member of a rather large family group. The code shows how it is carried out. After the agreement is made, a month elapses while a high official proclaims three times throughout the city of Ashur that such and such a one desires to acquire a certain property from such a one, and if any person has a claim against it, let him present it to the proper official. He is to be assisted by the delegate, the city scribe, the recorder, the mayor, and three of the official nobility. If no one appears, the judges shall draw up three copies of the proclamation for preservation with the recorder.[1]

[1] O. Schroeder, *Keilschrifttexte aus Assur, Verschiedenen Inhalts*, 1 ff.; 143 f.; 193. Jastrow, *JAOS.*, XLI, 1 ff.; Scheil, *Recueil des Lois Assyriennes;* Luckenbill, *AJSL.*, XXXIX, 56 ff.

CHAPTER XLIII

THE ARTS AND LIFE

EXCAVATORS of Assyrian sites must all have been monarchists. While in Babylonia and Palestine and Egypt we are rather well acquainted with the life of the every-day citizen, in Assyria we are largely confined to the palaces. We may make ourselves at home in their courts, we can reconstruct their past life through the letters and documents; when we would inquire of the commons, we must depend on the analogies of the palaces or on supposed parallels from Babylonia.

A life of the utmost plainness was lived by the countryman, the serf; civilisation in Assyria was essentially urban. Great differences existed in detail between imperial capital and hamlet, but the fundamental contrast between city and country lay in the greater complexity found in the former.

City man lived behind walls, which cramped him, yet not to the degree noticeable in the mediæval cities of Europe. The circuit of his walls was great and there was room within for gardens and open spaces if the city was large; if it was small, the open country was near; in any case he possessed estates outside the walls and yet within the legal limits of the municipality. Pleasant meeting-places were the gates and the squares behind where visitors must perforce enter, and thus could not escape the curiosity of the residents who congregated there for gossip, for business, for judgment, or, in the modern phrase, simply to "smell the air."

Since the twentieth pre-Christian century at least, Babylon had employed the checker-board system of streets; Ashur too employed the system with the streets diagonal to the compass points for shade, and Dur Sharrukin likewise used it. In the later days, when Ashur decayed, the system was abandoned and we have one short stretch where the street turns five times at right angles. Streets proper ranged from ten to twelve

555

feet wide, alleys half of that; they were paved with blocks of
stone or cobbles and were well drained. Outside the walls,
the royal road was paved and had mile-stones.

Abutting directly upon the street or opening off a small
court or a narrow alley were the houses. No sight could be
duller than a street in the residential section with its staring
blank walls of mud brick. Very interesting is the group of

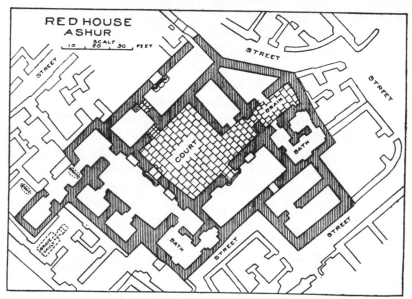

MAP 10. THE "RED HOUSE" AT ASHUR.

residences built over the ruins of Tukulti Urta's palace in the
seventh century. The builders as a rule dug down to the level
of the royal terrace, upon that was laid adobe, then the stone
foundations, and finally the clay walls. The walls are rarely
more than one stone thick, say about a foot, and a second
story is virtually excluded.

One entered the house through a small vestibule which shut
out the interior from prying eyes; in the case of one early residence, the visitor must pass down a long narrow corridor,
then around the corner directly back again, and then forward
to the court. In the centre was the courtyard, paved with

stones and brick or with cobbles in squares, rosettes, and various other geometric designs.   Around the court were the rooms.
In the more pretentious, there were separate units for each
sex.   Each possessed a large reception-room, whose walls were

covered with a mixture
of clay and chaff, with a
preparation of gypsum,
or perhaps there was a
band of red or a base-
board of black bitumen.
Rich rugs and hangings
broke the room's monot-
ony, and niches set in
the side walls provided
storage by day for cush-
ions and bedclothes.
Only the bathroom, with
its asphalted floor and
walls and with its drain,
showed further sign of
specialisation.

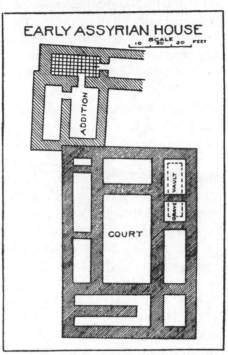

After all, house inte-
riors were for the rare
days when cold or rain
drove one indoors, or for
the escape from the mid-
day sun.   Family life

MAP 11.   EARLY ASSYRIAN HOUSE AT
ASHUR.

centred around the open court by day, by night one ascended
the stairs to the flat roof for repose.   When a man departed to
his eternal rest, it was only to be fixed the more closely in his
earthly home, for he was buried under its floor.

In the corner of every court was a rubbing-stone on which
the grain was ground into flour.   A hot fire of thorns or a slower
one of charcoal or dung was placed inside a jar laid on the
side, the dough was pasted on, and immediately it was ready,
thin and delicate.   Ordinarily the bread was of barley; on feast-
days the more expensive wheat was made into the cakes so beloved of the women in the days of Jeremiah.   Garden-truck

was brought in from the gardens just outside the walls, and with barley bread formed the main support of the people. Dates did not ripen so far north, but might be imported from Babylonia where they were the chief staple.

Meat was rarely eaten, save by the highest classes. Beef was virtually unknown, for the ox was too expensive to be used other than in agriculture. Mutton was the food of the better off, goat's flesh or even the unclean and rather dangerous swine of the lower classes, who, however, found their meat rather in ducks and geese. If the cock had been introduced, he was still little known. At times meats were boiled in a huge kettle; more often they were roasted or the fire was raked out of the jar already used for baking, the flesh placed inside, and the mouth closed. Roast kid from this fireless cooker was of a most gratifying delicacy. Dairy products were common, in general derived from goat's milk, and sesame, honey, and fruit syrups took the place of sugar in the preparation of dainties.

A well in the courtyard of each house at Ashur furnished water, farther north cisterns were more popular. Jugs and goat-skins brought water from the river until canals led cold water from the mountains. Cow's milk was an undreamed luxury, but goats, sheep, and camels furnished a scanty supply. Barley beer was borrowed from Babylonia, where the common people complained that it was too diluted to have much intoxicating power, though for a man of wealth it might be secured "extra strong." Date and other brandies were imported chiefly from the south, but neither beer nor brandy was in much esteem in Assyria. No grapes were pressed in the Triangle, but the near-by mountains furnished a supply of cheap wine. We shall not soon forget the pleasure of Ashur-nasir-apal as he "looks upon the wine when it is red," or the manner in which the helpers of Sennacherib found their hearts drenched with wine.[1] Already it had been observed that the strong drink which caused men to stagger also possessed the faculty of making them see double.

When the Assyrian went abroad, his first choice was the

[1] Cf. pp. 107, 324.

market. We may attempt its reconstruction from its modern descendant, a series of narrow roofed streets, to keep out the sun and perchance conceal defects in the goods offered. Various articles were sold, each in its separate street, with the merchants squatting on a low platform, their goods around them till nightfall, when they would be locked into the little box of a room in the rear. One of these quarters, that of the metalworkers, we can locate at the northwest corner of the city of Ashur, for its greatest gate bore their name. Travelling merchants of the better class displayed their wares at Ashur in what corresponds to the modern khan, where, around a great court paved with rough stones, were the sleeping-rooms and the long narrow stalls with many bronze bits to testify to the former presence of horses.

Manufacture was almost literally "handiwork." There was a little simple machinery, the spindle and loom for cloth, the wheel and the oven for pottery, but beyond this the craftsman had barely passed. Now and then the craft was carried on at home, but more regularly the work would be done in little shops just off the market, and the articles were sold by the man who made them. Each craft had its guild with its patron saint and its chief who was its direct representative with the government.

Once Ashur had followed the simple fashion of the Shumerian, but those days were long gone. The skirt of primitive times had changed into a dress slung from the left shoulder, and this in turn into a sleeved tunic with long skirt. Shumerians did not scruple to appear nearly or quite naked; the Semitic sense of shame increased the body-covering, which reaches its extreme in the dress of the Assyrian monarch where even the leg is concealed. In the few cases where we have women of the upper classes represented, as in the case of the queen of Ashur-bani-apal,[1] they dressed with even greater elaborateness.

Wool was the ordinary material for clothing. It was very cheap, since the steppe was filled with sheep, but it was not

[1] Cf. p. 502.

well adapted to so hot a climate. Against the summer sun, it did furnish needed protection, but it was too heavy for strenuous labour and it was none too cleanly. After the wool had been carded and the thread spun with spindle and whorl, it was woven at home on a simple loom.

For inside use, the higher classes preferred linen, which had long since been imported from Egypt, though now some flax was grown in western Asia. A king of the northern Judah boasts that in his days fine linen became extremely common, and he takes to himself the credit, since he ruled justly; credit should rather be given to the closer connection of the age with Egypt.[1] Cotton, to us the cheapest of materials, was first known in the reign of Sennacherib, and we may be quite sure that only members of his immediate entourage received dresses made from the trees whose wool they shred.[2]

Preparation of the clothing for the palace was an important industry, in whose manufacture and yearly transportation the highest officials took part. Kurban on the northeast frontier was a noted centre of weaving, and the weavers of Ishtar of Arbela were equally famous. Pure-white garments were required for many ceremonies and the fuller's art was much appreciated. More often the garments were dyed in what we should consider the most glaring colours, though they fitted well enough the clear southern sunshine. Purples prepared from the shells of the murex and similar varieties by the Phœnicians were the most fashionable. Each shell when broken provided but the tiniest pin-point of moisture, and the further preparation and fixing of the colour was a most intricate and delicate process. Because of this expensiveness, the tribute lists are full of its mention.

Many are the references to leather-working and many the representations of sandals. A tablet of 702 found in Carchemish seems to be an agreement with a group of Aramæans from the old Mitanni region to furnish oak and sumach for the purpose of tanning.[3] In addition, skins were prepared for parchment.

[1] Cf. p. 184.   [2] Cf. p. 331.   [3] Thompson, *Carchemish*, 135 ff.

Fig. 159. ASSYRIAN VASE WITH RELIEF.
(Nies Collection.)

Of the implements used in the average house, the most necessary were the work of the potter's art. Babylonia was probably the home of the wheel, which was known in the earliest
time, but the great majority of the coarser vessels were made
by hand. These were generally of the crude clay and in the
sickly greenish colour of nature. Their interior, especially if
they were to contain liquids, was coated with a thick layer of
coal-black bitumen. Turned on one side, they formed the

Fig. 160. GLASS AND ALABASTER VESSELS WITH NAME OF SARGON.

oven or the fireless cooker; placed in supports in the ground,
the jars might be filled with wine.

Earlier strata at Ashur give fine polished vases, or white
paint on black or a dark violet in geometrical designs. Kalhu
presents spirals, honeysuckles, cones, and tulips in black on
a pale ground. For our finest examples, thin egg-shell bodies
and delicate painting or even white dusting, we must go to
such provincial centres as Nasibina. Fragments have been
found in the capitals of a white glaze so fine that earlier writers
called it true porcelain, and that it was a native production
is proved by the discovery of crucibles and slag.

Pottery did not develop as it did, for example, in Greece, because Assyria was not so poor and so limited in materials; indeed, in historical times it was almost entirely supplanted by the metals and the various stones for all but the commonest uses. At the very doors of Nineveh alabaster could be had for the digging, and was easily worked when newly excavated. Passed through the skilful hands of the craftsman, it appeared in most attractive form and with the most beautiful translucence. A glimpse of the elaborate drinking-cups in the ban-

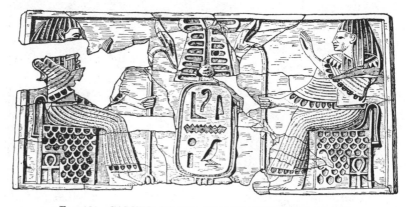

Fig. 161. CARVED IVORY IN THE EGYPTIAN STYLE.

queting scenes at Dur Sharrukin will show why the highest art of the craftsman was not lavished on vases, and how the Greeks imitated the metal rhytons in the less expensive clay. Pottery found another rival in glass, which had been imported from Egypt. Its perishable nature has permitted few examples to survive entire, but one glass jar from Kalhu has long been famous because, in addition to a lion, it bears the name of Sargon in cuneiform.

Doubtless a large part of the bazaars was filled with weapons, but the ceremonial sword of Adad-nirari I is our one first-class example of the armourer's art. For the rest, we must go to the sculptures or to the elaborate account of the chased and inlaid weapons Sargon found in Musasir.[1] Here

[1] Cf. p. 239.

too we may make mention of the inlaid ivories, with their mingling of Assyrian and Egyptian motifs.[1]

No great step was felt by the Assyrian to be taken when one passed from the crafts to what we should call the arts. He considered the architect or the sculptor as much a craftsman as the shoemaker or potter, and not one enjoyed a high position in society. None the less, through their honest craftsmanship these unknown artists produced results which to-day challenge our admiration.

Servile copying of Babylonia is an oft-repeated reproach; it is never more false than in the fundamental art, that of architecture. Babylonian foundations there were, to be sure, but not to the extent assumed. A very peculiar condition of affairs has lessened the fame of Assyria in this respect, the fact that so much more is known of Assyrian than of Babylonian architecture! Since both used mud brick to so great an extent, and burned brick to a lesser degree, it was perfectly natural to assume that the Assyrian technic would be found in Babylonia when it had been as fully excavated as Assyria.

Even yet, we know too little of Babylonian architecture to make comparison with the Assyrian entirely safe. Virtually the only city of the alluvium which has been adequately laid bare is the Babylon of Nebuchadnezzar. By that time Assyrian kings had built for almost a thousand years in Babylonia, and we have repeated accounts of temples, palaces, roads which they constructed. Much as the Assyrians learned in the process, it is unthinkable that Babylonians learned nothing in return, conservative as their temperament had become. Many of the elements in the Babylon of Nebuchadnezzar point to foreign influence.

Babylonia built her cities of mud bricks, that is, of carefully worked clay pressed in moulds, sometimes with a little chopped straw to hold them together, and then baked in the midday sun. Bricks were usually laid while still soft and made a solid mass, bound together, if at all, with a thin wash of the

[1] For the first half of the chapter, cf. especially B. Meissner, *Babylonien und Assyrien*, 1920.

same mud that formed the main body. Burnt bricks were in use from very early date, and then bitumen might be employed as mortar, but the difficulty of securing wood for burning made burnt bricks rare. There was never a real foundation, and the walls were of necessity thick to support the huge mass of the crude mud. Stone to face the walls was all but unknown.

The Assyrians took over the mud technic. This has regularly been cited as sufficient proof of Assyrian lack of originality. Such an argument is absurd, for at all times and in all portions of the Near East the majority of buildings have been erected of mud brick. Who, for example, does not recall the mud city walls of early Athens?

Ashur was not particularly well placed for the use of stone. The surrounding conglomerate was not adapted for building, and methods for transport of huge masses of stone were not to be derived from Babylonia; they must be invented or imported from Syria or Asia Minor or Egypt. As illustration, the sandstones employed in Eridu came from nearer home than the limestones used in Nineveh. Mud brick, on the other hand, was as near Ashur as Babylon, that is, one had only to go to the clayey fields. No difficult problems of transportation, no unmanageable masses, need be here considered. Building material cost nothing but the labour of carrying, and the most inexperienced slave, incapable of higher thought, could be trained in an hour to turn out quantities limited only by his physical strength. With the huge masses of captive labour at the disposal of an Assyrian king, there was every inducement to use crude brick. Further encouragement for its employment came from the intense heat, little less about Ashur than in the alluvium, for crude brick is simply earth, and earth is the ideal non-conductor.

While the Assyrians did cling to the use of crude brick as material for the mounds on which their structures were erected and for the walls of the buildings themselves, they utilised stone to a degree undreamed in the south. Their military sense taught them what it took centuries to teach the Greek, that city walls of mud were at the mercy of any invader who

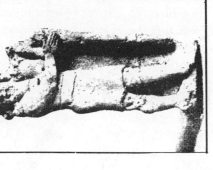

Fig. 164. ASSYRIAN DEITY. (Louvre.)

Fig. 163. GOD ON ANIMAL. (Louvre.)

Fig. 166. BRONZE BRACELET. (Louvre.)

Fig. 165. TERRA-COTTA ANTEFIX TO BUILDING. (Louvre.)

Fig. 162. ASSYRIAN DEMON. (Louvre.)

FIG. 167. PHŒNICIAN SHIELD FOUND IN CRETE, EGYPTIAN DESIGN.

could direct a stream against them, and that they were easily breached with the newly invented artillery. Reproach for mere imitation must hesitate in the presence of the massive stone circumvallation, later imitated by Nebuchadnezzar in Babylon. Nor was it imitation which produced the dado of sculptured reliefs which would not have been preserved for the modern objector had they not been covered by the ruins of the same mud-brick walls.

Two remarkable discoveries, the arch and its natural development, the dome, had been made in Babylonia; as in the case of so many inventions, it was a new country which made them its own. The arch was regularly used in underground drains which displayed a sense for the need of sanitation not again met until we come to Rome. It was also used in the burial-vault. The direct ancestor of the Roman triumphal arch is the triple-arched gateway of the Assyrian palace. As for the dome, it would appear to have been everywhere in Assyria, as it is in the present-day Orient, while the transitional form between arch and dome, the barrel vault, covered many of the long, narrow rooms.

Assyrian reliefs furnish some of our best evidence for the early use of the column, but in virtually every instance they represent a foreign scene or an imported building. Egypt was doubtless its inventor, and early examples from Babylonia are entirely lacking. At least as early as the first Tiglath Pileser, we find polygonal columns in basalt with capitals which are as original as they are ugly. Later, we find bases of stone and beautifully modelled, and at times winged lions were used for that purpose, while the columns were of wood, as they are in the houses of Assyria at the present. All in all, however, the column was a foreign device which was never fully naturalised. Assyria used it sparingly, save in the imported *bit hilani* of the Hittites.

Modern students of art who attempt an understanding of Assyrian æsthetics suffer from severe limitations. Art does not speak the same language throughout the ages. Its purpose is not primarily to hold the mirror up to nature, rather it attempts to afford æsthetic satisfaction through the medium of convention. The modern critic looks on art with eyes trained to Greek convention, or, to put it more accurately, what our ancestors believed to be Greek convention. Now it is true that Greek art was based on the art of the earlier Orient, that it used much the same technical methods, and that it was never free from some indication of such influence; it is even truer that from its earliest Minoan forms the spirit of Greek art was a thing apart, and this spirit quickly showed itself in new conventions.

At the very beginning of our study, then, we must free ourselves as far as may be possible of these preconceptions as to what true art must be. The last century has seen a more sympathetic study of such art as is not influenced to any degree by Greek convention, Chinese, Japanese, or Muslim, and we have even come to appreciate the folk art of lower-class Europe or the primitive art of less-cultured peoples, but in spite of these concessions to a broader æsthetics, it is not an easy matter for us to look upon Assyrian art with the same eyes as those of the men who rejoiced in its beauties.

Assyrian art was folk art, that is, it was nationalistic, and that in turn means that it was not the art of individuals. For twenty-five centuries, the study of art has been dominated by the idea of the "masters," individuals who lived a definite personal life of which we may learn many intimate details, and who made a definite, personal contribution to its development. Such a state cannot be reached until there has been a long period of folk art, and it is to this period of folk art, well towards its end, that Assyrian art must be assigned.

Continuity is the outstanding factor in such folk art. Freed from the disturbing influence of the individual genius, it passes through a normal development with few marked epochs. Its greatest devotees have no social standing, and such an atmosphere is not conducive to variation. A high-class artisan will feel it his business to reproduce the best in the ages gone before, not to invent new ideas or new processes. A national art which transcends these limitations, which avoids the ever-present danger of stagnation and overconventionalisation, which is most lifelike in its latest stage—such an art possesses a vitality which cannot but awaken our admiration.

Assyrian art may be based on that of Babylonia, but it breathes a spirit as different as that of Greece. Early Shumerian art is simply hopeless. The typical Lagash sculptures, whether we consider the Vulture Stele of Eannatum or the statues in the round of Gudea, are so inferior in execution to those of contemporary Egypt that their inferiority must be explained, not by a lack of technic which might have easily been learned on the Nile, but by simple lack of an artistic soul. That it was not lack of technical resources is shown by the sudden bloom when the Sargonid dynasty won Babylonia, and these Semites, not too distantly separated in race from the later Assyrians, produced the magnificent stele of Naram Sin or the lovely seal cylinders whose mature beauty is in such contrast to the conventionalised line-drawings of a few generations before.

At first sight, the earliest sculptures found at Ashur are pure Shumerian. Sitting figures remind one of the Gudea statues from Lagash, standing ones of Lugal-dalu from Adab. The ordinary dress is the flounced skirt leaving the upper half of the body nude, in general face and head are shaven, the body is short and stumpy. Closer examination shows peculiarities in countenance, in method of treating the hair, even to full beard for the men and massed hair for the women, fashions in dress which are not found in the south. But it is a very serious question if any artistic influences survived the bloody downfall of the men who are represented in these statues.

After a long period of artistic inactivity, sculptures begin to appear once more. A new race was now settled at Ashur and their art was their own. The few remains from before the time of Tiglath Pileser I are only too fragmentary, but they suffice. A headless statue, doubtless of some monarch from the middle of the second millennium, stands in sharp contrast to those of the "Shumerian" period. Its proportions are more normal, the almost grotesquely squat bodies of a thousand years earlier contrast with its well-built solidity, the arm muscles are not fat almost to the point of dropsy but are heavily muscled, it is evidently a portrait of a rather heavily built but well-proportioned man of medium height. His head is missing but his long beard falls to his breast, he wears a necklace around his short neck, his hands are folded one above the other, a simple, heavy robe completely envelops his lower body, so that not one bit of the flesh appears. A nude figure of Ishtar which bears the dedication of Ashur-bel-kala has lost head, arms, and feet, but in spite of the rough modelling is a not inadequate representation of a woman of the same muscular type. It is already evident that the Assyrians did not overemphasise muscular development because of any idea of greater power—they simply presented their men and women as they were.

The art was in full development by the reign of Tiglath Pileser I, whose obelisk relief, rock-cut royal figure, and palace-entrance animals already show all the chief peculiarities of the later centuries. Its first bloom is in the ninth century. The splendid reliefs of Ashur-nasir-apal, the somewhat less impressive figures in the round of that monarch and of his successor Shalmaneser III, the bronze gates, the work in faience, all testify to an art which leaves little to be desired for architectural effect, once we have admitted convention which appeared nature itself to contemporaries.

Political decay in the next century resulted quite naturally in artistic decadence, and the few reliefs of the last Tiglath Pileser are in many respects inferior to those of Ashur-nasir-apal, though a certain realism quite in accordance with his nature is to be noted. Sargon's sculptures may be more conventional but they are marked by a perfection of finish. Realism returns with Sennacherib. A greater use of background, a careful utilisation of preliminary sketches to secure accurate local colour, the constant contrast of scenes from every-day life with scenes of cruelty and horror, the beginnings of perspective when the figures in the background are smaller than those in front—all these mark distinct advance.

Highest excellence is reached with the sculptures of Ashur-bani-apal. Details are even more emphasised than in the case of Sennacherib, and where his reliefs may be compared side by side with those in Sennacherib's palace, the finish is seen to be superior. More ambitious compositions were attempted, and the grouping of the lion-hunt produced a masterpiece whose full effect has been lost by the scattering of the slabs. In the animal figures, and the lions in particular, Assyrian art gave its finest to the ancient world, and their influence was felt as far west as Greece. The sudden crash of the empire allowed no opportunity for decline, and Assyrian art was snuffed out in its prime. Much of the virility of Chaldæan art, still more of the Persian, something even of the Greek, came from the art of Assyria.

Artistically, the Assyrian period is the era of sculpture, but in making an estimate we must never forget that virtually all sculpture was used for architectural effect, rather than by and for itself. Nor must we forget the part played by colour. The material available for the sculptures, a gypseous alabaster with a uniform, rather dirty gray, left much to be desired. Details were picked out in colour. It is not certain whether the earlier reliefs were entirely polychrome, for no traces have been found on the background, but only on the hair, eyes, and sandals; in the time of Sargon, the background was a light-yellow ochre, reds and blues were especially beloved, and the brighter the better.

Above the dado of sculptured slabs, six to eight feet high, were plastered walls painted in tempera. As seen by the excavators, the colours were still bright, but they quickly faded on exposure to the air, and the unstable backing of mud brick contributed to their destruction. The colours have been analysed: the white was tin oxide, the yellow—Naples yellow it would be called nowadays—was an antimonate of lead with some tin, the blue was copper oxide, the greens came from the same source, the dark brown was an iron, and the red was a suboxide of copper. Numerous and elaborate as were the frescos, they were, in general, designs rather than figures or scenes. Dados of black, horizontal bands of various colours, rosettes or other floral subjects were on the walls where there were no sculptured reliefs. More rarely we find such a grouping as that of two white bulls, traced in black on a yellow ground with dark-blue decorations above, or a blue bull with eagle's wings. One composition was still more elaborate, a richly decorated horse with attendants which came from Dur Sharrukin.

After all, the traveller who knows his present-day Orient will not look for the best colour-effects in painting. Tiling has always been one of the best-known products of the Near East. Our first examples date from Ashur-nasir-apal, when we have captives in yellow tunics, blue overgarments, and white fringes outlined in black on a yellow ground, or guilloches in red and blue with white borders and black-and-white centres, between alternate palm-cones, palmettos, and pomegranates in red, white, and blue, in black and yellow. The highly elaborate design of his son Shalmaneser III receiving his commander-in-chief has already been described in detail.

The greater portion of the tile-work belongs to the period of the Sargonids. To Sargon himself belong the Dur Sharrukin representations. Here the ground is regularly blue, while the figures are in yellow, for since their purpose was primarily architectural, no attempt was made to represent the figures in the colours of life. White rosettes with raised centres mark the beginning of the technic which was to culminate in the raised bricks of the Chaldæan period. Blue, yellow, and white were the colours most beloved by Sargon's architects, though we find green employed for the leaves of the trees and part of the head-dress. Red also is rare, but appears in one brilliant tile, two white-faced men, with a horse's head and elaborate trappings between, on a green ground, and above a complicated design in which red, white, green, and yellow appear in turn.

A few fragments dating probably from the reign of Sennacherib complete the collection. On a pale-yellow ground appear yellow captives with shaven heads and necks roped together;

Fig. 168. PHŒNICIAN SHIELD FOUND IN CRETE, ASSYRIAN DESIGN.

two of them wear white loin-cloths, two long white garments, open down the front. Again, two blue horses are depicted on an olive-green background, and an Assyrian soldier is seen with an enemy, armed still with a dagger but wounded, who is clad only in a blue loin-cloth. A third presents yellow horses with blue harness on an olive-green ground. An enemy with white loin-cloth is shot by two arrows and a white scaled fish in blue swims in yellow water. Another enemy, naked save for fillet and feather, is pierced in the neck by an arrow, while blue horses hitched with white harness to a yellow chariot pass over the foe. Two soldiers with yellow helmets and shields of blue edged with yellow and blue squares have their faces outlined in white with the olive-green of the background showing through.[1]

Metal-working was likewise a highly developed art. From the most archaic period we have a female statuette in bronze, her close-fitting clothes draped over her left shoulder, with an elaborate mass of hair looped from her crown to her neck. Ashur-nasir-apal has left us fragments of bronze repoussé work on the hinges of the great palace door, and his son Shalmaneser III enlivened the record of his conquests with numerous scenes in the same fashion. Sargon, too, employed this form of decoration. Bits of the bronze-work from the throne of Ashur-nasir-apal show winged lions and bulls, or deities before the sacred tree. Lion weights from the time of Shalmaneser V to that of Sennacherib illustrate an interesting development in style. Bronze bowls from Kalhu show much the same fusion of Assyrian and Egyptian motifs as the Cretan shields from the same period which are generally attributed to the Phœnicians. But a small part of the metal wealth of Assyria has survived the repeated plunderings of the capitals; only when we read the accounts of the annals, such as the inventions of Sennacherib, the list Sargon gives of the metallic booty from Musasir, do we gain a fair idea of the high state of metallurgy.

Still less has been preserved of the precious metals. Plates

[1] Cf. Handcock, *Mesopotamian Archæology*, 281 f.

of gold placed under foundations and with cuneiform inscriptions are now known in considerable numbers, a huge thunderbolt in gold over a wooden core which once was held by Adad hints at the glitter of the divine statues and of their homes, earrings and amulets in the same precious metal have been seen in the hands of the dealers. For ornaments, however, we must in general go to the sculptures, where we are fairly bewildered by the number of earrings, necklaces, pendants, rings, bracelets, worn by the king and the higher officials. Such ornaments as have survived are mostly of the less-precious stones. Richly carved cylinder seals were still hung around the necks of men until they were needed to authenticate their business agreements, though the stamp seal was already in use. Agates, garnets, and the like appear fairly frequently, and even amber had travelled the long route from the Baltic. Poorer people must content themselves with shells or with beads from glass paste which is found in the earliest graves in Ashur. But it is a poor selection of what was once in the Assyrian palaces.

CHAPTER XLIV

THE REED STYLUS OF THE SCRIBE

Six thousand years ago the Shumerians in Elam drew crude pictographs roughly similar to those just coming into use among their distant neighbours of Egypt. The Shumerian language was agglutinative, that is, in structure it was somewhat similar to the modern Turkish, with each separate element a single syllable; it was therefore not difficult to adjust a given pictograph to the verbal form or to another grammatical element of similar sound.

A little of the pictured original survived to the earliest known inscriptions, and sample characters of still more primitive appearance were preserved through the curiosity of later-day scholars. Unlike the Egyptians, the inhabitants of Elam had already passed beyond the pictographic stage when they entered the Tigris-Euphrates region.

The next stage was the linear, when simple lines were cut on the stone records of the early monarchs and the few business documents might be incised on flat stone tablets. By this time, the great majority of the signs had forever lost any resemblance to the objects commemorated and had become arbitrary symbols. As the use of writing became more widely spread, stone proved insufficient in quantity; Babylonia had only mud as a substitute, but certain layers of the mud furnished the finest of clay for the potter and brick-maker. A genial thought of some scribe led to the use of this clay in the place of the less-convenient and scarcer stone.

Experience soon showed that straight lines pulled up the clay in inconvenient ridges; another genial idea was the use of a reed stylus. Instead of a character formed by a single pull of the implement, there was a series of short lines stamped into the moistened clay. The stylus was of wood, about the size of a small pencil, with four flat sides and with one end

bevelled. This was pressed gently into the clay, one end sinking
more deeply than the other, and thus there was made the wedge
from which the writing secured the name of cuneiform.   The
stylus was laid down on the sharp edge.   If the tip was de-
pressed deeply, a short, deep, broad character, a true wedge,
was formed; if laid lightly, a long, narrow line was the result.
A large number of these short strokes was needed to represent
a single sign.   Economy of effort soon lessened the number of
such strokes, the last remnants of picture-writing disappeared,
and the signs became purely conventional.

No system of writing was possessed by the Semites.   As
they began to veneer themselves with the superior civilisation
of their neighbours, they wrote in their language, but Akkadian was an inflected language like our own, Shumerian an
agglutinative language, imperfectly understood in its finer
details, and it needed only the Sargonid supremacy to adapt
the signs to the language of the conquerors.

The difficulty of the task and the imperfectness of the fit
may be imagined.   Large numbers of the signs had been used
to represent objects or ideas; these were taken over en bloc,
but read with their Semitic translation.   Thus were formed
the ideographs.   Certain of the signs had already been used
as simple syllables, free from any relation to their original
meaning as pictographs.   All these were accepted, and to this
already long list of values was added the Shumerian pronunciation of the more important of the ideographs.   Certain of
the ideographs were likewise used for determinatives, the upright wedge was placed before the name of the man, another
sign stood before that of a woman, the star, still recognisable
as such, indicated that the name of a deity followed.

A rather elaborate literature had already been produced
by the Shumerians.   Records of the kings were brief, the praise
of a god, a mere reference to conquests, a somewhat fuller description of the building.   Letters were not infrequent and
business records were a commonplace.   Pure literature in our
sense did not exist; the nearest approach was found in the
religious writings, a hymn of praise to a god who must be con-

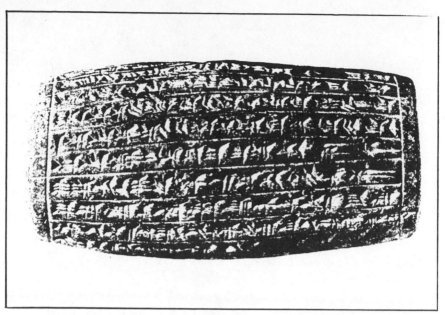

FIG. 169. CYLINDER OF ESARHADDON. (Yale Babylonian Collection.)

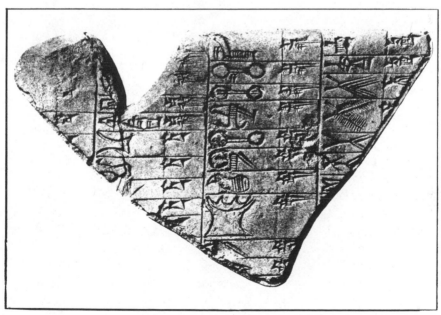

FIG. 170. LATE COPY OF THE EARLIER PICTOGRAPHS FROM WHICH
DEVELOPED THE CUNEIFORM WRITING.

ciliated, an incantation to drive away sickness. A few legends glorified the gods and answered such questions as how the universe came into being or attempted to satisfy the first speculations as to the entrance of evil into the world.

Each city praised its local god in this literature, and there were as many different creation stories and creating deities as there were independent city-states. Most prominent was Eridu, on a branch of the Persian Gulf, whose god Enki was ruler of the great abyss. His was the knowledge by which the evil spirits might be put to rout, in his honour was penned the prototype of the Hebrew Job. By the date of our first preserved records, the supremacy of Eridu was in the dim past, but traces of her influence are to be found throughout the whole later literature, and even the Greeks remembered how it was Oannes coming from the sea who gave Babylonia its first wisdom.

Also in times before written record was the political supremacy of Nippur, whose god Enlil through his divine "Word" gave the right to rule the alluvium to our oldest known conquerors. For a thousand years, Enlil remained the "lord" of Babylonia, in spite of changing dynasties. Anu, the sky-god, through the temporary supremacy of Uruk, was placed at the head of the pantheon, but he always remained far distant from the thoughts of the average Babylonian, and the accession of the Sargonids found Enlil still the real ruler of the country.

A Shumerian reaction brought the dynasty of Ur into power, and a perfect Renaissance of Shumerian literature ensued. To this period, in fact, may be traced the earliest surviving edition of many of the most important works. Then came the invasion of the west Semites, and the Semitic Akkadian became supreme.

Hammurabi and his colleagues brought about the greatest change in the history of Babylonian literature, the change from Shumerian to Akkadian; as, for instance, when he wrote down the laws in the tongue of the land. Shumerian still remained the sacred language, somewhat as was Latin in the Middle

Ages of Europe, and royal inscriptions placed it side by side with Akkadian. Shumerian formulas were retained in the business documents as Latin of a legal character is used to-day, until it is sometimes difficult to say whether a particular document is written in one or the other language.

This is the great age of translation. Huge dictionaries, the so-called "syllabaries," were prepared for the aid of the translators, and they have made possible for us the decipherment of the older language. Formal grammar was far in the future, but phrase-books afforded a control of the various forms. Sometimes translations were given by themselves, at others we have interlinear "trots" which are not always more accurate than those used by the lazy student of to-day. The genius of the Shumerian was quite different from the Akkadian, and the more advanced insight of a scientific philology often shows complete failure to grasp the finer distinctions.

No ancient scribe could be trusted to make a straight copy. Aside from mistranslations, of which there are sufficient, he must adapt his text to the new political and religious conditions. The rulers of the first dynasty of Babylon had a somewhat perverted patriotism which insisted that all literature should celebrate the glory of their city and of their city-god Marduk. Originally a minor solar deity, he was made the "father of all the gods."

The most famous of the creation stories, that of Nippur, honoured Enlil. His honour was rudely taken from him and handed over to Marduk; this required explanation, and the legend in its latest form told in detail the manner in which Enlil, after the other gods had refused the perilous task, assigned to Marduk the destruction of Tiamat, the chaos monster. Quite naturally, it was Marduk who completed the work of creation. Incantations, too, were to be said in the name of Marduk, though the Babylonian must always go to Ea, the successor of Enki of Eridu, for the exact prescription.

In the midst of this glorification of Marduk, the Assyrians slipped away from southern control. In their minds, therefore, Marduk remained the chief divinity of the alluvium and

Babylon was the chief city. Such literature as they had known was in the version which honoured Marduk. The result to literature was no less important than it was to political theory.

Assyria took over the signs in use under Hammurabi. Already they had been somewhat reduced in number and in complexity, and the process continued in the new state, but the Assyrians were less business men, their scribes were less in a hurry, their minds were more conservative along certain lines, and soon their forms were more complex than those used by the Babylonian merchant in his daily transactions.

The Assyrian language was a near neighbour of the Akkadian but not a mere dialect. There were important phonetic differences; for instance, when an Assyrian wished to say "from" he used *ishtu* instead of *ultu*. Differences in vocabulary were marked and the syntax was not always quite the same. The differences were something like those between English and Dutch. The average Assyrian could read Babylonian without much difficulty, though Ashur-bani-apal found it as necessary to have special instruction in Akkadian as in Shumerian.

Good honest Assyrian was the language of every-day life; in it were published the laws; even letters to the court were in pure vernacular, and their nervous, direct, picturesque style makes us regret that the scribes did not condescend to use it in their literary productions. Instead of developing their own language, they attempted to write Akkadian, and the result was the fearful and wonderful mixture of the royal annals. Assyrian scholars never quite succeeded in writing pure Babylonian, and the records of Ashur-nasir-apal in particular have a large infusion of native forms and phrases. In time, their Akkadian improved.

In language, the royal annals might be a queer compound of the two languages, the style was purely Assyrian, and they are the greatest glory of the Assyrian literature. In a very real sense, true history begins with the Assyrians. Their predecessors in Babylonia had been quite content with the barest reference to their conquests or their buildings, though a few rare exceptions do pass beyond this. Annals were not quite unknown, and the practical necessities of business demanded a certain attention to chronology, but the scribes of Hammurabi had barely gone beyond the line or two that described a successful war or a religious ceremony which was used to date the year. Hittites and Egyptians had annals of a sort, and the former often prefixed a historical introduction of some literary pretensions to their treaties.

Arik-den-ilu is the author of the first truly annalistic history in Assyria. Coming so soon after Assyrian relations with these two countries, we may suspect a certain influence, but the chief basis was Babylonian. The three main divisions, invocation to the gods, account of the conquests, statement of the building operations, remained the three chief divisions to the last edition. The invention of the cylinder, or hexagon, with its crowded lines of script, permitted a longer narrative, and with the inscription of Tiglath Pileser I we have the annals full grown.

Historians up to very recent times have considered foreign wars the chief if not the only subject worthy of their pens, and the Assyrian scribes were not in advance of their successors. In fact, they were the first to prepare detailed narratives of their military expeditions, and a too close following of their annals by modern writers has created the impression that the Assyrians were more warlike than the other imperial races of history. After all, history must be written on the basis of the extant records, which is why even the present volume is too largely a record of war.

The Assyrian scribe was almost a fanatic for exact chronology, and the system by which each year received its name from some high official was a great aid. As pious introduction and conclusion dealing with building grew ever longer, many facts of cultural interest crept in, and they are never absent from the main narrative. Sometimes the annals are dull lists of formulas, as in those of the last Tiglath Pileser, but even the dullest has its flashes of genius, its quotable phrases, its apt comparisons, its keen appreciation of nature.

The highest flights of which it was capable are seen in the great tablet inscription composed for Sargon or in the literary exercises of Ashur-bani-apal. Constant quotation in the preceding pages will have shown how effective from the literary standpoint is much of this historical material.

Unfortunately it is true, though quite understandable in these days of historian propagandists, that the neutral historian cannot praise his predecessor as much for accuracy of fact as for vividness of expression. These scribes were no cold-blooded scientists, willing to tell the truth, however unpleasant or however derogatory to their country's fame. They were state officials, with all the opportunity to know the truth which comes from official position and all the inducements to tell the story as their master wished which influenced nineteenth-century "nationalistic" history or the franker twentieth-century official propaganda. Success in glossing over unpleasant facts meant promotion, too great truthfulness might lose their heads. Patriotism demanded that records inscribed on the walls to be read by ambassadors or subject princes should teach the folly of resistance to Assyrian demands. Thus royal annals were of the same character as the recent productions which have shown so often that our boasted scientific writing of history is one more of the great illusions.

Each year an important conquest was made saw a new edition prepared. The first edition more closely approximated the truth as it was known to contemporaries, though with many gaps and not a few misstatements of facts. This portion was much abbreviated in the next edition and "improvements" were introduced which seriously vitiated its accuracy. Finally, and this is especially true of Ashur-bani-apal, honesty is thrown to the winds and whole campaigns are stolen from the father to add to the glory of the son.

Statistics were the special joy of the Assyrian historian and he could perform wonders with their aid. A favourite trick was to retain the original number of enemies killed or prisoners and booty taken, and to prefix to this a huge round number. This operation can be traced from edition to edition, as when

the original account of the sheep taken at Musasir says 1,235
and the official annals composed seven years later says 100,-
225.   When, therefore, we find Sennacherib claiming the capture of 200,150 from Hezekiah of Judah, it is natural to assume that the real number was 150.

So well did the Assyrians handle their histories, at least
from the literary point of view, that we expect great things in
the other categories of the ancient literature, but we are doomed
to disappointment.   Only in the literature centring about
Ashur do we have a purely religious and native development.
There was a creation story which gave the honour to Ashur,
and the hymns to Ashur are native compositions, however
they may have been modelled on the Babylonian.   The prophecies of Ishtar of Arbela have real literary merit and often
remind us of Biblical parallels in the later literature of consolation to degraded and captive Israel.   Here and there in
the Babylonian compositions found in Nineveh we may detect Assyrian interpolations.

The Assyrian genius for religious composition was unfortunately overwhelmed by the enormous mass of Babylonian
literature already available.   The ever-increasing waves of
Babylonianisation in the last Assyrian century made the Babylonian gods, with Marduk at their head, and by his side Nabu,
the god of the writing stylus, more prominent than ever.   With
them came their literature.   The libraries were filled from
Babylonia, though it may be questioned what was the influence of the tablets brought in so late as the time of Ashur-
bani-apal.

While Ashur-bani-apal was filling his library with tablets
from the earlier literature, there was going on a struggle which
was quite unnoticed by contemporaries, and no historian has
sung the warfare.   At least five thousand years before, the
Egyptians had invented an alphabet, in which the various
consonantal sounds were represented by a single sign.   Their
invincible conservatism had prevented extensive use of the
new system, and more particularly since the older pictographic
writing was a shorter and more convenient method of abbre-

viation—after the scribe had learned the large number of signs. It was therefore used principally for spelling out foreign names and words.

About the middle of the second millennium, Semites borrowed the alphabet and abandoned the remainder of the complicated system. Our first traces of this, the first true alphabet the world had ever seen, are found in the Sinaitic peninsula, but exactly who its authors were has not yet been discovered. Some have argued that Arab nomads have the honour, but it is far more probable that the traditional attribution is true, for the Phœnicians were just coming into their own as international traders. By the middle of the ninth century, the alphabet is in extensive use in Syria, as is testified by the Kalamu and Zakir inscriptions in the north, by the stele of Mesha in Moab, by the jar writings of Ahab's palace, and by the numerous seals, such as that which bears the name of the second Jeroboam. So extensive an employment can only be explained by a fairly long use of the alphabet in Phœnicia, especially as the characters all show the effect of much cursive writing.[1]

Though written in the Phœnician character and language, the names of the individuals who prepare them and the slips in the language show the north Syrian inscriptions the work of Aramæans. In the next century, the records are in the Aramæan language itself. Thus by the middle of the eighth century the two commercial peoples of the empire were using the alphabet. This is the very period when Aramæans were settling in every corner of Babylonia and Assyria; it is just in this middle of the eighth century that we chance upon our first Aramaic "docket" on a cuneiform tablet, and a half-century later they begin to make their appearance in Assyria. Business documents are still written in the cuneiform Assyrian, without which the transaction would not be valid, but on the edge of the tablet would often be found a notation in Aramaic, brief, but sufficient to identify it. The writer is obviously

[1] Gardiner, *Jour. Egypt. Archæology*, III, 1 ff.; Luckenbill, *AJSL.*, XXXVI, 27 ff.

accustomed to Aramaic as his native language. Soon the
court found it necessary to possess an Aramaic scribe. Matters had gone so far in the reign of Ashur-bani-apal that two
high officials could send an official letter to one another, not
in cuneiform on a clay tablet, but as an Aramaic ostracon.

The end of the Assyrian Empire saw the advantage still on
the side of the cuneiform, and in the last years of Ashur-bani-
apal Assyrian business documents were prepared in Gezer
of Palestine. Throughout the whole Chaldæan period they
continue to be so written, but Aramaic indorsements increase,
and there are no tablets from the west. Darius the Persian afforded the last opportunity to the cuneiform, when his scholars
adapted the writing to the Iranian language, and a real alphabet, though less perfect than the Semitic, was prepared. Only
Darius himself left full records in the new writing, his successors used it most sparingly. Another century saw the Aramaic adopted as the official language of the Persian Empire.
Egypt is full of Aramaic papyri, including those from the Jewish community at Elephantine; Jewish leaders in Palestine
preferred it to the antiquated, if sacred, Hebrew; natives of
Asia Minor wrote in it or used its characters for their own
language; the Phrygians borrowed it towards the end of the
eighth century, the Lydians used it side by side with their own,
the Greeks took over the Phœnician form in the seventh or
sixth century. It became the accepted character of Europe
and has retained its place to this day, with still ever-increasing
range, while both character and language were the common
possession of the Near East for a thousand years till the neighbour Arabic came to hold its sway to the present.

The cuneiform was now confined to Babylonia. Conservatism continued to employ it through Persian and Hellenistic and into the Arsacide period. The last tablets date from
the first century before our era. The final battle of the cuneiform had been fought and lost, and the script became for nineteen hundred years the great mystery of western Asia.

Side by side was waged another battle of culture. Like the
cuneiform writing, the clay tablet had its day of victory. To-

gether they had spread to Mesopotamia, to Armenia, to Asia Minor, to Syria and Palestine, to Egypt, and the Minoans of Crete, though they had invented a new system of writing of their own, retained the clay tablet.

When the Minoans fell before the Indo-Europeans, the tablet disappeared. About the same time, it ceased to be employed in Asia Minor, and Egypt knew it no more after it ceased to be longer needed to communicate with Syrian vassals. Examples are found in Palestine to the days of Ashur-bani-apal, but its fate had by now been settled.

Papyrus had already reached Phœnicia in the days of Wenamon, who found the archives of the Zakkalu chief thus written. Its progress was much slower than that of the alphabet, or even of pen and ink. Ink first appears on the margin of the clay tablet, then it was used on the potsherd. Papyrus did not grow in western Asia, it must be exported long distances, it was easily broken. A substitute was therefore discovered, the prepared skins of beasts. Skins of cattle and of white lambs are assigned to the priests of Gula and Ishtar, to the city scribe and the scribe of the temple.[1] The new writing material first appears under Tiglath Pileser III, and thereafter every expedition has its two scribes, the chief with stylus and tablet, his assistant with papyrus roll or parchment and Egyptian pen.

After the Chaldæan period, the tablet was confined to Babylonia. Pen and paper had won the fight against the clumsy tablet, but the tablet had its revenge; the papyri and parchments of western Asia have disappeared as completely as will our paper, but the clay tablets survive the centuries.[2]

[1] Schroeder, *OLZ.*, XX, 204.
[2] Cf. Breasted, *Physical Processes of Writing in the Early Orient, AJSL.*, XXXII, 230 ff.

CHAPTER XLV

DIVINE MYSTERIES

SCIENCE, the pursuit of knowledge for its own sake, made no appeal to the ancient Oriental mind; it was wisdom, the knowledge that produces a practical result, which in Biblical language was more precious than rubies. Like the Biblical wisdom, it was of divine origin and closely associated with things divine; it was the wisdom of the fathers and it was confined to the learned class. The Oriental attitude could not be better summed up than by the heading prefixed to one of the astrological works: "Let wise man tell wise man, the fool shall not behold it, for it is a mystery of the gods Anu and Enlil."

Great discoveries might have been expected in wisdom from the curious and versatile Semitic mind; the Assyrian aristocracy was interested in other, and to them more important, matters than natural science. In general, they were content to take their wisdom ready-made.

Primitive man early begins to speculate concerning the sensible world about him and to inquire how the universe came into being. Each city-state of Babylonia possessed its story of origins in which its divine king played the part of creator. With their usual patriotic acquisitiveness, the scribes of Babylon worked up all the earlier material into the seven tablets which show all the other gods, in fear of the dread chaos monster Tiamat, handing over their rights in the creative process to Marduk in recognition of his bravery. Most Assyrian scholars accepted this as the orthodox theory of creation.

Contact with Babylonia made the Assyrians conscious that they too needed a local creation story. Now in the seven tablets, immediately after the chaos monsters, appeared Anshar and Kishar, parents of the sky-god Anu, and the first deities to represent order. Even the epic in honour of Marduk admitted that they got the better of the forces of disorder. The Assyrians therefore went back of Marduk and identified Ashur with Anshar.   It was Anshar and not his successor of Babylon who destroyed the chaos monster by creating a mighty wind which was thrust up her nostrils and thus killed her, it was Anshar whom the gods celebrated and who assigned them their places.   The last, and naturally the most important, of Anshar's creative acts was the establishment of a copy of Esharra, the pronouncing the name of the city of Ashur, whose was to be the rule over whatever his hands had created, over the earth that his hands had created.   At the prediction, the gods rejoiced.[1]

Sennacherib was not satisfied with even this concession to Babylonian thinking. To him Ashur alone was the sole creator.   He was not only king of all the gods and father of the gods, lord of the whole body of gods, king of heaven and earth —he was creator of the gods, creator of Anu's heaven and of the abode of the dead, maker of all peoples; he fixed their fates. Sennacherib retold the story of the struggle with Tiamat. Before Ashur went the Mesopotamian gods, Sharur, Shargaz, the messenger Gaga, Nusku, Shulmanu, Tishpak, Urta of the wall, Azag-suga, Hani, Sibitti; after him marched Ninlil, Sherua, Sin, Ningal, Shamash, Aia, the Mistress, Anu and Antum, Adad and Shala, Ea and Damkina, the Mistress of the gods, and Urta.   Marduk, Nabu, and their consorts are conspicuously missing.   Mounted on a chariot with Amurru as his driver, he raised his bow against Tiamat and the monsters her progeny, he drew up his battle-line of gods in chariots and afoot, he loosed against her the deluge.   The gods who were on foot bound Tiamat and brought her to Ashur, her progeny fled seeking a safe place, but were put to death.[2]

After creation, primitive man demands a series of demigods to explain how various facts of life came to be. Such a myth as that of Adapa breaking the wings of the west wing,

---

[1] *CT.*, XIII, 24 f.; Rogers, *Cuneiform Parallels*, 54 ff.
[2] Craig, *Religious Texts*, I, 83; Meissner-Rost, *Bauinschriften*, pl. 16; Rogers, *Parallels*, 57 ff.

his ascent to heaven, his being cheated by a trick of eternal life, answered the very practical question as to why man does not live forever. The same question is raised in the great epic, that of Gilgamesh, which is in truth a series of etiological myths.

Incorporated in this was the story of the world flood, which, starting from Babylonia and closely copied in Palestine, followed the south of Asia, crossed the Pacific by its chain of islands, and divided into both North and South America. Two widely differing stories had been incorporated in the epic, one from Shuruppak, whose hero was Atrahasis, the other centring about Pir-napishtim of Sippar. The Assyrian addition was characteristic.

The original author placed the landing-place of the ark on Mount Nisir, the "Mount of Salvation," and by this he undoubtedly meant one of the peaks of the near-by mountains of Elam. Ashur-nasir-apal identified it with the magnificent isolated mountain he found east of his own country. The opening up of this territory moved the ark still farther into the unknown, and in the later years of the empire it was supposed to have rested on the mountains of Urartu. This last century of Assyrian rule, especially during the long reign of the pro-Assyrian Manasseh, was the period when the legends of the Tigris-Euphrates region were being worked over by the Hebrew scribes. Although the Hebrew editor cleansed the flood story of all its polytheistic elements, he still retained the "mountains of Ararat" as the resting-place of Noah's ark. After the Christian Era, Josephus locates it in the Kurdish mountains, and a few hours' climb north of Mosul will still show the tourist its supposed remains. The restless ark had still one more move to make. Post-Christian identification was with the magnificent mountain still farther north, the highest in western Asia, though the native Armenians retain the knowledge that it really should be called Mount Masis, and that Airarat was a province far to the south.

The practical Assyrian mind desired knowledge of the past that he might understand the present, but still more did he wish to predict the future. No branch of wisdom could be more important, for no action of king or people might be carried out contrary to the expressed will of the gods. As a by-product followed the beginnings of many of the sciences.

Like all peoples of early culture, the Shumerians discovered the expression of the divine will in all the manifestations of nature. Their religion was saturated with ideas not far from the animistic, and every object around them might have a spiritual reason for its activity. Each action of bird and animal and insect was carefully observed, the more so if it were at all out of the ordinary, and with it a result which had been actually noted or one which had been deduced logically. Scores of tablets with these observations were copied for Ashur-bani-apal, but we rarely find them connected with historical happenings.

Careful note of such facts in nature had its reaction on the minds of the observers. Animals were divided into classes, "living beings," that is, men, vertebrates, birds, and "worms," fish, true worms, and the lower animals. Species and varieties were rather closely distinguished, and there was the beginning of a crude zoology.

Liver divination was the method of unveiling the future most in use at the Assyrian court. Throughout the whole world, at a certain stage of knowledge, the liver is conceived as the seat of the emotions, and the story of the last Assyrian century has shown how this belief survived side by side with the more familiar identification of this centre with the heart. While this belief was still dominant, Shumerian scholars had worked out an elaborate system of prediction based on the assumption that the future might be foretold by the most "knowing" part of the sacrificed sheep, the liver.[1]

Later this highly animistic belief was combined with a purely Semitic custom, the appeal to Shamash, the sun-god, as the lord of destiny. As substitute for the sacred lot cast in Arabia, a tablet was prepared and laid before Shamash, and he was besought to give faithful decision through the sacrificed sheep.

[1] Cf. especially Jastrow, *Religion*, II, 203 ff.; *Aspects of Religious Belief*, 147 ff.

After this concession to a higher power, the actual result was obtained from a minute study of the liver. Every line or protuberance was marked and a special science grew up. Actual happenings played some small part in its development, as when the correlation of signs with the events in the elder Sargon's life was attempted. Rigid logic formed its chief basis. All signs on the left were unfavourable, those on the right were propitious. Lines which resembled the things of earth had similar meaning on the liver, and the size of the objects concerned afforded appropriate indication. We have seen how often this method was used in a national crisis, and how valued is the light cast on the narrative history.

We should expect that such minute study of the internal organs would result in comparisons with those of a man, that some start would be made towards anatomy and medicine. It is a fact that the vocabulary devoted to human anatomy is extraordinarily large. Medicine was still encumbered with the whole paraphernalia of hocus-pocus derived from a remote and animistic past, but despite this severe handicap, something had been learned in medicine and hygiene. The letters dealing with the health of Ashur-bani-apal's family furnish an excellent picture of the medical art in the seventh century.

More typical of Babylonian wisdom is astrology, the forecasting of the future from the motions of the heavenly bodies. Of all the pseudosciences, astrology is the most worthy of respect, as is proved by the lateness of its survival and by the eminence of the scientists who have believed in the influences of the stars.

So austere a cult can hardly have grown from the rank soil of Shumerian animism or from the vaporous marshes of the alluvium. The stars indeed appear with Shumerian names, and some part of it may have been developed in the mountains of Elam. It is the thin air of the desert which gives a brilliance to the heavenly host not found in moister lands; the long night marches inevitable to avoid the day's heat afford unmeasured leisure to observe the only objects visible in the black dark. It is easy to discover that the path through the trackless desert may be directed by the stars, it is an easy transition to believe that one's march through life may be determined by these same heavenly orbs. Traces of the popular astronomy of the Arab have survived the invasion of Greek terminology.

The sun in his various manifestations is the chief god of the Semites. His path through the heavens is the ecliptic, and by him is determined the natural year. On his annual journey, he passes through the twelve constellations which give their names to the zodiac, names which have survived almost unchanged to our day. His withdrawal through an eclipse is a terrible calamity, likely to stir up revolt and worthy mention as the most important event of the year.

Sin, the moon-god, was the ruler of the night, when desert men must work, and there was always a tendency evident to place him on an even higher throne than the sun. His appearances and disappearances formed a convenient and obvious method of keeping time, and twelve of his months gave a year which could be adjusted to the solar year by the use of an occasional intercalated month, for no cycle had yet been invented whereby the adjustment might be regularised. His chief means of foretelling the future was through his eclipses. It was recognised that eclipse must take place at the full moon, but the sar, or period of six thousand five hundred and eighty-five days, a little over eighteen years, after which eclipses recur, had not yet been discovered.

Each full moon was carefully watched, and report was made as to whether the awaited eclipse took place or not. Since the greater number of the lunar eclipses are partial, special attention was directed to such cases. The moon's disk was divided into four sections, one each attributed in the celestial geography to Akkad, Elam, Subartu, and Amurru. Reference to the Amorite land fixes an upper limit, the failure to mention Assyria determines the lower date, with the result that the system must have been put in use about the time of Hammurabi.

Assyrian scholars took the system over without change, and

in their letters regularly cite verbatim the Anu-Enlil series. Akkad became a foreign land, and Assyria desired its fate to be good when it was united with Assyria, bad when disjoined. Subartu was identified with Assyria, as an explanatory note from one of the astronomers informs the king. Elam and Amurru were regularly enemy lands. The omen was repeated in its ancient form, but the scribes did not hesitate to add an explanation in terms of the present-day situation.

While the opposition of sun and moon was carefully watched for eclipses of the moon, the conjunction was observed for another purpose. By it and by the first appearing of the new moon, the new month was ritually established and all was happiness once more, since the god had reappeared. The ritual first of the month was determined by actual observation—that the letters prove; but the business documents show that there was also a standard artificial month.

At the conjunction of sun and moon they had learned that solar eclipses might be expected, though they did not know just when. Solar eclipses are far less in numbers, but the three great total eclipses of the sun, August 15, 831, April 2, 824, and June 15, 763, all within the space of a man's life of threescore years and ten, must have given a powerful impulse to the study as it impressed the Hebrew prophet Amos and the editor of the Assyrian Chronicle. Mar Ishtar relates how the moon disappeared on the 27th, how they kept watch on the 28th, 29th, and 30th for the eclipse of the sun, but it passed by until the moon appeared on its proper day, the 1st of July, and fixed the new month. The king has written Balasi: "Is there anything in the heavens? Do thou observe." His eyes are steadfast, he sees nothing at all; this is the reason he has sent nothing to the king, for there is nothing to interpret. It is now the month to expect an eclipse of the sun-god, and watch will be kept on the 26th of November and the 26th of December. The expected eclipse did not take place; the king will hear the news with a sad heart. An eclipse was calculated but was not visible in Ashur, for as it approached that city, behold there were clouds everywhere and it was impossible to discover if the eclipse took place. Let the king send to the cities of Babylonia, surely it was seen in those cities, and so the king may secure reliable information. The abarakku and the magicians had calculated the sign of the eclipse, it was to come in May or April. Although the king had not abandoned the freeing incantations against the eclipse, which in fact are performed to make good any sin whatsoever, the great gods who dwell in the king's city overcast the sky and did not permit him to behold the eclipse, for they said: "Let the king realise that this eclipse is not hostile to the king or to his land." Let the king rejoice; in the month of April the weather-god Adad will grant peace and the seed-grain will be restored.[1]

Munnabitum sends the king a letter about the lunar eclipse, instead of reporting by word of mouth. The month, the day, the watch, the exact point where the eclipse began and withdrew are the points to be considered in fixing its evil. The month of June refers to Amurru and a decision is given to Ur; its evil applies to the fourteenth day, since they declare: "The fourteenth is Elam." The exact point where it began is unknown, but it withdrew to the southwest, which predicts evil for Elam and Amurru; as it was bright to the east and north, it is propitious for Subartu and Akkad, it says they shall win favour. The omen for all lands: The right of the moon is Akkad, the left Elam, the upper part is Amurru, the lower is Subartu. Jupiter stood in the eclipse, it signifies peace for the king, his name will be honoured and without a rival.[2]

On the thirtieth day the moon was high; let the king wait before the city of Ashur, let the king establish the day. Sin has set his face for favour, it is the beginning of the month, but it is not good to plan a thing for this day. His light is bright on the 13th, it is auspicious for a military expedition, on the 14th moon and sun are together, a favourable day will be opened up.[3]

With the sun and moon went the five other planets, "stars that alter their positions and cross the heavens." Morning

[1] H. 744; 687; 895.   [2] H. 1006; cf. H. 137.   [3] H. 894; 352; 76.

and evening stars were recognised as identical and considered as Ishtar, the predecessor of Venus in the skies as in the hearts of men and women. Mercury was the abode of Nabu, and because of its closeness to the sun was most carefully observed and with surprisingly accurate results. Mars was identified with Nergal, the destroying sun-god, doubtless because of its fiery red colour, and was naturally hostile to those who saw it. As the star of Elam, ever an enemy of the alluvium, it was the robber star, the star that deals death. Jupiter was the royal star and was identified by the citizens of Babylon with Marduk; the "terribly bright and great star" was on the whole favourable but with the qualifications due to an earthly monarch who was essentially just but humanly capricious. We have seen what a part his favourable movements played in the restoration of Babylon by Esarhaddon.[1] Saturn, the black star, was the guardian of right and justice, and since it reached its culmination in the "Scales," these came to be accepted as symbols of justice.

Mar Ishtar has written the king that Jupiter appears in the path of Anu, in the region of the star of the faithful shepherd, Orion; it is low in the haze, he does not understand yet its interpretation. Now it is lifted up, it stands below the constellation of the Chariot in the path of Enlil, and its interpretation is completed for this position but not for the earlier. When Jupiter meets eclipse, it will be well with the king, the family of the nobility will be powerful, the decrepit will cease. Venus has established its appearance at sunrise, it is fixed, it entered in the middle of April. Rites for Dilbat or Venus are regularly carried on in conjunction with those for other goddesses. The king has inquired about Mercury; yesterday Ishtar-shum-eresh proclaimed in the palace its going forth to Nabu-ahe-eriba. The signs of the rest day have come, all have been observed, they have passed off. Such is the report of Balasi. Mars is dominant, its brilliance is increasing; if the crown prince should enter before the king, some harm might befall.[2]

[1] See p. 378.   [2] H. 744; 46; 82; 23; 993; 354; 356.

Each of the seven planets had its own path in the heavens, though all were close together. Perhaps each had a separate sphere. Beyond them were the stars proper, and all were in a sort of celestial sphere, or perhaps rather three spheres. The description of the celestial sphere as it is taught to beginners to-day would have been intelligible in large part to the ancient Babylonians. They would have understood horizon and meridian, celestial equator and poles, and they knew the path of the ecliptic. Right ascension and declination would have puzzled them rather as terms than as factors of measurement, for they too knew the vernal equinox with which they logically began their year, and one of their systems of measurement divided the celestial sphere into three hundred and sixty degrees. This last we have been unable to improve. They knew that only at the two equinoxes were day and night equal, and they had calculated the average at other periods. Since the earliest observations, the equinoxes had made a long movement; while the vernal equinox in Assyrian times was in the sign of the Ram, there were plenty of observations before the first dynasty of Babylon when it was in the sign of the Bull, and one at least, that on the so-called astrolabe, was in the sign of the Twins.

We best realise the likeness to our own "Astronomy without the Telescope" when we turn to the stars. The "astrolabe" in its present badly copied form dates from the time of Ashur-bani-apal, but the star positions have been calculated for 4864 or thereabouts. The chief fixed stars are arranged in three concentric circles, belonging to Anu, Enlil, and Ea, respectively. Around the edge are the names of the twelve months, and each month has three stars attributed to it, one for each heaven and god. Each star is given its proper degree; in the outer ring this is based on a complete circle of two hundred and forty degrees, in the middle of one hundred and twenty, in the inner of sixty. More generally, the circle of three hundred and sixty degrees is used, as in the case of the "trip among the stars," in which distances from one constellation to another are given within five degrees and with a really remarkable exactness, once the changed position of the stars is reckoned with. Fragments of star maps draw lines in accordance with those on our maps to-day or stars are grouped into triangles, squares, or "wagons."

Superficial examination is enough to indicate that these are no rough estimates made by the eye alone. The meridian was very simply learned by means of a ziqpu instrument through which the north star was sighted, naturally quite another than ours, for about the time of Hammurabi it was alpha of the Dragon. The observer took his position just before sunrise, facing the south, and noted that at this moment a certain star culminated "in the midst of heaven," that is, on the meridian, or was just rising heliacally. Stars which might thus be observed were called specifically ziqpu stars and belonged to the Enlil way. By computing stellar distances, the other stars might be placed, especially by noting those which rose or set at the moment the determining star was at the meridian.

A second machine was the water-clock, which was probably already in operation in the Assyrian period. For a complete day of twenty-four hours, a talent or something like sixty pounds of water was permitted to flow through. Measurement of elapsed time was then reckoned in weight, down to ten shekels of water, the equivalent of four minutes. Time was in turn translated into degrees, the same as ours, on the circle of three hundred and sixty, and in this manner the right ascension of stars along the equator was found.

Some other machine must further be assumed, perhaps some sort of an armilla, for we have equally close reckonings of the stars along the ecliptic which could have been secured only by some such means. For instance, a fragmentary tablet exists with pictures of the zodiacal signs, of which are preserved the Virgin, winged and with the ears of grain, the Scales, and the Scorpion, also with the appropriate symbols. Each has thirty vertical lines, corresponding to the thirty degrees included within the signs. The position of a star is marked by a horizontal line over one of these vertical lines. The sign for the Scales is over what would correspond to one hundred and eighty-six degrees, and this is exactly where the chief star of the Scales was about 800.

Not content merely to reckon in degrees, Babylonian astronomers must often have asked the same question which is regularly put to their successors: "What is the star distance in units whose meaning we can grasp?" So they translated the degrees into double hours, each degree containing one thousand eight hundred, with a total of six hundred and fifty-five thousand two hundred. If these are taken as earthly measurements and if we estimate the average double hour as something between seven and eight miles, the circuit of the ecliptic and therefore the circumference of the universe comes to little less than five million miles. Modest as it is in comparison with the modern light-year, this was a tremendous and awe-inspiring universe. Astronomers who were accustomed to calculate distances between two such closely connected stars as the Twins at over fifty thousand miles would be easily brought to a mood where they might exclaim with the Hebrew psalmist: "What is man that thou art mindful of him?"

Turning to the star map, there are many old friends. Individual mistakes in identification there may well be and not all are accepted by all the little group which has studied Babylonian astronomy, but in recent years men of different schools have come to a substantial agreement in most respects. Cassiopeia is already close to the Pole, a somewhat different Pole, to be sure, she "stands the whole year in the heavens," though she is the "Irrigator," and the Dipper bears its alternate name of the Wain. The Capricorn, with his human head and fishy tail, is there, as in the seacoast sculptures of Sargon or as he was cast into the sea by Sennacherib. The Snake and the Scorpion threaten from the heavens, as do the Lion, the Wolf, and the Eagle; the various Fish may still be caught, the Twins are together.

These are easily identified. Others appear under unfamiliar names, but we begin to be certain of their location. Sirius is the Arrow; the Sirius year is very early in Babylonia, and there may be connection with the similar year of Egypt. The Star pre-eminently is the Pleiades, Orion is the True Shepherd of the Heaven, the Lynx was earlier the Boar, Aldebaran is the Fire. These seem certain, but the list might be much extended did we accept plausible identifications.

Planets and stars are in the distant vault of heaven; what is their relation to the earth? The earth, so a Babylonian map reveals to us, was conceived of as a flat object, cut by the Persian Gulf and the two great rivers, and encircled by the waters of death, whence came the springs of the earth, and beyond were the lands of mythology. Below was the underworld, above were the heavens, quite literally in the plural. Some of the stars never left their place above, others descended for known periods into the underworld, thence to emerge in due season.

The question now arises how much was known in the Assyrian period and what of new was then produced. Already the wisdom of the ancients had been largely codified, but we dare not judge the astronomical knowledge of the time by the minimum of any given tablet, since the scribes copied records of various ages without discrimination, and often the position of the stars can be shown to belong to a far earlier century. But a reading of the whole of the preserved literature shows a fair number which belong by computation to our era. The tablet with the zodiacal signs must be placed about 800, and in the last Assyrian century belongs the so-called planisphere, with its seven stars of Cassiopeia and its plan of the Twins and the Bull. On the other hand, we must exclude certain improvements made under the Chaldæan dynasty and the still greater changes after contact with the Greeks.

Some of the astronomical texts approach closely to pure science, but the practical purpose of star study was not to give direction or to correct the calendar, but to predict the future. Our documents show scarcely a trace of the usage, so common among the "Chaldæans" of late Greek or Roman times, of securing the horoscope of the individual from the stars. Earlier generations were convinced that such mysterious, far-distant, powerful beings could be interested only in the fate of nations, and the preceding extracts from the letters will show how often the stars were consulted for this purpose.[1]

[1] There is no trustworthy account of Babylonian astronomy in English. The more purely astronomical texts are collected by Weidner, *Beiträge zur Kenntniss den babylonischen Astronomie,* to which must be added the letters in the Harper collection, translated by Professor Waterman, and those in Thompson, *Reports of the Astrologers and Magicians.* The huge astrological corpus has been collected by Virolleaud, *Astrologie chaldéenne.* Kugler, *Sternkunde,* is primarily devoted to the post-Assyrian period.

CHAPTER XLVI

OUR LORD KING

No monarch rules the Arabian waste. Each little tribal group has its chief, a man of good family and some wealth who enjoys the empty honour of offering hospitality to all and sundry who may seek his tent. When there is talk of a raid, he may be chosen leader if he is thought worthy; otherwise, the best warrior will lead the raiders. The war-chief has the higher honour and a larger portion of the spoil, but there is no guarantee that he will hold the chief place. Should at any time any individual resent the leadership of his chief, he has only to remove his tent from the encampment and be first man among such as may be persuaded to accept his own. The desert knows no laws and ordinances, only immemorial custom, enforced by weight of public opinion. It is the mother of self-help, individualism, and democracy.

The conquest of the Fertile Crescent brought the nomad into contact with a totally different theory and practice. We of the present find it extremely difficult to understand the psychical environment in which king-worship can grow up. For its full fruition somewhat peculiar conditions are required. The reign of primitive spirits must be left behind, the gods must be clear-cut, a hierarchy and a king of the gods are demanded. From a very early time the Shumerians had possessed conceptions which gave promise of such a development. City-state and god were identical. In the Shumerian writing, Nippur is "town of the god Enlil," the chief god of Lagash is the "lord of Girsu," one of its component parts, Nannar is called "king of Ur." One of the commonest phrases in the royal dedications is "To such and such a god, my king."

Since the local deity was the ruler of the state, nay, the very state itself, he was naturally conceived as owner as well as ruler of all that it possessed. In so many words, we are told that the various states are the property of their respective deities. Not temples alone are erected for his divinity; city walls and new suburbs likewise increase his patrimony. Under these circumstances, the patesi is but the deputy of the god, the chosen of the divinity, the beloved of his heart, whose name has been called by him.

As yet, there was little loss to the ruler in this dependence upon the god. The priesthood was not predominant, religion was still in large part a mere department of the state, and the patesi was the personal representative of the god. As such, his welfare was identified with that of the deity himself and of the state under his rule, and rebellion against him was rebellion against the deity. Since all things material belonged to the city-god, by the same process of reasoning all things material belonged to his deputy. In this conception we have the ancestor and prototype of the manorial system, according to which the land is the personal property of the monarch, and its tillers pay him rent and not taxes.

Strange as it may seem, there is no proof that the Shumerians took the final step which brought about king-worship. It was the Semitic invaders, with the zeal of new converts, who made themselves deities in every sense of the word. They placed before their names the star which marked divinity and accepted such statements as "Naram Sin is the god of Agade." The time came when human kings ruled over more than the alluvium, over more than was included in the land once ruled by the supreme god Enlil himself. It was an easy step to argue that the mighty hero was at least the equal of the gods. Political and personal considerations undoubtedly contributed to the movement. Vassals might not believe in the immortality of rulers they saw eating and drinking and suffering like themselves, but flattery might secure promotion; kings might not be quite sure of their divinity, but it eased the difficulties of government. And it is a truism that men soon come to belief in their own hocus-pocus.

When men acted as though their monarchs were gods, it was not long before they or their children were persuaded

that there was something of the divine in the hero who had
conquered distant lands and had given them internal peace.
The ruler likewise soon came to believe that had he not in him
something of the divine, far above the average of the common
herd, he could not have been the hero he undoubtedly was.

Under the Ur dynasty and in the reign of Dungi, we have
the culmination of the idea of the deification of the reigning
monarch.　Servile courtiers named their children from him,
identifying him with the god Babbar or giving them such names
as "The god Dungi is my god," "The god Dungi is my creator." His official inscriptions call him "god of his land," to
him was erected the temple E Dungi, the appointment of his
chief priest dated the year as did the installation of a priest
for any of the great gods, a feast was celebrated in his honour
and from it was named a new month, and offerings were presented at his shrine.　In his honour men recited hymns blessing
him as the Lord who made glad the land, who caused songs of
peace to be sung in the Lower Land, and wailing in the Upper.
The god Dungi is the "God-King," whose name excels every
other name, whether the name of Enlil, of Enzu, or of Babbar.[1]

With the west Semitic dynasty of Nisin, the kings continue
to be considered gods. One of its kings, Idin Dagan, is married through his statue with the statue of the mother goddess.
In one of the liturgies, five kings from Idin Dagan to Bur Sin
are identified with the sleeping Tammuz and no fruit grows
in the gardens.　Hammurabi not only receives his law code
from Shamash, as Moses did from Yahweh; he is himself the
"Shamash of Babylon," the "god of kings"; his subordinates
say of him "Hammurabi is god."

Assyria took over the custom as a matter of course.　Tiglath Pileser's statue is listed among those of the gods and the
sign for god often preceded the king's statue.　Ashur-nasir-
apal's statue has actually been found with its altar before it.[2]
Ahaz of Judah set up the altar to the Assyrian king in Jerusalem, and it must be included among the images worshipped

by Manasseh.[1] Installation of a statue of the king by the side of Ashur is noted throughout the history. Tammaritu speaks of the king's spirit in terms equivalent to those which would be used by a Roman when speaking of the emperor's genius.[2] Even the crown prince was felt to possess this same sacredness, for we have the proper name Mar-sharri-belia, "the crown prince is my god." On the long road from prehistoric kinggodship to the divine ruler of Hellenistic or imperial Roman times and to the divine right of kings so sadly shattered in our own day, one of the most significant stopping-places is the Assyrian Empire.

In Babylonia the priests had long since won the upper hand, in Assyria the god-king was more powerful and his country never became priest-ridden. In the south palace and temple were in separate quarters, in the north the temple was frequently a mere adjunct to the palace. Certain of the kings, Tiglath Pileser III and Sennacherib in particular, were distinctly antihierarchical in their attitude.

Yet it was not all pleasure to be the god-king and the head of the official religion; there were duties as well as privileges. For example, the 7th, 14th, 19th, 21st, and 28th days of the month are evil days when the "shepherd of a mighty people" is not permitted to eat any food that is cooked, clothe himself with a clean garment, or ride in his chariot. He may not even make an offering until evening when he shall pour a libation, and the lifting up of his hands will then please the gods and goddesses to whom the particular day is dedicated.

On these days, the seer should not give an oracle, even in a secret place; the physician should not lay his hand on a sick man—even for laying a curse it is unsuitable. The remarkable coincidence of four of these with the Hebrew seven-day week, the possible explanation of the nineteenth as a week of weeks, seven times seven from the first of the previous month, has often been observed. It has been found that the middle of the month was called Shabatum and this may be the same word as the Sabbath, since it is called a "day of rest for the heart,"

[1] Cf. pp. 198, 379.   [2] *H*. 943; cf. p. 463.

a "day of atonement," and this seems to have been the character of the Shabbathon, the predecessor of the Hebrew Sabbath. The interest of these speculations should not prevent our realising the part these ceremonies play in reducing the despotism of the king.[1]

New Year's Day was a particularly unpleasant time, when he must play the peasant and fast for the good of his people till the new moon appeared. We can fairly see the two religious leaders with their tongues in their cheeks when the opportunity is presented to read a lesson of religious control to the young Ashur-bani-apal. Though the day has ended, the new moon has not yet been seen; the king may not eat or drink until it does appear, and there is more than a hint of insolence veiled behind the obsequiousness of the formulas when they suggest that after the moon is really observed he may eat bread and drink wine the whole year through.[2]

Closely connected with his position as head of religion was that of judge. As we have seen in a preceding chapter,[3] there was an elaborate and distinctive law code, where self-help was strictly limited, where royal officials were in large part necessary to legal action, where crimes were often punished by induction into the royal service. The few tablets which have survived to present the legal side of the Assyrian life show the functioning of a chief judge or sartennu, as well as the judicial activities of the majority of the higher officials. The king always remained the ultimate court of appeal, and the letters frequently show such appeal to the king and his taking over the case.

No doubt, the typical Assyrian felt that his monarch was primarily a general, just as the Roman received his title of emperor from the imperator. No campaign of importance should be waged without the presence of the king in person, and if he were not present, courtly fiction still preserved the pretence. There was no regular army in the earlier days, for the levy was called out each year. When a crisis appeared, the whole available force of citizens might be summoned to

[1] IV R., 32 f.; Rogers, *Parallels*, 189.   [2] *H*. 78.   [3] Cf. p. 550.

Fig. 172. UNDERGROUND STAIRS.
(Fort in Asia Minor.)

Fig. 171. ASSYRIAN CAMP AND SOLDIERS.
(Louvre.)

march under the royal standard. Normally, there was no regret at the call, the levies were protecting their own crops from the wandering people of steppe or mountain, there was booty to be secured, individuals might be chosen to settle new posts and as colonists to lord it over the native population.

Peasants were liable to the levy until the end of the empire, but the state grew too large for the blood tribute to be inflicted without serious disorganisation of agriculture and trade. Governors raised the armies they needed for local operations or sent their troops to the aid of their sovereign, and now and then client princes forwarded their contingents. But the extent of the empire made revolt a certainty unless this was supplemented by a regular standing army. Our first indication that such an army was in process of formation comes in the reign of the last Tiglath Pileser, but it was Sargon who brought the "royal army" to perfection.

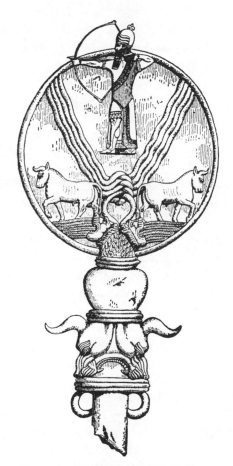

FIG. 173. ASSYRIAN STANDARD.

Closest to the royal person were his "Companions," the highest nobility of the land. Special detachments of bodyguards surrounded the king, the queen mother, the queen consort, the crown prince. Often they were used for special services, as bearers of royal rescripts, for transport of prisoners, for anything which demanded a confidential mission. A thousand picked soldiers were the troops "of his feet," so called because literally at the feet of the monarch as he rode his high chariot.

Chariots had been the main force of the king in the first Assyrian Empire, and the charioteers remained the elite corps throughout the whole history. As the Assyrians began to penetrate the mountains, they found it necessary to cut roads for the chariots, and even then it was not always possible to lead them into the innermost recesses. Horses were becoming better known, and by the time of Ashur-nasir-apal cavalry appear in great numbers. A majority of the troops was made up of foot-soldiers, bowmen and lancers, with partners to hold the heavy shields before them. Pioneers formed a very important part of the army, and we have had frequent occasion to note their labours; less is said of the commissariat, but this was in large part secured on the spot, for the Assyrians were past masters in the art of making war pay for itself.

The squad of ten under a non-commissioned officer was the smallest unit, but the normal tactical unit was the *kisru*, or company, of from fifty to perhaps two hundred, under the *rab kisir*, or captain. At the head of the army was the *rab shaqe*, unless the turtanu or the king took charge of the expedition in person.

Whatever part the native levies played in the standing army, it tended more and more to be filled with foreigners. Constant warfare had killed off the old sturdy peasantry, and their place was ill taken by deported captives. The necessity of keeping down the native population, the guarding against revolt by too efficient nobles, the danger of banditry or worse from the dispersal of conquered armies, led Assyrian kings, from Sargon onwards, to incorporate wholesale enemy forces into their own. Preceding pages afford frequent examples of such incorporation, and letters and documents show numerous cases where soldiers and even officers bear foreign names or are frankly recognised as belonging to some foreign country. Such a name as "He knew not his father" is especially significant when we find it assigned to a Chaldæan who was body-guard, equally so when we learn of the promotion of a man from Tabal to a captaincy.

Assyrian sculptures show us the equipment of these warriors. The bow was the chief weapon of offence, whether the soldier rode in a chariot, was on horseback, or on foot. A small proportion only bore lances, a few were slingers. Swords were rare, the common weapon being a dagger. Shields grew ever larger until one demanded the whole attention of a squire to protect his companion. Pointed helmets and coats of mail were worn by man and beast.

Warfare as carried on by the Assyrians would not be complete without account of the "artillery," the battering-rams and tanks, so often represented in the sculptures. Escalade formed a common method of attack and Sennacherib boasts of the "great flies of the walls." Mounds of circumvallation were commonly used, as were wooden banks against the city. We know little of Assyrian tactics, although we may sure they were superior, but the strategy we can test from the topography. Under geographical compulsion, their campaigns were often exact prototypes of those fought in the Near East in the last century.

Division of function between military and civil officials can scarcely be said to have existed in Assyria. The turtanu corresponded in a very real sense to the grand vizier of the Arab or Turkish Empire, who in turn was something of a chancellor or prime minister, but he also was in earlier days commander-in-chief of the army when the king was not himself in charge, and he was the governor of Harran, the former kingdom of Mitanni. When the turtanu became too powerful, his position as commander-in-chief was taken by the rab shaqe, whose title literally means "chief cupbearer." In the lists of eponyms, the king and the turtanu are followed by the rab bappiri, or "chief cellarer," or the nagir ekalli, the "chamberlain of the palace," and they by the abarakku, perhaps the lotion-maker, while less-important offices were filled by the chief cook or the chief trencherman. More specifically head of the court proper was "he who was over the palace."

The great advance made by the Assyrians in administration was the development of a provincial system. Empires before them had been formed by the personal union of two or more states, over each of which the king ruled by a separate royal title. Less-closely held states were governed by local kings with considerable autonomy, though under the Ur dynasty these patesis sunk to mere governors. Assyrian kings still pacified the most ancient states of the alluvium by this pretence of home rule and by the assumption of the particular royal title connected with that particular city-state, and they also called themselves "kings of kings," for they did rule subordinate kings of the buffer states on the frontier. Such dependent kings were controlled by a qepu, or "resident," who might deliver orders from home, or by a wife who had been a member of the Assyrian king's harem.

Provinces already existed as early as the middle of the second millennium. First in rank was the shakin mati, or "governor of the land," who ruled Ashur; then, as each conquered territory was reduced to provincial form, its ruler was placed in the list of eponyms. The second period of provincial government begins with the reign of Shalmaneser III, and the number and character of the provinces continued virtually unchanged until Tiglath Pileser III, who much reduced their size and importance, until their area barely reached that of the subdivisions of a province in the previous period. Thus the danger of revolt from an overvigorous governor was lessened, but there still remained too many cities of the first class, too many frontiers with the most serious problems to completely debase the provincial power, and the letters in nearly every case witness to the high position and skilful action of these governors. Occasionally, after a crisis, we find a Belibni who is viceroy in all but name.

Powerful as these governors sometimes were, the court kept careful check upon them. Shamash, through the liver omens, was regularly consulted about their appointment, and unfortunate indeed was the official when the sacrificed sheep possessed a liver with marks of ill omen. Once in his province, he was not left to slumber in peace or to oppress the provincials or to prepare revolt. He must report each event, no matter how unimportant, to his royal master, and the delay of a single day demanded a painful excuse. His subordinates were always ready to point out his shortcomings or sins in the hope of obtaining promotion for themselves, and his subjects made their complaints direct to the king, who then would send a sharp "royal word" to the luckless official. At any moment, a member of the king's body-guard might turn up with a reprimand, with the order for recall, or with instructions to put him quietly out of the way. Ashur-bani-apal's quarrels with Bel-ibni will illustrate every phase of a governor's worries.

Chief among the duties of the governor was the collection of the tribute. He must see that the subject kings on his borders brought in their yearly gifts of grain or animals, he must oversee in person the collection of those many taxes under which the serf or the member of the lower classes groaned. He must pay all the expenses of his own government, and still have enough for the dues to the great temples of the Assyrian capitals and for the upkeep of the court. One list has preserved the yearly contributions of a few of the provinces. Carchemish must pay the truly enormous sum of two talents of gold and a hundred of silver. Arpad and Que pay thirty talents of silver and Megiddo and Mansuate the half of that amount. Centre Nineveh gave thirty talents, Suburb Nineveh twenty, the New Quarter ten, the Queen's House twenty. New Kalhu paid but five and Suburb Kalhu but four, showing how Kalhu had fallen since it was abandoned by Sennacherib.[1]

A letter from an unknown correspondent indicates how the taxes from one province were divided. Two talents, twenty pounds of silver, clothing and elephant hides, fifty chitons and gowns, three jars of the lesser measure containing fish, twenty vessels of fish, one hundred fish, these are the tribute (madattu), while a crown of gold, twenty plates of silver, four

[1] J. 951; 953.

large gowns, fifteen tent covers from Hasa, ten chitons, ten large gowns, these are the taxes (nahartu) of the palace. Lesser amounts go to the "palace lady," and still less to the various court officials.[1]

Assyrian imperialism was in several respects quite different from what we know by that name to-day. Religious imperialism has disappeared, though agnostic statesmen may proclaim a war in the name of the national God and the protection of missionaries may be the excuse for filching a province. We must at the least credit the Assyrian with honesty when he carried on war in the name of Ashur, for to him the whole progress of Assyrian expansion was the triumph of the deified fatherland. To the extent that all states must acknowledge Ashur chief and father of the gods, the Assyrians were perfectly prepared to act the armed missionary. Beyond this, they cared little to impose their own culture. We have not a trace of any effort to enforce by law uniformity in language and custom. Once Ashur was accepted as chief god and taxes were regularly paid, the conquered or deported were reckoned good Assyrian citizens. Aramaic was used willingly by all officials, from the commander-in-chief to the humblest scribe, and it was employed on the estates of the crown prince. When a prince subject to Assyria wished to tell the world how much he was in favour with his Assyrian master, he used the Aramaic language.

Inevitably no subject state could be retained within the empire without becoming to a large extent Assyrianised, but no conscious effort brought this about. Narrow localism, such as obtained in the petty states of Syria, developed into a broader cosmopolitanism, but it was a healthy development. There was clash enough between the nationalism of the small states and the imperial ideal; we may sympathise with the former, but we cannot condemn the empire for an overzealous attempt to enforce uniformity.

It is universally admitted that the chief impulse to modern imperialism is the economic, and this in no broad sense, the

[1] *J*. 810.

betterment of the entire people, but narrowly commercial.
In the most primitive sense, Assyrian wars had an economic
basis, for they secured booty in the field and taxes thereafter
on which the governing classes might live. It cannot be sufficiently emphasised that commercial considerations in the
ordinary meaning of the word made absolutely no appeal.
There is no indication that the commercial classes had the
slightest influence on the foreign policy of the government,
and there is much evidence that the merchants were looked
upon with suspicion. Commercial cities were captured for
their booty, their taxes, their military situation, never as rivals
of merchant cities in Assyria proper.

No reader can peruse the letters without a very real admiration for the government as an administrative machine. Considering the circumstances under which they were written and
the proved fact that the majority which can be definitely assigned belong to periods of crisis, the whole impression is that
of remarkable efficiency. Graft is not entirely eliminated;
Adad-shum-usur, for example, has fallen so low that he cannot
even bribe a member of the court to take up his cause and,
therefore, must appeal to the king in person.[1] Inefficiency
and insubordination are sometimes asserted by rivals and
now and then are proved, but our feeling is that on the whole
the machine ran as smoothly as does the modern. There was
close inspection from above, but no serious loss of initiative
seems to have resulted.

It is not uncommon to assert that an ethical attitude towards
the ruler's subjects is the result of Christianity. We shall
certainly not look for a high development among the militaristic Assyrians. To be perfectly fair, however, we should note
the frequent occurrence of language implying something of this
attitude. The Good Shepherd was not first discovered by
Christians; the "faithful shepherd," the "true shepherd," the
"shepherd of the four world regions," are among the titles
the kings apply to themselves. If in practice there was more
stress on the worth of the sheep to the shepherd when sheared

[1] *H*. 2.

and eaten, enlightened self-interest demanded that the sheep be well fed and well treated and protected against the wolves, "the rulers and princes who hate me," the officials thinking only of their own welfare.

He may be a god himself, but he is also a pious follower of the great gods. With the aid of his helper gods, Ashur and Shamash, he walks righteously and it is their decrees which he carries out. He bears a sceptre of righteousness, which overwhelms all lands. Sargon's cylinder inscription is full of his claims of righteous action. Sennacherib is the watchful or the powerful shepherd, who fears the great gods, who guards the truth, who loves the right, who renders help, coming to the aid of the weak, and his expressed care for the groaning workmen and other signs of sentiment have already been noticed. Ashur-bani-apal in his messianic passages tells how happy was his land. The letters are as usual proof that this care was exercised in detail, if here too the figure of the calculating shepherd is somewhat in the foreground.

After all, the ultimate test of a government is not the good intentions of its rulers but what they accomplish. Judged by this test, the Assyrian can claim about as considerable a success as the next. Before the advent of the Assyrians, western Asia was in a state of chronic warfare between petty states; Assyria gave peace to a large portion of this area, a peace which was cheaply earned by isolated frontier wars or by taxation.

The material basis for Assyrian development was by no means of the best. Babylonia was of course extremely fertile, when it was administered from Assyria and was not inundated by nomads. Assyria proper was by no means rich in soil, for much was rocky and much could not be irrigated. Mesopotamia was fertile but denied water, Syria and Palestine were distinctly inferior. There was great mineral wealth just outside the borders of the empire, but little of this mining territory could ever be brought within.

That Assyria was the success she undoubtedly was must be attributed to two facts. First, her governing classes made the Assyrian peace. Taxation might be grinding but war was stopped, and such resources as the area possessed were allowed to develop. Second, these governing classes might look down on trade and commerce as such, but their peace permitted the development of the industrial possibilities of a population in the highest degree of technical efficiency. Add to this the trading ability of Babylonians and Aramæans, of Phœnicians and Greeks, who took advantage of the imposing imperial structure to make its treasures accessible to the races of the then civilised earth. The imperial structure was buttressed by industry and in its turn permitted a degree of industrialism which was unique in the world's history.

CHAPTER XLVII

ASHUR, THE KING–GOD

ASHUR was in many respects the precursor of Yahweh. In their beginnings, they had the same desert background. When their followers pressed forward into the same Fertile Crescent, they were faced by the same agricultural religion, and each took for his worship some of its least pleasing elements. Each became the supreme national god to a degree undreamed elsewhere, and each was attacked from without and about the same time. Each was about the same period well on the road towards monotheism. And then came the parting of the ways: Yahweh entered upon that unexampled development which led to the Christian Jehovah; Ashur succumbed to the miasma from Shumer.

In his first desert home, Ashur was a sun-god, a first cousin of Re of Egypt, Shamash of Sippar, Nergal of Kutu, and Marduk of Babylon. The desert sun is not a kindly deity who wakens the flowers from their winter sleep; he is the fierce god beneath whose blazing shafts pasturage withers, streams disappear, flocks and herds and man himself come to an untimely end. His fellow clansmen may not lightly take his name in vain, but he is a terror to their enemies. He is well fitted to be a leader of warriors.

The fierce Semites of the desert found in the Fertile Crescent a high agricultural civilisation whose peaceful exponents were interested, not in successful war, not in the flocks and herds, but in the growth of plants. Women had begun the primitive hoe culture, and it was only natural that the mysterious life-giving power inherent in woman should be transferred to what she cultivated. Thus there had grown up that cult of the mother goddess which is the basal religion of the Near East. There was much to be commended in this worship of the divine mother, but she was not always wedded and many of her rites were most repulsive to the modern man.[1]

Re of Egypt soon fell under the influence of the Nile valley, and the Nile himself, Osiris, handed over many of his attributes until Re might even be invoked as the god of the after-life. So Nergal in Babylonia added to his maleficent attributes as scorching sun-god the sway of the grim underworld, though legend long commemorated his descent into the home of the dead where by brute force he compelled the native goddess who then ruled it to accept him as her consort. Shamash took the oversight of the liver omens, while the name of Marduk was substituted wholesale for the elder Enlil, and only the reference of the cause and cure of disease to his "father" Ea preserved the proof that Marduk was not originally the god of healing magic.

Ashur was of sturdier build. He did borrow the symbol of his cousin Re, the winged sun-disk, and scholars identified him with the Anshar of the Shumerian creation myth. Such scholarly identification had little effect on king and noble.

Ashur, or rather Ashir, the earlier form of his name, was a well-known god to the colonists who settled in Cappadocia some twenty-four centuries before Christ, but otherwise he appears as a purely local deity. God, city, nation, all bore the same name, and were closely united. As Assyria expanded, his worship followed, and when the empire exceeded the limits of the nation, his image was still placed in every provincial capital or capital of a subject ally. Always, however, the original house in the capital of his name was his true home.

Not alone in temples was he worshipped. His chief symbol was the winged sun's disk with the bust of an archer; placed on a support and carried into battle, it meant the living presence of the god in camp and conflict. Yet the presence of this standard was something a little less material than an image, something of the same feeling existed as was indicated by the empty ark of Yahweh.

Through the presence of this symbol, Ashur himself brings

[1] Cf. p. 9.

the king aid. It is with his weapons that every ruler wins his battles, his are the Assyrian soldiers, the enemy are hostile to him in the first instance. It is Ashur who commands that the boundary of his land should be extended, the tax and tribute are of the lord Ashur, when the heavy yoke of the king's lordship is placed on newly conquered peoples, it is in reality to the lord Ashur they are made subject, to him they were not submissive, and when subdued they are numbered with those subject before the lord Ashur.

In peace, he is still all-powerful. He is the great lord, who rules the whole assembly of the gods, who bestows sceptre and crown, who establishes royal rule. It is the great lord Ashur who calls the new king by name, increases his kingdom over the kings of the four world quarters, magnifies his name, intrusts his weapons unsparing to his lordly power.

To be sure, it is recognised that he has colleagues, or rather subordinates. Sometimes they appear as the "great gods," sometimes they form a group, rarely they appear without him. But they are definitely his inferiors. Ashur is "father of the gods," and in the stern Semitic family life this implies a greater elevation above his sons than would be recognised in America. Before his all-embracing fatherhood, the great gods are scarcely more powerful than that other son of Ashur, the king. So he is likewise "king of the gods," or the "leader of the gods" against the chaos monster. And in the end, the other great gods tend to be remade in his image, to be simply Ashurs on a small scale, almost, we might say, they sink to the level of angels.

So Ashur remains an isolated god, stern, savage, passionless, aloof from human kind. He is, and there is none beside him. So stern is his isolation that even a wife is missing, his children have no known mother. Once only does he subject himself to human frailties, when he indulges in the great delight of his children, for like Yahweh he is a "man of war." Even here, he is supernatural in size and in distance, his very presence in war makes him all the more remote from the ordinary affairs of life.

Fig. 174 PROCESSION OF ASSYRIAN GODS.

No sooner were his people settled in the fertile countries than they were exposed to the same insidious influences from the agricultural religion as were the Hebrews. The Hebrew tribal God was early identified with the Baals, the agricultural lords of fertility, as Marduk of Babylon became the Bel, the Lord, par excellence. Ashur unbent so far as to accept the title of "great lord," but there is no proof of such yielding to the seductions of the nature-worship as are postulated by the golden bull of the Aaron story or by those set up at Bethel and at Dan. To the end Ashur remained in an isolation never attained by any of the gods of Babylonia.

Ashur remained unchanged but his followers were not immune to the lures of the lascivious rites employed in the worship of the goddess of fertility. The oldest temple at Ashur was that of the Assyrian Ishtar, and two other Ishtars took their names from the near-by cities of Nineveh and Arbela. Her cult remained unchanged though her name was Semitised. The mother goddess at Arbela was more fortunate than she of Delphi, for she never was forced to surrender to a god her right to predict the future and many were the occasions when Esarhaddon and Ashur-bani-apal invoked her aid. She did have a serious masculine rival, Shamash, with his liver omens, but his abode was not at Arbela.

Ishtar of the fertility rites was not the Ishtar of the kings. So far as there was a goddess to stand by the side of Ashur, it was Ishtar, not the "mother of mortals," but the "first among the gods, the lady of ruin, who looses the terrors of battle." Once she is called the "beloved wife of Ashur," as once he has a consort Ashuritum and again Ninlil is bracketed with him. In actual practice, Ishtar is a sister rather than a wife. It is not Ishtar, the goddess of unrestricted love with whom we deal, but the Bedawi matron of proved chastity and savage enough to lead her tribe into battle.

Like Israel again, the Assyrians did not have to reckon only with the native gods whose rights to the soil the invading deities were usurping. There was equal threat to Ashur from the higher material culture from without. Assyria had learned

Marduk as a suzerain in the earliest days of her existence, and this at the very era when Marduk was usurping all the rights of the other gods of Babylonia. The freedom of Ashur marked the decline of Marduk, but not for long. Assyria was always peculiarly susceptible to Babylonian influence, and, as it grew, the influence of Marduk grew with it. Then, too, the Assyrian monarchs were always hoping the day might come when Babylon should be an integral part of the Assyrian domain. When this was secured, Marduk was placed on an equality, an "equal brother" of Ashur was the way Ashur-bani-apal put it. Together they divided the world, but Ashur was always the chief of the two. How strong was this influence among the nobility is shown by the huge number of purely Assyrian officials whose names are compounded with Marduk.

Strangely enough, there was never the slightest danger to Ashur's position from Marduk. As early as Adad-nirari I, we find the Babylonian sky-god, Anu of Uruk, who had already usurped first place in the Adad temple and now was placed before Ashur. Anu, however, was even more ethereal than Ashur, and there was no aftermath. Ashur-nasir-apal does indeed place Ashur at the head in some of his inscriptions, but his annals are dedicated to Urta. We can scarcely understand how he can place Ashur first and still call Urta "the chief of the gods, the chief of the four world regions, who grants sceptre and sway to all cities, the lord of lords," but his many other titles simply show him a specialised Ashur. Shalmaneser III especially praises Shamash, and his son Shamshi-Adad V renews the praises of Urta, but neither was a rival of Ashur. The strange tendency to a near monotheism in the name of Nabu during the rule of Sammuramat has already been discussed.[1]

With the flood of Babylonian influence which followed the coronation of Tiglath Pileser III in Babylon, Nabu comes into his own. Nabu names lead all others in frequency, fifty of the letter-writers alone having names compounded with that of the god. The formula of greeting, "To the king my

[1] Cf. p. 164.

lord, thy servant so and so," is in ninety per cent of the cases followed by "May Nabu and Marduk be gracious to the king my lord." Our only exceptions are letters from cities with strongly individualised deities, and Ashur appears only in those from the city which bore his name. Now of course no king would have accepted such a greeting did it not correspond to his own feelings. That Marduk has supplanted his rivals may be explained on grounds set forth above; that Nabu, god of a comparatively unimportant suburb of Babylon, should have the precedence demands a reason. The discovery that a large proportion of the tablets in Ashur-bani-apal's library bear a confession that it was he who made the king learned may explain his particular case, why did the other Sargonids prefer Nabu to Ashur? Is it possible that after all they did have some appreciation of the "wisdom" of which Nabu was master?

From the west country, the Assyrians brought Adad, the weather-god, with his bellowing bull and his thunderbolt. His was the very early temple at Ashur later shared with the usurper Anu, his the golden thunderbolt recovered in the excavations. As Hadad, he was well known in Syria; it was the Adad of Aleppo who gave the sovereignty of that territory to Shalmaneser III, it was Hadad to whom Panammu I of the northern Judah set up a statue. Adad appears frequently in Assyrian historical records, but generally in metaphor, for it was in his likeness that the kings overwhelmed their enemies as with a flood, like Adad the mountains thundered after the retreating foe, but it was likewise Adad whose showers permitted the millennial happiness of Ashur-bani-apal's reign.

Two favourite Assyrian deities were Shamash and Sin, the sun and moon gods, who were worshipped in a double temple, similar to and across the square from the double temple of Anu and Adad. Its date, at least as early as the reign of Ashir-nirari I, proves the antiquity of their worship.

After Ashur had sloughed off his solar characteristics and had become the father of the gods, Shamash represented the sun. Judging from the royal names, he was extremely popular

in early times, and that popularity never lessened. He represented the more genial aspects of the sun, as they had been
learned in agriculture, he was the great lawgiver, the judge
who demanded righteousness, the supporter of the highest
ethical ideals. In the records of our period, however, his chief
function is the unveiling of the future through the liver omens.
It is a queer method of divination for a sun-god.

An altar from Ashur throws some light on solar conceptions.
On the base, the god faces his double, each standing on his
mountain. Behind each, attendants bear loads across the hills
and the procession is closed by the horse, who as "ass of the
mountains" to the east very appropriately comes from the
sunrise. The centre of the main composition is the king, bareheaded and barefooted; clad in the antique garment which
left one shoulder bare, his hand in the gesture of adoration.
On either side stands the sun-god, in his most archaic form,
head and upper body facing the spectator, lower body in pro-
file. He wears the short garment of the early Semite, with a
dagger in the girdle, but his hair is elaborately puffed out on
all sides and his beard is square and in individual curls. In
his hand he grasps his standard, a long pole with the crescent
moon, from which hang two tassels; above triple rings is the
sun's disk, within are eight rays, alternately waved and straight.
Similar disks on rings rest on the sun-god's head and fill the
corners made by the "horns" of the altar.[1]

Sin's chief abode was Harran, the capital of the old Mesopotamian kingdom. From the days of Shalmaneser III, Assyrian kings frequented his shrine and glorified it, and Ashur-
bani-apal has left us a full description of his temple. Thanks
to its influence, Harran was the only city outside Assyria and
Babylonia which boasted a charter as an imperial free city.
The business records with their frequent references to oaths
by or penalties to Sin of Harran, and the numerous names in
Si, the Mesopotamian equivalent, in the Harran Census, show
how popular was his rule.

We have now mentioned the chief gods worshipped in As-

[1] Jordan, *MDOG.*, XLIX, 33 ff.

syria. Only Ashur was purely Assyrian, the others were common Semitic in origin, and each was paralleled in Babylonia. Or rather, they were parallel in name, for as time went on, each of the imports from Babylonia grew to be more and more like Ashur, who still retained his aloofness. But, while they lost their own peculiar characteristics, they did the damage. Men in Assyria felt the need of deities who were more human than the far-away Ashur. With the flood of Babylonian deities in the last Assyrian century, all possibility of monotheism disappeared, and with that all possibility of a cosmopolitan religion. Ashur became more and more an abstract form of the Assyrian people, and when the end of the empire suddenly came, Ashur sank back into a purely local deity.[1]

Official worship was directed towards these gods and towards Ashur in particular. For them were the great temples, whose foundation went back to so remote a past and whose restoration by pious monarchs we have so often quoted. One at least, that of Ishtar at Ashur, was of prehistoric date, and already possesses the long narrow throne-room with the cult statue in the niche at the upper end which distinguished the Assyrian temple from the Babylonian with its broad shallow room. In many respects, this earliest of our temples affords our best picture of what an Assyrian temple was like.[2] Later, the Shumerian influence became more evident. Temple names are always in the Shumerian form, and the Shumerian word for "house," E, regularly precedes. From the south came also the temple tower, the huge mass of solid brickwork which was the ancestor of our church steeple. Imported into the alluvium by the mountain-loving Shumerians, it was rather out of place in Assyria, where it was dwarfed by near-by hills.

Aside from the statues, of which we may obtain some glimpses from the débris at Ashur or at Kalhu, we know little of their furniture and even less of their cult. Sacrifices there were, but the majority of our references are to the food and

---

[1] Cf. especially Jastrow, *Religion Babyloniens und Assyriens*, I, 201 ff., for the Assyrian pantheon.
[2] Cf. p. 17.

other supplies needed by the priests and attendants. Ceremonies likewise we may mention, but here again we walk in
darkness. The chief ceremonies seem to have been carried
out on New Year's Day, the day of the spring equinox, when
Ashur feasted his gods, and when the fates of mankind were
decided. Various gods had their various days, and in particular do we learn of the feast-days when the divine bridegroom went out to spend the day with his bride.[1]

With the vast mass of "religious texts," it is indeed a matter
for surprise that we can answer so few of the questions as to
the official cult. Soon the reason appears: there were two
religions at Ashur. The cult thus far discussed is the old
Semitic religion, and its gaps may be filled out without much
danger of error from the forms employed elsewhere among the
Semites. There was another religion, whose roots went back
to the most primitive magic and which had been imported
entire from Shumer. Gods of the proper Semitic type were
late-comers into this system; the real possessors were the spirits. Early Shumerians were not far from the animistic stage.
Their world was filled with spirits, thousands upon thousands
of them, and for the most part malignant. Group after group
of them were named, and still there remained others who were
unknown. Among the most terrible were the ghosts of the
dead, especially those who had died by violence. Terrible in
particular were those who brought disease, such as those who
transmitted tuberculosis, or those who threatened women when
a new life was coming into the world.

Fortunately, there were means of overcoming these evil
spirits. Long, long ago, the god of wisdom and of the cleansing
water, Ea of Eridu, had discovered the charms, the incantations, the hymns, the magical mixtures, which might cure the
sick or ward off the evil. Marduk later robbed him of this
office, but he still must go to the older god for advice.

Assyria was flooded with these Shumerian spirits, and every
citizen was open to their attacks. Ashur and the great gods
were far off, their interest was chiefly in the state and the kings;

[1] Cf. p. 371.

private individuals were more concerned with the good and especially the evil of their own lives. Their practical religion was therefore largely magic. The house of the magician at Ashur was one of the chief of the private residences, and from its halls has come a large number of "religious texts" which in reality represent a rather low grade of magic. Ashur-bani-apal's library was filled with texts prepared for the same purpose.

Magic is so low a form of religion that famous scholars have denied it the name of religion at all. Strangely enough, from this magical soil often spring the finest flowers of religion and of ethics. Nowhere is this more true than in Assyria. The magical texts themselves are naïvely primitive, simple adjurations to the evil spirit to depart, meaningless syllables and scarcely more meaning concoctions. Suddenly, in the midst of such a bit of hocus-pocus, we chance upon a hymn of extreme beauty, with an elevation of religious spirit so great that the Hebrew psalms are often brought into comparison.[1] Sin is often of purely ceremonial character, yet the sense of sin is there; nowhere in all the world's literature will there be found so close a resemblance to the penitential psalms of the Hebrews or the mediæval hymns which sing the wrath of God. Not all sin is ceremonial, there are inquisitions as to moral delinquencies. Has the sinner incited one member of a family against another, has he wrongly held men prisoner, has he used false weights or demanded the wrong price, has he removed the landmark or set up the boundary stone falsely, has he entered his neighbour's house and approached his neighbour's wife, has he shed his neighbour's blood, has he stolen his neighbour's garment, did he vow and not fulfil?[2] Here is much the same condemnation of unethical action as is found in the words of the Hebrew prophet Amos; indeed, the coincidences are almost verbal.

The final test of a religion is its ethics. No Assyrian wrote a treatise on formal ethics, none even prepared a hymn in praise of morality. We can discuss Assyrian morals only on

[1] Cf. p. 472.   [2] Rogers, *Parallels*, 170 ff.

the basis of practical action, and without mention of any ideals, any dreams of perfection. We have but to consider for a moment how our civilisation would be judged if only actions and not ideals were allowed in the balance, or we may perhaps view ourselves in the none-too-flattering mirrors set up by non-Christian Asiatics. Then, properly humble, we may search for traces of Assyrian morality.

Assyrians were religious, that we must grant, and they worshipped gods who demanded righteousness. In their published records, Assyrian monarchs boast their regard for the divine rules, and officials say the same in their correspondence. Doubtless they told the truth as often as do men of the present.

Was their ideal of righteousness the same as ours? In one respect it certainly was not, for to them righteousness meant following out certain ceremonial practices; we consider quite another group of practices pleasing in the eyes of the Deity. After ceremonial righteousness has been eliminated, there remains the more strictly ethical righteousness. Our chief sources for Assyrian history are the royal annals with their very practical purpose of presenting to the after-world a flattering portrait of the ruler and of persuading enemies that war was unwise. They are filled with imperialism of the frankest sort and they recite cruelties of a horrible character. Closer analysis often proves that bloodthirstiness must be lessened at the expense of their veracity, but even at that, the chief difference between their annals and those of the "nationalist" historians of the present is that the latter buttress their imperialism with fine phrases about the "white man's burden" or "our good old national God" while the Assyrians simply declared they were doing the service of their god and that was the end of it. As to the cruelties, what nation among their contemporaries did not use the same methods, what later empire has not concealed much the same crimes?

But we wrong the Assyrian when we derive our ideas of his ethics from his imperialist propaganda quite as much as when we typify Christian civilisation by the imperialist story-teller who praises the "god of the things that are" against the "God of things as they should be" preached by the Christian missionary. Turning to the letters, the laws, and the business documents, we are in exactly the same moral atmosphere which we find in the earlier parts of the Bible. Perhaps the legalistic tinge is stronger than it is in the earlier Hebrew records, though it is less strongly marked than in Babylonia. Our whole impression is that of a community quietly going about its own business, docilely bowing to written law, but quite willing to search for twilight regions where sharp dealing was justified. Yet it is not quite fair to say that the Assyrians had only the virtues of sharp shopkeepers. The kindly treatment of slaves, the advance of funds to serfs without interest, the care for the orphan and the widow, the regulations for the woman deserted by her husband, the provision that sons shall take their mother to their homes to be cherished as the bride that one loves, all this shows a humanity we should never suspect from the war annals.

There are blots on the picture, especially if we compare Assyrian practice with Christian ideal. Slavery existed, but it was less severe than what existed all over the Christian world a hundred years ago; serfdom must be acknowledged, but in most parts of Europe it was still defended as of divine institution one or two centuries since. Woman had a lower position in Assyria than she had in Babylonia, but at that she had more privileges than were hers legally in most parts of the Christian world a century ago. Polygamy was occasionally practised, by those who could afford it, divorce was easy for the man, much easier than in Babylonia, and it was virtually denied to the wife, prostitution was a recognised institution, regulated by the state, but adultery was severely punished, and the man in the case suffered the same penalty as the woman. With our vice reports and our six months' residences for divorces, it is doubtful if we have much advanced. The latest Assyrians lived six hundred years or more before the Christian era; needless to say, the peculiar virtues taught by the Christ and sometimes practised by his followers were not observed.

And yet, one cannot live with these men year after year without feeling how human they all were. They suffered their gusts of passion and they had their calculating meanness, they had their outbursts of cruelty, and at times the truth was not in them. All in all, they seem pretty decent folks, not so very different from the men of our block, in spite of different clothes, different speech, and a religion which never reached the Christian ideal. There were no saints among them, their religion was not of that type, but few of them appear such terrible sinners, if we judge them by twentieth-century practice and not by first-century preaching.

After life came death, but no hope of future bliss contributed to the ethical development of the Assyrian. He was regularly buried in the house in which he had lived, that he might still be at hand, but his was not a benign spirit. Sometimes he was simply placed in the earth, or his coffin might be two jars placed mouth to mouth. Family graves came to be prepared, large-sized vaults such as were used for the last resting-place of the kings of the middle period.[1] Sarcophagi were of stone or of clay; sometimes the last body only occupied its safety, the skeletons which had preceded would be broken up and deposited in the corners, or the sarcophagus would be crammed with the bones. Always the lamp was left in a niche, and even the smoke can still be seen. A large water-jar, a jug, and several dishes formed the remainder of the equipment needed for the after-life, but occasionally ornaments or even money were left behind by the mourners. Burning of corpses came late, and is found only in the graves with dish-cover coffin and a rock on top.

The spirit existed after death, but only as a vague ghost, harmful to the relatives if not properly placed in the grave, dangerous to passers-by in the dark when it must secure its livelihood from the offal of the streets. More fortunate if laid away with due ceremony, there was still little to hope for, mere existence in the vast gloomy underworld, such as that pictured by Ezekiel,[2] where no conscious joy might be

[1] Cf. p. 70.   [2] Cf. p. 643.

expected, where at best one drank pure water and did not actually suffer. With so gloomy a prospect for the future, one could not blame the Assyrian if he said: "Let us eat, drink, and be merry, for to-morrow we die." Yet his gloomy religion did not seriously affect his life. By temperament, he was less lively than the Egyptian, in his more serious quality he was akin to the men of the north, but his letters show him a normal, cheerful individual, accepting without complaint the hard lot assigned him by his divine rulers.

CHAPTER XLVIII

TRAGEDY

WITH startling suddenness, our records cease about 640. No longer do we enjoy the detailed narrative of the last few years, we must patch together with much theory the few fragments time has spared. Business, we can see, continued as usual, since we have documents from virtually every year, but they show nothing of the march of events.

The long reign of Ashur-bani-apal finally came to an end in 626. Of the circumstances of his death and of the events which followed we are entirely ignorant. A stray business document mentions a certain Nabu-rihtu-usur who sells by proxy his daughter for sixteen shekels of silver; the girl was to be a cheap wife for the son of the buyer, and the seller must have been in desperate straits.[1] A little later, Nabu-rihtu-usur is a candidate for the throne of Assyria and supported by Sin-shar-ibni, governor of Te, by the mass of Assyrian citizens, and by the inhabitants of Ashur in particular. Opposed to him was a young son of Ashur-bani-apal, who bore the same name as did Esarhaddon before his accession, Ashur-etil-ilani. After severe fighting, the true heir made good his claim, and in gratitude for the aid furnished by his commander-in-chief, Sin-shum-lishir, granted him large estates. Not content with this scant recognition of his services, the king-maker revolted and for a few short days was himself a king in Nippur.[2]

Deficient as were the resources of the kingdom, Ashur-etil-ilani must have his individual palace at Kalhu. On the southeast edge of the palace mound, above the ruins of Esarhaddon's New House, he erected his meagre residence. In place of the magnificent approaches of the earlier structures, with their bristling lions and bulls, simple terraces to the west found their only ornament in the thick cement with which the walls were covered. The area included was small and the ground

[1] J. 307.　　　　[2] J. 650; 807; Moldenke, *Texts*, II, No. 1.

plan extraordinary. Squares, pentagons, quadrangles, triangles, were the forms assumed by the rooms, while the largest, tiny enough as compared with its predecessors, resembled nothing so much as a huge question-mark. Naturally, the walls were of very varying thickness. No ornament marked the interior. Breast-high, there were coarse, roughly hewn slabs; above, the bare plaster wall without colour extended over the mud brick to the roof twenty feet above the limestone pavement. Niches in the wall and a rough cornice on the door-posts completed the sorry picture. Ezida, the Nabu temple in Kalhu, was rebuilt, and the brick inscriptions detailing this fact afford our most frequent souvenirs of this monarch.[1]

In his last desperate effort to retain Babylonia, Ashur-etililani made an extraordinary concession to the Dakkuru, still a power to be reckoned with. The body of their former king, that Shamash-ibni whom Esarhaddon had so viciously attacked with scorching proverbs in his letter to the non-Babylonians,[2] was brought from the mountains to find a resting-place in his home land, and was entombed in the midst of the fortress house. Ashur-etil-ilani is careful to state that no legal process may be raised against his action, and he calls upon Marduk, Nabu, and Nergal to punish the ruler or official who may disturb the remains. It was the last known official act of an Assyrian in Babylonia, though at least four full years of rule (626–622) are witnessed by the business documents from Nippur.[3]

In or after 622, he was succeeded by Sin-shar-ishkun, whose authority was recognised for at least two years in Sippar and in Uruk for seven. Ashur-etil-ilani had shown his affection for the Nabu of Kalhu by rebuilding his temple, his successor restored that at Nineveh and erected a new one at Ashur. But new temples to the Assyrian gods would not restore the Assyrian provinces.

[1] Layard, *Nineveh and its Remains*, II, 37; *Nineveh and Babylon*, 655; I. R. 8, 3; Streck, *Assurbanipal*, 380 ff.

[2] Cf. p. 352.   [3] Clay, *Misc. Ins.*, No. 43.

How the former provinces slipped away may be illustrated by the case of Judah. The long reign of Manasseh had come to an end, but the Egyptian tendencies indicated by the name of the chief god of the Nile valley did not make his son Amon less willing to serve Assyria. Amon likewise followed his father in his religious conservatism. After two years, he was put to

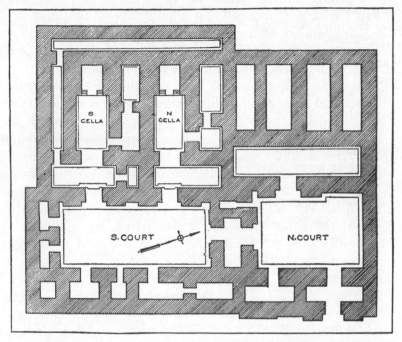

MAP 12. NABU TEMPLE OF SIN-SHAR-ISHKUN AT ASHUR.

death in his own house by the reformers, but the countryside had not been infected by the new doctrines which were again being preached in the capital; it was the men from the rural districts who avenged his murder, did justice on his assassins, and placed on the throne his eight-year-old son Josiah.[1]

Conservatism continued during the first years of Josiah. When in his thirteenth year of reign, prophetic commission was

[1] II Kings 21: 19 ff.

given to Jeremiah, he must still condemn the burning of incense to other gods, the immorality of the high places, the going after the Baals. Other nations, whose gods were not even alive, have refused to abandon them, but Judah has made her gods more numerous than her towns. Like the prophets of old, Jeremiah expected attack from Assyria; he saw a boiling caldron facing the north, for "out of the north is evil impending upon all the inhabitants of the land. All the ruling families of the north shall come, every one shall set its throne at the entrance to the gates of Jerusalem, and against all its walls and against all the cities of Judah."

"Blow the trumpet in the land, cry aloud: 'Let us gather together and enter the fortified cities.' Raise a signal against Zion, flee, delay not; calamity is coming from the north and great destruction. A hot wind from desert heights is coming against my daughter's people; not to winnow or to cleanse, it is a full and mighty wind. Behold, it comes like the clouds, its chariots are like the whirlwind; its horses are swifter than eagles, woe is us, we are ruined. Bandits come from afar, they shout at the cities of Judah; ambush they lay in the fields, on all sides they surround her. The whole land is in flight, from the noise of the horsemen and bowmen; they enter the thickets and caves, they climb the rocky places. A nation I bring from afar, a mighty and ancient nation; whose speech thou knowest not, nor understand their talking. An open tomb is their quiver, all are mighty warriors; they shall eat thy vines and thy fig-trees, thy forts beat down like olives; shepherds shall come with their flocks, their tents they shall pitch about her." [1]

Zephaniah, the great grandson of Hezekiah, found it necessary to threaten the cutting off of the shaveling priests and the remnant of Baal from Jerusalem, those who worship the heavenly host on the housetops, those who swear in turn by Yahweh and the king of Assyria. Yahweh will therefore utterly consume all from the face of the ground, man and beast, the birds of the heaven, the fish of the sea. Let all hold their peace

[1] Jer. 1–6.

in the presence of the Lord Yahweh, for at hand is the day of Yahweh.

Yahweh hath prepared a sacrifice, he hath consecrated his guests. He will punish the princes and king's sons, and those clothed in foreign apparel. "Near is the great day of Yahweh, it is near and hastens greatly; lo, the sound of Yahweh's day, bitterly cries the hero. That day is a day of wrath, a day of distress and trouble, a day of wasteness and desolation, a day of darkness and gloom, a day of clouds and thick darkness, a day of the trumpet and alarm, against the fortified cities and against the high battlements. And I will bring distress against men, that they should walk like the blind, since they have sinned against Yahweh; their blood shall be poured out as dust and their flesh as excrement. Neither their silver nor their gold shall deliver them in the day of Yahweh's wrath, but the whole land shall be devoured by the fire of his jealousy; for he will make an end, a terrible end, of all that dwell in the land." "For Gaza shall be forsaken and Ascalon a desolation; they shall drive out Ashdod at noon day and Ekron shall be rooted up. Woe to the men of the seacoast, the nation of the Cretans; Yahweh's word is against thee, Canaan, land of the Philistines, I will destroy thee, there shall be no inhabitant." [1]

In the thirteenth year of Josiah, that momentous 626 in which Ashur-bani-apal died, the Judæans were already planning revolt against Assyria. They have changed their foreign policy, declares Jeremiah, but it will avail them nothing; as they have already suffered disgrace through Assyria, so now will it be suffered through Egypt. With hand on head, bewailing their disgrace, shall they set forth, for Yahweh hath rejected all in whom they trust. [2]

The movement for independence came to a head in 621. While the repair of the temple was under way, the chief priest Hilkiah found a book; attributed to Moses, it bears evident traces of having been composed no long time previously. Much alarmed to discover that they had not been following the decrees of the great lawgiver, Josiah immediately summoned an

---

[1] Zeph. 1 f.   [2] Jer. 2 : 36 ff.

assembly at which king and people solemnly bound themselves to observe this code.

Since Judah was now proclaiming her independence as a nation, her God Yahweh likewise must cast off his foreign companions, and a long step was taken towards monotheism. Definite refusal of the Assyrian overlordship was marked by the destruction of the altars which Manasseh had erected in the two temple courts for Ashur and the Assyrian king; their ashes were thrown into the Kidron as were the altars on the roof of the upper chamber of Ahaz, to be connected with the sun-dial ascribed to the same monarch. In the same fire perished the chariots of the sun-god Shemesh, whom the Assyrians knew as Shamash, though Solomon himself had contrasted Shemesh with Yahweh at the dedication of his temple.[1] Human sacrifices had been celebrated to the king-god Melech in the valley of the children of Hinnom; the site of Topheth was defiled and so were the high places on the right of the mount of destruction where Solomon had built altars for the Sidonian Astart, the Moabite Chemosh, and the Ammonite Milcom. At the entrance to the city, where was the gate of the mayor Joshua, had been high places for the minor spirits of the countryside; within the very precincts of Yahweh's house dwelt sacred prostitutes who wove tunics for the Asherah, the column connected with the worship of the deities of fertility. High places and residences were torn down, the vessels for Baal, the Asherah, and the host of heaven were brought out and with the Asherah were committed to the flames in the Kidron; the ashes were scattered over the graves of the lower classes who had worshipped such foreign gods, the place where they had stood was filled with dead men's bones. All those who had offered incense to Baal, the sun and the moon, the zodiacal signs and the heavenly bodies, were slain, in particular the shaveling priests who had sacrificed in the villages round about; the other priests were brought from their now defiled village shrines and were assigned a subordinate position in Jerusalem.

Josiah's reforms were not confined to Judah; Bethel and

[1] I Kings 8 : 12 f. as preserved in the Greek translation.

its companion shrines felt his heavy hand in the next thirteen years. By the incorporation of the former Assyrian province of Samaria, the territory of the little kingdom was more than doubled in population and in wealth. In the eyes of the reformers; Yahweh was but rewarding his faithful servant for his obedience to the long-forgotten law; Jeremiah, however, opposed the introduction of the new code, insisting, "I spake not with your fathers concerning burnt offerings," and he flatly declared: "The false pen of the scribe has wrought falsely." [1] There were many to echo his words as they thought of the desecration of the age-old shrines of Bethel and Beersheba and Hebron, where Yahweh had appeared to the fathers; perhaps some also perceived the complete divorce that was soon to come between the official religion and the daily life of the villagers.[2]

The records of Sin-shar-ishkun close with the well-known appeal: "May a future prince, of the kings my descendants, when this temple has become ruined, restore its ruins, with his writings may he place the writing of my name; but may he who changes the tablet with the writing of my name, does not inscribe it on the tablet which has the writing of his own name, may the gods destroy his name, his seed, and his posterity."[3] But no son of his was to sit upon the throne in Ashur, it was his son and his posterity which was to be destroyed, his name to be forgotten or remembered only as an effeminate weakling who cumbered the ground, while his conquerors were to be among the best-known heroes of the ancient history.

Already, there had been established in Babylon a certain Nabu-apal-usur, better known to us by the Greek form of Nabopolassar. In abasement before his god Marduk, the pious monarch calls himself the "son of a nobody," "the little, unknown among the people"; he seems in reality to have been none other than the son of our old friend, Bel-ibni, whom we last saw consolidating Chaldæan power as viceroy of the Sealands. Nabopolassar was thus a descendant of that great

---

[1] Jer. 7 : 22; 8 : 8.   [2] II Kings 23; cf. *Amer. Hist. Rev.*, XX, 566 ff.
[3] Scheil, *Prisme*, 51 ff.

family of Iakin, which had so dominated Babylonia since its
first appearance more than two centuries before, and whose
Merodach Baladan had set an example which his successors
could but strive to emulate.

Like his father before him, Nabopolassar began his career as
administrator of the Sealands, when Sin-shar-ishkun had
learned that an army was coming up from the sea to attack
him.[1] The difficulties which followed the death of Ashur-bani-
apal permitted him to secure his position in Babylon and from
this year 626 he acted as independent ruler and ordered his
subjects to date their business records by his year as king of
Babylon. While still King of the Sealands, and therefore hostile to Uruk, he had carried off from that city as spoil a tablet
containing the "Exaltation of Ishtar."[2] A tablet of 615 is
dated at Uruk by the rule of Sin-shar-ishkun, but five years
before a partisan of Nabopolassar in Uruk had used the date of
his royal master.

By 616, all Babylonia was under his control, and in that year
he began the invasion of Mesopotamia. His first advance was
up the Euphrates where the men of Suhi and Hindanu paid
tribute without fighting. This was in May; three months
later it was reported that an Assyrian army was found in the
city of Qablinu. Nabopolassar marched up to meet them and
on the 12th of August the city was taken after a great battle,
and with it the Assyrian nobles and the Mannai who had come
from far-away Urumia to their aid. In the same month, Mane,
Sahiru, and Balihi, in the region of the river Balih were secured;
in the next Nabopolassar returned to Babylon.

Nabopolassar had reason for his haste. Early in his reign,
Psammetichus I (664–610) had been a vassal of Ashur-bani-
apal; then he had revolted and had freed Egypt; next he had
assisted Shamash-shum-ukin in his unfortunate revolt; now,
full of years, and with an Egypt prosperous as never since the
days of the Eighteenth Dynasty, he had begun to dream of

---

[1] Berossus, in Euseb., *Chron.*, 35.
[2] Thureau-Dangin, *RA.*, XI, 142; it was carried back from Elam in Seleucid
times.

following their example in a conquest of Syria. Assyrian power was no longer felt along the Mediterranean and after twenty-nine years of siege, Ashdod fell into his hands.[1] Nothing was to be feared from Assyria, but a renewed Babylonia was quite contrary to his calculations; so the empire which had called him vassal in his youth was supported in his old age as a buffer state against the rising power of another former Assyrian vassal! With the news that Mesopotamia had been invaded, Psammetichus put his troops in motion and only the hasty departure of the Babylonians prevented their being overtaken at Qablinu (October, 616).

Foiled on the Euphrates, Nabopolassar tried the line of the Tigris, and in the following March a Babylonian detachment secured Madanu in Arrapha and drove back the Assyrians to the Lower Zab. From here, it was an easy step across the Tigris to Ashur. The inner wall of the old sacred city had long since been covered with houses, the outer was ruinous. More recently, the exposed northwest corner had been masked by a rough wall at the level of the moat and touching the older line of circumvallation. We may still follow the walk by which the sentry paced the summit, ascend the steps up which the soldiers passed to hurl their spears, hide behind the battlements where they took refuge, peer through the narrow apertures like upright arrows through which the archers shot. The siege was begun in May, and in June the city was assaulted; in the meantime, the Assyrian king had mustered his army, the siege was raised, and the Babylonians were pursued as far as the Tekrits (Takritain), where they took refuge in the Birtu, or citadel. In his turn, Nabopolassar was besieged ten days, but Sin-shar-ishkun had no better fortune and the Assyrian armies returned home.

Thus far, conditions were not unauspicious for the future; Sin-shar-ishkun had a powerful ally in Psammetichus, Nabopolassar had been checked on both Euphrates and Tigris. Unfortunately for Assyria, this was the moment chosen by another enemy to enter the struggle. Median tribes had long

[1] Herod., ii, 157.

ago been familiar to the Assyrian provincial governors, but no one dreamed of serious danger from their presence on the frontier. Later Median tradition made their first great king a certain Deioces; in reality he was a petty village chief bested by Sargon.[1] After him they placed Fravartish, or Phraortes. He was reported to have brought under his yoke the various peoples of Asia, including the then little-regarded Persians,[2] but he is unknown to the inquiries of the sun-god. He was next said to have attacked Assyria, but was defeated and killed in battle with the loss of the greater part of his followers.

Authentic history is first reached with Huvakhshatara or Cyaxares. His feudal levies were reorganised and made a modern army with separation of the various arms. By November of 615 he was ready to act and descended into Arrapha, where he secured a city.

Encouraged by this success, Cyaxares appeared before Nineveh in August of 614. He was unable to force the walls and must content himself with the capture of Tarbisu, the childhood home of Ashur-bani-apal. He then passed down the Tigris to Ashur, where a thin wall of limestone with small towers had been extended into the ditch; it was still unfinished when Cyaxares appeared before it. Nabopolassar had no desire to see all his efforts wasted and their fruits in the hands of a probable rival; he hurried off his troops "to the aid of the Median," but Cyaxares had no more desire to see the old Assyrian capital, which had given its name and its god to the empire, in alien hands. So the city was at once assaulted; the Babylonian historian specially notes the evil treatment meted out to its chief men. So when Nabopolassar arrived with his army, he was faced by an accomplished fact. Now that he was in possession of the ancient capital and had thus delimited the bounds of his future acquisitions, Cyaxares was quite willing to come to terms with the master of a formidable body of soldiers. Amid the ruins of Ashur, friendship and alliance was established, and to seal the agreement, Nebuchadnezzar,

---

[1] Cf. p. 243.   [2] Herod., i, 103.

son of Nabopolassar, was married to Amyitis, daughter of Cyaxares's son Astyages.[1]

By this time, Suhi had returned to the Assyrian overlordship. In June, Nabopolassar took Rahilu in the midst of the Euphrates by a stone dike built out from the shore. Anat was next invested with siege-engines and a direct assault was made, but the assault failed and when Sin-shar-ishkun appeared in person, the Babylonians again retreated within the alluvium. It may be that the tradition is correct which tells how the Assyrians had called in the Scythians, long their allies against the Cimmerians, for their leader is said to have been Madyas, son of Protothyes, and this is that Bartatua who had been an ally so desirable that Esarhaddon had given him his daughter in marriage.[2] But therë is no contemporary evidence for the further statement that the Scythians defeated the Medes, ruled Asia for twenty-eight years, and were then deprived of their leaders at a treacherous banquet given by the Median king,[3] and the tradition remains doubtful.

All was ready for the final assault upon Nineveh by June of 612. Nabopolassar and Cyaxares, here called the "king of the Umman Manda," mustered their forces and marched up the Tigris. Three battles were fought from June to August, and then the city was assaulted. The main attack was directed from the northeast and the brunt fell upon the Hatamti Gate at this corner. To the south of the gate, the moat is still filled with fragments of stone and of mud bricks from the walls, heaped up when they were breached. Within the gate are traces of the counter-wall raised by the inhabitants in their last extremity, on the line where ran the city defences before the rebuilding by Sennacherib. Our chronicler tells of the great slaughter made of the Assyrian nobles; the ash heaps and calcined sculptures still show how intense was the fire in which the palaces and temples met their doom at the hands of the Indo-European barbarians.

"In those days did Sin-shar-ishkun" begins the chronicle,

---

[1] Berossus, in Euseb., *Chron.*, 29, 35.
[2] Cf. p. 360.
[3] Herod., i, 103 ff.

but what Sin-shar-ishkun did is lost in the break. Tradition related that, like the unhappy Shamash-shum-ukin, he heaped up a funeral-pile and burned himself with all his most cherished possessions. Not all the Assyrians were so hopeless. A certain noble named Ashur-uballit escaped from before the Babylonian troops. Cyaxares returned home the 20th of September, and Nabopolassar remained yet another month in Assyria to collect the wealth brought in from Nasibina and Rasappa. Thus Ashur-uballit was enabled to assume the title "king of Assyria" in a new capital, that Harran which had once been chief city of Mesopotamia.

So it was necessary for Nabopolassar to march against this new "land of Assyria" in 611. Three cities were taken, the last Rugguliti near Til Barsip on the 28th of November. The Babylonians were back in May of the next year and claim they "marched around victoriously in Assyria," but they accomplished nothing and were obliged to call in the Medes, who arrived in November. Ashur-uballit and his allies were driven out and fled across the Euphrates. Harran was thoroughly plundered of all its enormous accumulation of treasure, and the temple of Sin, chief shrine of Mesopotamia, was left in ruins by the Median barbarians.[1]

Even the loss of Harran did not damp the spirit of the unconquered Ashur-uballit. With a great army of Egyptians sent to his aid by Necho II, who had ascended the Egyptian throne the previous year, he appeared again in Mesopotamia in July of 609. The Euphrates was crossed, a Babylonian garrison cut off, and up to September assault after assault was made on Harran. Nabopolassar now came to the help of his troops and defeated Ashur-uballit in battle. In the same year, Nabopolassar secured Izalla and Urashtu. This is the last reference to Urartu or Haldia.[2]

---

[1] Cf. Nabu-naid, Langdon, *Königsinschriften*, 218, 272 ff., 284.

[2] In place of the traditional account, given in the late classical writers, we now have the contemporary record, published by C. J. Gadd, *The Fall of Nineveh*, 1923. That this record could be utilised at the last moment for my book, I owe to the friendly offices of Professors J. H. Breasted and Leroy Waterman, who sent information and the book from England immediately upon its publication.

Of the fate of Ashur-uballit, we know nothing more. But the very next year, 608, Necho appeared in Syria in person. Josiah, trusting to his righteousness in following the long-lost law of Moses, was defeated and killed in the battle of Megiddo, and Necho swept on to the Euphrates. In all probability, Ashur-uballit was in the army.[1]

An echo of these operations is found in two letters from the Babylonian commander-in-chief: "As for the land of Assyria, the day the king my lord does not mobilise the land, the people of Kar Duniash will revolt. The treasure of the land according to thy word have I taken, the treasure of the land according to thy word have I not taken, not without thy orders have I taken the city of Urizu, I have thy tablet and thy seal. Not without thy orders have I taken the city of Rimishu, I have thy tablet and thy seal. Not without thy orders have I taken the cities of Kur and Madaru, I have thy tablet and thy seal. The son of Zikri, who dwells in Ur, is but a slave, yet has he injured me; as I have informed my lord king, he has not done me justice. I and Uzub-shilu are the chief officials of the lord king, yet he has detained me, and my brothers he has beaten with a stick.

"As for what my lord king has inquired, 'Shall I go down after Kamu and the rest?' the king has given, let the king take away. The king has ordered: 'Send the incense grains which you have received from the hands of Ardia, son of Zikri, who dwells in Ur.' I would do all that he might desire, but he has not brought it. If it please the lord king, let me give instructions to bring it from the land of Kumina and give it to my lord king. The day the king went to Bel-malki-denu, before the face of the king he ate food, date-wine and grape-wine for his thirst he drank, oil he took."

Nabopolassar has ordered: "To his cities fire, to his cities fire do thou set, in city and field make desolation." "As the king my lord has said, so have I done. To his cities fire, to his cities fire I have set, in city and field have I made desolation. The captivity of Ashur have I dragged through the desert.

[1] II Kings 23: 29 ff.

When I seized them, I struck down their house, the head of the prince I cut off, to the king my lord I sent it. When I turned my face to the fortresses, the commanders of the fortresses cried out: 'The king, where is he? Tell us, the king, where is he? The road for our feet establish.' I replied: 'The king has pitched his camp at Baghdad, it is to his commanders he gives orders.' I set my face against the Assyrians." [1]

Briefly and almost contemptuously Nabopolassar writes the epitaph of the overthrown empire: "I slaughtered the land of Subarum, I turned the hostile land into heaps and ruins." "The Assyrian, who since distant days had ruled over all the peoples and with his heavy yoke had brought injury to the people of the Land, their feet from Akkad I turned back, their yoke I threw off." [2]

A generation later, the last Babylonian ruler, himself about to be overthrown by Iranian kinsmen of the Medes, drew the moral from the sins of Assyria, and told how the brave king of the Umman Manda "destroyed the shrines of the Assyrian gods entirely, and the cities of Akkad which had been hostile to the king of Akkad and had not brought him aid, so that he destroyed their shrines and laid them desolate like the storm wind." [3]

Nowhere did the events of this stirring time make a deeper impression than in Judah. Zephaniah cries out: "Yahweh will stretch forth his hand against the north and will destroy Assyria, he will make Nineveh a desolation and dry like the wilderness. Herds shall lie down in the midst of her, all the beasts of the nations. The pelican and the porcupine shall lodge in her capitals, the owl shall hoot in the windows, ravens shall be on the thresholds. This is the daughter of joy that abode without care, that said in her heart: 'I alone am alive, none is like unto me.' How is she become desolate, a place for beasts to lie down in! Each passer-by shall hiss and shake his fist at her." [4]

[1] *CT.*, XXII, 46 ff.; Thompson, *Late Bab. Letters*, No. 247 f.; Martin, *Lettres*, No. 247 f.

[2] Nabopolassar, 1, 3, 4; Langdon, *Königsinschriften*, 60 ff.

[3] Nabu-naid, *Prism*, II, 2 ff.; Langdon, *Königsinschriften*, 272 ff.

[4] Zeph. 2 : 13 ff.; cf. p. 486.

Nahum's whole prophecy is a savage rejoicing over the downfall of Assyria, for Nahum was an Israelite settled in exile at Elkosh, under a mountain slope north of Nineveh:

"He that shatters in pieces has come up against thee; keep the wall, guard the way, gird thy loins, make thy strength the utmost. The shield of his heroes is red, his warriors are clad in scarlet; they prepare the chariots today, the chariot horses are eager. The chariots rage in the fields, they rush to and fro in the plazas; their appearance is like that of torches, they dart about like the lightenings. He reads out the list of his nobles, in their eagerness they stumble; they hasten to reach the walls, the battering ram is made ready.

"The river sluices are opened, the palace walls are crumbling; the queen is stripped of her clothing, they are leading her away captive; her handmaidens moan like doves, upon their breasts they are beating. Nineveh was a tank of water, from it they are now escaping; 'Stand, stand,' they cry, not one of them looks backward. Take ye the spoil of silver, take ye the spoil of gold; there is no end to the store, an abundance of all goodly objects. She is empty and void and waste, hearts melt, knees shake; there is pain in all loins and pale have waxed all the faces.

"Where is the den of lions, the cavern of young lions; where prowled the king of beasts, and his whelp with none to affright them? Enough he tore for his whelps, enough for his mate he strangled; he filled his caves with prey, he filled his dens with ravin.

"Behold, I am against thee, saith Yahweh of Hosts; thy lair I will burn with smoke, thy young the sword shall devour. I will cut off thy prey from the earth, no more be heard thy messenger's voices.

"Woe to the bloody city, full of lies and rapine; the crack of the whip and the thunder of the rumbling wheels, the prancing horse and the bounding chariot, the horseman mounting and the flash of sword, the gleam of spear and a mass of the slain, a heap of corpses, there is no end of dead bodies.

"For the many infidelities of the well favored harlot, the

mistress of incantations, who sold states for her wicked deeds and clans through her incantations, behold, saith Yahweh of Hosts, I am against thee, I will strip thee of thy clothing, and show thy shame to the nations. Filth I will cast upon thee and disgrace thee, I will set thee up as a warning, all who see thee shall flee, shall cry: 'Desolate Nineveh, who shall bewail her?'

"Better art thou than No Ammon, that lay midst the rivers, the sea was her rampart, her wall was the water? Ethiopia was her strength, Punt and the Libyans her allies; yet she was carried away, they led her into exile. At the head of each street were her children, beaten to pieces; lots they cast for her nobles, her leaders they bound in fetters. Thou too shalt be drunken, thou too shalt be faint thou likewise shalt seek refuge.

"All thy forts are like fig trees, like the first ripe figs thy defenders; if they be shaken they fall right into the mouth of the eater. Thine the men who have changed into women,[1] open the gates of thy land to the enemy, the bars of thy gates hath the fire devoured.

"Water draw for the siege, thy forts do thou strengthen; descend to the clay pits, tread clay, lay hold of the brick mould. There shall the fire devour thee, the sword shall cut thee off. Make thyself many as the locusts, multiply as the grasshopper; above stars of the heavens increase thy traders, make thy guards as the locusts, thy scribes as the grasshoppers, that camp on cold days in the hedges; when comes the sun, they flee and no one knows their abode. Thy shepherds are in slumber, thy nobles have found rest; thy people are scattered in flight on the mountains, none is there to bring them together. For thy hurt is no healing, thy wounds are all mortal, all that hear of thy fate smite their hands in rejoicing, for on whom hath not thy iniquity constantly fallen?" [2]

Nahum spoke in anger; still more impressive is the epitaph

[1] Cf. p. 174.
[2] Nahum 2 f.; cf. J. M. P. Smith, "Nahum," in *International Critical Commentary*.

FIG. 175. REPUTED TOMB OF THE PROPHET NAHUM AT ELKOSH,
NEAR NINEVEH.

FIG. 176. DESCENDANTS OF THE "LOST TEN TRIBES" IN THEIR
HOME IN MESOPOTAMIA.

prepared by Ezekiel as he recalls to the Egyptian king the fate of the empire he would rival:

"Ashur was a cedar in Lebanon, and fair were his boughs; high was he in stature, in the clouds was his summit. He was nourished by waters, the deep made him grow; its streams encircled his garden, to all the field went its channels. Above all trees of the field was his stature exalted, many were his boughs; wide spread his branches, because of the many waters. All birds of the sky made their nest in his boughs; all beasts of the field bore their young 'neath his branches. Thus was he fair in his height and in the length of his branches; for his root was by many waters. Cedars in God's garden could not compare with him, fir trees were not like his boughs; plane trees were not like his branches, no tree in God's garden equalled his beauty.

"Since he was lofty in stature and his top was among the clouds, I gave him to the hands of the foreign hero who destroyed him. Strangers, most frightful of nations, hacked him down, left him fallen on the mountains; in all valleys his branches lie fallen, by all streams his boughs lie broken. On his ruin perch all birds of the sky, dwell all beasts of the field on his branches; that none of the trees by the waters should exalt themselves in their stature. That they lift not their tops to the clouds, that their mighty stand not up in their height, all those that drink water. They all are delivered to death, to the nethermost parts of the earth; in the midst of frail children of men, with them that descend to the Pit.

"On the day he went down to Sheol, I made the deep mourn him; its streams I restrained, I stayed the assemblage of waters. For him I made Lebanon dark, I made nations to quake at his fall, when I thrust him down to Sheol. All the trees of Eden, the choicest and best of Lebanon, all that drink water were comforted, in the nethermost parts of the earth. They too go with him to Sheol, to them that are slain by the sword; yea, his helpers shall perish, that dwelt in his shade mid the nations.

"Ashur is there with his comrades, the graves are round

about him; all slain they have fallen by the sword, in the depths of the Pit are their graves. Round about his grave are his comrades, all of them slain; fallen are they by the sword, who caused fear in the land of the living." [1]

[1] Ezek. 31: 3 ff.; 32 : 22 ff.; cf. C. H. Toy, *Ezekiel.*

CHAPTER XLIX

THE "ASSYRIAN WOLF"

"THE Assyrian came down like a wolf on the fold." It is needless to continue, for we all received our first impression of Assyrian character from Byron's ringing lines. If our youthful mind found the sermon too dull and we turned to the Bible left carelessly in the pew, we read of "the den of lions," "the bloody city, full of lies and rapine," "that caused fear in the land of the living." Such were some of the indictments hurled by the Hebrew prophets against their oppressors.

In our maturity, we open the pages of a book by a distinguished Orientalist and learn that "Assyria was the nest of the bird of prey whence, during nearly ten centuries, set forth the most terrible expeditions which have ever flooded the world with blood. Ashur was its god, plunder its morality, material pleasure its ideal, cruelty and terror its means. No people was ever more abject than those of Ashur; no sovereigns were ever more despotic, more covetous, more vindictive, more pitiless, more proud of their crimes. Assyria sums up in itself all the vices. Aside from bravery, it offers not a single virtue. One must leave over the whole of the world's history to find here and there, in the most troubled periods, public crimes whose frightfulness may be compared with the horrors daily committed by the men of Nineveh in the name of their god. The Assyrian is not an artist, not a man of literature, not a lawgiver; he is a parasite, basing his organisation of pillage on a formidable military power. As far as he extended his empire, he ruled but he did not govern; his appetites were without limit. In him is incarnate, to the highest degree, the defects and vices of Asiatic political systems." [1]

Nahum is indeed out-Heroded. What we have read is a triumph of the rhetorical art—but does it represent the sober verdict of history?

[1] De Morgan, *Premières Civilisations*, 1909, 340 ff.

Now the professional historian is suspicious by nature. He has learned to his discomfort that the ancient cynicism, "History is a lie agreed upon," applies with full force to many of the popular beliefs concerning the past. He is temperamentally shy of extreme views, knowing that truth generally takes the middle course. As *he* leaves over the pages of universal history, whether for troubled or untroubled periods, he finds in the original sources such an amazing recital of public and private frightfulness as would never be dreamed by the casual reader of our popular manuals. These examples seem to be somewhat evenly divided among races and peoples; none are found free from stain, all furnish much that appeals to his very human sympathy. The historian's task is neither to whitewash nor to blacken, it is to understand; it is worth our while to look at the facts, to see whether the Assyrian is an exception to the general run of historical individuals.

"The Assyrian was cruel." So he was. But it is something more than a rhetorical question when we inquire whether he was more cruel than others have been in times past and present. For example he cut off heads, while the Egyptians preferred hands or phalloi and our own Indians scalps; the English came nearer the Assyrian custom with their rotting heads of traitors spiked on Tower Gate in London. Where the Assyrian impaled, the Roman crucified, the Englishman quartered and drew; if the Assyrians burned youth and maidens in the fire, for each recorded example in the Assyrian annals, we can literally give a thousand cases of witches, another thousand of heretics burned by Christian orders. War is after all nothing but war, a reversion to savagery; there is not an Assyrian atrocity which has not its parallel or its equivalent in the civilised history of the last hundred years. We may with perfect justice condemn war and its cause, imperialism; as a warrior and an imperialist, the Assyrian was no better and no worse than his present-day descendants.

In his own records, one type of atrocity is conspicuous for its absence. The Old Testament has made us only too familiar with unmentionable crimes against women, and we never have been able to accept the blessing the pious psalmist invokes upon those who dash the little ones of the enemy against the stones. No student of war would dare assert that such crimes were not committed by battle-crazed Assyrians; the fact that there is not a single mention of such action in the royal records shows the same sense of decency which refuses to represent nude captive women in the sculptures. In ancient times, the theory held that captive women were to satisfy lust and then were to be killed or cast away, or at best retained as slaves; the newly discovered code provides specifically and in detail the ceremonies by which the Assyrian soldier might make the captive woman his legal wife. How great an advance is marked by this law will be appreciated by any one who knows the ancient theory and practice.

"No sovereign was ever more pitiless." It seems hardly possible that the author of this statement had ever read the Assyrian annals. Example after example may be cited from the preceding pages where enemies, nay, even rebels, were forgiven, were granted rings and clothes of honour, their gods were repaired and restored, their territory increased.[1] That these men frequently permitted their patriotism or their ambition to get the better of their gratitude, that costly wars resulted from misplaced mercy, did not deter the Assyrians from continuing the practice. The majority of Biblical critics are confident that the story the poor old Chronicler tells of Manasseh's rebellion and forgiveness[2] is made out of whole cloth. They would not be so confident if they realised that only seven years after Manasseh's rebellion Ashur-bani-apal did exactly the same thing, down to details, when he forgave Necho of Egypt.[3]

"No sovereign was more proud of his crimes." This is quite true. The Assyrian in his records makes himself out a very bad fellow indeed. He was in fact quite as human as the rest of us; it is human nature to desire to be thought worse, as well as better, than we really are. Besides, there was a very practical reason for a recital of frightfulness, the prevention of revolt.

[1] Cf. p. 377. [2] Cf. p. 384. [3] Cf. p. 416.

The Assyrian has been a very successful liar indeed, for his statements have been regularly accepted at face value. There is no excuse for the display of so touching but childlike a faith on the part of the Orientalist, for the official Assyrian records demand as drastic a higher criticism as has ever been inflicted upon any part of the Old Testament. We may compare one record with another, one edition with an earlier, an Assyrian statement with that of a Hebrew, the pictorial with the written, and at every stage we shall have plentiful examples of untruth.

Assyrians have been accused of spilling oceans of blood; they did so—in their statistics. All historians know that statistics of enemy loss are enormously overestimated, even in these days of statistical associations and professors of statistics. Yet it has been the fashion of many Orientalists, not merely to accept Assyrian statistics at face value, but, if there was a choice of numbers, to take the higher! We may recall a few illustrations of what the Assyrian statistician could make his figures perform.

Consider, for example, the case of the six thousand Aramæans defeated by Ashur-nasir-apal, with a loss of six thousand five hundred, leaving enough to be twice more defeated with heavy loss and a remnant to die of thirst in the wilderness.[1] Ahab and his allies at Qarqara undoubtedly checked the advance of Shalmaneser III. Observe the statistics: at first fifteen thousand of the enemy were killed; as later editions were prepared, the careful scribe increased the numbers to twenty thousand five hundred, and then, twenty-five thousand, while the last effort brought it up to twenty-nine thousand.[2] Recall the feat of the scribes of Sargon who in seven short years increased the sheep captured in a little mountain settlement from one thousand three hundred and twenty-five to one hundred thousand two hundred and twenty-five.[3]

During the larger part of the ten centuries cited by our Orientalist, Assyria was in no condition to wage offensive war. We do have the record of every year for a quarter of that time,

[1] Cf. p. 92.   [2] Cf. p. 136.   [3] Cf. p. 242.

from 890 to 640, and this is the great age of Assyrian imperialism. Of these two hundred and fifty years, wars are listed for one hundred and eighty. No wonder the unwary student jumps to the conclusion that the Assyrians were naught but "birds of prey" whose only business was to wage war.

A little analysis will show how few were the really important wars. Out of the hundred and eighty, at the most liberal estimate the king and the royal army were present in not over fifty, and half that number would probably be nearer the truth. Take as an illustration the campaign against Ashdod in 713. This has always been considered a major operation, one of those which deluged the world with blood. The Hebrew prophet Isaiah proves that the king was not in charge at all, and an inscription which is not generally known to scholars shows that just four hundred and twenty men made up the attacking force. This is a major operation among these years of warfare!

Nor were these one hundred and eighty years of war all devoted to offensive operations. The Haldian annals, for example, show that the majority of those listed against that country were to meet Haldian attacks, one of which penetrated to within twenty-five miles of Nineveh. A whole group were due to attacks or intrigues by Babylonia, by Elam, by Egypt, by Phrygia. The letters cover less than a hundred years but they show that not a few of the listed campaigns were of a hundred or so men sent out by the provincial governor against Medes or Arabs who were continuously harassing the settled agriculturalists. Not a few were necessitated by the ravages of the Aramæan nomads in Babylonia.

A single generation is covered by the inquiries of the sun-god. Not only do they support the letters in showing that Esarhaddon and Ashur-bani-apal were not engaging in wars of offence on the north and east frontiers, they prove a terrible danger, threatening the very existence of the empire, and they justify the frantic fear which was only masked in public by the pompous claims of victories. Had we equally full records from the other periods, it would doubtless be shown that a

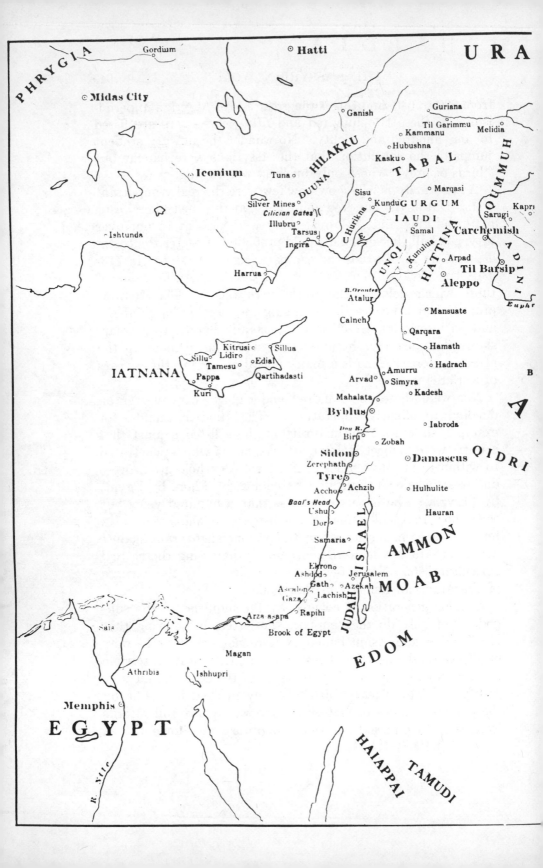

THE NEAR EAST

1000-600 B. C.

very small proportion indeed of the years in these ten centuries were devoted to wars of pure offence. As well might we call Rome a "bird of prey" because the temple of Janus was rarely closed, or apply the same term to the empire on whose flag the sun never sets because there is always some frontier war, or to the United States, with its almost uninterrupted series of Indian conflicts. On a rational evaluation of the evidence, it may be doubted whether the total killed in all the Assyrian wars equalled the number destroyed in those same lands during the Great War alone.

"As far as he extended his empire, he ruled but he did not govern." Here, at least, is an accusation which will not be supported by the majority of Orientalists, for it is generally recognised that the Assyrian Empire marks the first great advance in efficient imperialism. Before Assyrian times, empire was of the simplest, the greatest conqueror was merely a "king of kings," the so-called empire was simply an agglomeration of organically separate states. All that was needed was a weak ruler at the head and the empire separated automatically into its former components.

Assyria passed beyond that stage at a very early date. For the first time in history, we have a real empire with its subdivisions no longer potential states but administrative units, whose organisation was not based on historical accident but on administrative efficiency. At its head was no longer a subject king, but an Assyrian official, in daily communication with the capital, under close supervision, acting under detailed and definite orders, and subject to immediate recall and punishment. This was the system transmitted to the Persians, to the successors of Alexander, to Rome, and so to the moderns. Whether we admire imperialism or not, it is the simple fact that modern empires owe their government of dependencies to Assyria.

"No sovereign was ever more despotic." In theory, Assyria might have a god-king, the practice was far removed from despotism. The king must rule under the iron reign of laws, of religion, of society, of political theory, and when he departed from them, he did so at his peril. The last Shalmaneser, for instance, revoked the privileges of the old capital Ashur; he died the death and the usurping Sargon restored these privileges.[1] Priestly control is well illustrated by the letter in which the hungry and thirsty Ashur-bani-apal is told he must fast for the good of his people on the New Year's Day until the new moon appears to end his sufferings.[2] Adad-shum-usur flatly tells Esarhaddon to his face that when he divides his kingdom he is doing what the gods would not do in heaven.[3] Ashur-bani-apal must humbly appeal to the citizens of Babylon not to support his rebel brother and recite the good he has done them.[4]

"No people was more abject." We turn from these letters to the imperial free cities, with their charters of freedom from taxes, their chartered rights, their trading permitted to the four corners of the earth and to all tongues. We listen to the citizens of Babylon bluntly standing up for their rights.[5] As well might we say that the citizens of the imperial free cities of the Middle Ages were abject subjects of a pitiless despotism.

The statement that there was no Assyrian lawgiver is unfortunate rather for the author than for the Assyrians, for we now possess important fragments of a law which on the face of it was prepared by Assyrians and to meet Assyrian conditions. Some of its laws are as grim as those which disgraced our American statute-books a century ago; on the other hand, we find here the surprising belief that the woman taken in war may be made a wife with full privileges. Here too we learn of the destitute widow whose sons are to support her with food and drink; as the bride whom one loves shall they bind themselves to her. We do not expect romance in a law code, yet what visions of conjugal and filial love are conjured up by this one sentence.

"The Assyrian was not an artist." The Assyrian might proudly have made reply: "If you wish an answer, look about

[1] Cf. p. 206.   [2] Cf. p. 602.   [3] Cf. p. 397.
[4] Cf. p. 442.   [5] Cf. p. 432.

you." In the rather large ignorance of the material side of Babylonian civilisation which has endured almost to our own day, it has been taken for granted that the Assyrians were the mere copyists of their predecessors. Now that we have the evidence from both sides, the question may be considered settled. Much of their technic was borrowed from Babylonia, much from the Hittites, the Haldians, or the Egyptians. The result was not a mere physical but a chemical mixture, it was Assyrian to the core. Particularly must we admire the bas-reliefs, which a high authority in art once stated were the best the world produced before Phidias; he might not verify this statement to-day, but the very fact that it could be made sufficiently recognises the high quality of Assyrian art.

"The Assyrian was no man of literature." The argument seems to be about as follows: Ashur-bani-apal copied Babylonian works for his libraries, therefore, there was no native Assyrian literature. With this attitude general, it is natural that no attempt has been made to isolate the products of Assyria from those brought from the south. Yet one need not read far before one finds additions made by Assyrian scribes, native Assyrian myths, prayers of Assyrian princes, and as to the letters, some present the colloquial Assyrian, pure and undefiled, and with a tang which makes them real literature.

It seems strange that any one could read the royal annals and still deny literary sense to the Assyrians. Babylonians were not historically minded and few are the annals. Assyria produced the first literary historians. The average annals inscription is a detailed, fairly sober recital, shot through with occasional flashes which remind us that we are still dealing with a people akin to those who produced the *Arabian Nights*. Now and then they lapse into pure literature, as in the case of the gorgeous purple patches of the Tablet Inscription of Sargon. Would we deny literary value to the descriptions of the millennium which ensued when Ashur-bani-apal became king, we must deny it to the millennial prophecies of the Hebrews, so modelled on the Assyrian.

"Ashur was its god, plunder its morality, material pleasure

its ideal, cruelty and terror its means." Ashur was indeed the Assyrian god, and, like the god of every warrior people, he led his followers into battle. But he was something more, for in the best Assyrian days, the worship of Ashur approached monotheism. To the end, he stood in solitary state, a rather grim, somewhat chilly deity, but free from most of the ordinary failings, just to his friends, a good hater of those who opposed his people. The latent tendencies towards monotheism were swamped by the flood of religious customs from the south; more was the pity that Babylonian polytheism prevailed and prevented a parallel development to what was going on in the little states of Palestine.

Nothing marks more the superiority of Assyrian religion over Babylonian than the respective treatment of Ishtar. The Assyrians had the misfortune to settle in a country where sacred prostitution was a heritage from the age-long, non-Semitic worship of the mother goddess. The contemporaries of Amos in Israel were not able entirely to cast off its evil influence, even in the worship of Israel's God. The contemporaries of Amos in Assyria were no more successful. Yet compare the Ishtar of the Shumerians and Babylonians with the Ishtar of Nineveh or of Arbela. No longer is she primarily a belated excuse for immorality, she is the fierce Arab matron, loving and tender to her children, in whose defence she will fight with all the fierceness of outraged mother-love. Ishtar no longer represents soft and civilised sin, but bold, hardy, natural instinct of life.

Must we call the Assyrian a wolf? Not if by that we mean that he was a mere savage whose contribution to civilisation was negligible. The preceding pages have been perused in vain if it has not been made amply clear that his culture was his own, however much it may have been based on that of others, and it should be equally clear that he passed on much to posterity. If, after all, we tend to think first of his administrative activities, we will not have in mind the wolf but perhaps the shepherd-dog, savage towards his enemies, never permitting his sheep to stray. The shepherd-dog is not loved by his sheep; there be many, in the Philippines even, who do not agree with our interpretation of the "white man's burden," and the whole reaction of east against west is simple present-day comment on the text at the beginning of the sentence.

Centuries after the warder of the flock is dead, the impartial historian proves that the sheep have gained from his wardship. Roman provincials, for example, hated the Eternal City, and not without cause; with all her faults, with her numberless abuses, it is now universally recognised that the Roman Empire did a great work for civilisation. Nothing could be more evil than Cæsar's conquest of Gaul, for a million of lives were destroyed, probably more than all men put to death by all the Assyrian kings; who to-day would have the foundations of France other than Roman?

In their day, the Assyrians were the shepherd-dogs of civilisation. The great majority of their wars were wars of civilisation, either to bring within the range of cultural influences savage tribes or to hold back these savage tribes from destroying the thin line of civilisation in the Fertile Crescent. They failed tragically, and when they fell much of the older culture of western Asia was irretrievably lost. They failed, but they had held back the savages from the Arabian wastes or the equally backward Indo-Europeans from the northern grasslands until they had been at least varnished with the elements of the older culture.

Assyria was too small a state to bear the heavy burden of imperialism. For the moment, the Assyrian won great glory and much financial return, but he was bled white in the process, and his collapse was without hope of recovery.

What must be the final verdict of history? As his epitaph we must write, not that "In him is incarnate, to the highest degree, the defects and vices of Asiatic political systems," but the more charitable, more sympathetic, more historically just, "The Assyrian was a human being; being such, he was very much like ourselves. He was sometimes good and sometimes bad, he was cruel and he was forgiving, he was wise and then he blundered, he had capabilities for certain work, he had none for others. All in all he was a man, and a capable man; he suffered the usual human limitations, he was a child of his age. The empire he founded marked a mile-stone in the long and heartbreaking advance towards a higher civilisation. He was the shepherd-dog of civilisation, and he died at his post." Such an epitaph is sadly lacking in rhetorical art, but it is the sober truth of history.

INDEXES

INDEX OF PROPER NAMES

Names of kings of important countries or city-states are in small capitals; names of countries or cities ruled are abbreviated as follows: A = Assyria; B = Babylonia; D = Damascus; Eg = Egypt; El = Elam; H = Hittite; I = Israel; J = Judah; M = Mitanni; T = Tyre; U = Urartu. Other proper names are thus indicated: C = city; G = god; L = land; M = mountain; R = river; T = tribe.

INDEX OF SUBJECTS